EYEWITNESS

A LIVING DOCUMENTARY OF THE AFRICAN AMERICAN CONTRIBUTION TO AMERICAN HISTORY

Revised and Updated

WILLIAM LOREN KATZ

A TOUCHSTONE BOOK
PUBLISHED BY SIMON & SCHUSTER

New York   London   Toronto   Sydney   Tokyo   Singapore

TOUCHSTONE
Rockefeller Center
1230 Avenue of the Americas
New York, NY 10020

First Touchstone Edition 1995

TOUCHSTONE and colophon are registered trademarks
of Simon & Schuster Inc.

Designed by Irving Perkins Associates
Manufactured in the United States of America

10   9   8   7   6   5   4   3   2   1

Library of Congress Cataloging-in-Publication Data
Katz, William Loren.
    Eyewitness: a living documentary of the African American contribution to American history /
William Loren Katz. — 1st Touchstone ed.
    p.   cm.
    "Revised and updated."
    "A Touchstone book."
    Includes bibliographical references and index.
    1. Afro-Americans — History — Sources.   2. Afro-Americans — Biography.   I. Title.
E184.6.K38   1995
973'.0496073 — dc20   95-8287
                                                                                                        CIP
ISBN 0-684-80199-X

The author has made every effort to obtain permission for the
reprinting of all selctions contained herein. If any owner of
copyrighted material is not acknowledged herein, please contact
the publisher for proper acknowledgement in all future editions
or reprintings of this book.

*The author gratefully acknowledges the cooperation of the following institutions and individuals that
provided many of the illustrations used in this book.* Friedman Abeles; The Associated Publishers,
Inc.; Association for the Study of Negro Life and History; Bancroft Library; The Bettman Archive,
Inc.; Brown Brothers; Helen Buckler; California State Library; Chicago Historical Society; Culver Pic-
tures; Denver Public Library Western Collection; Department of the Army; Department of State; De-
troit Public Library; Explorers Club; Kansas State Historical Society; Library of Congress; Los Angeles
County Museum; Minnesota Historical Society; Charles Moore from Black Star; National Archives;
Nebraska State Historical Society; New York Public Library Picture Collection; The New York Times;
Oregon Historical Society; Professor Kenneth Wiggins Porter; Schomburg Collection of the New York
Public Library; Student Nonviolent Coordinating Committee; United Nations; United Press Interna-
tional Photo; United States Air Force; United States Signal Corps; University of Oklahoma, Division of
Manuscripts; Valentine Museum, Richmond, Virginia; World Wide Photo.

We do not believe that things will always continue the same. The time must come when the Declaration of Independence will be felt in the heart, as well as uttered from the mouth, and when the rights of all shall be properly acknowledged and appreciated. God hasten that time. This is our home, and this is our country. Beneath its sod lie the bones of our fathers; for it, some of them fought, bled, and died. Here we were born, and here we will die.

Meeting of African American New Yorkers, 1831

PREFACE

This book first appeared in 1967, but it began to take shape many years before the modern civil rights movement, in my high school days during World War II and my research in the origins of American jazz music. This research took on a deeper meaning in 1955 when I became a teacher of American history in New York public secondary schools. School courses routinely distorted the role of African Americans, picturing them as content under slavery and bewildered by freedom. Young citizens were fed such stereotypes as historical truth. The school curriculum, I began to realize, had been a major if subtle obstacle to racial understanding and peace in America. My response as a teacher was to introduce eyewitness accounts from my own collection that highlighted the African American gift to America. A few white parents grumbled, but not many, and students of every race responded enthusiastically to the new material. As the era of McCarthyism lifted, I was able to introduce even more accounts of this fascinating history.

My first acknowledgment must go to my students at Woodlands High School, for they helped select many of the accounts and pictures included. Beginning with the time this project was only a handful of dittoed sheets for my teenage students, I was assisted by the New World Foundation, the New York State Department of Education, and a host of teacher friends, especially Kenneth Haskins, Dan Smith, and Bernard Gaughran.

As *Eyewitness* progressed from manuscript to book, it received aid and comfort from Martin Luther King, Jr., James M. McPherson, Mrs. George

E. Haynes, Ernest Kaiser, Dorothy Porter, Ralph Bunche, Jerome S. Ozer, and Warren Halliburton. To Dr. Sara D. Jackson of the National Archives, this author is so deeply indebted that appreciation cannot be adequately expressed. Each step of the way Ben Katz offered his fatherly encouragement and poured in his finely honed research skills and Phyllis Katz her many editing talents.

The new edition owes a special thanks to editor Sheila Curry; the NAACP, Klanwatch, and the National Urban League's Ernie Johnson, Jr.; the editors of *Interrace, Essence,* and *Race and Poverty;* Scott Minerbrook of *U.S. News and World Report, Daily News* columnist Playthell Benjamin, and George Tooks and editor Dawad Philip of the *Daily Challenge,* which also provided key photographs. Jean Carey Bond of the ACLU proved to be the project's best friend by offering important leads, data, and hours of inimitably pointed, witty, and sage criticism.

A few months after the original work appeared, the superintendent of a major urban school system held aloft its red cover and announced, "If we use this book, blood will run in our corridors." It was not used in his schools, but blood flowed in his corridors anyway. Traditional Eurocentric blinders still hide much of this inspiring tale of the New World's first freedom fighters. The results are unfortunate. For people of color a proud and worthy legacy has been lost or buried. White Americans have inherited a flawed perspective on the past, one that continues to determine racial attitudes and shape government policy.

This is *Eyewitness's* first new edition since 1974. This one not only reflects new scholarship but has been brought up in time to the Clinton administration and issues of the "post–civil rights era."

For the most part, this story is told in the words of those who made history. Each quotation in the narrative, as well as in the eyewitness sections, is by a person contemporaneous with the events or people described. Documents have been edited without changing meaning, and original spelling has been preserved. The author has largely let the participants define the issues, chart the course, and speak for themselves. My organizing principle has been a typical course in American history. Any errors of fact or judgment remain mine alone.

I have attempted to tell this American story in unadorned prose, avoiding moral preaching and special pleading. To the extent I have succeeded in this, mind has conquered heart, for this project has been, from its first moments, a labor of love.

WILLIAM LOREN KATZ, February 1995

CONTENTS

Contents

Contents

Contents

Contents

22   SURVIVING REAGANOMICS, 1980–1992   543

23   URBAN POLITICS IN THE REAGAN-BUSH ERA   577

24   THE CLINTON ADMINISTRATION   612

1 THE OPENING OF NEW WORLDS

FOR ALL WHO CAME TO THESE SHORES, America was a land of freedom, hope, and opportunity. For all—except Africans. They came in chains and for hundreds of years had to fight just to be free. With few friends, and against almost hopeless odds, African American men and women struggled to stay alive, to obtain their freedom, and to share in the American dream of human dignity and justice for all.

The African came to America as a slave who had been captured—captured, as Frederick Douglass wrote, by "a band of successful robbers who had left their homes, and gone to Africa, and stolen us from our homes, and in a strange land reduced us to slavery." For more than four centuries this trade drained Africa of its healthiest sons and daughters.

Slavery had been a part of civilization since the day when man first learned to plant, harvest crops, and develop a surplus. The ancient Egyptians, Greeks, Romans, and Africans had both held and been slaves during the course of history, and slavery was described in and sanctioned by the Bible. Even white Christians had been enslaved by their fellow Europeans as well as other peoples. Before the African slave trade, the slave was usually a prisoner of war or a criminal paying his or her debt to society. He or she was often protected in certain rights by both laws and customs, although an outcast and not an accepted member of society. Many bondsmen were allowed their liberty after years of faithful service. Only the slavery of North America denied the humanity of the slave and called the African inferior because of skin color.

The trade that began in 1442 when ten Africans were brought to Prince Henry of Portugal and the discovery of the New World a half century later were both part of a single historical movement. They were two aspects of the bold European explorers' conquests during the fifteenth and sixteenth centuries. And they grew out of a strange combination of religious zeal and greed for new land and cheap labor.

The Europeans needed a labor force to develop the mines, forests, and fertile fields of the New World. In Africa they found a hearty people, familiar with agriculture and used to hard work, who could turn the abundant natural resources of the Americas into staggering profits. Using the most advanced weapons of the time and a diplomacy based on deceit, the conquerors exploited the resources of both regions.

This new source of wealth from Africa attracted nobles as well as pirates. The duke of York, who captured New Amsterdam from the Dutch in 1664, had two years earlier formed a "Company of Royal Adventurers" that captured people in the African kingdom of Guinea and sold them for gold. So much money poured into the British treasury from this trade that the king issued a new coin called the *guinea.*

The enormous profits of the slave trade became the most convincing argument for its continuation despite its known horrors. The European and American merchants who profited from this trade justified themselves by

An African chief sells prisoners of war to European slave merchants. Slavery was common in Africa; it was used as a punishment for crimes or making war. However, African slavery protected the basic rights of the prisoner and allowed her or him to own property, marry (even a member of the owner's family), and eventually gain freedom. Slavery in the New World would be very different.

pointing out that Africans were not Christians. Since the idea of enslaving non-Christians was generally acceptable, the slave traders became wealthy and respected members of their communities. They built universities and churches and even gave their ships such names as *Jesus* and *Grace of God*. The New World, they claimed, offered the Africans contact with both Christianity and civilization in place of "African savagery."

The real Africa was very different from the Africa described by the slave trader. For one thing, it could no more be spoken of as one unified continent than Europe could. Africa was a land of many languages, religions, colors, and stages of development. In the years before the arrival of the Europeans, Africans achieved a cultural progress equal to and often superior to that of Europe. During the African metal age that began five hundred years before the birth of Christ, the African people began to cultivate the soil, build great cities, develop their arts, smelt and work iron ore, and build complex social systems. African craftsmen were skilled in leather, wood, glass, gold, ivory, copper, tin, silver, and bronze. In the kingdom of the Congo, every clan had its special crafts such as weaving, wine making, pottery, and smithery. Each craft sent representatives to the national council that advised the monarch. For centuries, African kings combined religion and business by making pilgrimages to Mecca in huge caravans that displayed their enormous riches.

The kingdom of Songhay in West Africa had developed a banking system, a school system, and a complete code of laws by the fifteenth century,

Ancient bronze statue of an African hunter carrying home an antelope. Considered a masterpiece, this statue was found in Benin City in 1897 and is now on display at the British Museum.

Congo knives. While Africans were a diverse population of many tribes, all shared a great skill in handicrafts and created some of the world's greatest art. However, beautiful weapons were no match for European rifles and cannons.

and instituted economic reforms that made it prosperous. It traded with European and African nations, and its University of Sankoré at Timbuktu offered courses in surgery, law, and literature to African, Asiatic, and European scholars. Leo Africanus, a highly educated Spanish Moor who visited Timbuktu, noticed a "great store of doctors, judges, priests, and other learned men, [and] . . . manuscripts or written books . . . which are sold for more money than any other merchandise." In the year that Columbus discovered the New World, Songhay ruled an empire that was larger than all of Europe. The slave traders of Portugal, Spain, Holland, Denmark, France, and England wrecked much of this civilization as they plundered Africa for slaves and battled each other for control of the slave trade.

While Africans came to the New World as prisoners, they did not leave their homeland without a struggle or submit easily to bondage. Captain Philip Drake, a slave trader for fifty years, reported, "The Negroes fought like wild beasts. . . . Slavery is a dangerous business at sea as well as ashore." A seaman aboard a slave ship wrote in his diary, "If care not be taken they [the slaves] will mutiny and destroy the ship's crew in hopes to get away. To prevent such misfortunes we visit them daily, narrowly searching every corner between decks, to see whether they have . . . any pieces of iron, or wood or knives." Clearly, the seething human cargo packed below the decks of the slavers made the trip dangerous.

Insufficient food and water and the outbreak of epidemics took many lives among both slaves and crew. The seamen kept away from their human cargo and its special misery. Slaver Thomas Branagan described how the prisoners

Gezo, king of Dahomey. Wealth and education were not uncommon in the urban centers of Africa before and during the slave trade era.

Crewmen aboard a slaver force an African to eat. Many tried to starve themselves to death.

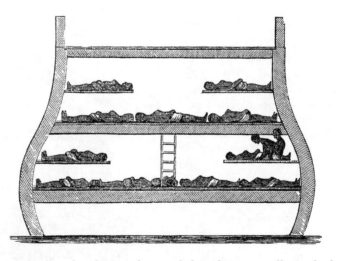

Cross section of a slave ship showing the crowded conditions. Insufficient food and water, crowding, and disease often left the slaves too weak to revolt. But more than one hundred slave mutinies took place on board the ships bringing Africans to the New World.

"struggle, they resist; but all in vain. No eye pities; no hand helps." But through their own efforts slaves successfully revolted more than a hundred times on the high seas. Resistance to tyranny began at the birth of tyranny.

Spanish and Portuguese Explorations

Africans served the European conquerors in many ways. Some traveled as seamen and officers to the Americas. They traveled with Columbus and, in 1513, thirty marched with Balboa to the Pacific and built the first ships on that coast. Six years later, three hundred Africans dragged the heavy Spanish artillery that Cortés used to defeat the Aztecs of Mexico. The first wheat crop in the New World was planted and harvested by one of Cortés's Black men. Others accompanied Pizarro in his conquest of Peru, and in 1565 they built St. Augustine, America's first city.

The best-known African explorer with the Spanish expeditions was Estevanico. A man of rare courage and ability, Estevanico served as an advisor to Cortés, and as a guide to Cabeza de Vaca and Father Marcos de Niza. He explored Florida, Mexico, and parts of Arizona and New Mexico. During a Florida expedition in 1528, Estevanico, Cabeza de Vaca, and two companions were captured by Indians. They escaped, only to spend eight years wandering through swamps and forests trying to find their way to the Spanish headquarters in Mexico. It was during this time that the four explorers first heard of Cibola from the Indians. Cibola, or the "Seven Cities of Gold," was said to lie somewhere north of Mexico. The attempt to reach this legendary land was to lead to Estevanico's last journey.

Estevanico (right) and his three companions trade with the Indians. (Courtesy Denver Public Library Western Collection.)

In 1539, the Spanish explorer Father Marcos de Niza led an expedition to search for the Seven Cities of Gold, and his scout was Estevanico. A member of the group told how important Estevanico was to the expedition: "It was the Negro who talked to them [the Indians] all the time; he inquired about the roads we should follow, the villages; in short, about everything we wished to know." Estevanico was sent ahead with two large greyhounds and a group of Indian guides. In his earlier trip Estevanico had posed as a medicine man in order to survive among the Indians. This time he again assumed this disguise and carried a large gourd decorated with strings of bells and a red and a white feather. The gourd was supposed to be either a source of magic or a symbol of peace.

Father Marcos had instructed Estevanico to send back wooden crosses to show his progress. The closer he got to Cibola the larger the crosses were to be. Excitement rose in Father Marcos's camp when one by one large white crosses began to arrive almost immediately and, with them, news of Estevanico's fast progress. News came of gifts of leather and turquoise that were being showered on the explorer. As many as three hundred Indian men and women joined Estevanico's group on its march to Cibola. Every few days another large cross arrived for Father Marcos.

Then no word. Weeks later an Indian staggered in with news of Estevanico's murder and the massacre of his party by the Indians surrounding the Seven Cities of Gold. Father Marcos's party fled back to Mexico, but the story of Estevanico's discovery spurred De Soto, Coronado, and other Spanish explorers to search for Cibola. Hundreds of years after Estevanico's death, the Zuñi Indians, whose villages he was approaching when he met his death, still told stories about a strange Black man who had once entered their land.

The vast majority of Africans brought by the Spanish adventurers came not as explorers like Estevanico, but as laborers. Less than fifty years after Columbus first landed in the New World, the Spanish governor of Mexico wrote that Africans were "indispensable for the cultivation of the land and the royal revenue." The letters of King Ferdinand of Spain show a lively interest in the economic value of Black slaves.

But keeping Africans in slavery was a difficult and dangerous business. They "fled among the Indians and taught them bad customs and never would be recaptured," wrote the governor of Mexico in 1502. The first settlement within the present borders of the United States, near the Pedee River, was the scene of a successful slave uprising. In the winter of 1526, in this South Carolina colony of five hundred Spaniards and one hundred Africans, slaves rebelled and fled to the Indians. Enslaved together, Africans and Indians, from California to Argentina, escaped together.

The pattern of resistance to slavery continued for centuries. In the early nineteenth century, slave trader Philip Drake wrote of the Spanish colonies, "In Barbadoes, Trinidad, and St. Thomas, the whites lived in constant fear of massacre." Three hundred years after the first slave revolt in a Spanish colony, Rio de Janeiro slaves set fire to crops, smashed machinery, and were only defeated (although not captured) by the use of troops. They were led by an Ashanti warrior named Quobah who was never found.

Runaway slaves began their own "maroon" colonies, the largest being the Republic of Palmares in northeastern Brazil. This colony sheltered twenty thousand people within its three great walls. The runaways grew beans, cane, and bananas which they traded with other villages. Courts of justice carried out the many laws of its government and many of the customs of Africa were kept alive during the ninety years of the city's existence. One of its leaders, Zambi, was described as "a Negro of singular courage, great presence of mind, and unusual devotion." Twenty-five Portuguese attempts to crush Palmares ended in failure. One of the defeated officers described the city as "so well fortified as to be lacking only in ar-

Africans accompanied the Spaniards on their major New World expeditions.

tillery." An overwhelming army of Portuguese was finally able to capture and destroy the city in 1697. According to legend, the defeated soldiers, led by their ruler, hurled themselves from a cliff rather than surrender.

The slavery that developed in the Spanish and Portuguese colonies was different, in a number of important respects, from the system of bondage developed in North America. In Latin America, a powerful Catholic Church, interested in the soul of the African, protected him or her from many abuses. In America, no church or any other power dared tell a slaveholder how to treat his or her slaves. The Church in Latin America encouraged owners to liberate slaves who became Christians. Marriages between Africans and whites were not opposed by the Church, and Latin American slavery was not infected with racial prejudice. The South American slave was thought of as a member of the human race and not as part of an "inferior race." Slaves who were severely beaten could protest to the court, and some even won their liberty from cruel owners. In Brazil, a slave could purchase his or her freedom by raising the amount of money which had originally been paid for him or her. In Cuba, slaves were allowed to buy their freedom on the installment plan, paying their masters a down payment and a set amount each month.

An example of how high an African might rise in New Spain was provided by Brother Martín de Porres. Born in Lima, Peru, in 1579, this tall, soft-voiced young man became a surgeon's apprentice and later a doctor. Brother de Porres is noted for starting Peru's first orphanage, and today it still carries on the work he began. Made a member of the Dominican Order before his death in 1639, de Porres often said, "I could do nothing without Christ." Two centuries later Pope Gregory XVI bestowed the title of "Blessed" on Brother de Porres. In 1962 Brother Martín de Porres became the world's first African American saint.

Vicente Guerrero, of African and Indian parentage, was a Mexican revolutionary leader who in 1829 became President of Mexico. He wrote Mexico's Constitution and freed its slaves.

In 1696, European and Black troops clashed near the Republic of Palmares.

The Dutch Colonies

The Dutch colony of New Amsterdam, founded in 1626, included eleven male slaves. Women slaves were brought to the colony a few years later. Slaves were considered so necessary to the settlement that the Dutch would not execute six Africans who had taken part in a murder. Instead, the six were told to draw lots so that one could be chosen for hanging. When the man chosen, a giant in size, broke the hangman's ropes, he was freed, to the general delight of the community.

Slaves were important to the Dutch colony of New Amsterdam. Their extensive use in agriculture pushed fur trapping into second place in the colonies' economy. Governor Peter Stuyvesant owned forty slaves, making him the largest slaveholder in the colony. The slave laws were lenient, allowing bondsmen "half-freedom." During the Indian wars, Black bondsmen were issued arms and fought alongside the Dutch. In court cases African Americans were allowed to testify against whites.

As in the Spanish and Portuguese colonies, slaves worked in a variety of trades. They built forts and public projects and even served as armed deputies to rent collectors. While the colony's Jews were not allowed to serve in the militia or to own land, African Americans were. The legislature three times passed laws to keep settlers from aiding slaves fleeing their masters. Slaves' petitions for freedom were often accompanied by petitions of whites supporting their rights to be free.

In 1644, the Dutch liberated a dozen slaves and gave them "their freedom on the same footing as other free peoples." Obviously the Dutch placed Africans on the same level with other indentured servants who were set free after a specified amount of service. In 1661, the first American slave petition for freedom came from a slave couple in New Amsterdam and was sent to Peter Stuyvesant. Its plea was for the liberty of a son—and it was granted. But when the British captured the colony a few years later, African American servants were declared to be held in *perpetual* slavery. The fact that the duke of York was a leader in the Royal African Company of slave traders undoubtedly was an important reason for this change and for the sharp increase in the number of Africans brought as slaves to New York.

The French Colonies

Jean Baptiste Pointe Du Sable. (Courtesy Chicago Historical Society.)

The earliest French explorers of the New World brought Africans along on their expeditions. They journeyed down the Mississippi River to the Indian settlements with Marquette and Joliet. The French Jesuit colony in

Kaskaskia, Illinois, included seventy African Americans. They served as farmers, blacksmiths, carpenters, brewers, and masons. In 1720, Philippe Renault, a Paris banker, brought white and Black laborers to work in the lead, copper, and silver mines of New France.

The best-known African explorer of the French expeditions was Jean Baptiste Pointe du Sable, a tall, handsome man who had been educated in Paris. He came to New France in 1765 and later built a trading post at the mouth of the Chicago River. Like many other French traders and trappers, du Sable married an Indian woman. His trading post spread out to include a forty-foot house, bakehouse, dairy, smokehouse, workshop, stable, and barn. Eventually it became the site of the city of Chicago. The Indians joked that the first white man to come to Chicago was a Black man.

The French colony of Haiti in the Caribbean was the scene of the only successful slave revolt in human history. The revolution began in August 1791, when a half million slaves rose against their French masters. They were joined by thousands of free Africans who lived on the island. For ten years, French, Spanish, and English armies tried in vain to crush the rebellion. The invaders, including Napoleon's powerful armies, were driven into the sea. The Haitian forces were led by Toussaint L'Ouverture, a short, slight ex-slave coachman of fifty with a remarkable knowledge of military

Toussaint L'Ouverture, liberator of Haiti.

Slave revolt in Haiti. Armed slaves drive back foreign troops.

tactics. In 1803, the revolutionists declared their freedom and announced, "Restored to our primitive dignity, we have asserted our rights; we swear never to yield them to any power on earth."

Emperor Napoleon had learned an important lesson from his defeat in Haiti—how impossible it was to hold colonies so far from France. When a delegation from Thomas Jefferson, president of the United States, arrived to discuss the purchase of New Orleans, Napoleon surprised them by offering to sell the entire Louisiana territory, from the Gulf of Mexico to the Canadian border. The Americans gladly agreed, and this $15,000,000 bargain (four cents an acre) doubled the size of the United States.

AFRICA DURING THE SLAVE TRADE

[*What was Africa like during the slave trade? What were the Africans like? A slave trader, Captain Theodore Canot, tells about the town of Timbo in West Africa, and of a visit he made to a tribe called the Bagers.*]

. . . It was the height of the dry season, when everything was parched by the sun, yet I could trace the outlines of fine plantations, gardens, and rice-fields. Every where I found abundance of peppers, onions, garlic, tomatoes, sweet potatoes, and cassava, while tasteful fences were garlanded with immense vines and flowers. Fowles, goats, sheep, and oxen stalked about. . . .

. . . I strolled repeatedly through the town. I became excessively familiar with its narrow streets, low houses, mud walls, cul-de-sacs [dead-end streets], and mosques. I saw no fine bazaars, marketplaces, or shops. The chief wants of life were supplied by peddlers. Platters, jars, and baskets of fruit, vegetables, and meat, were borne around twice or thrice daily. Horsemen dashed about on beautiful steeds towards the fields in the morning, or came home at nightfall at a slower pace. *I never saw man or woman bask lazily in the sun.* Females were constantly busy over their cotton and spinning wheels when not engaged in household occupations; and often have I seen an elderly dame quietly crouched in her hovel at sunset reading the Koran. Nor are the men of Timbo less thrifty. Their city wall is said to hem in about ten thousand individuals, representing all the social industries. They weave cotton, work in leather, fabricate iron from the bar, engage diligently in agriculture, and, whenever not laboriously employed, devote themselves to reading and writing, of which they are excessively fond.

[*When it became known in Timbo that Canot was a slave trader, he found "a personal dread of me in the town. . . . I was Death now!"*]

When I took my usual morning walk the children ran from me screaming. . . . The poor regarded me as the devil incarnate. Once or twice, I caught women throwing a handful of dust or ashes towards me, and uttering an invocation from the Koran to avert the demon or save them from his clutches. Their curiosity was merged in terror. *My popularity was over.*

[*Captain Canot visited the Bager people to check on a chest of his goods that had been left among them.*]

I opened the chest, which, to my surprise, was unlocked, and found it nearly full of the merchandise I had placed in it. I shook the cask, and its weight seemed hardly diminished. I turned the spiggot, and lo! the rum trickled on my feet. . . .

"Good!" said the chief, "it is all there,—is it not? We Bagers are neither Soosoos, Mandingoes, Foulahs, nor *Whitemen*, that the goods of a stranger are not safe in our towns! We work for a living; we want little; big ships never come to us, and we neither steal from our guests nor go to war to sell one another!"

. . . [The chief] then sent a crier through the town, informing the women that a white stranger would be their guest during the night; and, in less than half an hour, my hut was visited by most of the village dames and damsels. One brought a pint of rice; another some roots of *cassava;* another, a few spoonfuls of palm oil; another a bunch of peppers; while the oldest lady of the party made herself particularly remarkable by the gift of a splendid fowl. . . .

There was nothing peculiar in this exhibition of hospitality, on account of my nationality. It was the mere fulfillment of a Bager law; and the poorest *black stranger* would have shared the rite as well as myself. I could not help thinking that I might have travelled from one end of England or America to the other, without meeting a Bager *welcome*. Indeed, it seemed somewhat questionable, whether it were better for the English to civilize Africa, or for the Bagers to send missionaries to their brethren in Britain!

Brantz Meyer, ed., *Captain Canot, or Twenty Years of an African Slaver* (New York, 1854), 120–22; 177–80.

A SLAVER DESCRIBES THE AFRICAN TRADE

[*Long after the slave trade had been outlawed by the nations of the world, it continued openly. It was a dangerous but highly profitable business. Captain James Smith was one of the few traders convicted, and his sentence was only two years in prison and a $1,000 fine. He answered the questions of a newspaper editor.*]

"New York," said Captain Smith, "is the chief port in the world for the Slave Trade." He repeated two or three times, "*It is the greatest place in the universe for it.* Neither in Cuba nor in the Brazils is it carried on so extensively. Ships that convey Slaves to the West Indies and South America are fitted out from New York. Now and then one sails from Boston and Philadelphia; but New York is our headquarters. My vessel was the brig 'Julia Moulton.' I got her in Boston, and brought her here, and sailed from this port direct for the coast of Africa."

"But do you mean to say that this business is going on now?"

"*Yes, all the while. Not so many vessels have been sent out this year—perhaps not over twenty-five. But last year there were thirty-five.*"

"Are there large shipping-houses engaged in it?"

"Yes; I can go down to South Street, and go into a number of houses that help to fit out ships for the business. I don't know how far they own the vessels, or receive the profits of the cargoes. But these houses know all about it. . . ."

"But when you reach the African coast, are you not in great danger from British Ships-of-War?"

"Oh, no, we don't care a button for an English squadron. *We run up the American flag, and if they come aboard, all we have to do is to show our American papers, and they have no right to search us.*". . .

"How many Slaves could you carry on your vessel?"

"We took on board 664. We might have stowed away 800. If she had been going to the Brazils, we should have taken that number. She would carry 750 with ease. The boys and women we kept on the upper deck. But all the strong men—those giant Africans that might make us trouble—we put below on the Slave deck."

"Did you chain them or put on handcuffs?"

"No, never; they would die. We let them move about."

"Are you very severe with them?"

"We have to be very strict at first—for a week or so—to make them feel that we are masters. Then we lighten up for the rest of the voyage."

"How do you pack them at night?"

"They lie down upon the deck, on their sides, body to body. There would not be room enough for all to lie on their backs."

"Did many die on the passage?"

"Yes. I lost a good many the last cruise—more than ever before. *Sometimes we find them dead when we go below in the morning.* Then we throw them overboard."

"Are the profits of the trade large?"

"Yes, sir, very large. My Brig cost $13,000 to fit her out completely. My last cargo to Cuba was worth $220,000."

"Did you ever get chased by the English ships?"

"Yes; once a Man-of-War chased two of us. The mate betrayed me. I never liked the man. He was scared. He had no heart. You see, it takes a man of a particular constitution to engage in our business. . . . We belong to no country. We are under the protection of no law. We must defend ourselves. A man must have a great deal of nerve in such a situation when he is liable to be chased by ships-of-war, or perhaps, finds himself suddenly in the midst of a whole fleet.". . .

"But are you not tired of this business?"

"Why, I didn't want to go out the last voyage. I tried to get another Captain to take charge of my ship. I wanted to stay at home and get married. But *good men* in our business are scarce. And I had to go."

Geo. W. Carleton, *The Suppressed Book About Slavery!* (New York, 1864), 408–11.

Stephan Dorantez (Estevanico) Finds the Seven Cities of Gold—and Death!

[*Estevanico, or "Little Stephan," had been chief scout in the 1528 Cabeza de Vaca expedition into Florida. In 1539, he went with Friar Marcos de Niza into the American Southwest in search of the Seven Cities of Gold (Ceuola or Cibola) supposed to be hidden there. Father de Niza, leader of the expedition, tells of Estevanico's last adventure.*]

. . . I sent Stephan Dorantez the Negro another way, whom I commaunded to goe directly northward fiftie or threescore leagues, to see if by that way hee might learne any newes of any notable thing which wee sought to discover, and I agreed with him, that if hee found any knowledge of any peopled and riche Countrey which were of great importance, that hee should goe no further, but should returne in person, or shoulde sende mee certaine Indians with that token which wee were agreed upon, to wit, that if it were but a meane thing, hee shoulde sende mee a White Crosse of one handfull long; and if it were any great matter, one of two handfuls long; and if it were a Countrey greater and better than Nueva Espanna, hee should send mee a great crosse. So the sayde Stephan departed from mee on Passion-sunday after dinner: and within foure dayes after the messengers of Stephan returned unto me with a great Crosse as high as a man, and they brought me word from Stephan, that I should forthwith come away after him, for hee had found people which gave him information of a very mighty Province, and that he had sent me one of the said Indians. This Indian told me, that it was thirtie dayes journey from the Towne where Stephan was, unto the first Citie of the sayde Province, which is called Ceuola. Hee affirmed also that there are seven great Cities in this Province, all under one Lord, the houses whereof are made of Lyme and Stone, and are very great . . . and that in the gates of the principall houses there are many Turques-stones cunningly wrought. . . .

[*After days of additional travel and more messages from Estevanico, Father Marcos saw another of his slave's Indian guides.*]

[The guide] came in a great fright, having his face and body all covered with sweat . . . and he told mee that a dayes journey before Stephan came to Ceuola [and sent his gourd] and two feathers one white and another red, in token that he demanded safe conduct, and that he came peaceably. . . .

[*The magistrate refused the peace offer and forbade Stephan's entrance. Two other Indians stumbled into Father Marcos's camp with the final details.*]

These wounded Indians I asked for Stephan, and they agreeing in all poynts with [what] the first Indian sayd, that after they had put him into the . . . house without giving him meat or drinke all that day and all that night, they took from Stephan all the things which hee carried with him. The next day when the Sunne was a lance high, Stephan went out of the house [and suddenly saw a crowd of people coming at him from the city,] whom as soone as hee sawe he began to run away and we likewise, and foorthwith they shot at us and wounded us, and certain men fell dead upon us . . . and after this we could not see Stephan any more, and we thinke they have shot him to death, as they have done all the rest which went with him, so that none are escaped but we onely.

Richard Hakluyt, *Hakluyt's Collection of the Early Voyages, Travels, and Discoveries of the English Nation* (London, 1810), 438–45.

St. Malo Leads a Slave Revolt in New Spain

[*A description of a slave revolt leader in Spanish New Orleans is preserved in this song, "The Dirge of St. Malo," still sung many years later (in 1880) by "old Madeline," an African American woman from New Orleans. The "Cabildo men" mentioned were the Spanish judges, police, and jailers.*]

Alas! young men, come, make lament
For poor St. Malo in distress!
They chased, they hunted him with dogs,
They fired at him with a gun,

. . . .

They hauled him from the cypress swamp
His arms they tied behind his back,
They tied his hands in front of him;
They tied him to a horse's tail,
They dragged him up into the town.
Before those grand Cabildo men
They charged that he had made a plot
To cut the throats of all the whites.
They asked him who his comrades were;
Poor St. Malo said not a word!
The judge his sentence read to him,
And then they raised the gallows-tree.
They drew the horse—the cart moved off—
And left St. Malo hanging there.
The sun was up an hour high
When on the Levee he was hung,
They left his body swinging there,
For carrion crows to feed upon.

George W. Cable, "Creole Slave Songs," *Century Magazine* 31 (April 1886): 814–15.

2 THE ENGLISH COLONIES

In 1619 the new English colony of Jamestown was the scene of two events of great importance in the history of American democracy. Twenty African laborers were brought into the port and sold by the captain of a Dutch ship, and the House of Burgesses, America's first representative assembly, met for the first time. For close to 250 years, Africans would be used as forced labor in the world's first representative democracy.

Slave Life in Colonial America

The cargo of Africans was purchased to help relieve Jamestown's labor shortage. In that same year, one hundred London boys were brought to the colony for the same purpose. Both Africans and whites were freed following an agreed-upon number of years of labor—for they were indentured servants rather than slaves. Members of both groups became landowners and slaveholders. In fact, the first runaway slave case in Virginia involved an African American master.

Two generations later, however, the House of Burgesses passed laws making newly arrived Africans, and the children born to them, slaves forever. The excuse for enslaving them was that they were neither Christian nor white. As soon as a few became Christians, Virginia adopted a law de-

This slave was placed in an iron collar for attempting to run away.

claring "that baptisme of slaves doth not exempt them from bondage."

Indians had been used as slaves but they had proved unsuited to plantation labor. They died from the white man's diseases or from the rigors of the slave system. Many escaped to the woods which they knew better than their captors, or to their tribes. A few remained in slavery and were subjected to the same rules as Africans. Unlike the Indian, Africans were used to agricultural labor. Furthermore, they were thousands of miles from home and friends, so that even when they managed to escape, their skin color made them an easy target for recapture in a land of whites.

The Southern Colonies

Slaves in the Southern colonies worked largely on the rice, tobacco, and sugar cane crops. A British officer described their working day as lasting from "daybreak" to "late in the evening." At night, "they sleep on a bench, or on the ground, with an old scanty blanket, which serves them at once for bed and covering,"

As a surveyor, George Washington used Black and white assistants.

Not all the Southern slaves worked in the fields. Some were skilled craftsmen, and others became servants in the "big house" of their masters. Slaves built the mansions of Mount Vernon and Monticello. Some worked as chimney sweepers in Charleston, where, in 1763, they combined to protest their working conditions. Others helped to protect the city from Indian attacks in 1708 by serving as cowboy patrols. George Washington saw slave "pioneers or hatchet men" employed on the Virginia frontier. Abel, a talented Virginia slave who escaped, was described by his owner in glowing terms: "He plays on the violin . . . a pilot for the York River and the Bay. He can write so as to be understood. He has gone off in a boat with two masts, schooner rigged. . . . A white lad went off with him." Abel may have been one of the many Africans who worked alongside white indentured servants and free laborers.

While slave labor was important in all of the English colonies, it became vital to the development of the Southern colonies. Even Georgia, which began with a ban on slavery, gave up the restriction after a generation. "All unanimously agree," wrote one of its leaders in 1740, "that without Negroes Georgia can never be a colony of any consequence." By the time the American Revolution began, the slave population exceeded the free population in many areas of the South. Slaves comprised 65 percent of South Carolina's total population. The fear of rebellion led to strict "slave codes" in regions of dense slave populations.

The colonial period, however, even in the South, was marked by a more tolerant attitude toward people of color than the pre–Civil War period.

Black and white apprentices were treated in much the same manner in South Carolina. As early as 1740, Alexander Garden of Charleston proposed a school for slaves. His unique idea included the suggestion that its instruction "must be by Negro schoolmasters . . . equally property as other slaves, but educated for this service. . . ." Garden's plan was accepted, and he selected two slave boys of fifteen, Andrew and Harry, for training as schoolmasters. In 1743 the school opened under the direction of Harry, whom Garden called a "genius." Within a year Harry was instructing sixty slave scholars, mainly in "the principles of our holy religion." The school continued until Harry's death in 1764.

The Middle and New England Colonies

The farther north one went the smaller was the slave population. New England's slaves never numbered more than 2 percent of the total population. Slavery in the North often was more humane than in the South. New York City provided schools for African Americans in 1705 and Philadelphia did so in 1758. Puritan minister Cotton Mather insisted that masters treat their slaves "according to the rules of humanity" as persons with "immortal souls in them and . . . not mere beasts of burden."

Life for the New England slave was rarely as burdensome as it was for his Southern brother. Puritan masters thought it wrong to work their slaves on the Sabbath. They also made sure African Americans were admitted to the white hospitals when ill. Cotton Mather formed a society to instruct African Americans in Christianity and performed slave marriages with Christian dignity. He told other ministers to preach "Thy Negro is thy neighbor" to their congregations. Furthermore, he practiced what he preached: "I would remember, that my servants are in some sense my children. . . . Nor will I leave them ignorant of anything, wherein I may instruct them to be useful to their generation." He added that "I will put Bibles and other good and proper books into their hands."

Slaves took part in every phase of the diverse economic life of the North. Twenty-four slave women worked in a Rhode Island creamery. The famous Touro Synagogue in Newport, an excellent example of colonial New England architecture, was built during the French and Indian War with the aid of hired African American craftsmen. Prince Fowle was a slave who served as a pressman on New Hampshire's first newspaper. Many of New England's sailors were Black. Quaker Anthony Benezet, who began a school for Black children in Philadelphia, reported, "I have found amongst the Negroes as great variety of talents as amongst a like number of whites." Benezet stated that the belief "that the Blacks are inferior in their capacities, is a vulgar prejudice, founded on . . . pride or ignorance." The Quaker devoted the rest of his life to African American education.

It was easier for the New England slave to improve his condition or gain his freedom than it was for his Southern brother. Slave soldiers received the same pay and treatment as whites. More than a few slaves successfully sued their owners for their freedom. In 1769 a slave named James took his master to court in Concord, claiming he had "restrained him of his liberty and held him in servitude." When he lost the case, James took it to a higher court and finally won. Owners such as Cotton Mather freed their slaves out of kindness or Christian principle.

The free New England African American was, at times, able to rise high in the colonial society of the eighteenth century. Newport Gardner of Rhode Island opened a music school for African Americans and whites, and his former master took lessons at his studio. Since his rise did not protect him from prejudice, he finally left America to settle in Africa.

Discrimination did keep people of color from rising as far as they might have. A French traveler to New England wrote:

Tituba, a Salem house slave, delighted and frightened Puritan teenagers with strange stories and "sorcery." Accused of witchcraft, her testimony tore the community apart—leading to the Salem witch-hunt of 1692.

> Those Negroes who keep shops live moderately and never augment their business beyond a certain point. The reason is obvious. The whites . . . like not to give them credit to enable them to undertake any extensive commerce nor even give them the means of [a] common education. . . .

Lucy Terry and her husband, Abijah Prince, were remarkable examples of slaves who became free and prosperous in colonial New England. Miss Terry was kidnapped from Africa when she was an infant and lived in Deerfield, Massachusetts, from the age of five. It was here that she met Prince. In 1746 she witnessed a bloody Indian massacre in her village and wrote a rhymed description of it. It was the first poem written by an African on American soil.

Prince was freed and given land by the terms of his master's will. In 1756 the couple was married before a justice of the peace and Prince purchased Lucy's freedom. Another settler left him more land in Vermont in his will. When he became a charter member of the town of Sunderland in Vermont, he was granted still more land.

The Princes had six children, and when Cesar, the oldest boy, was ready for college, Lucy Prince tried to enroll him in Williams College. For three hours she addressed the trustees, trying to persuade them to change their policy of not admitting people of color. Despite the fact that she quoted "an abundance of law and Gospel, chapter and verse," she was unsuccessful. Cesar was one of the thousands of African Americans to serve in the Revolution. He probably marched with the Green Mountain Boys under

Colonel Ethan Allen, who lived across the creek from the Prince family.

Lucy Prince went to court when a neighbor in Sunderland claimed part of the Prince farm as his land. She argued her case all the way from the court in her small town to a United States Supreme Court Justice. According to this authority, Justice Samuel Chase told her she had made a better argument than any he had ever heard from a Vermont lawyer, and she won her case. For eighteen years, until she died at the age of ninety-one, Lucy Prince rode horseback over the Green Mountains each year to visit her husband's grave.

The Fight Against Bondage

Slaveholders in all the colonies lived an uneasy life with their "property" often in revolt or flight. In 1657 Indians and African Americans attacked Hartford, Connecticut, and burned homes. In 1690 Connecticut towns instituted a nine-o'clock curfew for all people of color. Some towns passed laws that forbade this group to come out of doors during fires. In 1727 Indians and Africans attacked Virginia settlements. Obviously a number of Black men had made common cause with red men. Clearly the enemy of both the slave and the Indian was the same, the white man. When Natchez Indians massacred whites in 1730 they spared 106 African Americans. A Boston law forbade red or Black people from carrying a stick or cane, day or night, which could "be fit for . . . fighting or anything of that nature."

Hunting runaway slaves. George Washington thought slaves were a "very troublesome" kind of property because they ran away or planned revolts. Slaves owned by Washington, Patrick Henry, and George Mason, "father of the Bill of Rights," ran away to find freedom.

In 1721, Virginia's governor had the Five Civilized Nations sign treaties promising to return fugitive slaves. In 1726, New York's governor forced the same promise from the Iroquois Confederacy. In 1746, the Hurons made this promise and the next year the Delawares did as well. None of them returned a single slave.

From New England to Georgia, slaveholders had to be constantly alert to the escape of their slaves. Slaves ran away from all kinds of masters, both mean and kind. Even a strict but gentle master such as George Washington sold one of his slaves, Tom, because he had run away repeatedly. Washington advised Tom's new owner to keep him "handcuffed, lest he should attempt to escape."

Even the "Society of Negroes," which Cotton Mather began in 1693, aimed at curtailing slave resistance as well as fostering the Puritan gospel. Its members had to pledge themselves to provide runaways *"no Shelter"* and see they were "discovered and punished."

Slave resistance took many forms. In 1723 Boston slaves were accused of setting a dozen fires in one April week. In 1740 New York slaves were accused of trying to poison the water supply. The following year, the city crushed a revolt that included whites and more than a hundred African Americans. Carolina slaves attacked a warehouse and seized guns and ammunition. A white eyewitness described the scene: "Being thus provided with arms, they elected one of their number captain, and agreed to follow him, marching toward the southwest, with colors flying and drums beating, like a disciplined company." Troops smashed this revolt.

Rebellions marked the era of British colonial rule but little was heard about them. In 1774 James Madison said of one slave revolt, "It is prudent that such attempts should be concealed as well as suppressed."

When they could not flee or revolt, the bondsmen kept in touch with each other in many secret ways. John Adams wrote in 1775, "The Negroes have a wonderful art of communicating intelligence among themselves; it will run several hundred miles in a week or a fortnight."

Opposition to slavery did not come from people of color alone. The persecuted Quakers of the middle colonies, who rejected war and violence, were the first group of white people to come to the aid of the slave. They saw slavery as a form of violence and freed their own slaves, before asking others to do the same. In 1688, the Germantown, Pennsylvania, Quakers issued the first group protest against slavery in America. They said, "What thing in the world can be done worse to us, than if men should rob or steal us away, and sell us for slaves to strange countries." After thus identifying themselves with the slaves, the Quakers asked if Africans did not have "as much right to fight for their freedom, as you have to keep them slaves?"

Many important colonial figures were opposed to slavery. Samuel

Martha Washington views her slave women at the spinning wheel.

Sewall, Roger Williams, James Otis, and John Woolman were among outstanding colonial leaders who denounced human bondage. The first of Thomas Paine's articles to be published in America (March 1775) was a scathing attack on slavery and the African trade. A month later Paine and Benjamin Franklin helped found the first antislavery society in America.

Defending the Colonies

African Americans played an important role in defending frontier settlements. One Virginia slave fired a gun full of nails to disperse an Indian raid on a fort. Another unknown hero barked orders and answered them himself to convince Native Americans that his fort had many men. Although he was the only man present in the fort, his trick worked and they retreated. One night in 1788, slave Dick Pointer "saved the lives of many citizens" at Fort Donnelly, Virginia, by fighting off a surprise attack single-handedly until the garrison awoke and came to his rescue.

The colonial militias often called African Americans into service, and some slaves won their freedom by serving in the army. South Carolina promised freedom to any slave who slew or captured an enemy in battle. So many soon qualified that the offer was changed to ten pounds in cash. In 1747, South Carolina officially thanked its colored militiamen, who "in times of war, behaved themselves with great faithfulness and courage, in repelling the attacks of His Majesty's enemies." While paying them this compliment, the legislature limited the number of Black militiamen to one-third of the total force. This made certain that there would always be more whites than African Americans with guns.*

The Spanish in St. Augustine tried to turn the slaves in the English colonies against their masters. They accepted those who managed to escape to Florida and invited others to leave the English. In 1687 eight men and two women fled their South Carolina plantation for St. Augustine. A dozen years later a Spanish decree promised protection "to all Negro deserters from the English who fled to St. Augustine and became Catholics." Many took up the offer of liberty and Catholicism. An English sea captain was astounded to find his runaway slaves walking the streets of St. Augustine. They made faces and laughed at him.

Cultural Growth in Colonial America

Both slaves and free people of color contributed to the cultural growth of the English colonies. Jupiter Hammon, a Long Island slave, published religious poems. Gustavus Vasa, captured in Nigeria, wrote a moving account of his life in Africa, his capture, and slave life in Virginia. His autobiography sold eight editions in America and England. As a free man, Vasa presented a petition against the slave trade to Parliament.

Gustavus Vasa was brought to America from Africa during Colonial times. After he gained his freedom, he wrote a book telling of his capture and mistreatment.

Several African Americans contributed to the medical and scientific knowledge of the colonies. A South Carolina slave named Cesar developed a series of cures for poisons that were successfully used. He was granted his freedom and an annuity of one hundred pounds for his discoveries.

James Derham, a slave in the post-Revolutionary period, was sold to a New Orleans physician who taught him to prepare drugs and gave him lessons in French and Spanish. When he was twenty-one, Derham became a physician and practiced in New Orleans. Dr. Benjamin Rush, surgeon general of the Continental army, and a signer of the Declaration of Independence, reported on his meeting with Dr. Derham:

> I have conversed with him upon most of the acute and epidemic diseases of the country where he lives, and was pleased to find him perfectly acquainted with

---

* Slaves and free African Americans served in Queen Anne's War (1702–1713), King George's War (1744–1748), and the French and Indian War (1754–1763). They fought and died alongside General Braddock and George Washington in 1755 and took part in the capture of Fort Ticonderoga and Crown Point in 1758. They also served aboard practically every ship in the colonial navy, receiving the same pay, food, and treatment as white sailors.

the modern simple mode of practice in those diseases. I expected to have suggested some new medicines to him; but he suggested many more to me. He is very modest and engaging in his manners.

The colonial period was blessed with men like Thomas Jefferson and Benjamin Franklin, whose capabilities ranged from political affairs to science. Benjamin Banneker, a Maryland free African American, contributed to the fields of science, mathematics, and political affairs. A man of dignified dress and appearance (friends said he looked like Benjamin Franklin), Banneker began his studies as a teenager. Using crude tools, he constructed a clock, the first one made entirely with American parts.

Banneker educated himself with books borrowed from a Quaker neighbor. His interest in scientific matters soon brought him to the attention of Thomas Jefferson, who sent samples of *Banneker's Almanac* to French scientists. Banneker then suggested that Jefferson lend his "aid and assistance" in helping to end slavery if Mr. Jefferson was impressed with his work. Jefferson promised that he would.

For a decade before his death, Banneker authored a popular almanac

Benjamin Banneker, a Maryland free African American. A farmer and scientist, he was chosen by President George Washington to serve on the commission that planned the city of Washington, D.C.

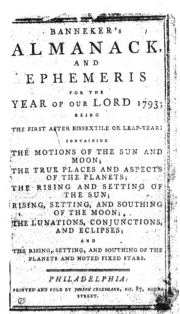

Banneker's Almanac for 1793. For ten years Banneker published an almanac that provided information about the sun, moon, and tides. Thomas Jefferson was so impressed with it that he sent copies to French scientists and wrote to Banneker telling of his high regard for his work. Banneker answered that if African Americans were free, many others could contribute to American life and culture.

that included antislavery essays as well as carefully prepared tables giving information about the tides, moons, crops, and sun. But he is best remembered for the part he played in the commission of three that planned the city of Washington, D.C. Banneker was appointed to the commission upon Jefferson's suggestion to President Washington. With his Quaker friend, George Ellicott, Banneker chose the sites for the White House, the Capitol, and many other important government buildings.

Phillis Wheatley, poet, from a portrait published in her 1773 book of verse. Her work was encouraged by her kind Boston mistress, who finally liberated her.

When the French commission head quit and took the printed plans with him, Banneker and Ellicott were able to reconstruct them from memory. By the time Banneker died, in 1806, Thomas Jefferson was the occupant of the White House in the city that Banneker had helped to plan. Three years before his death, however, the state of Maryland passed a law forbidding free people of color, such as Banneker, from voting in any election.

Phillis Wheatley, kidnapped from Africa at the age of nine, was sold to a kind master in Boston. Her master's wife encouraged the sensitive young lady to develop her poetic talents, and she began writing poems when she was a teenager. Her first book of poems, published in London in 1773, was the second volume of poetry published by a woman in America.

Miss Wheatley's poems drew favorable comments from Voltaire, John Hancock, Benjamin Franklin, and George Washington. When she sent a poem to Washington praising him as commander in chief of the Revolutionary army, he wrote to her and asked her to visit him at his Cambridge headquarters. The slave poet and the general met in 1776, but there is no record of what they said to each other about either poetry or liberty.

LIFE ON BOARD A COLONIAL SLAVE SHIP

[*Gustavus Vasa was only eleven when he was captured in Benin, Africa, and taken by slave ship to Virginia. This is his account of the trip.*]

The first object which saluted my eyes when I arrived on the coast was the sea, and a slaveship, which was then riding at anchor, and waiting for its cargo. These filled me with astonishment, which was soon converted into terror, which I am yet at a loss to describe, nor the then feelings of my mind. When I was carried on board I was immediately handled, and tossed up, to see if I were sound, by some of the crew; and I was now persuaded that I had got into a world of bad spirits, and that they were going to kill me. . . .

I was not long suffered to indulge my grief; I was soon put down under the decks, and there I received such a salutation in my nostrils as I had never experienced in my life; so that, with the loathsomeness of the stench, and crying together, I became so sick and low that I was not able to eat, nor had I the least desire to taste anything . . . but soon, to my grief, two of the white men offered me eatables; and, on my refusing to eat, one of them held me fast by the hands, and laid me across, I think, the windlass, and tied my feet, while the other flogged me severely. . . .

In a little time after, amongst the poor chained men, I found some of my own nation, which in a small degree gave ease to my mind. I inquired of them what was to be done with us? they gave me to understand we were to be carried to these white people's country to work for them. I then was a little revived, and thought, if it were no worse than working, my situation was not so desperate: but still I feared I should be put to death, the white people looked and acted, as I thought, in so savage a manner; for I had never seen among any people such instances of brutal cruelty; and this not only shewn towards us blacks, but also to some of the whites themselves. One white man in particular I saw, when we were permitted to be on deck, flogged so unmercifully with a large rope near the foremast, that he died in consequence of it; and they tossed him over the side as they would have done a brute. This made me fear these people the more; and I expected nothing less than to be treated in the same manner. . . .

The stench of the hold while we were on the coast was so intolerably loathsome, that it was dangerous to remain there for any time, and some of us had been permitted to stay on the deck for the fresh air; but now that the whole ship's cargo were confined together, it became absolutely pestilential. The closeness of the place, and the heat of the climate, added to the number in the ship, which was so crowded that each had scarcely room to turn himself, almost suffocated us. . . ,

The shrieks of the women, and the groans of the dying, rendered the whole a scene of horror almost inconceivable. Happily perhaps for myself I was soon reduced so low here that it was thought necessary to keep me almost always on deck; and from my extreme youth I was not put in fetters. In this situation I expected every hour to share the fate of my companions, some of whom were almost daily brought upon deck at the point of death which I began to hope would soon put an end to my miseries. . . .

One day, when we had a smooth sea, and moderate wind, two of my wearied countrymen, who were chained together (I was near them at the time), preferring death to such a life of misery, somehow made through the nettings, and jumped into the sea; immediately another quite dejected fellow, who, on account of his illness, was suffered to be out of irons, also followed their example; and I believe many more would very soon have done the same, if they had not been prevented by the ship's crew, who were instantly alarmed. Those of us that were the most active were in a moment put down under the deck; and there was such a noise and confusion amongst the people of the ship as I never heard before, to stop her, and get the boat out to go after the slaves. However, two of the wretches were drowned, but they got the other, and afterwards flogged him unmercifully, for thus attempting to prefer death to slavery. In this manner we continued to undergo more hardships than I can now relate; hardships which are inseparable from this accursed trade. . . .

Gustavus Vasa, *The Interesting Narrative of the Life of Olandah Equiano or Gustavus Vasa, Written by Himself* (London, 1793), 46–53.

THE COLONIAL SLAVE CODE

[*A "slave code," designed to establish the rules of human bondage, was promulgated by each colonial legislature beginning in the 1660s. The following portions of these Southern laws indicate the conditions and problems faced by American slaves.*]

[*A Virginia law of 1669.*] . . . if any slave resist his master (or other by his master's order correcting him) and by the extremity of coercion could chance to die, that his death shall not be accounted felony, but the master (or that other person &c.) be acquitted from molestation, since it cannot be presumed that prepensed malice (which alone makes murder a felony) should induce any man to destroy his own estate.

John Codman Hurd, *The Law of Freedom and Bondage,* 1 (New York, 1858), 232.

[*A South Carolina law of 1740.*] Whereas many owners of slaves, and others who have the care, management, and overseeing of slaves, do confine them so closely to hard labor that they have not sufficient time for natural rest, Be it therefore enacted, That if any owner of slaves, or other persons, who shall have the care, management or overseeing of slaves, shall work or put such slave or slaves to labor more than fifteen hours in twenty-four hours . . . every such person shall forfeit a sum not exceeding twenty pounds nor under five pounds current money, for every time he, she, or they shall offend [the law]. . . .

William Goodell, *The American Slave Code* (New York, 1853), 128–29.

THE FIRST WRITTEN ANTISLAVERY PROTESTS

[*The first known antislavery statement was made in February 1688 by Pennsylvania Quakers. Its antislavery arguments left little room for improvement.*]

. . . There is a saying, that we should do to all men like as we will be done ourselves. . . . Here [in America] is liberty of conscience, which is right and reasonable; here ought to be likewise liberty of the body. . . . But to bring men hither, or to rob and sell them against their will, we stand against. . . . Pray, what thing in the world can be done worse towards us, that if men should rob or steal us away, and sell us for slaves to strange countries; separating husbands from their wives and children. . . .

. . . have these poor Negroes not as much right to fight for their freedom, as you have to keep them slaves?

George H. Moore, *Notes on the History of Slavery in Massachusetts* (New York, 1866), 75–77.

[*In 1788 there appeared the first known African American protest against slavery to be published. Its author, "Othello," has left no history.*]

. . . In you [whites] the superiority of power produces nothing but a superiority of brutality and barbarism. Weakness, which calls for protection, appears to provoke your inhumanity. Your fine political systems are sullied by the outrages committed against human nature and the divine majesty.

When America opposed the pretensions of England, she declared that all men have the same rights. After having manifested her hatred against tyrants, ought she to have abandoned her principles? . . .

H. Gregoire, *An Enquiry Concerning the Intellectual and Moral Faculties, and Literature of Negroes,* translated by D. B. Warren (Brooklyn, 1810), 185–86.

SLAVE REVOLT IN COLONIAL SOUTH CAROLINA

[*Periodic revolts were a part of colonial life, particularly in the South where the slave population was most numerous. The following description by a Southern white eyewitness is of a rebellion in Stono, South Carolina, around 1740.*]

. . . A number of Negroes haveing assembled together at Stono, first surprised and killed two young men in a warehouse, and then plundered it of guns and ammunition. Being thus provided with arms, they elected one of their number captain, and agreed to follow him, marching towards the southwest, with colours flying and drums beating, like a disciplined company. . . . *they plundered and burnt every house, killing every white person they found in them, and compelling the Negroes to join them.*

Governor Bull returning to Charleston from the southward, met them, and observing them armed, spread the alarm, which soon reached the Presbyterian Church at Wiltown. . . . By a law of the province, all Planters were obliged to carry their arms to Church, which at this critical juncture proved a very useful and necessary regulation. The women were left in Church trembling with fear, while the militia, under the command of Captain Bee, marched in quest of the Negroes, who by this time had become formidable, from the number [of slaves] that joined them.

They had marched about twelve miles, and *spread desolation through all the plantations in their way.* They halted in an open field, and began to sing and dance, by way of triumph. During these rejoicings, the militia discovered them . . . One party advanced into the open field and attacked them, and, having killed some Negroes, the remainder took to the woods and dispersed. Many ran back to their plantations, in hopes of escaping suspicion from the absence of their masters; *but the greater part were taken and tried.* Such as had been compelled to join them, contrary to their inclination, were pardoned, but all the chosen leaders and first insurgents suffered death.

Cited in Edwin C. Holland (ed.), *A Refutation of the Calumnies Circulated Against the Southern and Western States, Respecting the Institution and Existence of Slavery Among Them* (Charleston, 1822), 70–71.

A SLAVE REPORT IN RHYME ON THE ATTACK ON OLD DEERFIELD, AUGUST 25, 1746

[*Slave Lucy Terry wrote this description of a battle in her Massachusetts village. It is considered to be one of the best accounts of the event.*]

August 'twas the twenty-fifth
Seventeen hundred forty-six
The Indians did in ambush lay
Some very valient men to slay
Twas nigh unto Sam Dickinson's mill,
The Indians there five men did kill
The names of whom I'll not leave out
Samuel Allen like a hero fout
And though he was so brave and bold
His face no more shall we behold

Eleazer Hawks was killed outright
Before he had time to fight
Before he did the Indians see
Was shot and killed immediately
Oliver Amsden he was slain
Which caused his friends much grief and pain
Simeon Amsden they found dead
Not many rods off from his head.
Adonijah Gillet, we do hear
Did lose his life which was so dear
John Saddler fled across the water
And so escaped the dreadful slaughter
Eunice Allen see the Indians comeing
And hoped to save herself by running
And had not her petticoats stopt her
The awful creatures had not cotched her
And tommyhawked her on the head
And left her on the ground for dead.
Young Samuel Allen, Oh! lack-a-day
Was taken and carried to Canada.

George Sheldon, "Negro Slavery in Old Deerfield," *The New England Magazine* 8 (March 1893): 56.

A QUAKER SPEAKS OF SLAVES AND SLAVERY

[*John Bartram was a Quaker farm boy during the eighteenth century who became botanist to the king of England. In the following passage he explains to a visitor why his servants look so well and happy.*]

Though our erroneous prejudices and opinions once induced us to look upon them as fit only for slavery, though ancient custom had very unfortunately taught us to keep them in bondage; yet of late, in consequence of the remonstrances of several Friends, and of the good books they have published on that subject, our society treats them very differently. With us they are now free. I give those, whom thee didst see at my table, eighteen pounds a year, with victuals and clothes, and all other privileges which the white men enjoy. Our society treats them now as the companions of our labours; and, by this management as well as by means of the education we have given them, they are in general become a new set of beings. Those, whom I admit to my table, I have found to be good, trusty, moral, men; when they do not what we think they should do, we dismiss them, which is all the punishment we inflict. Other societies of Christians keep them still as slaves, without teaching them any kind of religious principles. What motive beside fear can they have to behave well? . . . We gave them freedom, and yet few have quitted their ancient masters. The women breed in our families; and we become attached to one another. I taught mine to read and write; they love God, and fear his judgements. The oldest person among them transacts my business in Philadelphia with a punctuality from which he has never deviated. They constantly attend our meetings, they participate in health and sickness, infancy and old age in the advantages our society affords. Such are the means we have made use of to relieve them from that bondage and ignorance in which they were kept before.

J. Hector St. John (Crèvecoeur), Letter 11 of *Letters from an American Farmer* (London, 1782), 262–63.

PHILLIS WHEATLEY'S POEM ON HER OWN SLAVERY

[*Phillis Wheatley seldom mentioned herself in her poetry. But in* Poems on Various Subjects, *published in 1773, a portion of one poem tells about her own life. As a child she was kidnapped in Africa and brought to Boston.*]

To the Right Honourable WILLIAM, Earl of Dartmouth, His Majesty's Principal Secretary of State for North America, and company.

> No more *America* in mournful strain
> Of wrongs, and grievance unredress'd complain,
> No longer shall thou dread the iron chain,
> Which wanton *Tyranny* with lawless hand
> Has made, and which it meant t'enslave the land.
>   Should you, my lord, while you pursue my song,
> Wonder from whence my love of *Freedom* sprung,
> Whence flow these wishes for the common good,
> By feeling hearts alone best understood,

I, young in life, by seeming cruel fate
Was snatch'd from *Afric's* fancy'd happy seat:
What pangs excruciating must molest,
What sorrows labour in my parent's breast?
Steel'd was the soul and by no misery mov'd
That from a father seiz'd his babe belov'd
Such, such my case. And can I then but pray
Others may never feel tyrannic sway?

Phillis Wheatley, *Poems on Various Subjects* (London, 1773), 74.

A Slave Is Invited to Visit General Washington

[*In the first year of American independence, General George Washington wrote this letter to the slave-poet, Phillis Wheatley, thanking her for the poem which she had written about him. The two met shortly thereafter, at Washington's Cambridge, Massachusetts, headquarters.*]

Miss. Phillis: Your favour of the 26th of October did not reach my hands 'till the middle of December. Time enough, you will say, to have given an answer ere this. Granted. . . .

I thank you most sincerely for your polite notice of me, in the elegant lines you enclosed; and however undeserving I may be of such encomium and panegyrick, the style and manner exhibit a striking proof of your great poetical Talents. In honour of which, and in a tribute justly due you, I would have published the Poem, had I not been apprehensive, that, while I only meant to give the World this new instance of your genius, I might have incurred the imputation of Vanity. This and nothing else, determined me not to give it place in the public prints.

If you should ever come to Cambridge, or near Head Quarters, I shall be happy to see a person so favoured by the Muses, and to whom Nature has been so liberal and beneficent in her dispensations. I am, with great Respect, etc.

Letter of February 28, 1776, in John C. Fitzpatrick, ed., *The Writings of George Washington from the Original Manuscript Sources 1754–1799,* 4 (Washington, 1938): 360–61.

GEORGE WASHINGTON'S POSITION ON SLAVERY

[This 1786 letter written by George Washington to Robert Morris reveals the difficulties faced by a slaveholder—even one with good will and humanitarian beliefs. It also contains history's first mention of the Underground Railroad.]

Dear Sir: I give you the trouble of this letter at the instance of Mr. Dalby of Alexandria; who is called to Philadelphia to attend what he conceives to be a vexatious lawsuit respecting a slave of his, whom a Society of Quakers in the city (formed for such purposes) have attempted to liberate. . . . And if the practice of this Society of which Mr. Dalby speaks, is not discountenanced, none of those whose *misfortune* it is to have slaves as attendants, will visit the City if they can possibly avoid it; because by so doing they hazard their property; or they must be at the expence (and this will not always succeed) of providing servants of another description for the trip.

I hope it will not be conceived from these observations, that it is my wish to hold the unhappy people, who are the subject of this letter, in slavery. I can only say that there is not a man living who wishes more sincerely than I do, to see a plan adopted for the abolition of it; but there is only one proper and effectual mode by which it can be accomplished and that is by Legislative authority; and this, as far as my suffrage will go, shall never be wanting. But when slaves who are happy and contented with their present masters, are tampered with and seduced to leave; when a conduct of this sort begets discontent on one side and resentment on the other, and when it happens to fall on a man, whose purse will not measure with that of the Society, and he looses [sic] his property for want of means to defend it; it is oppression in the latter case, and not humanity in any, because it introduces more evils than it can cure.

John C. Fitzpatrick, ed., *The Writings of George Washington from the Original Manuscript Sources 1754–1799*, 28 (Washington, 1938): 407–408.

THE EPITAPH OF A PROUD MAN

[A Concord, Massachusetts, man who died in colonial times had this epitaph carved on his gravestone.]

GOD
Wills us free;
Man
Wills us slaves,

I will as God wills,
God's will be done.

Here lies the body of JOHN JACK,
A native of Africa, who died March, 1773,
Aged about *sixty years.*

Tho' *born* in a land of *slavery,*
He was born *free;*
Tho' he lived in a land of *liberty,*
He lived a *slave. . . .*

Tho' not long before
Death, the grand Tyrant,
Gave him his final emancipation,
And set him on a footing with kings. . . .

AMERICA'S FIRST AFRICAN AMERICAN MASON
DISCUSSES DISCRIMINATION

[*Prince Hall devoted his life to making America a better place in which to live. After his enlistment petition went to John Hancock and George Washington, he was accepted in the Revolutionary army. As a Boston landowner and voter, he demanded that his state free and educate its slaves. He soon established a school in his own home. In 1797, he addressed America's first Black social order on the discrimination which they faced and on how they should respond.*]

. . . Patience I say, for were we not possessed of a great measure of it you could not bear up under the daily insults you meet with in the streets of Boston; much more on public days of recreation, how are you shamefully abus'd, and that at such a degree, that you may be truly said to carry your lives in your hands . . . [since many have been attacked] by a mob of shameless, low-lived, envious, spiteful persons, some of them not long since, servants in gentlemen's kitchens. . . .

My brethren, let us not be cast down under these and many abuses we at present labour under: for the darkest is before the break of day. . . .

Although you are deprived of the means of education; yet you are not deprived of the means of meditation. . . .

Live and act as Masons, that you may die as Masons; let those despisers see, altho' many of us cannot read, yet by our searches and researches into men and things, we have supplied that defect . . . [and] give the right hand of affection and fellowship to whom it justly belongs [and] let their colour and complexion be what it will: their nation be what it may, for they are your brethren.

Prince Hall, *A Charge Delivered to the African Lodge,* 24 June 1797, 10–13.

3 BUILDING OF A NATION

AT THE END OF THE FRENCH AND INDIAN WAR, the British increased the taxes on the thirteen colonies and sent officials and soldiers to collect these taxes. Boston became a center of resistance to both the taxes and the British soldiers. Irritation grew on both sides.

Colonists burn British stamps and stamp paper.

The Revolution

On the snowy winter night of March 5, 1770, the inevitable happened. A group of Boston patriots met a company of British soldiers, but this time the usual name-calling, scuffling, and throwing of snowballs ended in bloodshed.

The leader of the crowd of Boston men and boys was Crispus Attucks, a tall runaway slave who had become a seaman. When Attucks waved his cordwood club and urged the crowd forward, someone gave the order to fire, and the British muskets cut down Attucks and four other Bostonians. Unlike Attucks, whose death made him the first martyr to American independence, another African American named Andrew fled into a doorway as bullets flew that fateful evening. Andrew lived to tell a court exactly what happened.

This "Boston Massacre" was the first battle of the American Revolution.

The Boston Massacre. British troops fire on a Boston mob led by runaway slave Crispus Attucks. A monument to Attucks and the four other American martyrs now stands in Boston.

Lemuel Haynes. A minuteman who fought at Concord Bridge. He later became minister to a white New England congregation.

Before the War for Independence ended at Yorktown, eight thousand more African Americans would fight to help build the new nation.

As the British and colonial forces moved toward full-scale war, "minutemen" drilled everywhere. When the British advanced on Lexington and Concord, Lemuel Haynes was among those who answered Paul Revere's and William Dawes's call to arms. Haynes was only one of the several African American minutemen who, at Concord Bridge on April 19, 1775, fired some of those shots "heard round the world."

A few weeks later Haynes, Primas Black, and Epheram Blackman had joined Ethan Allen and his Green Mountain Boys in the capture of Fort Ticonderoga.

In the next battle of the war, Bunker Hill, African Americans and whites, whose ammunition included nails and scraps of iron as well as musket balls, cut down advancing forces of the British army twice and retreated only when all the ammunition was gone. When the British commander, Major Pitcairn, appeared suddenly in front of the colonial lines and called on the rebels to surrender, "his commanding air at first startled the men immediately before him. They neither answered nor fired." Except for one man. "At this critical moment, a Negro soldier [Peter Salem] stepped forward, and aiming his musket directly at the major's bosom, blew him through."

Another patriot, Salem Poor, was singled out for special commendation by Colonel William Prescott, the colonial field commander in the battle. Prescott (who early in the battle had shouted the immortal words, "Don't fire until you see the whites of their eyes!") now, with thirteen other officers, commended "a Negro man named Salem Poor," who "behaved like an experienced officer, as well as an excellent soldier."

A Hessian soldier wrote, "No regiment is to be seen in which there are not Negroes in abundance and among them are able-bodied, strong, and brave fellows." They served with Francis Marion, the Swamp Fox, in the Carolinas, and in the United States Navy with John Paul Jones. At fourteen, James Forten sailed with Stephen Decatur aboard the *Royal Louis* as a powderboy. When he was captured and offered a chance to go to Eng-

At the Battle of Bunker Hill, Peter Salem (left) kills Major Pitcairn (center).

land, the boy answered "I AM HERE A PRISONER FOR THE LIBERTIES OF MY COUNTRY. I *NEVER, NEVER, SHALL PROVE A TRAITOR TO HER INTERESTS.*"

Other African Americans served as spies and won praise and, sometimes, their liberty for repeatedly going behind enemy lines to obtain military information. James Armistead was a spy for General Lafayette and was granted his freedom at the Frenchman's request. Black soldiers froze in Washington's army at Valley Forge. In the boats crossing the Delaware with their commander were Prince Whipple, an African slave, and Oliver Cromwell, a New Jersey freeman. On that Christmas night of 1776, they took part in the surprise attack and capture of the British garrison of Hessians at Trenton, New Jersey.

African Americans served in the Revolutionary army and navy in spite of attempts by some Americans to keep them out. Slaveholders in the Continental Congress had George Washington halt enlistments of Blacks. But steps taken by the British soon led to a change in this policy. The British governor of Virginia, Lord Dunmore, offered freedom to any slaves reaching his lines. Many made the attempt. The Continental army decided to accept African Americans rather than see them used by the enemy. Northern colonies formed special Black regiments, and a white soldier named Harris witnessed a battle in which they took part:

James Armistead. This slave repeatedly entered British lines to spy for General Lafayette. In 1786, the Virginia legislature granted him his freedom because he had aided the American cause "at the peril of his life."

> Had they been unfaithful, or given way before the enemy all would have been lost. *Three times in succession* they were attacked, with most desperate valor and fury, by well disciplined and veteran [British] troops, and *three times* did they successfully repel the assault, and thus preserve our army from capture. They fought through the war. They were brave, hardy troops. They helped gain our liberty and independence.

African Americans marched in every patriot army.

In 1779, when the scene of warfare shifted from the North to the South, Virginians began to accept free people of color and even slaves into the patriot army. These soldiers became part of regular combat units, where they ate and fought alongside white soldiers. Many served on the sea, some as ship pilots. Caesar Tarrant served four years as pilot of the *Patriot* and the ship captured a British vessel while under his command. Others served aboard the *Liberty* during its twenty battles with the enemy.

Saul Matthews, a Black Virginian, entered a British garrison in 1781 on a spy mission. He not only brought back valuable information for his fellow Americans but led a raid on the British troops that same night. His amazing courage was highly praised by Baron Von Steuben, Lafayette, and General Nathaniel Greene.

Many of the slaves enlisted when they were promised their freedom. But the slaves who had fled to Lord Dunmore were often betrayed and were sent, still slaves, to the West Indies. Some American slaveholders also refused to keep their word. But others did, and many a former slave soldier enjoyed some of the freedoms he helped to establish.

The role which people of African descent from other lands played in the American Revolution is comparatively unknown. Yet like Lafayette, Von Steuben, Pulaski, and Kosciusko, the Fontages Legion from Haiti served gallantly with the Continental army. At the battle of Savannah on October 9, 1779, more than five hundred of these Haitian freemen held back a fierce British attack that might well have wiped out the French and American armies. One of those wounded in the battle was Sergeant Henri Christophe. He returned to his country and later became second in command to Haiti's "George Washington," Toussaint L'Ouverture. After L'Ouverture's death, Henri Christophe became emperor of Haiti.

Two months after the ringing words of the Declaration of Independence had sounded in the colonies, the Massachusetts legislature issued a proclamation calling slavery "utterly inconsistent with the . . . struggle for liberty." Before America's first year of independence drew to a close, several Massachusetts towns voted to end slavery. For the first time in the history of the human race, governments voted to end human bondage. It was an important beginning.

The Critical Period Leads to the Constitution

In the years that followed the Revolution, the poor who had fought in the struggle for independence sought a greater measure of the liberty that they had helped to win. It was an era of turbulence, marked by the revolt of debtor farmers in western Massachusetts, led by a Revolutionary hero,

Daniel Shays. Among Shays's men, indicted a year later, was Moses Sash, a five-foot-eight Black soldier of the Revolution, the only man of the group to be indicted twice. Sash was charged as "a Captain" and a member of Shays's "Councill," and his indictment read:

> . . . that Moses Sash of Worthington . . . a Negro man and labourer being a disorderly, riotous & seditious person [did] . . . promote, incite, & maintain riots, mobs, tumults, [and] insurrections in this Commonwealth . . . to disturb, impede, & prevent the Government . . . and to prevent the Courts of justice from sitting as by Law [and] . . . did procure guns, bayonets, pistols, swords, gunpowder, bullets, blankets, & provisions & other warlike supplies.

When John Hancock was elected governor of Massachusetts, he pardoned Shays, Sash, and the other revolt leaders.

While the Confederation Congress lacked the power to suppress Shays's rebellion, it did establish a democratic government for the states being formed out of the Northwest territory. It also forbade slavery there in its famous Northwest Ordinance, issued in 1787. In that same year, American leaders in Philadelphia met to draw up a new Constitution. What would they do about slavery?

The Founding Fathers had opposed slavery and the slave trade. "Among my first wishes," Washington had written, "is to see some plan adopted by which slavery in this country may be abolished." Jefferson had predicted that "nothing is more certainly written in the Book of Fate, than that this people shall be free." Patrick Henry said about slavery: "I will not, I cannot justify it." Benjamin Franklin became a leader of Pennsylvania's Society for Promoting the Abolition of Slavery, and Alexander Hamilton became a founder and leader of the New York Manumission Society.

The men who met at Philadelphia to write a new Constitution, however, came to build a strong and united country, not to solve the slavery question. To keep the loyalty of the slaveholders and slave traders in the North and South, they agreed to protect slave property in three separate sections of the Constitution:

1. They gave the African slave trade twenty more years in which to cease operations.
2. They provided that all runaway slaves had to be returned to their owners.
3. Because slaveholders were to be taxed for their slaves, as property, they were allowed three votes for every five slaves owned.

In spite of this bargain with those who traded in men, women, and children, most of the delegates left the convention convinced that slavery was dying. They thought the Northwest Ordinance proved that Congress had the power to halt slavery's growth forever. They reasoned that the end of the slave trade in twenty years would dry up the source of the evil. And they knew that several states had already ended human bondage and that others had banned the slave trade. They felt sure that their compromises were a temporary arrangement, at worst.

Certainly they could not foresee the invention of the cotton gin which took place just six years later. The fifty-five men at Philadelphia could not realize that slaveholders, made wealthy and greedy by profits from cotton, would use these compromises to shield slavery and protect its growth. The practical result of these compromises was that slave merchants continued to import Africans, ignored the Constitution, and violated all legal attempts to halt the trade.

Richard Allen, African American civic and religious leader. During the War of 1812, Allen and Jones, at that time leaders of America's first Black church, raised a force of 2,500 men to protect Philadelphia from the British. Shortly before his death in 1831, Allen wrote, "This land, which we have watered with our tears and our blood, is now our mother country."

The United States Constitution provided for an end to slave trading after 1807. But the Southern planters always needed more laborers, and the traders were unwilling to give up their profitable business. Although slave trading was considered piracy after 1808, it continued until the Civil War. The death penalty was not carried out against any slave trader until 1862, when Nathaniel Gordon was found guilty of the crime and hanged.

Black and white U.S. seamen being led off the *Chesapeake*.

The War of 1812

On a June morning in 1807, the British man-of-war *Leopard,* a few miles outside of Norfolk harbor, fired upon the United States Navy's *Chesapeake,* killing three and wounding eighteen men. British officers speedily boarded the *Chesapeake* and seized four men, whom they charged with desertion from the Royal Navy. One *was* a deserter and he was promptly executed. But Daniel Martin, William Ware, and John Strachan, all African American seamen, were able to prove they were Americans and were finally freed. The attack on the *Chesapeake* and the attempt to seize its sailors became the best-known instance of thousands of such foreign seizures of American seamen.

By the War of 1812, at least one of every six members of the United States Navy was an African American. In the war they fought on privateers as well as ships of the line. They won praise from both Captain Perry, who at first had doubted their ability, and Commodore Chauncey, who never had. When Perry objected to the Black sailors that Chauncey sent him, the commodore answered that they "are not surpassed by any seamen we have in the fleet and I have yet to learn that the color of the skin or the cut and trimming of the coat can affect a man's qualifications or usefulness. I have nearly fifty blacks on board of this ship, and many of them are among the best men." After his triumph at Lake Erie, Perry admitted that his African American sailors were among the bravest men on his ship.

The Battle of New Orleans

When Andrew Jackson heard that a large British force was moving toward New Orleans, he made a special appeal for help to the city's free African Americans. Four hundred volunteered to fight when Jackson promised them equality of treatment and pay. One battalion was made up of merchants, craftsmen, and laborers and the other of refugees from Santo Domingo. Slaves from nearby plantations volunteered to help build the American defenses.

At 7:00 A.M. on January 8, 1815, General Edward Pakenham led his British troops forward toward the American lines. Facing Pakenham's trained soldiers were the two African American battalions, a group of New Orleans business and professional men called "Beale's Famous Rifles"—Mississippi riflemen who were unshaven, had long hair, and carried knives and tomahawks—Jean Lafitte's pirates rounded up from his hideout and from the New Orleans jail, regular army troops, Choctaw Indians in full war paint, and Kentucky draftees in ragged clothes and carrying old muskets. A sharp two-hour battle began in a heavy fog. Although outnumbered two to one, Jackson's "integrated" army killed and wounded more than 1,500 of Pakenham's men and lost only a handful of their own. Never again would a foreign army attempt to invade the United States.

Emperor Napoleon of France was so astounded by the American victory that he wrote for information about it. Andrew Jackson wrote this description of the death of Pakenham: "I have always believed he fell from the bullet of a free man of color, who was a famous rifle-shot. . . ."

When an army paymaster held up pay for the Indians and African Americans, Jackson told him to pay all "without inquiring whether the troops are white, black, or tea." Jackson's order was quickly obeyed.

All New Orleans turned out to honor Jackson and his troops after their glorious victory. Loud cheers greeted the free men of color and Jordan B. Noble, their young drummer boy. But for many years afterward the Black veterans were not permitted to march in the annual celebration. Slaveholders had become fearful of Black heroes. In 1862, with New Orleans under the control of the Union army, Noble the drummer boy marched again—at the head of a victorious Union army.

CRISPUS ATTUCKS AND THE BOSTON MASSACRE OF 1770

[*When Crispus Attucks, leading a crowd of Boston patriots against British soldiers, was shot down, he became one of the first martyrs to American independence. This eyewitness description of the event, given at the trial of the British soldiers, is by a slave named Andrew.*]

Andrew (Mr. Oliver Wendell's Negro)—sworn

On the evening of the 5th of March I was at home, I heard the bells ring, and went to the gate, and saw one of my acquaintances, and we run down to the end of the lane and saw another acquaintance coming up, holding his arm; I asked him what's the matter, he said the soldiers were fighting, had got cutlasses, and were killing everybody, and that one of them had struck him on the arm, and almost cut it off: He told me I had best not go down; I said a good club was better than a cutlass. . . . I went to the Town House, saw the Sentinels placed at the main guard standing by Mr. Bowe's corner; numbers of boys on the other side of the way were throwing snow balls at them; the Sentinels were enraged and swearing at the boys: the boys called them lobsters, bloody backs, and hallooed who buys lobsters. . . .

I turned about and saw the officer standing before the men, and one or two persons engaged in talk with him. A number were jumping on the backs of those that were talking with the officer, to get as near as they could. Upon this I went as close to the officer as I could; one of the persons who was talking with the officer turned about quick to the people, and said, Damn him, he is going to fire; upon that they gave a shout, and cried out, fire and be Damn'd, who cares for you, you dare not fire, and began to throw snow balls and other things which then flew very thick.

Q. Did they hit any of them?

A. Yes, I saw two or three of them hit, one struck a grenadier on the hat, and the people who were right before them had sticks; and as the soldiers were pushing with their guns back and forth, they struck their guns, and one hit a grenadier on the fingers. At this time, the people up at the Town House called again, come away, come away. . . . The people seemed to be leaving the soldiers, and to turn from them, when there came down a number from Jackson's Corner, huzzaing and crying, damn them, they dare not fire, we are not afraid of them; one of these people, a stout [heavyset] man with a long cordwood stick, threw himself in, and made a blow at the officer; I saw the officer try to ward off the stroke, whether he struck him or not I do not know; the stout man then turned round, and struck the grenadier's gun at the captain's right hand, and immediately fell in with his club, and knocked his gun away, and struck him over the head, the blow came either on the soldier's cheek or hat. This stout man held the bayonet with his left hand, and twitched it and cried kill the dogs, knock them over; this was the general cry; the people then crowded in, and upon that the grenadier gave a twitch back and relieved his gun, and he up with it and began to pay away on the people. I was then betwixt the officer and this grenadier, I turned to go off, when I heard the word fire; at the word fire I thought I heard the report of a gun, and upon my hearing the report, I saw the same grenadier swing his gun, and immediately he discharged it.

Q. Do you know who this stout man was, that fell in and struck the grenadier?

A. I thought and still think, it was the Mulatto who was shot.

Q. Do you know the grenadier who was thus assaulted and fired?

A. I then thought it was Killroy, and I told Mr. Quincy so the next morning after the affair happened, I now think it was he from my best observation but I can't positively swear it.

Q. Did the soldiers of that party, or any of them, step or move out of the rank in which they stood to push the people?

A. No, and if they had they might have killed me and many others with their bayonets.

Q. Did you, as you passed through the people towards Royal-Exchange lane and the party, see a number of people take up any and every thing they could find in the street, and throw them at the soldiers?

A. Yes, I saw ten or fifteen round me do it.

Q. Did you yourself pick up everything you could find and throw at them?

A. Yes, I did.

Q. After the gun fired, where did you go?

A. I run as fast as I could into the first door I saw open, which I think was Mr. Dehon's, I was very much frightened.

The Trial of the British Soldiers of the 29th Regiment of Foot for the Murder of Crispus Attucks, Samuel Gray, Samuel Maverick, James Caldwell, and Patrick Carr on Monday Evening, March 5, 1770 (Boston, 1824), 71–73.

CONGRESSMAN EUSTIS DESCRIBES AFRICAN AMERICAN SOLDIERS

[*Congressman William Eustis, who served throughout the Revolution as an army surgeon, and later became governor of Massachusetts, indicates why many in the North favored ending slavery.*]

At the commencement of the Revolutionary War, there were found in the Middle and Northern States, many blacks, and other people of color, capable of bearing arms; a part of them free, the greater part slaves. The freemen entered our ranks with the whites. The time of those who were slaves was purchased by the States; and they were induced to enter the service in consequence of a law, by which, on condition of their serving in the ranks during the war, they were made freemen. In Rhode Island, where their numbers were more considerable, they were formed, under the same considerations, into a regiment commanded by white officers; and it is required, in justice to them, to add, that they discharged their duty with zeal and fidelity. The gallant defence of Red Bank, in which this black regiment bore a part, is among the proofs of their valor.

Among the traits which distinguished this regiment was their devotion to their officers: when their brave Col. Greene was afterwards cut down and mortally wounded, the sabres of the enemy reached his body only through the limbs of his faithful guard of blacks, who hovered over him and protected him, every one of whom was killed, and whom he was not ashamed to call his children. . . .

The war over, and peace restored, these men returned to their respective states; and who could have said to them, on their return to civil life, after having shed their blood in common with the whites in the defense of the liberties of the country: "You are not to participate in the rights secured by the struggle, or in the liberty for which you have been fighting"? Certainly no white man in Massachusetts.

George Livermore, *An Historical Research Respecting the Opinions of the Founders of the Republic on Negroes as Slaves, as Citizens and as Soldiers, Annals of Congress,* 16th Cong., 2nd sess. (Boston, 1862), 154.

AFRICAN AMERICANS IN PHILADELPHIA STAGE A "KNEEL-IN"

[*The Right Reverend Richard Allen tells of the incidents leading up to the establishment of the African Methodist Episcopal Church of Philadelphia.*]

A number of us usually attended St. George's Church in Fourth street; and when the colored people began to get numerous in attending the church, they moved us from the seats we usually sat on, and placed us around the wall, and on Sabbath morning we went to church and the sexton stood at the door, and told us to go in the gallery. He told us to go, and we would see where to sit. We expected to take the seats over the ones we formerly occupied below, not knowing any better. We took those seats. Meeting had begun, and they were nearly done singing, and just as we got to the seats, the elder said, "Let us pray." We had not been long upon our knees before I heard considerable scuffling and low talking. I raised my head up and saw one of the trustees, H——— M———, having hold of the Rev. Absalom Jones, pulling him up off of his knees, and saying, "You must get up—you must not kneel here." Mr. Jones replied, "Wait until prayer is over." Mr. H——— M——— said, "No, you must get up now, or I will call for aid and force you away." Mr. Jones said, "Wait until prayer is over, and I will get up and trouble you no more." With that he [Mr. H——— M———] beckoned to one of the other trustees, Mr. L——— S——— to come to his assistance. He came, and went to William White to pull him up. By this time prayer was over, and we all went out of the church in a body, and they were no more plagued with us in the church.

Richard Allen, *The Life, Experience and Gospel Labors of the Rt. Rev. Richard Allen, Written by Himself* (Philadelphia, 1887), 14–15.

HALTING THE YELLOW FEVER EPIDEMIC IN PHILADELPHIA

[*In 1793 Philadelphia was swept by a yellow fever epidemic that drove President Washington and other government officials from the city. African American leaders Absalom Jones and Richard Allen offered the aid of the city's Black community. This is their account of the epidemic.*]

In order the better to regulate our conduct, we called on the mayor next day, to consult with him how to proceed, so as to be most useful. The first object he recommended was a strict attention to the sick, and the procuring of nurses. This was attended to by Absalom Jones and William Gray. . . . Soon after, the mortality increasing, the difficulty of getting a corpse taken away, was such, that few were willing to do it, [even] when offered great rewards. The black people were looked to. We then offered our services in the public papers, by advertising that we would remove the dead and procure nurses. Our services were the production of real sensibility;—we sought not fee nor reward. . . . It was very uncommon, at this time, to find any one that would go near, much more, handle, a sick or dead person.

. . . Here it ought to be remarked . . . that two thirds of the persons who rendered these essential services, were people of colour. . . . May the Lord reward them, both temporally and spiritually.

When the sickness became general, and several of the physicians died, and most of the survivors were exhausted by sickness or fatigue; that good man, Doctor Rush, called us more immediately to attend upon the sick . . . and accordingly directed us where to procure medicine duly prepared, with proper directions how to administer them, and at what stages of the disorder to bleed. . . . This has been no small satisfaction to us; for, we think, that when a physician was not attainable, we have been the instruments in the hand of God, for saving the lives of some hundreds of our suffering fellow mortals.

A. J. and R. A. [Absalom Jones and Richard Allen], *A Narrative of the Proceedings of the Black People During the Late Awful Calamity in Philadelphia, in the Year 1793* (Philadelphia: William W. Woodward, 1794), 4–5.

[*Dr. Benjamin Rush, America's most noted medical man of the time, describes his work during the epidemic.*]

Dear Sir. . . . The only information which I am capable of giving you relates to the conduct of the Africans of our city. In procuring nurses for the sick, Wm. Grey and Absalom Jones were indefatigable, often sacrificing for that purpose whole nights of sleep without the least compensation. Richard Allen was extremely useful in performing the mournful duties, which were connected with burying the dead. Many of the black nurses, it is true, were ignorant, and some of them were negligent, but many of them did their duty to the sick with a degree of patience and tenderness that did them great credit.

During the indisposition and confinement of the greatest part of the Physicians of the City, Richard Allen and Absalom Jones procured copies of the printed directions for curing the fever—went among the poor who were sick—gave them the mercurial purges—bled them freely, and by these means, they this day informed me, they had recovered between two and three hundred people.

I am the more pleased with the above communication as it sheweth the safety and simplicity of the mode of treating the disease, which they politely said was generally successful. . . .

The Amazing Benjamin Banneker

[*Benjamin Banneker was a respected mathematician and scientist whose work came to the attention of Thomas Jefferson and, through Jefferson, to the Marquis de Condorcet of the French Academy of Science. In 1790, Banneker was chosen to serve on the commission of three that planned the federal city at Washington, D.C. Mrs. Martha Ellicott Tyson, a friend of Banneker's, tells of the commission's work.*]

After the adoption of the Constitution of the United States, the States of Maryland and Virginia ceded a portion of their territory to constitute a seat for the metropolis of the country. . . . The survey [of the area] subsequently, in the year 1790, devolved upon Major Andrew Ellicott, of Ellicott's Upper Mills.

Major Ellicott selected Benjamin Banneker as his assistant upon this occasion, and it was with his aid that the lines of the Federal Territory, as the District of Columbia was then called, were run.

It was the work, also, of Major Ellicott, under the orders of General Washington, then President of the United States, to locate the sites of the Capitol, [the] President's house, [the] Treasury, and other public buildings. In this, also, Banneker was his assistant.

"Banneker, the Afric-American Astronomer," in *The Posthumous Papers of Martha E. Tyson,* edited by her daughter (Philadelphia, 1884), 36–37.

[*In 1791 Banneker sent a handwritten copy of an almanac he was about to publish to Thomas Jefferson, then secretary of state. Here is Jefferson's letter in reply.*]

Philadelphia, Aug. 30, 1791

Sir,—I thank you sincerely for your letter of the 19th instant and for the Almanac it contained. No body wishes more than I do to see such proofs as you exhibit, that nature has given to our black brethren, talents equal to those of the other colors of men, and that the appearance of a want of them is owing merely to the degraded condition of their existence, both in Africa & America. I can add with truth, that no body wishes more ardently to see a good system commenced for raising the condition both of their body & mind to what it ought to be, as fast as the imbecility of their present existence, and other circumstances which cannot be neglected, will admit. I have taken the liberty of sending your Almanac to Monsieur de Condorcet, Secretary of the Academy of Sciences at Paris, and member of the Philanthropic society, because I considered it as a document to which your whole colour had a right for their justification against the doubts which have been entertained of them. I am with great esteem, Sir Your most obed[t] humble serv[t].

[On that same day, Jefferson sent Banneker's almanac to the head of France's Academy of Science with the letter that follows.]

Philadelphia. Aug. 30, 1791

To the Marquis de Condorcet

Dear Sir, . . . I am happy to be able to inform you that we have now in the United States a Negro, the son of a black man born in Africa, and of a black woman born in the United States, who is a very respectable mathematician. I procured him to be employed under one of our chief directors in laying out the new federal city on the Potowmac, & in the intervals of his leisure, while on that work, he made an Almanac for the next year, which he sent me in his own hand writing, & which I inclose to you. I have seen very elegant solutions of Geometrical problems by him. Add to this that he is a very worthy & respectable member of society. He is a free man. I shall be delighted to see these instances of moral eminence so multiplied as to prove that the want of talents observed in them is merely the effect of their degraded condition, and not proceeding from any difference in the structure of the parts on which intellect depends. . . .

Present my affectionate respects to Madame de Condorcet, and accept yourself assurances of the sentiments of esteem & attachment which I have the honour to be Dear Sir your most obed[t] & most humble serv[t].

Paul Leicester Ford, *The Writings of Thomas Jefferson*, 5 (New York and London: G. P. Putnam's Sons, 1895): 377–78, 378–79.

ANDREW JACKSON APPEALS TO BLACK NEW ORLEANS

[As British forces approached New Orleans in the last days of the War of 1812, Andrew Jackson issued this appeal for help on September 21, 1814.]

PROCLAMATION
To the free colored inhabitants of Louisiana.

Through a mistaken policy you have heretofore been deprived of a participation in the glorious struggle for national rights in which our country is engaged. This no longer shall exist.

As sons of freedom, you are now called upon to defend our most inestimable blessing. As Americans, your country looks with confidence to her adopted children, for a valorous support, as a faithful return for the advantages enjoyed under her mild and equitable government. As fathers, husbands, and brothers, you are summoned to rally round the standard of the Eagle, to defend all which is dear in existence.

Your country, although calling for your exertions, does not wish you to engage in her cause, without amply remunerating you for the services rendered. Your intelligent minds are not to be led away by false representations.—Your love of honor would cause you to despise the man who should attempt to deceive you. In the sincerity of a soldier, and the language of truth I address you.

To every noble hearted, generous, freeman of color, volunteering to serve during the present contest with Great Britain, and no longer, there will be paid the same bounty in money and lands, now received by the white soldiers of the U. States, viz. one hundred and twenty-four dollars in money, and one hundred and sixty acres of land. The non-commissioned officers and privates will also be entitled to the same monthly pay and daily rations, and clothes furnished to any American soldier.

On enrolling yourselves in companies, the major-general commanding will select officers for your government, from your white fellow citizens. Your non-commissioned officers will be appointed from among yourselves.

Due regard will be paid to the feelings of freemen and soldiers. You will not, by being associated with white men in the same corps, be exposed to improper comparisons or unjust sarcasm. As a distinct, independent battalion or regiment, pursuing the path of glory, you will, undivided, receive the applause and gratitude of your countrymen.

To assure you of the sincerity of my intentions and my anxiety to engage your invaluable services to our country, I have communicated my wishes to the governor of Louisiana, who is fully informed as to the manner of enrolment, and will give you every necessary information on the subject of this address.

> *Head quarters*, 7th military district,
> Mobile, Sept. 21st 1814
> *Andrew Jackson*,
> Maj-gen, commanding

Niles' Weekly Register 7, (3 December 1814): 205.

[*As the British prepared for their final attack on New Orleans, General Jackson reviewed the six thousand troops under his command. Of this force, about five hundred were African Americans in two battalions. After the review, Jackson read the address that follows:*]

TO THE MEN OF COLOR

Soldiers—. . . you surpass my hopes. I have found in you, united to those qualities, that noble enthusiasm which impels to great deeds.

Soldiers—The President of the United States shall be informed of your conduct on the present occasion, and the voice of the representatives of the American nation shall applaud your valor, as your general now praises your ardor. The enemy is near; his "sails cover the lakes;" but the brave are united; and if he finds us contending among ourselves, it will be for the prize of valor and fame its noblest reward.

By command, *Thomas L. Butler,* Aid-de-camp.

Niles' Weekly Register 7 (28 January 1815): 346.

GENERAL ANDREW JACKSON DESCRIBES THE BATTLE OF NEW ORLEANS

[*In a letter written to Napoleon Bonaparte, Jackson gave this firsthand description of his famous victory at New Orleans.*]

The battle commenced at a very little before 7 A.M., January 8, 1815, and as far as the infantry was concerned it was over by 9 A.M. My force was very much mixed. I had portions of the Seventh and Forty-fourth regular infantry regiments, Kentucky and Tennessee riflemen, creoles, United States marines and sailors, Baratarian men [Lafitte's Pirates] . . . and two battalions of free Negroes. . . . The British strength was almost the same as mine, but vastly superior in drill and discipline. Of their force my riflemen killed and wounded 2117 in less than an hour, including two general officers (both died on the field, each a division commander), seven full colonels, with seventy-five line and staff officers. I lost 6 killed and 7 wounded. . . .

There was a very heavy fog on the river that morning, and the British had formed and were moving before I knew it. . . .

. . . "God help us!" I muttered, watching the rapidly advancing line. Seventy, sixty, fifty, finally forty yards, were they from the silent kneeling riflemen. All of my men I could see was their long rifles rested on the logs before them. . . . not a shot was fired until the redcoats were within forty yards. I heard Coffee's voice as he roared out: "Now, men, aim for the center of the crossbelts: Fire!" . . . in a few seconds after the first fire there came another sharp, ringing volley. . . . The British were falling back in a confused, disorderly mass, and the entire first ranks of their column were blown away. For two hundred yards in our front the ground was covered with a mass of writhing wounded, dead, and dying redcoats. By the time the rifles were wiped the British line was reformed, and on it came again. This time they were led by General Pakenham in person, gallantly mounted, and riding as though he was on parade. . . . I heard a single rifle-shot from a group of country carts we had been using, about one hundred and seventy-five yards distant, and a moment thereafter I saw Pakenham reel and pitch out of his saddle. I have always believed he fell from the bullet of a free man of color, who was a famous rifle-shot, and came from the Atakappas region of Louisiana [probably Major Savory of the Santo Domingo battalion]. . . .

They sent a flag to me, asking leave to gather up their wounded and bury their dead, which, of course, I granted. I was told by a wounded officer that the rank and file absolutely refused to make a third charge. "We have no chance with such shooting as these Americans do," they said.

William Hugh Robarts, "Napoleon's Interest in the Battle of New Orleans," *Century Magazine* 53 (January 1897): 360–61.

SERVING AT SEA IN THE WAR OF 1812

[*Commander Nathaniel Shaler of the United States privateer* Gov. Tompkins *wrote this letter on January 1, 1813, describing a sea battle and the heroism of his mixed crew.*]

. . . At sunrise, three ships were discovered ahead. We made all sail in chase. The wind being light, we came slowly up with them. On a nearer approach, they proved to be two ships and a brig.—One of the ships had all the appearance of a large transport. . . . At 3 P.M. . . . before I could get our light sails in, and almost before I could turn round, I was under the guns, (not of a transport) but of a large *frigate!*—and not more than a quarter of a mile from her.

I immediately . . . commenced a brisk fire from our little battery; but this was returned with woful interest. Her first broadside killed two men and wounded six others. . . .

The name of one of my poor fellows who was killed ought to be registered in the book of fame, and remembered with reverence as long as bravery is considered a virtue; he was a black man by the name of *John Johnson;* a 24 lb. shot struck him in the hip and took away all the lower part of his body; in this state the poor brave fellow lay on the deck, and several times exclaimed to his shipmates, *"Fire away my boy, no haul a color down."* The other was also a black man, by the name of *John Davis,* and was struck in much the same way: he fell near me, and several times requested to be thrown overboard, saying, he was only in the way of others.

While America has such tars, she has little to fear from the tyrants of the ocean.

Niles' Weekly Register 5 (26 February 1814): 430.

4 FRONTIERSMEN CONQUER THE WILDERNESS, 1800–1860

PIONEER EXPLORERS, TRAPPERS, MISSIONARIES, and settlers opened the vast American continent from the Atlantic to the Pacific coasts in the years before the Civil War. Despite hunger, epidemics, storms, droughts, stampedes, wild animals, freezing cold, and blazing heat, they established a civilization in the wilderness. This hearty breed of men and women was made up of all sorts of Americans. African Americans, as slave laborers or free men and women, moved with each wave.

Slave Frontiersmen

Most African Americans who went West followed the wagons of their masters, sometimes in chains. They prodded cattle onward, searched for water, or hunted for game. Later they cleared the land and built the cabins. Slaves raised crops in Mississippi, dug gold in California, roped and branded cattle in Texas. Some ran off at the first opportunity, sensing that man was meant to be free in this beautiful new country.

Others stood by their masters, even during Indian raids. Jim Bowie, inventor of the famous throwing knife, and his slave were in a party that fought off a Comanche attack near San Antonio in 1831. During the long battle, shielded by the fire of white men, the big slave darted to a spring and brought water back to the thirsty men. Another slave, Bob Anderson, and his master were surprised by Native Americans while working near their cabin. Both men were saved by the women of the family who came to their rescue with blazing shotguns. A teenage slave named Smith was attacked by three Indians as he worked in his master's cornfield. With a butcher knife in one hand and a pistol in the other, he fought back, killing one, wounding another, and sending the third screaming to the woods.

Bold and decisive action brought liberty to some frontier slaves. For example, a slave named Tom won his freedom in Texas for his courageous defense of his master. The two men were ambushed by Apaches while prospecting. When the master was badly wounded, Tom had to drive off the Indians alone. Afterward, he carried his master thirty miles to a doctor.

Red People Meet Black People

Mandan Indians examine York. They thought his black color might rub off.

The Lewis and Clark Expedition into the vast Louisiana territory benefited from the strong muscles and fine mind of York, Clark's slave. Well over six feet in height and two hundred pounds in weight, York was an excellent swimmer, fisherman, and hunter. Along with Sacajawea, the Indian guide, he proved to be of great help in making friends with the Indians. Lewis reported that tribesmen came from all over to see this Black giant with short curly hair. An agile man despite his size, York delighted the Indians with the wild leaps and bounds which he called dancing. The tribes, wrote Lewis, "seemed as anxious to see this monster as they were the merchandize which we had to barter for their horses." Although York "spoke bad French and worse English," according to another member of the expedition, he and Sacajawea acted as interpreters for the party. Clark freed York at the end of the two-and-one-half-year trip.

York's unusual success with the Indians was matched by other slaves. Native Americans were quick to note that the Black slaves and the red men had a common enemy—the white man. African Americans were admitted to many nations.

The acceptance of slaves by Indian villages infuriated many whites on the frontier. A United States Army survey of the Choctaw Indians in 1831 showed that the tribe included 512 Blacks. The Pamunky Indians of Virginia included so many African Americans that whites petitioned the government to take their land away, claiming they were no longer "Indians at all, but Negroes." The Shawnees and the Cherokees used their villages as stations for runaway slaves on the famous underground railroad that led to Canada.

In many instances African Americans rose to leadership in various tribes. During an Indian raid in Texas in 1839 the settlers were surprised to find that the leader was "a big French Negro, weighing about two hundred pounds." "This Negro," reported a settler, "claimed to have always been free, but would not acknowledge any allegiance to the Texas government." He was promptly shot.

In some instances Indian nations held African Americans (and whites) as slaves, but it seems to have been a very different form of slavery from that in the South. A European visitor to Oklahoma in 1853 told how Indians had learned to keep slaves by observing whites. "But these slaves receive from their Indian masters more Christian treatment than among the Christian whites." He noted that African Americans were treated like other members of the village "and [that] the Negro is regarded as a companion and helper, to whom thanks and kindness are due when he exerts himself for the welfare of the household."

Free African Americans as Trappers and Missionaries

"The old fur traders," Colonel James Stevenson, an old trapper, recalled, "always got a Negro, if possible, to negotiate for them with the Indians, because of their 'pacifying effect.' They could manage [the Indians] better than the white men, and with less friction."

George Bonza.

Many of these early Black trappers married into Indian nations. Pierre Bonza, one of this hearty breed, married a Chippewa and lived in her village. Their son George followed in his father's footsteps and became a wealthy man working for the American Fur Company and later serving as an interpreter for Governor Lewis Cass of the Michigan territory. George Bonza laughingly told his friends he was one of "the first two white men that came into this country."

The most important African American frontiersman of this period was James Beckwourth, a handy man with a Bowie knife, gun, or hatchet. He headed west from St. Louis when he was nineteen, leaving a life of slavery. He quickly picked up the skills necessary for survival on the frontier. Beckwourth was a pugnacious, short-tempered fellow, and a reporter who knew him in 1860 called him "the most famous Indian fighter of this generation."

Beckwourth lived a life full of daring adventures and unusual opportunities. When an old Indian woman claimed Beckwourth was her long-lost son, he was taken into the Crow tribe and named "Morning Star." He soon became their chief and led them into many battles shouting, "I will show

Photograph of James Beckwourth. The man who helped him write his life story said, "Probably no man ever lived who has met with more personal adventure involving danger to life." Made chief of the Crow Indians, Beckwourth was called "Morning Star."

you how to fight." Often, he reported, "my battle-axe was red with the blood of the enemy." His reputation prompted General Stephen Kearny to ask for Beckwourth's assistance in California's war for independence: "You like war, and I have good use for you now."

But Beckwourth's claim to a place in history does not rest upon his exploits as a patriot, a wilderness fighter, or an Indian chief. In April 1850, James Beckwourth discovered a pass through the Sierra Nevadas that became an important gateway to California during the Gold Rush. The pass still bears his name. By 1852 Beckwourth established a hotel and trading post in Beckwourth Valley, but he was not destined to live out his life as a peaceful innkeeper.

The Crows, according to one legend, invited Beckwourth to a village feast, intent on convincing him to lead them again. When Beckwourth turned them down, he was poisoned. According to this version of his death, if the Crows could not have him as a live chief, they intended to keep Beckwourth in the tribal burial ground.

At the same time Beckwourth started west, determined to master the ways of the frontier, two gentle African American missionaries came west to preach the Christian gospel to the Indians. John Marrant of New York instructed Cherokees, Creeks, and others in the word of God. John Stewart, a Virginia Baptist minister, brought his message of salvation to the Wyandot: "Pray to the Lord both day and night with a sincere heart and

He will uphold you in all your trials and troubles." Marrant managed to convert the Cherokee chief and his daughter, and Stewart was so successful that his church sent additional ministers to assist in his important work.

Following the trappers and missionaries west were the settlers. In 1833 a party of 385 men, women, and children left a life of slavery in Virginia's Roanoke River Valley for a life of freedom on their own land in Ohio. They had been set free by the terms of Senator John Randolph's will, and this kind master had also provided them with parcels of land to divide in Mercer County. After a long trip by wagon and boat, the slaves were stunned to find that they had been cheated out of their land by their master's relatives. In their search for jobs and homes some pushed on into Indiana and some migrated to other parts of Ohio. Some met white citizens who offered them the help needed to begin their new life.

The United States Acquires Florida

Hundreds of Africans crossed the American border into Spanish Florida to escape slavery. The swamps and forests became their home. People built houses and raised families in this hidden and fertile land. For fifty miles along the banks of the Appalachicola River, their cornfields supplied them with food and their horses and cattle grazed in the clearings.

Many fugitives joined the Seminoles, a nation that had left the Creek Indians (Seminole means *runaway*). America's first foreign treaty (1790) demanded that the Creeks "deliver" those slaves who lived among them. But the Indians continued to protect their new Black friends in defiance of all authority. Generation after generation of African Americans lived in this quiet valley.

By the time the War of 1812 ended, the furious slaveholders demanded that force be used to eliminate Florida as "a perpetual harbor for our slaves," as General Andrew Jackson called it. Jackson dispatched two gunboats, an army regiment, and five hundred Creeks to subdue the Seminoles and their African allies. The immediate objective of this expedition was a powerful wooden fort abandoned by the British and left to the Black leader, Garcia. As the gunboats approached it, the sailors noted that it still flew the British flag. After a few shots to determine the distance, one of the gunboats hit the fort's powder magazine with a heated cannonball. "The explosion was awful and the scene horrible beyond description," wrote an American officer. Most of the fort's three hundred men, women, and children were killed, and only three were uninjured. Those who survived the explosion were either put to death or sold into slavery.

This daring invasion of Spanish soil was a powerful argument in convinc-

Runaway slave
in Florida.

Creek Indians hired by the United States took part in the invasion of Florida in 1816. After the destruction of "Fort Negro," they marched the survivors back to Georgia.

ing Spain to sell Florida before Jackson merely took it. But the sale of Florida in 1819 did not end the problem of slave runaways and their Indian friends. Three Seminole Wars were necessary to move the Seminoles to Oklahoma. Throughout the conflict the ex-slaves were the most determined fighters. John T. Sprague, an American soldier in the third Seminole War, noted, "The Negroes exercised a wonderful control [over the Seminoles]. . . . It was not until the Negroes capitulated that the Seminoles ever thought of emigrating."

This second Seminole War lasted eight years (1835–1842) and cost the United States 1,500 men and $40,000,000; it was the most expensive Indian war waged by this country until this time. After the war had been under way for a year, General Thomas Jesup of the American forces stated: "This, you may be assured, is a Negro, not an Indian war."

Louis Pacheco, a slave hired by the Americans, took on the role of a counterspy. He notified the Seminoles of the path he would use for the

Negro Abraham (center) served as an interpreter for the Seminole Indians in their 1825 negotiations with the United States in Washington, D.C. One army officer described him as having "the crouch and spring of a panther." He admitted bitterly that Abraham had "ruled all the councils and actions of the Indians in this region." In 1838 Abraham tried to convince the tribes to accept the United States demand that they move to Oklahoma: "We do not live for ourselves only, but for our wives and children, who are as dear to us as those of any other men." But it was the overwhelming United States force that finally convinced most of the Seminoles and their African American allies to accept the new location.

United States troops and then led them into an ambush. After this famous "Dade massacre," Pacheco lived on with his Seminole and Black friends. While some Seminoles moved to the West, others stayed on and never surrendered to American authority.

Defenders of the Lone Star Republic

When the Mexican government offered Americans Texas land, slaveholders and their human property followed Stephen Austin into the Texas plains. Many of these slaves served as cowhands and years later drove cattle up the trails to Kansas.

One was Bose Ikard. Charles Goodnight, founder of the Goodnight-Loving trail from Texas to Montana, brought Ikard to Texas when he was five. Goodnight remembered him as one of his strongest cowboys, one who "surpassed any man I had in endurance and stamina. There was a dignity, a cleanliness, and a reliability about him that was wonderful." Ikard, wrote his boss, "was very good in a fight and he was probably the most devoted man that I ever had. I have trusted him farther than any living man. He was my detective, banker, and everything in Colorado, New Mexico, and the other wild country I was in."

Other African Americans rode into Texas as free men, summoned by Stephen Austin's promise of cheap land and a chance to begin a new life. Greenbury Logan, who answered Austin's call in 1831, was one of those to receive both land and Texas citizenship. Logan later wrote that he "loved the country" and stayed because he felt himself more a free man "than in the States." He was among the first to volunteer in the war for Texan independence. He fought in many battles, and his severe wounds left him disabled.

From the Alamo to the final battle at San Jacinto, African Americans took part in the fight for the Lone Star Republic. Some were slaves whose bravery on the battlefield won them their freedom. Others were free men such as Hendrick Arnold, who served as a scout for three American armies.

As soon as the war ended with the surrender of Santa Anna to Sam Houston, however, the Black patriots were forgotten. As Texas became an important slaveholding region, the legislature tried to eliminate the state's free people of color. Greenbury Logan, too disabled to work his farm, was denied tax exemption. He and others found their rights restricted and their presence no longer wanted in the land they had helped to defend.

Some free people of color stayed on through the efforts of their white friends in the Texas legislature. One was Aaron Ashworth, who went to Texas in 1833. Seventeen years later he owned 2,570 head of cattle and a large ranch and employed a white tutor for his children. The Ashworth family continued to contribute to the development of Texas for many years. Another free man, Isham Hicks, stayed on to supervise the construction of the First Methodist Church in Comanche county.

Oregon

William Owen Bush, son of George Owen Bush, was the only Black man elected to the first Washington legislature (1889).

Among early American explorers of the Oregon territory was a free man of color, George Washington Bush, who fought at the battle of New Orleans under Andrew Jackson. Bush and his white companions found their way from the Mexican border to the Columbia River Valley. When they heard that any African American who entered the Oregon territory would be whipped, all of the members of the company decided to fight to protect him. The law was never carried out.

In 1844 Bush, his wife, and five children led several white couples in the trip to the Columbia River. One of Bush's companions remembers him giving the men of the wagon train this advice: "Boys, you are going through a hard country. You have guns and ammunition. Take my advice: Anything you see as big as a blackbird, kill it and eat it." Bush's group became the first American settlers north of the Columbia River. Although African Americans were denied the right to homesteads, Bush's friend, Colonel Michael Simmons, a member of the Oregon legislature, had Congress pass a special act granting Bush a 640-acre plot.

The Bush family became wealthy, but often divided their crops with other less fortunate white settlers. One of Bush's sons raised a prize wheat crop (a sample of which was placed in the Smithsonian Institution) and another was twice elected to the state legislature. Bush is remembered today as one of the leading pioneers of Oregon and Washington, and Bush Prairie is named after him.

On to California

Jacob Dodson, like Bush, was a free man of color who jumped at the chance to explore the West. United States Army Colonel John C. Frémont, "the Pathfinder," and scout Kit Carson took Dodson with them on three expeditions into California and Oregon. At the time of their first trip, Frémont described his young expert with the lariat and the horse as "only eighteen, but strong and active and nearly six feet in height." Dodson fought alongside Frémont and Carson in California's war for independence.

William A. Leidesdorff.

Very few pioneers of any race became as wealthy as Alexander Leidesdorff, who sailed his 106-ton schooner, *Julia Ann,* to California from New Orleans in 1841. Leidesdorff soon owned a 35,000-acre California estate he called *Rancho Americano.* He introduced the first steamboat to California as well as the first horse race. He served as an American government consul and built San Francisco's first hotel, but died before California joined the Union.

The discovery of gold brought many slaveholders to California, and they brought their bondsmen to take care of the necessary labor. Some slaves such as Alvin Coffey and Daniel Rogers won their freedom by their work in the gold fields. Daniel Rogers was cheated out of his liberty by his master, but whites from his native Arkansas responded by raising money to purchase his freedom and presented him with a certificate that praised his "honesty, industry and integrity."

Thousands of free African Americans were among the "forty-niners" who flocked to California seeking instant wealth. There were a thousand of them by 1850, and two years later the number had doubled. One became manager of the Frisbie Hotel in Sonoma. Two others became Pony Express riders, carrying the mail in California: George Monroe, whose route was from Merced to Mariposa, and William Robinson, who rode from Stockton to the mines. In one county 86 out of 123 free African Americans were listed as miners, and in another it was 52 out of 62 people. More than a few became rich, for by 1855 California's Black population had amassed $2,375,000, so that it was America's wealthiest Black community. Along with the increased wealth came a large number of churches, many of which operated schools.

Many Californians of all races were helped through the efforts of two

Black gold miners and white gold miners. This photograph was taken at Spanish Flat, California, in 1852.

George Monroe, Pony Express rider.

Mrs. Biddy Mason.

Black reformers, Biddy Mason and J. B. Sanderson. Mrs. Mason trudged to California behind the three hundred wagons of her Mississippi master. Her job was to make sure the livestock stayed with the caravan. In California, Mrs. Mason and her three daughters won their freedom. They settled in Los Angeles when it was a small town with eight white families and one other African American family. Through hard work, saving, and shrewd business sense, Mrs. Mason soon became a rich landowner and was soon well known to the poor, to the imprisoned, and to those left destitute by floods. Her generosity seemed unbounded. She purchased land for churches, built schools for nurses, and aided children of the poor.

Sanderson devoted his talents to starting schools for those children who were not admitted to the public schools. From San Francisco to Sacramento, he founded schools for Asian, African, and Native Americans. He taught in most of them until a replacement could be found.

In California, as elsewhere in the United States, Black settlers took action to secure their civil rights. A "Franchise League" was formed in the state to campaign for repeal of the law forbidding people of color the right to testify in trials involving whites. At an 1856 Black convention, one delegate asked, "When will the people of this state learn that justice to the colored man is justice to themselves?" Five hundred white San Franciscans signed the petitions of the Franchise League, and so did whites in five other counties. Under the leadership of Mary E. Pleasant, a former Georgia slave, the campaign achieved success by 1863. The following year Mrs. Pleasant put the law to practical use, successfully suing a streetcar company for rude treatment and winning a judgment of $600.

Mary E. Pleasant, early California civil rights leader.

Democracy and Slavery in the West

The westward movement can be credited with spreading the American ideals of democracy, brotherhood, and equality. On the frontier, man was judged by his skills rather than by his ancestors. Women played a key role in frontier homes and, therefore, demanded a larger voice in many decisions. Cooperation was necessary to build homes and bring in the crops.

But the democracy that flowered on the frontier was lily white. Because the free person of color was associated with his slave brother and sister, he faced greater hardships than other settlers. In no land of the Western plains could a Black vote. To enter Iowa in 1839 he or she had to present a five-hundred-dollar bond and proof of freedom. Few had such proof, and even fewer had five hundred dollars. By 1844 Iowans announced that they would "never consent to open the doors of our beautiful state" to people of color, for equality would lead to "discord and violence."

When Illinois passed restrictions on its free African Americans, one of the Black men who turned away in disgust was named George Washington. In 1855 he pushed westward into Washington, where he became the first settler in what became the city of Centralia.

While white Westerners opposed the free Black, they battled slavery with equal vigor. Abraham Lincoln said that the new land must be kept "for homes of free white people. This cannot be, to any considerable extent, if slavery shall be planted within them." Lincoln pointed out that slave labor reduces the dignity of all labor and drives out "poor white people." Westerners resented both the slaveholder who did no work, and his slaves who were forced to work.

Congressman David Wilmot, whose famous proviso would have banned slavery in the Southwest, argued for a white man's West: "I plead the cause and the rights of white freemen. I would preserve to white labor a fair country, a rich inheritance, where the sons of toil of my own race and own color can live without the disgrace which association with Negro slavery brings upon free labor."

But the Southern masters desperately needed new land to expand their

Mifflin W. Gibbs, editor of California's first Black newspaper. During the Gold Rush, he led in the drive for civil rights.

slave economy. "Whenever slavery is confined . . . its future is doomed," said a Southern congressman. Slavery used farming methods which tended to ruin the most fertile soil. Mississippi entered the Union in 1818, and by 1856 a soil expert reported "a large part of the state is already exhausted; the state is full of old deserted fields."

The most successful Southern attempt to take new land in the West involved the United States in a war with Mexico. The war was denounced by many in the North as caused by the greed of slaveholders. Ulysses S. Grant, who served in the war, said, "I do not think there was ever a more wicked war than that waged by the United States on Mexico." Henry David Thoreau went to jail rather than pay his taxes during the war. Congressman Abraham Lincoln thought that President Polk had sent American troops into Mexican land to provoke war. According to the terms of the peace treaty signed in 1848, Mexico lost one-half of her national territory.

The Southern drive for new land continued during the 1850s. In 1853 William Walker of Tennessee tried to capture lower California from Mexico but failed miserably. He had greater success a few years later when he took over Nicaragua and had himself elected president. He restored slavery and looked forward to "a formal alliance with the seceding States." By the time that eleven Southern states had left the Union, Walker had been captured and shot by a South American firing squad of three races

From the bitter arguments over Missouri in 1819 to the savage warfare that engulfed Kansas in the 1850s, the West was slavery's battleground. Slowly but surely the West became allied with the free North. It would be no accident of history that the president who ended slavery was born in a Kentucky log cabin, or that the first Black troops to bear arms in defense of the Union were fugitive slaves living on the Kansas plains. They rode into Missouri to free their brothers and sisters in bondage.

JAMES BECKWOURTH, FRONTIERSMAN

[James Beckwourth was a runaway slave, a tough frontier scout, and chief of the Crow Indians. Dacotah Indian Paul Dorion describes Beckwourth's battle with Blackfoot Indians.]

"You are all fools and old women," he [Beckwourth] said to the Crows; "come with me, if any of you are brave enough, and I will show you how to fight."

He threw off his trapper's frock of buckskin and stripped himself naked, like the Indians themselves. He left his rifle on the ground, took in his hand a small light hatchet, and ran over the prairie to the right, concealed by a hollow from the eyes of the Blackfeet. Then climbing up the rocks, he gained the top of the precipice behind them. Forty or fifty young Crow warriors followed him. By the cries and whoops that rose from below he knew that the Blackfeet were just beneath him; and running forward he leaped down the rock into the midst of them. As he fell he caught one by the long loose hair, and dragging him down tomahawked him; then grasping another by the belt at his waist, he struck him also a stunning blow, and, gaining his feet, shouted the Crow war-cry. He swung his hatchet so fiercely around him, that the astonished Blackfeet bore back and gave him room. He might, had he chosen, have leaped over the breastwork and escaped; but this was not necessary, for with devilish yells the Crow warriors came dropping in quick succession over the rock among their enemies. The main body of the Crows, too, answered the cry from the front, and rushed up simultaneously. The convulsive struggle within the breastwork was frightful; for an instant the Blackfeet fought and yelled like pent-up tigers, but the butchery was soon complete, and the mangled bodies lay piled together under the precipice. Not a Blackfoot made his escape.

Francis Parkman, *The Oregon Trail* (Boston, 1872), 125.

[*The following passage is Beckwourth's own description of the discovery of the pass over the Sierra Nevada mountains that still bears his name.*]

We proceeded in an easterly direction, and all busied themselves in searching for gold; but my errand was of a different character; I had come to discover what I suspected to be a pass.

It was the latter end of April when we entered upon an extensive valley at the northwest extremity of the Sierra range. . . . Swarms of wild geese and ducks were swimming on the surface of the cool crystal stream, which was the central fork of the Rio de las Plumas, or sailed the air in clouds over our heads. Deer and antelope filled the plains and their boldness was conclusive that the hunter's rifle was to them unknown. Nowhere visible were any traces of the white man's approach, and it is probable that our steps were the first that ever marked the spot. We struck across this beautiful valley to the waters of the Yuba, from thence to the waters of the Truchy. . . . This, I at once saw, would afford the best waggon-road into the American Valley approaching from the eastward, and I imparted my views to three of my companions in whose judgment I placed the most confidence. They thought highly of the discovery, and even proposed to associate with me in opening the road. We also found gold, but not in sufficient quantity to warrant our working it. . . .

On my return to the American Valley, I made known my discovery to a Mr. Turner, proprietor of the American Ranch, who entered enthusiastically into my views; it was a thing, he said, he had never dreamed of before. If I could but carry out my plan, and divert travel into that road, he thought I should be a made man for life. Thereupon he drew up a subscription-list, setting forth the merits of the project, and showing how the road could be made practicable to Bidwell's Bar, and thence to Marysville. . . . He headed the subscription with two hundred dollars.

When I reached Bidwell's Bar and unfolded my project, the town was seized with a perfect mania for the opening of the route. The subscriptions toward the fund required for its accomplishment amounted to five hundred dollars. . . . While thus busily engaged I was seized with erysipelas, and abandoned all hopes of recovery; I was over one hundred miles away from medical assistance, and my only shelter was a brush tent. I made my will, and resigned myself to death. Life still lingered in me, however, and a train of waggons came up, and encamped near to where I lay. I was reduced to a very low condition, but I saw the drivers, and acquainted them with the object which had brought me out there. They offered to attempt the new road if I thought myself sufficiently strong to guide them through it. The women, God bless them! came to my assistance, and through their kind attentions and excellent nursing I rapidly recovered from my lingering sickness, until I was soon able to mount my horse, and lead the first train, consisting of seventeen waggons, through "Beckwourth's Pass.". . .

In the spring of 1852 I established myself in Beckwourth Valley, and finally found myself transformed into a hotel-keeper and chief of a trading-post. My house is considered the emigrant's landing-place, as it is the first ranch he arrives at in the golden state, and is the only house between this point and Salt Lake.

James Beckwourth, *The Life and Adventures of James Beckwourth, Mountaineer, Scout, Pioneer, and Chief of the Crow Nation of Indians,* written from his own dictation by T. D. Bonner (London, 1892), 424–27.

THE DESTRUCTION OF FORT NEGRO, 1816

[Shortly after the end of the War of 1812, the United States government, prodded by angry slaveholders, began military operations against Spanish Florida. While the overall objective was the incorporation of this rich and fertile land into the United States, an immediate goal was the capture of hundreds of slaves who had taken refuge in Florida. Many had married into or joined the Seminoles, and more than a few were leaders. A fort on the Appalachicola River was the first target of the U.S. forces.]

[Letter of General Andrew Jackson, of May 16, 1816, to General Gaines.] I have little doubt of the fact, that this fort has been established by some villains for the purpose of rapine and plunder, and that it ought to be blown up, regardless of the ground on which it stands; and if your mind shall have formed the same conclusion, destroy it and return the stolen Negroes and property to their rightful owners.

Joshua R. Giddings, *The Exiles of Florida* (New York, 1863), 37.

[Report of Colonel Clinch.] At two o'clock on the morning of the 20th we landed within cannon shot of the Fort. . . . Finding it impossible to carry my plans into execution without . . . artillery, I ordered Major McIntosh to keep up an irregular fire.

. . . In the evening a deputation of chiefs went into the Fort and demanded its surrender, but they were abused and treated with the utmost contempt. The Black Chief [Garcia] heaped much abuse on the Americans, & said he had been left in command of the Fort by the British Government and that he would sink any American vessels that should attempt to pass it, and would blow up the Fort if he could not defend it. The chiefs also informed me that the Negroes had hoisted a red flag, and that the English Jack was flying over it. . . .

In the course of the evening after consulting with the commanding officer of the convoy I directed him to move up the two gun vessels at day light the next morning.

Report of Col. Clinch of the destruction of Fort Negro, on the Appalachicola, July 29, 1816 (Washington: War Records Office, National Archives).

[Report of Sailing-Master Loomis.] At 4 A.M. on the morning of the 27th, we began warping the gun vessels to a proper position; at 5, getting within

gun shot, the fort opened [fire] upon us which we returned; and after ascertaining our real distance with cold shot, we commenced with hot [heated cannon balls] . . . the *first* one of which entering their magazine, blew up, and completely destroyed the fort.

J. Loomis, *Letter of 13 August 1816,* in House Documents, 15th Cong., 2nd sess., 16–17.

[*Report of Colonel Clinch.*] The explosion was awful and the scene horrible beyond description. Our first care on arriving at the scene of destruction was to rescue and relieve the unfortunate beings that survived the explosion.

The war yells of the Indians, the cries and lamentations of the wounded, compel'd the soldier to pause in the midst of victory, and to drop a tear for the sufferings of his fellow beings, and to acknowledge that the great ruler of the Universe must have used us as an instrument in chastising the blood thirsty murderous wretches that defended the Fort. The Fort contained about one hundred effective men (including twenty five Choctaws) and about two hundred women and children not more than one sixth part of which number were saved. . . .

. . . The greater part of the Negroes belonged to the Spaniards and Indians. The American Negroes had principally settled in the river and a number of them had left their fields and gone over to the Seminoles on hearing of our approach. Their corn fields extended nearly fifty miles up the river and their numbers were daily increasing. The chief passed sentence of death on the outlawed Choctaw chief and the black commandant [Garcia] . . . and the sentence was immediately carried into execution.

Report of Col. Clinch, *op. cit.*

SEMINOLES AND SOLDIERS ARGUE

[*Beginning in the early days of the Republic, Indians and American army officers exchanged bitter notes and letters about the Indians' protection of runaway slaves or the attacks on Native American villages by slave catchers. Part of that war of words is revealed in American State Papers from 1818 to 1835.*]

[*General Gaines to the Seminole Chiefs.*] Your Seminoles are very bad people. . . . You have murdered many of my people, and stolen my cattle and many good horses, that cost me money; and many good houses that cost me money you have burnt for me; and now, that you see my writing, you'll think I have spoken right, I know it is so; you know it is so. . . .

I tell you this, that if you do not give me up the murderers who murdered my people, I say I have got good strong warriors, with scalping-knives and tomahawks. You harbor a great many of my black people among you at Sahwahnee. If you give me leave to go by you against them, I shall not hurt any thing belonging to you.

[*King Hatchy Answers General Gaines.*] You charge me with killing your people, stealing your cattle and burning your houses; it is I that have cause to complain of the Americans. While one American has been justly killed, while in the act of stealing cattle, more than four Indians while hunting have been murdered by these lawless freebooters. I harbor no Negroes. When the Englishmen were at war with America, some [Negroes] took shelter among them; and it is for you white people to settle those things among yourselves, and not trouble us with what we know nothing about. I shall use force to stop any armed Americans from passing my towns or my lands.

American State Papers 1 (Washington, 1832), 723.

[*Chief Emachutochustern, Seminole, to General Thompson, Indian Agent, 1835.*]

Dear Sir: I am induced to write you in consequence of the depredations making and attempting to be made on my farm by a company of men, Negro stealers, some of whom are from Columbus [Georgia]. . . . It is reported and believed by all the white people around here that a large number of them will very shortly come down here and attempt to take off Billy, Jim, Rose and her family, and others. These same men have been engaged in the same business up in the "Creek Nation." I should like to have your advice how I should act. I dislike to make any trouble, or to have any difficulty with any of the white people; but if they will trespass on my premises and on my rights, I must defend myself in the best way I can. . . . But is there no *civil law* that will protect me? Are the free Negroes and the Negroes belonging in this town to be stolen away publicly—in the face of all law and justice carried off and sold to fill the pockets of these worse than "land pirates"? Certainly not. I know you will not suffer it. Please direct me how to act in this matter. . . .

American State Papers, Military Affairs 4 (Washington, 1861): 463.

DELAWARE INDIANS, WHITE RELIGION, AND BLACK SLAVERY

[A revealing picture of how Native Americans viewed slavery is contained in this report by two white missionaries. Sent to convert the Delaware nation before its removal to the West, they entered this report into the church records.]

They rejoiced exceedingly at our happiness in thus being favored by the Great Spirit, and felt grateful that we had condescended to remember our red brethren in the wilderness. But they could not help recollecting that we had a people among us, whom, because they differed from us in color, we had made slaves of, and made them suffer great hardships, and lead miserable lives. Now they could not see any reason, if a people being black entitled us thus to deal with them, why a red color should not equally justify the same treatment. They therefore had determined to wait, to see whether all the black people amongst us were made thus happy and joyful before they would put confidence in our promises: for they thought a people who had suffered so much and so long by our means, should be entitled to our first attention; and therefore they had sent back the two missionaries, with many thanks, promising that when they saw the black people among us restored to freedom and happiness they would gladly receive our missionaries.

William Henry Smith, *A Political History of Slavery,* Volume 1 (New York, 1903): 11. Quoted from *The Star in the West* (n.p., n.d.), 232.

ADVICE FROM A SETTLER IN INDIANA

[During the 1820s and 1830s African Americans who had intermarried with Cherokees in North Carolina came to Indiana by covered wagon. By 1832 they formed the Roberts settlement in Hamilton County. This community later produced its share of lawyers, doctors, dentists, teachers, ministers, and Civil War soldiers. But in 1830, when settler Willis Roberts told his cousin "Long" James Roberts that he was thinking of returning to North Carolina, "Long" James wrote him this letter.]

After leaving you on the 15th day of February, 1830, I feel it a duty for me to write a few lines to inform you of my mind on what you are going to do. . . .

It seems very plain to me that you are now going to make one of the worst mistakes that you ever made, in many ways. The first is that you are taking your children to an old country that is worn out and to slave on. . . .

. . . To think that you are going to take your small children to that place and can't tell how soon you may be taken away from them and they may come under the hands of some cruel slave holder, and you know that if they can get a colored child they will use them as bad again as they will one of their own slaves; it is right that parents should think of this, most especially if they are going to the very place and know it at the same time.

I would not this night, if I had children, take them to such a place and there to stay for the best five farms in three miles around where we came from, for I think I should be going to do something to bring them to see trouble and not enjoy themselves as free men but be in a place where they are not able to speak for their rights. . . .

I cannot do myself justice to think of living in such a country. When I think of it I can't tell how any man of color can think of going there with small children. It has been my intention ever since I had notice of such if I lived to be a man and God was willing I would leave such a place.

I wish you well and all your family and I hope that you all may do well, as much so as any people I ever saw or ever shall see, and I hope that you may see what you are going to do before it is too late. This is from the heart of one who wishes you well. . . .

[*Willis Roberts did visit North Carolina but returned to Indiana to live.*]

Letter from James Roberts to Willis Roberts, the Roberts Settlement Collection (Washington: Library of Congress, Manuscript Collection).

GREENBURY LOGAN AND THE LONE STAR REPUBLIC

[*Greenbury Logan came to Texas at the invitation of Stephen Austin and fought in its war for independence. Disabled from wounds received in the war, he wrote to a member of the Texas legislature asking for tax relief. His letter also mentions his special burdens as a Black Texan. The Texas legislature refused to pass a tax-relief bill for Logan.*]

I hope you will excuse me for taking the liberty of riting to you. I knew not of you being in the county until the night before you left for Austin. it was my wish to see you from the time you was elected but in consiquence of your absence I co[u]ld not. I presume it is unecessary to give you eny informasion abought my coming to Texas. I cam[e] here in 1831 invited by Col. Austin. it was not my intention to stay until I had saw Col. Austin who was then in Mexico. after se[e]ing him on his return and conversing with him relitive to my situation I got letters of sittizen ship. having no famoly with me I got one quarter League of land insted of a third. but I love the country and did stay because I felt myself mower a freeman then in the states. it is well known that Logan was the man that lifted his rifle in behalf of Texas as of fremans righted. it is also known that Logan was in everry fite with the Maxacans during the camppain of 35 until Bexhar was taken in which event I was the 3rd man that fell. My discharge will show the man[n]er in which I discharged my duty as a free man and a sol[d]ier but now look at my situation. every previleg dear to a freman is taken a way and logan liable to be imposed upon by eny that chose to doo it. no chance to collect a debt with out witness, no vote or say in eny way, yet liable for Taxes [as] eny other [person]. . . . I am on examination found perment injurd and can nom[o]re than support by myself now as every thing that is deare to a freman is taken from me. the congress will not refuse to exempt my lands from tax or otherwise restoure what it has taken from me in the constitution. to leave I am two poor and imbarrased and cannot leav honerable as I came. I am tow old and cr[i]ppled to go on the world with my famaly recked. if my debts was payd I wo[u]ld be willing to leav the land though my blood has nearly all been shed for its rights—now my dear friend you are the first man I hav ever spoken to for eny assistance. I hombely hope you as a gentleman . . . will look into this errur and try if you cannot effect—something for my relief. I know I have friends in the house if a thing of the kind was brought up. . . . please euse your best exertions. . . . G. Logan

Harold Schoen, "The Free Negro in the Republic of Texas," Part IV, *Southwestern Historical Quarterly* 41 (July 1937): 84–86. Reprinted with permission.

GEORGE BUSH LEADS A PARTY TO OREGON

[*Among the early settlers in the Oregon territory was a freeman, George Bush. In Bush's party on the Oregon Trail were a group of white men, David Kindred, Gabriel Jones, and Colonel Michael T. Simmons. Later Simmons got a grant of 640 acres of farmland for his friend Bush. John Minton, a white pioneer who had*

*met Bush in Missouri at the wagon train's starting point, met him again on the
way west. The date was September 5, 1844.*]

I struck the road again in advance of my friends near Soda Springs. There
was in sight, however, G. W. Bush, at whose camp table Rees and I had received the hospitalities of the Missouri rendezvous. Joining him, we went
on to the Springs. Bush was a mulatto, but had means, and also a white
woman for a wife, and a family of five children. Not many men of color left
a slave state so well to do, and so generally respected; but it was not in the
nature of things that he should be permitted to forget his color. As we went
along together, he riding a mule and I on foot, he led the conversation to
this subject. He told me he should watch, when we got to Oregon, what
usuage was awarded to people of color, and if he could not have a free
man's rights he would seek the protection of the Mexican Government in
California or New Mexico. He said there were few in that train he would
say as much to as he had just said to me. I told him I understood. This conversation enabled me afterwards to understand the chief reason for Col.
M. T. Simmons and his kindred, and Bush and Jones determining to settle
north of the Columbia [River]. It was understood that Bush was assisting
at least two of these to get to Oregon, and while they were all Americans,
they would take no part in ill treating G. W. Bush on account of his color.

[*As a matter of fact, when the party heard that any African American trying to
enter Oregon might be whipped, they decided that every one of them would fight
to protect Bush.*]

No act of Colonel Simmons as a legislator in 1846 was more creditable
to him than getting Mr. Bush exempt from the Oregon law, intended to deter mulattoes or Negroes from settling in Oregon—a law, however, happily
never enforced.

John Minton, "Reminiscences of Experiences on the Oregon Trail in 1844," *The Quarterly
of the Oregon Historical Society* 2 (September 1901): 212–13.

A FORTY-NINER MAKES A NEW LIFE IN CALIFORNIA

[*After Alvin Coffey and his master came to California during the Gold Rush, the
master took away both the $5,000 which Coffey had earned for him in the mines
and the $700 which the slave had earned for himself working nights. Then he sold*

Coffey to a new master. Coffey convinced his new owner that he could earn enough in the mines to buy his freedom as well as the freedom of his wife and three children. The master agreed, and by 1860 Coffey's family were united free and prosperous in Tehama County—and one of the noted pioneer families of California. Here is Coffey's story of his first trip westward.]

I started from St. Louis, Missouri, on the 2nd of April in 1849. There was quite a crowd of neighbors who drove through the mud and rain to St. Joe to see us off. About the first of May we organized the train. There were twenty wagons in number and from three to five men to each wagon.

We crossed the Missouri River at Savanna Landing on or about the 6th, no the 1st week in May. . . . At six in the morning, there were three more went to relieve those on guard. One of the three that came in had cholera so bad that he was in lots of misery. Dr. Bassett, the captain of the train, did all he could for him, but he died at 10 o'clock and we buried him. We got ready and started at 11 the same day and the moon was new just then.

We got news every day that people were dying by the hundreds in St. Joe and St. Louis. It was alarming. When we hitched up and got ready to move, [the] Dr. said, "Boys, we will have to drive day and night." . . . We drove night and day and got out of reach of the cholera. . . .

We got across the plains to Fort Larimie, the 16th of June and the ignorant driver broke down a good many oxen on the trains. There were a good many ahead of us, who had doubled up their trains and left tons upon tons of bacon and other provisions. . . .

Starting to cross the desert to Black Rock at 4 o'clock in the evening, we traveled all night. The next day it was hot and sandy. . . .

A great number of cattle perished before we got to Black Rock.

. . . I drove our oxen all the time and I knew about how much an ox could stand. Between nine and ten o'clock a breeze came up and the oxen threw up their heads and seemed to have new life. At noon, we drove into Black Rock. . . .

We crossed the South Pass on the Fourth of July. The ice next morning was as thick as a dinner-plate.

[The wagon train went on through Honey Lake to Deer Creek in Sacramento Valley and then to Redding Springs on 13 October 1849.]

On the morning of the 15th we went to dry-digging mining. We dug and dug to the first of November, at night it commenced raining, and rained and snowed pretty much all the winter. We had a tent but it barely kept us all dry. There were from eight to twelve in one camp. We cut down pine trees for stakes to make a cabin. It was a whole week before we had a cabin to keep us dry.

The first week in January, 1850, we bought a hundred pounds of bear meat at one dollar per pound.

Alvin Coffey, *Reminiscences,* taken from the bound unfolioed manuscript copy of *Reminiscences of Society Members* with the special permission of the Society of California Pioneers, San Francisco.

CALIFORNIA'S FIRST BLACK NEWSPAPER

[*In 1855, Mifflin W. Gibbs began California's first Black paper,* Mirror of the Times. *He issued this call for Black unity.*]

A new Governor, hostile to all our interests is soon to be inaugurated, and a Legislature of the same stripe is about to assemble, and we are quarreling among ourselves instead of uniting on the subject of our rights, and devising some general plan of operation for the good of the whole people. . . .

We have enemies enough to contend with among the corrupt politicians in this State, and the Colored man who is satisfied with his condition, and would unite with his oppressors rather than spend a dollar, or make any sacrifice to secure his own protection, is so low in the scale of manhood, that he ought to be drummed out of decent society, and his passage paid to some of the Southern States where he may be able to obtain a master. We call upon every man who wears a dark skin to come up and unite on this question—do his whole duty—let there be no faltering or quibbling in the premises.

Mirror of the Times, 12 December 1857.

5 THE SOUTH WHEN COTTON WAS KING

Masters and Slaves

By the time rebel guns opened fire on Fort Sumter in April 1861, the South had become a backward agricultural region. It had few railroads, industries, schools, or libraries. While the writers of New England were blazing new paths in American literature, life among the slaveholders was pictured by one of their servants:

> Quarrels and brawls of the most violent description were frequent . . . and whenever they became especially dangerous, and glasses were thrown, dirks drawn, and pistols fired, it was the duty of the slaves to rush in, and each one drag his master from the fight, and carry him home.

Williams G. Simms, a noted South Carolina novelist and historian, described the effect of slavery on literature in these words: "No, sir, there never will be a literature worth the name in the Southern States so long as their aristocracy remains based on so many head of Negroes and so many bales of cotton."

Meanwhile, poor whites like Hinton Helper of North Carolina were complaining:

We are compelled to go to the North for almost every article of utility or adornment, from matches, shoe-pegs, and paintings to cotton-mills, steamships, and statuary . . . we are dependent on Northern capitalists for the means necessary to build our railroads, canals and other public improvements.

Even the cotton gin, the invention that turned the South white with cotton and dark with slaves, was devised by Eli Whitney, a Massachusetts schoolteacher.

Whitney's invention changed the course of Southern history. At a time when slavery appeared to be dying, a machine was invented which did the work previously done by fifty slaves. Cotton prices dropped, and world demand rose. The slave population leaped from less than a million in 1793 to four million just before the Civil War. More land was planted for cotton and still more was needed. The price of slaves rose from two hundred to two thousand dollars each. Cotton production soared from a few million to two billion bales. The cotton frontier moved west from the Carolinas into Alabama, Texas, southern Kansas, and California.

For slaves, the changes brought by the cotton gin were unfortunate. They became cogs in the vast, driving machine that piled up cotton for the world market. Masters and overseers, a planter admitted, treated both slave and land as something to be "worn out, not improved." The life span of the field slave fell as cotton production rose.

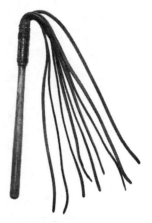

The cat-o'-nine-tails, used on every plantation, was manufactured in the North.

The cotton gin. As it drove down the price of cotton garments, it increased the need for more slaves and more land for cotton planting.

A slave coachman. Skilled or house slaves were better treated than field hands.

Seven out of eight slaves worked on the Southern plantations, mainly in the Deep South. Their working day was from early sunrise to late sunset. Every plantation owner or overseer set the working conditions and served as judge and jury over his slaves. According to one Southerner, overseers, who were paid according to how much was produced, "care for nothing but to make a large crop." Slaves were not human—they were property. As property, they could be bought and sold at auctions, willed to relatives, rented out, lost at cards, or won in raffles.

Slaves did far more than labor in the fields. Some were house servants—butlers, cooks, maids, and nurses—and these were better treated than field slaves. Some were made overseers and given positions of trust. For example, Joe Anderson helped Cyrus McCormick invent his famous reaper. And Irish visitor Isaac Weld, touring the South at the end of the eighteenth century, noticed that slaveholders "have nearly everything they can want on their own estates. Amongst their slaves are found taylors, shoemakers, carpenters, smiths, turners, wheelwrights, weavers, tanners. . . ." A Georgia doctor admitted in 1837 that "without a population of blacks the whole country would become a desert."

The Slaveholder Justifies Slavery

To the white Southerner, slavery was a social as well as a labor system. To justify it, masters developed elaborate theories. Alexander H. Stephens of Georgia said that "equality of the races is fundamentally wrong" and proclaimed "the great truth that the Negro is not equal to the white man; that slavery—subordination to the superior race—is his natural and normal condition." John C. Calhoun of South Carolina claimed that slaveholders took "low, degraded and savage" Africans and "civilized" and "improved" them. George Fitzhugh of Virginia said that slaves were "perhaps the happiest and the freest people in the world."

The slaveholders carefully taught poor whites and their slaves this myth of superior and inferior races. Through this myth and their wealth, three thousand leading slaveholders were able to control the South's eight million whites and four million Blacks. In 1866, President Andrew Johnson, who had been a poor white, told Frederick Douglass, "There were twenty-seven nonslaveholders to one slaveholder [in Tennessee], and yet the slave power controlled the state." Ministers, editors, teachers, scientists, and sheriffs followed their wishes. "There is no legislation except for the benefit of slavery and slaveholders," wrote Hinton Helper, a poor white from North Carolina. The South was organized to protect slave property, and so the interests of the majority of its citizens were neglected. The economic progress and growth of democracy that took place on the free soil of the West and North left the South untouched. "We meet multitudes of poor whites on all our great roads, seeking new homes to the West or the

A slave is auctioned off to the highest bidder. Whites and Blacks alike were dehumanized by participating in and seeing such scenes.

South," wrote a South Carolina planter. "Slavery," concluded Hinton Helper, "destroys whatever it touches."

Although they suffered deeply from competition with slave labor, poor whites supported this system that called them superior because of their white skins. They served in the nightly slave patrols for six cents an hour and hunted runaways for the rewards. Only a few of them helped slaves escape or took part in the many slave conspiracies and revolts.

The Slave in Southern Cities

Not all slaves were beaten, and few were beaten this badly, but all slaves knew that at any given time they could be subjected to whipping.

Half a million slaves worked in Southern cities and towns by 1860. They became ship pilots, lumberjacks, printers, or factory workers. They built bridges in Mississippi, hotels in Alabama, roads in Louisiana, and ships in Georgia and Maryland. One was a locomotive engineer. Another was a laboratory assistant in the United States Naval Academy in Maryland. When, in 1847, white workers of the Tredegar Iron Works of Virginia went on strike to protest the use of slaves, the manager replaced the strikers with more slaves. When the foreman who was making the Statue of Freedom for the Capitol in Washington went on strike, he was replaced by a slave. The *New York Tribune* reported, "The black master builder lifted the ponderous masses and bolted them together, joint by joint, piece by piece, till they blended into the majestic freedom." Many skilled whites migrated to the free lands of the West rather than face competition with slaves.

In the decades before the Civil War, masters increasingly trained their slaves in various trades so that they could rent them out at high rates. The slave preferred either skilled or city work to plantation work because of the freedom and dignity it gave him. When slave Emanuel Quivers was hired out to work at the Tredegar Iron Works, he persuaded the owner to buy him. Then Quivers worked extra hours for pay—and in four years was able to buy himself, his wife, and four children. As a free man he went to California during the Gold Rush and lived to see his children educated. His son became a foreman in a factory in Stockton.

City slaves enjoyed greater liberty than plantation hands. They learned self-reliance and often earned money for themselves by working extra hours. Slave Lunsford Lane had agents in three North Carolina cities selling his specially prepared pipe tobacco in fifteen-cent packages. Lane soon made enough money to purchase his freedom and that of his large family. Citizens of Charleston bitterly resented the urban slaves because they were "in every way . . . conducting themselves as if they were not slaves." Another white warned that city slaves "get strange notions into their heads

Lunsford Lane.

Henry Brown emerging from the small box that carried him to freedom. The white Southerner who helped Brown escape was sent to prison.

and grow discontented," which was true. In Richmond, Henry Brown, who worked in a tobacco factory, found a white man who was willing to seal him in a box and ship him to Philadelphia. In Baltimore, Frederick Douglass learned how to read and write from white playmates and later escaped to New York with a pass from a Black seaman.

The Free African American Population

A quarter of a million free people of color lived in the South by 1860. Despite severe restrictions, several achieved outstanding success. In 1846 Norbert Rillieux of New Orleans perfected a vacuum pan that revolutionized the sugar refining industry in Europe and America. Sent by his wealthy father to France to study, Rillieux taught applied mechanics in Paris and published many scientific papers by the time he was twenty-four. Dr. Charles Browne, of the United States Department of Agriculture, said, "Rillieux's invention is the greatest in the history of American chemical engineering, and I know of no other invention that has brought so great a saving to all branches of chemical engineering." Rillieux submitted a complicated proposal for a sewerage system for his city, but it was not accepted. He returned to Paris, where he lived for the rest of his life.

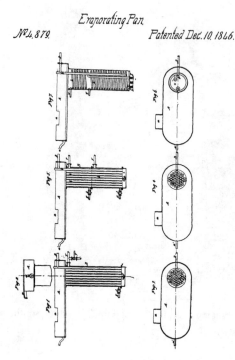

Norbert Rillieux's evaporating pan for sugar refining. This invention revolutionized the sugar-refining industry.

There were other African American inventors from the South, but it is difficult to determine how many since, under existing laws, they could be refused permission to patent their creations. However, Henry Blair of Maryland patented a seed planter for corn in 1834, and in 1854 Henry Sigler of Galveston, Texas, patented an improved fishhook and later sold his patent for only $625.

Patent drawing for Henry Blair's seed-planter, 1834. It is the first patent to be held by an African American. The master held patents for anything slaves invented. There may have been a considerable number of inventions by slaves because the Southern Confederacy thought it necessary to include a section in its Constitution stating that the owner of a slave also controlled his invention.

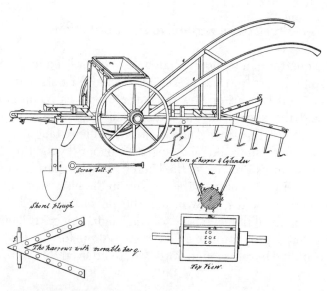

A large number of educated and talented New Orleans African Americans contributed to a book of French verse, *Les Cenelles,* edited in 1845 by Armand Lanusse. By 1816, the New Orleans Opera House established a segregated section in the upper tier for the many people of color who attended it.

Although the teaching of slaves—and sometimes of free African Americans—was forbidden by law, some schools operated illegally, two of them with Black principals. One of these principals, John Chavis of North Carolina, instructed whites during the day and African Americans at night (at lower fees). Daniel A. Payne, a South Carolina free Black, established a school with a curriculum that included arithmetic, literature, science, chemistry, botany, zoology, astronomy, and geography, as well as reading and writing. Payne had taught himself these subjects as well as Greek, Latin, and French. Later, at Wilberforce, Payne would become the first African American college president in America.

Bishop Daniel A. Payne of the African Methodist Episcopal Church.

To most whites, the free people of color were a dangerous third force in a society built for two—slave and master. "The superior condition of the free persons of color," complained a group of whites in Charleston in 1822, "excites discontent among our slaves, who continually have before their eyes, persons of the same color, many of whom they had known in slavery . . . freed from the control of masters, working where they please, going whither they please. . . ." Seeing these freemen, "the slave pants for liberty."

Despite the fact that the free Blacks were carefully watched, they helped slaves escape. Their homes and stores were often the Southern stations of the Underground Railroad. Some forged passes for slaves, and others contributed money to help them escape. Samuel Martin of Mississippi, an ex-slave who became wealthy, bought six slaves and, in 1844, led them to the free soil of Pennsylvania. Four thousand other free people of color owned slaves, usually family members or close friends, that the law would not allow them to liberate.

Day-to-Day Resistance to Bondage

The South became a battleground in the slaves' daily struggle to improve their lot, to live in dignity, or to escape to freedom. With courage and ingenuity, African Americans made protection of the family their first line of defense. Family strength was the psychological base that launched other kinds of resistance. "My mother often hid us in the woods," wrote Moses Grandy, "to prevent master selling us." Alabama slave Cudjo Lewis reported that slave women "overpowered and soundly thrashed" an overseer

Ellen Craft dressed as a young slaveholder. With her darker husband serving as her "coachman," the couple rode to freedom in high style, stopping at the best Southern hotels. They moved to England, where they entered school.

who had insulted one of them. The slaves who labored in the fields destroyed tools and crops and sometimes tried to poison masters and overseers. They set so many fires that some companies refused to insure homes in the slave states. The slaves pretended to be lame, sick, blind, or insane, and they often pretended stupidity or clumsiness to avoid work.

Dr. Samuel Cartwright of New Orleans, a respected Southern medical man, was convinced that African Americans suffered from special diseases. He called one *dysaethesia aethiopica* and claimed that it caused Blacks to "break, waste, and destroy everything they handle." His other discovery was *"drapetomania, or the disease causing negroes to run away."* This "disease of the mind" was sometimes cured, he said, by "whipping the devil out of them." To those who claimed that slavery was such a happy life and so "natural" to African Americans, their resistance could only be viewed as *a disease peculiar to negroes."*

Each year, thousands escaped to Southern cities, free states, Mexico, or Canada. Entire colonies lived in the woods or the swamps from Virginia to Florida. America's first treaty under the constitution asked the Creek Indians to return slaves who were being hidden in their villages in Georgia.

Slaves fled their masters long before the Underground Railroad was developed. They set out into an unknown land where every white face was a possible enemy. They hid in trees, tall grass, hollow logs, churches, schools, attics, and woods. They escaped aboard ships, sleds, horses, and wagons. Some got away in barrels, sacks, and coffins. Sometimes they had to battle slave catchers on the road. On Christmas Eve 1855, a group of young Black people escaped by wagon from Virginia. They were well armed and

Ann Wood and other young slaves drive off slave catchers.

A slave gallops to freedom on his master's horse. "Don't be afraid to take the best horse, you're entitled to it," a group of runaways wrote to their friends in slavery.

led by young, determined Ann Wood. When a posse surrounded them in Maryland, Ann Wood dared the whites to fire, holding "a double-barreled pistol in one hand and a long dirk knife in the other, utterly unterrified and fully ready for a death struggle." The posse retreated, and the proud young people reached Philadelphia in safety.

To prevent flight, planters took every precaution. They kept all knowledge of the outside world from their bondsmen. State laws provided severe punishments for anyone who taught a slave to read or write. "The increase of knowledge [among slaves] is the principal agent in evolving the spirit we have to fear," wrote a Carolina planter in 1800. Slaves who worked near water were "not allowed to learn the art of swimming," wrote slave Solomon Northrup. Slave patrols guarded the countryside at night. Savage dogs, valued at three hundred dollars each, were kept in readiness to hunt runaways. White ministers preached to slaves that "they must always obey their masters." Rebellious slaves were publicly whipped or sold farther South so that the price of resistance would be clear to all.

In many parts of the South, slaves waged a battle to learn to read and write, to practice religion, or even to hear what was going on outside the plantation. "My father and other boys used to crawl under the house an' lie on the ground to hear massa read the newspaper to missus," recalled one. Another told how her mistress would spell out words she did not want the

Despite every effort to control slaves, they fled to the swamps or planned revolts.

slave to know, but "I ran to uncle an' spelled them over to him, an' he told me what they meant."

Slave Booker T. Washington told how slaves "kept themselves informed of events by what was termed the 'grapevine' telegraph." Frederick Douglass conducted a Sunday school in the woods until he was warned that he would be killed if he did not stop.

The Slave Revolts

The greatest fear of the slaveholder was not the escape of his slaves but possible revolts. A Carolina planter warned a friend, "The love of freedom, sir, is an inborn sentiment . . . it springs forth and flourishes with a vigor that defies all check. There never have been slaves in any country, who have not seized the first favorable opportunity to revolt." It was not surprising, then, when a visitor to the South reported that "I have known times here when not a single planter had a calm night's rest. They never lie down to sleep without . . . loaded pistols at their sides."

Slave revolts were planned, or took place, in Southern cities, on plantations, or aboard ships. Except for those at sea, none could succeed, for the entire armed might of the local and state militia and the armed forces of

Africans were raffled off during slavery along with horses and cattle.

Nat Turner surrenders.

the federal government stood ready to crush any rebellion. But plots and revolts marked the entire history of slavery in the United States. They were a last, hopeless, and desperate battle against a system that held lives in contempt and destroyed human dignity.

In 1800, Gabriel Prosser, a Virginia slave, prepared thousands of his fellow bondsmen to attack Richmond. A violent storm saved the city. It washed out bridges and flooded roads, and before Gabriel could regroup his men, the plot was betrayed by two house slaves. The leaders were arrested, tried, and sentenced to death. One told the court that he had only done for his people what George Washington had done for America: "I have ventured my life . . . to obtain the liberty of my countrymen."

In Charleston, South Carolina, in 1822, a vast slave plot was uncovered. Its leader was a tall, muscular carpenter, Denmark Vesey, who spoke several languages. As a young man, Vesey had bought his own liberty when he won a $1,500 raffle. The conspiracy had been planned for four years, and the slaves involved had hidden away weapons and ammunition. The authorities, given information by two house slaves, arrested 131 suspects. An attempt to rescue the slaves was feared. Federal troops stood by to protect the city as the leaders were led to the gallows. Before the traps were sprung, the doomed men called on slaves everywhere to revolt until freedom was theirs.

It was the Nat Turner revolt of 1831 which so frightened the South that at least one state considered giving up slavery. Turner led his small band of Virginia slaves from plantation to plantation, murdering slaveholding families and recruiting their slaves. Before the rebellion was finally smashed, federal troops, artillery, and state forces had to be called in. For two months a panic-stricken Virginia legislature talked seriously of ending slavery. But the lawmakers decided, instead, to crush all slave resistance with more severe laws and tighter controls over slaves. Since Nat Turner was a preacher and an educated man, Southern states increased their control of Black preachers and the education of slaves. "To see you with a book in your hand, they would almost cut your throat," recalled one slave.

A member of the Virginia legislature admitted how far they would go to keep slaves from learning.

> We have, as far as possible, closed every avenue by which light might enter their minds. If you could extinguish the capacity to see the light, our work would be completed; they would then be on a level with the beasts of the field, and we should be safe! . . .

The spirit of defiance among slaves did not end with the death of Nat Turner. "We are living on a volcano," warned one slaveholder. Two mu-

Africans aboard the *Amistad* seize control.

tinies aboard the ships of the slave trade were successful. In 1839, Cinque, son of an African king, led fifty-four slaves in a revolt aboard the *Amistad*. "I would not see you serve the white men," he told them. "You had better be killed than live many moons in misery. . . . I could die happy if by dying I could save so many of my brothers from the bondage of the white men." Cinque and his men seized the ship and tried to sail it back to Africa. By the treachery of the slave dealers, whose lives they had spared, they were landed on the Long Island coast and captured. Cinque and others were finally freed by the Supreme Court of the United States after a lengthy battle by ex-president John Quincy Adams, who served as their lawyer.

In 1841, a slave named Madison Washington led a revolt aboard the *Creole* that also succeeded. Washington rescued his wife, who was held below decks with other slave women. The lives of the white crew had been spared on promises of good behavior. However, the crew proved to be treacherous, and the slaves wanted to execute them. At this point, Washington said, "We have got our liberty, and that is all that we have been fighting for. Let no more blood be shed." The free men and women of the *Creole* sailed to the West Indies, and lived out their lives in freedom.

Until Emancipation Day, slave men and women battled for their dignity and freedom in ways that appeared most practical. Many demonstrated the same raw bravery and stubborn courage as the minutemen at Concord, or the ragged armies at Valley Forge.

A Slave Picks Cotton

[*Solomon Northup was a free man who was kidnapped in Washington, D.C., and sold into slavery. He worked for twelve years as a plantation slave before he finally won his freedom. He describes cotton picking on a Louisiana plantation, in late August, the cotton-picking season.*]

When a new hand, one unaccustomed to the business, is sent for the first time into the field, he is whipped up smartly and made for that day to pick as fast as he can possibly. At night it is weighed, so that his capability in cotton picking is known. He must bring in the same weight each night following. If it falls short, it is considered evidence that he has been laggard, and a greater or less number of lashes is the penalty.

An ordinary day's work is two hundred pounds. A slave who is accustomed to picking, is punished, if he or she brings in a less quantity than that. There is a great difference among them as regards this kind of labor. Some of them seem to have a natural knack, or quickness, which enables them to pick with great celerity, and with both hands, while others, with whatever practice or industry, are utterly unable to come up to the ordinary standard. Such hands are taken from the cotton field and employed in other business. . . .

The hands are required to be in the cotton field as soon as it is light in the morning, and, with the exception of ten or fifteen minutes, which is given them at noon to swallow their allowance of cold bacon, they are not permitted to be a moment idle until it is too dark to see, and when the moon is full, they often times labor till the middle of the night. They do not dare to stop even at dinner time, nor return to the quarters, however late it be, until the order to halt is given by the driver.

The day's work over in the field, the baskets are "toted," or in other words, carried to the gin-house, where the cotton is weighed. . . . This done, the labor of the day is not yet ended, by any means. Each one must then attend to his respective chores. One feeds the mules, another the swine—another cuts the wood, and so forth; besides, the packing is all done by candlelight. Finally, at a late hour, they reach the quarters, sleepy and overcome with the long day's toil. Then a fire must be kindled in the cabin, the corn ground in the small hand-mill, and supper, and dinner for the next day in the field, prepared. All that is allowed them is corn and bacon, which is given out at the corncrib and smokehouse every Sunday morning. Each one receives, as his weekly allowance, three and a half pounds of bacon, and corn enough to make a peck of meal. That is all—no tea, coffee, sugar, and, with the exception of a very scanty sprinkling now and then, no salt. . . .

S. Northrup, *Twelve Years a Slave* (Philadelphia, n.d.), 165–69.

MASTER AND SLAVE RELATIONSHIPS

[*Along with the cruel and heartless masters, there were also some kind and trusting owners. In this last will of Judge Upshur one can see the kind of feeling that existed between this master and his slave of twenty-four years.*]

I emancipate and set free my servant, David Rice, and direct my executors to give him *one hundred dollars.* I recommend him in the strongest manner to the respect, esteem, and confidence of any community in which he may happen to live. He has been my slave for twenty-four years, during all which time he has been trusted to every extent, and in every respect; my confidence in him has been unbounded; his relation to myself and family has always been such as to afford him daily opportunities to deceive and injure us; yet he has never been detected in any serious fault, nor even in an unintentional breach of decorum of his station. His intelligence is of a higher order, his integrity above all suspicion, and his sense of right and propriety correct, and even refined. I feel that he is justly entitled to carry this certificate from me in the new relations which he must now form; it is due to his long and most faithful services, and to the sincere and steady friendship which I bear to him. In . . . twenty-four years, I have never given him, nor had occasion to give him, one unpleasant word. I know of no man who has fewer faults or more excellences than he.

Harriet Beecher Stowe, *The Key to Uncle Tom's Cabin* (Boston, 1854), 39–40.

[Josiah Henson tells us of a completely different kind of relationship between a master and a slave. The kind of life which this master led made it necessary for him to place a good deal of faith in his slave.]

. . . My master's habits were such as were common enough among the dissipated planters of the neighborhood; and one of their frequent practices was to assemble on Saturday or Sunday, which were their holidays, and gamble, run horses, or fight game-cocks, discuss politics, and drink whiskey and brandy and water all day long. Perfectly aware that they would not be able to find their own way home at night, each one ordered his body-servant to come after him and help him home. I was chosen for this confidential duty by my master; and many is the time I have held him on his horse, when he could not hold himself in the saddle, and walked by his side in darkness and mud from the tavern to his house. Of course, quarrels and brawls of the most violent description were frequent consequences of these meetings; and whenever they became especially dangerous, and glasses were thrown, dirks drawn, and pistols fired, it was the duty of the slaves to rush in, and each one drag his master from the fight, and carry him home. To tell the truth, this was a part of my business for which I felt no reluctance. I was young, remarkably athletic and self-relying, and in such affrays I carried it with a high hand, and would elbow my way among the whites,—whom it would have been almost death for me to strike—seize my master and drag him out, mount him on his horse, or crowd him into his buggy, with the ease with which I would handle a bag of corn. I knew that I was doing for him what he could not do for himself, and showing my superiority to others, and acquiring their respect in some degree, at the same time.

Josiah Henson, *Truth Stranger Than Fiction, Father Henson's Story of His Own Life* (Boston, 1858), 31–33.

FREDERICK DOUGLASS: LIFE AS A BATTLE

[Edward Covey, a professional "slave breaker" for masters with hard-to-handle slaves, had already beaten Frederick Douglass several times when Douglass decided to resist. This is his story of the fight.]

The fighting madness had come upon me, and I found my strong fingers firmly attached to the throat of my cowardly tormentor; as heedless of consequences, at the moment, as though we stood as equals before the law. The very color of the man was forgotten. I felt as supple as a cat, and was ready for the snakish creature at every turn. Every blow of his was parried, though I dealt no blows in turn. I was strictly on the *defensive,* preventing him from injuring me, rather than trying to injure him. I flung him on the ground several times, when he meant to have hurled me there. I held him so firmly by the throat, that his blood followed my nails. He held me and I held him.

All was fair, thus far, and the contest was about equal. My resistance was entirely unexpected, and Covey was taken all aback by it, for he trembled in every limb. *"Are you going to resist,* you scoundrel?" said he. To which, I returned a polite "yes sir." . . . He called for his cousin Hughes, to come to his assistance. . . . I was still *defensive* toward Covey, but *aggressive* toward Hughes; and, at the first approach of the latter, I dealt a blow, in my desperation, which fairly sickened my youthful assailant. He went off, bending over with pain, and manifesting no disposition to come within my reach again. . . .

By this time, Bill, the hired man, came home. . . . "What shall I do, Mr. Covey?" said Bill. "Take hold of him—take hold of him!" said Covey. With a toss of his head, peculiar to Bill, he said . . . "My master hired me here, to work, and *not* to help you whip Frederick." It was now my turn to speak. "Bill," said I, "don't put your hands on me." To which he replied "My God! Frederick, I aint goin' to tech ye," and Bill walked off, leaving Covey and myself to settle matters as best we might.

But, my present advantage was threatened when I saw Caroline (the slavewoman of Covey) coming to the cow yard for milk, for she was a powerful woman, and could have mastered me very easily, exhausted as I now was. As soon as she came into the yard, Covey attempted to rally her to his aid. Strangely—and, I may add, fortunately—Caroline was in no humor to take a hand in any such sport. . . . Caroline answered . . . precisely as Bill had answered, but in *her,* it was at greater peril so to answer; she was the slave of Covey. . . .

Covey at length [two hours had elapsed] gave up the contest. Letting me go, he said—puffing and blowing at a great rate—"now, you scoundrel, go to your work; I would not have whipped you half so much as I have had you not resisted." The fact was, *he had not whipped me at all.* . . .

During the whole six months that I lived with Covey, after this transaction, he never laid on me the weight of his finger in anger. . . .

[*In the Baltimore shipyard where Douglass worked as a caulker, white and free Black carpenters were feuding. Though Douglass was a slave, the ill feeling in the yard drew him into the fight.*]

The spirit . . . was one of malice and bitterness, toward colored people *generally,* and I suffered with the rest, and suffered severely. . . . Edward North, the biggest in everything . . . ventured to strike me, whereupon I picked him up, and threw him into the dock. Whenever any of them struck me, I struck back again, regardless of consequences. I could manage any of them *singly;* and, while I could keep them from combining, I succeeded very well. In the conflict which ended my stay at Mr. Gardiner's, I was beset by four of them at once. . . . Two of them were as large as myself, and they came near killing me, in broad day light. The attack was made suddenly, and simultaneously. One came in front, armed with a brick; there was one at each side and one behind, and they closed up around me. I was struck on all sides. . . . It was impossible to stand against so many. . . .

After making my escape from the ship yard, I went straight home, and related the story of the outrage to [my] Master Hugh Auld. . . .

. . . His indignation was really strong and healthy; but, unfortunately, it resulted from the thought that his rights of property, in my person, had not been respected, more than from any sense of the outrage committed on me *as a man.* . . . He related the outrage to the magistrate [Mr. Watson] . . . and seemed to expect that a warrant would, at once, be issued for the arrest of the lawless ruffians. . . .

"Mr. Auld, who saw this assault of which you speak?"

"It was done, sir, in the presence of a ship yard full of hands."

"Sir," said Watson, "I am sorry, but I cannot move in this matter except upon the oath of white witnesses."

"But here's the boy; look at his head and face . . . *they* show *what* has been done."

But Watson insisted that he was not authorized to do anything, unless *white* witnesses . . . would come forward, and testify to what had taken place. . . .

Frederick Douglass, *My Bondage and My Freedom* (New York and Auburn, 1855), 242–46, 312–17.

THE BREAKUP OF SLAVE FAMILIES

[*Josiah Henson describes the auction sale at which his family was broken up.*]

. . . the remembrance of the breaking up of McPherson's estate is photographed in its minutest features in my mind. The crowd collected round the stand, the huddling group of Negroes, the examination of muscle, teeth, the exhibition of agility, the look of the auctioneer, the agony of my mother—I can shut my eyes and see them all.

My brothers and sisters were bid off first, and one by one, while my mother, paralyzed by grief, held me by the hand. Her turn came, and she was bought by Isaac Riley of Montgomery county. Then I was offered to the assembled purchasers. My mother, half distracted with the thought of parting forever from all her children, pushed through the crowd, while the bidding for me was going on, to the spot where Riley was standing. She fell at his feet, and clung to his knees, entreating him in tones that a mother could only command, to buy her *baby* as well as herself, and spare to her one, at least, of her little ones. Will it, can it be believed that this man, thus appealed to, was capable not merely of turning a deaf ear to her supplication, but of disengaging himself from her with such violent blows and kicks, as to reduce her to the necessity of creeping out of his reach, and mingling the groan of bodily suffering with the sob of a breaking heart? As she crawled away from the brutal man I heard her sob out, "Oh, Lord Jesus, how long, how long shall I suffer this way!" I must have been then between five and six years old. I seem to see and hear my poor weeping mother now. This was one of my earliest observations of men; an experience which I only shared with thousands of my race. . . .

Josiah Henson, *Truth Stranger Than Fiction, Father Henson's Story of His Own Life* (Boston, 1858), 11–13.

EFFORTS TO REUNITE THE SLAVE FAMILY

[*During the entire period of American slavery, slaves made efforts to rejoin loved ones sold away. These attempts to reunite families can be seen in the reward notices printed by owners in Southern newspapers.*]

Macon (Ga.) Messenger, November 23, 1837. $25 Reward.—Ran away, a Negro man, named Cain. He was brought from Florida, and has a wife near Mariana, and probably will attempt to make his way there.

Richmond (Va.) Compiler, September 8, 1837. Ran away from the subscriber, Ben. He ran off without any known cause, and I suppose he is aiming to go to his wife, who was carried from the neighborhood last winter.

Richmond (Va.) Enquirer, February 20, 1838. Stop the Runaway!!!—$25 Reward. Ran away from the Eagle Tavern, a Negro fellow named Nat. He is no doubt attempting to follow his wife, who was lately sold to a speculator named Redmond. The above reward will be paid by Mrs. Lucy M. Downman, of Sussex County, Va.

Savannah (Ga.) Republican, September 3, 1838. $20 Reward for my Negro man Jim.—Jim is about 50 or 55 years of age. It is probable he will aim for Savannah, as he said he had children in that vicinity.

Lexington (Ky.) Observer and Reporter, September 28, 1838. $50 Reward.—Ran away from the subscriber, a Negro girl, named Maria. She is of a copper color, between 13 and 14 years of age—bare headed and bare footed. She is small of her age—very sprightly and very likely. She stated she was going to see her mother at Maysville.

Theodore Dwight Weld, *American Slavery As It Is. Testimony of a Thousand Witnesses* (New York, 1839), 164–66.

SOLD TO LOUISIANA

[*Slaves feared being sold to states of the Deep South. One slave describes the scene as a group is taken to a railroad depot.*]

. . . the victims were to take the cars from a station called Clarkson turnout, which was about four miles from master's place. The excitement was so great that the overseer and driver could not control the relatives and friends of those that were going away, as a large crowd of both old and young went down to the depot to see them off. Louisiana was considered by the slaves as a place of slaughter, so those who were going did not expect to see their friends again. While passing along, many of the Negroes left their master's fields and joined us as we marched to the cars; some were yelling and wringing their hands, while others were singing little hymns that they were accustomed to for the consolation of those that were going away, such as,

> When we all meet in heaven,
>   There is no parting there;
> When we all meet in heaven,
>   There is parting no more.

We arrived at the depot and had to wait for the cars to bring the others from the Sumterville Jail, but they soon came in sight, and when the noise of the cars died away we heard wailing and shrieks from those in the cars. While some were weeping, others were fiddling, picking banjo, and dancing as they used to do in their cabins on the plantations. Those who were so merry had very bad masters, and even though they stood a chance of being sold to one as bad or even worse yet they were glad to be rid of the one they knew.

While the cars were at the depot, a large crowd of white people gathered, and were laughing and talking about the prospect of Negro traffic; but when the cars began to start and the conductor cried out, "all who are going on this train must get aboard without delay," the colored people cried out with one voice as though the heavens and earth were coming together, and it was so pitiful, that those hardhearted white men who had been accustomed to driving slaves all their lives, shed tears like children. As the cars moved away we heard the weeping and wailing from the slaves, as far as human voice could be heard; and from that time to the present I have neither seen nor heard from my two sisters, nor any of those who left Clarkson depot, on that memorable day.

Jacob Stroyer, *Sketches of My Life in the South* 1 (Salem, 1879): 29–31.

WHY THE SLAVES SANG

[In 1855 Frederick Douglass explained why slaves were expected to sing and why their sad songs were so much a part of slavery.]

... slaves are generally expected to sing as well as to work. A silent slave is not liked by masters or overseers. *"Make a noise," "make a noise,"* and *"bear a hand,"* are the words usually addressed to the slaves when there is silence amongst them. This may account for the almost constant singing heard in the Southern states. There was, generally, more or less singing among the teamsters, as it was one means of letting the overseer know where they were, and that they were moving on with the work. But, on allowance day, those who visited the great house farm were peculiarly excited and noisy. While on their way, they would make the dense old woods, for miles around, reverberate with their wild notes. These were not always merry because they were wild. On the contrary, they were mostly of a plaintive cast, and told a tale of grief and sorrow. In the most boisterous outbursts of rapturous sentiment, there was ever a tinge of deep melancholy. I have never heard any songs like those anywhere since I left slavery, except when in Ireland. There, I heard the same wailing notes, and was much affected by them. It was during the famine of 1845–6. . . .

I did not, when a slave, understand the deep meaning of those rude, and apparently incoherent songs. I was myself within a circle, so that I neither saw nor heard as those without might see and hear. They told a tale which was then altogether beyond my feeble comprehension; they were tones, loud, long, and deep, breathing the prayer and complaint of souls boiling over with the bitterest anguish. Every tone was a testimony against slavery, and a prayer to God for deliverance from chains. The hearing of those wild notes always depressed my spirits, and filled my heart with ineffable sadness. The mere recurrence, even now, afflicts my spirit, and while I am writing these lines, my tears are falling. To those songs I trace my first glimmering conceptions of the dehumanizing character of slavery. I can never get rid of that conception. Those songs still follow me, to deepen my hatred of slavery, and quicken my sympathies for my brethren in bonds.

Frederick Douglass, *My Bondage and My Freedom* (New York and Auburn, 1855), 97–99.

A SLAVE INVENTOR

[*In this letter, to one of those who had given money to buy the freedom of slave Benjamin Bradley, we learn of a remarkable inventor. Bradley helped pay for his own freedom and paid back those who had helped him.*]

Dear Sir:—I am very happy to inform you that the freedom of the slave Benjamin Bradley has been accomplished by the payment of $1,000, to which you contributed the final $122 necessary to make it up. . . .

Bradley was owned by a master in Annapolis, Maryland. Eight years ago he was employed in a printing office there. He was then about sixteen, and showed great mechanical skill and ingenuity. With a piece of gun-barrel, some pewter, a couple of pieces of round steel, and some materials, he constructed a *working model of a steam engine.*

His master soon afterwards got him the place of a helper in the department of Natural and Experimental Philosophy in the Naval Academy at Annapolis. He sold his first steam engine to a Midshipman. With the proceeds, and what money he could lay up (his master allowing him five dollars a month out of his wages), he built an engine large enough to drive the first cutter of a sloop-of-war at the rate of sixteen knots an hour. . . .

Professor Hopkins, of the Academy, says that he gets up the experiments for the lecture-room very handsomely. Being shown once how to line up the parabolic mirrors for concentrating heat, he always succeeds afterwards. So with the chemical experiments. He makes all the gasses, and works with them, showing the Drummond light, &c. Prof. Hopkins remarks of him that "he looks for *the law* by which things act."

He has been taught to read and write, mainly by the Professor's children; has made very good progress in arithmetic, and will soon take hold of algebra and geometry.

The Anglo-African Magazine 1 (November 1859): 367. Reprinted from the *Journal of Commerce.*

A CHARLESTON SCHOOLMASTER

[*Daniel A. Payne, a free Black of Charleston, opened his first school in 1829. He taught three children during the day and three adult slaves at night. Each pupil paid fifty cents a month. As his expenses mounted, he became discouraged and quit. Then a white man told him that the difference between a master and slave was "nothing but superior knowledge," and Payne decided to reopen his school.*]

On the first of the year 1830 I re-opened my school, which continued to increase in numbers until the room became too small, and I was constrained to produce [a larger] place. This in turn became too small, and one was built for me. . . .

During the three years of my attendance at the school of Mr. Thomas S. Bonneau I learned how to read, write, and spell; also arithmetic as far as the "Rule of Three." Spelling was a delightful exercise of my boyhood. In this I excelled. . . . History was my great delight. Of geography and map-drawing, English grammar and composition I knew nothing, because they were not taught in any of the schools for colored children. . . . [He then managed to find a geography and atlas for his classes.]

. . . at the same time with geography I studied and mastered English grammar. . . . I therefore added that to my curriculum.

Having now the groundwork, I began to build the superstructure. I commenced with "Playfair's Euclid," and proceeded as far as the first five books. The next thing that arrested my attention was botany. . . . Descriptive chemistry, natural philosophy, and descriptive astronomy followed in rapid succession. . . .

Then, on a Thursday morning, I bought a Greek grammar, a lexicon, and a Greek Testament. On the same day I mastered the Greek alphabet; on Friday I learned to write them; on Saturday morning I translated the first chapter of Mathew's Gospel from Greek into English. My very soul rejoiced and exulted in this glorious triumph. Next came the Latin and the French. Meanwhile I was pushing my studies in drawing and coloring till I was able to produce a respectable flower, fruit, or animal on paper and on velvet.

My researches in botany gave me a relish for zoology; but as I could never get hold of any work on this science, I had to *make books* for myself. This I did by killing such insects, toads, snakes, young alligators, fishes, and young sharks as I could catch. I then cleaned and stuffed those that I could, and hung them upon the walls of my school-room. . . .

My enthusiasm was the inspiration of my pupils. I used to take my first class into the woods every Saturday in search of insects, reptiles, and plants, and at the end of five years I had accumulated some fine specimens of each of these. . . .

. . . it was also one of my methods in order to interest my pupils to erect several gymnastic instruments, that they might develop their muscular systems and find amusement to break the monotony of the school-room; but in all their sports I led them in person. . . .

Bishop Daniel Alexander Payne, *Recollections of Seventy Years* (Nashville, 1888), 19–25.

THE CHRISTMAS SEASON ON THE PLANTATION

[*Ex-slave Jacob Stroyer describes the Christmas holidays when slaves had days off, visited relatives, and were not required to work.*]

Both masters and slaves regarded Christmas as a great day. When the slaveholders made a large crop they were pleased, and gave the slaves from five to six days, which was much enjoyed by the Negroes, especially by those who could dance. Christmas morning was held sacred both by master and slave, but in the afternoon or in a part of the next day the slaves were required to devote themselves to the pleasure of their masters. Some of the masters would buy presents for the slaves, such as hats and tobacco for the men, handkerchiefs and little things for the women, these things were given after they had been pleased with them, after either dancing or something for their amusement.

When the slaves came up to their master and mistress the latter would welcome them, the men would take off their hats and bow and the women would make a low courtsy. There would be two or three large pails filled with sweetened water with a gallon or two of whisky in each, this was dealt out to them until they were partly drunk; while this was going on those who could talk very well would give tokens of well wishing to master and mistress, and some who were born in Africa would sing some of their songs, or tell different stories of the customs in Africa. After this they would spend half a day in dancing in some large cotton house or on a scaffold, the master providing fiddlers who came from other plantations if there were none in the place, and who received from fifteen to twenty dollars on these occasions.

A great many of the strict members of the church who did not dance would be forced to do it to please their masters, the favorite tunes were *The Fisher's Hornpipe*, *The Devil's Dream* and *Black-eyed Susan*. . . .

After the dancing was over we had our presents, master giving to the men, and mistress to the women, then the slaves would go to their quarters and continue to dance. . . .

Jacob Stroyer, *Sketches of My Life in the South* 1 (Salem, 1879): 34–35.

THE DENMARK VESEY PLOT OF 1822

[*Denmark Vesey, a free man living in Charleston, South Carolina, planned to capture the city. Before his slave followers struck, the plot was betrayed and the leaders arrested. First, Rolla, the slave of the governor, tells his story to the court.*]

I know Denmark Vesey, on one occasion he asked me, what news? I told him, none. He replied, we are free, but the white people here won't let us be so; and the only way is, to raise up and fight the whites. I went to his house one night, to learn where the meetings were held. . . . Vesey told me, he was the leader in this plot. . . . Vesey induced me to join. When I went to Vesey's house, there was a meeting there, the room was full of people, but none of them white. That night, at Vesey's, we determined to have arms made, and each man to put in twelve and a half cents towards that purpose. . . . At this meeting, Vesey said, we were to take the guardhouse and magazines, to get arms; that we ought to rise up against the whites to get our liberties. He was the first to rise up and speak, and he read to us from the bible, how the *children of Israel were delivered out of Egypt from bondage;* he said, that the rising would take place last Sunday night week (the 16th June), and that Peter Poyas was one [leader].

[*Jesse, a slave.*] I was invited to Denmark Vesey's house, and when I went, I found several men met together, among whom was Ned Bennett, Peter Poyas, and others, whom I did not know. Denmark opened the meeting by saying, he had an important secret to communicate to us, which we must not disclose to any one, and if we did, we should be put to instant death. He said, we were deprived of our rights and privileges by the white people, and that our church was shut up, so that we could not use it, and that it was high time for us to seek for our rights, and that we were fully able to conquer the whites, if we were only unanimous and courageous, as the St. Domingo people were. He then proceeded to explain his plan, by saying, that they intended to make the attack by setting the governour's mills on fire, and also some houses near the water, and as soon as the bells began to ring for fire, that they should kill every man, as he came out of his door. . . .

[*A Black man reporting his talk with Peter Poyas.*] I asked what was the plan? . . . I am the captain, said he, to take the lower guardhouse and arsenal. But, I replied, when you are coming up, the sentinel will give the alarm. He said, he would advance a little distance ahead, and if he could only get a *grip at his throat he was a gone man,* for his sword was very sharp. . . . I then said, that this thing seems true. My man, he said, God has a hand in it, *we have been meeting for four years, and are not yet betrayed.* I told him, I was afraid, after all, of the white people from the back country, and Virginia, &c. He said that the blacks would collect so numerous from that country, we need not fear the whites from the other parts, for when we have once got the city we can keep them all out. . . .

James Hamilton, Jr., *Negro Plot—An Account of the late intended insurrection among a portion of the Blacks of the City of Charleston, South Carolina published by the Authority of the Corporation of Charleston* (Boston, 1822), 35, 36, 42.

THE NAT TURNER REBELLION, 1831

[The plantation rebellion led by preacher Nat Turner in August 1831 is described here from the point of view of the slave master, and then of the slaves.]

[*A master.*] I have a horrible, a heart-rending tale to relate. . . .

. . . a band of insurgent slaves (some of them believed to be runaways from the neighboring swamps), had turned out on Sunday night last, and murdered several whole families, amounting to 40 or 50 individuals. . . .

The insurrection was represented as one of a most alarming character. . . . Unfortunately a large number of the effective male population was absent at camp meeting in Gates county, some miles off . . . and the panic which they [the slaves] struck at the moment prevented the assembling of a force sufficient to check their career.

As soon as this intelligence was received, our authorities met, and decided on making an immediate application to col. *House,* commanding at Fortress Monroe, who at 6 o'clock this morning embarked on board the steam boat *Hampton,* with three companies and a piece of artillery for Suffolk. These troops were re-inforced in the roads by detachments from the U.S. ships *Warren* and *Natchez,* the whole amounting to nearly 300 men.

. . . the few [slaves] who have thus rushed headlong into the arena, will be shot down like crows or captured and made examples of. The militia are collecting in all the neighboring counties, and the utmost vigilance prevails. . . .

Niles' Weekly Register 40 (27 August 1831): 455–56.

Gen. Eppes, who is in command of the troops, reports under date of the 28th ult. [of August] that all the insurgents except Nat Turner, the leader, had either been taken or killed. On the 29th Gen. Broadnax reports to the governor that all was quiet and free from visible marauders; he thinks all have been killed or taken except four or five. He states that Nat, the ringleader, who calls himself general, and pretends to be a Baptist preacher, declares to his comrades that he is commissioned by Jesus Christ, and proceeds under his inspired directions . . . he is not taken, and the account of his being killed at the affair of the bridge is not correct. . . .

Niles' Weekly Register 41 (3 September 1831): 5.

[*Nat Turner tells how he hid himself and was captured.*] . . . I gave up all hope for the present, and on Thursday night, after having supplied myself with provisions . . . I scratched a hole under a pile of fence rails in a field, where I concealed myself for six weeks, never leaving my hiding place but for a few minutes in the dead of night to get water, which was very near. . . . I know not how long I might have led this life if accident had not betrayed me. A dog in the neighborhood passing by my hiding-place one night while I was out, was attracted by some meat I had in my cave, and crawled in and stole it, and was coming out just as I returned. A few nights after, twó Negroes having started to go hunting with the same dog . . . discovered me. . . . On making myself known they fled from me. Knowing then they would betray me, I immediately left my hiding place, and was pursued almost incessantly until I was taken a fortnight afterwards by Mr. Benjamin Phipps, in a little hole I had dug out with my sword . . . under the top of a fallen tree.

T. R. Gray, *The Confession, Trial and Execution of Nat Turner* (Petersburg, Virginia, 1881), 17–18.

[*Charity Bowery, an old slave woman.*] At the time of the old Prophet Nat, the colored folks was afraid to pray loud; for the whites threatened to punish 'em dreadfully, if the least noise was heard. The patrols was low drunken whites, and in Nat's time, if they heard any of the colored folks praying or singing a hymn, they would fall upon 'em and abuse 'em, and sometimes kill 'em afore master or missis could get to 'em. The brightest and best was killed in Nat's time. The whites always suspect such ones. They killed a great many at a place called Duplon. They killed Antonio, a slave of Mr. J. Stanley, whom they shot; then they pointed their guns at him, and told him to confess about the insurrection. He told 'em he didn't know anything about insurrection. They shot several balls through him, quartered him, and put his head on a pole at the fork of the road leading to the court. It was there but a short time. He had no trial. They never do. In Nat's time, the patrols would tie up the free colored people, flog 'em, and try to make 'em lie against one another, and often killed them before anybody could interfere. Mr. James Cole, High Sheriff, said, if any of the patrols came on his plantation, he would lose his life in defense of his people. . . .

Thomas Wentworth Higginson, "Nat Turner's Insurrection," *Atlantic Monthly* 8 (August 1861): 180.

[*Moses Grandy, another slave.*] Formerly slaves were allowed to have religious meetings of their own; but after the insurrection which I spoke of before, they were forbidden to meet even for worship. Often they are flogged if they are found singing or praying at home. They may go to the places of worship used by the whites; but they like their own meetings better. My wife's brother Isaac was a colored preacher. A number of slaves went privately into a wood to hold meetings; when they were found out, they were flogged, and each was forced to tell who else was there. Three were shot, two of whom were killed, and the other was badly wounded. For preaching to them, Isaac was flogged. . . .

Moses Grandy, *Narrative of the Life of Moses Grandy* (Boston, 1844), 35–36.

"SLAVERY IS RUINOUS TO THE WHITES . . ."

[*After the Nat Turner rebellion of 1831 had been crushed, the future of slavery was debated in the Virginia legislature. One of many delegates who attacked the system was T. Marshall, who pointed out its evil effect on whites.*]

Slavery is ruinous to the whites—retards improvement—roots out industrious population, banishes the yeomanry of the country—deprives the spinner, the weaver, the smith, the shoemaker, the carpenter of employment and support. The evil admits of no remedy—it is increasing, and will continue to increase, until the whole country[side] will be inundated with one black wave, covering its whole extent, with a few white faces here and there floating on the surface. The master has no capital but what is invested in human flesh—the father instead of being richer for his sons, is at a loss how to provide for them; there is no diversity of occupations, no incentive to enterprise. Labor of every species is disreputable because performed mostly by slaves. Our towns are stationary, our villages almost everywhere declining—and the general aspect of the country[side] marks the curse of a wasteful, idle, reckless population who have no interest in the soil, and care not how much it is impoverished. Public improvements are neglected, and the entire continent does not present a region, for which nature has done so much and art so little. . . .

Niles' Weekly Register 43 (8 September 1832): 23.

THE DREAM OF LIBERTY

*[What are the thoughts of a slave as he plans escape? Lewis Clarke, a Kentucky
slave in the 1840s, tells the worries and fears that went through his mind when he
was about to make a break for freedom. Clarke made good his escape.]*

I had long thought and dreamed of LIBERTY; I was now determined to
make an effort to gain it. No tongue can tell the doubt, the perplexities,
the anxiety, which a slave feels when making up his mind upon this subject. If he makes an effort and is not successful, he must be laughed at by
his fellows, he will be beaten unmercifully by the master, and then
watched and used the harder for it all his life.

And then, if he gets away, *who, what,* will he find? He is ignorant of the
world. All the white part of mankind that he has ever seen are enemies to
him and all his kindred. How can he venture where none but white faces
shall greet him? The master tells him that abolitionists *decoy* slaves off into
the free states to catch them and sell them to Louisiana or Mississippi;
and, if he goes to Canada, the British will put him in a *mine under ground,
with both eyes put out, for life.* How does he know what or whom to believe? A horror of great darkness comes upon him, as he thinks over what
might befall him. Long, very long time did I think of escaping before I
made the effort.

At length the report was started that I was to be sold for Louisiana.
Then I thought it was time to act. My mind was made up.

Harriet Beecher Stowe, *The Key to Uncle Tom's Cabin* (Boston, 1854), 21–22.

TROUBLES ON THE ROAD TO FREEDOM

*[After their escape, two teenage slaves, William and Charles Parker, ran into diffi-
culties on the way from Maryland to Pennsylvania.]*

The first place at which we stopped to rest was a village on the old York
road, called New Market. There nothing occurred to cause us alarm; so,
after taking some refreshments, we proceeded towards York; but when

near Logansville, we were interrupted by three white men, one of whom, a very large man, cried—

"Hallo!"

I answered,—"Hallo to you!"

"Which way are you travelling?" he asked.

We replied,—"To Little York."

"Why are you travelling so late?"

"We are not later than you are," I answered.

"Your business must be of consequence," he said.

"It is. We want to go to York to attend to it; and if you have any business, please attend to it, and don't be meddling with ours on the public highway. We have no business with you, and I am sure you have none with us."

"See here!" said he; "you are the fellows that this advertisement calls for," at the same time taking the paper out of his pocket, and reading it to us.

Sure enough, there we were, described exactly. He came closely to us, and said,—"You must go back."

I replied,—"If I must, I must, and you must take me."

"Oh, you need not make any big talk about it," he answered; "for I have taken back many a runaway, and I can take you. What's that you have in your hand?"

"A stick."

He put his hand into his pocket, as if to draw his pistol, and said,—"Come! give up your weapons."

I said again,—" 'Tis only a stick."

He then reached for it, when I stepped back and struck him a heavy blow on the arm. It fell as if broken; I think it was. Then he turned and ran, and I after him. As he ran, he would look back over his shoulder, see me coming, and then run faster, and haloo with all his might. I could not catch him, and it seemed, that, the longer he ran, the faster he went. The other two took to their heels at the first alarm,—thus illustrating the valor of the [Southern] chivalry!

At last I gave up the chase. The whole neighborhood by that time was aroused, and we thought best to retrace our steps to the place whence we started. Then we took a roundabout course until we reached the railroad, along which we travelled. For a long distance there was unusual stir and commotion. Every house was lighted up; and we heard people talking and horses galloping this way and that way, with other evidences of unusual excitement. This was between one and two o'clock in the morning.

William Parker, "The Freedman's Story," *Atlantic Monthly* 17 (February 1866): 158–59.

HENRY "BOX" BROWN IS *SHIPPED* TO FREEDOM

[*Brown climbed into a box in Richmond, Virginia, in 1848 and had a white friend
send him by express to Philadelphia. Here is his story of the trip.*]

. . . I took my place in this narrow prison, with a mind full of uncertainty as
to the result. It was a critical period of my life, I can assure you, reader; but
if you have never been deprived of your liberty, as I was, you cannot realize
the power of that hope of freedom. . . .

I laid me down in my darkened home of three feet by two, and . . . resigned myself to my fate. My friend was to accompany me but he failed to
do so; and contented himself with sending a telegraph message to his correspondent in Philadelphia, that such a box was on its way to his care.

I took with me a bladder filled with water to bathe my neck with, in case
of too great heat; and with no access to the fresh air, excepting three
small . . . holes, I started on my perilous cruise. I was first carried to the express office, the box being placed on its end, so that I started with my head
downwards, although the box was directed, "this side up with care." From
the express office, I was carried to the depot, and from thence tumbled
roughly into the baggage car, where I *happened* to fall "right side up," but
no thanks to my transporters. But after a while the cars stopped, and I was
put aboard a steamboat, *and placed on my head.* In this dreadful position,
I remained the space of an hour and a half, it seemed to me, when I began
to feel of my eyes and head, and found to my dismay, that my eyes were almost swollen out of their sockets, and the veins on my temple seemed
ready to burst. I made no noise however, determining to obtain *"victory or
death,"* but endured the terrible pain, as well as I could, sustained under
the whole by the thoughts of sweet liberty. About half an hour afterwards,
I attempted again to lift my hands to my face, but I found I was not able to
move them. A cold sweat now covered me from head to foot. . . . One-half
hour longer and my sufferings would have ended in that fate, which I preferred to slavery; but I lifted up my heart to God in prayer, believing that
he would yet deliver me, when to my joy, I overheard two men say, "We
have been here *two* hours and have travelled twenty miles, now let us sit
down, and rest ourselves." They . . . turned the box over, containing my
soul and body, thus delivering me from the power of the grim messenger
of death, who a few moments previously had aimed his fatal shaft at my
head, and had placed his icy hands on my throbbing heart. One of these
men inquired of the other, what he supposed that box contained, to which
his comrade replied, that he guessed it was the mail. "Yes," I thought, "it is
a *male*, indeed, although not the *mail* of the United States."

Soon after this fortunate event, we arrived at Washington, where I was thrown from the wagon, and again as my luck would have it, fell on my head. . . . Pretty soon, I heard some one say, "there is no room for this box, it will have to remain behind." I then again applied to the Lord, my help in all my difficulties, and in a few minutes I heard a gentleman direct the hands to place it aboard, as "it came with the mail and must go on with it." I was then tumbled into the car, my head downwards again, as I seemed to be destined to escape on my head. . . . We had not proceeded far, however, before more baggage was placed in the car, at a stopping place, and I was again turned to my proper position. No farther difficulty occurred until my arrival in Philadelphia. I reached this place at three o'clock in the morning, and remained in the depot until six o'clock A.M., at which time, a waggon drove up. . . . I was soon placed on this waggon, and carried to the house of my friend's correspondent, where quite a number of persons were waiting to receive me. They appeared to be some afraid to open the box at first, but at length one of them rapped upon it, and with a trembling voice, asked, "Is all right within?" to which I replied, "All right." The joy of these friends was excessive . . . each one seized hold of some tool, and commenced opening my grave. At length the cover was removed, and I arose, and shook myself . . . and I swooned away.

George Stearns, *Narrative of Henry Box Brown by Himself* (Boston, 1849), 60–62.

THE CONTENTED SLAVE WHO RAN AWAY

[James Christian had all that a person could want—except his freedom. He served the family of President Tyler in the White House, was always treated with kindness and generosity, had as much spending money as he wanted, and lived well. Yet even he ran away and was interviewed at the Philadelphia station of the Underground Railroad.]

"I have always been treated well; if I only have half as good times in the North as I have had in the South, I shall be perfectly satisfied. Any time I desired spending money, five or ten dollars were no object." . . . with regard to food also, he had fared as well as heart could wish, with abundance of leisure time at his command. His deportment was certainly very refined and gentlemanly. . . . He had been to William and Mary's College in his younger days, to wait on young master James B. C. where, through the kindness of some of the students, he had picked up a trifling amount of book learning. . . . On the death of the old Major [Christian, his owner] James fell into the hands of his son, Judge Christian. . . . Subsequently he fell into the hands of one of the Judge's sisters, Mrs. John Tyler (wife of ex-President Tyler), and then he became a member of the President's domestic household, was at the White House, under the President, from 1841 to 1845. . . .

"How did you like Mr. Tyler?" said an inquisitive member of the Vigilance Committee. "I didn't like Mr. Tyler much," was the reply. "Why?" again inquired the member of the Committee. "Because Mr. Tyler was a poor man. I never did like poor people. I didn't like his marrying into our family, who were considered very far Tyler's superiors." "On the plantation," he said, "Tyler was a very cross man, and treated the servants very cruelly; but the house servants were treated much better, owing to their having belonged to his wife, who protected them from persecution, as they had been favorite servants in her father's family." James estimated that "Tyler got about thirty-five thousand dollars and twenty nine slaves, young and old, by his wife."

What prompted James to leave such pleasant quarters? It was this: He had become enamored of a young and respectable free girl in Richmond, with whom he could not be united in marriage solely because he was a slave. . . . So . . . the resolution came home to him very forcibly to make tracks for Canada.

William Still, *The Underground Rail Road* (Philadelphia, 1872), 69–70.

Varieties of Slave Resistance

[A Virginia farmer describes some ways slaves fought their masters.]

The slave, if he is indisposed to work, and especially if he is not treated well, or does not like the master who has hired him, will sham sickness—even make himself sick or lame—that he need not work. But a more serious loss frequently arises, when the slave, thinking he is worked too hard, or being angered by punishment or unkind treatment, "getting the sulks," takes to "the swamp," and comes back when he has a mind to. . . .

"But, meanwhile, how does the Negro support life in the swamp?" I asked.

"Oh, he gets sheep and pigs and calves, and fowls and turkeys; sometimes they will kill a small cow. We have often seen the fires; where they were cooking them, through the woods, in the swamp yonder. If it is cold, he will crawl under a fodder-stack, or go into the cabins with some of the other Negroes, and in the same way, you see, he can get all the corn, or almost anything else he wants."

"He steals them from his master?"

"From anyone; frequently from me. I have had many a sheep taken by them."

"It is a common thing, then?"

"Certainly, it is, very common, and the loss is sometimes exceedingly provoking. One of my neighbors here was going to build, and hired two mechanics for a year. Just as he was ready to put his house up, the two men, taking offense at something, both ran away, and did not come back at all, till their year was out, and then their owner immediately hired them out again to another man."

These Negroes "in the swamp," he said, were often hunted after, but it was very difficult to find them, and, if caught, they would run again, and the other Negroes would hide and assist them. Dogs to track them he had never known to be used in Virginia.

Frederick Law Olmsted, *A Journey in the Seaboard Slave States* (New York, 1856), 100–101.

"I Do as I Am Bid"

[*John Capehart explains his special service for slaveholders.*]

Q. Mr. Capehart, is it a part of your duty, as a policeman, to take up colored persons who are out after hours in the streets?

A. Yes, sir.

Q. What is done with them?

A. We put them in the lock-up, and in the morning they are brought into Court and ordered to be punished—those that are to be punished.

Q. What punishment do they get?

A. Not exceeding thirty-nine lashes.

Q. Who gives them these lashes?

A. Any of the Officers. I do, sometimes.

Q. Are you paid *extra* for this? How much?

A. Fifty cents a head. It used to be sixty-two cents. Now, it is only fifty. Fifty cents for each one we arrest, and fifty more for each one we flog.

Q. Are these persons you flog Men and Boys only, or are they Women and Girls also?

A. Men, Women, Boys, and Girls, just as it happens . . .

Q. Is your flogging confined to these cases? Do you not flog Slaves at the request of their Masters?

A. Sometimes I do. Certainly, when I am called upon.

Q. In these cases of private flogging, are the Negroes sent to you? Have you a place for flogging?

A. No; I go round, as I am sent for.

Q. Is this part of your duty as an Officer?

A. No, sir.

Q. In these cases of private flogging, do you inquire into the circumstances to see what the fault has been, or if there is any?

A. That's none of my business. I do as I am bid. The Master is responsible.

Geo. W. Carleton, *The Suppressed Book About Slavery* (New York, 1864), 193–95.

DR. CARTWRIGHT DESCRIBES "NEGRO DISEASES"

[*Dr. Samuel Cartwright of the University of Louisiana was a highly respected medical man widely published in Southern journals.* De Bow's Review *printed this account of two slave diseases the doctor had discovered.*]

DRAPETOMANIA, OR THE DISEASE
CAUSING NEGROES TO RUN AWAY

DRAPETOMANIA is from [a Greek word meaning] a runaway slave, and [another Greek word meaning] *mad or crazy*. It is unknown to our medical authorities, although its diagnostic symptom, the absconding from service, is well known to our planters and overseers. . . . The cause in most of the cases, that induces the Negro to run away from service, is as much a disease of the mind as any other species of mental alienation, and much more curable as a general rule. With the advantages of proper medical advice, strictly followed, this troublesome practice that many Negroes have of running away, can be almost entirely prevented, although the slaves be located on the borders of a free state, within a stone's throw of the abolitionists. . . .

Before Negroes run away, unless they are frightened or panic-struck, they become sulky and dissatisfied. The cause of this sulkiness and dissatisfaction should be inquired into and removed, or they are apt to run away or fall into Negro consumption. When sulky and dissatisfied with cause, the experience of those [overseers and owners] on the line and elsewhere, was decidedly in favor of whipping them out of it, as a preventive measure against absconding, or other bad conduct. It was called whipping the devil out of them.

DYSAETHESIA AETHIOPICA, OR HEBETUDE
OF THE MIND AND OBTUSE SENSIBILITY
OF BODY—A DISEASE PECULIAR TO NEGROES—
CALLED BY OVERSEERS, "RASCALITY"

From the careless movements of the individuals affected with the complaint, they are apt to do much mischief, which appears as if intentional, but is mostly owing to the stupidity of mind and insensibility of nerves induced by the disease. Thus, they break, waste, and destroy everything they handle—abuse horses and cattle,—tear, burn, or rend their own clothing, and, paying no attention to the rights of property, steal others, to replace what they have destroyed. . . . They slight their work,—cut up corn, cane, cotton, or tobacco when hoeing it, as if for pure mischief. They raise disturbances with their overseers and fellow-servants, and seem insensible to pain when subjected to punishment. . . .

Dr. Cartwright of New Orleans, "1. Diseases and Peculiarities of the Negro Race," *De Bow's Review* 11 (September 1851): 331–34.

A SERMON FOR SLAVES

[Slaves attended religious services conducted by white ministers who included sermons on loyalty. Bishop Meade of Virginia wrote this slave sermon.]

. . . Having thus shown you the chief duties you owe to your great Master in heaven, I now come to lay before you the duties you owe to your masters and mistresses here upon earth. And for this you have one general rule, that you ought always to carry in your minds; and that is to do all service for them as if you did it for God himself.

Poor creatures! you little consider, when you are idle and neglectful of your masters' business, when you steal, and waste, and hurt any of their substance, when you are saucy and impudent, when you are telling them lies and deceiving them, or when you prove stubborn and sullen, and will not do the work you are set about without stripes and vexation—you do not consider, I say, that what faults you are guilty of towards your masters and mistresses are faults done against God himself, who hath set your masters and mistresses over you in his own stead, and expects that you would do for them just as you would do for him. And pray do not think that I want to deceive you when I tell you that your masters and mistresses are God's overseers, and that, if you are faulty towards them, God himself will punish you severely for it in the next world. . . .

Frederick Law Olmsted, *A Journey in the Seaboard Slave States* (New York, 1856), 119.

STEALING AN EDUCATION

[*In the South it was unlawful to teach a slave to read or write. Yet Susie King Taylor and Frederick Douglass learned to read. Taylor obtained her education in Savannah, Georgia, and this is her story.*]

I was born under the slave law in Georgia, in 1848, and was brought up by my grandmother in Savannah. There was three of us with her, my younger sister and brother. My brother and I being the two eldest, we were sent to a friend of my grandmother, Mrs. Woodhouse, a widow, to learn to read and write. She was a free woman and lived on Bay Lane, between Habersham and Price streets, about half a mile from my house. We went every day about nine o'clock, with our books wrapped in paper to prevent the police or white persons from seeing them. We went in, one at a time, through the gate, into the yard to the kitchen, which was the schoolroom. She had twenty five or thirty children whom she taught, assisted by her daughter, Mary Jane. The neighbors would see us going in sometimes, but they supposed we were there learning trades, as it was the custom to give children a trade of some kind. After school we left the same way we entered, one by one, when we would go to a square, about a block from the school and wait for each other.

Susie King Taylor, *Reminiscences of My Life in Camp* (Boston, 1902), 5.

[Frederick Douglass had begun to learn his ABCs from his master's wife. Her husband, discovering this, warned her that it was illegal and that, furthermore, education "would forever unfit him for the duties of a slave."]

From this time I was most narrowly watched. If I was in a separate room any considerable length of time, I was sure to be suspected of having a book, and was at once called to give an account of myself. . . . The plan which I adopted, and the one by which I was most successful, was that of making friends of all the little white boys whom I met in the street. As many of these as I could, I converted into teachers. With their kindly aid, obtained at different times and in different places, I finally succeeded in learning to read. When I was sent on errands, I always took my book with me, and by going one part of my errand quickly, I found time to get a lesson before my return. I used also to carry bread with me, enough of which was always in the house, and to which I was always welcome; for I was much better off in this regard than many of the poor white children in our neighborhood. This bread I used to bestow upon the hungry little urchins, who, in return, would give me that more valuable bread of knowledge. I am strongly tempted to give the names of two or three of those little boys, as a testimonial of the gratitude and affection I bear them; but prudence forbids;—not that it would injure me, but it might embarrass them; for it is almost an unpardonable offense to teach slaves to read in this Christian country. It is enough to say of the dear little fellows, that they lived on Philpot Street, very near Durgin and Bailey's [Baltimore] ship-yard. . . .

Frederick Douglass, *Narrative of the Life of Frederick Douglass* (Boston, 1845), 38.

6 INDUSTRIAL AND CULTURAL GROWTH IN THE FREE NORTH

AS THE SOUTH TURNED TO COTTON AND SLAVES, the North entered into a period of industrial, commercial, and cultural growth. This growth, however, was fed by profits made by trading in cotton and slaves. Colonial New England's largest industry had been the distilling of the rum used to purchase slaves in Africa. New England merchants built factories and centers of learning with the fortunes they made in the slave trade. In Rhode Island the Brown brothers founded a university with their profits, and Abraham Redwood endowed a library. But Northern factories also produced the whips and chains used by Southern slaveholders to control their restless slave population. Daniel Webster of Massachusetts said, "I hear the sound of the hammer, I see the smoke of furnaces where manacles and fetters are forged for human hands." He was standing in Boston when he spoke.

The North Chooses Free Labor

The North had liberated its slaves soon after the Revolution. Some argued that slavery was wrong in a country that called itself "the land of the free," and others were impressed with the courageous role of African American soldiers both in the Revolution and in the War of 1812.

There was a strong economic reason for the North's abolition of slavery, however, that had nothing to do with sentiment: it did not pay. To use slaves on farms where there was little work for them during the long Northern winters was a waste of the money it cost to clothe and feed them. While a free laborer could be "laid off" when there was no work, a slave had to be cared for every day. And white mechanics refused to compete with slaves. Vice President John Adams wrote in 1795 that if Northern employers "had been permitted to hold slaves, the common white people would have put the slaves to death, and their masters too, perhaps."

Each Northern state liberated its slaves but refused them equality with whites. Gerritt Smith, a New York abolitionist in the 1840s, said:

> Even the noblest black is denied that which is free to the vilest white. The omnibus, the car, the ballot-box, the jury box, the halls of legislation, the army, the public lands, the school, the church, the lecture room, the social circle, the table, are all either absolutely or virtually denied to him.

A passenger is asked to leave a Philadelphia railway car in 1856 and sit in the car set aside for African Americans. Through individual and group action, segregated traveling facilities were eliminated from some Northern towns and states before the end of the Civil War.

In 1819, in New York's African school, a teenager asked his graduating class these questions:

> What are my prospects? To what shall I turn my hand? Shall I be a mechanic? No one will employ me; white boys won't work with me. Shall I be a merchant? No one will have me in his office. Can you be surprised at my discouragement?

This student may have known that the TB rate was twice as high for people of color as for whites and that families moving into white neighborhoods became targets of arsonists and mobs.

Even wealthy African Americans suffered because of Northern prejudice.* Charlotte Forten's father could afford to send her to a private school near Boston. In school the teenager found the white girls friendly, but outside "they feared to recognize me." In 1854 she confided to her diary that:

---

*One can contrast prejudice in the Northern states with the attitude of the Canadian government during the same period of time. In 1829, a delegation of Cincinnati Blacks, seeking refuge after being driven from the town by whites, interviewed Sir James Colebrook, governor of Upper Canada. His answer to their plea included the following: "Tell the republicans on your side of the line, that we royalists do not know men by their color. Should you come to us you will be entitled to all the privileges of the rest of His Majesty's subjects." A sizable number of African Americans did migrate to Canada at this time, and formed the settlement of Wilburforce.

New York mobs destroy an African American Orphan Home in 1863. Anti-Black rioting rocked many Northern cities before, during, and after the Civil War.

Black children in the North are denied admission to a white school.

It is hard to go through life meeting contempt with contempt, hatred with hatred, fearing with too good reason, to love and trust hardly any one whose skin is white—however lovable, attractive, and congenial. . . . In the bitter, passionate feelings of my soul again and again there rise the questions "When, oh! when shall this cease?" "Is there no help?" . . . Let us take courage; never ceasing to work—hoping and believing that, if not for us, for another generation there is a better, brighter day in store. . . .

Although all immigrant groups who came to America faced discrimination at first, they were eventually able to enjoy better jobs, finer homes, and the friendship of their neighbors. African Americans, however, were forced to remain, permanently, on the bottom rung of the social ladder.

Edward W. Blyden. Before and after the Civil War, he became a leading spokesperson for Black resettlement in Africa.

The North Becomes a Business Center

At the time when many rich merchants in the North were piling up wealth in the African slave trade, Paul Cuffe was a notable exception. Cuffe was born in 1759 and became a sailor aboard a whaling ship at sixteen. In a few years he was building his own ships. A tall, muscular, and serious young man, Cuffe and other Black taxpayers of Massachusetts protested in 1780 to the Revolutionary government against "taxation without representa-

In 1780, Paul Cuffe and eight other Massachusetts African Americans protested to their state government against taxation without representation. They noted Blacks "have cheerfully entered the field of Battle in Defense of the Common Cause," American independence from England.

William Lloyd Garrison began his *Liberator* with funds supplied by African Americans. For years they were three-fourths of his readership.

tion." Three years later a Massachusetts court ruled that African Americans did have the right to vote if they paid taxes.

By 1806 Cuffe's wealth included large parcels of New England land and many vessels. He sailed as captain on his own ships, established cultural relations with Africa, taught navigation in Sierra Leone, and brought African products to Europe and America. Cuffe used his own funds and ships to carry Black settlers to Africa. "I furnished them provisions . . . without fee or reward—my hope is in a coming day," he wrote in his diary. Cuffe died in 1817, a respected Quaker member of his New Bedford community.

New England's shipbuilding and fishing industries were able to make important strides because of the work of Black inventors. Lewis Temple, a New Bedford blacksmith, surprised his friends when he invented a toggle harpoon. They thought the thin Black workman was interested in baseball and little else. But Temple's harpoon became the standard one in the industry. A recent authority has called it "the most important single invention in the whole history of whaling." Because it did not slip out, it resulted in the capture of a greater proportion of the harpooned whales than had been previously possible.

James Forten of Philadelphia invented a device that aided in the control of sails. This veteran of the United States Navy, who had served in the Revolution, became wealthy and built a sail factory employing fifty Black and white workers. Forten used the money his invention earned to further the abolitionist cause. He contributed a considerable sum to William Lloyd Garrison's *Liberator* during the first crucial years of its publication and was an important influence on the white editor. Forten became president of Philadelphia's Moral Reform Society, won a citation for saving a number of people from drowning, and helped recruit 2,500 African Americans to defend his city during the War of 1812.

Long before the Civil War, several African Americans were owners of growing Northern businesses. Thomas L. Jennings, a New York tailor, invented a process for cleaning clothes, patented it, and made a fortune. One of his sons became a New Orleans dentist and another a successful Boston businessman. Jennings, like Forten, used his money to finance antislavery groups.

John Jones. From a painting. (Courtesy Chicago Historical Society.)

John Jones came to Chicago from North Carolina as a young man with only $3.50 in his pocket. He made a great deal of money in the tailoring business and used it to finance both the Underground Railroad and the fight against discrimination in his state. His efforts helped repeal Illinois's "Black Laws" that denied legal equality to his people in that state until 1865. Later he also secured the passage of a law that opened the Cook County (Chicago) schools to people of color. After the Civil War, he was twice elected Cook County commissioner.

Early Civil Rights Campaigns

The North's quarter of a million free Black men and women demanded full citizenship rights long before the Civil War. By 1860, when the Brooklyn Board of Education called Black pupils "mere grinning caricatures of humanity," there were African American literary, reading, and educational societies. There had been eighteen Black newspapers by 1860. The first, *Freedom's Journal,* begun in 1827, announced its purpose: "We wish to plead our own cause. Too long have others spoken for us. Too long has the publick been deceived by misrepresentations in things which concern us dearly." Charles B. Ray, editor of *The Colored American* in New York, took a leading part in exposing the city's inferior education for Black students. He pointed out that while there were only 2.5 times as many white students as Black, the board of education had spent a mere $1,000 for new Black schools compared to $1,600,000 for new schools for whites.

In 1821, when the New York Constitutional Convention delegates, led by Martin Van Buren, restricted African American voting rights to men who owned more than $250 in landed property, Black men organized to repeal this injustice. In 1837, petitions reached the state legislature from New York City, Oswego, Albany, and Genesee counties. When the legislature still refused the change, a mass protest meeting was held. By 1860, Brooklyn's eighteen and Manhattan's forty-eight Black suffrage clubs campaigned against this "cruel and heavy hand laid upon us." But in a referendum that year, white New Yorkers voted overwhelmingly to keep the discriminatory provision.

It was ironic that the Jacksonian reform movement ("era of the common man"), while it removed all property restrictions for white voters, actually increased suffrage restrictions for Black people. Between 1807 and 1837, five Northern states cut down Black voting rights. In 1841, Frederick Douglass and white abolitionists campaigned successfully in Rhode Island against the Dorr Constitution, which would have repealed Black voting power. And in 1855, John Mercer Langston, elected to a town council in Brownheim, Ohio, became the first African American elected to office in the United States. But these were two rare electoral victories.

John M. Langston, first African American elected to public office, served in the Brownheim, Ohio, council in 1855. It was the beginning of a career in public service that later led to a diplomatic post in Haiti and a place in the United States Congress.

One of the earliest civil rights activists was James W. C. Pennington, an escaped Maryland slave blacksmith. Although the brilliant young man was refused formal admission to Yale University, he was permitted to attend classes. He was denied the right to participate in discussions or to take books from the library, but learned to read and write English, German, Latin, and Greek anyway. In 1842, he wrote a textbook history of African Americans. He also became the first man of African descent to receive a doctor of divinity degree from Heidelberg University. "This pronounces the universal brotherhood of humanity," said a university official as he handed Reverend Pennington his diploma. The minister returned to his congregation in New York and led them in some of America's earliest nonviolent civil rights demonstrations.

Elsewhere African Americans used legal maneuvers or demonstrations to try to win their rights. A Black newspaper in New York advised its readers to combat discrimination in white churches: "Stand in the aisles, and rather worship God on your feet, than become a party to your own degradation. You must shame your oppressors, and wear out prejudice by this holy policy." In 1808, to celebrate the law prohibiting the slave trade, Black New Yorkers held three huge parades. Marchers carried signs reading, "Am I not a man and a brother." Rather than celebrate the Fourth of July, African Americans celebrated the First of August, honoring the day in 1833 when England abolished slavery in all of its overseas possessions.

Rev. James W. C. Pennington. He fled slavery to become a noted minister, abolitionist, and writer.

Throughout the North, education for students of color was offered, if at all, on a separate and unequal basis. But in Boston, the Black campaign to desegregate the schools achieved success. A lawsuit in 1849 was instituted by the father of Sarah Roberts, a six-year-old pupil who had to walk past five white schools to reach her inferior Black one. The defense lawyers were Charles Sumner, a white abolitionist, and Robert Morris, a Black attorney. They argued forcefully that a caste system in schools was dangerous in a democracy, but they lost the case. Then, in 1855, mounting African American and abolitionist pressure convinced the Massachusetts legislature to abolish Boston's school segregation. "Tomorrow," rejoiced one Black student, "we are like other Boston boys!"

There were people of color who used passive resistance and others who fought back with fury against those who denied them their rights. But no matter which way they resisted unjust laws, many Northern African Americans believed with their great leader Frederick Douglass, "If there is no struggle, there is no progress."

Development of an Intellectual Class

William Whipper, who ran a successful lumberyard in Columbia, Pennsylvania, was a leading member of a Black intellectual class that had begun to develop long before the Civil War. He used his own funds and money he collected from local whites to help fugitive slaves on their way to Canada. For more than a dozen years, he spent one thousand dollars on this dangerous work, then contributed another five thousand dollars to the Union cause during the Civil War. In 1870 he wrote, "I would prefer to be penniless in the streets, rather than have withheld a single hour's labor or a dollar from the sacred cause of liberty, justice, and humanity."

William Whipper, an early advocate of passive resistance to unjust laws.

Whipper was also vitally interested in the elevation of the North's free Black population and spoke before several of their "Reading Societies" which were springing up in Northern cities. In 1837 he delivered "An Address on Non-violent Resistance to Offensive Aggression," speaking in favor of the theory of nonviolent resistance to evil. This was a dozen years before Henry David Thoreau wrote his famous essay on civil disobedience and a hundred years before Mahatma Gandhi in India and Martin Luther King made this theory famous. Whipper claimed, as did Gandhi and King, that nonviolence "is not only consistent with reason, but the surest method of obtaining a speedy triumph of the principles of universal peace."

William Wells Brown was a runaway slave who taught himself to read and write. Brown helped rescue other runaways from slave catchers and saw them transported to safety in Canada aboard Great Lake boats. Brown

William Wells Brown, writer.

was one of the best-known abolitionist speakers here and in Europe. "My religion," he said, "was to help do away with the curse of American slavery."

Brown never lost his sense of humor. Once, when telling what it meant to try to give a speech to a crowd that included twenty-seven "babies in their mothers' arms," he wrote, "But they give us rice pudding out here for breakfast, and that gives me strength to meet the babies." Brown was America's first African American novelist (1853) and playwright (1858) and later wrote three travel books and several short histories of his people.

Martin R. Delany became a fiery advocate for African American manhood in the years before, during, and after the Civil War. This short, stocky Black militant attended Harvard Medical School until prejudice forced him out. His hatred of racism led him to consider both the use of force and resettlement in Africa as solutions to the problems of slavery and discrimination. Delany named each of his eleven children after famous Black heroes, and he woke every morning, thankful, he said, that God had made him "a Black man." He advocated violence to halt slave catchers, and in his 1852 history of African Americans he insisted, "We must make an Issue, Create an Event, and Establish a National Position for Ourselves." He not only proposed a Black exodus to Africa but in 1860 explored the continent for a suitable site.

During the Civil War, Delany visited Abraham Lincoln with a plan for an army unit staffed with Black officers and men. The president had "this most extraordinary and intelligent Black man" appointed the first African

Martin R. Delany, a militant spokesperson for Black liberation, was willing to consider any path to that goal—including violence or Black migration to Africa. He named his children after Black figures in history and woke every morning delighted that he was Black and alive.

American major in the Union army. After the war, Delany lived in South Carolina, urging ex-slaves to use guns if necessary to protect their freedom, and insisting, "Black men must have Black leaders." Toward the end of his life, he again advocated resettlement in Africa.

Henry Highland Garnet also became a leading militant voice. He was born in slavery and at ten was carried to liberty by an uncle and his father. At nineteen, he made his first antislavery speech. Later he attended the World Peace Conference in Frankfurt and the Antislavery Convention in London. He aided fugitives in the Underground Railroad, claiming "one hundred and fifty, in a single year, have lodged under my roof." In 1843, he electrified a Black convention with a call for massive slave uprisings.

Reverend Henry H. Garnett.

Dr. James McCune Smith, a respected New York physician, used his vast knowledge of science and history in an attempt to destroy the myth that African Americans were physically or mentally suited to slavery. On two occasions he challenged the leading spokesman for slavery, John C. Calhoun. Calhoun had used the 1840 census statistics to prove that Blacks in the free states were more inclined to madness than Southern slaves. Dr. Smith was among those who found some important errors in the census figures. He found, for example, that the census listed nineteen insane Blacks in six Maine towns where only one lived and reported this in *The Liberator.* "To make 19 crazy men out of one man, is pretty fair calculation, . . ." he laughed. Then he became serious: "Freedom has not made us mad; it has strengthened our minds by throwing us upon our own resources, and has bound us to American institutions with a tenacity which nothing but death can overcome." Dr. Smith, on another occasion, demolished another Calhoun statement, that slaves lived longer than free Blacks, illustrating that the opposite was true.

Dr. Smith wanted people of color themselves to play a leading part in the fight for justice. In 1855 he told a Black convention in New York:

> The time is come when our people must assume the rank of a first-rate power in the battle against caste and Slavery; it is emphatically our battle; no one else can fight it for us, and with God's help we must fight it ourselves.

Smith practiced what he preached, leading the fight for civil rights in New York until his death in 1865.

One of the most outstanding contributions to world culture in the mid-nineteenth century was made by the actor Ira Aldridge, the son of a New York minister. To avoid riots by whites who resented serious theater performed by people of color, Aldridge and the other New York actors of the

Surgeon A. T. Augusta of the Union army challenged Washington, D.C., streetcar segregation during the Civil War.

"African Company" used comedy skits between the acts of their production of Shakespeare. Aldridge went to Europe to study under the well-known English actor Edmund Kean, and in 1833 both men opened at London's famous Covent Garden Theatre in *Othello.* Aldridge played the title role, and his teacher played the role of the evil Iago.

Aldridge not only achieved worldwide fame as Othello, the Moor, but played white parts as well, using white makeup. His acting was acclaimed from Ireland to Russia, and he received medals from the kings of Prussia and Austria. A French drama critic who saw Aldridge perform in Russia wrote, "I have never seen an artist identify himself so perfectly with the character he represents. . . . Everybody, men and women, wept."

But Americans had no chance to see this famous actor. Because of public prejudice against a Black actor appearing with a white cast, Aldridge had been forced to cancel an appearance in Baltimore. In 1867, with slavery abolished, the actor planned to return and tour with his own Shakespearean company, but he died before he could complete plans.

Beginning in 1830 Black leaders met in national conventions to chart their campaigns against both slavery in the South and discrimination in the North. Almost every free state also had its conventions where African American delegates debated courses of action against poor jobs, segregated schools and streetcars, prohibitions against Blacks serving in the militia or voting in elections. Petition campaigns, mass meetings and court cases were part of the assault on these conditions.

Some African American leaders rejected integration into white society. In 1854 a National Emigration Convention advocated a Black exodus from America. It pointed to the twin horrors of slavery and bigotry and said people must do what is necessary to survive. H. Ford Douglass, a leader from Illinois, told the 101 delegates:

In 1833 Prudence Crandall, a Quaker school principal, opened her exclusive Connecticut girls' school to African Americans. The townspeople refused to sell her merchandise, jailed her, and finally set fire to the school and forced its closing.

I can hate this Government without being disloyal because it has stricken down my manhood, and treated me as a saleable commodity. I can join a foreign enemy and fight against it, without being a traitor, because it treats me as an ALIEN and a STRANGER. . . .

Such militancy would recur often in African American history.

Ira Aldridge, actor.

Paul Cuffe, Merchant and Philanthropist

[Paul Cuffe climbed high on America's ladder of success. He was one of ten children born to an ex-slave who died when Paul was fourteen. Though he never attended a day of school, Cuffe became a businessman at twenty-one. His great interest in Africa led to many interesting projects: he learned navigation in two weeks so that he could captain his Traveller *to Africa with thirty-eight settlers; he taught in Africa and brought its products to America, England, Russia, and the West Indies. Cuffe's letters and* Journal *have been preserved.]*

I have for some years had it impressed on my mind to make a voyage to Sierra Leon in order to inspect the situation of the country, and feeling a real desire that the inhabitants of Africa might become an enlightened people and be so favored as to give general satisfaction to all those who are endeavoring to establish them in the true light of Christianity. And as I am of the African race I feel myself interested for them and if I am favored with a talent I think I am willing that they should be benefited thereby.

Letter of June 6, 1808, in Paul Cuffe Papers (New Bedford Library).

[After his 1811 trip to Africa, Cuffe returned to America. He recorded this 1812 incident in his Journal.]

Embarked this morning at 5 o'clock [from Washington]. . . . Arrived in Baltimore at 3 in the afternoon. When I took my seat, being the first in I took the after seat. When the passengers came,—in came a blustering powder headed man with stern countenance. [He said,] "Come away from that seat."

I . . . sat still. He then bustled along and said, "I want to put my umbrella in the box." I arose. He then put his umbrella in. He then said "You must go out of this for there is a lady coming in." I entered into no discourse with him, but took my seat; he took his beside me but showed much evil contempt. At length the women and a girl made their appearance. I then arose and invited the women into the seat after saying "We always give way to accommodate the women." We set forward on our journey. On our way at the tavern I was overtaken by Wm Hunter member of Congress. He was very free and conversant, which this man above mentioned observed. Before we got to Baltimore, he became loving and openly accosted me "Captain take the after seat," but from the common custom I thanked him and wished him to keep his seat.

I believe if I am favored to keep my place, my enemies will become friendly. I note this for encouragement and memory.

When I arrived in Baltimore they utterly refused to take me in at the tavern or to get me a dinner unless I would go back among the servants. This I refused, not as I thought myself better than the servants, but from the nature of the case. I found my way to a tavern where I got my dinner.

Paul Cuffe, *Journal,* entry for 5 May 1812, in Paul Cuffe Papers (New Bedford Library).

JAMES FORTEN TO PAUL CUFFE: THE COLONIZATION QUESTION

[*In 1817 few Americans were as wealthy as James Forten. After attending a Quaker school, Forten became an apprentice to a sailmaker. His invention of a sailing device made him about $100,000. But his goal was the salvation of his people, and he became a leader in Philadelphia's African American community. He came to the conclusion that people of color would be better off in Africa and corresponded with Paul Cuffe about his efforts to bring people to Africa. But during a large meeting in January, Forten discovered that the city's poor African Americans rejected the idea of going to Africa.*]

Esteemed friend . . .

The African Institution met at the Rev. R. Allens the very night your letter came to hand. I red that part to them that wished them a happy New Year, for which they desired me to return you many thanks. I must now mention to you that the whole continent seems to be agitated concerning Colonising the People of Colour. . . . Indeed the People of Colour, here was very much fritened at first. They were afrade that all the free people would be Compelled to go, particularly in the southern States. We had a large meeting of Males at the Rev. R. Allens Church the other evening Three thousand at least attended, and there was not one sole that was in favour of going to Africa. They think that the slave holders want to get rid of them so as to make their property more secure. However it appears to me that if the Father of all mercies, is in this interesting subject . . . the way will be made strate and clear. We however have agreed to remain silent, as the people here both the white & colour are decided against the measure. My opinion is that they will never become a people until they com out from amongst the white people, but as the majority is decidedly against me I am determined to remain silent, except as to my opinion which I freely give when asked. . . .

I remain very affectionately,
Yours unalterably,
James Forten

[*In less than a year Forten altered his views, perhaps as a result of this unanimous opposition to colonization. He became a leading abolitionist and is credited with convincing William Lloyd Garrison that colonization in Africa did nothing for African Americans but remove them from their homeland.*]

James Forten, Letter of 25 January, 1817, in Paul Cuffe Papers (New Bedford Library).

A PLEA TO ABOLISH SLAVERY IN THE NORTH

[*At New York's Constitutional Convention of 1821, delegate Clarke argued that the bravery of African American soldiers in the Revolution and in the War of 1812 entitled them to freedom.*]

In the War of the Revolution, these people helped to fight your battles by land and by sea. Some of your States were glad to turn out corps of colored men, and stand "shoulder to shoulder" with them.

In your late war [of 1812], they contributed largely towards some of your most splendid victories. On Lakes Erie and Champlain, where your fleets triumphed over a foe superior in numbers and engines of death, they were manned, in a large proportion, with men of color. And, in this very House, in the fall of 1814, a bill passed, receiving the approbation of all the branches of your government, authorizing the Governor to accept the services of a corps of two thousand free people of color. Sir, these were times which tried men's souls. In these times, it was no sporting matter to bear arms. . . . They were not compelled to go; they were not drafted. No; your pride had placed them beyond your compulsory power. But there was no necessity for its exercise; they were volunteers; yes, Sir, volunteers to defend that very country from the inroads and ravages of a ruthless foe, which had treated them with insult, degradation, and slavery.

Wm. C. Nell, *The Colored Patriots of the American Revolution* (Boston, 1855), 148–49.

IRA ALDRIDGE, WORLD-FAMOUS ACTOR

[Ira Aldridge achieved stardom for his roles in Shakespearean dramas. This is how his performances were received by European critics.]

[London Weekly Times] Mr. Aldridge is an African of Mulatto tint, with wooly hair. His features are capable of much expression, his action is unrestrained and picturesque, and his voice clear, full, resonant. His powers of energetic declamation are very marked, and the whole of his acting appears impulsed by a current of feeling of no inconsiderable weight and vigor, yet controlled and guided in a manner that clearly shows the actor to be a person of much study and a great stage experience.

H. G. Adams, *God's Image in Ebony* (London, 1854), 158.

[*The St. Petersburg correspondent for* Le Nord] . . . The success of the Negro actor, Ira Aldridge has been wonderful. At his *debut,* people were curious to see an Othello who needed [nothing] . . . to blacken his face. . . . From his appearance on the stage the African artist completely captivated his audience by his harmonious and resonant voice, and by a style full of simplicity, nature, and dignity.

[*Russian reporter for the* New York Herald] . . . An American Negro, named Ira Aldridge, has been performing at the Imperial Theater in several of Shakespear's pieces, and has met with great applause. His principal character, of course, is Othello, and he portrays the jealous African with . . . truth and energy. . . .

The Anglo-African Magazine 1 (February 1859): 63.

INTERVIEW WITH A YOUNG SCULPTRESS

[Edmonia Lewis or Wildfire was the first Black woman to achieve fame in the field of sculpture. She attended Oberlin College and was trained in the studio of Edmund Brackett of Boston. Writer Lydia Maria Child interviewed her.]

One of the most interesting individuals I met at the reception was Edmonia Lewis, a colored girl about twenty years of age, who is devoting herself to sculpture. . . . I told her I judged by her complexion that there might be some of what was called white blood in her veins. She replied, "No; I have not a single drop of what is called white blood in my veins. My father was a full-blooded Negro, and my mother was a full-blooded Chippewa." . . .

"And have you lived with the Chippewas?"

"Yes. When my mother was dying, she wanted me to promise that I would live three years with her people, and I did."

"And what did you do while you were there?"

"I did as my mother's people did. I made baskets and embroidered moccasons and I went into the cities with my mother's people, to sell them." . . .

"But, surely," said I, "you have had some other education than that you received among your mother's people, for your language indicates it."

"I have a brother," she replied, "who went to California, and dug gold. When I had been three years with my mother's people, he came to me and said, 'Edmonia, I don't want you to stay here always. I want you to have some education.' He placed me at a school in Oberlin. I staid there two years, and then he brought me to Boston, as the best place for me to learn to be a sculptor. I went to Mr. Brackett for advice; for I thought the man who made a bust of John Brown must be a friend to my people. Mr. Brackett has been very kind to me."

She wanted me to go to her room to see . . . a head of Voltaire. "I don't want you to go to praise me," she said; "for I know praise is not good for me. Some praise me because I am a colored girl, and I don't want that kind of praise. I had rather you would point out my defects, for that will teach me something."

L. Maria Child, "Letter," *The Liberator* (19 February 1864), 31.

Prejudice Destroys a School in Connecticut

[*In 1833 Principal Prudence Crandall decided to admit Sarah Harris, an African American pupil, to her Connecticut school. The white community of Canterbury rebelled. Miss Crandall describes events.*]

. . . The reason for changing my school of white pupils for a school for colored girls is as follows: I had a nice colored girl, as help in my family, and her intended husband regularly received the "Liberator." The girl took the paper from the office and loaned it to me. Having been taught from early childhood the sin of slavery, my sympathies were greatly aroused. Sarah Harris, a respectable young woman and a member of the church, called often to see her friend Marcia, my family assistant. In some of her calls I ascertained that she wished to attend my school, and board at her own father's house at some little distance from the village. I allowed her to enter as one of my pupils. By this act I gave great offense. The wife of an Episcopalian clergyman who lived in the village told me that if I continued that colored girl in my school, it could not be sustained. I replied to her, *That it might sink, then, for I should not turn her out!*

I very soon found that some of my school would leave, not to return, if the colored girl was retained. Under these circumstances, I made up my mind that if it were possible I would teach colored girls exclusively.

Wendell Phillips Garrison, "Connecticut in the Middle Ages," *Century Magazine* 9 (September 1885): 780.

[*Reverend Samuel J. May, a white minister who tried to help Miss Crandall, describes what happened next.*]

Undismayed by the opposition of her neighbors and the violence of their threats, Miss Crandall received early in April fifteen or twenty colored young ladies and misses from Philadelphia, New York, Providence, and Boston. At once her persecutors commenced operations. All accommodations at the stores in Canterbury were denied her; so that she was obliged to send to neighboring villages for her needful supplies. She and her pupils were insulted wherever they appeared in the streets. The doors and door-steps of her house were besmeared, and her well was filled with filth. Had it not been for the assistance of her father and another Quaker friend who lived in the town, she might have been compelled to abandon "her castle" for the want of water and food. But she was enabled to "hold out," and Miss Crandall and her little band behaved somewhat like the besieged in the immortal Fort Sumter. The spirit that is in the children of men is usually roused by persecution. I visited them repeatedly, and always found teacher and pupils calm and resolute. . . .

Samuel J. May, *Some Recollections of Our Antislavery Conflict* (Boston, 1869), 50.

[*One of the Black students wrote on 24 May 1833 of new events.*]

. . . There are thirteen scholars now in the school. The Canterburians are *savage*—they will not sell Miss Crandall an article from their shops. . . . But the happiness I enjoy here pays me for all. The place is delightful; all that is wanting to complete the scene is *civilized men.* Last evening the news reached us that the new Law [against the school] had been passed. The bell rang, and a cannon was fired for half an hour. Where is justice? In the midst of all this Miss Crandall is unmoved. When we walk out, horns are blown and pistols fired.

The Liberator, 22 June 1833, 99.

[Reverend May describes the end of the story.]

. . . About twelve o'clock, on the night of the 9th of September, Miss Crandall's house was assaulted by a number of persons with heavy clubs and iron bars; five window sashes were demolished and ninety panes of glass dashed to pieces.

I was summoned next morning to the scene of destruction and the terror-stricken family. Never before had Miss Crandall seemed to quail, and her pupils had become afraid to remain another night under her roof. The front rooms of the house were hardly tenantable; and it seemed foolish to repair them only to be destroyed again. After due consideration, therefore, it was determined that the school should be abandoned. The pupils were called together, and I was requested to announce to them our decision. Never before have I felt so deeply sensible of the cruelty of the persecution which had been carried on for eighteen months, in that New England village against a family of defenceless females. Twenty harmless, well-behaved girls, whose only offence against the peace of the community was that they had come together there to obtain useful knowledge and moral culture, were to be told that they had better go away, because, forsooth, the house in which they dwelt would not be protected by the guardians of the town, the conservators of the peace, the officers of justice, the men of influence in the village where it was situated. The words almost blistered my lips. My bosom glowed with indignation. I felt ashamed of my country, ashamed of my color. . . .

Samuel J. May, *Some Recollections of Our Antislavery Conflict* (Boston, 1869), 71.

CANAAN, NEW HAMPSHIRE, AND BLACK STUDENTS

[Black students Alexander Crummell, Henry H. Garnet, and Thomas Sidney of New York were invited to attend school in Canaan, New Hampshire, in 1835. Alexander Crummell tells their story.]

It was a long and wearisome journey, of some four hundred and more miles; and rarely would an inn or a hotel give us food, and nowhere could we get shelter. . . . The sight of three black youths, in gentlemanly garb, traveling through New England was, *in those days, a most unusual sight;* started not only surprise, but brought out universal sneers and ridicule. We met a most cordial reception at Canaan from two score white students, and began, with the highest hopes, our studies. But our stay was the briefest. . . . On the 4th of July, with wonderful taste and felicity, the farmers, from a wide region around, assembled at Canaan and resolved to remove the academy as a public nuisance. On the 10th of August they gathered together from the neighboring towns, seized the building, and with ninety yoke of oxen carried it off into a swamp about a half mile from its site. They were two days in accomplishing this miserable work.

Meanwhile, under Garnet, as our leader, the boys in our boarding house were moulding bullets, expecting an attack upon our dwelling. About eleven o'clock at night the tramp of horses was heard approaching, and as one rapid rider passed the house and fired at it, Garnet quickly replied by a discharge from a double-barrelled shotgun which blazed away through the window. At once the hills, from many miles around, reverberated with the sound. Lights were seen in scores of houses on every side, and the towns and villages far and near were in a state of great excitement. But that musket shot by Garnet doubtless saved our lives. The cowardly ruffians dared not attack us. . . .

Alexander Crummell, *The Eulogy on Henry Highland Garnet* (Washington, 1882), 12–13.

WILLIAM WELLS BROWN FOILS A KIDNAPPING

[*Northern African Americans, in constant fear of being captured by kidnappers and sold into Southern slavery, formed organizations patterned after the minutemen. William Wells Brown describes how his group managed to rescue the Stanford family of New York from kidnappers.*]

. . . One man got on the track of the carriage, and followed it to the ferry at Black Rock, where he heard that it had crossed some three hours before. He went on to Buffalo, and gave the alarm to the colored people of that place. . . . The alarm was given just as the bells were ringing for church. . . . We started on a run for the livery-stable, where we found as many more of our own color trying to hire horses to go in search of the fugitives. . . .

We travelled on at a rapid rate, until . . . we met a man . . . who made signs for us to stop. . . . he informed us that the carriage we were in pursuit of was at the public house. . . .

We proceeded to the tavern, where we found the carriage standing in front of the door, with a pair of fresh horses ready to proceed on their journey. . . . We all dismounted, fastened our horses, and entered the house. We found four or five persons in the bar-room who seemed to rejoice as we entered.

One of our company demanded the opening of the door, while others went out and surrounded the house. The kidnappers stationed one of their number at the door, and another at the window. They refused to let us enter the room, and the tavern-keeper, who was more favorable to us than we had anticipated, said to us: "Boys, get into the room in any way that you can; the house is mine, and I give you the liberty to break in through the door or window." This was all that we wanted, and we were soon making preparations to enter the room at all hazards. Those within had warned us that if we should attempt to enter they would "shoot the first one." One of our company, who had obtained a crowbar, went to the window, and succeeded in getting it under the sash, and soon we had the window up, and the kidnappers, together with their victims, in full view.

One of the kidnappers, while we were raising the window, kept crying at the top of his voice, "I'll shoot, I'll shoot!" but no one seemed to mind him. As soon as they saw that we were determined to rescue the slaves at all hazards, they gave up, one of their number telling us that we might "come in."

The door was thrown open, and we entered, and there found Stanford seated in one corner of the room, with his hands tied behind him, and his clothing, what little he had on, much stained with blood. Near him was his wife, with her child, but a few weeks old, in her arms. Neither of them had anything on except their night clothes. They had been gagged, to keep from alarming the people, and had been much beaten and bruised when first attacked by the kidnappers. Their countenances lighted up the moment we entered the room.

William Wells Brown, *Narrative of William W. Brown* (London, 1849), 112–15.

PREJUDICE IN OHIO IN 1834

[*Students from Lane Seminary, near Cincinnati, investigated the conditions of free people of color. Here is a part of their report.*]

A respectable master mechanic stated to us . . . that in 1830 the President of the Mechanical Association was publicly tried by the Society for the crime of assisting a colored young man to learn a trade. Such was the feeling among the mechanics that no colored boy could learn a trade, or colored journeyman find employment. A young man of exceptional character and an excellent workman purchased his freedom and learned the cabinet making business in Kentucky. On coming to this city, he was refused work by every man to whom he applied. At last he found a shop carried on by an Englishman, who agreed to employ him—but on entering the shop, the workmen threw down their tools and declared that he should leave or they would. . . . The unfortunate youth was accordingly dismissed.

In this extremity, having spent his last cent, he found a slaveholder who gave him employment in an iron store as a common laborer. Here he remained two years, when the gentleman finding he was a mechanic, exerted his influence and procured work for him as a rough carpenter. This man, by dint of perseverance and industry, has now become a master workman, employing at times six or eight journeymen. But, he tells us, he has not yet received a single job of work from a native born citizen of a free state.

This oppression of the mechanics still continues. One of the boys of our school last summer sought in vain for a place in this city to learn a trade. . . .

The combined oppression of public sentiment and law reduce the colored people to extreme misery.

Proceedings of Ohio Anti-Slavery Convention (Cincinnati, 1835), 19.

"OHIO'S NOT THE PLACE FOR ME"

[*By the 1850s, thousands of African Americans had fled to Canada. One runaway slave, Henry Bibb, published a newspaper,* Voice of the Fugitive, *from Canada. He pledged its pages to combating slavery, supporting "moral reforms," and advocating migration to Canada. He insisted, "We shall oppose the annexation of Canada to the United States." In his second issue, Bibb published a song for fugitive slaves, sung to the tune of "Oh Susannah."*]

I'm on my way to Canada,
    That Cold and dreary land;
The dire effects of Slavery
    I can no longer stand.

My soul is vexed within me so,
    To think that I'm a slave,
I've now resolved to strike the blow,
    For freedom or the grave.

    O! Righteous Father
    Wilt thou not pity me.
    And aid me on to Canada
    Where colored men are free? . . .

[Sixth verse]

Ohio's not the place for me;
    For I was much surprised
So many of her sons to see
    In garments of disguise.
Her name has gone throughout the world,
    Free Labour, Soil and Men—
But slaves had better far be hurled
    Into the Lion's Den.

    Farewell, Ohio!
    I'm not safe in thee;
    I'll travel on to Canada,
    Where colored men are free.

"Away to Canada!" *Voice of the Fugitive* 1, no. 2 (15 January 1851): 4.

FREDERICK DOUGLASS'S FREEDOM RIDE

*[Northern railroads restricted African Americans to "Jim Crow" cars. Frederick
Douglass tells how this practice was ended in Massachusetts.]*

. . . Attempting to start from Lynn, one day, for Newburyport, on the eastern railroad, I went, as my custom was, into one of the best railroad carriages on the road. The seats were very luxuriant and beautiful. I was soon
waited upon by the conductor, and ordered out; whereupon I demanded
the reason for my invidious removal. After a good deal of parleying, I was
told that it was because I was black . . . I was soon waited on by half a
dozen fellows of the baser sort, (just such as would volunteer to take a bull-

dog out of a meeting-house in time of public worship,) and told that I must move out of that seat, and if I did not, they would drag me out. I refused to move, they clutched me, head, neck, and shoulders. But, in anticipation of the stretching to which I was about to be subjected, I had interwoven myself among the seats. In dragging me out, on this occasion, it must have cost the company twenty-five or thirty dollars, for I tore up seats and all. So great was the excitement in Lynn, on the subject, that the superintendent, Mr. Stephen A. Chase, ordered the trains to run through Lynn without stopping, while I remained in that town; and this ridiculous farce was enacted. For several days the trains went dashing through Lynn without stopping. At the same time that they excluded a free colored man from their cars, this same company allowed slaves, in company of their masters and mistresses to ride unmolested.

After many battles with the railroad conductors, and being roughly handled in not a few instances, this proscription was at last abandoned; and the "Jim Crow car"—set up for the degradation of colored people—is nowhere found in New England. This result was not brought about without the intervention of the people, and the threatened enactment of a law compelling railroad companies to respect the rights of travelers. . . .

Frederick Douglass, *My Bondage and My Freedom* (New York and Auburn, 1855), 399–400.

DR. PENNINGTON'S RESISTANCE TO NEW YORK STREETCAR SEGREGATION

[*In the 1850s Black New Yorkers were compelled to ride on the front platform of Sixth Avenue horse-drawn streetcars. One of many instances of opposition to that policy was the direct action of Reverend James W. Pennington. John P. Early, a white merchant, told the Superior Court of New York of Pennington's efforts.*]

. . . as the doctor took his seat on the right side of the car, the [white] passengers near him rose up and left a vacant space on both sides of him for three or four seats. A number of the passengers went to the conductor and requested him to turn Dr. P. out. [*Pennington denied this.*] He was approached and asked civilly to take a seat on the front platform, as that was the regulation on the road. He declined, but the conductor insisted on his leaving his seat to which he replied that he would maintain his rights. . . .

The conductor then asked the driver to stop the car, and remove the doctor. He stopped, took Dr. P. in his arms, embraced him, and carried him backward through the car, the doctor apparently making all the resistance in his power. He was, however, forced through the car, over the platform and into the street, near the sidewalk. . . .

New York Daily Tribune, 19 December 1856.

DR. JAMES MCCUNE SMITH CALLS ON ALL AFRICAN AMERICANS TO JOIN THE BATTLE FOR CIVIL RIGHTS

[*Dr. James McCune Smith, a scholar and physician who had earned his bachelor of arts, master of arts, and medical degrees at the University of Glasgow, urged his people to fight their own battles at a Black convention in New York City in 1855.*]

The influence of our land and its institutions reaches to the uttermost parts of the earth; and go where we may, we will find American prejudice, or at least the odor of it, to contend against. It is easiest, as well as manliest, to meet and contend with it here at the fountain head. . . . But the hour has come for us to take a direct and forward movement. We feel and know it. . . . We are awakened, as never before, to the fact that if Slavery and caste are to be removed from the land, we must remove them ourselves; others may aid and assist if they will, but the moving power rests with us. . . . We must act up to what we declare. . . . And from the mere act of riding in public conveyances, up to the liberation of every slave in the land do our duties extend—embracing a full and equal participation, politically and socially, in all the rights and immunities of American citizens. If our duties are weighty, we have the means to perform them. . . . [Some states have] made movements toward recognizing our rights as citizens thereof. But efforts on our own part have helped toward this good result: in Massachusetts mainly by the efforts of some colored citizens, led by a member of this Council, both houses of the Legislature, have done their share toward granting us equal suffrage, and the Governor has strongly recommended the same. In New-York, through the efforts of a member of this Council and the President of our State Council, aided by the moving eloquence of another member of our council, the Legislature passed a vote of equal suffrage. . . . In Pennsylvania strong and able effort has been made to obtain the franchise by our colored brethren, and not without some signs that the labors of her intelligent and energetic colored citizens have not been in vain. . . . The time is come when our people must assume the rank of a first-rate power in the battle against caste and Slavery; it is emphatically our battle; no one else can fight it for us, and with God's help we must fight it ourselves.

New York Daily Tribune, 9 May 1855, 6–7.

7 THE AGE OF REFORM, 1820–1860

Boston's Vigilance Committee—formed to battle slave catchers coming from the South to capture runaways—included, at one time, writer James Russell Lowell, lawyer and novelist Richard Henry Dana, educator and humanitarian Samuel G. Howe, and Reverend Theodore Parker, the city's outstanding minister. Ex-presidents John Adams and John Quincy Adams served without fee as lawyers for fugitive slaves seized in Massachusetts. Northern writers such as Melville, Hawthorne, Emerson, Thoreau, Whittier, Longfellow, Bryant, and the Alcotts wrote, spoke or took action against slavery. Women's rights leader Susan B. Anthony opened her Rochester, New York, home to slaves fleeing to Canada and demanded that the North "prove to the South, by her acts, that she fully recognizes the humanity of the black man." In one of his poems Walt Whitman, poet of American democracy, spoke of his identification with the slave—"I am the hounded slave, I wince at the bite of the dogs."

The Great Reformers

This was the great age of reform in U.S. history, and many white and Black philosophers, writers, ministers, orators, and editors spoke out for justice for all who were mistreated or denied the common rights of humanity. This movement in America was linked with a worldwide interest in reform that included such men as Richard Cobden in England, Daniel O'Connell in Ireland, and Victor Hugo in France. It sought to reshape the nation and the world along humanitarian lines—peace, concern for the unfortunate, an end to slavery, equality, education for all, and justice for men and women regardless of color.

In America this era included Horace Mann's campaign for public schools and Dorothea Dix's fight for understanding and help for those in jails and insane asylums. Samuel G. Howe sought to prove that the deaf, dumb, and blind could be educated, and Susan B. Anthony and Elizabeth Cady Stanton battled for equal rights for women. Black leaders such as William Wells Brown, Frederick Douglass, and Sojourner Truth fought for increased education, women's rights, and universal peace—and several toured Europe to support these causes in England, Ireland, and France.

It was the time of Sojourner Truth, a tall former New York slave, whose vibrant voice stirred antislavery meetings with moving stories of the wrongs heaped upon her people. Although illiterate, she spoke for women's rights simply and clearly against men far more educated than herself. And she battled segregation on the streetcars of Washington by simply refusing to leave the white section, or creating a scene which convinced conductors that it was wiser to leave her alone.

Sojourner Truth, a former New York slave, spoke for Black freedom and women's rights. Though unable to read or write, she became a masterful orator.

Frederick Douglass

No one better represented the age of reform than a tall, broad-shouldered young runaway slave named Frederick Douglass. While a boy in Baltimore, Douglass learned to read and write despite his master's vigilance and the laws making it a crime for slaves to learn to read and write. When a slave breaker named Covey tried to whip him into submission, Douglass—then a teenager—fought him off for two hours and won. After his escape from Maryland, Douglass lectured for the antislavery cause and published the story of his life.

In the 1840s Douglass toured Europe to raise funds and make friends for the abolitionist cause. He also spoke out for Irish freedom, world peace, and political rights for all regardless of sex, wealth, or color. He told a London audience in 1846, "You may rely upon me as one who will never desert the cause of the poor, no matter whether black or white."

Douglass spent five weeks lecturing in Ireland on home rule for the Irish and emancipation for the African American. He was introduced to

An English magazine's picture of Frederick Douglass addressing a British audience. Douglass spoke against slavery and for women's rights, Irish freedom, federal aid to education, and the right of the oppressed everywhere to equal protection under the law.

Irish audiences by orator Daniel O'Connell as "the Black O'Connell of the United States." Seventy thousand citizens of Ireland had previously signed a petition calling on the American Irish to support the antislavery cause and treat Black people as equals.

He returned to America to publish his own newspaper, the *North Star.* His editorials demanded the end of capital punishment, mistreatment of Chinese immigrants and American Indians, and neglect of education for the poor. For fifty years he wrote and spoke for justice and human rights. Douglass described his opposition to slavery in these words:

> I have held all my life, and shall hold to the day of my death, that the fundamental and everlasting objection to slavery, is not that it sinks a Negro to the condition of a brute, but that it sinks a *man* to that condition.

He also pointed out a simple truth when he said, "Let us not forget that justice to the Negro is safety to the nation."

Douglass did more than speak for justice—he placed himself in the thick of the battle. He refused to leave Northern railroad cars set aside for whites and reported, "I was often dragged out of my seat, beaten, and severely bruised, by conductors and brakemen." In Indiana a mob broke his arm when he spoke out against slavery. His Rochester home was a station for the Underground Railroad, and his sons became conductors for fugitives traveling to Canada, and then Civil War soldiers.

During the Civil War, Douglass urged Lincoln to free the slaves and arm African American men. When Lincoln finally adopted these policies, he asked Douglass to serve as his adviser. Douglass raised troops for the Union army, his two sons among the first to enlist. After the war Douglass continued his battles. He urged Congress to enact "a great national system of aid to education" and a laws that would protect the rights of the liberated African Americans. He died in 1895 shortly after delivering a speech on behalf of women's rights. A mental and physical giant, he had helped pull his country and people from the depths of slavery.

The Rise of Militant Abolitionism

The fight against slavery had been going on since the first slave ship left Africa. Flight was the most common form slaves used to end their bondage. Even when recaptured, they tried to break away. Josiah Quincy, a New England Federalist, was the lawyer for the first fugitive captured under the laws of the new Constitution. The case, however, was never ruled upon because his client knocked down two policemen and made his escape from the court.

Many early white organizations formed to help slaves believed that the

To dramatize the horror of slavery, one Sunday Reverend Henry Ward Beecher "sold" a slave named Sarah in his Brooklyn church.

only solution to the problem was the deportation of slaves to Africa. Even many slaveholders could support this idea. In 1821 the American Colonization Society, supported largely by slaveholders, with the aid of the United States Congress, established a colony in Liberia. Some twelve thousand African Americans were sent there, mostly slaves liberated on the condition that they accept this deportation.

But the most uncompromising fight against bondage began with the slaves themselves as well as their free relatives. In 1829, David Walker, a Boston agent for the first Black newspaper, issued an *Appeal* to those in bondage. His message was simple: if you are not given your liberty, rise in bloody rebellion. When copies of his *Appeal* were found in Southern cities from Virginia to Louisiana, slaveholders panicked. They offered a reward for Walker's capture, dead or alive. He died mysteriously the following year, but the fight went on.

Growing White Support

When twenty-six-year-old William Lloyd Garrison came to Boston and began to publish his famous *Liberator* on January 1, 1831, he found that his main support came from African American abolitionists. Rich Blacks contributed money, Black newsboys sold the paper on the streets, and three-quarters of his readers were African Americans. This determined young man was the first of his race to look at the African American's problem

William Still, secretary of the Underground Railroad in Philadelphia. He decided to keep careful records when he discovered that a runaway he was interviewing was his brother.

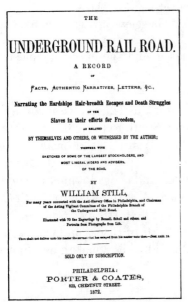

from the African American's point of view. "In your sufferings I participate," he told Boston's Black community. He fiercely denounced slavery as a sin and violation of human rights and forcefully proclaimed that there would be no compromise with it. Garrison said the government was protecting the evil and publicly burned a copy of the Constitution—"a blood-stained document"—because it regarded humans as property. "He will shake our nation to its center," said a minister who heard him for the first time, "but he will shake slavery out of it."

A number of whites had joined Garrison and the African Americans of the antislavery movement by the 1830s. Levi Coffin, Indiana Quaker and banker, began using his Newport home to hide runaways even earlier when he found that the Black people of the town who had been hiding them lacked the money and resources to do it well. Coffin was soon called the "president of the Underground Railroad."

This "railroad" developed its own language. The "trains" were the large farm wagons that could conceal and carry a number of fugitives. The "tracks" were the back country roads which were used to escape the slave catchers. The "stations" were the homes where the slaves were fed and cared for as they moved from station to station. The "conductors" were the fearless men and women of both races who led the slaves toward freedom, and the "passengers" or "parcels" were the slaves who dared to break for liberty. Passengers paid no fare and conductors received no pay.

This strange railroad had many ways of moving slaves. Twenty-eight slaves walked in a funeral procession from Kentucky to Ohio. Calvin Fairbank, a white minister who spent fourteen years in jail for his part in aiding runaways in the 1850s, described his work in these words:

> I piloted them through the forests, mostly at night; . . . boys dressed as girls, and girls as boys; on foot and on horseback, in buggies, carriages, common wagons, in and under loads of hay, straw, old furniture, boxes, and bags . . . or in boats or skiffs; on rafts, and often on a pine log. And I never suffered one to be recaptured.

The most daring and successful conductor was Harriet Tubman, a former slave. She made nineteen trips into the South to bring three hundred relatives, friends, and strangers to freedom. Wanted dead or alive in the South, she was never captured and never lost a passenger. A determined worker, Tubman carried a gun for protection and drugs to quiet the crying babies in her rescue parties. During the Civil War, she went to South Carolina to guide Union raids deep into Confederate territory.

The Underground Railroad united the efforts of Blacks and whites in its dangerous work. Thomas Garrett, a gentle old white Quaker, and Samuel

For many years William Lambert helped run the Detroit station of the Underground Railroad. His organization was called "African Mysteries: The Order of the Men of Oppression." It utilized a complicated system of signals, oaths, and procedures.

"General Moses," John Brown had called her. Before she died at ninety-three Harriet Tubman had led three hundred slaves to freedom, directed Union raiding parties during the Civil War, and built a home for ex-slaves who were too old or too ill to work.

Burris, a young Black man, ran the station in the slave state of Delaware during the 1840s. Garrett paid out a fortune in court fines for his crime of aiding fugitives but said to a judge:

> Thee hasn't left me a dollar, but I wish to say to thee, and to all in the court-room, that if anyone knows of a fugitive who wants shelter, and a friend, *send him to Thomas Garrett* and he will befriend him.

Burris was captured and was punished by being auctioned off as a slave. No one knew that the highest bidder was sent by Thomas Garrett to buy him and return him to freedom.

Quaker Thomas Garrett (left) and Samuel Burris (right) ran a station of the Underground Railroad in slave Delaware.

The threat of losing millions of dollars invested in slave property brought a furious response from slaveholders, their Northern business associates, and their friends in the federal government. Abolitionists were driven from the South, their printing presses wrecked, and their literature burned. The federal government, from the early 1800s until the election of Lincoln in 1860, favored the minority of slaveholders who ruled the Southern states. In 1835, President Andrew Jackson forbade the Post Office to deliver abolitionist mail in the South. Congress, in clear violation of the Bill of Rights, decided not to accept any antislavery petitions. This "Gag Rule" was finally defeated after an eight-year Congressional battle led by then congressman (former president) John Quincy Adams.

In the North, abolitionists faced mobs of ruffians urged on by men whose business depended upon Southern slavery. In the forty-eight hours of October 21 and 22, 1835, abolitionist meetings in New York, Massachusetts, and Vermont were broken up by white gangs. William Lloyd Garrison was almost killed by a mob led by "respectable" Boston merchants. Reverend Elijah Lovejoy was killed by an Illinois mob two years later.

The antislavery crusaders were made of strong Yankee metal that did not bend and rarely broke. Though never a majority of the American people, they aimed their appeal directly at the American conscience. They were ready, in the words of one, "to fight against slavery until Hell freezes and then continue the battle on the ice." Many white citizens felt that the white abolitionists threatened the nation's peace, but African Americans saw them in a different light. A convention of fugitive slaves held in 1850

Boston aristocrat Wendell Phillips joined the abolitionists after seeing a mob almost lynch William Lloyd Garrison. He became one of America's greatest orators and radical reformers. His speaking style was described as "easy and graceful, but powerful as the soft stretching of a tiger's paw." After the Civil War he continued his campaign for Black rights, women's suffrage, and the right of trade unions to strike.

sent these words to their brothers in bondage: "The abolitionists act the part of friends and brothers to us and our only complaint against them is, that there are so few of them."

While the abolitionists were fearless and determined, they were rarely united. "Meetings were a disorderly convention, each [member] having his own plan or theory," wrote one minister. Ex-presidents and ex-slaves, poets and politicians, men of God and atheists tried to set a common program. William Lloyd Garrison drove large numbers of Black and white abolitionists out of the American Antislavery Society when he demanded that they refuse to vote in elections. James G. Birney, an Alabama slaveholder who had become an abolitionist, led a large number of Western abolitionists away from Garrison into the Liberty Party, which ran antislavery men for office. Frederick Douglass's newspaper supported Birney and urged African Americans to use political action to end slavery in America.

President Abraham Lincoln, a week before his death, said, "I have only been an instrument. The logic and moral power of Garrison, and the antislavery people of the country and the Army, have done all."

THE PHILOSOPHY OF A GREAT AMERICAN REFORMER

[The creed of Frederick Douglass is embodied in a speech delivered in 1857.]

Let me give you a word of the philosophy of reform. The whole history of the progress of human liberty shows that all concessions yet made to her august claims, have been born of earnest struggle. The conflict has been exciting, agitating, all-absorbing, and, for the time being, putting all other tumults to silence. It must do this or it does nothing. If there is no struggle there is no progress. Those who profess to favor freedom and yet deprecate agitation, are men who want crops without plowing up the ground, they want rain without thunder and lightning. They want the ocean without the awful roar of its many waters.

This struggle may be a moral one, or it may be a physical one, and it may be both moral and physical, but it must be a struggle. Power concedes nothing without a demand. It never did and it never will. Find out just what any people will quietly submit to and you have found out the exact measure of injustice and wrong which will be imposed upon them, and these will continue till they are resisted with either words or blows, or with both. The limits of tyrants are prescribed by the endurance of those whom they oppress. In the light of these ideas, Negroes will be hunted at the North, and held and flogged at the South so long as they submit to those devilish outrages, and make no resistance, either moral or physical. Men may not get all they pay for in this world, but they must certainly pay for all they get. If we ever get free from the oppressions and wrongs heaped upon us, we must pay for their removal. We must do this by labor, by suffering, by sacrifice, and, if needs be, by our lives and the lives of others.

Two Speeches by Frederick Douglass (Rochester, 1857), 21–22.

DAVID WALKER'S CALL FOR ACTION

[David Walker, born free in North Carolina, in his fiery pamphlet, written in 1829, concluded that slave revolts were justified and he advised his people to take action. He also had words of advice for all Americans.]

. . . Remember, Americans, that we must and shall be free and enlightened as you are, will you wait until we shall, under God, obtain our liberty by the crushing arm of power? Will it not be dreadful for you? I speak Americans for your good. We must and shall be as free I say, in spite of you. You may do your best to keep us in wretchedness and misery, to enrich you and your children, but God will deliver us from under you. And wo, wo, will be to you if we have to obtain our freedom by fighting. Throw away your fears and prejudices then, and enlighten us and treat us like men, and we will like you more than we do now hate you, and tell us now no more about colonization [to Africa], for America is as much our country, as it is yours.— Treat us like men, and there is no danger but we will all live in peace and happiness together. For we are not like you, hard hearted, unmerciful, and unforgiving. What a happy country this will be, if the whites will listen. . . . But Americans, I declare to you, while you keep us and our children in bondage, and treat us like brutes, to make us support you and your families, we cannot be your friends. You do not look for it, do you? Treat us then like men, and we will be your friends. . . .

David Walker, *Walker's Appeal, in Four Articles* (Boston, 1830), 79–80.

A White Quaker Builds a "Station"

[Levi Coffin, born and brought up in North Carolina, was a member of the Society of Friends and always opposed slavery. His work for the Underground Railroad began in earnest when he moved to Newport, Indiana.]

. . . Soon after we located at Newport, I found that we were on a line of the U.G.R.R. [Underground Railroad]. Fugitives often passed through that place, and generally stopped among the colored people. . . . I learned that the fugitive slaves who took refuge with these people were often pursued and captured, the colored people not being very skillful in concealing them, or shrewd in making arrangements to forward them to Canada. . . . I was willing to receive and aid as many fugitives as were disposed to come to my house. I knew that my wife's feelings and sympathies regarding this matter were the same as mine, and that she was willing to do her part. . . .

In the winter of 1826–27, fugitives began to come to our house, and as it became more widely known on different routes that the slaves fleeing from bondage would find a welcome and shelter at our house, and be forwarded safely on their journey, the number increased. Friends in the neighborhood, who had formerly stood aloof from the work, fearful of the penalty of the law, were encouraged to engage in it when they saw the fearless manner in which I acted, and the success that attended my efforts. . . .

. . . the Underground Railroad business increased as time advanced, and it was attended with heavy expenses, which I could not have borne had not my affairs been prosperous. I found it necessary to keep a team and a wagon always at command, to convey the fugitive slaves on their journey. Sometimes, when we had large companies, one or two other teams and wagons were required. These journeys had to be made at night, often through deep mud and bad roads, and along by ways that were seldom traveled. Every precaution to evade pursuit had to be used, as the hunters were often on the track, and sometimes ahead of the slaves. . . .

I soon became extensively known to the friends of the slaves, at different points on the Ohio River, where fugitives generally crossed, and to those northward of us on the various routes leading to Canada. . . . Three principal lines from the South converged at my house: one from Cincinnati, one from Madison, and one from Jeffersonville, Indiana. The roads were always in running order, the connections were good, the conductors active and zealous, and there was no lack of passengers. Seldom a week passed without our receiving passengers by this mysterious road. . . .

Levi Coffin, *Reminiscences of Levi Coffin* (Cincinnati, 1876), 107–12.

NEW YORK MERCHANTS VS. THE ABOLITIONISTS

[*Many wealthy and important Northerners opposed the abolitionist groups. Reverend Samuel J. May found out why one day in 1835.*]

At the annual meeting of the American Antislavery Society in May, 1835, I was sitting upon the platform of the Houston Street Presbyterian Church in New York, when I was surprised to see a gentleman enter and take his seat who, I knew, was a partner in one of the most prominent mercantile houses in the city. He had not been seated long before he beckoned me to meet him at the door. I did so. "Please walk out with me, sir," said he; "I have something of great importance to communicate." When we had reached the sidewalk he said, with considerable emotion and emphasis: "Mr. May, we are not such fools as not to know that slavery is a great evil, a great wrong. But it was consented to by the founders of our Republic. It was provided for in the Constitution of our Union. A great portion of the property of the Southerners is invested under its sanction; and the business of the North, as well as the South, has become adjusted to it. There are millions upon millions of dollars due from Southerners to the merchants and mechanics of this city alone, the payment of which would be jeopardized by any rupture between the North and South. We cannot afford, sir, to let you and your associates succeed in your endeavor to overthrow slavery. It is not a matter of principle with us. It is a matter of business necessity. We cannot afford to let you succeed. And I have called you out to let you know, and to let your fellow-laborers know, that we do not mean to allow you to succeed. We mean, sir," said he, with increased emphasis—"we mean, sir, to put you Abolitionists down—by fair means if we can, by foul means if we must."

Samuel J. May, *Some Recollections of Our Antislavery Conflict* (Boston, 1869), 127–28.

ABOLITIONISTS MOBBED IN NEW ENGLAND IN 1835

[*The antislavery fight often became a battle for free speech, press, and assembly. William Lloyd Garrison describes his capture by, and escape from, a white Boston mob.*]

. . . on seeing me, three or four of the rioters, uttering a yell, furiously dragged me to the window, with the intention of hurling me from that height to the ground, but one of them relented and said—"Don't let us kill him outright." So they drew me back, and coiled a rope about my body—probably to drag me through the streets. I bowed to the mob, and requesting them to wait patiently until I could descend, went down upon a ladder that was raised for that purpose. I fortunately extricated myself from the rope, and was seized by two or three powerful men [abolitionist friends]. . . . They led me along bareheaded, (for I had lost my hat), through a mighty crowd ever and anon shouting, "He shant be hurt! You shant hurt him! Don't hurt him! He's an American!" I was thus conducted through Wilson's Lane into State-street, in the rear of the City Hall, over the ground that was stained with the blood of the first martyr's in the cause of *Liberty* and *Independence,* by the memorable massacre of 1770. . . . My offense was in pleading for liberty—liberty for my enslaved countrymen, colored though they be. . . .

William Lloyd Garrison, *The Liberator,* 7 November 1835, 179.

[*Reverend Samuel J. May describes the breaking up of his New England speaking tour by white mob violence.*]

. . . I had spoken about fifteen minutes, when the most hideous outcries, yells, from a crowd of men who had surrounded the house startled us, and then came heavy missiles against the doors and blinds of the windows. I persisted in speaking for a few minutes, hoping the blinds and doors were strong enough to stand the siege. But presently a heavy stone broke through one of the blinds, shattered a pane of glass and fell upon the head of a lady sitting near the centre of the hall. She uttered a shriek and fell bleeding into the arms of her sister. The panic-stricken audience rose *en masse,* and began a rush for the doors. Seeing the danger, I shouted in a voice louder than I ever uttered before or since,

Sit down, every one of you, sit down! . . . If there is any one here whom the mob wish to injure, it is myself. I will stand here and wait until you are safely out of the house. But you must go in some order as I bid you.

To my great joy they obeyed. . . .
When the house was nearly empty I took on my arm a brave young lady, who would not leave me to go through the mob alone, and went out. Fortunately none of the ill-disposed knew me. So we passed through the lane of madmen unharmed, hearing their imprecations and threats of violence to the ——— Abolitionist when he should come out.
It was well we had delayed no longer to empty the hall, for at the corner

of the street above we met a posse of men more savage than the rest, dragging a cannon, which they intended to explode against the building and at the same time tear away the stairs; so furious and bloodthirsty had "the baser sort" been made by the instigation of "the gentlemen of property and standing."

In October it was thought advisable for me to go and lecture in several of the principal towns of Vermont. I did so, and everywhere I met with contumely and insult. I was mobbed five times. In Rutland and Montpelier my meetings were dispersed with violence. . . .

Samuel J. May, *Some Recollections of Our Antislavery Conflict* (Boston, 1869), 152–53.

A CALL TO SLAVES

[*Reverend Henry H. Garnet of New York at eleven escaped to the North and graduated from Oneida Institute in 1840. Three years later, at twenty-seven, at a Black convention in Buffalo, New York, he issued a call for slaves to revolt.*]

Brethren, it is as wrong for your lordly oppressors to keep you in slavery as it was for the man thief to steal our ancestors from the coast of Africa. You should therefore now use the same manner of resistance as would have been just in our ancestors when the bloody foot prints of the first remorseless soul-thief was placed upon the shores of our fatherland. . . .

Brethren, the time has come when you must act for yourselves. It is an old and true saying that, "if hereditary bondsmen would be free, they must themselves strike the blow." You can plead your own cause, and do the work of emancipation better than any others. . . . Think of the undying glory that hangs around the ancient name of Africa—and forget not that you are native-born American citizens, and as such, you are justly entitled to all the rights that are granted to the freest. Think how many tears you have poured out upon the soil which you have cultivated with unrequited toil and enriched with your blood; and then go to your lordly enslavers and tell them plainly, that you *are determined to be free*. Appeal to their sense of justice, and tell them that they have no more right to oppress you than you have to enslave them. . . . Inform them that all you desire is FREEDOM and that nothing else will suffice. Do this, and forever after cease to toil for the heartless tyrants, who give you no other reward but stripes and abuse. If they then commence work of death, they, and not you, will be responsible for the consequences. You had far better all die—*die immediately*, than live slaves, and entail you wretchedness upon your posterity. If you would be free in this generation, here is your only hope. However much you and all of us may desire it, there is not much hope of redemption without the shedding of blood. If you must bleed, let it all come at once—rather *die freemen than to live to be slaves. . . .*

Brethren, arise, arise! Strike for your lives and liberties. Now is the day and the hour. Let every slave throughout the land do this, and the days of slavery are numbered. You cannot be more oppressed than you have been—you cannot suffer greater cruelties than you have already. *Rather die freemen than live to be slaves.* Remember that you are FOUR MILLIONS!

[*The convention turned down Garnet's appeal for slave revolts by a single vote. After the Civil War Garnet became president of Avery College in Pennsylvania and served as United States Minister to Liberia, where he died.*]

A Memorial Discourse by Rev. Henry Highland Garnet, James McCune Smith, ed. (Philadelphia, 1865), 48–59.

FREDERICK DOUGLASS: EARLY ABOLITIONIST DAYS

[*Three years after his escape from slavery, Frederick Douglass joined the abolitionists as a speaker. He describes these early days.*]

Among the first duties assigned to me, on entering the ranks, was to travel, in company with Mr. George Foster, to secure subscribers to the *Anti-slavery Standard* and the *Liberator*. With him I traveled and lectured through the eastern counties of Massachusetts. Much interest was awakened— large meetings assembled. Many came, no doubt, from curiosity to hear what a Negro could say in his own cause. I was generally introduced as a "*chattel*"—a "*thing*"—a piece of southern "*property*"—the chairman assuring the audience that *it* could speak. Fugitive slaves, at that time, were not so plentiful as now [1855]; and as a fugitive slave lecturer, I had the advantage of being a "*brand new fact*"—the first one out. Up to that time a colored man was deemed a fool who confessed himself a runaway slave, not only because of the danger to which he exposed himself of being retaken, but because it was a confession of a very *low* origin. . . . The only precaution I took, at the beginning, to prevent Master Thomas from knowing where I was, and what I was about, was the withholding of my former name, my master's name, and the name of the state and county from which I came. During the first three or four months, my speeches were almost exclusively made up of narrations of my own personal experience as a slave. "Let us have the facts," said the people. . . . "Tell your story, Frederick," would whisper my then revered friend, William Lloyd Garrison, as I stepped upon the platform. I could not always obey, for I was now reading and thinking. New views of the subject were presented to my mind. It did not entirely satisfy me to *narrate* wrongs; I felt like *denouncing* them. . . .

Frederick Douglass, *My Bondage and My Freedom* (New York and Auburn, 1855), 360–62.

The Underground Railroad in the South

[*This letter, dated 13 June 1858, from Camden, Maryland, indicates some of the problems faced by free people of color helping others to escape.*]

Mr. Still:—I writ to inform you that we stand in need of help if ever we wonted help it is in theas day, we have Bin trying to rais money to By a hors but there is so few here that we can trust our selves with for fear that they may serve us as tom otwell [a traitor] served them when he got them in dover Jail. But he is dun for ever, i wont to no if your friends can help us, we have a Road that more than 100 past over in 1857. it is one we made for them, seven in march after the lions had them [the seven runaways that Tom Otwell had turned over to the Dover police] there is no better [Road] in the State, we are 7 miles from Delaware Bay. you may understand what i mean. I wrote last december to the anti Slavery Society for James Mot and others concerning of purchasing a horse for this Bisnes if your friends can help us the work must stil go on for ther is much frait pases over this Road, But ther has Ben but 3 conductors for sum time. you may no that there is but few men, sum talks all dos nothing, there is horses owned by Collard peopel but not for this purpose. We wont one for to go when called for, one of our best men was nigh Cut [caught] By keeping of them too long, By not having means to convay them tha must Be convad if they pass over this Road safe tha go through in 2 nights to Wilmington, for i went there with 28 in one gang last November, tha had to ride for when thea com to us we go 15 miles, it is hard Road to travel i had sum conversation with mr. Evens and wos down here on a visit. pleas try what you can do for us this is the place we need help, 12 mile i live from mason and Dixson Line. I wod have come but cant have time, as yet there has been some fuss about a boy ho lived near Camden, he has gone away, he ses me and my brother nose about it but he dont. . . .

. . . Ancer this letter.

Pleas to writ let me no if you can do anything for us. I still remain your friend.

William Still, *The Underground Rail Road* (Philadelphia, 1872), 448–49.

John Fairfield, A Southern White Conductor

[*Levi Coffin, known as the president of the Underground Railroad, tells of a young man from a slaveholding family who became a daring conductor on the Underground Railroad.*]

. . . When quite a young man, he decided to make a visit to the State of Ohio, and seek his fortune in a free State. Thinking that it would be a good opportunity to put his anti-slavery principles into practice, he planned to take with him one of his uncle's slaves, a bright, intelligent young man, about his own age, to whom he was much attached. John and this young colored man had played together when young boys, and had been brought up together. They had often discussed plans by which Bill, the slave, could make his escape to Canada, but no attempt had been made to carry them out, until young Fairfield determined to visit Ohio. The arrangement was then made for Bill to take one of his master's horses, and make his escape the night before Fairfield started, and wait for him at a rendezvous appointed. This plan was carried out, and Bill traveled as Fairfield's servant until they reached Ohio. Not feeling safe in that State, he went on to Canada. . . .

When Fairfield told me the story, some years afterward, I asked him if he did not feel guilty of encouraging horse-stealing, as well as Negro-stealing. I knew that death was the penalty for each of these crimes, according to the laws of Virginia and North Carolina.

The reply was: "No! I knew that Bill had earned several horses for his master, and he took only one. Bill had been a faithful fellow, and worked hard for many years, and that horse was all the pay he got. As to Negro-stealing, I would steal all the slaves in Virginia if I could." . . .

He was an inveterate hater of slavery, and this feeling supplied a motive for the actions of his whole life. He believed that every slave was justly entitled to freedom, and that if any person came between him and liberty, the slave had a perfect right to shoot him down. He always went heavily armed himself, and did not scruple to use his weapons whenever he thought the occasion required their use. He resorted to many stratagems to effect his object in the South, and brought away numbers of slaves from nearly every slave State in the Union. . . .

I reproved him for trying to kill any one. I told him it was better to suffer wrong than to do wrong, and that we should love our enemies.

"Love the devil!" he exclaimed. "Slaveholders are all devils, and it is no harm to kill the devil. I do not intend to hurt people if they keep out of the way, but if they step in between me and liberty, they must take the consequences. When I undertake to conduct slaves out of bondage I feel that it is my duty to defend them, even to the last drop of my blood."

I saw that it was useless to preach peace principles to John Fairfield. He would fight for the fugitives as long as his life lasted. . . .

[*In the following selection, Levi Coffin tells what a slave, one of a party of ten that Fairfield had led to freedom, told him about the young Southerner and their escape.*]

. . . "I never saw such a man as Fairfield. He told us he would take us out of slavery or die in the attempt, if we would do our part, which we promised to do. We all agreed to fight till we died, rather than be captured. Fairfield said he wanted no cowards in the company; if we were attacked and one of us showed cowardice or started to run, he would shoot him down."

They were attacked several times by patrolers, and fired upon, but always succeeded in driving the enemy and making their escape, keeping near their leader and obeying his commands. Fairfield said that they had a desperate battle one moonlight night with a company of armed men. They had been discovered by the patrolers, who had gathered a party of men and waylaid them at a bridge.

Fairfield said: "They were lying in ambush at each end of the bridge, and when we got fairly on the bridge they fired at us from each end. They thought, no doubt, that this sudden attack would intimidate us and that we would surrender, but in this they were mistaken. I ordered my men to charge to the front, and they did charge. We fired as we went, and the men in ambush scattered and ran like scared sheep."

"Was anybody hurt?" I asked.

In reply Fairfield showed me several bullet holes in his clothes, a slight flesh wound in one arm, and a slight flesh wound on the leg of one of the fugitives.

"You see," he said, "we were in close quarters, but my men were plucky. We shot to kill, and we made the devils run."

[*In another exploit, Fairfield gathered together a party of light-skinned slaves from Maryland, the District of Columbia, and Virginia and brought them out of slavery to relatives in Canada.*]

. . . After gaining their confidence and making them acquainted with his plans, Fairfield went to Philadelphia and bought wigs and powder. These cost him eighty dollars. . . . His first experiment with these articles of disguise was made at Baltimore. Having secretly collected the mulatto slaves of that city and vicinity, whom he had arranged to conduct to the North, he applied the powder and put on the wigs. The effect was satisfactory; the slaves looked like white people.

Fairfield bought tickets for them and they took the evening train to Harrisburg, where he had made arrangements for another person to meet them, who would accompany them to Cleveland and put them aboard the boat for Detroit.

Fairfield, having seen his party safely on the way, returned immediately to Washington City for another company, who, by the aid of wigs and powder, passed for white people. He put these fugitives on the train, and accompanied them to Pittsburg. I received a letter from a friend in Cleveland informing me of the arrival of both these parties. . . .

[*Just before the Civil War, after years as a conductor on the Underground Railroad, after many pitched battles with slaveholders, and numerous terms in Southern jails, John Fairfield mysteriously disappeared.*]

Levi Coffin, *Reminiscences of Levi Coffin* (Cincinnati, 1876), 429–45.

THE STRUGGLE FOR WOMEN'S RIGHTS

[*The Seneca Falls Convention of 1848 launched the U.S. women's rights movement. One pioneer leader was Elizabeth Cady Stanton. It was a tense moment when she decided to submit her motion proposing women be given the right to vote. She told her husband what she intended to do.*]

. . . "You will turn the proceedings," replied her husband, "into a farce; I wash my hands of the whole business. . . ." Lucretia Mott [another leader] also . . . said, "Lizzie, thou wilt make the convention ridiculous." But Lizzie was of a different opinion; and she withstood Mrs. Mott with modest courage and independence. . . . Mrs. Stanton . . . found only one person among the delegates who was willing from the first to champion her novel demand. This was the brave and high-souled Frederick Douglass, to whom she successfully appealed, saying,

> You, like myself, belong to a disenfranchised class, and must see that the root of all our social and legal disabilities lies in our deprivation of the right to make laws for ourselves. Will you urge the convention to adopt this protest against injustice? I have never spoken in public, and cannot defend my own resolutions. I want your help.

"You shall have it," was the reply. Mr. Douglass, with his ready genius as an orator, proved more than equal to the occasion. Mrs. Stanton, too, greatly to her surprise, found that her tongue was loosed, and that she could rise and reply to objections with happy success. . . .

[*This historic resolution was passed, and Douglass continued to fight for women's rights.*]

Laura Curtis Bullard, "Elizabeth Cady Stanton," in *Our Famous Women* (Hartford, 1884), 613–14.

THE PARIS PEACE CONGRESS OF 1849

[*The unity of European and American reform movements during the pre–Civil War period is shown in this report by William Wells Brown.*]

. . . Victor Hugo took the chair as President of the Congress, supported by vice-presidents from the several nations represented [England, France, Germany, Switzerland, Greece, Spain, and the United States]. Mr.

Richard, the secretary, read a dry report of the names of societies, committees, etc. which was deemed the opening of the Convention.

The president then arose, and delivered one of the most impressive and eloquent appeals in favor of peace that could possibly be imagined. . . . Victor Hugo concluded his speech amid the greatest enthusiasm on the part of the French, which was followed by hurras in the old English style. . . .

Well, at the close of the first sitting of the convention, and just as I was leaving, Victor Hugo, to whom I had been introduced by an M.P., I observed near me a gentleman with his hat in hand, whom I recognized as one of the passengers who had crossed the Atlantic with me in the *Canada*, and who appeared to be the most horrified at having a Negro for a fellow-passenger. This gentleman, as I left M. Hugo, stepped up to me and said, "How do you do, Mr. Brown?"

"You have the advantage of me," said I.

"O, don't you know me? I was a fellow-passenger with you from America; I wish you would give me an introduction to Victor Hugo and Mr. Cobden."

I need not inform you that I declined introducing this pro-slavery American to these distinguished men. I only allude to this, to show what a change came over the dreams of my white American brother by crossing the ocean. . . .

William Wells Brown, *Sketches of Places and People Abroad* (Boston, 1855), 59–61.

HARRIET TUBMAN'S LAST TRIP

[Harriet Tubman returned to the South nineteen times to free three hundred other slaves. Quaker conductor Thomas Garrett describes her last trip.]

Respected Friend:—William Still:—I write to let thee know that Harriet Tubman is again in these parts. She arrived last evening from one of her trips of mercy to God's poor, bringing two men with her as far as New Castle. I agreed to pay a man last evening, to pilot them on their way to Chester county; the wife of one of the men, with two or three children, was left some thirty miles below, and I gave Harriet ten dollars, to hire a man with carriage, to take them to Chester county. She said a man had offered for that sum, to bring them on. I shall be very uneasy about them, till I hear they are safe. There is now much more risk on the road, till they arrive here, than there has been for several months past, as we find that some poor, worthless wretches are constantly on the look out on two roads, that they cannot well avoid more especially with carriage, yet, as it is Harriet who seems to have had a special angel to guard her on her journey of mercy, I have hope.

Thy Friend
Thomas Garrett

William Still, *The Underground Rail Road* (Philadelphia, 1872), 530.

[*After the Civil War, Frederick Douglass wrote to Harriet Tubman.*]

. . . I have had the applause of the crowd and the satisfaction that comes of being approved by the multitude, while the most that you have done has been witnessed by a few trembling, scarred, and foot-sore bondmen and women, whom you have led out of the house of bondage, and whose heart-felt *"God bless you"* has been your only reward. The midnight sky and the silent stars have been the witnesses of your devotion to freedom and of your heroism. Excepting John Brown—of sacred memory—I know of no one who has willingly encountered more perils and hardships to serve our enslaved people than you have. Much that you have done would seem improbable to those who do not know you as I know you. . . .

Sarah Bradford, *Harriet, The Moses of Her People* (New York, 1886), 135.

SOJOURNER TRUTH SPEAKS FOR WOMEN'S RIGHTS

[*The leaders of a women's rights convention in May 1851 saw a tall, gaunt Black woman march toward the speaker's platform. Sojourner Truth, mother and former New York slave, had listened to male speakers state that women need not be given rights since they were mentally inferior to men.*]

. . . At her first word there was a profound hush. She spoke in deep tones, which, though not loud, reached every ear in the house, and away through the throng at the doors and windows.

"Wall, chilern, whar dar is so much racket dar must be somethin' out o' kilter. . . . What's all dis here talkin' 'bout?

"Dat man ober dar say dat womin needs to be helped into carriages, and lifted ober ditches, and to hab de best place everywhar. Nobody eber helps me into carriages, or ober mud-puddles, or gibs me any best place!" And raising herself to her full height, and her voice to a pitch like rolling thunder, she asked: "And a'n't I a woman? Look at me! Look at my arm! (and she bared her right arm to the shoulder, showing her tremendous muscular power). I have ploughed and planted, and gathered into barns, and no man could head me! And a'n't I a woman? I could work as much and eat as much as a man—when I could get it—and bear de lash as well! And a'n't I a woman? I have borne thirteen chilern, and seen 'em mos' all sold off to slavery, and when I cried out with my mother's grief, none but Jesus heard me! And a'n't I a woman?

"Den day talks 'bout dis ting in de head; what dis dey call it?" ("Intellect," whispered someone near.) "Dat's it, honey. What's dat got to do wid womin's rights . . . ? If my cup won't hold but a pint, and yourn holds a quart, wouldn't ye be mean not to let me have my little half measure full?" And she pointed her significant finger, and sent a keen glance at the minister who had made the argument. The cheering was long and loud.

"Den dat little man in black dar, he say women can't have as much rights as men, 'cause Christ wan't a woman! Whar did your Christ come from?" Rolling thunder couldn't have stilled that crowd, as did those deep, wonderful tones, as she stood there with outstretched arms and eyes of fire. Raising her voice still louder, she repeated, "Whar did your Christ come from? From God and a woman! Man had nothin' to do wid Him." . . .

. . . She ended by asserting: "If de fust woman God ever made was strong enough to turn de world upside down all alone, dese women togedder (and she glanced her eye over the platform) ought to be able to turn it back, and get it right side up again! And now dey is asking to do it, de men better let 'em." Long-continued cheering greeted this. . . .

Amid roars of applause, she returned to her corner, leaving more than one of us with streaming eyes, and hearts beating with gratitude. She had taken us up in her strong arms and carried us safely over the slough of difficulty turning the whole tide in our favor. . . .

Frances D. Gage, "Reminiscences by Frances D. Gage," in Elizabeth Cady Stanton, Susan B. Anthony, and Matilde Joselyn Gage, eds., *History of Woman Suffrage* 1 (Rochester, 1887): 115–17.

8 STEPS TO CIVIL WAR

O<small>N</small> M<small>AY</small> 14, 1857, Frederick Douglass told a New York meeting, "My hopes were never brighter than now." Supreme Court Chief Justice Roger Taney, a Maryland slaveholder, had just handed down the Dred Scott decision, which opened new land to slavery. But Douglass, a former Maryland slave, pointed out that:

> Judge Taney can do many things, but he cannot perform impossibilities. He cannot bale out the ocean, annihilate this firm old earth, or pluck the silvery star of liberty from our Northern sky.

To prove that the Dred Scott decision could not fasten bondage on the country permanently, Douglass pointed to past compromises. He said the slavery issue had not been settled by the Missouri Compromise, the war with Mexico, the Compromise of 1850, or the opening of Kansas to slavery. "The fact is, the more the question has been settled, the more it has needed settling." Douglass had an ability to see beyond the defeats of the moment to later victories.

Dred Scott.

The Fugitive Slave Law

Douglass was right. Ever since the birth of the United States, Americans had tried in every way possible to settle the slavery issue once and for all.

But each agreement had only led to additional demands by the slaveholders. The Compromise of 1850 was called by some "a final settlement." It included a strong fugitive slave law, a penalty of six months' imprisonment, and a $1,000 fine for anyone caught helping a slave to escape. Southerners thought that this tough measure would be sufficient to halt the escape of their slaves. The Northern reaction to this law shocked them.

Black and white members of the Underground Railroad went into action. Lewis Hayden of Boston, who had escaped slavery and hid many fugitives in his house, placed two kegs of explosives in his cellar and announced he would blow up the house rather than let slave catchers enter. The fiery editor Martin R. Delany said:

> Sir, my house is my castle. . . . If any man approaches that house in search of a slave—I care not who he may be, whether constable or sheriff, magistrate or even judge of the supreme Court . . . —if he crosses the threshold of my door, and I do not lay him a lifeless corpse at my feet, I hope the grave may refuse my body a resting place. . . .

Lewis Hayden, a runaway slave leader in the Boston Vigilance Committee.

A group of Ohio Quakers said they would continue to aid runaways "in defiance of all the enactments of all the governments on earth." White abolitionist Wendell Phipps told a cheering Boston audience that "Law or no law, Constitution or no Constitution, humanity shall be paramount."

A group of Canadians who had escaped from slavery held a convention in New York and wrote "our enslaved brethren" to "be prayerful, be brave—be hopeful." Many of these Canadians then joined the Underground Railroad to bring others out of bondage.

Abolitionists posted notices describing slave catchers who entered Northern cities. Some followed these Southerners into stores and streetcars and pointed them out to all. Prominent lawyers volunteered, or were hired, to defend fugitives caught in the web of the new law. In some cases defendants, with the help of abolitionists, escaped from courtrooms.

A Congressional committee reported that the effort to recapture fugitives in the North "often leads to most unpleasant, if not perilous collisions." President Millard Fillmore decried this resistance "by lawless and violent mobs." But opposition mounted.

In 1851, a Black vigilance committee in Pennsylvania killed two members of a posse who had come to claim two runaways. Together Black and white abolitionists broke into jails and attacked United States marshals to free slaves to be returned to their masters. It took twenty-two military units including marines, cavalry, and artillery to hold back the thousands of Bostonians who, in 1854, were bent on freeing slave Anthony Burns. A

CAUTION!!
COLORED PEOPLE
OF BOSTON, ONE & ALL,
You are hereby respectfully CAUTIONED and advised, to avoid conversing with the
Watchmen and Police Officers
of Boston,
For since the recent ORDER OF THE MAYOR & ALDERMEN, they are empowered to act as
KIDNAPPERS
AND
Slave Catchers,
And they have already been actually employed in KIDNAPPING, CATCHING, AND KEEPING SLAVES. Therefore, if you value your LIBERTY, and the Welfare of the Fugitives among you, Shun them in every possible manner, as so many HOUNDS on the track of the most unfortunate of your race.
Keep a Sharp Look Out for
KIDNAPPERS, and have
TOP EYE open.
APRIL 24, 1851.

Slave catchers driven off by a vigilance committee in Christiana, Pennsylvania. William Parker and his band then escaped to Canada with the help of Frederick Douglass.

Anthony Burns, captured in Boston, was returned to slavery in Virginia in 1854.

mere twenty years earlier, a Boston mob had almost lynched William Lloyd Garrison for denouncing slavery. Times had changed. John Brown noted that the Fugitive Slave Law made "more abolitionists than all the lectures we have had for years." Brown always preferred action to lectures.

A War of Words Leads to Violence

Moved by the plight of slave runaways under the new law, Harriet Beecher Stowe in 1852 wrote a novel to dramatize the evils of slave life. *Uncle Tom's Cabin* became a worldwide best-seller and brought the evils of slavery home to any American who could read. Samuel Green, a free African American, was sentenced to ten years in prison by a Maryland court for having a copy of the book in his possession.

In 1854, Congress, under the leadership of Senator Stephen A. Douglas, passed the Kansas-Nebraska Act, opening that territory to slavery. Armed settlers from the North and South entered Kansas to fight out the slavery issue. When one slaveholder tried to auction a slave boy at Iowa Point, a bloody clash occurred. "It was a bunch of 'free soilers' who were determined to break up the auction," recalled the boy.

> A man leading a riderless horse rushed up to me and shouted: "The moment your feet touched Kansas soil, you were a free man," and, then, he ordered me to mount the horse and we rode at a fast gallop, leaving the groups to fight it out.

"Some one planned to assassinate me," reported Governor John W. Geary of Kansas, but added, "I am perfectly cool . . . but I am more vigilant than ever."

Violence flared over the Kansas issue in the United States Senate. Abolitionist Senator Charles Sumner, seated behind his Senate desk, was beaten bloody and unconscious by the slashing cane of Congressman Preston Brooks of South Carolina. Brooks explained that Sumner had insulted slaveholders in a speech he made on "Bleeding Kansas." While Sumner became a martyr to the North, Brooks was applauded in the South. Other abolitionists "should catch it next," wrote a Richmond, Virginia, paper, and Southerners sent Brooks more canes.

Out of the fighting in bloody Kansas rose a new party pledged to halt the growth of slavery—the Republican party. One of the new party's leaders, Abraham Lincoln, asked in 1855, "Can we as a nation continue *permanently forever*—half slave and half free?"

An iron-willed white man named John Brown stood watching Lawrence, Kansas, set ablaze by proslavery night riders and gave his answer: "I have only a short time to live—only one death to die, and I will die fighting for this [antislavery] cause." Much earlier he had pledged his family to a crusade against slavery in a ceremony in his family kitchen. John Brown, Jr., then about eighteen, recalled:

> After prayer he [John Brown] asked us to raise our right hands, and then he administered to us an oath [that] bound us to secrecy and devotion to the purpose of fighting slavery by force and arms to the extent of our ability.

John Brown. Because he was willing to defy any authority in his war on slavery, he has been called mad. A few years after his death, Union soldiers sang "The John Brown Song" as they marched into battle.

In 1859, John Brown completed his plans for a raid on the government arsenal at Harpers Ferry. It was to be his first step in the creation of a headquarters and an African American republic in the Virginia mountains. Frederick Douglass had spent hours trying to convince Brown that he was entering "a perfect steel trap." But the old man had made up his mind. Only illness kept Harriet Tubman from joining the invaders.

Leading a group of nineteen men that included five Blacks and his own sons, Brown launched his attack. The assault bogged down and, within hours, it was overwhelmed by marines led by Robert E. Lee. Tried and convicted, Brown and his men, knowing their cause to be just, calmly faced death. "I have thirteen children, and only four are left," said Mrs. Brown, "but if I am to see the ruin of my house, I cannot but hope that Providence may bring out of it some benefit for the poor slave."

The slaves continued to flee North during the 1850s. Despite the greater vigilance of Southerners, more escaped than ever before.

More white hands than ever reached out to aid fleeing slaves and hinder their pursuers. Representative Joshua Giddings proudly told Congress he defied the law by helping runaways. "I fed them, I clothed them, gave them money for their journey and sent them on their way rejoicing."

This decade that began with a compromise with slaveholders concluded with an election that spelled the end of compromise. Abraham Lincoln, dedicated to halting the growth of slavery, defeated a Democratic party that was split over the slavery issue. Americans had finally elected a president opposed to the extension of slavery.

Osborne Perry Anderson. One of five Black men with John Brown. He escaped and wrote a book on the Harpers Ferry raid.

A wounded John Brown faces the court that condemned him to death.

Abolitionist Wendell Phillips rejoiced. "For the first time in our history, the *slave* has chosen a President of the United States. . . . Lincoln is in *place*, Garrison is in *power.*" (By 1863 the logic of events made this exaggeration come true!) But one thing was certain in 1860. The masters of the salves were no longer the masters of the United States.

As slave states began to leave the Union, a tense nation prayed that Mr. Lincoln would measure up to the great challenge. By Lincoln's inauguration as president eleven southern states had formed a confederacy based on the notion that as its vice president, Alexander Stephens said, "freedom is not possible without slavery." Slaves added their voices to the debate when sixty marched through New Castle, Kentucky, shouting Republican slogans and singing political songs. Said a white Texan, "We sleep on our arms and the whole country is deeply excited."

CHALLENGING THE 1850 FUGITIVE SLAVE LAW

[*Dr. Martin R. Delany, lecturer, world traveler, medical man, and abolitionist editor and orator, spoke to a Pittsburgh meeting which included the mayor.*]

Honorable mayor, whatever ideas of liberty I may have, have been received from reading the lives of your revolutionary fathers. I have therein learned that a man has a right to defend his castle with his life, even unto the taking of life. Sir, my house is my castle; in that castle are none but my wife and my children, as free as the angels of heaven, and whose liberty is as sacred as the pillars of God. If any man approaches that house in search of a slave—I care not who he may be, whether constable or sheriff, magistrate or even judge of the Supreme Court—nay, let it be he who sanctioned this act to become a law [President Millard Fillmore], surrounded by his cabinet as his body-guard, with the Declaration of Independence waving above his head as his banner, and the constitution of his country upon his breast as his shield,—if he crosses the threshold of my door, and I do not lay him a lifeless corpse at my feet, I hope the grave may refuse my body a resting-place, and righteous Heaven my spirit a home. O, no! he cannot enter that house and we both live.

Frank A. Rollin, *The Life and Public Services of Martin R. Delany* (Boston, 1883), 76.

[Reverend Jarmain Loguen of Syracuse, New York, an escaped slave who used his home and church to hide runaways, announced his determination to resist the new law before a public meeting in his city on 4 October 1850.]

. . . The time has come to change the tones of submission into tones of defiance,—and to tell Mr. Fillmore and Mr. Webster, if they propose to execute this measure upon us, to send their bloodhounds. . . .

. . . I don't respect this law—I don't fear it—I won't obey it! It outlaws me, and I outlaw it, and the men who attempt to enforce it on me. I place the government officials on the ground that they place me. I will not live a slave, and if force is employed to re-enslave me, I shall make preparations to meet the crisis as becomes a man.

J. W. Loguen, *The Rev. J. W. Loguen, As a Slave and As a Freeman* (Syracuse, 1859), 392–93.

THE RECEPTION AND TREATMENT OF KIDNAPPERS

[The following suggestions were published in the abolitionist Liberator.*]*

As soon as the arrival of one or more slave-hunters is known, let the Vigilance committee appoint a sub-committee of the most active and devoted friends of liberty, sufficiently numerous for the thorough accomplishment of the following purposes, namely:

To keep themselves informed, by active, open, personal supervision, of every step the kidnappers take, every act they do, and every person they visit, as long as they remain in the place:

By personal interference, and calling aloud upon the citizens for rescue, to prevent them from seizing any man or woman as a slave:

To point them out to the people, wherever they go, as Slave-hunters: and, finally,

When to leave the town, to go with them and point them out to members of the Vigilance committee or other friends of freedom in the first place in which they stop, that similar attention may be paid them there. . . .

As soon as the kidnappers arrive in any town, large handbills should be posted in all the public places, containing their names, with a description of their persons and the business on which they come.

An attempt should be made to induce the landlord of any hotel or boarding-house to which they may go, to refuse them entertainment, on the ground of their being persons infamous by profession, like pickpockets, gamblers, or horse-stealers.

If this proves unsuccessful, some of the committee . . . should take lodgings in the same house with the kidnappers, and take, if possible, sleeping rooms and seats at a table directly opposite to them.

The doors of the house should be watched carefully, day and night, and whenever they go out, two resolute, unarmed men should follow each of them wherever he goes, pointing him out from time to time with the word SLAVE-HUNTER. . . . He should not have a moment's relief from the feeling that his object is understood, that he cannot act in secret, that he is surrounded by those who loathe his person and detest his purpose, and who have means always at hand to prevent the possibility of success. . . .

C. K. W., "Reception and Treatment of Kidnappers," *The Liberator*, 31 January 1851, 20.

Boston Defies the Law in 1851

[*Boston's Black community freed the first man under the new law. White Reverend Thomas Wentworth Higginson tells how the rescue of Shadrach was engineered by Robert Morris, a Black lawyer.*]

. . . on the day of the arraignment of the alleged fugitive, the fact was noted in a newspaper by a colored man of great energy and character, employed by a firm in Boston and utterly unconnected with the Abolitionists. He asked leave of absence, and strolled into the Court-House. Many colored men were at the door and had been excluded; but, he, being known and trusted, was admitted, and the others, making a rush, followed in behind him with a hubbub of joking and laughter. There were but a few constables on duty, and it suddenly struck this leader, as he and his followers passed near the man under arrest, that they might as well keep on and pass out at the opposite door, taking among them the man under arrest, who was not handcuffed. After a moment's beckoning the prisoner saw his opportunity, fell in with the jubilant procession, and amid continued uproar was got outside the Court-House, when the crowd scattered in all directions.

It was an exploit which . . . was treated at Washington as if it had shaken the nation. Daniel Webster called it "a case of treason"; President Fillmore issued a special proclamation; and Henry Clay gave notice of a bill to lend added strength to the Fugitive Slave Law. . . .

Thomas Wentworth, *Cheerful Yesterdays* (Boston and New York, 1898), 135–36.

THE DISAPPEARING DEFENDANT

[*Levi Coffin describes the first important Ohio case under the new Fugitive Slave Law. A runaway named Louis had been captured and tried in Cincinnati in 1853. One of his two volunteer defense lawyers was Rutherford B. Hayes, president of the United States after the Civil War.*]

When the time set for the decision arrived, the court-room was crowded with interested listeners, white and Black. . . . The judge was slow and tedious in reviewing the evidence, and as he spoke in a low tone, and the auditors were anxious to hear they leaned forward much absorbed, trying to catch every word, as they expected every moment to hear the Negro consigned to slavery.

Louis was crowded, and to gain more room, slipped his chair back a little way. Neither his master nor the marshal noticed the movement, as they were intently listening to the judge, and he slipped in his chair again, until he was back of them. I was standing close behind him and saw every movement. Next he rose quietly to his feet and took a step backward. Some abolitionists, friendly to his cause, gave him an encouraging touch on the foot, and he stepped farther back. Then a good hat was placed on his head by some one behind, and he quietly and cautiously made his way around the south end of the room, into the crowd of colored people on the west side, and, through it, toward the door. I and several other abolitionists had our eyes on him, and our hearts throbbed with suppressed excitement and anxiety lest he should be discovered. The door and passage were crowded with Germans, through whom Louis made his way, and passing down stairs, gained the street. He was well acquainted with the different streets, and made his way quickly, though with not enough haste to attract attention, through an alley, across the canal, through the German settlement, and by an indirect route to Avondale, where he knew the sexton of the colored burying ground. About five minutes after he left the court-room his absence was discovered, and created a great sensation. The marshal cried, "Louis is gone!" and made a rush for the door and down stairs, followed by his supporters to search for the fugitive who had slipped through their fingers. Louis' friends were all delighted, of course. . . . A vigorous search was made for Louis by the marshal and the pro-slavery party, but he could not be found.

I, and other abolitionists, learning of his whereabouts, decided that he was not safe on the outskirts of the city, and the following night we disguised him in woman's apparel, brought him into the city, and took him to the house of one of his colored friends, on Broadway, near Sixth Street. He was placed in an upper room and the door locked, and here he remained about a week. . . .

Reminiscences of Levi Coffin (Cincinnati, 1876), 550–52.

THE CHRISTIANA "RIOT"

[*Slaveholder Gorsuch, accompanied by United States Marshal Kline and a posse, arrived in Christiana, Pennsylvania, in the morning of 11 September 1851 to recapture two of Gorsuch's slaves. William Parker, who was hiding the runaways in his house, describes what happened as the United States marshal entered his house and came up the stairs, followed by the posse.*]

. . . I met them at the landing, and asked "Who are you?"

The leader, Kline, replied, "I am the United States Marshal."

I then told him to take another step, and I would break his neck.

He again said, "I am the United States marshal."

I told him I did not care for him nor the United States. At that he turned and went downstairs. . . .

I told them all not to be afraid, nor to give up to any slaveholder, but to fight until death.

"Yes," said Kline, "I have heard many a Negro talk as big as you, and then have taken him; and I'll take you."

"You have not taken me yet," I replied; "and if you undertake it you will have your name recorded in history for this day's work." . . .

While they were talking, I came down and stood in the doorway, my men following behind. . . .

"Old man, you had better go home to Maryland," said Samuel [Thompson, Gorsuch's slave].

"You had better give up, and come home with me," said the old man.

Thompson took Pinckney's gun from him, struck Gorsuch, and brought him to his knees. Gorsuch rose and signalled to his men. Thompson then knocked him down again, and he again rose. At this time all the white men opened fire, and we rushed upon them; when they turned, threw down their guns, and ran away. We, being closely engaged, clubbed our rifles. We were too closely pressed to fire, but we found a good deal could be done with empty guns. . . .

When the white men ran, they scattered. I ran after Nathan Nelson, but could not catch him. I never saw a man run faster. . . .

The riot, so called, was now entirely ended. The elder Gorsuch was dead; his son and nephew were both wounded, and I have reason to believe others were,—how many, it would be difficult to say. Of our party, only two were wounded. . . .

William Parker, "The Freedman's Story," *Atlantic Monthly* 17 (March 1866): 283–88.

THE ATTEMPT TO FREE ANTHONY BURNS, 1854

[*Boston's Black and white abolitionists—those who believed in direct action—were determined to free a slave being held prisoner in a Boston courthouse. Reverend Thomas Wentworth Higginson, who spearheaded the attack, tells the story.*]

. . . Mingling with the crowd, I ran against Stowall, who had been looking for the axes, stored at a friend's office in Court Square. He whispered, "Some of our men are bringing a beam up to the upper stairway." Instantly he and I ran round and grasped the beam; I finding myself at the head, with a stout [strong] Negro opposite me. The real attack had begun.

What followed was too hurried and confusing to be described with perfect accuracy of details, although the main facts stand out vividly enough. Taking the joist up the steps, we hammered away at the southwest door of the Court-House. It could not have been many minutes before it began to give way. . . . There was room for but one to pass in. I glanced instinctively at my Black ally. He did not even look at me, but sprang in first, I following. . . . We found ourselves inside, face to face with six or eight policemen, who laid about them with their clubs, driving us to the wall and hammering away at our heads. Often as I had heard of clubbing, I had never before known just how it felt, and to my surprise it was not half so bad as I had expected. I was unarmed, but had taken boxing lessons at several different times . . . but hands were powerless against clubs, although my burly comrade wielded his lustily. . . . I did not know that I had received a severe cut on the chin, whose scar I yet carry, though still ignorant how it came. Nor did I know till next morning . . . that, just as the door sprang open, a shot had been fired, and one of the marshal's deputies, a man named Batchelder, had been killed. . . .

There had been other fugitive slave rescues in different parts of the country, but this was the first drop of blood actually shed. In all the long procession of events which led the nation through the Kansas struggle, past the John Brown foray, and up to the Emancipation Proclamation, the killing of Batchelder was the first act of violence. It was, like the firing on Fort Sumter, a proof that war had really begun. . . .

[*Although the attempt to free Anthony Burns failed, a few months after his return to the South the young slave was purchased by Northern abolitionists. He became a minister in Canada.*]

T. W. Higginson, "Cheerful Yesterdays," *Atlantic Monthly* 79 (March 1897): 350–52.

Harriet Tubman's Troy, New York, Raid

[*Harriet Tubman, with a crowd in the thousands, helped free Charles Nalle in 1859. Martin Townsend, Nalle's white lawyer, describes the scene.*]

When Nalle was brought from Commissioner Beach's office into the street, Harriet Tubman, who had been standing with the excited crowd, rushed . . . to Nalle, and running one of her arms around his manacled arm, held on to him without even loosening her hold through the more than half-hour's struggle . . . to the dock, where Nalle's liberation was accomplished. In the mêlée she was repeatedly beaten over the head with policemen's clubs, but she never for a moment released her hold. . . .

True, she had strong and earnest helpers in her struggle, some of whom had white faces as well as human hearts. . . . But she exposed herself to the fury of the sympathizers with slavery, without fear, and suffered their blows without flinching. Harriet crossed the river with the crowd, in the ferry-boat, and when the men who led the assault upon the door of Judge Stewart's office were stricken down, Harriet and a number of other colored women rushed over their bodies, brought Nalle out, and putting him in the first wagon passing, started him for the West.

Sarah Bradford, *Harriet, The Moses of Her People* (New York, 1886), 126–27.

"A SUCCESSFUL FARCE"

[*Southern bitterness over obstruction of the Fugitive Slave Law appears in a editorial in the Augusta, Georgia,* Republican.]

Massachusetts owes to the South the fugitive slaves within her limits; efforts have been made to get several of them back. We lost the two Crafts and Shadrach, and recovered Sims. A faithful execution of the law indeed! . . . Sims was the fugitive slave of Mr. Potter, beyond dispute; yet the case was kept in court, and before a commissioner, for a whole week. It was necessary to guard him with a heavy police [guard] in the third story of the Court House. The building was surrounded by a barricade of chains, and hundreds of the military had to be kept on guard to prevent his forcible rescue. The whole case looks more like a successful farce than anything else. Look at some of the incidents. Mr. Fletcher Webster is imprisoned, Marshal Tukey is held to bail in the sum of a thousand dollars; Mr. Bacon and Mr. De Lyon, the agents of Mr. Potter, were arrested on a charge of conspiracy to kidnap, and had to give bail to the amount of $10,000—one of the agents narrowly escaped being struck on the head by a Negro named Randolph. . . . This is faithful execution of the law! . . . It was such an execution of it as will prevent nineteen persons out of twenty from attempting to rescue their slaves at all. . . .

Austin Bearse, *Reminiscences of Fugitive-Slave Law Days in Boston* (Boston, 1880), 30.

SENATOR CHARLES SUMNER IS BEATEN IN THE SENATE

[*On 22 May 1856, Senator Charles Sumner, a New England abolitionist, spoke in the Senate about the war in "bleeding Kansas." He blamed slaveholders and named some of his Senate colleagues by name. The next day, as Senator Sumner sat writing at his desk, he was beaten unconscious with a cane wielded by Representative Preston Brooks of South Carolina. Three editorials in Virginia newspapers illustrate the Slaveholders' reaction to the incident.*]

[The Richmond Whig] A glorious deed! a most glorious deed!! Mr. Brooks, of South Carolina, administered to Senator Sumner, a notorious Abolitionist, from Massachusetts, an effectual and *classical* caning. We are rejoiced. The only regret we feel is that Mr. Brooks did not employ a Slave-whip, instead of a stick. We trust the ball may be kept in motion. Seward and others should catch it next.

[The Petersburg Intelligencer] We entirely concur with *The Richmond Whig,* that if a thrashing is the only remedy by which the Abolitionists can be controlled, that it will be well to give Senator William H. Seward a double dose at least every other day until it operates freely on his political bowels.

[The Richmond Examiner] Good!—good!!—very good!!! The Abolitionists have been suffered to run too long without collars. They must be lashed into submission. Sumner, in particular, ought to have nine-and-thirty [lashes] early every morning. . . . Senator Wilson . . . [is] absolutely dying for a beating. Will not somebody take him in hand? . . . If need be, let us have a caning or cowhiding every day.

George W. Carleton, *The Suppressed Book About Slavery* (New York, 1864), 368–69.

Abraham Lincoln Sees No Peaceful End of Slavery

[*Lincoln was slow to realize slavery's dangers to the country. In this 1855 letter, he appears to have understood the violent course that the slave power would take.*]

Hon. Geo. Robertson, Lexington, Ky.

My Dear Sir: . . . [you] once spoke of "the peaceful extinction of slavery" and used other expressions indicating your belief that the thing was, at some time, to have an end. Since then we have had thirty-six years of experience; and this experience has demonstrated, I think, that there is no peaceful extinction of slavery in prospect for us. . . . On the question of liberty, as a principle, we are not what we have been. When we were the political slaves of King George, and wanted to be free, we called the maxim that "all men are created equal" a self-evident truth; but now when we have grown fat, and have lost all dread of being slaves ourselves, we have become so greedy to be *masters* that we call the same maxim "a self-evident lie." The Fourth of July has not quite dwindled away; it is still a great day for burning fire-crackers!

That spirit which desired the peaceful extinction of slavery has itself become extinct with the *occasion* and *men* of the Revolution. . . . The Autocrat of all the Russians will resign his crown and proclaim his subjects free republicans, sooner than will our American masters voluntarily give up their slaves.

Our political problem now is, "Can we as a nation continue together *permanently—forever—*half slave, and half free?" The problem is too mighty for me. . . .

John G. Nicolay and John Hay, *Abraham Lincoln* 1 (New York, 1890): 390–91.

THE RAID OF JOHN BROWN'S MEN

[*John Brown's band struck terror in slaveholders. With courage, Brown and his men faced the gallows in Virginia. John Copeland, one of the African Americans in the band, wrote to his brother shortly before his execution.*]

I am not terrified by the gallows, which I see staring me in the face, and upon which I am soon to stand and suffer death for doing what George Washington was made a hero for doing. . . . While, for having lent my aid to a general no less brave, and engaged in a cause no less honorable and glorious, I am to suffer death. Washington entered the field to fight for the freedom of the American people—not for the white man alone, but for both black and white. The blood of black men flowed as freely as that of white. . . . It was a sense of the wrongs which we have suffered that prompted that noble but unfortunate Captain Brown and his associates to attempt to give freedom to a small number, at least, of those who are now held by cruel and unjust laws, and by no less cruel and unjust men. . . . I fully believe that not only myself, but also all three of my poor comrades who are to ascend to the same scaffold (a scaffold already made sacred to

the cause of freedom by the death of that great champion of human freedom, Captain John Brown), are prepared to meet our God.

Richard J. Hinton, *John Brown and His Men* (New York and London, 1894), 509–10.

[*The high regard in which people of color held John Brown is seen in this report of his execution in a Black magazine.*]

As he stepped out of the door, a black woman, with a little child in her arms, stood near his way. . . . He stopped for a moment in his course, stooped over, and with the tenderness of one whose love is as broad as the brotherhood of man, kissed the child affectionately. . . .

"The Execution of John Brown," *The Anglo-African Magazine* 1 (December 1859): 398.

THE ELECTION OF 1860 AND SECESSION

[*Frederick Douglass evaluated the election of Abraham Lincoln.*]

What, then, has been gained to the anti-slavery cause by the election of Mr. Lincoln? Not much, in itself considered, but very much when viewed in the light of its relations and bearings. For fifty years the country has taken the law from the lips of an exacting, haughty and imperious slave oligarchy. The masters of slaves have been masters of the Republic. Their authority was almost undisputed, and their power irresistible. They were the President-makers of the Republic, and no aspirant dared to hope for success against their frown. Lincoln's election has vitiated their authority, and broken their power. It has taught the North its strength, and shown the South its weakness. More important still, it has demonstrated the possibility of electing, if not an Abolitionist, at least an *anti-slavery reputation* to the Presidency.

[*As Southern states seceded and war began, Douglass predicted it would lead to the abolition of slavery.*]

. . . Any attempt now to separate the freedom of the slave from the victory of the Government, . . . any attempt to secure peace to the whites while leaving the blacks in chains . . . will be labor lost. The American people and the Government at Washington may refuse to recognize it for a time; but the "inexorable logic of events" will force it upon them in the end; that the war now being waged in this land is a war for and against slavery; and that it can never be effectually put down till one or the other of these vital forces is completely destroyed.

Douglass' Monthly 3 (December 1860): 371, and (May 1861): 450.

9 THE CIVIL WAR

THE SOUTH CAROLINA TROOPS who manned the guns facing Fort Sumter asked Edmund Ruffin, a Virginia slaveholder and hater of Yankees, if he would like the honor of firing the first shot. That evening he wrote in his diary, "Of course I was highly gratified by the compliment and delighted to perform the service—which I did. The shell struck the fort. . . . The firing then proceeded." Ruffin had no idea that his action would lead to the end of the slavery he had so long defended. Few Americans did.

The War to Preserve the Union, 1861–1863

African Americans immediately answered President Lincoln's call for seventy-five thousand volunteers to suppress the rebellion but were turned away. One hundred and fifteen students from Wilberforce University rushed to enlist. "We were told," recalled Richard Cain, who became a South Carolina congressman after the war, "that this was a white man's war and that the Negro had nothing to do with it." When Jacob Dodson, who had explored the West with Kit Carson and John C. Frémont, offered to raise a force of three hundred others to defend Washington, D.C., he was turned down by Secretary of War Simon Cameron.

Edmund Ruffin.

From the beginning, President Lincoln made clear that his purpose was to preserve the Union. He assured North and South he would not meddle with slavery. Lincoln was concerned with keeping the loyalty of the four slave states that had remained in the Union. He also knew that most Northerners would not support a war fought to end slavery.

Whatever he did against slavery or for Black people, he did to help the Union. In 1862 he wrote, "If I could save the Union without freeing *any* slave, I would do it." The President, despite his life-long personal hatred of slavery, tried mightily to do just that.

To prevent slavery from becoming an issue in the conflict, the president and the War Department ordered Union generals to return slaves who were coming into their lines. General George McClellan announced he would crush any slave revolts that took place in his sector. He also ordered the Hutchinson family of folksingers out of his camp because of the anti-slavery songs they sang to the troops. When John Frémont tried to liberate slaves in Kentucky and General Hunter tried to enlist ex-slaves in the Union army, Lincoln brought both actions to a halt.

This slave family rode to the Union lines in their master's wagon.

But the slavery issue would not die. Black men, women, and children kept entering Union lines seeking freedom. They insisted that the blue-coats were their friends long before emancipation became a Union policy.

The Union soldier, trapped behind Confederate lines, found the slaves to be of invaluable assistance. "The Negroes were fairly jubilant at being able to help genuine Yankees," wrote John Ransom, a Union private. He described how a few led him and his buddies through a Confederate fortress one night, "actually stepping over the sleeping rebels." Said another Union soldier, "To see a Black face was to find a true heart."

The Union spy system relied heavily upon information supplied by former slaves. Allen Pinkerton, chief of the Union Secret Service, "found the Negroes of invaluable assistance." John Scobel, a Mississippi slave, became one of Pinkerton's most trusted agents, repeatedly crossing into Confederate territory to bring back military information.

An outstanding example of help to the Union forces was provided by Robert Smalls, the African American pilot of a Confederate gunboat, the *Planter*. In May 1862 Smalls and his slave crew sailed the ship out of Charleston harbor and surrendered it to the Union fleet. "I thought the *Planter* might be of some use to Uncle Abe," he explained. Smalls and his crew were rewarded by Congress for their bold exploit, and Smalls was asked to Washington to meet President Lincoln. When the Union flag was again raised over Fort Sumter in April 1865 it was the *Planter*, with Smalls at the helm, that brought more than two thousand African Americans to the ceremony. After the war, Smalls served five terms as a South Carolina congressman.

An ex-slave serves as scout for Union troops.

The crew of the *Planter*. The pilot, Robert Smalls, later met with President Lincoln.

The closer the bluecoats came to the plantations, the more difficult it became for masters to control their slaves. Slave patrols were doubled during the war, but discontent continued to grow. Forty slaves were killed in Mississippi for plotting a rebellion. Others took to the woods to form guerrilla bands. Most, however, waited for the approach of the federal troops. Union General Rufus Saxton told of resistance as bluecoats captured the Sea Islands in 1861:

> They [the slaveholders] tried to take their Negroes with them but they would not go. They shot down their Negroes in many instances because they would not go with them. They tied them behind their wagons, and tried to drag them off; but the Negroes would not go. The majority of Negroes remained behind and came into our lines.

"Contrabands" build fortifications for Union army near Alexandria, Virginia.

These slaves soon established their own schools, tended the soil, built roads and homes for a community of thousands. They later formed the First South Carolina Volunteers, the first slave regiment to go into action against the Confederacy.

The Union policy toward the slaves slowly began to change. On 23 May 1861, General Ben Butler of the Union army was holding three slaves who had fled to Fortress Monroe after they had been forced to build Confederate defenses. When a Confederate officer came to get them, Butler refused to give them up. Since they had been used by the enemy he considered them in the same light as captured guns or ammunition—*contraband of war*. With that phrase Butler began the official freeing of slaves.

News of liberty always traveled fast among slaves—in two months, Butler's post had nine hundred "contrabands" working for the Union army. Soon these ex-slaves were performing most of the various services needed around the army camps. Many tried to get the bluecoats to teach them the magic of reading and writing.

The War to End Slavery, 1863–1865

Before the year 1862 was half over, President Lincoln saw the need for a further change in Union policy. He told a member of his cabinet that he had "come to the conclusion that it was a military necessity, absolutely necessary for the salvation of the nation, that he must free the slaves. . . ." By the time he issued the Emancipation Proclamation on 1 January 1863, African American regiments in Louisiana, Missouri, and South Carolina had clashed with their former masters.

The Emancipation Proclamation opened the United States armed

Even before the Emancipation Proclamation, Black troops were fighting Confederates. In 1862 the First South Carolina Volunteers met and drove back an attack by Confederate soldiers and their bloodhounds.

During the Civil War, slave patrols throughout the South were increased. This contemporary drawing shows slaves complying with a patrol request to see their passes, but with attitudes that range from apparent meekness to obvious disdain.

African American troops in North Carolina liberating slaves.

forces to African Americans, slave and free. Before the war ended, more than two hundred thousand entered the army and navy. "Brothers! The hour strikes for us. . . ." wrote a Black New Orleans paper in both French and English. Said Frederick Douglass, "The day dawns—the morning star is bright upon the horizon."

The Black Soldier

Sergeant William H. Carney, one of the twenty-two Black Medal of Honor recipients during the Civil War, took part in the battles to recapture Fort Sumter.

Many in the North and South were surprised to find that African Americans, especially those who had been slaves, made good soldiers. "The idea of their doing any serious fighting against white men is simply ridiculous," said one Southern newspaper. The reports from the battlefields soon ended the laughter. In more than two hundred battles, they fought bravely and won praise from both friends and enemies. Twenty-three won the Medal of Honor, American's highest military honor. At Milliken's Bend Black troops faced an attacking force of Texans twice the size of their own. Though recently inducted into the army and largely untrained, the Black troops defended their position. *Harper's Weekly* reported some early battles in these words:

> At Helena, they bore the brunt of the fighting, and defeated a superior force of the enemy. At Port Hudson, they led . . . General Bank's unsuccessful attack upon the place, and left half of their number on the field. At Charleston, the colored regiment from Massachusetts, led by the heroic Colonel Shaw, was

placed in the front, and sacrificed itself to make a way for the white troops who followed. Wherever the Negroes have had a chance they have given evidence of the most exalted gallantry.

In the U.S. Army, there were 178,958 African Americans, who fought in 39 major battles and 449 engagements. In the U.S. Navy, there were 29,000, one-fifth of the total. Black troops liberated Charleston, Petersburg, Richmond, and Wilmington, North Carolina. Without his Black troops, Lincoln admitted, "we would be compelled to abandon the war in three weeks."

Just one year after the Emancipation Proclamation, President Lincoln wrote to General Wadsworth that the African American troops had "heroically vindicated their manhood on the battlefield."

The contributions of the Black soldier were remarkable in light of the disadvantages under which he served. He was placed in segregated units under white officers who were often prejudiced. African American regiments were sent into battle with less training than white regiments and with weapons inferior to those issued to whites. Their medical facilities were worse, and their doctors fewer. They suffered greater casualties than whites for all of these reasons. For more than a year, the War Department paid Black soldiers half as much as whites. Until their pay was made equal,

U.S.S. *Mendota's* Black and white crew. There were thirty thousand Black Union sailors. Six won the Medal of Honor.

An ex-slave is transformed into a Union soldier. More than two hundred thousand African Americans served in the Union army and navy.

some regiments refused to accept any pay at all. However, they all continued to fight.

The worst hazard which Black troops faced was capture by the Confederates. The South sold some into slavery and put others to death. At Fort Pillow, Tennessee, African American troops were massacred after their surrender on 12 April 1864. Ransome Anderson of the United States Colored Heavy Artillery described the scene to Congress:

> Most all the men that were killed on our side were killed after the fight was over. They [the Confederates] called them out and shot them down. Then they put some in the houses, and shut them up, and then burned the houses.

When Lincoln warned the Confederacy that he would take action against their soldiers for such deeds, this brutality stopped.

The Confederacy dared not arm its slaves. "If slaves make good soldiers," said Confederate Senator Howell Cobb, "then our whole theory of slavery is wrong." When New Orleans free Blacks volunteered to fight, they were issued broomsticks instead of guns. After the city was captured by federal troops, General Butler provided these soldiers with guns, and they went into action against the Confederacy.

Black women as well as white women served the troops behind the lines and organized relief societies. Susie King was one of many nurses who worked with Clara Barton tending the sick and wounded. Mrs. Elizabeth

Like many a young Yankee soldier, this bluecoat sat for his photograph with an American flag as his background.

Black infantrymen rout Confederates in Virginia and capture their cannons. Northerners and Southerners were surprised to find that ex-slaves made courageous soldiers. Even President Lincoln had had his doubts.

Keckley, the White House seamstress, began a relief society for the freed-men who now poured behind Union lines or spilled over the countryside in the wake of General Sherman's march through Georgia. In Nashville and other Southern cities held by Union troops, African American men and women organized their own committees for relief.

The Home Front

The war quickened Black demands for equality in the North—and led to marked advances. After long campaigns, Illinois and California dropped their "Black Laws" that denied equal rights. Illinois repealed a law that punished African Americans for merely entering the state. Congress voted to allow African Americans to testify in federal cases and approved the hiring of Black mail carriers.

While these advances were being made, the Northern home front exploded in violence. In New York City, the poorest whites, many of them recent Irish immigrants who blamed Black people for the war and resented their competition for jobs, rioted for four days. Roving bands attacked and lynched African American men, women, and children. A Black orphans' home was set ablaze. An Irish fireman led some twenty Black children to safety. The entire city police force as well as United States troops had to be called to restore order and halt the murders.

The End of the War

But the war was coming to a close. In February 1865 African American troops entered Charleston, and the white Colonel of the Fifty-fifth Massachusetts Regiment wrote of their reception:

> The few white inhabitants left in the town were either alarmed or indignant, and generally remained in their houses; but the colored people turned out *en masse*. . . . Cheers, blessings, prayers, and songs were heard on every side. Men and women crowded to shake hands with men and officers. . . . The glory and the triumph of this hour may be imagined, but can never be described. . . .

Many slave songs reflected the new mood. "No more driver's lash for me, no more, no more," slaves sang in secret. In Georgetown, South Carolina, slaves were jailed for openly singing "We'll soon be free, When the

Lord will call us home." A Black boy admitted they meant the "Yankees" when they sang "the Lord." The victorious Black Union soldiers also sang. The First Arkansas Volunteers marched to this song:

> We are going out of slavery,
> We're bound for freedom's light.
> We mean to show Jeff Davis
> How Africans can fight.

Edmund Ruffin, who fired the first shot of the war, heard the news of surrender. His South had lost and his slaves had gone to freedom. Ruffin took his gun and fired another shot—ending his own life.

Just before the war ended, General Ben Butler told his Black troops, "With the bayonet you have unlocked the iron-barred gates of prejudice, opening new fields of freedom, liberty, and equality to yourselves and your race forever." The general had spoken too soon. The war was over, but the fight for rights was only beginning. When Abraham Lincoln's funeral took place in Washington, African American troops were left out of the vast army of sorrowing soldiers and civilians who marched behind his coffin. Only in New York City and after they had protested bitterly were they allowed to march with the other mourners.

The Fifty-fifth Massachusetts Colored Infantry liberating Charleston on 21 February 1865. Colonel Charles B. Fox (riding horse) wrote, "It was one of those occasions which happen but once in a lifetime, to be lived over in memory for ever."

"The Union Dead" as pictured by *Harper's Weekly*, 1865.

BLACK VOLUNTEERS ARE REJECTED

[Jacob Dodson had served with General Frémont on his famous explorations of the West. In this letter of 23 April 1861, addressed to Secretary of War Cameron, Dodson answers Lincoln's call for volunteers.]

Sir: I desire to inform you that I know of some three hundred of reliable colored free citizens of this City, who desire to enter the service for the defence of the City.

I have been three times across the Rocky Mountains in the service of the Country with Frémont and others.

I can be found about the Senate Chambers, as I have been employed about the premises for some years.

Yours respectfully,
Jacob Dodson,
(Colored)

[Mr. Dodson received this reply. It was dated 29 April 1861.]

Sir: . . . I have to say that this Department has no intention at present to call into the service of the government any colored soldiers.

Simon Cameron
Secretary of War

Elon A. Woodward, ed., *The Negro in the Military Service of the United States* 2 (Washington: National Archives, 1888): 803, 807.

RUNAWAYS AND UNION TROOPS

*[It was government policy that runaway slaves coming into army lines were to be
returned to their masters, but this congressional investigation found that some
Union troops refused to return the slaves. In this passage, General Daniel E. Sick-
les is being questioned.]*

Q. We have been directed by the House of Representatives to inquire into the
treatment of contrabands coming within your lines. What has been the custom
of dealing with them in your division . . . ?

A. . . . My own practice has been, when contrabands come into my lines from
Virginia, crossing the river, to examine them and obtain what information was
practicable. When I found them intelligent and well behaved I have retained
them in camp, sometimes in the quartermaster's department, sometimes in
[the] charge of suitable persons near my headquarters, that they might be employed as scouts and guides . . . [and] when no objection has been made they
have been employed, in a few instances, by officers as servants. . . .

. . . In September and October last, and perhaps as late as November, in two
or three instances, orders came from the headquarters of the army of the Potomac, directing that such and such persons—naming them—claiming to have
slaves within one of my camps . . . should be permitted to search the camp and
reclaim their slaves. I addressed a communication . . . stating that such steps
would be likely to lead to disorder and mischief in the camps; because in several instances the sympathies of the men had been excited by seeing slaves, re-
claimed under such circumstances, very harshly treated. . . .

Q. Was that communication sent to General McClellan?

A. Yes, sir. . . .

Q. You spoke of the barbarous treatment these men [the slaves] had received
sometimes when they had been surrendered; what can you state about that
more than you have already stated?

A. Lieutenant Colonel Benedict reported to me one or two instances that had
come under his notice, where Maryland owners had obtained possession of
their slaves, and would immediately set to work flogging them in view of the
troops; and the result would be that the soldiers would go out and rescue the
Negro, and in some instances would thrash the masters. . . . It was a regiment
of excellent soldiers, but they were resolute, desperate men; they were all fire-
men of New York City—the 2nd regiment of Fire Zouaves—and they came to
the conclusion . . . that they would not permit any man to come within their
lines upon a similar mission. . . .

Q. You spoke of some orders of General Hooker directing that certain men who
were disloyal should be permitted to go into [your] camp and search for their
men.

A. Some of them were disloyal.

Q. Was any inquiry made as to that matter?

A. No, sir; not that I know of. I know that Posey [one of the slave owners] was under arrest in Washington for some time, for using his house as a signal station for the enemy. . . .

    The most valuable and reliable information of the enemy's movements in our vicinity that we have been able to get we have derived from Negroes who have come into our lines. They have been frequently employed by me as scouts, sometimes singly and sometimes in parties of two or three. Sometimes they have been sent as guides with our troops when it was not deemed proper to hazard them unattended; and they have uniformly, whether employed as scouts or guides, proved faithful. In many instances they have proved to be persons of remarkable intelligence. . . .

Q. Were these colored, who rendered you these services, slave or free?

A. All of them slaves, I presume. I will mention one instance particularly, where a colored man named Jim . . . was sent on a number of scouting expeditions, both for the army and the navy, for the Potomac flotilla and for myself. And one duty that he performed was attended with so much danger, and was performed with so much fidelity and ability, that I recommended that he should be allowed one hundred dollars for it. My recommendation was complied with, and he received that sum. That is but one of twenty services that he has rendered the government, all of more or less magnitude. . . .

Q. Do you know of any instance where they have been treacherous to the Union cause?

A. No, sir; not one. . . . They will submit to any privation, perform any duty, incur any danger. I know an instance in which four of them recently carried a boat from the Rappahannock river, passing through the enemy's pickets successfully, to the Potomac and crossed over to my camp and reported themselves there. They gave us information of the position of the enemy's force which was communicated to headquarters; a service upon which it would be difficult to fix a price. These services rendered by these men are known to the soldiers, and contribute, I presume, largely to the sympathy which they feel for them. . . .

[*Lieutenant Joseph L. Palmer, Jr. gave the following testimony.*]

Q. What do you know in relation to parties owning slaves coming into your camps after them . . . ?

A. . . . There was one case in the 5th regiment where a man named Cox claimed some slaves. He was very badly treated by the soldiers. He came there with an order from division headquarters for two or three slaves. He pointed out who they were, and undertook to take them away; but the soldiers pounced upon him and beat him severely, injuring him considerably. The officers interfered, and saw him safely out of the camp, but not until he had been considerably injured. He went away without his slaves. . . .

    With our people, there was a feeling of indignation against it, from the lowest to the highest; it was the universal feeling. Some of the officers would turn away, saying to these claimants "you can take your property if you will, but I will have nothing to do with it," and then walk into their tents and pay no more attention to them. Sometimes they would allow their men to treat these people very roughly, until they were obliged to interpose to prevent their being seriously injured.

Report of the Joint Committee on the Conduct of the War, Report 108, Part 3, 37th Cong., 3rd sess., 632–45.

LINCOLN DECIDES ON EMANCIPATION

[*In his diary, Gideon Wells, Lincoln's secretary of the navy, noted the first time that the president spoke of emancipation.*]

On Sunday, the 13th of July, 1862, President Lincoln invited me to accompany him in his carriage to the funeral of an infant child of Mr. Stanton. Secretary Seward and Mrs. Frederick Seward were also in the carriage. . . . It was on this occasion and on this ride that he first mentioned to Mr. Seward and myself the subject of emancipating the slaves by proclamation in case the rebels did not cease to persist in their war on the Government and the Union, of which he saw no evidence. He dwelt earnestly on the gravity, importance, and delicacy of the movement; said he had given it much thought, and had about come to the conclusion that it was a military necessity, absolutely essential for the salvation of the nation, that we must free the slaves or be ourselves subdued, etc., etc. This was, he said, the first occasion where he had mentioned the subject to anyone . . . and before separating, the President desired us to give the subject special and deliberate attention, for he was earnest in the conviction that something must be done. It was a new departure for the President, for until this time, in all our previous interviews, whenever the question of emancipation or the mitigation of slavery had been in any way alluded to, he had been prompt and emphatic in denouncing any interference by the General Government with the subject. . . . But the reverses before Richmond, and the formidable power and dimensions of the insurrection, which extended through all the slave States and had combined most of them in a confederacy to destroy the Union, impelled the Administration to adopt extraordinary measures to preserve the national existence. . . .

John G. Nicolay and John Hay, *Abraham Lincoln, a History* 6 (New York, 1890): 121, 122.

The Georgia Sea Islands Celebrate Emancipation

[The following two descriptions are of the Emancipation Day celebration that took place at the Sea Island headquarters of the First South Carolina Volunteers on 1 January 1863. The first is by Charlotte Forten, the young Black school-teacher working on the island, and the second is by white Colonel Thomas Wentworth Higginson.]

The celebration took place in the beautiful grove of live-oaks adjoining the camp. It was the largest grove we had seen. I wish it were possible to describe fitly the scene which met our eyes as we sat upon the stand, and looked down on the crowd before us. There were the black soldiers in their blue coats and scarlet pantaloons, the officers of this and other regiments in their handsome uniforms, and crowds of lookers-on—men, women, and children, of every complexion, grouped in various attitudes under the moss-hung trees. . . .

Charlotte Forten, "Life on the Sea Islands," Part 2, *Atlantic Monthly* 13 (June 1864): 668–69.

[Higginson, the commander of the Carolina Volunteers, describes the celebration's climax.]

. . . the colors were presented to us by the Rev. Mr. French, a chaplain who brought them from the donors in New York. All this was according to the programme. Then followed an incident so simple, so touching, so utterly unexpected and startling, that I can scarcely believe it on recalling, though it gave the key-note to the whole day. The very moment the speaker had ceased, and just as I took and waved the flag, which now for the first time meant anything to these poor people, there suddenly arose, close beside the platform, a strong male voice (but rather cracked and elderly), into which two women's voices instantly blended, singing, as if by an impulse that could no more be repressed than the morning note of the song-sparrow,—

> My Country, 'tis of thee,
> Sweet land of liberty,
> Of thee I sing!

People looked at each other, and then at us on the platform, to see whence came this interruption, not set down in the bills. Firmly and irrepressibly the quavering voices sang on, verse after verse; others of the colored people joined in; some whites on the platform began, but I motioned them to silence. I never saw anything so electric; it made all other words cheap; it seemed the choked voice of a race at last unloosed. Nothing could be more wonderfully unconscious; art could not have dreamed of a tribute to the day of jubilee that should be so affecting; history will not believe it; and when I came to speak of it, after it was ended, tears were everywhere. . . . Just think of it!—the first day they had ever had a country, the first flag they had ever seen which promised anything to their people, and here, while mere spectators stood in silence, waiting for my stupid words, these simple souls burst out in their lay [song], as if they were by their own hearths at home! When they stopped, there was nothing to do for it but to speak, and I went on; but the life of the whole day was in those unknown people's song.

Thomas Wentworth Higginson, *Army Life in a Black Regiment* (Boston, 1882), 40–41.

THE FIRST SLAVE REGIMENT

[Colonel Higginson writes about his experience as commander of the first official regiment of ex-slaves.]

. . . I had always had so much to do with fugitive slaves, and had studied the whole subject with such interest, that I found not much to learn or unlearn as to this one point. Their courage I had before seen tested; their docile and lovable qualities I had known; and the only real surprise that experience brought me was in finding them so little demoralized. . . .

. . . In almost every regiment, black or white, there are a score or two of men who are naturally daring, who really hunger after dangerous adventures, and are happiest when allowed to seek them. Every commander gradually finds out who these men are, and habitually uses them; certainly I had such, and I remember with delight their bearing, their coolness, and their dash. Some of them were Negroes, some mulattoes. One of them would have passed for white, with brown hair and blue eyes, while others were so black you could hardly see their features. These picked men varied in other respects too; some were neat and well-drilled soldiers, while others were slovenly, heedless fellows,—the despair of their officers at inspection, their pride on a raid. They were the natural scouts and rangers of the regiment; they had the two-o'clock-in-the-morning courage, which Napoleon thought so rare. The mass of the regiment rose to the same level under excitement, and were more excitable, I think, than whites, but neither more nor less courageous. . . .

. . . I do not remember ever to have had the slightest difficulty in obtaining volunteers, but rather in keeping down the number. . . . There were more than a hundred men in the ranks who had voluntarily met more dangers in their escape from slavery than any of my young [white] captains had incurred in all their lives. . . .

. . . As to the simple general fact of courage and reliability I think no officer in our camp ever thought of there being any difference between black and white. . . .

. . . They had more to fight for than the whites. Besides the flag and the Union, they had home and wife and child. They fought with ropes round their necks, and when orders were issued that the officers of colored troops should be put to death on capture, they took a grim satisfaction. It helped their *esprit de corps* immensely. With us, at least, there was to be no play-soldier. Though they had begun with a slight feeling of inferiority to the white troops, this compliment substituted a peculiar sense of self-respect. And even when the new colored regiments began to arrive from the North my men still pointed out this difference,—that in case of ultimate defeat, the Northern troops, black or white, would go home, while the First South Carolina must fight it out or be re-enslaved. . . .

. . . Inexperienced officers often assumed that, because these men had been slaves before enlistment, they would bear to be treated as such afterwards. Experience proved the contrary. The more strongly we marked the difference between the slave and the soldier the better for the regiment. One half of military [duty] lies in obedience the other half in self-respect. A soldier without self-respect is worthless. Consequently there were no regiments in which it was so important to observe the courtesies and proprieties of military life as in these. I had to caution the officers to be more than usually particular in returning the salutations of the men . . . and on no account to omit the titles of the non-commissioned officers. . . .

. . . All now admit that the fate of the Confederacy was decided by Sherman's march to the sea. Port Royal was the objective point to which he marched, and he found the Department of the South, when he reached it, held almost exclusively by colored troops. Next to the merit of those who made the march was that of those who held open the door. That service will always remain among the laurels of the black regiments.

Thomas Wentworth Higginson, *Army Life in a Black Regiment* (Boston 1882), 243–63.

LINCOLN DEFENDS EMANCIPATION

[*In this letter of 26 August 1863, President Lincoln answers a letter by a man opposed to emancipation.*]

I know, as fully as one can know the opinions of others, that some of the commanders of our armies in the field, who have given us our most important successes, believe the emancipation policy and the use of the colored troops constitute the heaviest blow yet dealt to the rebellion, and that at least one of these important successes could not have been achieved when it was but for the aid of black soldiers. . . .

You say you will not fight to free Negroes. Some of them seem willing to fight for you—but no matter. Fight you, then, exclusively to save the Union. I issued the proclamation on purpose to aid you in saving the Union. Whenever you shall have conquered all resistance to the Union, if I shall urge you to continue fighting, it will be an apt time then for you to declare you will not fight to free Negroes. I thought that in your struggle for the Union, to whatever extent the Negroes should cease helping the enemy, to that extent it weakened the enemy in his resistance to you. Do you think differently? I thought that whatever Negroes can be got to do as soldiers leaves just so much less for white soldiers to do in saving the Union. Does it appear otherwise to you? But Negroes, like other people, act upon motives. Why should they do anything for us, if we will do nothing for them? If they stake their lives for us, they must be prompted by the strongest motive, even the promise of freedom. And the promise, being made, must be kept. . . .

Peace does not appear so distant as it did. I hope it will come soon, and come to stay; and so come as to be worth the keeping in all future time. . . . And then there will be some black men who can remember that with silent tongue, and clenched teeth, and steady eye, and well-poised bayonet they have helped mankind on [to] this great consummation; while I fear there will be some white ones unable to forget that with malignant heart and deceitful speech they strove to hinder it.

John G. Nicolay and John Hay, *Abraham Lincoln, a History* 7 (New York, 1904): 382–84.

THE BATTLE OF MILLIKEN'S BEND, LOUISIANA

[*On 6 June 1863 about one thousand African American troops were surprised in camp by a rebel force of about two thousand men. An eyewitness reported.*]

. . . a force of about one thousand Negroes and two hundred men of the Twenty-third Iowa . . . was surprised in camp by a rebel force of about two thousand men. Before [their] colonel was ready, the men were in line, ready for action. As before stated, the rebels drove our force toward the gunboats, taking colored men prisoners and murdering them. This so enraged them that they rallied and charged the enemy more heroically and desperately than has been recorded during the war. It was a genuine bayonet charge, a hand-to-hand fight, that has never occurred to any extent during this prolonged conflict. Upon both sides men were killed with the butts of muskets. White and black men were lying side by side, pierced by bayonets, and in some instances transfixed to the earth. In one instance, two men, one white and the other black, were found dead, side by side, each having the other's bayonet through his body. If facts prove to be what they are now represented, this engagement of Sunday morning will be recorded as the most desperate of this war. . . . it was a contest between enraged men: on the one side from hatred to a race; and on the other, desire for self-preservation, revenge for past grievances, and the inhuman murder of their comrades. One brave man took his former master prisoner, and brought him into camp with great gusto. A rebel prisoner made a particular request, that *his own* Negroes should not be placed over him as a guard. Dame Fortune is capricious! His request was *not* granted. Their mode of warfare does not entitle them to any privileges.

George W. Williams, *History of the Negro Race in America* 2 (New York, 1883): 326–27.

SERGEANT WILLIAM CARNEY WINS THE CONGRESSIONAL MEDAL OF HONOR AT FORT WAGNER

[*On 18 July 1863, the Fifty-fourth Massachusetts Volunteers—first Black Northern regiment—distinguished themselves in their attack on Fort Wagner, off the South Carolina coast. In a letter, written on 15 October 1863, Colonel M. S. Littlefield reports on Sergeant William Carney's heroism.*]

When the Sergeant arrived to within about one hundred yards of the fort—he was with the first battalion, which was in the advance of the storming column—he received the regimental colors, pressed forward to the front rank, near the Colonel [Shaw], who was leading the men over the ditch. He says, as they ascended the wall of the fort, the ranks were full, but as soon as they reached the top, "they melted away" before the enemy's fire "almost instantly." He received a severe wound in the thigh, but fell only upon his knees. He planted the flag upon the parapet, lay down on the outer slope, that he might get as much shelter as possible; there he remained for over half an hour, till the 2nd brigade came up. He kept the colors flying until the second conflict was ended. When our forces retired he followed, creeping on one knee, still holding up the flag. It was thus that Sergeant Carney came from the field, having held the emblem of liberty over the walls of Fort Wagner . . . and having received two very severe wounds, one in the thigh and one in the head. Still he refused to give up his sacred trust until he found an officer of his regiment.

When he entered the field hospital, where his wounded comrades were being brought in, they cheered him and the colors. Though nearly exhausted with the loss of blood, he said, "Boys, the old flag never touched the ground."

Of him as a man and soldier, I can speak in the highest term of praise.

George W. Williams, *History of the Negro Race in America* 2 (New York, 1883): 330–31.

AFRICAN AMERICAN TROOPS IN BATTLE

[This is a white journalist's description of the first battle by the Black troops commanded by General Hinks near Petersburg, Virginia, in June 1864.]

. . . The Rebel cannon opened. The sons of Africa did not flinch, but took their positions with deliberation. They had been slaves; they stood face to face with their former masters, or with their representatives. The flag in front of them waving in the morning breeze was the emblem of oppression; the banner above them was the flag of the free. . . .

The Rebels were on a knoll in the field, and had a clear sweep of all the approaches. The advancing troop must come out from the woods, rush up the slope, and carry it at the point of the bayonet, receiving the tempest of musketry and canister.

Hinks deployed his line. At the word of command the colored men stepped out from the woods, and stood before the enemy. They gave a volley, and received one in return. Shells crashed through them, but, unheeding the storm, with a yell they started up the slope upon the run. They received one charge of canister, one scathing volley of musketry. Seventy of their number went down, but the living hundreds rushed on. The Rebels did not wait their coming, but fled towards Petersburg, leaving one of the pieces of artillery in the hands of their assailants, who leaped over the works, turned it in a twinkling, but were not able to fire upon the retreating foe, fleeing in consternation towards the main line of entrenchments two miles east of the city.

The colored troops were wild with joy. They embraced the captured cannon with affectionate enthusiasm, patting it as if it were animate, and could appreciate the endearment.

"Every soldier of the colored division was two inches taller for that achievement," said an officer describing it. These regiments were the Fifth and Twenty-second United States colored troops, who deserve honorable mention in history.

Charles Carleton Coffin, *Four Years of Fighting* (Boston, 1866), 356.

SHERMAN'S MARCH THROUGH NORTH CAROLINA

[*General Sherman's march to the sea was joined by thousands of slaves. Sherman's aide, Major George E. Nichols, talked to a slave family in Fayetteville.*]

As in other parts of the South which we have visited, the masters have run away, taking with them all the able-bodied slaves; but the Negroes who were able escaped, and have returned to join our column. . . .

An intelligent old quadroon woman, whose mother, eighty-six years of age, sat near, and who was surrounded by her daughters and grandchildren—four generations in one group—said to me today:

"There, sir, are my two sons-in-law. Yesterday morning their master tried to take them away, offering them their freedom if they would go into the army voluntarily; but they knew better than that. They never would fire a gun against the Federals."

"No," interposed one of the young men; "I would not fight for the man who is my master and my father at the same time. If they had forced me into the army, I would have shot the officer they put over me the first time I got a chance."

The old grandmother, who, with her family, spoke with no trace of the Negro dialect, continued:

"No, sir; the slaves know too well what it means; they'd never put muskets in the slaves' hands if they were not afeared that their cause was gone up. They are going to be whipped; they are whipped now. . . ."

"Indeed, sir," they all broke out with one accord, "if we can only get to any place where we can be free, and able to work for ourselves, we shall be thankful."

Brevet Major George Ward Nichols, *The Story of the Great March* (New York, 1865), 236–39.

DEMAND FOR A SOLDIER'S PAY

[Corporal James Henry Gooding of the Fifty-fourth Massachusetts Colored Regiment wrote this letter to protest the fact that Black soldiers received less pay than whites. His regiment refused to accept any pay for eighteen months until the War Department stopped this discrimination. By the time pay was equalized, however, Corporal Gooding was dead. Captured in battle, he died in Andersonville prison.]

Morris Island, Department of the South, September 28, 1863.

Your Excelency Abraham Lincoln:

Your Excelency will pardon the presumtion of an humble individual like myself, in addressing you, but the earnest Solicitation of my Comrades in Arms, besides the genuine interest felt by myself in the matter is my excuse, for placing before the Executive head of the Nation our Common Grievance: On the 6th of the last Month, the Paymaster of the department informed us, that if we would decide to receive the sum of $10 (ten dollars) per month, he would come and pay us that sum [white soldiers were paid $13]. . . . Now the main question is, Are we *Soldiers* or are we LABOURERS. We are fully armed, and equipped, have done all the various Duties, pertaining to a Soldiers life, have conducted ourselves, to the complete satisfaction of General Officers, who were, if any, prejediced *against* us, but who now accord us all the encouragement, and honour due us: have shared the perils, the Labour, of Reducing the first stronghold, that flaunted a Traitor Flag: and more, Mr. President, Today, the Anglo Saxon Mother, Wife, or Sister, are not alone, in tears for departed Sons, Husbands, and Brothers. The patient Trusting Decendants of Africs Clime, have dyed the ground with blood, in defense of the Union, and Democracy. Men too your Excellency, who know in a measure, the cruelties of the Iron heel of oppression, which in years gone by, the very Power, their blood is now being spilled to Maintain, ever ground them in the dust. But When the war trumpet sounded o'er the land, when men knew not the Friend from the Traitor, the Black man laid his life at the Altar of the Nation,—and he was refused. When the Arms of the Union, were beaten, in the first year of the War, And the Executive called [for] more food, for its ravaging maws, again the black man begged, the privelege of Aiding his Country in her need, to be again refused. And now, he is in the War: and how has he conducted himself? Let their dusky forms, rise up, out of the mires of James Island, and give the answer. Let the rich mould around Wagners parapets be upturned, and there will be found an Eloquent answer. Obedient and patient, and Solid as a wall are they, all we lack, is a paler hue, and a better acquaintance with the Alphabet. Now your Excellency We have done a Soldiers Duty. Why cant we have a Soldiers pay? . . .

We appeal to You, Sir: as the Executive of the Nation, to have us Justly Dealt with. The Regt, do pray, that they be assured their service will be fairly appreciated, by paying them as american Soldiers, not as menial hierlings. Black men You may well know, are poor, three dollars per month, for a year, will supply their needy Wives, and little ones, with fuel. If you, as Chief Magistrate of the Nation, will assure us, of our whole pay, we are content, our Patriotism, our enthusiasm will have a new impetus, to exert our energy more and more to Aid Our Country. Not that our hearts ever flagged, in Devotion, spite the evident apathy displayed in our behalf, but We feel as though, our Country spurned us, now we are sworn to serve her.

Please give this a moments attention.

Letter of Corporal James Henry Gooding to President Abraham Lincoln (Washington: National Archives, War Records Office), 1–4.

THE LIBERATION OF THE *PLANTER*

[*Robert Smalls, slave pilot of the Confederate* Planter, *and his slave crew seized the ship and sailed it to freedom. In 1864 he addressed a Black audience.*]

. . . Although born a slave I always felt that I was a man and ought to be free [Applause], and I would be free or die. While at the wheel of the "Planter" as Pilot in the Rebel service, it occurred to me that I could not only secure my own freedom but that of numbers of my comrades in bonds, and moreover, I thought that the "Planter" might be of some service to "Uncle Abe." I was not long in making my thoughts known to my associates, and to my dear wife. . . .

I reported my plans for rescuing the "Planter" from the Rebels' Captain to the crew (all colored) and secured their secrecy and cooperation. On May 13, 1862 we took on board several large guns at the Atlantic Dock. At evening of that day the Captain went home, leaving the boat in my care, with instructions to send for him in case he should be wanted. As I could not get my family safely on board at the Atlantic Dock, I took them to another dock, and put them on board a vessel loading there, "The Ettaone."

At half past 3 o'clock in the morning of the 14th of May 1862 I left the Atlantic Dock with the "Planter," went to the "Ettaone," took on board my family, and several other families, then proceeded down Charleston River slowly. When opposite Fort Johnson I gave the signal and on reaching Fort Sumter at 4 A.M. I gave the signal which was answered from the fort, thereby giving permission to pass. I then made speed for the [Union] blockading fleet. When entirely out of range of Sumter's guns, I hoisted a white flag, and at 5 A.M. reached a Union blockading vessel, commanded by Capt. Nichols, to whom I turned over the "Planter."

The A.M.E. Church Review (Philadelphia, January–March 1955), 23.

SUSIE KING TAYLOR AND THE UNION ARMY

[*Ex-slave Susie K. Taylor married a soldier and went to work for the army, one of thousands of Black women, free or slave, who served as nurses, teachers, and cooks.*]

I taught a great many of the comrades in Company E. to read and write, when they were off duty. Nearly all were anxious to learn. My husband taught some also when it was convenient for him. . . .

About four o'clock, July 2 [1864], the charge was made. The firing could be plainly heard in camp. I hastened down to the landing and remained there until eight o'clock that morning. When the wounded arrived, or rather began to arrive, the first one brought in was Samuel Anderson of our company. He was badly wounded. Then others of our boys, some with their legs off, arm gone, foot off, and wounds of all kinds imaginable. They had to wade through creeks and marshes, as they were discovered by the enemy and shelled very badly. A number of the men were lost, some got fastened in the mud and had to cut off the legs of their pants, to free themselves. The 103d New York suffered the most, as their men were very badly wounded.

My work now began. I gave assistance to try to alleviate their sufferings. I asked the doctor at the hospital what I could get for them to eat. They wanted soup, but that I could not get; but I had a few cans of condensed milk and some turtle eggs, so I thought I would try to make some custard. . . . This I carried to the men, who enjoyed it very much. My services were given at all times for the comfort of these men. I was on hand to assist wherever needed. I was enrolled as company laundress, but I did very little of it, because I was always busy doing other things through camp, and was employed all the time doing something for the officers and comrades.

Susie King Taylor, *Reminiscences of My Life in Camp* (Boston, 1902), 21, 34–35.

BLACK TROOPS TAKE OVER CHARLESTON

[*On 17 February 1865, the Fifty-fifth Regiment of Massachusetts Volunteers marched triumphantly into the rebel city singing "Babylon Is Falling" and the "Battle-Cry of Freedom." Correspondent Charles Coffin described their reception and their duties.*]

While dining we heard the sound of drums and a chorus of voices. Looking down the broad avenue we saw a column of troops advancing with steady step and even ranks. It was nearly sunset, and their bayonets were gleaming in the level rays. It was General Potter's brigade, led by the Fifty-Fifth Massachusetts,—a regiment recruited from the ranks of slavery. Sharp and shrill the notes of the fife, stirring the drum-beat, deep and resonant the thousand voices singing their most soul-thrilling war-song,—

"John Brown's body lies a mouldering in the grave."

Mingling with the chorus were cheers for Governor Andrew [of Massachusetts] and Abraham Lincoln!

They raised their caps, hung them upon their bayonets. Proud their bearing. They came as conquerors. Some of them had walked those streets before as slaves. Now they were freemen,—soldiers of the Union, defenders of its flag.

Around them gathered a dusky crowd of men, women, and children, dancing, shouting, mad with every joy. Mothers held up their little ones to see the men in blue, to catch a sight of the starry flag, with its crimson folds and tassels of gold. . . .

The deepest humiliation to the Charlestonians was the presence of Negro soldiers. They were the provost guard [Military Police] of the city, with their head-quarters in the citadel. Whoever desired protection papers or passes, whoever had business with the marshal or the general commanding the city, rich or poor, high-born or low-born, white or black, man or woman, must meet a colored sentinel face to face and obtain from a colored sergeant permission to enter the gate. They were first in the city, and it was their privilege to guard it, their duty to maintain law and order.

A Rebel officer who had given his parole, but who was indiscreet enough to curse the Yankees, was quietly marched off to the guard-house by those colored soldiers. It was galling to his pride, and he walked with downcast eyes and subdued demeanor.

Charles Carleton Coffin, *Four Years of Fighting* (Boston, 1866) 481–82.

A NEW LIFE FOR SLAVES

[*When the Union army and navy freed slaves in the Georgia and South Carolina Sea Islands, Charlotte Forten, from New England, was one of many who came to help teach new ways.*]

Christmas night, the children came in and had several grand shouts. They were too happy to keep still.

"Oh, Miss, all I want to do is to sing and shout!" said our little pet, Amaretta. And sing and shout she did, to her heart's content.

She read nicely, and was very fond of books. The tiniest children are delighted to get a book in their hands. Many of them already know their letters. The parents are eager to have them learn. . . .

They are willing to make many sacrifices that their children may attend school. One old woman, who had a large family of children and grandchildren, came regularly to school in the winter, and took her seat among the little ones. She was at least sixty years old. Another woman—who had one of the best faces I ever saw—came daily, and brought her baby in her arms. . . .

While writing these pages I am once more nearing Port Royal. . . . I shall dwell again among "mine own people." I shall gather my scholars about me, and see smiles of greeting break over their dusk[y] faces. My heart sings a song of thanksgiving, at the thought that even I am permitted to do something for a long-abused race, and aid in promoting a higher, holier, and happier life on the Sea Islands.

Charlotte Forten, "Life on the Sea Islands," Part 2, *Atlantic Monthly* 13 (June 1864): 667–76.

The Death of President Lincoln

[*Frances Ellen Watkins Harper, a widely known Black poet, expressed the feelings of many in this letter written a few days after the assassination.*]

Sorrow treads on the footsteps of the nation's joy. A few days since the telegraph thrilled and throbbed the nation's joy. To-day a nation sits down beneath the shadow of its mournful grief. Oh, what a terrible lesson does this event read to us! . . . Well, it may be in the providence of God this blow was needed to intensify the nation's hatred of slavery, to show the utter fallacy of basing national reconstruction upon the votes of returned rebels, and rejecting loyal black men. . . . Moses, the meekest man on earth, led the children of Israel over the Red Sea, but was not permitted to see them settled in Canaan. Mr. Lincoln has led [us] up through another Red Sea to the table land of triumphant victory, and God has seen fit to summon for the new era another man . . . Let the whole nation resolve that the whole virus shall be eliminated from its body; that in the future slavery shall only be remembered as a thing of the past that shall never have the faintest hope of resurrection.

William Still, *The Underground Rail Road* (Philadelphia, 1872), 766–67.

10 PRESIDENTIAL RECONSTRUCTION

F REE AT LAST! In 1865 African Americans in America became free. As a result of the Union victory, aided, said Frederick Douglass, "by its strong Black arm" and the Thirteenth Amendment to the Constitution, Black liberty was a new law of the land. It was a time for rejoicing and a time to search for lost relatives and for a job, an education, a home, some land of one's own. But there were many whites who refused to accept the new situation. According to one visitor to the South, as the freedman reached for his rights he received "a hundred cuffs for one helping hand."

The Freedmen's Bureau

A Northern schoolmistress teaches ex-slaves.

Long before schoolmistresses arrived from New England, or the government thought of a Freedmen's Bureau, Blacks were helping each other enjoy the fruits of freedom. In 1861 on a portion of soil near Jamestown, Virginia, Mary S. Peake, from Norfolk, Virginia, ran the first school for ex-slaves. Soon thousands of ex-slaves who had settled along the South Carolina and Georgia seacoast were learning to read and write from Black and white teachers sent by Northern missionary societies. Even before the newcomers had arrived, seventeen carpenters were building houses and schools and ex-slaves were teaching the young.

In 1865 the federal government organized a Freedmen's Bureau to deal with the problems of reconstruction in the South. In a meeting between General Oliver O. Howard and the secretary of war, the general recalled that "Mr. Stanton held out to me a great basket full of papers, saying, 'There is your bureau, General, take it.' I took my bureau and walked out with it. I think now that God led me and assigned that work to me." Missionary zeal would guide many in the bureau. Corruption would touch others.

In the five years it existed the bureau built 4,300 schools and hired 3,300 teachers. Although constantly under attack from whites who feared educated and skilled African Americans, the schools proved a great success. A bureau official, J. W. Alvord, described this North Carolina scene in 1866: "A child six years old, her mother, grandmother, and great-grandmother, the latter over 75 years of age . . . commenced their alphabet together and each one can read the Bible fluently." A white Tennessee official reported, "The colored people are far more zealous in the cause of education than

Returning soldiers are discharged at Little Rock, Arkansas.

Standing outside their Arlington, Virginia, school, their new textbooks in front of them, a group of ex-slave children prepare to learn the magic of reading.

the whites. They will starve themselves, and go without clothes, in order to send their children to school." Many schools had night classes for adults who labored each day in the fields.

The Freedmen's Bureau was responsible for providing relief and other important services to ex-slaves and ex-masters. More whites than Blacks lined up for its relief supplies. "We have fed with government charity rations sixty-four whites to one colored person," reported one official. To a section that had rested on slave labor, the bureau tried to bring understanding and fair contracts to both Black laborer and white landlord.

White anger at Black progress often struck at bureau officials. Some were indicted or arrested on flimsy charges, and others were beaten or driven from the state. "Only the presence of the military," reported Colonel York from Kentucky, "controlled the passions against the bureau." In some cases freedmen armed to protect their schools and teachers.

Despite poor management and some corrupt officials, the bureau brought relief, health, and education to the liberated. It reduced the death rate from 38 to 3 percent and raised literacy from 5 to 25 percent. The universities of Howard, Fisk, Storer, Hampton, and many others still stand as living monuments to its success.

One of the problems the agency failed to solve was the distribution of land. In five years the bureau gave out a million acres of land, while the federal government in the West handed out hundreds of millions of acres to white homesteaders. Most Southern land was returned to the original owners as they were granted pardons by the president. The failure to distribute land more evenly left poor families of the South helpless. Without land of their own, the poor were at the mercy of the landowners who hired and fired them. The plantation owners' hold on the land afforded them the same kind of power they once commanded as slave masters.

In vain African Americans appealed for "forty acres and a mule" as their reward for centuries of toil. Reverend Richard Cain toured the South and found that, like the North, it needed a "system of small farms." If the poor "possess lands, they have an interest in the soil, in the State, in its commerce, its agriculture, and in everything pertaining to the wealth and welfare of the State." But nothing as radical as dividing the huge plantations was done. Northern businessmen and Southern planters opposed it. This failure, Frederick Douglass noted, left the Black man "on his knees."

The Freedman's Bureau, as pictured in this *Harper's Weekly* political cartoon, served as a mediator between Southern rebels and ex-slaves.

The Black Codes

The relationship between master and slave proved harder to remove than the debris of war. "I never did a day's work in my life, and I don't know where to begin," said a Mississippi planter. "I think the Negro is about two degrees below the white man," said Reuben Davis, cousin of Jefferson Davis. "I think the Negro is by nature dishonest; I think the Negro is by nature destitute of all ideals of virtue, and I think the Negro is capable of being induced to commit any crime whatever, however violent, especially if he was encouraged by bad white men."

Throughout the South whites reacted to Black liberty with unreasoning hatred and fear. Carl Schurz, who toured the South for President Andrew Johnson after the war, was told by a Union general, "Wherever I go—the street, the shop, the house, the hotel, or the steamboat—I hear the people talk in such a way as to indicate that they are yet unable to conceive of the Negro as possessing any rights at all." Whites who were honorable in dealing with other whites "will cheat a Negro without feeling a single twinge of their honor. To kill a Negro, they do not deem murder. . . ."

African Americans were ambushed by ex-Confederates as they strolled along the roads. Some were attacked simply "because they have been in the [Union] army," reported a Southern judge. In Nashville, Tennessee, General Clinton Fiske described the city's young whites: "You see young men standing on street corners with cigars in their mouths and hands in their pockets, swearing Negroes won't work." He added, "In this city it is the Negroes who do the hard work."

In 1866 Frederick Douglass and a Black delegation asked President Johnson to protect Blacks' voting rights as the surest protection for all their other rights. He refused, telling Douglass that these rights were a state matter.

Cartoon showing President Andrew Johnson falsely promising a Black veteran his protection. At this very moment African Americans in New Orleans and Memphis were massacred as they tried to assert their rights. Johnson, a Southern poor white, resented both slaveholders and slaves and favored "white supremacy."

Immediately after the war, Southern legislatures passed "Black Codes" to replace the "Slave Codes." The spirit of slavery lived on in the new laws. Mississippi simply changed the word "slave" to "Black." In South Carolina a person of color needed a license for any job other than servant or farmer, and the license cost up to $100. African Americans could not own guns, city property, testify in court, or otherwise act like citizens. They could be arrested for "being impudent" to or "insulting" whites. States provided for the arrest of any Black man as a vagrant who did not have a job.

But the jails were never full. Prisoners were soon rented out (their former masters getting first choice) to work off their sentences and fines through labor. Members of the Seventy-fourth United States Colored Infantry were arrested the day after their discharge from the army because they did not have employment certificates. A new slavery had replaced the old. Before slaves were held by individual owners. Now, noted one Southerner, "the white community as a whole controls the Blacks as a group."

President Andrew Johnson

Many in the North looked at the Black Codes and wondered who had won the war. But not President Andrew Johnson. A poor white who had been an indentured servant in Tennessee, Johnson hated slaveholders, slavery, and slaves. Since the war ended slavery, he felt a choice must be made between ex-slaves and their ex-masters. As he believed in the supremacy of the white race, he felt they should rule. In vetoing the Freedmen's Bureau bill, he said Blacks "are an inferior race" who "have learned in slavery all that they know in civilization." He suggested that Black people look to him as a "Moses" to lead them to a promised land.

The new president began granting pardons to Confederate leaders and restoring their power. When anti-Black outbreaks exploded, he was more convinced than ever that whites should control the South.

In February 1866, Frederick Douglass led an African American delegation to see the president about conditions in the South. That week ex-rebel soldiers in Kentucky were robbing freedmen after the local marshal forced returning Black soldiers to surrender their guns. A Freedman's Bureau official wrote, "I am powerless to accomplish anything without soldiers."

Douglass, John Jones, and George T. Downing tried to convince the president that he must protect African American lives and grant them the vote. No, said Johnson, that would lead to "a war of the races." Whites in the South, not laws, will protect the freedmen, he insisted. Blacks had no "natural right" to vote and should migrate to the North if conditions were bad. Douglass told the president, "You enfranchise your enemies and disfranchise your friends." But President Johnson could not believe that even Black men who fought to save the Union were "friends." The delegation left knowing that in leaving Black rights in the hands of Southern whites, Johnson was delivering them into the hands of old enemies.

In the summer of 1866, whites in Memphis and New Orleans rioted against Blacks. Hundreds were killed, mainly by police bullets, as they sought to organize for political action. General Sheridan said of the New Orleans attack ordered by the mayor, "It was an absolute massacre by the police." While President Johnson pressed his campaign of leniency toward ex-Confederates, "outrages upon the Freedmen have greatly increased," reported a white officer.

To further his program of reconstruction, the president used his pardoning power. Land taken from ex-Confederates was returned with their pardons. Some of this land had been given or sold to ex-slaves who had no intention of surrendering it. At James Island ex-Confederates who tried to reclaim their land were driven back three times. Their lives were spared only because a government official pleaded for them.

General Saxton, commanding United States troops in the South, protested to Congress, "The faith of the government has been pledged to these freedmen to maintain them in the possession of their homes, and to break its promise in the hours of its triumph is not becoming to a just government." He pleaded in vain for Congress to leave the land in the hands of the freedmen. "On some islands," he wrote, "the freedmen have established civil governments with constitutions and laws, with all the different departments of schools, churches, building roads, and other improvements." But in spite of protests the land was restored to the original owners.

The men who led the South toward secession and war had secured power again. Through the Black Codes they were once again in control of the Black labor lost by emancipation. As before, they ran the state governments of the South. They even had a friend in the White House. It was time to return to their former position in the United States Congress. The first Southern representative elected after the war included fifty-eight Confederate congressmen, six Confederate cabinet members, nine Confederate army officers, and Confederate vice president Alexander H. Stephens.

If President Johnson was not unhappy, Congress was. It refused to seat the new congressmen from the South. A Mississippi planter admitted that the ex-Confederates had moved too quickly. "Yes, it was unwise, *at this time. We showed our hand too soon.* We ought to have waited till the troops were withdrawn, and our representatives admitted to Congress; then we could have had everything our way."

A Soldier Asks for the Vote

[*John Cajay of the Eleventh United States Colored Heavy Artillery felt that the African Americans' courage on the battlefield entitled them to the vote. He wrote to a Black newspaper on 5 June 1865 from Louisiana.*]

. . . I see, as peace and reconstruction make their progress, the predominant feeling, which [kept] . . . us from rising upon a level with other citizens, shows itself more plainly as the rebellion is being brought to a close. If we did not merit this suffrage, or had done anything detrimental to the good of the country, then I would think such proceedings were just; but when we have done all we could to help sustain the government, and assisted, with other loyal citizens, to crush this rebellion, I think it no more than right that we should have the rights of suffrage. . . .

. . . These self same people who are opposed to our right [to vote], are those who have been tutored from their cradles to look upon the Negro as their inferior, and are taught to persecute us. . . .

The Anglo-African Magazine, 5 August 1865, 1.

[President Abraham Lincoln had written in January 1864.]

How to better the condition of the colored race has long been a study which has attracted my serious and careful attention; hence I think I am clear and decided as to what course I shall pursue . . . regarding it as a religious duty, as the nation's guardian of these people who have so heroically vindicated their manhood on the battlefield, where, in assisting to save the life of the republic, they have demonstrated in blood their right to the ballot. . . .

The Liberator, 29 December 1865.

THE ASPIRATIONS OF FREE MEN

[In the months following the end of the Civil War, African Americans met in Southern states to formulate their plans. A group at the First Baptist Church of Norfolk, Virginia, on 1 December 1865, drew up these resolutions.]

. . . we are a peaceable and law abiding people and that the stories so industriously circulated against us That we are contemplating and preparing for insurrection and riotous and disorderly proceedings are vile falsehoods designed to provoke acts of unlawful violence against us. . . .

   . . . we have faith in God and our Country and in the justice and humanity of the American people for redress of all our grievances but that we will not cease to importune and labor in all lawful and proper ways for equal rights as citizens until finally granted.

   . . . we appoint [a committee] to proceed to Washington to urge upon Congress such legislation as will secure to the lately rebellious states a republican form of Government and the consequent protection to ourselves of life, liberty, and property and of the granting to our people in those states of the right to testify in the Courts and of equality of suffrage the same as to white citizens. That said committee be empowered to represent us before the Freedman's Bureau at Washington . . . to secure if possible the selection and nomination . . . of the local agents by the Freedmen themselves. . . .

Freedmen's Bureau files (Washington, D.C., National Archives), Record Group 92.

When Freedom Came

[*In late 1861 thousands of slaves were freed when Union forces captured Port Royal, South Carolina. President Lincoln directed Edward L. Pierce to handle their problems. After ex-slaves were provided with food and clothing, Pierce established schools. He reported this conversation with one class.*]

"Children, what are you going to do when you grow up?"
"Going to work, Sir."
"On what?"
"Cotton and corn, Sir."
"What are you going to do with the corn?"
"Eat it."
"What are you going to do with the cotton?"
"Sell it."
"What are you going to do with the money you get for it?"
One boy answered in advance of the rest—
"Put it in my pocket, Sir."
"That won't do. What's better than that?"
"Buy clothes, Sir."
"What else will you buy?"
"Shoes, Sir."
"What else are you going to do with your money?"

There was some hesitation at this point. Then the question was put,—

"What are you going to do Sundays?"
"Going to meeting."
"What are you going to do there?"
"Going to sing."
"What else?"
"Hear the parson."

"Who's going to pay him?".

One boy said,—"Government pays him;" but the rest answered,—"We's pays him."

"Well, when you grow up, you'll probably get married, as other people do, and you'll have your little children; now what will you do with them?"

There was a titter at this question; but the general response came,—

"Send 'em to school, Sir."
"Well, who'll pay the teacher?"
"We's pays him."

One who listens to such answers can hardly think that there is any natural incapacity in these children to acquire, with maturity of years, the ideas and habits of good citizens. ·

Edward L. Pierce, "The Freedmen at Port Royal," *Atlantic Monthly* 12 (September 1863): 306–7.

"I NEVER BEFORE SAW CHILDREN SO EAGER TO LEARN"

[*Charlotte Forten, an African American teacher who went South to teach exslaves, describes her first days teaching on the Georgia Sea Islands.*]

. . . I never before saw children so eager to learn, although I had had several years' experience in New-England schools. Coming to school is a constant delight and recreation to them. They come here as other children go to play. The older ones, during the summer, work in the fields from early morning until eleven or twelve o'clock, and then come to school, after their hard toil in the hot sun, as bright and as anxious to learn as ever.

Of course there are some stupid ones, but these are in the minority. The majority learn with wonderful rapidity. Many of the grown people are desirous of learning to read. It is wonderful how a people who have been so long crushed to the earth . . . can have so great a desire for knowledge, and such a capacity for attaining it. . . .

After the lessons, we used to talk freely to the children, often giving them slight sketches of some of the great and good men. Before teaching them the *John Brown* song, which they learned to sing with great spirit, Miss T. told them a story of the brave old man who had died for them. I told them about Toussaint [L'Ouverture, the Black liberator of Haiti], thinking it well they should know what one of their own color had done for his race. They listened attentively, and seemed to understand. . . .

Charlotte Forten, "Life on the Sea Islands," *Atlantic Monthly* 13 (March 1864): 591.

IDEAS THAT DID NOT DIE WITH THE CONFEDERACY

[In 1865 a Mississippi planter speaks to a Northern visitor.]

"We can't feel towards them as you do; I suppose we ought to, but it isn't possible for us. They've always been our owned servants, and we've been used to having them mind us without a word of objection, and we can't bear anything else from them now. If that's wrong, we're to be pitied sooner than blamed, for it's something we can't help. I was always kind to my slaves. I never whipped but two boys in my life, and one of them I whipped three weeks ago."

"When he was a free man?"

"Yes; for I tell you that makes no difference in our feeling towards them. I sent a boy across the country for some goods. He came back with half the goods he ought to have got for the money. . . ."

J. T. Trowbridge, *The South* (Hartford, 1866), 291–92.

BLACK POWER IN 1865: BLACK AND WHITE VIEWS

[When Major Martin R. Delany addressed an outdoor meeting of six hundred ex-slaves on St. Helena Island, he was not aware that a white officer from his own regiment was spying on him. Their different interpretations of Black power have a familiar ring. Delany's speech was recorded by Lt. Edward M. Stoeber.]

. . . As before the whole South depended upon you, now the *whole country* will depend upon you. I give you an advice how to get along. Get up a community and get all the lands you can—if you cannot get any singly.

. . . Now you understand that I want you to be the producers of this country. It is the wish of the Government for you to be so. We will send friends to you, who will further instruct you how to come to the end of our wishes. You see that by so adhering to our views, you will become a wealthy and powerful population.

Now I look around me and notice a man, barefooted, covered with rags and dirt. Now I ask, what is that man doing, for whom is he working. I hear that he works for that and that farmer, "for 30 cents a day." I tell you that must not be. That would be slavery over again. I will not have it, the Government will not have it, and the Government shall hear about it. I will tell the Government. I tell you slavery is over, and shall never return again. We have now 200,000 of our men well drilled in arms and used to Warfare and I tell you it is with you and them, that slavery shall not come back again, and if you are determined it will not return again.

[Lt. Stoeber then added his own evaluation.]

My opinion of the whole affair is, that Major Delany is a thorough hater of the white race and excites the colored people unnecessarily. . . .

He tells them to remember, "that they would not have become *free,* had they *not armed themselves* and *fought for their independence.*" This is a falsehood and a misrepresentation. Our President Abraham Lincoln declared the colored race free, before there was even an idea of arming colored men. . . .

The mention of having two hundred thousand men well drilled in arms:—does he not hint to them what to do?; if they should be compelled to work for employers?

In my opinion of this discourse he was trying to encourage them, to break the peace of society and force their way by insurrection to a position he is ambitious they should attain to.

Report of Lt. Edward M. Stoeber (Washington, D.C., National Archives, 24 July 1865), Record Group 94.

GENERAL SWAYNE REPORTS ON TEXAS

[United States General W. Swayne reported on Texas reconstruction.]

The entire crop raised in Texas—cotton, corn, sugar, and wheat—was gathered and saved by the 1st of December. Most assuredly no white man in Texas had anything to do with the gathering of the crops, except perhaps to look on and give orders. Who did the work? The freedmen, I am well convinced, had something to do with it; and yet there is a fierce murmur of complaint against them everywhere that they are lazy and insolent. . . .

Two-thirds of the freedmen in the section of the country which I traveled over have never received one cent of wages since they were declared free. A few of them were promised something at the end of the year, but instances of prompt payment of wages are very rare.

I saw freedmen east of the Trinity River who did not know that they were free until I told them. There had been vague rumors circulated among them that they were to be free on Christmas day, and that on New Year's there was to be a grand division of all the property, and that one-half was to be given to the black people. . . .

Public speakers in different portions of the State declared and insisted that the only object the Yankees had in continuing the war was to free the Negroes, and that if the southern people were beaten, all the lands and property would be taken from them and given to the blacks, and that the poor whites and rich people alike would be enslaved. It is not strange that the freedmen hearing this matter talked of publicly for four years by men of influence and standing should finally believe there was some truth in it. . . .

Report of the Joint Select Committee to Inquire into the Condition of Affairs in the Late Insurrectionary States, 42nd Cong., 2nd sess., 1872.

The Rebel Spirit Lives On

[President Andrew Johnson allowed whites to deny justice to the freedmen—as can be seen in these two reports of the Florida Freedmen's Bureau.]

[Andrew Mahoney from Lake City, Florida, 1 May 1866.] . . . the system here is when a freedman is found guilty of a crime for stealing he is fined and if he cannot pay the fine, his services are sold to the highest bidder for the shortest period of time, this is according to the Law of the State and there is no other means of punishing Criminals. In my district there are a great many freed people suffering such sentences throughout this part of the State. . . .

The blessings of Freedom have neither made them [the Negroes] vain nor indolent, on the Contrary—as it naturally should, for they are not so unappreciative, or benighted as their late groveling condition would seem to warrant the belief, it has infused into them a feeling of manliness, and enterprising industry, which, if properly nurtured will raise them as far above their late conditions, as in that condition they were beneath Freemen, in a marvelously short time.

[*T. W. Osborn from Tallahassee, Florida, 8 May 1866.*] We have unfortunately had some cases of personal violence in the State. One freedman in Madison Co. killed by a white man. The murderer has made his escape without arrest. One freedman shot in Alachua County by a white man who was arrested and afterwards released from the guard by an armed mob. Other cases of violence have occurred. . . .

The freed people are working well throughout the State and the agricultural prospects of the State are now excellent. Vagrancy among the colored people is almost unknown, and no assistance is required by them. . . .

The schools are in a prosperous condition and have thus far been successfully conducted. . . .

[*Mr. Osborn did report, however, that Black children in a bureau school were attacked by the children from a white school for singing* Rally Round the Flag *(a Union army song) and other patriotic songs.*]

Office of the Adjutant General, Letters Received 4 (Washington: National Archives, War Records Office, 1866).

TROUBLE FOR THE FREEDMEN'S BUREAU IN KENTUCKY

[*Lieutenant-Colonel York reports on difficulties he faced in 1866.*]

. . . the rampant disloyalty of the people in that portion of the State [Livingston County], seems to demand immediate attention. The enemies of the Gov't, acting under a misapprehension of the action of President Johnson, have recently been more violent in denouncing the Bureau, and I am convinced that outrages upon the Freedmen, have greatly increased, from the same cause.

Mr. Furman, who was sent from this office to investigate the Bucker case, passed several days in Livingston and Lyons Counties, and reports that the Union people are alarmed by the fierce demonstrations of the rebels, who openly denounce the Freedmen's Bureau, who seek in every

way to harass the Union people, and illtreat and oppress the Freedmen—
that meetings are called ostensibly to endorse the President [Andrew
Johnson], but in reality to denounce the Gov't. . . . In this place the same
malignant spirit of disloyalty is held in check, only by the presence of the
military. During the present week the windows of the Freedmen's School
house have been broken by parties unknown. . . . I have been indicted by
the Grand Jury of McLenacken Co. upon a charge of having furnished
false passes to slaves, and the Sheriff has a warrant to arrest me and confine me in the Co. jail in default of my giving bail in the sum of Five Hundred Dollars. . . . I would respectfully request instruction as to the action
most proper in this case.

   . . . it is with pleasure that I report the condition of the old [Black] people in this place as steadily improving. All they require is an opportunity
and proper encouragement to become good and useful citizens.

Office of the Adjutant General, Letters Received 4 (Washington: National Archives, War
Records Office, 1866).

THE FREEDMEN'S BUREAU COURTS

[*The Freedmen's Bureau brought the South a new kind of justice. A Northern visitor describes a few hours in a Freedmen's Bureau Court.*]

The freedmen's court is no respecter of persons. The proudest aristocrat
and the humblest Negro stand at its bar on an equal footing. . . .

   A great variety of business is brought before the Bureau. Here is a Ne-
gro-man who has printed a reward offering fifty dollars for information to
assist him in finding his wife and children, sold away from him in times of
slavery: a small sum for such an object, you may say, but it is all he has, and
he has come to the Bureau for assistance. . . . Yonder is a white woman,
who has been warned by the police that she must not live with her husband because he is black, and who has come to claim protection in her
marriage relation, bringing proof that she is really a colored woman. . . .
Yonder comes an old farmer with a stout colored boy, to get the Bureau's
sanction to a contract they wish to make. "Pull off your hat, Bob," says the
old man; "you was raised to that"; for he was formerly the lad's owner. . . .
He is very grateful for what the officers do for him, and especially for the
good advice they give the boy. "I'll do well by him, and larn him to read, if
he'll do well by me."

As they go out, in comes a powerful, short-limbed black in tattered over-coat. . . . He has made a crop; found everything—mules, feed, implements; hired his own help,—fifteen men and women; managed everything; by agreement he was able to have one half; but, owing to an attempt to swindle him, he has had the cotton attached and now it is not on his account he has come, but he is owing his men wages, and they want something for Christmas, which he thinks reasonable, and he desires the Bureau's assistance to raise three hundred dollars. . . . "For I'm bound," he says, "to be liberal with my men."

Here is a boy, who was formerly a slave, to whom his father, a free man, willed a sum of money, which the boy's owner borrowed, giving his note for it, but never repaid,—for did not the boy and all that he had belong to his master? The worn and soiled bit of paper is produced; and now the owner will have that money to restore, with interest. Lucky for the boy that he kept that torn and dirty scrap carefully hidden all these years! . . .

J. T. Trowbridge, *The South* (Hartford, 1866), 340–44.

DEFENDING THE NIGHT SCHOOL

[*This 1866 letter by Brevet Captain C. M. Hamilton describes how African Americans in Marianna, Florida, met threats against their school and white teacher.*]

The night school has been frequently disturbed. One evening a mob called out of the school house, the teacher, who on presenting himself was confronted with four revolvers, and menacing expressions of shooting him, if he did not promise to quit the place, and close the school.

The freedmen promptly came to his aid, and the mob dispersed.

About the 18th or 19th of the month, I was absent . . . when quite a formidable disturbance took place at this school. The same mob threatened to destroy the School that night, and the freedmen learning this, assembled at their . . . place of instruction in a condition of self-defence.

I understand that not less than forty colored men armed to protect themselves, but the preparations becoming known to the *respectable rowdies,* they only maneuvered about in small squads, and were wise enough to avoid a collision.

It is to be lamented that such bitterness and anarchy should exist, and on my return I discountenanced the movement, even on the part of those who only sought self-protection. Yet I am gratified to report that the result of this affair has been quite salutary on the disposition of the people, for it seems to have infused a terror into them, and they now see the fearful necessity for *law* to rule, instead of mobs and riots.

Office of the Adjutant General, Letters Received 4 (Washington: National Archives, War Records Office, 1866).

"THE PRESIDENT . . . SEEMED TO FORGET"

[*President Johnson used his pardoning power to restore the lands of former Confederates. A Northern visitor in Hampton, Virginia, described the changes.*]

I found it a thrifty village, occupied chiefly by freedmen. The former aristocratic residences had been replaced by Negro huts. . . . There was an air of neatness and comfort about them which surprised me, no less than the rapidity with which they were constructed. One man had just completed his house. He told me that it took him a week to make the poles for it and bring them from the woods, and four more days to build it.

A sash-factory and blacksmith's shop, shoemakers' shops and stores, enlivened the streets. The business of the place was carried on chiefly by freedmen, many of whom were becoming wealthy, and paying heavy taxes to the government.

Every house had its wood-pile, poultry and pigs, and little garden devoted to corn and vegetables. Many a one had its stable and cow, and horse and cart. The village was surrounded by freedmen's farms, occupying the abandoned plantations of recent Rebels. The crops looked well, though the soil was said to be poor. Indeed, this was by far the thriftiest portion of Virginia I had seen.

In company with a gentleman who was in search of laborers, I made an extensive tour of these farms, anxious to see with my own eyes what the emancipated blacks were doing for themselves. I found no idleness anywhere. Happiness and industry were the universal rule. I conversed with many of the people, and heard their simple stories. They had but one trouble: the owners of the lands they occupied were coming back with their pardons [from the President] and demanding the restoration of their estates. Here they [the freedmen] had settled on abandoned Rebel lands, under the direction of the government, and with the government's pledge, given through its [army] officers, and secured by an act of Congress, that they should be protected in the use and enjoyment of those lands for a term of three years, each freedman occupying no more than forty acres, and paying an annual rate to the government not exceeding six per cent. of their value. Here, under the shelter of that promise, they had built their little houses and established their humble homes. What was to become of them? On one estate six hundred acres there was a thriving community of eight hundred freedmen. The owner had been pardoned unconditionally by the President, who, in his mercy to one class, seemed to forget what justice was due to another.

J. T. Trowbridge, *The South* (Hartford, 1866), 220–21.

11 CONGRESSIONAL RECONSTRUCTION

To some in Congress, it was obvious that radical measures were necessary to halt disloyalty in the South. Two abolitionists, Thaddeus Stevens in the House and Charles Sumner in the Senate, led the "Radicals" of Congress to enact new laws. Over the vetoes of President Johnson, Congress passed legislation that provided for military control of the South, gave equal rights to former slave men, and canceled the rights of ex-Confederate leaders.

Reconstruction in the South

In the South, this "Radical Reconstruction" led to the beginning of a new social order. The freedmen's right to vote was protected by the Fourteenth and Fifteenth amendments to the Constitution. In an 1864 letter to General Wadsworth of New York, President Lincoln had said that he felt that Black soldiers "have demonstrated in blood their right to the ballot, which is but the human protection of the flag they have so fearlessly defended." Congressman Thaddeus Stevens saw the vote of freedmen as absolutely necessary to protect their rights and keep the South loyal. "If it be just," he said, "it should not be denied; if it be necessary, it should be adopted; if it be punishment to traitors, they deserve it." Although the majority of ex-slaves could neither read nor write, neither could many white Southern voters or millions of European immigrants who voted in Northern cities.

Now African Americans and poor whites began rebuilding their state governments. They drew up new constitutions, approved the Fourteenth and Fifteenth amendments, returned their states to the Union, and elected men to Congress. Although Black voters outnumbered whites in several states, they never sought to control any government at any time. Though they held offices from local sheriff to state governor, they were always willing to support white candidates. One Black, P. B. S. Pinchback, served forty-three days as governor of Louisiana when the white governor was removed by impeachment.

At South Carolina's Constitutional Convention African Americans played a decisive role—there were 76 of them among the 131 delegates. Among the delegates were such brilliant figures as Francis Cardoza and Robert B. Elliott, both educated at British universities. But it was another college graduate and Black delegate, Reverend Richard Cain, who proclaimed the great purpose of the convention.

P. B. S. Pinchback continued to fight discrimination long after he was forced from high office in Louisiana.

> I want a constitution that shall do justice to all men. I have no prejudices and feel above making any distinctions. . . . I hope we will take hold high upon the highway of human progress. . . . I want to see internal improvements, the railroads rebuilt, and, in fact, the whole internal resources of the State so developed that she shall be brought back more happy and prosperous than she ever was.

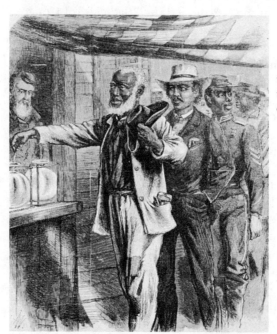

Under the protection of the Fourteenth Amendment and federal troops, Southern African Americans began to vote.

The Constitution drawn up by the Blacks and whites of the state of South Carolina brought the great reforms of the North to the South. Louis F. Post, who was to serve Woodrow Wilson for eight years as assistant secretary of labor, was present in South Carolina and recalled:

> By every truly democratic test, that Negro-made constitution of South Carolina stands shoulder high above the white man's Constitution which it superseded.

The state lowered the taxes on the poor, abolished imprisonment for debt, granted voting rights to all regardless of property or race. The state's first public school system was established. Women were granted greater rights than ever before. Presidential electors were chosen directly by the people. Courts, county governments, hospitals, and charitable and penal institutions were built or reorganized.

Years later Congressman Joseph Rainey, a former slave who escaped during the Civil War, pointed with pride to the justice of the South Carolina Constitution:

> Our convention which met in 1868, and in which Negroes were in a large majority . . . adopted a liberal constitution, securing alike equal rights to all citizens, white and black, male and female, as far as possible. Mark you, we did not discriminate, although we had a majority. Our constitution towers up in its majesty with provisions for the equal protection of all classes of citizens.

Reverend Richard Cain took part in South Carolina's Constitutional Convention of 1868 and in the government that developed from it. He was twice elected to the United States Congress.

In Mississippi, too, "a state government had to be organized from top to bottom" and this "important task was splendidly, creditably, and economically done," reported John R. Lynch, later Mississippi's first African American Congressman.

Vast political changes were taking place from Virginia to Texas. Edward King, a prejudiced Northern writer touring the South in 1873, found Black contributions to government remarkable for a people just released from slavery. In Virginia he found African American officeholders often had a "ludicrous" manner of speech, "but it was evident that all were acting intelligently." He visited a city council meeting and found it "as well conducted as that of any Eastern city." In Arkansas he found officials "of excellent ability." In Florida he found that the state superintendent of education was a Black "gentleman of considerable culture and capacity."

In Mississippi and South Carolina King saw large numbers of African American officials among the higher and lower officers of the states. He noted them in Natchez managing city affairs in "a very satisfactory" manner. In South Carolina King found that "the President of the Senate and the Speaker of the House, both colored, were elegant and accomplished

Congressman Joseph H. Rainey of South Carolina. He served two terms in the House of Representatives.

men, highly educated, who would have creditably presided over any commonwealth's legislative assembly." As King stood in the library of the state university, two Black senators were enrolling in the law classes. "I was informed that dozens of members were occupied every spare moment outside of the sessions in faithful study."

A new day had dawned in the South. In Natchez, Mississippi (which had an African American mayor), Black and white children played together in the streets. Louisiana School Superintendent Thomas Conway described school integration: "The children were simply kind to each other in the school-room as in the streets and elsewhere! . . ." But 99 percent of the Southern schools remained segregated. Black parents knew that school integration would lead to the closing of schools. They accepted education on a segregated level rather than this dread possibility.

A Black policeman in South Carolina in 1873. During Reconstruction there were African American sheriffs, mayors, judges, and representatives in the South.

Concluding the 1873–1874 session of the South Carolina legislature, the African American Speaker of the House, S. J. Lee, thanked the men of both races who had made it a success. He admitted that the group was little skilled in government but stated that they sincerely sought to serve the best interests of the state. He pointed out how they had reduced the debt from twenty to six million dollars, and said that they, "in a large degree, regained the confidence of the public." Turning to the future, he said, "The first thing necessary for us to do is to secure as much intelligence as we can. Intelligence, is *the* power, the controller of a nation's fate, and that we must secure at all hazards." He pointed with great pride to growing numbers of schools and the increasing number of "competent, well-trained teachers." New scholarships at the university were established for the poor and "the people are becoming daily more enlightened." "The colored people . . . are progressive and thrifty, and striving to educate themselves, and thereby become worthy and prosperous citizens." He ended by thanking them for electing him Speaker. "I felt my inexperience and the heavy re-

Black and white children play together during Reconstruction.

South Carolina legislators. For several years African Americans were a majority of the members of the state's lower house. Whites continued to control the Senate, courts, governorship, and most local offices.

sponsibility resting upon me. I have tried, and I hope successfully, to be impartial and just. If sometimes I failed," Mr. Lee admitted, "attribute it rather to the head than the heart. . . ."

Serving in Congress

From 1870 to 1901 twenty-two African Americans served their states as congressmen and sat in every Congress from the Forty-first to the Fifty-sixth, with one exception. Although half were former slaves, the group included brilliant and superb orators. Republican presidential candidate James G. Blaine, who served with many of these men, said of their abilities:

> The colored men who took seats in both the Senate and the House did not appear ignorant or helpless. They were as a rule studious, earnest, ambitious men whose public conduct . . . would be honorable to any race.

THE FIRST COLORED SENATOR AND REPRESENTATIVES.
In the 41ˢᵗ and 42ⁿᵈ Congress of the United States.

A Currier and Ives print of seven of the fourteen African American congressmen who served during Reconstruction (1870–1876).

Senator B. K. Bruce of Mississippi. A former runaway slave, Bruce once received six votes for the Republican vice-presidential nomination and was considered for a post in President Garfield's cabinet. He was appointed register of the treasury, and his signature on all United States paper money made it valid.

None of them, pointed out one former Confederate leader, had ever been touched by the corruption that had reached so many men in the federal government during this era of easy money and low public morality.

Half of the African American congressmen were college-educated and several held college degrees. Robert Smalls, who served five full terms as a South Carolina congressman, was the war hero who had delivered a Confederate gunboat to the Union army. All of the men were vitally interested in protecting the new rights of the free and battled long hours for passage of civil rights laws. The interest of these congressmen in civil rights often stemmed from their own bitter experiences on trains or in restaurants. Jefferson Long, Georgia's only Black congressman, spoke from personal experience against violence during elections. While seven of his supporters were shot in street fighting one Election Day, Long hid in a church belfry. These congressmen also demanded protection for the many whites in the South who faced violent attack for defending equality.

The twenty-two African American congressmen (two were senators from Mississippi) pursued a wide range of issues besides civil rights. As loyal Republicans they supported higher tariffs to protect American industry. Some favored soldiers' pensions, internal improvements, and federal aid to education. "I am true to my own race . . . but at the same time, I would not have anything done which would harm the white race," said one. South Carolina congressman Rapier, "in order to know something of the feelings of a free man—left home and travelled six months in foreign lands."

The Violent End of Reconstruction

The downfall of the biracial governments of the South was inevitable since people of color had few guns, little land, and less government protection. Organized violence was the main weapon of those who sought to restore the old order.

Congressman Jeremiah Haralson of Alabama in 1875 called for federal aid to education.

Masked night riders such as the Ku Klux Klan sprang up everywhere to terrorize Black voters and their white supporters. The main Klan targets were African American officials, teachers, and successful farmers. When freedmen "made good money and had a good farm, the Ku Klux went to work and burned 'em down," recalled one African American. In 1869 a Louisiana agent of the Freedman's Bureau reported: *Driving the freedmen from their crop* and seizing it themselves when it is grown, is a complaint against the planters that comes to us from every quarter." Each year, along with the "generous yield of nature, so welcome, so needed, so widespread, come, too, reports of injustice, outrage, violence, and crime," wrote a United States official.

The twenty-five thousand troops assigned to control the South—and guard the entire Mexican border—were not able to halt the Klan attacks. While some officers did their best, others made only token efforts. Striking at night, masked, and on fast horses, the Klan picked off the most competent and daring of Black leaders. No courts convicted the Klan leaders. "We are in the hands of murderers," wrote three hundred Vicksburg voters in 1875. "They say they will carry this election either by ballot or bullet." African Americans who were ready to fight back often had been stripped of their weapons by white sheriffs, or were too poor to afford guns. Abraham Burriss appealed to Governor Ames of Mississippi: "But give us guns and we will show the scoundrels that colored people *will fight.*" After thirty Blacks were massacred at Meridian, Mississippi, in 1871, Congress passed a law to end the Ku Klux Klan menace, but other organizations sprang up to take the Klan's place.

Ku Klux Klan members struck at night, killing or driving off Black leaders and the whites who stood by them.

African Americans reacted to the mounting violence in many ways. Black militia companies were formed, some sponsored by the state governments. Others warned of meeting violence with violence. Reverend Charles Ennis of Georgia explained the problem:

> We have no protection at all from the laws of Georgia. . . . A great many freedmen have told me that we should be obliged to rise and take arms and protect ourselves, but I have always told them this would not do; that the whole South would then come against us and kill us off, as the Indians have been killed off. I have always told them the best way was for us to apply to the Government for protection, and let them protect us.

The attacks on Black and white teachers and schools for freedmen did not cease. Samuel Allen, an African American teacher, was attacked by a mob in 1869 because he had "committed a great wrong; I had kept a Sunday school. . . ." Allen fought off the mob with a saber and fled to the woods. When a mob in Marianna, Florida, called a white teacher out of his Black school, "the freedmen came promptly to his aid, and the mob dispersed," reported a United States Army captain. When the mob returned

Anti-Black violence was designed to prevent African Americans from holding office, voting, and attending schools. Federal troops seemed powerless to halt the violence.

In 1873 Blacks barricaded a courthouse in Louisiana to fight off a white mob. In the next few years Blacks increasingly faced the choice of meeting violence with violence or losing their rights.

the next night, "forty colored men armed to protect themselves" and drove the mob off without firing a shot. In all Southern states, schools were set ablaze and teachers beaten or forced to leave the state.

Weapons more subtle than violence were used against the reconstruction governments. Their enemies charged them with fraud or misuse of public funds. Corruption of public officials during the postwar period reached into all levels of government: city, state, and federal. This was the era of the Credit Mobilier scandal, the Whiskey Ring, the salary grab, and the Tweed Ring. In New York the Tweed Ring stole $100,000,000 while it ran the city government. Members of President Grant's Cabinet fled the country to escape prosecution for misuse of public funds.

The reconstruction governments of the South also were often unable to halt those who used governmental power for personal gain. While public funds were misused by the reconstruction governments, Black participants did not inaugurate this practice. As a matter of fact, they benefited least from it. Corrupt Northern Carpetbaggers and Southern Scalawags and Democrats were able to steal far more than former slaves. Moreover, the Tweed Ring in New York managed to steal more money than all the reconstruction governments combined.

Those seeking to restore Southern "white supremacy" exaggerated the corruption and incompetence of African American lawmakers. Their real enemies were the many successful and competent farmers, merchants, and lawmakers who disproved their concept of white superiority.

White Southerners who supported the reconstruction governments were termed "Scalawags" and Northerners who came South to join them

Reverend Henry M. Turner, elected to the Georgia legislature, was denied his seat by the white lawmen. Toward the end of his life Turner came to believe that his people would be better off in Africa than in America.

were called "Carpetbaggers." Scalawags, Carpetbaggers, and "radical" African Americans could not find jobs easily. Wives and children of Republican Blacks were refused service by doctors or stores. Since there was no secret ballot, Mississippi papers printed the names of Republican voters in 1875 so that they could be fired from jobs, intimidated, or beaten.

Voting booths were secretly moved on Election Day or guarded by masked riders. When all else failed, Republican votes were given to the Democrats by election officials. In Georgia, the state legislature simply refused to seat the many Black elected representatives. A furious senator, Henry M. Turner, shouted, "I am here to demand my rights, and to hurl thunderbolts at the men who would dare to cross the threshold of my manhood." But it was no use. Turner and the others were refused entrance.

Restoration of White Supremacy

By 1876, only three Southern states—Florida, Louisiana, and South Carolina—had reconstruction governments. The fate of the South was finally sealed as part of the political "deal" that gave the 1876 presidential election to Rutherford B. Hayes. When it first appeared that he had lost to the Democrat, Tilden, Hayes said, "I don't care for myself; and the [Republican] party, yes, and the country, too, can stand it; but I do care for the poor colored man of the South." But a few weeks later he announced that he was convinced that "absolute justice and fair play to the Negro" could be gotten best "by trusting the honorable and influential whites." On Hayes's

Congressman Robert Brown Elliott speaking for the 1875 Civil Rights Bill. Elliott was answering Alexander H. Stephens, former vice president of the Confederacy. The law passed, but was declared unconstitutional in 1883 by the Supreme Court.

Inauguration Day, whites in Hamburg, South Carolina, attacked and killed scores of African American residents.

Although some Black men were elected to office during the following generation, for the vast majority the democracy of Reconstruction was over—and with it the schools and public facilities that had been opened to Black men, women, and children. President Grant looked at the government of Mississippi and said it "is governed today by officials chosen through fraud and violence such as would scarcely be credited to savages, much less to a civilized and Christian people."

In 1875 a tall, muscular African American farmer stood before Senator George Boutwell of Massachusetts and demanded that something be done about the murder of his people. He was considering killing the racists responsible, saying, "We could do it in a night." "No," answered Boutwell "we intend to protect you." The promise was never kept.

For the Black men and women and for the South the result was tragedy. The torch of democracy that had burned brightly for a short while was extinguished. And Southerners would live—from that day until the 1960s—in the darkness of tyranny, poverty, and ignorance.

THE SOUTH CAROLINA CONSTITUTIONAL CONVENTION OF 1868: "SHOULD RACE OR COLOR BE MENTIONED?"

[*Black delegates B. F. Randolph and F. L. Cardoza argue for the inclusion of a section saying, "Discrimination on account of race or color in any case whatsoever shall be prohibited. . . ."*]

Mr. B. F. Randolph. . . . In our Bill of Rights, I want to settle the question forever. . . .

Mr. C. P. Leslie. I would ask the delegate if it would not have been a little better for his theory if the Scriptures had added "without distinction of race or color."

Mr. B. F. Randolph. If the gentleman will tell me why Congress saw fit to say "all men are created equal," I may answer his question.

Mr. B. F. Whitmore. . . . We discussed this matter in Committee, and the determination arrived at was not to introduce the word color in the Bill of Rights. . . . The colored man was a citizen, his rights had been declared, and I propose to defend those rights whenever called upon. . . .

Mr. F. L. Cardoza. It is a patent fact that, as colored men, we have been cheated out of our rights for two centuries, and now that we have the opportunity, I want to fix them in the Constitution in such a way that no lawyer, however cunning or astute, can possibly misinterpret the meaning. If we do not do so, we deserve to be, and will be, cheated again. . . .

Proceedings of the Constitutional Convention of South Carolina 1 (Charleston, 1868): 353–55.

THE SOUTH CAROLINA CONSTITUTIONAL CONVENTION OF 1868: "LAND AND FREEDOM"

[*Reverend Richard Cain and Francis L. Cardoza give their views of poor people's need for land. Cardoza stresses breaking up plantations and distributing small farms to the landless. Born free in Charleston in 1837, Cardoza had studied at the University of Glasgow. He speaks first.*]

. . . What is the main cause of the prosperity of the North? It is because every man has his own farm and is free and independent. Let the lands of the South be similarly divided. . . . We will never have true freedom until we abolish the system of agriculture which existed in the Southern States. It is useless to have any schools while we maintain this stronghold of slavery as the agricultural system of the country. . . . If they [the lands] are sold, though a few mercenary speculators may purchase some, the chances are that the colored man and the poor [white] man would be the purchasers. I will prove this . . . by facts. About one hundred poor colored men of Charleston met together and formed themselves into a Charleston Land Company. They subscribed for a number of shares at $10 per share, one dollar payable monthly. They have been meeting for a year. Yesterday they purchased some 600 acres of land for $6,600 that would have sold for $25,000 or $50,000 in better times. . . . This is only one instance of thousands of others that have occurred in this city and State. . . .

[*Richard Cain, born free and educated at Wilberforce University, agreed.*]

. . . I believe the possession of lands and homesteads is one of the best means by which a people is made industrious, honest and advantageous to the State. . . . I have gone through the country and on every side I was besieged with questions: How are we to get homesteads, to get lands. . . . Give these men a place to work, and I will guarantee before one year passes, there will be no necessity for the Freedman's Bureau. . . .

. . . what we need is a system of small farms. Every farmer owning his own land will feel he is in possession of something. It will have a tendency to settle the minds of the people in the State and settle many difficulties. . . .

Proceedings of the Constitutional Convention of South Carolina 1 (Charleston, 1868): 117, 379–80.

THE SOUTH CAROLINA CONSTITUTIONAL CONVENTION OF 1868: "SCHOOLS AND EDUCATION"

[Delegates debated whether to make school attendance compulsory and whether or not to integrate schools. Each of the Black delegates who speaks later represented his state in Congress, except for Mr. Cardoza, who served for eight years as secretary of state and secretary of the treasury of South Carolina.]

Mr. R. C. De Large. . . . This section proposes to open these schools to all persons, irrespective of color, to open every seminary of learning to all. Heartily do I endorse the object, but the manner in which it is to be enforced meets my most earnest disapproval. . . . The schools may be opened to all, under proper provisions in the [state] Constitution, but to declare that parents "shall" send their children to them whether they are willing or not is, in my judgment, going a step beyond the bounds of prudence. . . .

Mr. A. J. Ransier. . . . Civilization and enlightenment follow fast upon the footsteps of the schoolmaster; and if education must be enforced to secure these grand results, I say let the compulsory process go on. . . .

Mr. F. L. Cardoza. . . . We only compel parents to send their children to some school, not that they shall send them with the colored children; we simply give those colored children who desire to go to white schools, the privilege to do so.

Mr. R. H. Cain. . . . To do justice in this matter of education, compulsion is not required. I am willing to trust the people. They have good sense, and experience itself will be better than all the force you can employ to instill the idea of duty to their children. . . .

Mr. R. B. Elliott.... [Another speaker] has said this law is to force the white and colored children into the public schools together. The only question is whether children shall become educated and enlightened, or remain in ignorance. This question is not white or black, united or divided, but whether children shall be sent to school or kept at home. If they are compelled to be educated, there will be no danger to the Union, or a second secession of South Carolina. . . .

Proceedings of the Constitutional Convention of South Carolina 2 (Charleston, 1868): 685–704.

PROGRESS AND CORRUPTION IN MISSISSIPPI

[*Henry W. Warren graduated from Yale in 1865 and headed south, first as a schoolteacher in Tennessee and later as a plantation owner and Speaker of the Mississippi legislature. He describes Mississippi's government.*]

. . . From the first there were plenty of Confederate generals and colonels in the Legislature. The manner of the blacks to the whites was habitually civil, and something of the slave's deference to the white man remained. I think the legislation was generally of reasonably good character. I knew positively of but little corruption. That there was some corruption and more extravagance, I have no doubt. But I have served in the Massachusetts Legislature, and I think the Southern State was but little worse than the Northern. The Negro members, though with some able and honest leaders of their own, like Bruce and Lynch, followed largely the prominent white men. . . . A "carpet-bagger" I hardly ever met, though no doubt there were some—but the name was given to all Northerners. As to expense, you must remember that the State had to be completely rehabilitated. The war had ruined everything; public buildings were destroyed or dilapidated; and under military rule things had simply been kept going. Everything had to be reconstructed. The slaves had become citizens, and that doubled the number to be provided for. There had been practically no public schools, and they were set up throughout the State. Taxes had fallen largely on slave property, now they came on land. So it was inevitable that there should be an increase in taxation. . . . In those years there was immense progress on the part of the Negroes,—political discussion was educational. I think if the Federal government had provided better school education, and had protected the voters at the polls, all might have gone well. That there was more or less extravagance on the part of the Legislature is not to be denied. So there is in Massachusetts. . . .

George S. Merriam, *The Negro and the Nation, a History of American Slavery and Enfranchisement* (New York, 1906), 338–40.

THE PURPOSES OF THE KU KLUX KLAN

[Klansmen tried to keep Southern Blacks ignorant and under white control, according to the sworn testimony of two African Americans, one a state senator from Mississippi and the other a teacher in North Carolina.]

[*State Senator Robert Gleed of Mississippi*] Well, sir, we have thought from their organization and from other indications we have had, that the . . . purposes of the [Klan] organization have been to remand the colored men of the country to as near a position of servitude as possible, and to destroy the Republican Party if possible; it has been, in other words, political. . . .

Do you think one of the objectives of the Ku Klux organization in its various visits has been to break down the growing spirit of independence in the black man?

Yes, sir; and to establish white supremacy in the South, and to destroy the republican party. . . .

Testimony Taken by the Joint Select Committee to Inquire into the Condition of Affairs in the Late Insurrectionary States, Mississippi (Washington, 1872): 722.

[*Samuel Allen, a teacher who beat off a Klan raid*] They [the Klansmen] said I had committed a great wrong; I had kept a Sunday-school which I was forbidden to do. They told me that this thing of teaching . . . was something they did not allow; that the church they belonged to never sanctioned any such thing; that it was not sanctioned by the neighborhood or the country and it must not be done, and finally they told me it should not be done and when I proceeded on with the Sunday-school, they said to me, "We gave you orders to stop, and you have continued against our orders; now you have got to stop."

Report on the Alleged Outrages in the Southern States by the Select Committee of the Senate (Washington, 1871), 49.

THE POWER OF THE KU KLUX KLAN

[*Throughout Reconstruction, masked racist gangs had a power greater than their numbers would indicate and influence that reached into every part of local and state government. Colonel George W. Kirk of the North Carolina state troops described Klan power in his state.*]

. . . I have spoken of their having the law and the courts all on their side. The juries were made up of Ku-Klux, and it was impossible for any of the loyal people to get justice before the courts. Not less than fifty or sixty persons have been killed by the Ku-Klux in the State, besides some three or four hundred whippings, and there has never been a man convicted that I have heard of. Out of all those that I arrested, against whom there was good proof as could possibly be given, enough to convict anybody before twelve honest men, I do not think one has ever been tried. They know very well when they commit these depredations that they will be cleared, and it just makes it that much worse for the loyal people. If they prosecute them for debt or for anything else they fail. Colored men cannot get justice, cannot get their hard earned money. They agree to give them part of the crop, and about the time of the harvest they charge them with something and run them off. They dare not say a word. . . .

Report on the Alleged Outrages in the Southern States by the Select Committee of the Senate (Washington, 1871), 10.

TEACHING SCHOOL IN GEORGIA IN 1870

[*This report in 1870 by an agent of the Freedmen's Bureau, J. K. Lewis, indicates the continuing attack on Black education.*]

In one half of the state there is little opposition to their schools and the respectable citizens give them their countenance and support. In many counties however there is still great bitterness of feeling against the schools and all those engaged in the work and bands of K.K.K. armed and disguised men, have committed most atrocious outrages. About the last of November Mr. R. H. Gladdings who has been teaching . . . at Greensboro,

Green Co. was driven away. The man with whom he boarded (a white man) was taken out of his house in the night and unmercifully whipped and Mr. Abram Colby (colored) a member-elect of the legislature and one of Mr. Gladdings strong supporters in the school work, was taken out of his house and beaten nearly to death. Mr. Gladdings was warned to leave and appealed to the Mayor for protection to prevent any outrage upon him, he was therefore obliged to leave. . . . Notwithstanding these difficulties the school work goes on with increased efficiency. The freemen pay more liberally than ever toward the support of their schools.

Office of the Adjutant General, Letters Received (Washington: National Archives, War Records Office, 1870).

"HIS INTENSE ZEAL FOR EDUCATION"

[*R. A. Seely, an official of the Freedmen's Bureau, wrote this report, in 1870, about an incident that occurred in his region.*]

On the fourth of October the [school] house was completely destroyed by fire, nothing being saved but a few benches, and the Sunday School Library. . . .

The fire was undoubtedly the work of an incendiary as it occurred at midnight and no fire had been kindled within the building. . . . The total loss was not less than ten thousand dollars.

It would be difficult for any one who does not know the poverty of the freedman and his intense zeal for education to conceive the disheartening effect of such a calamity upon the poor people who had denied themselves every luxury, and with unprecedented liberality had given one half their wages, week after week, for the construction of this house for themselves and their children. But words of cheer and friendly counsel were not wanting. And, thanks to the elastic temperament of the African, the general despondency soon gave way to new and more vigorous effort. And the work was re-commenced with resolution as firm as before. And with means and purposes broader than ever.

Office of the Adjutant General, Letters Received (Washington: National Archives, War Records Office, 1870).

LAWMAKERS GO TO COLLEGE

[Edward King, a white Northerner, visited the South Carolina legislature in 1873.]

The House, when I visited it, was composed of eighty-three colored members, all of whom are Republicans, and forty-one whites; the Senate consisted of fifteen colored men, ten white Republicans, and eight white Democrats. The President of the Senate and the Speaker of the House, both colored, were elegant and accomplished men, highly educated, who would have creditably presided over any commonwealth's legislative assembly. . . . The little knot of white Democrats, massed together in one section of the hall, sat glum and scornful amid the mass of black speakers. . . . There are men of real force and eloquence among the Negroes chosen to the House but they are the exception. In the Senate there was more decorum and ability among the members. Several of the colored senators spoke exceedingly well, and with great ease and grace of manner; others were awkward and lacked refinement. . . .

I visited the University a day or two after the revolution caused there by the entrance of the first colored student, the Secretary of State himself. In the library . . . I saw the book from whose lists the white students had indignantly erased their names when they saw the Secretary's round, fair script beneath their own. The departure of the old professors and scholars was the signal for a grand onward movement by the blacks, and a great number entered the preparatory and law schools. They have summoned good teachers from the North, and are studying earnestly. . . . While I was in the library a coal black senator arrived, with two members of the House, whom he presented to the head of the faculty as desirous of entering the law class. I was informed that dozens of members were occupied every spare moment outside of the session in faithful study. . . .

Edward King, "The Great South," *Scribner's Monthly* 8 (June 1874): 156–58.

A CONGRESSMAN DENOUNCES SEGREGATION

[Mississippi African American congressman John R. Lynch describes to Congress the indignities he suffered on an official trip to Washington. Lynch was born a slave in 1847, was elected Speaker of the Mississippi House when he was twenty-two, and was then elected to three terms in the United States Congress.]

. . . Think of it for a moment; here am I, a member of your honorable body, representing one of the largest and wealthiest districts in the State of Mississippi, and possibly in the South; a district composed of persons of different races, religions, and nationalities; and yet, when I leave my home to come to the capital of the nation, to take part in the deliberations of the House and to participate with you in making laws for the government of this great Republic, . . . I am treated, not as an American citizen, but as a brute. Forced to occupy a filthy smoking-car both night and day, with drunkards, gamblers, and criminals; and for what? Not that I am unable or unwilling to pay my way; not that I am obnoxious in my personal appearance or disrespectful in my conduct; but simply because I happen to be of a darker complexion. If this treatment was confined to persons of our own sex we could possibly afford to endure it. But such is not the case. Our wives and our daughters, our sisters and our mothers are subjected to the same insults and to the same uncivilized treatment. . . . The only moments of my life when I am necessarily compelled to question my loyalty to my Government or my devotion to the flag of my country is when I read of outrages having been committed upon innocent colored people and . . . when I leave my home to go travelling.

Mr. Speaker, if this unjust discrimination is to be longer tolerated by the American people . . . then I can only say with sorrow and regret that our boasted civilization is a fraud; our republican institutions a failure; our social system a disgrace; and our religion a complete hypocrisy. . . .

The Congressional Record 2, part 5, 43rd Cong., 1st sess., 4783.

A SENATOR DEFENDS HIMSELF

[*Many Blacks elected to Congress during Reconstruction were challenged by their Democratic opponents, and some were never able to take their seats. One was P. B. S. Pinchback, the famous Louisiana politician who served briefly as governor of that state. In this speech, given in 1873 while his case was under consideration by the Senate, he defended his election and record. Although he was not seated, the Senate paid his senator's salary.*]

. . . several Senators (I hope they are not Republicans) think me a very bad man. If this be true I fear my case is hopeless, for I am a bad man in the eyes of the democracy [and] weak-kneed Republicans. But of what does my badness consist [?] I am bad because I have dared on several important occasions to have an independent opinion. I am bad because I have dared at all times to advocate and insist on exact and equal justice to all Mankind. I am bad because having colored blood in my veins I have dared to aspire to the United States Senate, and I am bad because your representatives dared express the will of the people rather than obey the will of those who thought they were the peoples' Masters, when they elected me.

Friends I have been told that if I dared utter such Sentiments as these in public that I certainly would be Kept out of the Senate, all I have to say in answer to this, is that if I cannot enter the Senate except with bated breath and on bended knees, I prefer not to enter at all. . . .

P. B. S. Pinchback, *Pinchback's Handwritten Manuscript: Notes for a Speech,* from Howard University's Moorland Collection (Washington, 1873).

FINAL REPORT TO THE SOUTH CAROLINA HOUSE, 1874

[*Speaker S. J. Lee gives this report to the nine Black and thirty-four white members of the House of Representatives at the close of the regular session in 1874.*]

We have been condemned and maligned; our motives have been misconstrued, and our actions [too] . . . ; but notwithstanding the malignity of our enemies, every right thinking person must perforce admit that we have done well. While we are . . . perhaps, very little skilled in the science of government, many good and laudable enactments have emanated from us, and . . . we have sought in every instance to subserve all personal interests to those of the State. . . .

We cannot hide the fact that many things in our midst need pruning and reforming, but *we* can effect it. . . . We, as a people, are blameless of misgovernment. It is owing to bad men, adventurers, persons who, after having reaped millions from our party, turn traitors and stab us in the dark. Ingratitude is the worst of crimes, and yet the men we have fostered, the men we have elevated and made rich, now speak of our corruption and . . . charge us with every conceivable crime. They lay everything at our doors, and seek by letters, published in northern journals, to ruin our credit and blacken our prospects abroad. . . .

Permit me, now, to refer to our increased educational advantages. It is very pleasing, gentlemen, to witness how rapidly the schools are springing up in every portion of our State, and how the number of competent, well-trained teachers are increasing. . . . Our State University has been renovated and made progressive. New Professors, men of unquestionable ability and erudition, now fill the chairs once filled by men who were too aristocratic to instruct colored youths. A system of scholarships has been established that will, as soon as it is practically in operation, bring into the University a very large number of students. . . . The State Normal School is also situated here, and will have a fair attendance of scholars. We have, also, Claflin University, at Orangeburg, which is well attended, and progressing very favorably; and in the different cities and large towns of the State, school houses have been built, and the school master can be found there busily instructing the "young idea how to shoot." The *effects* of education can also be perceived; the people are becoming daily more enlightened; their minds are expanding, and they have awakened, in a great degree, from the mental darkness that hitherto surrounded them. . . .

Journal of the House of Representatives of the State of South Carolina, for the Regular Session of 1873–1874 (Columbia, 1874), 549–53.

A MISSISSIPPI ELECTION: VOTE STEALING

[*D. J. Foreman, a Black Republican leader, had three hundred Republican voters and only forty-seven Democrats in his district. He explains to a Senate committee, in 1875, how the district went to the Democrats.*]

. . . we held meetings but we did not hold them publicly. We used to go into the swamps to hold them, and we had a house off the road where we could meet, with no lamps or anything.

Q. What did you do at those meetings?
A. We would meet for the purpose of discussing what we were going to do at the election.
Q. What did you propose to do at the election?
A. Some said not to go to the polls; some said they would go; some said they were afraid to go, and some said they were not, and they would go if they got killed. . . .

Q. Are your people armed generally [?] . . .

A. No, sir; they are poorly armed. . . .

Q. When did you first know what the result was [in the 1875 election]?

A. I met Bazelius, clerk of the election, the next morning coming from Vicks-burgh, and I asked him what was the result of the election. He told me: "We beat you badly yesterday." I says, "No, you didn't; you polled forty-seven votes." He says, "It was you polled forty-seven votes, and we polled three hundred. You all voted democratic votes." . . .

Q. Do you know anything more about what took place at the election?

A. [The whites] . . . met the colored people, and would not allow them to come with arms; and the white people kept on theirs, and that scared the colored people. . . .

Q. And the democrats carried their arms?

A. Yes, sir; and Mr. Henderson told me that I would have to shut my mouth; and I told him that I thought they were going to let us have a fair election; and they said it was a fair election, only the fuss I was making. I told him I was making a fuss for something; that I thought as they did not allow colored people to bring their arms, that they ought not to have theirs.

Mississippi in 1875, Senate Report 527, part 2, 44th Cong., 1st sess. (Washington, 1876), 1380–83.

A MISSISSIPPI ELECTION: VIOLENCE

[*In 1875, these letters to Mississippi's Republican governor, Adelbert Ames, reveal mounting violence as Election Day approached. The first letter is from Senator Charles Caldwell, a Black Republican leader assassinated a few months later.*]

. . . The intimidation and threatening of colored voters continues uninter-rupted, and with as much system, determined purpose, and combination of effort as if it were a legitimate means of canvassing and the chief one to be relied on in controlling the colored element. . . .

In behalf of the people whom I represent, I appeal to your excellency for the protection which the laws of the State guarantee to every citizen re-gardless of party or race.

[*Letter from three hundred Vicksburg Negro voters.*] . . . we are intimi-dated by the whites. We wants to hold meetings, but it is impossible to do so; if we does, they will say we are making an invasion on the city and come out [to] kill us. When we hold church meetings, they breakes that up; our lives are not safe in our houses. Now we ask you who shall we look to for protection. . . . We are in the hands of murderers. There will not be peace here until troops come to unarm them. . . .

[*Letter of H. W. Lewis of Columbia, Mississippi.*] Dear Sir: Everything in this and adjoining counties is up to fever heat. The 24-pound cannon thunders forth every night. The brass band accompanies the democratic speakers, together with about 50 hot-headed young men, and assassination and bloodshed are openly encouraged. Our voters are very much over-awed, and [we] fear we cannot get out more than one-half of them. If troops could be sent here, even a "corporal's guard," it would act like magic, and we would sweep everything in this part of the State. As it is, it looks as though we should lose everything. . . .

If anything can be done, I know you will do it. If not, we shall do the best we can and try to meet the issue bravely.

[*Letter from a group of Black Republicans.*] Dear Governor: We here give you notice that the white people of this towne have jest received, by express from New Orleans, three boxes of guns and also some boxes of pistols for the porpus of a riot in this place, while we have not got a gun or do not want any desturbemenst, and we asks you for our protection or helpe some way or erther, knowing that you are our govnor and the only help for us. Please give us some helpe, we ask agin. . . .

[*William Canly writes from De Soto County.*] Governor Ames, DEAR SIR: We, as Republicans of the State of Mississippi, do ask you to tell us whether we are to be murdered by the whites of the State or not, without protection at all. . . .

. . . the whites are allowed to have war guns among us in time of peace, and we call all such as that unjust.

Now, when we was registering [to vote], I saw Mr. Jim Chamberlin turn away some men who was 23 years of age. Is that equal? No sir. . . . White men who were to young to work on the public roads could register. I call all such as that fraud.

[*A white Republican wrote this letter after the election had been held.*] Our election has been *broken* up by armed White-Leaguers. This morning, long before the opening of the polls in this city, the White-Leaguers came, cavalry, infantry, and artillery, and they drove the colored men before them, and compelled them to fly for their lives. No colored man was allowed to vote unless he voted the democratic ticket. They openly declared that if any republican tried to go the polls they would shoot him down. . . .

We have been slumbering on a volcano for ten days, but to-day it culminated at the ballot-box. It is no longer with them the number of votes but the number of guns.

"Documentary Evidence," *Mississippi in 1875,* Senate Report 527, part 2, 44th Cong., 1st sess. (Washington, 1876), 19–56.

RECONSTRUCTION'S IMPERISHABLE BLACK GIFTS

[In 1895, a new South Carolina Constitutional Convention met to restore white supremacy. As the majority of white delegates prepared to crush his rights, former congressman Thomas E. Miller spoke of the "imperishable gifts bestowed upon South Carolina during Reconstruction by Negro legislators." But his summary did not change the vote to deny Black men like himself equal rights.]

. . . in the administration of affairs for the [1873 to 1876] years, having learned by experience the result of bad acts, we immediately passed reformatory laws, touching every department of State, county, municipal and town governments. These enactments are today upon the state books of South Carolina. They stand as living witnesses of the Negro's fitness to vote and legislate upon the rights of mankind.

. . . We were eight years in power. We had built school houses, established charitable institutions, built and maintained the penitentiary system, provided for the education of the deaf and dumb, rebuilt the jails and court houses, rebuilt the bridges and re-established the ferries. In short, we had reconstructed the State and placed it upon the road to prosperity and, at the same time, by our acts of financial reform transmitted to the Hampton government an indebtedness not greater by more than $2,500,000 than was the bonded debt of the State in 1868, before the Republican Negroes and their white allies came into power.

The Suffrage, Speeches by Negroes in the Constitutional Convention (n.p., 1895), 13, 15.

12 AN AGE OF INVENTION AND INDUSTRIAL GROWTH

THE CIVIL WAR had swept away obstacles to America's industrial growth. Congress was no longer dominated by slaveholders who voted down high tariffs, grants to railroads, and measures for the protection or advancement of business. The hard-driving industrialist became the hero of the new age. The abolitionist was a figure of the past, and many who had had sympathy for the slave now showed little interest in former slaves.

The new change in interest could be seen in the actions of the federal government. Rutherford B. Hayes had served as a volunteer lawyer for fugitive slaves before the Civil War. Now, as president, he withdrew the last federal troops from the South, ending all protection of people of color. Instead of defending equal rights with federal troops, Hayes and other presidents used them to break strikes of railroad workers.

The Fourteenth Amendment to the Constitution, designed to shield the rights of former slaves, was used, instead, to protect corporations. Federal courts ruled that when the amendment stated that no state could "deprive any person of life, liberty, or property," this meant corporations as well as people. In the years that followed, the nation's industrial concerns received all the protection from the amendment that the African Americans in the South were being denied.

In an age of greed, the kind of men who cornered the United States gold market also stole the pennies that ex-slaves had deposited in the Freedmen's Bank. Money, after all, was money, and the only trick was getting it. There was little sentiment in these times, and even less concern, for the powerless. You had to be strong to survive, and if you were not, your troubles meant little. Those who did survive built a powerful industrial and commercial nation. Their raw materials included the brainpower of America's inventive minds, and the powerful arms and skills of its factory workers.

Inventors and Inventions

To meet the needs of faster communication and transportation, American companies sought out the best inventive minds. Many African Americans were among those who produced electrical, mechanical, and telephonic equipment. Before the turn of the nineteenth century they had patented hundreds of inventions. They produced everything from new kinds of elevators and photographic and telegraphic equipment to refrigerators, golf tees, and modern bathroom fixtures. They became part of the inventive thrust feeding the industrial revolution.

Elijah McCoy, the son of runaway slaves, played a prominent role in the development of transportation and factory machinery. In 1872 McCoy, educated in Scotland as a mechanical engineer, invented a lubricating cup that fed oil to parts of a machine while it was in operation. This made it possible for locomotives, steam boilers, and factory machinery to be oiled without interrupting their operations. Inventor McCoy received more than fifty patents for his various devices.

Elijah McCoy, son of runaway slaves, held many patents. His lubricating cup was the first "real McCoy."

Inventor Lewis Howard Latimer assisted
Bell and Edison.

Lewis Howard Latimer, who worked with both Alexander Graham Bell and Thomas Edison, was born to a poor Boston family in 1848. To help support the family, and at the same time further the cause of emancipation, he sold copies of William Lloyd Garrison's *The Liberator* on the streets. When he was sixteen, Latimer joined the United States Navy and served aboard the U.S.S. *Massasoit* during the Civil War. After the war, he returned to Boston, where he began work as an office boy in a company of patent lawyers. He rose to the position of chief draftsman for the firm.

Around the year 1876 Latimer, then an expert electrical engineer and draftsman, met Alexander Graham Bell. Some of the people who knew Latimer in the early days said, "It was Latimer who executed the drawings and assisted in preparing the applications for the telephone patents of Alexander Graham Bell."

He left Bell a few years later to join the United States Electric Lighting Company at Bridgeport, Connecticut, where, with the noted inventor Hiram S. Maxim, he invented an incandescent electric light and supervised the building of manufacturing plants in New York, Philadelphia, and Canada.

In 1884 Latimer joined the engineering staff of the Edison Electric Light Company. He worked for Edison for many years, becoming the only African American member of the famous Edison Pioneers, people who had worked with Edison before 1885. In 1890 he wrote a book explaining, to the general public, the use and workings of the electric light. Latimer

Jan Matzeliger, inventor of the machine that revolutionized the shoe industry and made Lynn, Massachusetts, the shoe capital of the world. Government experts, baffled by his patent drawings, sent a specialist to examine the machine. Matzeliger died young and poor after working ten years to develop his device.

also proved invaluable to the legal department of the Edison Company. Since he had usually drawn the original plans for Edison inventions, he was the company's star witness in patent cases that reached the courts. After he retired, Latimer published a volume of his poetry and gave more time to the study of literature.

Granville T. Woods directed his inventive talents toward improvements in the railroad and electrical industries. He invented a telegraph system that made it possible to send messages between moving trains, thus reducing the danger of accidents. His invention of an automatic air brake brought greater safety to the nation's railroads. Woods also contributed to the development of the "third rail" used in electrical railroads.

He invented devices which he sold to Bell, Edison, and Westinghouse. In two patent cases against the Edison Company, Woods was able to prove that he had had earlier rights to inventions claimed by Edison. After the second court victory, Thomas Edison offered Woods a position, which he turned down, preferring to be his own boss. In 1888 the *American Catholic Tribune* called Woods "the greatest electrician in the world." Though this would be hard to prove, it indicates that, though Woods is unknown today, he was highly thought of in his own time.

Unlike Granville T. Woods, Jan Matzeliger never received the recognition due an important inventor. In 1883, when he was thirty years old, he invented a machine which combined so many steps that it practically manufactured an entire shoe in one operation. A slender, erect young man, Matzeliger was well liked in his town of Lynn, Massachusetts. Neighbors found him cheerful and "quick to see the funny side of things," and a Lynn editor found him "a man not only of wonderful mechanical ability, but a man of equally wonderful energy and tenacity of purpose." His machine became the basis for the multimillion-dollar growth of the United Shoe Company, which bought the invention. Yet Matzeliger, like many other inventors, sold it for very little. At thirty-seven he died of tuberculosis.

The complete story of the early African American inventors cannot be told because bigotry has blurred the picture. When inventors found that many people would not accept their devices when it was learned their creators were Black, some concealed their identities. A naval cadet who left Annapolis because of racial prejudice, Henry E. Baker, assistant examiner of the United States Patent Office for many years, conducted a long and careful investigation of the matter. Although he found proof difficult to obtain in many cases, he turned up some 800 to 1,200 patents owned by men he identified as African American—before the year 1913.

In 1900 Henry Baker published his first findings in four giant volumes which included the actual drawings and plans submitted to the Patent Office by Black inventors prior to the turn of the century. Baker's findings are highly instructive because this contribution to America's early achievements in science and invention has been almost totally neglected.

Henry E. Baker. He conducted the first great search for Black inventors in America. In 1913 his research uncovered a thousand patents held by Black men.

Baker's list includes these inventions patented by African Americans before 1900: a jet-propulsion balloon; a railroad crossing switch; an electric lamp; a self-setting animal trap; a telephone system; a cotton seed planter and fertilizer distributor; letter box; window cleaner; gauge; guitar; printing press; lifesaving device for ships; folding chair; fountain pen; safety gate for bridges; a rapid-fire naval gun; bicycle; steam boiler.

The most noted Black inventor of the modern period was Garrett A. Morgan. On 25 July 1916, an explosion in Tunnel Number Five, 228 feet below Lake Erie, trapped a dozen men. Morgan arrived with his newly invented gas mask. Putting on his mask, Morgan entered the gas-filled tunnel and rescued a number of men. In 1923 Morgan invented the traffic light, which straightened out the disorder of crowded city streets in the age of the automobile. A complicated device with a simple purpose, the invention has saved many lives from that day to this.

Great Fortunes

No people of color amassed great fortunes equal to those of John D. Rockefeller, J. P. Morgan, or Andrew Carnegie. But the first American woman to become a millionaire by her own efforts was the daughter of ex-slaves.

In 1905 Madam C. J. Walker, an orphan at six and a former laundry worker, developed a hair conditioner for Black women. Since whites ignored this market she also developed other cosmetics which were specifically designed for women of color. In a few years, the Madam C. J. Walker Manufacturing Company in Indiana was a vast industry and included a school to train salesmen and saleswomen. Before Madam Walker died in 1919 at the age of fifty-one, she built a school for girls in West Africa, provided it with a $100,000 grant, and gave a good deal of money to charity.

Charles C. Spaulding also followed the "rags to riches" trail. He entered the insurance business in 1898 and accepted a sixty-five-cent commission on a forty-dollar life insurance policy. A few days later the customer died, and Spaulding and his partners paid the policy out of their own pockets. Undismayed, Spaulding had to work harder than before to make a success of the business.

> When I came into the office in the morning, I rolled up my sleeves and swept the place as a janitor. Then I rolled down my sleeves and was an agent. And later I put on my coat and became general manager.

In an age of fierce competition and deep-seated prejudice, the most successful Black businesses and banks resulted from cooperative efforts. Some were sponsored by churches, for in African American life the house of worship was often a bulwark against all storms and an aid in all aspects of life. Early in the twentieth century, Mrs. Maggie L. Walker of Virginia

Andrew J. Beard invented a device for coupling railroad cars. Before the automatic coupler, railroad workers had to place a pin between cars as they moved together, and were often injured or killed. Beard received $50,000 for this invention.

In 1900, Booker T. Washington (seated second from left) formed the National Negro Business League to promote Black enterprises.

built a church-sponsored insurance business into a thriving enterprise. Mrs. Walker organized youth clubs and fostered interracial work with white women's clubs.

Early Labor Unions

It is not known whether John Henry of the famous folk song was a man of flesh or myth. But his race with a steam drill has come to symbolize man's attempt to resist the power of machines. Gigantic John Henry, according to the song, beat the machine—but died in the attempt. The worker in industrial society needed greater protection against the machine than his own arms. Some saw unions as one way to meet the new challenge. This type of organization was also the workers' response to the employer who now had so many workmen he rarely knew their names or skills.

Maggie L. Walker. This early businesswoman worked for unity among Black and white people in Virginia.

Most workmen in the postwar period faced severe competition and the determined opposition of their employers. The government usually took the employer's side against unions. To achieve any success, workers knew that they must be united. But this was difficult. The color prejudice that had separated Black workers from white ones during slavery continued to divide them after freedom. As late as 1934, in Pennsylvania, an African American steelworker said, "The jobs whites won't touch—we get them."

The early national unions tried to unite all workers, regardless of color. In 1866 the National Labor Union invited all to join. Isaac Myers of Baltimore, the outstanding African American labor leader of the time, assured the 1869 convention of the National Labor Union, "The white laboring men have nothing to fear from the colored laboring men. We desire to have the highest rate of wages that our labor is worth. . . ." Myers stressed, "American citizenship for the black man is a complete failure if he is proscribed from the workshops of the country." After the speech a majority of the white delegates voted to accept Black members—but in separate locals.

Isaac Myers had no choice but to begin a separate organization. By the end of 1869 he assembled two hundred delegates at the first convention of the National Colored Labor Union. They advocated the income tax, women's rights, cooperative associations, and the unity of workers regardless of color or belief. The following year Myers entered the South to organize workers of both races. He pleaded that to win success "the white and colored mechanics must come together and work together." But white unions still refused to accept Black members. And Black unions were too weak to bargain effectively with employers. Gradually Republican politicians used these unions for their own publicity purposes. In 1872 Myers' National Colored Labor Union admitted this when it said of the Re-

Black delegate Frank J. Farrell introduces President Terrence J. Powderly to a Virginia convention of the Knights of Labor. Farrell later became a leading socialist.

publican party, "By its success, we stand; by its defeat we fall." It soon fell.

The Knights of Labor, formed as a secret union in 1869, also made an effort to unite all workers. It opened its doors to "men and women of every craft, creed and color." With the help of Black organizers, its African American membership soon skyrocketed to sixty thousand. Southern states passed laws against the new union and drove out its organizers. In 1887 George and Henry Cox were among the leaders of ten thousand Black and white workers who went out on strike against Louisiana sugar plantations. The strike was violently crushed and the two brothers were among the score of union leaders killed.

At the first meeting of the American Federation of Labor in 1881, Black delegate Jeremiah Grandison warned the others that "it would be dangerous to skilled mechanics to exclude from the organization the common laborers." He pointed out that these men could be used to replace skilled men on strike. President Samuel Gompers and his new A.F. of L. paid no attention to Grandison's warning and ignored the unskilled workers in favor of the skilled craftsmen.

Although the unions of the A.F. of L. claimed to be open to all, African Americans were rarely accepted as members. Some were allowed to form segregated locals which had little power. Just as Grandison had predicted, this exclusion led workers of color to take work for less than union pay. When they did this Samuel Gompers scornfully called them "cheap men."

The only important Black A.F. of L. union of this early period came into being in August 1925. It was called the Brotherhood of Sleeping Car Porters, and it chose Asa Philip Randolph to be its president. A tall, scholarly man, Randolph was respected for his knowledge of history and economics as well as his abilities as an editor and public speaker. He rejected all efforts of the employers to frighten or bribe him and soon won pay increases for his eight thousand members. His union became part of the A.F. of L., and Randolph became the first of his race to hold a seat on its executive board, a position he used to prod union leaders who discriminated.

Despite isolated incidences of progress, few African Americans were in unions by 1900. Of twenty-two thousand Black carpenters, only one thousand were union members. White workers often tried to drive Blacks off jobs, and many strikes occurred in the North and South when they were hired to work alongside whites. Oscar DePriest, a Kansas painter who later became the North's first Black congressman, carried a pistol to warn those trying to drive him off jobs.

A. Philip Randolph.
For half a century, he
was labor's Black voice.

Even those Blacks whose skills were appreciated when they were slaves found little use for them in freedom. Discriminatory laws and customs gradually eliminated African Americans from the skilled trades. And whites refused to accept Black apprentices. The A.F. of L., by accepting only skilled laborers, thus automatically excluded the vast majority of Black workers, without even resorting to discrimination.

By keeping African Americans out of unions, the white workers turned them into competitors instead of allies. Employers were quick to seize on this division, and they used Black strikebreakers during labor conflicts. The famous Homestead Strike of 1892 and the 1919 steel strike were won by employers partly in this way. Many people of color were able to break into certain industries only when white workers went out on strike and they were offered the jobs.

Although the temptation to take a decent job was great, many African Americans stubbornly resisted being used as strikebreakers. In 1901, when three hundred Birmingham African Americans were brought to Chicago to break a steel strike, many attended the meeting called by the whites to protest strikebreaking. Black leader Henry Taylor told the meeting, "There is not a man in our party who will work . . . under a gun or in another's place. We don't want to fill strikers' places and we won't under guard." His men kept the pledge.

In several places, and even during strikes, Black and white workers proved themselves capable of unity—even in the Deep South. For example, the New Orleans Dock and Cotton Council's seventy-two union members included an equal number of African American and white union delegates. Its top officers were rotated so that each group would have a turn at running this central union body. When a strike of ten thousand of

Learning by doing at Hampton College, 1900. Black and Indian students gained a variety of industrial skills by working and building at the college. Ironically, this emphasis upon industrial education came when white artisans were forcing African Americans from the skilled trades. Nevertheless, most Black colleges continued to emphasize this type of education. (Collection, The Museum of Modern Art, New York. Gift of Lincoln Kirstein.)

these workers hit New Orleans at the turn of the century, the president of the Black longshoremen, E. S. Swan, commented, "The whites and Negroes were never before so strong cemented in a common bond and in my 39 years of experience on the levee, I never saw such solidarity." The strikers won their demands.

Before it was crushed, a 1908 strike in Birmingham, Alabama, showed that a remarkable degree of unity between Black and white mine workers was possible. They struck for a union shop and to oppose a wage cut. For two months these twenty thousand laborers held out against the opposition of local police, state troops, bombings, and a lynching. According to a Birmingham reporter, they attended meetings at which "Negroes as well as whites bore red flags, and black men were among the principal speakers." But they were finally beaten down by overwhelming force.

A New York union of streetworkers laid down their tools and went home when African American members were treated unfairly by the company. "Unless you give us a written guarantee to recognize all the members of our union, black as well as white," none would work, a white member told the company. The company gave in.

In most places, however, the prejudice against Black workers kept them from joining unions or receiving the support of white workers. The A.F. of L. also discriminated against Asian-American workers. In a booklet written in 1908 Samuel Gompers and other A.F. of L. leaders called for the exclusion of Asians from America by law or, if necessary, "by force of arms."

At this point reporter Ray Stannard Baker visited an Indianapolis hod-carriers union which was controlled by African Americans, though it did include white workers. When some Black members bullied a white worker, other Blacks reported this to the union. Several workmen were warned about their behavior, and one African American left the job when he was fined. The union then finished building a clubhouse for all of its members.

If other unions had wanted to solve the problems of discrimination this easily, the history of American racial relations might have been vastly different. And so might have been the history of American labor.

A Gary, West Virginia, coal mine in 1911. Black and white boys and men mined coal together. The United Mine Workers, one of few unions to admit African Americans, enrolled twenty thousand of all thirty thousand Black people in unions.

GRANVILLE T. WOODS, ELECTRICAL INVENTOR

[Granville T. Woods devised a system of communication between moving trains, but is best known for his invention of an automatic air brake. This article appeared in Cosmopolitan Magazine *in 1895.]*

Mr. Woods has taken out some thirty-five patents in various countries and has many still pending. He is the inventor of a telephone which he sold to the Bell Telephone Company, and of a system of telegraphing from moving railway trains, which was successfully tried on the New Rochelle branch of the New Haven road in 1885. Three years ago, an electric railway system of his invention was operated at Coney Island [New York]. It had neither exposed wires, secondary batteries, nor a slotted way. The current was taken from iron blocks placed at intervals of twelve feet between the rails, in which, by an ingenious arrangement of magnets and switches, the current was turned on to the blocks only as they were successively covered by the cars.

The most remarkable invention of Mr. Woods is for the regulation of electric motors. In almost all applications of electric power it is necessary at times to control the speed of the motors without changing the loads or disturbing the voltage at the source of supply. This has usually been done by introducing large dead resistances in series with the motors. These quickly become hot, and are extremely wasteful of electricity. Mr. Woods has, by his improvements, reduced the size of these resistances, so as to materially lessen the losses by them, and to remove other objectionable features. . . .

Certain features of this invention are now involved in interference proceedings in the United States Patent Office with five rival inventors. Of these, only one had the invention perfected to the extent of using a dynamotor. . . . The proceedings, however, showed that Woods completely developed his invention when there was no prior model to guide him, and when the others were at most only taking the preliminary steps which led them years later in the same direction. . . .

When a boy of ten, Mr. Woods was set to work at bellows blowing in an Australian railroad repair shop. He soon made himself familiar with all its departments, and with his spare earnings engaged private instruction from the master mechanic of the establishment. At the age of sixteen, Woods was brought by his parents to America, and he became a locomotive engineer on the Iron Mountain road, in Missouri. Later, he secured a position as engineer on the British steamer "Ironsides," and in 1880 established a repair shop of his own in Cincinnati.

Mr. Woods has a remarkably thorough knowledge of the intricate mathematics of electricity, and of legal practice respecting inventions. . . .

S. W. Balch, *Cosmopolitan Magazine* 18 (April 1895): 761–62.

A Member of the Edison Pioneers

[*Lewis H. Latimer was the only Black member of the Edison Pioneers, that early group of inventors who worked with Thomas Edison. When Latimer died on 11 December 1928, the Edison Pioneers issued this statement about his life.*]

Mr. Latimer was born at Chelsea, Mass., September 4th, 1848. . . . At the age of 16 he enlisted in the Naval service of the Federal Government, serving as a "landsman" on the U.S.S. *Massasoit* from which he was honorably discharged in 1865, when he returned to Boston and secured employment as an office boy in the office of Messrs. Crosby and Gould, patent solicitors. In this office he became interested in draughting and gradually perfected himself to such a degree as to become their chief draughtsman. . . . It was Mr. Latimer who executed the drawings and assisted in preparing the applications for the telephone patents of Alexander Graham Bell. In 1880 he entered the employ of Hiram S. Maxim, Electrician of the United States Electric Lighting Co., then located at Bridgeport, Connecticut. It was while in this employ that Mr. Latimer successfully produced a method of making carbon filaments for the Maxim electric incandescent lamp, which he patented. His keen perception of the possibilities of the electric light and kindred industries resulted in his being the author of several other inventions. . . . In 1884 he became associated with the Engineering Department of the Edison Electric Light Company. . . .

He was of the colored race, the only one in our organization, and was one of those to respond to the initial call that led to the formation of the Edison Pioneers, January 24, 1918. Broadmindedness, versatility in the accomplishment of things intellectual and cultural, a linguist, a devoted husband and father, all were characteristic of him, and his genial presence will be missed from our gatherings.

Lewis Howard Latimer, "Statement of the Edison Pioneers," 11 December 1928.

A CONGRESSMAN SPEAKS OF BLACK INVENTORS

[*George H. Murray, a former slave, spent two years at South Carolina University, until all people of color were expelled in 1876. In 1892 he was elected to the United States Congress, where he championed the causes of free silver and Black education. On 10 August 1894, he told his white colleagues in the House of Representatives of Black progress in the field of invention.*]

We have proven in almost every line that we are capable of doing what other people can do. We have proven that we can work as much and as well as other people. We have proven that we can learn as well as other people. We have proven that we can fight as well as other people, as was demonstrated in the late [Civil] war. There are still, however, traducers and slanderers of our race who claim that we are not equal to others because we have failed to produce inventors. . . .

. . . I hold in my hand a statement prepared by one of the assistants in the Patent Office, showing the inventions that have been made by colored men within the past few years. . . .

This statement shows that colored men have taken out patents upon almost everything, from a cooking stove to a locomotive. Patents have been granted to colored men for inventions and improvements in the workshop, on the farm, in the factory, on the railroad, in the mine, in almost every department of labor, and some of the most important improvements that go to make up that great motive power of modern industrial machinery, the steam engine, have been produced by colored men. . . .

. . . Mr. Speaker, the colored people of this country want an opportunity to show that the progress, that the civilization which is now admired the world over, that the civilization which is now leading the world, that the civilization which all the nations of the world look up to and imitate—the colored people, I say, want an opportunity to show that they, too, are part and parcel of that great civilization. . . .

Mr. Speaker, in conclusion I ask the liberty [of] appending to my remarks the statistics to which I referred.

There was no objection.

[*Congressman Murray then submitted the list of ninety-two patents. Eight of them were patents which he held.*]

The Congressional Record, 53rd Cong., 2nd sess., 8382.

THE DEMANDS OF FREE LABORERS, 1865

[*Shortly after Emancipation, Blacks in Richmond, Virginia, united to demand better working conditions.*]

Richmond, September 18, 1865 Dear Sirs We the Tobacco mechanicks of this city and Manchester is worked to great disadvantages. In 1858 and 1859 our masters hiered us to the Tobacconist at a price ranging from $150 to $180. The Tobacconist furnished us lodging food and clothing. They gave us tasks to performe. all we made over this task they payed us for. We worked faithful and they paid us faithful. They then gave us $2 to $2.50, and we made double the amount we now make. The Tobacconist held a meeting, and resolved not give more than $1.50 cts. per hundred, which is about one days work—in a week we make 600 lbs apece with a ste[a]mer. This weeks work then at $1.50 amounts to $9—the steamers wages is from $4 to $4.50 cts. which leaves from $5 to $4.50 cents per week about one half what we made when slaves. Now to Rent two small rooms we have to pay from $18 to 20. We see $4.50 cts or $5 will not more then pay Rent say nothing about food clothing medicin Doctor Bills. Tax and Co. They say we will starve through laziness that is not so. But it is true we will starve at our present wages. . . . give us a chance. . . . It is impossible to feed ourselves and family—starvation is Cirten unless a change is brought about.
 Tobacco Factory Mechanicks of Richmond and Manchester

J. T. Trowbridge, *The South* (Hartford, 1866), 230–31.

THE FIRST BLACK NATIONAL LABOR CONVENTION

[*Some two hundred delegates gathered to unite Black labor in 1869. The principal address was made by John M. Langston, who later became a dean at Howard University, and Virginia's only African American congressman.*]

The laboring class of any community, educated and united, constitute its strength. . . .

Among the colored men of this country there is no small amount of industrial capacity, native and acquired. All over the South and among the colored people of the North, workmen in gold, silver, brass, iron, wood, brick, mortar, and the arts, are found doing skillfully and at usual wages the most difficult tasks in their several departments of labor. . . . As illustrating this statement, it may be appropriately mentioned that perhaps the most accomplished gunsmith among the Americans is a black man, an ex-slave of North Carolina. . . . It is perhaps true, too, that the most finished cabinetmaker and blacksmith of our country is of the same class. And it is said to be the fact that the most valuable invention given us by the South, the cotton plough (the patentee of which formerly resided in Mississippi), was the creature of a slave's genius. . . .

Of the pilots and engineers running steamboats on the different rivers of this State, many of the very best are colored men. It is said that the two most trustworthy pilots in North Carolina are freedmen; one of whom is running a steamboat on Cape Fear river, and the other across Albermarle sound, and on the Chowan and Blackwater rivers. The former is paid $15 per month more than any other pilot on the river, because of his superior ability. The engineer on the boat run by this pilot, is also a freedman, and is said to be one of the best in the State.

. . . one of the most interesting sights which it was my good fortune to witness while in the State, was the building of a steamboat on Cape Fear river by a colored shipbuilder, with his gang of colored workmen. . . .

With a voting power under our present and just system of reconstruction of seven hundred and fifty thousand electors, and an actual laboring force of three millions, out of [a Negro population of] four millions and a quarter . . . we are an element in the industry of the country of importance, value, and power.

. . . our mottoes are liberty and labor, enfranchisement and education. The spelling-book and the hoe, the hammer and the vote, the opportunity to work and to rise . . . we ask for ourselves and our children. . . .

Proceedings of the Colored National Labor Convention Held in Washington (Washington, 1870), 16–18.

A BLACK MEMBER OF THE KNIGHTS OF LABOR

[In 1886, a Black member in Texas wrote to Terrence Powderly approving his efforts to build an interracial Knights of Labor.]

Dear Sir and Bro.

Your letter on the color line meets the approval of the colored people in this part of the South . . . and has help[ed] our cause here a great deal.

A good organizer and lectur[er] in this part of the country would increase the membership among the colored in this state and adjoining states supprisingly. Of course the prejudice in the south amonge the majority of the white laborers is quite strong against the Negro, some places in this state the white assembly will not admit the Negro . . . [and] this has given the weak kneed Negro a good chance to leave the order, and those not members to fight it. . . . I have been a faithful member since June 28th 85 I am highly pleased with its principles.

D. H. Black, *letter of 15 October 1886*, Terrence Powderly Papers (*Catholic University of America*).

THE BLACK MECHANICS OF ATLANTA

[*In 1902 seniors from Atlanta University investigated the conditions of the Black artisans of their city. This is the report of H. H. Pace.*]

The first person from whom I obtained any real information was a brickmason who received me cordially and who was inclined to talk. . . . He was a Union man and said that colored brickmasons were well received by the white unions "if they knew their business," although the initiation fee was larger for colored men and the sick and death benefits much smaller for them than for whites. I next saw a machinist who lived in a tumble down house in a rather poor locality. But he said he owned the house. I found a carpenter who was almost totally despondent. He couldn't get work. . . .

The next thing of particular interest to me was a gang of men, white and black, at work upon ten or twelve three-room houses. The person in charge of the work was a colored man who gave his name and address as Tom Carlton, Edgewood, Georgia. He talked to me himself but refused to let me talk to his employees. . . . He said he could join the white union now, they were after him every day to do so. But he wouldn't, because once awhile back when he was working for wages he was refused admission. . . .

Of the whole number questioned . . . all had worked at some time or did work sometimes with whites in the same work. The painters said that the white painters were not very friendly disposed toward them, and did not allow them to join their union under any circumstances. The plumbers were under somewhat the same ban.

Not one of the artisans in my territory had been to a trade school. Nearly every one simply "worked awhile under a first-class brickmason" or "carpenter," etc. Several had learned their trades during slavery and followed them ever since. . . . None answered "Yes" to the question of any "higher training."

The most interesting bit of information in regard to color discrimination was obtained from a colored fireman on the Southern Railway. He said the Company refused to sign a contract and wage scale with his union but did sign one with the white union. Moreover, he said:

If I take a train from here to Greenville, S.C., I get for that trip $2.60, the white engineer gets $6.00. But if that same train had the same engineer and a *white* fireman, the engineer would get his $6.00 just the same but the fireman would get $3.25. He gets 65 cts. more for doing the same work I do. . . .

W. E. Burghardt Du Bois, ed., *The Negro Artisan* (Atlanta, 1902), 115.

THE NATIONAL NEGRO BUSINESS LEAGUE

[*In 1900 Booker T. Washington, noting the rise of African American businesses and wishing to unite them for mutual gain, organized the National Negro Business League. In five years it had more than one hundred chapters. In 1905 the Colorado Springs, Colorado, chapter, spoke of its goals.*]

Whereas, we believe that the time has come for the colored people to enter more largely into business pursuits by means of individual as well as co-operative efforts as the surest and most speedy way to gain earnings from invested capital, and to afford employment for our race, and for the further purpose of stimulating our people in this community to engage in such industrial pursuits as may be practical and possible, therefore be it

Resolved, That we form a local business league . . . and invite the cooperation of all who desire to better the material condition of our people in this city.

Resolved, That we take steps to present the wonderful undeveloped agricultural and mineral resources of Colorado to desirable colored citizens who may be induced to settle in this state, bring with them capital, brains and pluck for the purpose of seeking permanent homes and helping to develop the natural resources of this state.

Newspaper clipping, *Booker T. Washington Papers* (Washington: Library of Congress Manuscript Collection), Box 847.

COMBATTING SEGREGATED STREETCARS

[*As Southern cities segregated streetcars, Blacks in Austin, Houston, Savannah, and New Orleans tried to organize their own transportation system. "Jim Crow" streetcar law in New Orleans in 1902 gave impetus to Black protest.*]

. . . An association of women attached to the Masonic Order proposed to run bus lines to accommodate Negro passengers, and issued a call to the fifty or more Negro organizations in New Orleans to send representatives to a meeting at which the question would be considered. Unfeasible as the scheme was, it nevertheless appealed strongly to the Negroes, and at the meetings representatives from nearly all the organizations were present.

It was apparent from the discussions that the "ruling passion" back of it all was a sense of deep humiliation that Negroes as a race should be considered unworthy to ride in conveyances with white people. The railway companies had announced their intention of putting wire screens in every car, and to have Negroes occupy the rear seats. This idea of sitting behind screens, as if they were wild or obnoxious animals, was another fact contributing to their mortification. Many of them, it was said, took pride in keeping clean, in wearing good clothes, and in behaving well, as much because they could feel at ease in decent company as because it gave them other personal satisfaction. To exclude such Negroes from compartments occupied by white people would, they said, be as unjust as it would be to force them to sit in compartments with unworthy representatives of their own race, whom they, as much as the white people, despised. It would be equally unjust to admit obnoxious white people to white compartments and exclude respectable Negroes from enjoying the same privilege.

Probably the next most pronounced sentiment of the meetings was a demand for Negroes to support one another in business enterprises. To the Negroes, the strongest argument in favor of a bus line was the fact that it would be a Negro enterprise supported by Negro capital and conducted for the general benefit of the race in New Orleans. Out of this assertion grew many an urgent appeal for Negroes to acquire property and contribute to the general welfare of other Negroes by patronizing them in their businesses. This sentiment is growing stronger and stronger every day, and the results of it are more and more apparent. Negroes no longer wish to send their children to white teachers; Negro patients demand the services of Negro physicians; drugstores, saloons, grocery-stores, coal and wood shops—in fact, almost every retail business in the city—are conducted on a small scale by Negroes, and patronized almost exclusively by members of that race.

Of course the plan to establish a bus line failed. Opposition to it grew as its impracticable features became known, and at the third or fourth meeting nothing more was heard of the idea. The prevailing statement then was that the meeting was for the purpose of devising means to better the Negro's condition in New Orleans. . . .

Several prominent Negroes have refused to be seen on a "Jim Crow" car. They prefer to walk. Others ride on the cars, but stand on the platforms rather than be forced to sit behind the screens. . . .

A. R. Holcombe, "The Separate Street-Car Law in New Orleans," *Outlook* (29 November 1902), 746–47.

13 THE LAST FRONTIER

LIFE IN THE WEST was dangerous until settlers filled in the last open spaces and law and order came to stay. Mobs calling themselves vigilantes often made laws and executed men they decided were guilty of crimes. Federal troops and marshals did their best to keep the peace, suppress the Indians, and prevent the outlaws from killing or terrorizing the law-abiding settlers who poured into the territories.

Many African Americans were among the farmers and riders of the last frontier. On average, a typical trail crew of eleven that drove cattle up the Chisholm Trail to Kansas after the Civil War included two or three Black cowboys. An estimated 8,000 African Americans were among the estimated 35,000 cowboys. Some had come West as slaves and were cowboys before they became free men. Thousands of others headed West after emancipation, seeking a new and free life where skill would count more than skin color. Some came to live by the law; others rode in to break it.

Black and white cowboys were part of the gun-twirling mayhem of Dodge City and Abilene. The first man shot in Dodge was a cowboy named Tex, an innocent bystander to a fight—and he was an African American. The first man arrested in Abilene was not innocent—and he was a Black man. His Black and white trail crew buddies were so infuriated by his arrest that they shot up the town and staged Abilene's first jailbreak to rescue him.

The Shores family, homesteaders in Custer County, Nebraska, in 1887.

Edwin P. McCabe. After being elected state auditor of Kansas, he left for Oklahoma to create a Black state. Thousands of African Americans followed him, but the effort failed.

Britton Johnson, a tall former slave, was known far and wide in Texas for his physical strength and courage and, mainly, for being one of the best shots on the Texas frontier. In 1864 a Comanche raiding party attacked his settlement, killing Johnson's young son and several other people. The Comanche carried off his wife, his three other children, and several white settlers. Johnson's plan for reuniting his family called for him to enter the Indian camp and gain their confidence by volunteering as a warrior.

Johnson was accepted by the Comanche, since they needed new warriors. One night he helped his wife, children, and the white prisoners escape. His trouble with the Comanche, however, did not end there.

In 1871 Johnson and a few other Black cowhands were attacked by twenty-five Comanche on the Texas plains. Johnson directed the men to kill their horses and use their bodies as breastworks. But the Indians repeatedly rode through the cowboys' defenses and picked the men off one by one. When Johnson found that he was the only one still alive, he gathered all the guns and loaded them during lulls in the battle so that he could pour a rapid fire into the attacking men. He faced charge after charge before he was finally cut down. A settler who found his body counted 173 shells near it.

Most of those who came West had neither the skill nor the bravery of Britton Johnson. Some were just simple people looking for a home and good farming land which they could call their own. Under the guidance of Edwin P. McCabe, tens of thousands of people of color arrived in Oklahoma, hoping to turn it into a refuge from Southern violence. Between 1890 and 1910 thirty all-Black towns sprouted in Oklahoma. Under the leadership of Black women schools were established and illiteracy was virtually abolished in a few years.

The rough life of the West created a number of wild men who lived by their own law. One of these was a former slave called Nat Love, better known as "Deadwood Dick." He claimed that he had ridden with Billy the Kid and Frank and Jesse James and that he had known Buffalo Bill and Bat Masterson.

In his 1907 autobiography, Nat Love wrote of his many adventures on the frontier. He was adopted by Indians, rode a hundred miles in twelve hours on an unsaddled horse, and tried to rope and steal a United States Army cannon. His good friend Bat Masterson got him out of that scrape. Love told how he rode into a Mexican saloon and ordered two drinks—one for him and one for his horse.

Nat Love won the title of "Deadwood Dick" in an 1876 rodeo.

Whether in town or out on the range, Love lived a life of wild fun and had amazingly good luck. "While our money lasted," he wrote of a trip into Dodge City, "we could certainly enjoy ourselves in dancing, drinking, and shooting up the town." Even the dangers of the plains were fun to him. "Horses were shot from under me, men killed around me, but always I escaped with a trifling wound at the worst."

In 1890, the year the United States Census showed that the last frontier had closed, Nat Love left the wild life of the cowboy for a peaceful berth on the railroad—as a Pullman porter. He did not see the "Iron Horse" as his enemy, or regret leaving the range.

It would be incorrect to conclude from the story of Nat Love's life that cowboys were always lucky or accurate shots. In 1869 a Black cowboy

Black, white, and red marshalls tried to keep the peace in Oklahoma. (From the left) Amos Maytubby (Indian), Zeke Miller (white), Neely Factor and Bob Fortune (African Americans).

named Ben and his white buddies went after a group of Indians who had stolen their horses. Ben was so angry that he charged alone into their village and shot it out with the man mounted on his horse. Only Ben's horse was killed.

The West had its share of men who killed neither by accident nor as a result of a fight. They were the desperadoes who robbed banks and trains, or jumped claims, or shot people down in cold blood. Some of these, such as Billy the Kid and Cherokee Bill, were mass murderers. Cherokee Bill was similar to Billy the Kid in almost everything but skin color. Both young men killed without regard to whether or not their victims were armed. Both died before they reached the age of twenty-one. Cherokee Bill told the happy crowd that turned out to see him swing at the end of a rope that he had no last words. He said that he had come to die for his crimes and not to make a speech.

However, most African American cowhands were ordinary, hard-working men who earned "$30 a month and grub."

Those Who Tamed the West

For many years the uneasy peace in the Western territories was kept by the United States Army, which included Black units—the Ninth and Tenth cavalries and the Twenty-fourth and Twenty-fifth infantries. They were stationed at various times from the Rio Grande to the Canadian border. They fought bandits as well as Apaches, Sioux, and Comanche. They took the field against Billy the Kid, Geronimo, and Crazy Horse. During the In-

Bill Picket invented the cowboy sport of "bulldogging," which involves leaping from a horse onto the horns of a steer and wrestling the beast to the ground. His assistants included Tom Mix and Will Rogers.

10TH CAVALRY

Tenth Cavalry Regimental Crest.

Soldiers of the Twenty-fourth Infantry.

Ninth Cavalry troops ride to the rescue in a sketch by the noted artist Frederick Remington. These Buffalo Soldiers had a reputation for arriving just in the nick of time to rescue settlers or other soldiers.

Henry O. Flipper, first African American graduate of West Point.

dian wars, fourteen of these Black soldiers won the nation's highest military decoration, the Congressional Medal of Honor.

The troopers of the Ninth and Tenth cavalries constituted a fifth of all the United States mounted troops assigned to protect the frontier. They were commanded by white officers who considered the assignment a professional honor. Lieutenant John J. Pershing led the Tenth in Montana, in the charge up San Juan Hill, in the Philippines, and during the punitive expedition into Mexico in 1916—and was nicknamed "Blackjack" Pershing. "We officers of the Tenth Cavalry," recalled the tough, emotionless Pershing, "could have taken our black heroes in our arms."

Isaiah Dorman rode into fame and death with General George Custer at the Little Big Horn. For many years Dorman had served as a courier for the War Department in the Dakota territory. In May of 1876 General Custer requested that Dorman be assigned to his command "and report for duty to accompany the expedition as Interpreter" into Montana. Dorman was part Sioux, which explains his ability to serve as interpreter.

On June 25 and 26 Dorman was among the 264 men who fought and died with Custer. For reasons never made clear, the Sioux did not scalp and mutilate Dorman as they did the white soldiers.

During the period of Reconstruction and extending into the 1890s, Black Texans were among those elected to the state legislature. They worked to protect cattlemen and build a more prosperous state. In 1870 a former slave named Richard Allen devised the Texas pension law for veter-

The Seminole Negro Indian Scouts, hardest-hitting United States Army unit of the 1870s, never lost a man in battle or had one seriously wounded. Four earned the Congressional Medal of Honor.

A Tenth Cavalryman sketch by Frederick Remington. Indians called the cavalrymen "Buffalo Soldiers"— after an animal they considered sacred.

ans. As chairman of the Committee on Roads and Bridges of the Texas legislature, Representative Allen helped link his vast state with a system of bridges and roads.

African American legislator Alexander Asberry sponsored a law to protect the grazing herds of cattle by holding the railroads responsible for cattle run down by their trains.

Texas State Senator Matt Gaines also worked hard. He proposed granting tax exemptions to libraries, schools, and churches. Concerned with the protection of the unfortunate, he sought to have the state assume responsibility for its mentally ill. Gaines and the other African American legislators battled without success against the laws that segregated students by race in Texas schools.

Helping Native Americans

In the days when white leaders said "the only good Indian is a dead Indian," the Black college at Hampton was the first to open its doors, in 1879, to more than a hundred Native Americans. An eager young ex-slave,

Black students and Indian students at Hampton Institute.

Indian orchestra at Hampton College, 1900. Acceptance of Indians at Hampton came during the period when most whites felt "the only good Indian is a dead Indian." (Collection, The Museum of Modern Art, New York. Gift of Lincoln Kirstein.)

Booker T. Washington, was placed in charge of this unique experiment to prove that Indians could and should be educated. When they finally gave up their blankets, long hair, and peace pipes for books, workshops, and the knowledge the college offered them, the experiment was called a success.

When Mr. Washington took one of his Native American students to the nation's capital, he found a strange color line. Aboard the steamboat the Indian was admitted to the dining room, while he was not. And in Washington a hotel manager accepted the pupil but not the teacher.

The "Exodus of 1879"

In 1879 African American women were the main organizers of a vast migration of Southern Blacks to the West. This "Exodus of 1879" was one of the most dramatic invasions of settlers that the West has ever known. Thousands upon thousands of poor Black farmers organized committees,

Exodus leader Benjamin "Pap" Singleton.

contributed their savings, and hired agents to arrange the trip West. In torn and tattered clothing, with their few belongings on their backs, they poured into Kansas. They were searching for liberty and opportunity and fleeing a brutal oppression. One settler told a congressional investigating committee why they left: "The whole South—every State in the South—had got into the hands of the very men that held us as slaves. . . . We said there was no hope for us and we better go."

This ragged band often found a helping hand. The governor of Kansas received a delegation of one hundred in 1879 and told them what they could expect by way of help in his state. A Freedman's Relief Association was organized. An eyewitness reported that "temporary shelter was speedily provided for them; food and the facilities for cooking it were furnished them in ample measure." Many whites in Kansas provided the "Exodusters" with jobs and homes.

"Exodusters" walking to Kansas.

Not all of the "Exodusters" were warmly welcomed into communities. A group of 150 from Mississippi was driven out of Lincoln, Nebraska. In Denver, Colorado, those who arrived "found that the owners of houses would not rent to them." But both prominent African Americans of the town and sympathetic whites sold them small houses.

The refugees from the South who poured into Nebraska built a number of small communities. But earlier, in 1867, when the state joined the Union, Black people were told to stay away from the polls in Nebraska City and were threatened with guns and knives when they came to vote in Omaha. By the 1880s, however, African Americans were among those graduating from Nebraska high schools and serving in the state legislature. David Patrick of Aurora carried the mail by Pony Express to Fort Kearny, and Tom Cunningham was a police officer in Lincoln. Dr. M. O. Ricketts, an ex-slave, graduated with honors from the University of Nebraska College of Medicine in 1884. The doctor was twice elected to the state legislature and five other African Americans followed in his footsteps to the state house.

Ex-slave Barney Ford ran the Inter-Ocean Hotel in Cheyenne, Wyoming. It catered to all—from presidents to prospectors.

African Americans contributed to the growth of the West throughout its last frontier days. A crew of three hundred Black laborers worked on the Union Pacific Railroad along with Irish, German, and Chinese laborers. Emmett J. Scott of Houston published the *Texas Freeman,* and W. J. Hardin served in the Wyoming legislature. Charles Pettit served as a United States deputy marshal in Wichita, Kansas. Black frontier women ran laundries, hotels, farms, and carting firms. They taught school, scrubbed floors, wrote for newspapers, and herded cattle. Their frontier grit helped transform sparsely settled lands into thriving, populous states. In Cascade, Montana, Mary Fields delivered the U.S. mail and drove a stagecoach. In Denver, Colorado, the funeral of pioneer Clara Brown, who began a church, was attended by the governor and mayor.

A Black cowboy named Williams taught Theodore Roosevelt how to break in a horse, while another named Clay taught comedian Will Rogers the art of roping. Others, far too numerous to mention, helped tame the West and found there a greater measure of equality than in the places from which they had come.

The Farmers' Rebellion

The prosperity which the Civil War brought to farmers began to end with the surrender of General Robert E. Lee. The farmers' economic troubles went from bad to worse as they waited for prices to rise. Debts came due, railroads and banks raised their rates, and as prices dropped, farmers obtained the money which they so desperately needed by taking out mortgages on their homesteads. In Kansas the number of mortgages increased 300 percent in the seven years following 1880. And the seven-year period was capped with the most devastating winter and broiling summer in the history of the Great Plains. The depressions of 1873 and 1893 drove the farmers even closer to desperation as they saw their friends and neighbors lose their homes and land to creditors.

Convict road gangs in North Carolina, 1910. The wagons were homes for Black convicts who were moved from place to place to labor for the state. Bloodhounds, whips, and guns were part of the control system over the prisoners.

In the South cotton prices began a rapid decline after the war. By 1868 the price of cotton had fallen from one dollar a pound to twenty-five cents. By 1894 the price was down to five cents.

Throughout the South, the sharecropping system grew. Poor whites and Blacks worked a landlord's acreage for a part of the crop. The landlord kept the records of sharecropper expenses and often falsified the record to keep them in never-ending debt. The average sharecropper, white or Black, had little chance before the law. But Black sharecroppers had even less chance than whites, because they had to face white sheriffs, judges, and juries.

Five out of six African Americans lived under a system of peonage. One of its victims told how it worked:

> I am not an educated man. I will give you the peonage system as it is practiced here in the name of the law.
>
> If a colored man is arrested here and hasn't any money, whether he is guilty or not, he has to pay just the same. A man of color is never tried in this country. It is simply a farce. Everything is fixed before he enters the courtroom. I will give you an illustration of how it is done:
>
> I was brought in a prisoner, to go through the farce of being tried. The whole of my fine may amount to fifty dollars. A kindly appearing man will come up and pay my fine and take me to his farm to allow me to work it out. At the end of the month I find that I owe him more than I did when I went there. The debt is increased year in and year out. You would ask, "How is that?" It is simply that he is charging you more for your board, lodging, and washing than they allow you for your work, and you can't help yourself either . . . because you are still a prisoner. . . .
>
> One word more about peonage. The court and the man you work for are always partners. One makes the fine and the other one works you and holds you, and if you leave you are tracked with bloodhounds and brought back.

Black Southern families were largely confined to laboring in the cotton fields.

The Populists

During the post–Civil War years farmers united to fight common enemies. At first they formed separate groups, as whites feared that advances for African Americans would be at their expense. A "Colored Farmers' Alliance" reached a million members by 1890. That year the white Farmers' Alliance invited the Blacks to a joint meeting in Florida. A Kansas farmer reported "the former slave owner and the former slave shook hands warmly."

From Kansas, south to the Rio Grande, Blacks and whites responded to the call of the People's or Populist party. Black Populists in Texas served on the party's executive committee from 1891 to 1900. One reported that "colored people are coming into the new party in squads and companies. They have colored third-party speakers and are organizing colored clubs." A Black delegate told the Texas Populist convention of 1892, "I am an emancipated slave of this state" and "my interest is yours and yours mine."

That same year ninety-two Black delegates attended the Populist National Convention. Populist Ignatius Donnelly predicted the party's victories "would wipe out the color line in the South."

One important Populist contribution to American democracy was its ability to unite farmers in the South. The Populist candidate for president in 1892, James B. Weaver, rode into Raleigh, North Carolina, in a parade of 350 Black and white horsemen. Tom Watson, a white Georgia congressman, told Black Southern farmers, "You are kept apart that you may be separately fleeced of your earnings. You are made to hate each other because upon that hatred is rested the keystone of the financial despotism which enslaves you both." An African American preacher named H. S. Doyle made sixty-three speeches for Watson despite threats against his life. In one town armed white farmers massed to protect Doyle from violence.

The Populists specifically appealed to Black voters by a willingness to nominate African American candidates and demands for a secret ballot and an end to the convict-lease system. The secret ballot would protect Black voters from intimidation by employers or other whites. The convict-lease system made slaves of Black workers, of which there were ten to every white victim of this forced-labor device.

The Populist convention of 1896 bitterly debated the idea of merging with the Democrats behind William Jennings Bryan. Reporter Henry Demarest Lloyd wrote, "The most eloquent speeches made were those of the whites and blacks explaining to the convention what the rule of the Democrats meant in the South." An African American delegate from Georgia, Lloyd reported, "told how the People's Party alone gave full fel-

Congressman George Henry White, who sponsored America's first antilynching bill, served North Carolina from 1897 to 1901. He spoke for equal rights during a time of maximum oppression.

lowship to his race, when it had been abandoned by the Republicans and cheated and betrayed by the Democrats." While the Populists voted to support Bryan for president, they nominated Tom Watson for vice president. Seconding Watson's nomination, a Black delegate said, "He has made it possible for the Black man to vote according to his conscience in Georgia." But with the defeat of the Populists and Democrats by Republican William McKinley, the Populist party began to decline.

The most noted African American politician during the Populist era was George H. White, a college graduate who held law degrees from two universities. This former slave served six years in the North Carolina legislature and eight years as a state prosecuting attorney. In 1896 and in 1898 voters elected him to Congress despite widespread racist violence.

In Congress and out Representative White sought to advance the industrial and agricultural interests of his state. As congressional interest turned to Cuba and the war with Spain, he warned his colleagues "the nation must care for those at home as well as abroad." The problem of racial injustice, he told Congress, must be met. "You will have to meet it. You have got this problem to settle, and the sooner it is settled the better it will be for all concerned. I speak this in all charity. I speak this with no hostility."

At every opportunity White denounced discrimination "by constitutional amendment and State legislation" or "by cold-blooded fraud and intimidation." He pointedly asked Congress, "How long will you sit in your seats and hear and see the principles that underlie the foundations of this Government sapped away little by little?"

Representative White was known for his pointed speeches and biting humor. The only African American in Congress for two terms, White never forgot that he spoke "as the sole representative for nine million people." He attacked every form of discrimination from racist jokes to the mounting number of lynchings. "We ask and expect a chance in legislation, and we will be content with nothing else," he told Congress, and insisted that the constitutional amendments protecting equal rights be enforced. On 20 January 1900, he introduced the first congressional bill to make lynching a federal crime. Petitions poured into White's office from all over the country supporting his bill, but it never came to a vote.

In his last speech, Representative White reminded Congress that his antilynching bill "still sweetly sleeps" in the Judiciary Committee. He entered a last plea for "the life, the liberty, the future happiness" of his people. African Americans were, he reminded all, "a rising people" and would in time send others to the United States Congress.

Violence and intimidation were the main methods used to drive the remaining Black Populists out of their offices. In North Carolina, where the Populist campaigns had led to the election of many African Americans, one newspaper screamed in 1898 about "NEGRO CONGRESSMEN, NEGRO SOLICITORS, NEGRO REVENUE OFFICERS, NEGRO COLLECTORS OF CUSTOMS, NEGROES in charge of white institutions . . ." "It is time for the shotgun to play a part, and an active one in the elections," said an opponent of equality. A bloody riot in Wilmington, North Carolina, drove out Black officeholders and many citizens. But the Wilmington riot was not the final stage of the "white supremacy" campaign. In 1900 the North Carolina constitution was amended to include a poll tax, a literacy test, and a "grandfather clause" that denied the suffrage to people of color.

The defeat of the Populists led to a systematic repression of the South's Black population. From 1890 to 1910 Southern states restricted the right to vote to whites and during this period segregation laws were passed. Many white Populists, such as Tom Watson, turned racist with a fury. Watson blamed Blacks for Populist defeats and backed every effort to deprive them of the right to vote. Watson stayed on in politics, using his bigotry to attract the votes of fellow white Georgians. His hate campaign was extended to Catholics and Jews. Early in the twentieth century, Watson called Catholic priests "murderers" and cheered a Georgia mob which had lynched an innocent Jewish man. By the time Watson died in 1922, he was a bitter racist and a United States senator from Georgia. The Ku Klux Klan sent an eight-foot cross of roses to his funeral.

The Farmers' Scientist

The greatest single gift to Southern agriculture after the Civil War came from the gentle hands of George Washington Carver. A slave boy who had once been exchanged for a horse, Dr. Carver gained national fame because of his scientific research at Tuskegee Institute.

After long years of experimentation, Dr. Carver found more than 350 uses for the Southern crops of peanuts, sweet potatoes, and pecans. He traveled through the Alabama countryside to bring his knowledge to farmers of both races. The crown prince of Sweden spent three weeks at the side of the Tuskegee scientist, watching him make things grow and discovering new ways of making them more useful. Henry Ford provided a laboratory in which Carver might expand his work. His students remember the great scientist as a kindly teacher who "would never embarrass you or get angry in public." Many years before Dr. Martin Luther King, Jr., asked his followers to meet hatred with love, Dr. Carver said, "no man can drag me down so low as to make me hate him."

For many years Dr. Carver worked for the United States government. At one time before Congress he was given fifteen minutes to explain his work, for no one thought that talk about peanuts or sweet potatoes need take any longer. His talk so aroused the interest of the committee that he was given almost an hour to finish. His findings, published by the U.S. Department of Agriculture, benefited farmers everywhere.

Dr. George Washington Carver and students in his Tuskegee laboratory.

Dr. Carver at work in his laboratory in the 1940s.

When Dr. Carver died in 1943, President Franklin D. Roosevelt and Vice President Henry A. Wallace led the nation in paying respect to the great scientist.

NAT LOVE, "DEADWOOD DICK," COWBOY

[*Nat Love, fifteen years old and a former slave, rode into the West seeking adventure, found it, and wrote about it in* The Life and Adventures of Nat Love, *published in 1907. His boastful tales are as believable as those told by Davy Crockett, Daniel Boone, Jim Beckwourth, and earlier Western hands and tall-tale spinners. Nat Love tells how he won the title of "Deadwood Dick" on 4 July 1876, in Deadwood City.*]

. . . Our trail boss was chosen to pick out the mustangs from a herd of wild horses just off the range, and he picked out twelve of the most wild and vicious horses that he could find.

The conditions of the contest were that each of us who were mounted was to rope, throw, tie, bridle and saddle, and mount the particular horse picked for us in the shortest time possible. The man accomplishing the feat in the quickest time [was] to be declared the winner.

It seems to me that the horse chosen for me was the most vicious of the lot. Everything being in readiness, the "45" cracked and we all sprang forward together, each of us making for our particular mustang.

I roped, threw, tied, bridled, saddled, and mounted my mustang in exactly nine minutes from the crack of the gun. The time of the next nearest competitor was twelve minutes and thirty seconds. This gave me the record and championship of the West, which I held up to the time I quit the business in 1890, and my record has never been beaten. It is worthy of passing remark that I never had a horse pitch with me so much as that mustang, but I never stopped sticking my spurs in him and using my quirt on his flanks until I proved his master. Right there the assembled crowd named me Deadwood Dick and proclaimed me champion roper of the western cattle country.

Nat Love, *The Life and Adventures of Nat Love, by Himself* (Los Angeles, 1907), 73, 93.

FIGHTING OFF A BANDIT AMBUSH

[*The Arizona sun beat down on a small detachment of the Twenty-fourth Infantry and Ninth Cavalry as they moved across the plains from Fort Grant to Fort Thomas guarding the army paymaster, Wham, and his strongbox. Outlaws had placed a boulder in their path and waited in ambush. The paymaster describes what happened when the soldiers investigated the boulder blocking the road.*]

They were nearly all at the boulder when a signal shot was fired from the ledge of rocks about fifty feet above to the right, which was instantly followed by a volley, believed by myself and the entire party to be fifteen or twenty shots.

A sharp, short fight, lasting something over thirty minutes, ensued during which time the . . . officers and privates, eight of whom were wounded, two being shot twice, behaved in the most courageous and heroic manner. . . .

Sergeant Brown, though shot through the abdomen did not quit the field until again wounded, this time through the arm.

Private Burge who was to my immediate right, received a bad wound in the hand, but gallantly held his post, resting his rifle on his fore-arm and continuing to fire with much coolness, until shot through the thigh and twice through the hat.

Private Arrington was shot through the shoulder, while fighting from this same position.

Privates Hams, Wheeler, and Harrison were also wounded, to my immediate left, while bravely doing their duty under a murderous cross-fire. . . .

The brigands fought from six well-constructed stone forts; the arrangements seemed thorough, the surprise complete. . . .

I was a soldier in Grant's old regiment, and during the entire war it was justly proud of its record of sixteen battles and of the reflected glory of its old Colonel, the "Great Commander," but I never witnessed better courage or better fighting than shown by these colored soldiers, on May 11, 1889, as the bullet marks on the robber positions to-day abundantly attest.

"Letter of J. W. Wham," *Medal of Honor File of Sergeant Benjamin Brown* (Washington: War Records Office, National Archives, 1889).

Senator Bruce Demands Justice for Indians

[*B. K. Bruce escaped from slavery during the Civil War and moved to Mississippi during Reconstruction. He became a teacher and a wealthy landowner, entered politics, and was elected to the United States Senate in 1874. His long fight for justice included a defense of open immigration and of Indian rights. During a Senate debate on 7 April 1880, Bruce took the floor to denounce the U.S. policy "that has kept the Indian a fugitive and a vagabond, that has bred discontent, suspicion, and hatred in the mind of the red man. . . ."*]

Our Indian policy and administration seem to me to have been inspired and controlled by a stern selfishness, with a few honorable exceptions. Indian treaties have generally been made as the condition and instrument of acquiring the valuable territory occupied by the several Indian nations, and have been changed and revised from time to time as it became desirable that the steadily growing, irrepressible white races should secure more room for their growth and more lands for their occupancy; and wars, bounties, and beads have been used . . . for the purpose of temporary peace and security for the whites, and as the preliminary to further aggressions upon the red man's lands, with the ultimate view of his expulsion and extinction from the continent. . . .

Now, sir, the Indian is a physical force; a half million of vigorous, physical, intellectual agents ready for the plastic hand of Christian civilization, living in a country possessing empires of untilled and uninhabited lands. The Indian tribes, viewed from this utilitarian standpoint, are worth preservation, conservation, utilization, and civilization, and I believe that we have reached a period when the public sentiment of the country demands such a modification in the Indian policy, in its purposes, and in its methods, as shall save and not destroy these people.

The Congressional Record, 46th Cong., 2nd sess., 2195–96.

PRIVATE HENRY JOHNSON'S STORY

[*Private Henry Johnson describes an action which won him the Congressional Medal of Honor at Milk River, Colorado, in October 1879.*]

[I] was on guard as Sergeant of the Guard, on or about the day and night of October 5th 1879, during which time there was almost continual firing from the enemy [Ute Indians] upon our men; that we had fortified ourselves into small pits known as rifle pits, and that the Indians outnumbered the soldiers by at least ten to one.

During the morning of the date above mentioned, [I] came out of the pit in which [I] had been fortified and went over to other pits to give necessary instruction to some of the members of [my] guard, during which time [I] was exposed to the fire from the Indians who were very near and at easy range of [me].

Some of Major Thornburg's men had been wounded, and were suffering from want of water, and that [I] was one of the party of men who formed a skirmish line by order of Capt. F. Dodge 9th Cavalry and fought their way back to the Creek (Milk River) for water for the wounded and themselves.

Deposition of Henry Johnson, Troop K, 9th Cavalry, 14 August 1890 (Washington: National Archives, War Records Office).

THE TENTH CAVALRY WITHOUT WATER

[*Lieutenant Charles L. Cooper of the Tenth Cavalry describes his unit's eighty-six-hour period without water on the Staked Plains of Texas.*]

[After several days of trailing a group of Indians the troops were] lost on the Staked Plains, without water and no prospects of getting any, as we did not know which way to go for it, and from our experience we knew the greater part of the country was "dry as a bone."

In the meantime our men had been dropping from their horses with exhaustion, as we had been nearly two days without water, and we were retarded greatly in endeavoring to keep the men together. . . . [By the next day] the men were almost completely used up, and the captain and I were not much better. Our men had dropped back, one by one, unable to keep up with us; their tongues and throats were swollen, and they were unable even to swallow their saliva—in fact, they had no saliva to swallow, that is if I judge of their condition from my own. My tongue and throat were so dry that when I put a few morsels of brown sugar, that I found in my pocket, into my mouth, I was unable to dissolve it in order to swallow it. During this time while lying on the ground, one of my private horses showed signs of exhaustion, staggered, and fell; so in order to relieve the men, I had his throat cut, and the blood distributed among them. The captain and I drank heartily of the steaming blood. . . .

This, our fourth day without water, was dreadful. . . . Men gasping in death around us; horses falling dead to the right and left; the crazed survivors of our men fighting each his neighbor for the blood of the horses. . . . We left camp at 8 o'clock at night, and travelled until about 3 the next morning. . . . The captain and I travelled some five miles . . . and finally reached Double Lake, completely exhausted. We found there six of the men of our company, whom we had missed, and immediately started them out with canteens of water for their suffering comrades. Our loss on the trip was four men died from thirst [out of 61]. . . .

The Daily Tribune, 8 September 1877 (Washington: National Archives, War Research Office).

A New Life in Leavenworth, Kansas

[In 1864 H. C. Bruce and his fiancée armed themselves and fled slavery in Missouri for the West. Bruce tells how they found life in Kansas.]

On March 31, 1864, I landed at Leavenworth, Kansas, with my intended wife, without a change of clothing and with only five dollars in cash, two of which I gave to Rev. John Turner, Pastor of the A.M.E. [African Methodist Episcopal] Church, who united us in marriage in his parlor that day. . . . The next day I was out hunting for work, which I obtained with a brick contractor, at two dollars and seventy-five cents per day. . . .

I remember the bitter feeling existing between the Irish and the Colored laborers in Leavenworth, Kansas, which had its beginning about the close of the war. They had several little conflicts, and on one occasion the civil authorities interfered to prevent bloodshed.

I recall an instance when the Colored people had been informed that the Irish were intent on surrounding the Baptist Church, corner Third and Kiowa streets, to "clane the nagurs out," on Sunday night. The Colored people prepared to meet them, by selecting Fenton Burrell as captain, and secreting nearly fifty armed men in a vacant lot in the rear of the church, to await the appearance of the Irish. Soon a squad of them came up Third street to within a hundred yards of the church, but after halting a few minutes marched back and dispersed. I learned afterwards that Col. D. R. Anthony, a recognized friend of both races, went in person to the leaders and informed them of the reception they would receive if they proceeded further, and advised them to disperse and go home, which they did.

H. C. Bruce, *The New Man* (York, Pa., 1895), 112, 119–20.

A SOUTHERN EXODUS REACHES KANSAS

[*In 1879 a vast migration of Southern African Americans, fleeing cruel oppression, poured into Kansas. An eyewitness describes the scene.*]

One morning in April, 1879, a Missouri steamboat arrived at Wyandotte, Kansas, and discharged a load of colored men, women and children, with divers barrels, boxes, and bundles of household effects. It was a novel, picturesque, pathetic sight. They were of all ages and sizes . . . ; their garments were incredibly patched and tattered, stretched, and uncertain; . . . and there was not probably a dollar in money in the pockets of the entire party. The wind was eager, and they stood upon the wharf shivering. . . . They looked like persons coming out of a dream. And, indeed, such they were . . . for this was the advance guard of the Exodus.

Soon other and similar parties came by the same route, and still others, until, within a fortnight, a thousand or more of them were gathered there at the gateway of Kansas—all poor, some sick, and none with a plan of future action. . . .

The case was one to appeal with force to popular sympathy. . . . So temporary shelter was speedily provided for them; food and facilities for cooking it were furnished them in ample measure. . . . Then came more of them. The tide swelled daily. . . .

The closing autumn found at least 15,000 of these colored immigrants in Kansas. Such of them as had arrived early in the spring had been enabled to do something toward getting a start, and the thriftier and more capable ones had made homestead-entries and contrived, with timely aid, to build cabins; in some cases, small crops of corn and garden vegetables were raised. . . .

. . . Numerous cabins of stone and sod were constructed while the cold season lasted; . . . in many cases, the women went to the towns and took in washing, or worked as house-servants . . . while the men were doing the building. Those who could find employment on the farms about their "claims", worked willingly and for small wages, and in this way supported their families, and procured now and then a calf, a pig, or a little poultry; others obtained places on the railroads, in the coal-mines, and on the public works at Topeka. Such as got work at any price, did not ask assistance; those who were compelled to apply for aid did it slowly, as a rule, and rarely came a second time. Not a single colored tramp was seen in Kansas all winter; and only one colored person was convicted of any crime. . . .

. . . their savings are not remarkable, to be sure, but they are creditable, and not to be lightly passed over. The wonder is that they have anything whatever to show for . . . twelve months of hand-to-mouth hardship and embarrassment.

Henry King, "A Year of the Exodus in Kansas," *Scribner's Monthly* 8 (June 1880), 211–25.

COUNTING THE BLACK VOTE

[Black men continued to vote after Reconstruction despite violence and fraud.]

In Southern Alabama, prominent leaders in democratic [party] politics said that in the "black districts" it was common to have, at each place of holding elections, two ballot-boxes, one for white voters, and the other for the Negroes. . . . If the blacks are present, and likely to vote in such numbers as to "threaten the overthrow of society," or give cause of alarm to the leading white citizens, the offered vote of some ignorant Negro is challenged. The gangway is filled behind him by a long line of Negroes, pressing forward in single file, and impatient to vote. The Negro selected to be challenged is always one who lives in a distant part of the township or district. Somebody is dispatched to summon witnesses from his neighborhood, or some other cause of delay is discovered. . . . Of course the other Negroes cannot vote until this case is decided. It comes to an end by and by, and the conclusion which is at last reached is, usually, that the challenged Negro has the right to vote, and his ballot is accepted. . . . When the hour for the closing of the polls arrives there has not been sufficient time for the full Negro republican [party] vote to be polled. . . .

"But," I often inquired, "what if the Negroes should become tired of this enforced waiting, and, understanding its purpose, should push forward, and demand that their votes shall be received?"

"Then," answered my informants, significantly, "there is a collision. The Negroes are the attacking party, and of course they will be worsted." . . .

In Southern Alabama and in Mississippi influential and prominent Democrats said to me: "Some of our people, some editors especially, deny that the Negroes are hindered from voting; but what is the good of lying? They *are* interfered with, and we are obliged to do it, and we may as well tell the truth."

J. B. Harrison, "Studies in the South," *Atlantic Monthly* 50 (July 1882): 103–4.

THE "FIRST AND DEAREST RIGHTS" OF BLACK FARMERS

[*African American Representative Thomas E. Miller of South Carolina was a lawyer before he entered Congress. In 1891 he addressed the House.*]

There are other things more important to us [than holding office]. First is the infernal lynch law. That is the thing we most complain of. It is a question whether when we go to work we will return or not. Second, they have little petty systems of justices who rob us of our daily toil, and we cannot get redress before the higher tribunals. Third, we work for our task-masters, and they pay us if they please, for the courts are so constructed that Negroes have no rights if these rights wind up in dollars and cents to be paid by white task-masters. . . .

Yes, gentlemen, we want office but the first and dearest rights the Negro of the South wants are the right to pay for his labor, his right of trial by jury, his right to his home, his right to know that the man who lynches him will not the next day be elected by the State to a high and honorable trust, his right to know that murderers shall be convicted and not elected to high office. . . .

The Congressional Record 22, part 2, 51st Cong., 2nd sess., 1216.

Congressman White Vows: We Will Return

[*In his farewell speech of 29 January 1901, Representative George H. White, the last Black congressman from the South, notified his fellow members that "one day we will break the bonds" for "we are climbing!" His speech summarized Black accomplishments in the first thirty-five years of freedom.*]

. . . we have reduced the illiteracy of the race at least 45 per cent. We have written and published near 500 books. We have nearly 300 newspapers, 3 of which are dailies. We have now in practice over 2,000 lawyers and a corresponding number of doctors. We have accumulated over $12,000,000 worth of school property and about $40,000,000 worth of church property. We have about 140,000 farms and homes, valued at in the neighborhood of $750,000,000, and personal property valued at about $170,000,000. We have raised about $11,000,000 for educational purposes, and the property per capita for every colored man, woman, and child in the United States is estimated at $75.

We are operating successfully several banks, commercial enterprises among our people in the Southland, including 1 silk mill and 1 cotton factory. We have 32,000 teachers in the schools of the country; we have built, with the aid of our friends, about 20,000 churches, and support 7 colleges, 17 academies, 50 high schools, 5 law schools, 5 medical schools, and 25 theological seminaries. We have over 600,000 acres of land in the South alone. The cotton produced, mainly by black labor, has increased from 4,669,770 bales in 1860 to 11,235,000 in 1899. All this we have done under the most adverse circumstances. We have done it in the face of lynching, burning at the stake, with the humiliation of "Jim Crow" cars, the disfranchisement of our male citizens, slander and degradation of our women, with factories closed against us, no Negro permitted to be conductor on the railway cars, whether run through the streets of our cities or across the prairies of our great country, no Negro permitted to run as engineer on a locomotive, most of the mines closed against us. Labor unions—carpenters, painters, brick masons, machinists, hackmen, and those supplying nearly every conceivable avocation for livelihood have banded themselves together to better their condition, but, with few exceptions, the black face has been left out. The Negroes are seldom employed in our mercantile stores. At this we do not wonder. Some day we hope to have them employed in our own stores. With all these odds against us, we are forging our way ahead, slowly perhaps, but surely. You may tie us and then taunt us for a lack of bravery, but one day we will break the bonds. You may use our labor for two and a half centuries and then taunt us for our poverty, but let me remind you we will not always remain poor. You may withhold even the knowledge of how to read God's word and learn the way from earth to glory and then taunt us for our ignorance, but we would remind you that there is plenty of room at the top, and we are climbing. . . .

This, Mr. Chairman, is perhaps the Negroes' temporary farewell to the American Congress; but let me say, Phoenix-like he will rise up some day and come again. These parting words are in behalf of an outraged, heart-broken, bruised, and bleeding, but God-fearing people, faithful, industrious, loyal people—rising people, full of potential force. . . .

The only apology that I have to make for the earnestness with which I have spoken is that I am pleading for the life, the liberty, the future happiness, and manhood suffrage of one-eighth of the entire population of the United States. [Loud applause.]

The Congressional Record, 56th Cong., 2nd sess., 1636–38.

14 REFORMERS MEET THE PROBLEMS OF THE MACHINE AGE

For many citizens, the most important products of America's factories were the social problems created by this new industrial power. Immigrants from Europe and Asia, and migrants fresh from the farms of the country-side, poured into the cities that began to spread out around the factories. In the last decades of the nineteenth century America changed from a nation of tiny towns and small farms to one of large cities. The stresses and strains were enormous. In Atlanta, Georgia, schools, four out of fourteen white children and five of every seven African American children had no seats or desks. Crowded cities led to slums and crime. Unemployment, strikes, and depressions hurt both workers and businessmen. Poverty lived down the street or across the railroad tracks from fabulous wealth.

The Great Reformers

Reformers pointed to problems of industrialism that had to be faced and solved. Men and women wanted security for their families, decent places in which to live, good schools for their children with playgrounds nearby.

Women wanted the right to vote. Immigrants wanted to share in the opportunity that America promised. People of color wanted the same pay, education, and rights that others received. Frederick Douglass said, before the Civil War, "I . . . would scorn to demand for my race a single right or privilege that I would not freely grant to you."

Long before the Civil War, Douglass's words and actions had made clear his interest in oppressed people everywhere. "I am not only an American slave, but a man, and as such, am bound to use my powers for the welfare of the whole human brotherhood." In a speech on patriotism, Douglass said, "My sympathies are not limited by my relation to any race. I can take no part in oppressing and persecuting any variety of the human family. Whether in Russia, Germany, or California, my sympathy is with the oppressed, be he Chinaman or Hebrew." Douglass's newspaper proudly fought for the rights of "the Indian, Mongolian, Caucasian."

In an age that looked on Asians and Indians as inferior or dangerous people, Black congressmen of the Reconstruction period spoke out for fair treatment of all persecuted groups. John O'Hara of North Carolina asked the government to provide relief for the Cherokees, and Senator B. K. Bruce of Mississippi demanded that the government deal justly with Indians. Bruce also told the Senate he opposed a law that restricted Asian immigration: "Representing as I do a people who but a few years ago were considered essentially disqualified from enjoying the privileges and immunities of American citizenship . . . I shall vote against this bill."

In the long but ultimately successful campaign to extend the right to vote to women, Black leaders had always played a part. In 1848 Frederick Douglass had led the fight, at the first women's rights convention, to pass the first resolution demanding that women be allowed to vote. Congressman Alonzo J. Ransier of south Carolina was an active campaigner for women's rights. William E. B. Du Bois, writing in *The Crisis* in 1919, called on "every black voter in the State of New York" to "cast his ballot in favor of woman suffrage" and all other Blacks "should do the same thing." When a 1913 women's rights parade in Washington, D.C., was heckled by males in the crowd, one of the women noted that the city's people of color "were quiet and respectable" and seemed "sorry for the indignities which were incessantly heaped upon us." She concluded, "I thank them in the name of all the women for their kindness."

Protection of American civil liberties had long been an interest of many important Americans. "To suppress free speech," said Frederick Douglass, "is a double wrong. It violates the rights of the hearer as well as those of the speaker." William E. B. Du Bois deplored the denial of rights to Sacco

Frederick Douglass, one of America's greatest reformers, battled for human rights until the day he died. His crusades for women's rights, universal peace, and equal rights for all took him all over America and Europe.

and Vanzetti, two Italian immigrants. When they were tried for murder in 1921, and put to death in 1927, people all over the world were convinced that they were found guilty only because they were radicals and foreigners. "We who are black," wrote Du Bois, "can sympathize with Sacco and Vanzetti and their friends more than other Americans. We are used to being convicted because of our race and opinions." As the Irish struggled to be free of English rule, Du Bois wrote, "God speedily grant the ultimate freedom of Ireland."

Lucy Parsons, born a slave in Texas in 1853, became a voice for women and the oppressed. A militant revolutionary from the 1870s to her death in 1942, she denounced lynching, capitalism, war, and low wages. In 1905 she urged a new kind of strike—workers should remain inside factories "and take possession of the necessary property of production." She was the first important Marxist woman of color.

Frances Ellen Watkins Harper, an early Black reformer, as a teenager helped slaves escape to Canada. As an adult she was a popular poet and speaker for temperance and women's rights.

The Urban Reformers

Many newcomers to cities were oppressed by poverty, slums, and crime. These problems drew the attention of such reformers as Jane Addams, Lillian Wald, Jacob Riis, and African American reformers as well. As early as 1865, a Black relief society in Nashville, Tennessee, provided aid to starving people without regard to color. By 1913 African Americans supported a hundred orphanages in the United States. Black "law and order" leagues rose to curb crime and regulate saloons in Georgia and Texas.

The African Americans who came North during the late nineteenth century faced a color line in housing. Jacob Riis, the Danish immigrant who became a New York reporter, described how landlords restricted Blacks to certain sections of the city in 1890. "Where he permits them to live, they go; where he shuts the door, stay out. By his grace they exist at all in certain localities." Riis found this "despotism . . . deliberately assigns to the defenceless Black that level for the purpose of robbing him. . . ."

Dr. George Haynes, a New York scholar who had long studied the problems of urban living, sought to reduce the crowding and poverty of people of color in the many industrial centers of the North and South. He knew that violence and fear lived in every ghetto. In 1911 Dr. Haynes, together with other Black and white reformers, organized the Urban League to improve health, housing, job opportunities, and recreation. A believer in racial harmony as a means of achieving progress for people of both races, Dr. Haynes explained the goals of the Urban League: "INTER-

Dr. George Edmund Haynes, a founder of the Urban League.

RACIAL COOPERATION was the basic principle on which the organization was to develop. White people were to be asked to work WITH Negroes for their mutual advantage and advancement rather than working for them as a problem."

The Era of Jim Crow

In 1894 a crusading Seattle editor named Horace Cayton called on all citizens to unite for progress and "smoke the pipe of everlasting peace." The young African American expressed his patriotism:

> Let there be one flag and one country for all manner of man that swears allegiance thereto. Let America be for Americans, without color or race distinctions cutting any figure in the contest.

Thomas Rice dressed as the stage character "Jim Crow."

Cayton's voice went unheard because he lived during the "Jim Crow" era.* This was the name given to the thousands of state laws, city ordinances, and local customs whose impassable color line kept people of color from opportunities which were open to whites.

In the period from 1890 to 1910, each Southern state wrote into law (often into their Constitutions) the many devices which kept black men and women from enjoying the rights and privileges of citizens.† And in the 1896 *Plessy* vs. *Ferguson* case, the United States Supreme Court laid down the "separate but equal" doctrine when it ruled that laws segregating people because of their race did not violate the United States Constitution.

From the time Mr. Homer Plessy was arrested for taking a seat in a "white" train until 1954, African Americans have been forced to live under a variety of humiliating Southern laws. Oklahoma segregated phone booths and Mississippi segregated Coca-Cola machines. In Atlanta, a

In 1886, August Tolton became the first African American to be ordained a Catholic priest. A son of slaves, Tolton had worked from dawn to dusk in a tobacco factory for twelve years.

---

*The phrase "Jim Crow" dates to 1830. Thomas Rice, a famous white entertainer, walked out of his Baltimore theater to observe a Black singer-dancer performing in the alley. Rice "borrowed" the man's dance routine and costume and enlarged on the song he was singing. He made the words famous all over the world—"wheel about, turn about, dance jest so— every time I wheel about I shout Jim Crow!" Like another white invention, "Uncle Tom," which Blacks used to describe a man afraid to stand up for his rights, "Jim Crow" came to mean the many kinds of racial discrimination Blacks faced in America.

†In 1883 the Supreme Court struck down the last of the civil rights laws (1875) passed by Congress after the Civil War. That same year Emma Lazarus, daughter of Jewish immigrants from Poland, wrote her stirring poem for the Statue of Liberty: "Give me your tired, your poor, your huddled masses yearning to breathe free. . . ."

Black witness was not allowed to swear to tell the truth on the same Bible that white witnesses used. In Birmingham, Alabama, Blacks and whites faced a penalty of six months in prison if they "did play together or in company with each other in any game of cards or dice, dominoes, or checkers."

Southern schools were totally segregated. But Florida thought it also necessary to segregate the textbooks of Black and white pupils while the books were in storage. Washington, D.C., African Americans found they could not bury their dead dogs in the same dog cemetery that whites used.

Blacks who faced the Southern court found a special kind of injustice. If one committed a crime against a white, he received exaggerated newspaper coverage and the full penalty of the law. Often, innocent men, because of their color, were accused of crime. And if a white committed a crime against an African American, the punishment (if the case was ever brought to court) was mild. Even if a Black committed a crime against a Black, Southern courts thought so little of Black life and property that his punishment was often a light one. For many years lynch mobs, often led by "respectable" white citizens, killed an average of almost two African Americans a week. The victims were often seized from the hands of the law, sometimes with the assistance of sheriffs and jailers. A study of this massive crime shows that Southern mobs preferred to burn their victims; Northern and Western mobs preferred hanging.

During the time when lynching and race riots were common, a grandfather points out the Liberty Bell to his grandchildren.

African Americans in the North found their opportunities restricted by custom rather than by law. A white writer in 1912 admitted that in Ohio "the Negro has nothing resembling equality with the white man." Neighborhoods, schools, unions, and public facilities were silently segregated. Jackie Robinson, who lived in Pasadena, California, during the 1920s recalled, "We saw movies from segregated balconies, swam in the municipal pool only on Tuesdays, and were permitted in the YMCA on only one night a week. Restaurant doors were slammed in our faces."

The intensity of racist feeling at the turn of the century can be measured by many white newspaper predictions that the race was dying. The Peoria, Illinois, *Journal* of 3 December 1899 headlined: RACE PROBLEM IS DISAPPEARING. STATISTICS SHOW NEGRO RACE WILL EVENTUALLY DISAPPEAR.

During this era of Jim Crow African Americans were degraded in magazines, newspapers, nursery rhymes, popular songs, cartoons, movies, and jokes. Men were referred to as "dangerous," "stupid," "humorous," or "childlike." In 1887, a South Carolina white wrote, "Southerners will call a Negro 'Senator Smith,' or 'Sheriff Smith,' or 'Colonel Smith,' to escape addressing him as 'Mr. Smith.'" A St. Louis Bible society published a book entitled *The Negro a Beast* which tried to prove that a person of color had no soul. It sold thousands of copies. People of color of this time had powerful enemies and few friends.

Resistance to Jim Crow

One of the heroic leaders of early battles against discrimination was Miss Ida Wells. At fourteen she had to bring up her four younger brothers and sisters. She did so and also put herself through college. She started her campaign against lynching in Tennessee at the age of nineteen. Her articles in the Memphis *Free Speech* exposed the mounting number of lynchings. Miss Wells, a forceful and attractive woman, carried two pistols for protection. In 1892 she published information showing that the lynching of three successful African American grocers was the work of their white competitors. Her press was wrecked, and she was driven from Memphis but she carried her crusade to Northern cities and to Europe. In 1898 she led a delegation of women and congressmen to President McKinley to protest the lynching of a Black postmaster. "We refuse to believe this country, so powerful to defend its citizens abroad, is unable to protect its citizens at home," she told the president. Nothing was done, however. In 1909 she became a founder of the NAACP and continued her campaign until her death in 1931.

African Americans, despite the danger, often took determined actions to halt Jim Crow practices. On the evening of 12 May 1871, a young boy launched a "sit-in" aboard a segregated Louisville horse-drawn streetcar. Screaming white teenagers cursed him and eventually dragged him from the car. When the youth finally fought back, he was arrested. In the days that followed, others—mostly young men—entered streetcars and sat stony and silent in the face of abuse. When drivers walked off the cars, these men who staged the 1871 "sit-ins" sometimes drove the cars from stop to stop. The Louisville company, in the face of mounting violence and opposition, agreed to integrate their street railway. The said "it was useless to try to resist . . . the claim of Negroes to ride in the cars."

Reporter Ray Stannard Baker told how the appearance of segregated streetcars in Savannah, Georgia, caused "violent protestations on the part of Negroes and a refusal by many of them to use the cars at all." In the years between 1898 and 1906, African American boycotts took place in New Orleans, Mobile, and Houston, but they were generally unsuccessful. The whites had all the power and Black people lacked economic independence and strong organizations. These would come a half century later.

In 1883 Black conventions were held in Kentucky, Arkansas, South Carolina, and Texas to protest against the denial of civil rights. Editor T. Thomas Fortune told his people to "fight fire with fire," and added, "It is time to face the enemy and fight inch by inch for every right he denies us."

Despite threats of violence and murder itself, Blacks in the South elected officials in various states until the turn of the century. In 1890, six-

Journalist John E. Bruce. In 1889 he said, "The only salvation for the Negro is to be found in a resort to force under wise and discreet leaders."

Ida B. Wells devoted her life to the fight against lynching and discrimination.

teen African American legislators served in the Louisiana assembly. Others served in Congress until 1901. Famous politicians such as Congressman George White and P. B. S. Pinchback (governor of Louisiana for forty-three days) continued to demand an end to violence and segregation.

In the Deep South African Americans used a variety of means to defend their rights during this period of maximum repression. Those in Liberty County, Georgia, had two representatives in the state legislature in 1899. That same year a thousand armed Blacks of the county liberated farmer Henry Delegal, who had been arrested for dating a white woman. Delegal and his army hid in the great Okefenokee swamp while the governor sent regiments of state militia after him and white newspapers pleaded, "There has never been the slightest danger that Henry Delegal would be lynched." Until matters were settled peacefully, Georgia residents trembled with the thought of a bloody race war. Two years later a Black conference in Alabama, concerned with the growing danger of violence, passed this resolution:

> Regardless of how others may act, we urge upon our race a rigid observance of the law of the land, and that we bear in mind that lawlessness begets crime and hardens and deadens not only the conscience of the law-breaker, but also the conscience of the community.

Blacks have traditionally resisted Jim Crow by migration. In the 1890s, thousands left the South for Oklahoma and points west. The group shown here left the West for New York City, seeking transportation to Africa.

Editor T. T. Fortune.

Alexander Crummel, a runaway slave who became a noted minister, author, and scholar. In 1897 he organized the first meeting of the American Negro Academy to develop scholarly studies of African American life.

Outnumbered African Americans had good cause to reject violence. From 1892 to 1901 African Americans were lynched at the rate of three or four a week. Usually the victims were the most forthright voices of their people or common citizens who were murdered to crush the fires of discontent. Some Black leaders simply disappeared from their homes. The white South had no use for Black leaders.

Successful African Americans such as Dr. Daniel Hale Williams often used their personal good fortune to help others. This fair-skinned, red-headed young doctor founded the first interracial hospital in America, Provident Hospital in Chicago. He also started a school to train Black nurses since they were not permitted to enter white nursing schools. In 1893, by performing the first successful heart operation in history, Dr. Williams became world famous. President Grover Cleveland appointed him head of the Freedmen's Hospital in Washington, D.C. Throughout the rest of his life, Dr. Williams continued to make medical history and to battle against the color line.

Dr. Daniel Hale Williams.

Booker T. Washington and His Age

During the era of Jim Crow laws African Americans were forced to live a life apart from the American mainstream. A white reporter in the 1880s was told by a Black businessman that he "got the respect of whites . . . by his ability and by making money . . . [and] he had ceased to expect that the colored race would get it any other way." Reporter Ray Stannard Baker, after investigating conditions in the cities of the South in 1909, concluded, "The struggle of the races is becoming more and more rapidly economic." In Illinois and in Oklahoma, Blacks formed their own towns to escape persecution and to prove that they could successfully manage their own affairs.

A philosophical ex-slave named Booker T. Washington carried this economic approach to racial problems much further. He became the leading spokesperson of Black vocational education and a living example of the heights an African American could reach in an era of savage repression.

Washington had taught himself to read after working all day in a West Virginia salt mine. He worked his way through Hampton Institute and then became the first president of Alabama's Tuskegee Institute. At Tuskegee he taught his students the importance of self-reliance, hard work, saving, and learning a trade. He proudly pointed out to visitors that most of the college's buildings had been built by its students.

On a hot afternoon in September 1895, Booker T. Washington came to the attention of the entire country. A skillful orator, Washington was asked

An 1866 orphan home in Memphis, Tennessee. Black organizations for self-help and self-improvement predate the United States Constitution.

to speak at the "Negro exhibit" at the Atlanta Exposition. Introduced by Governor Bullock of Georgia, Booker T. Washington called on his people to work hard for, and to accept, the friendship of the Southern white. In an age when racist persecution was fierce and unrelenting, the young educator offered a program to appease the white man. He said African Americans would not join unions or cause strikes. He emphasized that "the wisest among my race understand" that seeking "social equality is the extremest folly." Washington asked for help to secure better education for his people and offered in return this acceptance of segregation: "In all things that are purely social we can be as separate as the fingers, yet one as the hand in all things essential to mutual progress."

The speech was an immediate success. Governor Bullock "rushed across the platform and took me by the hand," and "I received so many and such hearty congratulations that I found it difficult to get out of the building." A letter of praise soon came from President Grover Cleveland.

Booker T. Washington made important white friends—Presidents Roosevelt and Taft and industrialists Andrew Carnegie and John D. Rockefeller. He soon became the main channel through which money for any

Booker T. Washington and his influential friends. On Washington's right is President William Howard Taft, and on his left is millionaire Andrew Carnegie.

Black educational purpose came, and he was able to build many schools for his people. He was consulted by presidents on matters relating to African American progress and was asked which Blacks should receive appointments to government posts. Booker T. Washington became a bridge between his oppressed people and the white world.

As a leader during the period of maximum oppression, Washington told Alabama farmers at the turn of the century, "We have got to be patient and long suffering." But Booker T. Washington's views were immediately challenged by other leaders. President John Hope of Atlanta University publicly asked, "If we are not striving for equality, in heaven's name for what are we living. . . . Yes, my friends, I want equality. Nothing else." For many, Booker T. Washington's compromises had gone too far. Later, Washington himself would realize that his appeasement had not gained any new rights for his people and he would secretly finance those who fought for an end to segregation. In his last article he said that segregation did nothing for African Americans but hold them back.

The Drive for Full Civil Rights

As it became increasingly clear that Booker T. Washington's program could not lead, even eventually, to civil rights, some prominent Blacks looked for another approach and a new leader. In 1903 Dr. William E. B. Du Bois challenged Washington in his book *The Souls of Black Folk*. A short, soft-spoken historian and sociologist, Dr. Du Bois had been the first Black to graduate from Harvard with a Ph.D. degree. His first demands were for equal political rights for his people. He pointed out that Washington "practically accepts the alleged inferiority of the Negro races," and "withdraws many of the high demands of Negroes as men and American citizens."

There were similarities as well as differences between the two men. Du Bois himself knew this. "Actually, Washington had no more faith in the white man than I do." Washington's theory, however, was: "When you head is in the lion's mouth, use your hand to pet him." Each man sought to advance the cause of his people but by different means. Wrote Du Bois:

> So far as Mr. Washington preaches Thrift, Patience, and Industrial Training for the masses, we must hold up his hands and strive with him . . . But so far as Mr. Washington apologizes for injustice, North or South, does not rightly value the privilege and duty of voting . . . and opposes the higher training and ambition of our brighter minds,—so far as he, the South, or the Nation does this—we must unceasingly and firmly oppose them.

Historian Carter G. Woodson, in 1915, founded the Association for the Study of Negro Life and History.

Both Du Bois and Washington were strong-willed, energetic men who overcame mountains of prejudice to gain success. Each man had a commanding influence on masses of African Americans. Washington did it through his mastery of oratory and a clear writing style; Du Bois through historical studies, poetry, novels, lectures, essays, articles, and philosophical discussions. Washington sought to advance his people by pacifying whites; Du Bois, by assailing their ears with protests and demands.

Du Bois began to gather other reformers to plan a more militant attack on discrimination. In 1905 they met at Niagara Falls, Canada. (The hotels on the New York side of the border would not accept them.)

Tragic events were soon to give the Du Bois "Niagara movement" important white support. In 1908 bloody racist rioting exploded in Springfield, Illinois. Blacks were killed within a few blocks of where Abraham Lincoln had once lived. William English Walling, a reporter, who went to investigate the story for his paper, described its horrifying details. He told his readers that the "spirit of Lincoln . . . must be revived." On the one hundredth anniversary of Lincoln's birth, a group of white and Black reformers, including Walling, called for resistance to racial attacks. Du Bois and his group were to play an important part in the organization that was formed—The National Association for the Advancement of Colored People (NAACP).

The list of NAACP supporters reads like a roster of the noted reformers

Dr. W. E. B. Du Bois in 1911.

of this period (1909). Among the whites were writers Lincoln Steffens, Ray Stannard Baker, and William Dean Howells; reformers Lillian Wald, Jane Addams, Mary White Ovington, and Rabbi Stephen S. Wise; and educator John Dewey. Among the famous African Americans were educators Mary Church Terrell and Mary McLeod Bethune, crusader Ida Wells, Du Bois, and churchmen Archibald H. Grimké and Alexander Walters.

The NAACP attacked discrimination on a broad front. Its staff of lawyers stood ready to defend those accused of crimes because of their color. Their first case involved a New Jersey Black man arrested for murder. "There was no evidence against him," recalled Mary White Ovington, "but he was black and had been near the scene of the crime." The NAACP won his release. Within ten years NAACP lawyers were winning significant cases before the United States Supreme Court.

The NAACP did not operate only on the legal front. Beginning in 1910 it published *The Crisis* magazine. Under the editorship of Du Bois its pages stressed African American accomplishments and publicized the practices of discrimination. African American poets were often given their first audience through the pages of *The Crisis*. In 1914 the NAACP announced it would award the Spingarn Medal to the outstanding African American of each year. By 1921, the NAACP had conducted a campaign to have an antilynching law passed by Congress. The law did pass the House by a two-to-one vote only to be talked to death by Southern senators.

The NAACP office in New York City marked every lynching by flying this flag.

In 1920 the NAACP hired a blond, blue-eyed young man as an investigator. His name was Walter White and despite his appearance he was a Black man and proud of it. Because of his looks, however, he was able to investigate forty-one lynchings and eight race riots. He met Klansmen, attended their meetings, and was once sworn in as a sheriff's deputy in Oklahoma. "Now you can go out and kill any nigger you see," another deputy told him, "and the law'll be behind you." But even with the evidence that White collected for ten years at the peril of his life, and photographs of actual murderers at particular scenes, no convictions resulted.

The editorial page of the first issue of *The Crisis* was largely devoted to a discussion of the evils of school segregation. "This is wrong," wrote editor Du Bois, "and should be resisted by black men and white." It would be no accident of history that one of the greatest reforms in American history—desegregation of the schools—would be carried to the United States Supreme Court in 1954 and won by three NAACP lawyers.

Walter White investigated anti-Black riots and lynchings.

JIM CROW FOLLOWS CADET SMITH TO WEST POINT

[J. W. Smith was the first Black to enter the United States Military Academy at West Point. What happened to him there is told by Smith himself, and by David Clarke, a white educator who helped the young recruit. Smith was finally forced out.]

[David Clarke.] Smith was a member of my household, and was the most truthful and correct boy in all his habits and deportment that I ever saw. He went [to West Point], and God only knows how much he has suffered from the day he trod that ground. . . . I have been there three times to look after him. He would have left in July had it not been for me. I had an interview with President [U.S.] Grant. . . . He said, "Don't take him away; the battle might as well be fought now as any time." So he was permitted to stay. Scarcely has a day passed when he has not been assaulted by words, or blows inflicted, to force him to do something for which they might expel him. . . .

New National Era, 26 January 1871, 2.

[Cadet J. W. Smith writes to a friend.] Your kind letter should have been answered long ere this, but really I have been so harassed with examinations and insults and ill treatment of these cadets that I could not write or do anything else scarcely. I passed the examination all right, and got in, but my companion Howard failed and was rejected. Since he went away I have been lonely indeed. And now these fellows appear to be trying their utmost to run me off, and I fear they will succeed if they continue as they have begun. We went into camp yesterday, and not a moment has passed since then but some one of them has been cursing and abusing me. . . . It is just the same at the table, and what I get to eat I must snatch for like a dog. I don't wish to resign if I can get along at all; but I don't think it will be best for me to stay and take all the abuses and insults that are heaped upon me. . . .

The New Era, 14 July 1870, 1.

[News account of a further incident.] The case of the colored cadet Smith who has been on trial before a court-martial at West Point for breaking a cocoanut dipper over the head of another cadet named Wilson has been closed. . . . He appears to have been too prompt in breaking the

cocoanut dipper over cadet Wilson's head: but that member doubtless represented to him for the time the collective heads of the white cadets who had subjected him to humiliating ill treatment. . . .

New National Era, 3 November 1870, 2.

An 1879 Plea for Federal Aid to Education

[*On 23 January 1879, Congressman Richard Cain of South Carolina, completing his second term in the House, spoke for federal aid to education.*]

. . . This Government can do no greater deed than to dedicate a part of the revenues accruing from the sale of public lands to the education of the people. There are millions of the citizens of this Republic who will not receive that education which everyone ought to have to make them worthy citizens unless the Government shall secure it to them. This should not be left entirely to the States, because they will not fully do this work.

. . . Education in the South will be more effective than a standing army. Educate the masses of the people and you open up the means for their higher and grander development. . . . but I also believe famine should be provided for before you expect schoolhouses.

The Congressional Record, 45th Cong., 3rd sess., 688.

The Demands of Nashville's Black Middle Class

[*In 1886 a group of African American businessmen told white writer Charles D. Warner what rights they expected as Americans.*]

. . . They were all solid, sensible business men, and all respected as citizens. They talked most intelligently of politics, and freely about social conditions. In regard to voting in Tennessee there was little to complain of; but in regard to Mississippi, as an illustration, it was an outrage that . . . the colored Republican vote did not count. What could they do? Some said that probably nothing could be done; time must be left to cure the wrong. Others wanted the Federal government to interfere, at least to the extent

of making a test case on some member of Congress that his election was illegal. . . .

Finally I asked this intelligent company . . . "What do you want here in
the way of civil rights that you have not?" The reply from one was that he
got the respect of the whites just as he was able to command it by his ability and by making money, and, with a touch of a sense of injustice, said he
had ceased to expect that the colored race would get it in any other way.
Another reply was—and this was evidently the deep feeling of all:

> We want to be treated like men, like anybody else, regardless of color. We don't
> mean by this social equality at all. . . . We want the public conveyances open to
> us according to the fare we pay; we want privileges to go to hotels and to the-
> atres, operas and places of amusement. We wish you could see our families and
> the way we live; you would then understand that we cannot go to the places as-
> signed us in concerts and theatres without loss of self-respect. . . .

Charles Dudley Warner, "The South Revisited," *Harper's New Monthly* 74 (March 1887):
640.

Self-Help in the South

*[Samuel J. Barrows, a New England reformer, traveled 3,500 miles in the South to
investigate Black progress.]*

. . . The Negroes are showing their awakened and eager interest in education by the zeal with which they are embracing their opportunities. Everywhere I found in colleges, normal institutes, and district schools fresh, live
interest. In some sections, the eagerness of the colored people for knowledge amounts to an absolute thirst. In Alabama, the state superintendent
of education, a former Confederate major, assured me that the colored
people in that State are more interested in education than the whites are.
Nothing shows better this zeal for education than the sacrifices made to secure it. President Bumstead, of Atlanta University, asks, "Where in the history of the world have so large a mass of equally poor and unlettered
people done so much to help themselves in educational work?" This challenge will long remain unanswered. The students of Atlanta University pay
thirty-four percent of the expenses of that institution. A letter from the
treasurer of Harvard College informs me that about the same proportion
of its expenses is paid from tuition fees. . . . It must be remembered, also,

that at Harvard tuition fees and other expenses are mostly paid by parents and guardians; at Atlanta they are paid by the students themselves, and to a large degree by personal labor. . . .

Another remarkable illustration is furnished by the Tuskegee Normal School. This institution was started in 1881 by a Hampton graduate, Mr. Booker T. Washington, on a state appropriation of $2000. It has grown from 30 pupils to 450, with 31 teachers. During the last year 200 applicants had to be turned away for want of room. Fourteen hundred acres of land and fourteen school buildings form a part of the equipment. . . . All the teachers are colored. Of the fourteen school buildings, eight have been erected, in whole or in part, by the students. . . .

One of the most important results of the excellent work done by Hampton, Atlanta, and Tuskegee is seen in the radiating influence they exert through the country in stimulating primary education. . . . In a district of Butler County, Alabama, the children formed a "one cent society." They brought to the teacher a penny a day. About thirty dollars was raised to buy land, and the school-teacher, a colored girl, helped to clear it and burn the brush. . . . In Lee County, the people "supplement" for an assistant teacher. One district school which I visited, eighteen miles from Tuskegee, taught by a graduate of its institute, well illustrated the advantage of industrial education. Having learned the carpenter's trade at the normal school, he was able, with the help of his pupils, to build a fine new schoolhouse. . . .

The interest in education is seen also in the self-denial and sacrifice which parents make to keep their children at school. This sacrifice falls chiefly on the mothers. . . . "I know mothers," said a student [at Tuskegee], "who get three dollars a month, and out of that pay one dollar for the rent, and yet send their children to school." To do this they wash all day and half the night. Said a colored clergyman in Chattanooga:

> Sometimes, when I go about and see how hard many of these mothers work, I feel almost inclined to say, "You ought to keep your child at home"; but they hold on with wonderful persistence. Two girls graduated from Atlanta University. Their mother had been washing several years to keep them in school. She came up to see them graduate. She was one of the happiest mothers I ever saw.

At Selma University, some of the students walk for ten to fifteen miles a day in going to and from the university. . . .

The colored people do more towards taking care of their unfortunate classes than is generally realized. . . . The colored orphan asylum established by Mrs. Steele in Chattanooga is, I am told, the only Protestant colored orphan asylum south of Washington. What, then, becomes of orphan children? They are adopted. I have met such children in many homes, and their love and respect for their foster parents refute the charge that the Negro is incapable of gratitude. . . .

In other respects the colored people have developed a laudable disposition to take care of their own poor. In addition to the Odd Fellows, Masons, and Knights of Pythias, benevolent and fraternal organizations are multiplying. The city churches are feeling a new impulse to such work. Brotherhoods, Good Samaritan societies, and mutual benefit organizations are established. Members of these organizations are allowed a regular stipend when sick. In New Orleans, the colored people have started a widow's home, and have collected enough money to buy a piece of ground and put up a respectable building. In Montgomery, I visited the Hale Infirmary, founded by the late Joseph Hale and his wife, leading colored citizens. It is a large two-story building, especially designed by the son-in-law of the founder for hospital purposes.

Samuel J. Barrows, "What the Southern Negro is Doing for Himself," *Atlantic Monthly* 57 (June 1891): 810–15.

"JUSTICE IS NOT DEAD IN THE REPUBLIC"

[*As Southern states stripped African American citizens of the right to vote, Louisiana ex-governor P. B. S. Pinchback made the following speech on the subject.*]

. . . Those laws not only deprive the colored citizens of "privileges and immunities" enjoyed by all other citizens in those States . . . but they impose a humiliating and degrading separation against, and a brand of inferiority upon, not only the colored people residing in said States, but upon every member of the entire race if they should have occasion to visit or pass through one of those States. It is an insult and a wrong which should be resisted by the whole race with every lawful means at its command. First and most important step in that direction in my opinion, is to secure a decision on the merits of the case from the Supreme Court of the United States as to the constitutionality of the so-called Constitutions recently arbitrarily and fraudulently adopted in several Southern States, under which wholesale disfranchisement is imposed upon the race solely on account of color. . . .

It is noticeable that wherever colored men have been deprived of the ballot, unjust class legislation has speedily followed, race antagonism has been intensified, and lawlessness and outrage against the race increased.

This is a grave condition. . . . It is truly said that eternal vigilance is the price of liberty. It will not do for you and me and others of the race who are not now under the immediate shadow of these unjust laws to be indifferent. It is the whole race which is assailed, and the whole race should protest against and oppose these wrongs to the last. . . . Our cause is just and must prevail if we manfully, earnestly, and judiciously appeal to the heart and conscience of the American people for redress of our grievances. Justice is not dead in the Republic. . . .

Speech delivered at a testimonial. Manuscript in P. B. S. Pinchback files, Howard University Moorland Collection. (No date is indicated, but mention of campaigning for McKinley places it between 1896 and 1900.)

BOOKER T. WASHINGTON'S "ATLANTA COMPROMISE"

[*The year 1895 brought important changes to African American life. Lynchings were increasing, and Southern states were rewriting their constitutions to eliminate equal rights. At this moment in history Booker T. Washington tried to conciliate the whites and act as mediator between them and his people. His speech at Atlanta brought him instant white approval.*]

. . . To those of my race who depend on bettering their condition in a foreign land or who underestimate the importance of cultivating friendly relations with the Southern white man, who is their next-door neighbor, I would say: "Cast down your bucket where you are"—cast it down in making friends in every manly way, of the people of all races by whom you are surrounded.

Cast it down in agriculture, mechanics, in commerce, in domestic service, and in the professions. . . . Our greatest danger is that in the great leap from slavery to freedom we may overlook the fact that the masses of us are to live by the productions of our hands, and fail to keep in mind that we shall prosper in proportion as we learn to dignify and glorify common labour and put brains and skill into the common occupations of life; shall prosper in proportion as we learn to draw the line between the superficial and the substantial, the ornamental gewgaws of life and the useful. No race can prosper till it learns that there is as much dignity in tilling a field as in writing a poem. It is at the bottom of life we must begin, and not at the top. Nor should we permit our grievances to overshadow our opportunities.

To those of the white race . . . were I permitted I would repeat what I say to my own race: "Cast down your bucket where you are." Cast it down among the eight millions of Negroes whose habits you know, whose fidelity and love you have tested in days when to have proved treacherous meant the ruin of your firesides. Cast down your bucket among these people who have, without strikes and labour wars, tilled your fields, cleared your forests, builded your railroads and cities, and brought forth treasures from the bowels of the earth. . . . Casting down your bucket among my people, helping and encouraging them as you are doing on these grounds, and to education of head, hand, and heart, you will find that they will buy your surplus land, make blossom the waste places in your fields, and run your factories. While doing this, you can be sure in the future, as in the past, that you and your families will be surrounded by the most patient, faithful, law-abiding, and unresentful people that the world has seen. As we have proved our loyalty to you in the past, in nursing your children, watching by the sick-bed of your mothers and fathers, and often following them with tear-dimmed eyes to their graves, so in the future, in our humble way, we shall stand by you with a devotion that no foreigner can approach, ready to lay down our lives, if need be, in defence of yours, interlacing our industrial, commercial, civil, and religious life with yours in a way that shall make the interests of both races one. In all things that are purely social we can be as separate as the fingers, yet one as the hand in all things essential to mutual progress.

There is no defence or security for any of us except in the highest intelligence and development of all. If anywhere there are efforts tending to curtail the fullest growth of the Negro, let these efforts be turned to stimulating, encouraging, and making him the most useful and intelligent citizen. Effort or means so invested will pay a thousand per cent interest. These efforts will be twice blessed—"blessing him that gives and him that takes." . . .

Nearly sixteen millions of hands will aid you in pulling the load upward, or they will pull against you the load downward. We shall constitute one-third and more of the ignorance and crime of the South, or one-third its intelligence and progress; we shall contribute one-third to the business and industrial prosperity of the South, or we shall prove a veritable body of death, stagnating, depressing, retarding every effort to advance the body politic. . . .

The wisest among my race understand that the agitation of questions of social equality is the extremest folly, and that progress in the enjoyment of all the privileges that will come to us must be the result of severe and constant struggle rather than of artificial forcing. No race that has anything to contribute to the markets of the world is long in any degree ostracized. It is important and right that all privileges of the law be ours, but it is vastly more important that we be prepared for the exercises of these privileges. The opportunity to earn a dollar in a factory just now is worth infinitely more than the opportunity to spend a dollar in an opera-house.

. . . I pledge that in your effort to work out the great and intricate problem which God has laid at the doors of the South, you shall have at all times the patient, sympathetic help of my race. . . .

Booker T. Washington, *Up from Slavery* (New York, 1901), 218–25.

DR. DU BOIS ANSWERS WASHINGTON

[*In his famous* The Souls of Black Folk *Dr. William E. B. Du Bois answered Booker T. Washington.*]

. . . in the history of nearly all other races and peoples the doctrine preached . . . has been that manly self-respect is worth more than lands and houses, and that a people who voluntarily surrender such respect, or cease striving for it, are not worth civilizing.

In answer to this, it has been claimed that the Negro can survive only through submission. Mr. Washington distinctly asks that black people give up, at least for the present, three things,—

First, political power,
Second, insistence on civil rights,
Third, higher education of Negro youth,—

and concentrate all their energies on industrial education, the accumulation of wealth, and the conciliation of the South. . . . As a result of this tender of the palm-branch, what has been the return? In these years [since Booker T. Washington's Atlanta speech] there have occurred:

1. The disfranchisement of the Negro.
2. The legal creation of a distinct status of civil inferiority.
3. The steady withdrawal of aid from institutions for the higher-training of the Negro.

These movements are not, to be sure, direct results of Mr. Washington's teachings; but his propaganda has, without a shadow of doubt, helped their speedier accomplishment. . . .

[Negroes] do not expect that the free right to vote, to enjoy civic rights, and to be educated, will come in a moment; they do not expect to see the bias and prejudices of years disappear at the blast of a trumpet; but they are absolutely certain that the way for a people to gain their reasonable rights is not by voluntarily throwing them away and insisting that they do not want them; that the way for a people to gain respect is not by continually belittling and ridiculing themselves; that on the contrary, Negroes must insist continually, in season and out of season, that voting is necessary to proper manhood, that color discrimination is barbarism, and that black boys need education as well as white boys. . . .

So far as Mr. Washington preaches Thrift, Patience, and Industrial Training for the masses, we must hold up his hands and strive with him. . . . But so far as Mr. Washington apologizes for injustice, North or South, does not rightly value the privilege and duty of voting, belittles the emasculating effects of caste distinctions, and opposes the higher training and ambition of our brighter minds— . . . we must unceasingly and firmly oppose them. By every civilized and peaceful method we must strive for the rights which the world accords to men, clinging unwaveringly to those great words which the sons of the [Founding] Fathers would fain forget: "We hold these truths to be self-evident: That all men are created equal; that they are endowed by their Creator with certain unalienable rights; that among these are life, liberty, and the pursuit of happiness."

W. E. Burghardt Du Bois, *The Souls of Black Folk* (Chicago, 1903), 51–59.

THE MISSION OF THE MEDDLER

[In both the North and the South a popular way of attacking reformers was to call them "do-gooders" or "meddlers." In a magazine article, Mary Church Terrell, an 1883 graduate of Oberlin College and first president of the National Association of Colored Women, defends "the meddler."]

Everybody who has tried to advance the interests of the human race by redressing wrongs or by inaugurating reforms has first been called a meddler. An acknowledged philanthropist or public benefactor may be defined as a meddler, whose labors have been crowned with success. . . .

In the United States there is an imperative need of meddlers today—active, insistent, and fearless meddlers who will spend their time investigating institutions, customs, and laws whose effect upon the citizens of any color or class is depressing or bad. The crying need of the whole wide world is meddlers. In Great Britain, Ireland is waiting for a large number of the aggressive, humane kind to appear. In Russia the dumb, driven cattle made in the image of God, but reduced to the level of brutes are in sore need of the meddler who has here a great and glorious work to perform. . . . In Russia and Germany and elsewhere as well the Jew needs the service of the meddler, who shall ask why the narrow and vicious of all races and creeds are permitted to pursue and persecute a people whose ability and whose virtues are so conspicuous and whose hand is raised against none.

. . . In the United States there is an imperative need of a host of meddlers who will . . . go so far as "to interfere officiously" if need be, where corruption of any kind is apparent and the transgression of the law is clear.

[*Shortly before her death, Mrs. Terrell was still one of America's important meddlers. In 1953 at the age of eighty-nine, she led a group into a restaurant in Washington, D.C., to protest its refusal to serve African Americans. The group was arrested but finally won their case in court.*]

Mary Church Terrell, "The Mission of the Meddler," *The Voice of the Negro* 2 (August 1905): 566–67.

TIME TO DENOUNCE LYNCHINGS

[*In 1894, two years after she was driven out of Memphis for exposing whites who had taken part in a lynching, fiery young Ida Wells published* A Red Record. *It was the first book to document the crime of lynching. This was her conclusion.*]

. . . We demand a fair trial by law for those accused of crime, and punishment by law after honest conviction. No maudlin sympathy for criminals is solicited, but we do ask that the law shall punish all alike. We earnestly desire those that control the forces which make public sentiment to join with us in the demand. Surely the humanitarian spirit of this country which reaches out to denounce the treatment of Russian Jews, the Armenian Christians, the laboring poor of Europe, the Siberian exiles, and the native women of India—will not longer refuse to lift its voice on this subject. If it were known that the cannibals or the savage Indians had burned three human beings alive in the past two years, the whole of Christendom would be roused, to devise ways and means to put a stop to it. Can you remain silent and inactive when such things are done in our own community and country? Is your duty to humanity in the United States less binding?

Ida B. Wells, *A Red Record* (Chicago, 1894), 97.

CONGRESSMAN WHITE INTRODUCES THE FIRST ANTILYNCHING BILL

[*Here are two versions of the same news story. One is by Congressman Griggs of Georgia, the other is by George White of North Carolina. As a result of the acceptance of the first version, a man named Hose was lynched. Representative White in his version shows that Griggs's facts may have been incorrect. Then Congressman White introduced the first antilynching bill into the United States Congress.*]

[*Representative Griggs.*] . . . A little family a few miles from the town of Newman were at supper in their modest dining room. The father, the young mother, and the baby were seated at the table. Humble though it was, peace, happiness, and contentment reigned in that modest house. A monster in human form, an employee on the farm [Hose], crept into that happy little home and with an ax knocked out the brains of that father, snatched the child from its mother, threw it across the room out of his way, and then by force accomplished his foul purpose. . . .

[*Representative White.*] The other side of this horrible story portrays a very different state of affairs. A white man, with no interest in Hose or his victim, declares upon oath that Hose did not commit this atrocious crime charged against him, but was an employee of Cranford [the husband], and had importuned him for pay due him for labor. This incensed his employer, who rushed upon Hose with a gun. Hose seized an ax and killed

Cranford instantly, in self-defense, and then fled to the woods with the greatest possible speed. I do not vouch for either side of this story, but only refer to it to show the necessity for trying all persons charged with crime, as the law directs. . . .

I tremble with horror for the future of our nation when I think what must be the inevitable result if mob violence is not stamped out of existence and law once more permitted to reign supreme.

To the end that the National Government may have jurisdiction over this species of crime [lynching], I have prepared and introduced the following bill. . . .

A bill for the protection of all citizens of the United States against mob violence, and the penalty for breaking such laws [death].

The Congressional Record, 56th Cong., 1st. sess., 2151–53.

DR. DU BOIS WRITES TO A SCHOOLGIRL IN 1905

[*The famous scholar took time out from his work to tell a schoolgirl how vital it is for everyone to take part in American life.*]

I wonder if you will let a stranger say a word to you about yourself? I have heard that you are a young woman of some ability but that you are neglecting your school work because you have become hopeless of trying to do anything in the world. I am very sorry for this. How any human being whose wonderful fortune it is to live in the 20th century should under ordinarily fair advantages despair of life is almost unbelievable. And if in addition to this that person is, as I am, of Negro lineage with all the hopes and yearnings of hundreds of millions of human souls dependent in some degree on her striving, then her bitterness amounts to a crime.

There are in the United States today tens of thousands of colored girls who would be happy beyond measure to have the chance of educating themselves that you are neglecting. If you train yourself as you easily can, there are wonderful chances of usefulness before you: You can join the ranks of 15,000 Negro women teachers, of hundreds of nurses and physicians, of the growing number of clerks and stenographers, and above all of the host of homemakers. Ignorance is a cure for nothing. Get the very best training possible and the doors of opportunity will fly open before you as they are flying before thousands of your fellows. On the other hand every time a colored person neglects an opportunity, it makes it more difficult for others of the race to get such an opportunity. Do you want to cut off the chances of the boys and girls of tomorrow?

Herbert Aptheker, ed., *A Documentary History of the Negro People in the United States* 2 (New York: The Citadel Press, 1951): 864. Reprinted by permission.

A RACIST VERSION OF HISTORY

[The Clansman *was a play that made heroes of the Ku Klux Klan and villains of the Black lawmakers of the Reconstruction South. This is a review of the play by an African American magazine in 1905.* The Clansman *later became the spectacular movie* Birth of a Nation.]

. . . To our way of thinking, Mr. Thomas Dixon, Jr., is one of those men walking about who should be incarcerated in a madhouse. Surely the man's mind is unhinged. . . . Mr. Dixon's two most prominent books, *The Clansman* and *The Leopard's Spots* are both manuals of deviltry and barbarism. They are full of wild, raging mobs and secret bands of marauders. It is the first time our public morals have been so low as to do open honor to anarchy. . . . A Negro is shown pursuing a little white girl for violent and unholy purposes. . . . The play was hissed in Richmond. In Columbia the whole performance was amid thunderous applause and hisses. . . . At Bainbridge . . . a mob, fired by the scenes in *The Clansman,* broke into a jail and lynched a Negro charged with murder. In Alabama, an organization known as "The Sons of the Clansmen" has been formed among the young whites. . . . Dr. Len G. Broughton, of [Atlanta], declared that:

"The whole show is a disgrace to Southern manhood and womanhood. . . . The devil of selfish greed is back of it all. It is doing the Negro harm and corrupting the people of our own race. It is un-Christian; it is un-American; it is unsound, and it is unsafe."

. . . The Rev. Richard Carroll, a Negro minister, witnessed the play by invitation at Columbia. He says, "From the beginning to the end the Negro was represented as a brute, a beast and a demon from hell. . . . It is the forerunner of much bloodshed and anarchy." . . .

The Voice of the Negro 2 (December 1905): 836.

A Boy Views the Atlanta Riot of 1906

[*During a racist political campaign in Atlanta, Georgia, white mobs invaded the Black ghetto killing ten men and women and wounding sixty others. Young Walter White, thirteen, discovered he was, despite his white skin, a Black man.*]

Father told Mother to take my sisters, the youngest of them only six, to the rear of the house, which offered more protection from stones and bullets. My brother George was away, so Father and I, the only males in the house, took our places at the front windows of the parlor. The windows opened on a porch along the front side of the house, which in turn gave onto a narrow lawn that sloped down to the street and a picket fence. There was a crash as Negroes smashed the street lamp at the corner of Houston and Piedmont Avenue down the street. In a very few minutes the vanguard of the mob, some of them bearing torches, appeared. . . . In a voice as quiet as though he was asking me to pass him the sugar at the breakfast table, [Father] said, "Son, don't shoot until the first man puts his foot on the lawn and then—don't you miss!"

In the flickering light the mob swayed, paused, and began to flow toward us. In that instant there opened up within me a great awareness; I knew then who I was. I was a Negro, a human being with an invisible pigmentation which marked me as a person to be hunted, hanged, abused, discriminated against, kept in poverty and ignorance, in order that those whose skin was white would have readily at hand a proof of their superiority, a proof patent and inclusive, accessible to the moron and the idiot as well as to the wise man and the genius. No matter how low a white man fell, he could always hold fast to the smug conviction that he was superior to two-thirds of the world's population, for those two-thirds were not white.

It made no difference how intelligent or talented my millions of brothers and I were, or how virtuously we lived. A curse like that of Judas was upon us, a mark of degradation fashioned with heavenly authority. There were white men who said Negroes had no souls, and who proved it by the Bible. Some of these now were approaching us, intent upon burning our house. . . .

Yet as a boy there in the darkness amid the tightening fright, I knew the inexplicable thing—that my skin was as white as the skin of those who were coming at me.

The mob moved toward the lawn. I tried to aim my gun, wondering what it would feel like to kill a man. Suddenly there was a volley of shots. The mob hesitated, stopped. Some friends of my father's had barricaded themselves in a two-story building just below our house. It was they who had fired. . . . Our friends, noting the hesitation, fired another volley. The mob broke and retreated up Houston Street.

In the quiet that followed I put my gun aside and tried to relax. But a tension different from anything I had ever known possessed me. I was gripped by the knowledge of my identity, and in the depths of my soul I was vaguely aware that I was glad of it. . . .

Walter White, *A Man Called White* (New York: The Viking Press, 1948), 9–12. Adapted from *A Man Called White*, by Walter White, copyright 1948 by Walter White, Reprinted by permission of The Viking Press, Inc.

A BLACK ILLINOIS TOWN IN 1908

[*During the Jim Crow era, some African Americans sought self-government in their own towns. A white college president describes Brooklyn, Illinois.*]

This municipal colonization of Afro-Americans apparently affords a striking refutation of the oft-repeated claim that Negroes are born to follow and never to lead—for it seems to have progressed to a degree of unusual prosperity, and its possibilities are yet only to be estimated. The executive heads boast, and county officials have been heard to say, that there is less crime, even fewer violations of the "city code," within the confines of this little corporation than in many of the larger towns of mixed population. . . .

Whites, as well as blacks, who have watched the place grow to its present population of 1,900, agree that a spirit of perfect harmony prevails there in every business walk; that the Negroes are law-abiding to an extreme, self-supporting, honest, and proud of their achievements. . . .

The town has an annual income, from all sources, amounting to more than $10,000, and may levy additional assessments for needed improvements. The present policy is not to incur needless expense. . . .

The mere handful of whites—probably fifty in number—who have habitation in the place live in evident peace with their colored brothers. There is never any race riot or even discord, but they have no voice in the municipal government other than to walk up to the polls each succeeding year and cast their ballots for chosen leaders. Only once . . . was a white man chosen to town office. That was several years ago, when an unpopular Negro was nominated to represent his ward. The citizens banded together and elected his [white] opponent by an overwhelming majority. . . .

Business is conducted by the Negro merchants in Brooklyn much the same as in any other place of like population, where the inhabitants depend upon their weekly or monthly wage to provide for their families. Accounts are run at the different stores and payments met with remarkable promptness. . . .

The labor element find employment at $1.50 to $2 a day, and, as the larger proportion own their homes, where they raise vegetables and poultry, their lot is far from a hard one.

At the head of the administration is Burton Franklin Washington. . . . While, in his opinion, it would be better to have complete isolation from the white race, he realizes that there will always be an element to invade the towns, and says there should never be any prejudice of the blacks against the minority. "There is none here," he said, "and there never will be. As an instance of the perfect harmony which has always existed in Brooklyn, a white man here shot and seriously wounded a respectable colored citizen without apparent cause. The assailant was locked up in our town jail, and altho the injured man hovered between life and death for many days, there was no attempt at violence upon the prisoner. We give the few whites that are here the same show that we have ourselves, if they are determined to stay with us. We pay their school teacher $80 a month, furnish them adequate police protection, and look after their interests as well as it can be done with our means." . . .

The picture is simply a case of the bottom rail being on top, where fate, fortune or whatever it may be termed has brought Afro-Americans together . . . and placed the whites under their control in a peaceable, satisfactory manner of living.

Iverson B. Summers, "A Negro Town in Illinois," *The Independent* 65 (27 August 1908): 464–69.

A BLACK PLAN TO SEIZE TEXAS

[*No book more clearly voiced Black frustration and rage during the era of lynch law than the first novel of Sutton E. Griggs. Beyond his stiff Victorian characters and melodramatic plot, Griggs at twenty-six was calling for a separate Black republic in America. His* Imperium in Imperio *described a secret African American government in Waco poised to seize Texas and wage war on the United States.*]

A PLAN OF ACTION FOR THE IMPERIUM IN IMPERIO

. . . Quietly purchase all Texas land contiguous to states and territories of the Union. Build small commonplace huts on these lands and place rapid-fire disappearing guns in fortifications dug beneath them. All of this is to be done secretly, the money to be raised by the issuance of bonds by the Imperium.

. . . Encourage all Negroes who can possibly do so to enter the United States Navy.

. . . Enter into secret negotiations with all of the foreign enemies of the United States, acquainting them of our military strength and men aboard the United States war ships.

. . . While the Governor is away, let the troops proceed quietly to Austin, seize the capitol and hoist the flag of the Imperium.

. . . We can then, if need be, wreck the entire navy of the United States in a night; the United States will then be prostrate before us and our allies.

. . . We will demand the surrender of Texas and Louisiana to the Imperium. Texas, we will retain. Louisiana we will cede to our foreign allies in return for their aid. Thus will the Negro have an empire of his own, fertile in soil, capable of sustaining a population of fifty million people.

Sutton E. Griggs, *Imperium in Imperio* (Cincinnati, 1899) 251–52.

15 AMERICA ENTERS THE TWENTIETH CENTURY

John Mercer Langston.

ON A WARM DAY IN 1877 the new United States minister to the republic of Haiti arrived at the Presidential Palace at Port au Prince to present his credentials. For the next eight years John Mercer Langston of Virginia, a former slave who had become head of Howard University's Law School, worked to build better relations between his country and the small Black nation. His careful studies of the island's economy enabled American exporters to penetrate the British and French monopoly on Haitian commerce. In a short time American calicoes appeared in Haitian shop windows and Americans were drinking Haitian coffee. Langston, along with Frederick Douglass and historian George W. Williams, was among the thirteen African American diplomats who served in foreign capitals before the Spanish-American War.

The Spanish-American War

American interest in the Caribbean islands, as well as those in the Atlantic and the Pacific, grew out of the industrial expansion that followed the Civil War. Interest in Cuba stemmed from American investments in its plantations and concern for a people savagely mistreated by its Spanish rulers.

The sinking of the battleship *Maine* in Havana harbor, with a loss of 260 white and Black sailors, brought a furious response from Americans. For months the public had been aroused by sensational news stories printed in American papers about Cuba. Often the stories were entirely or partially false—but they sold newspapers. Although it was never proved that Spain was responsible for the explosion aboard the *Maine*, U.S. newspapers claimed Spain was guilty and demanded an invasion of Cuba. Congress quickly passed a Declaration of War.

To speed African American enlistments, President William F. McKinley appointed one hundred Black officers to the army. The four regular Black

Troop C, Ninth Cavalry, leading the charge up San Juan Hill, from a painting by Fletcher C. Ransom.

units, the Ninth and Tenth cavalries and the Twenty-fourth and Twenty-fifth infantries, were sent to Cuba, but aboard ship they were kept in the hold and forbidden to mingle on deck with white soldiers. In port they were denied shore leave. America's highest ranking African American officer, Major Charles Young, was allowed to do little more than make his appearance in Cuba. President McKinley once had advised African Americans, "Be patient, be progressive, be determined, be honest, be God-fearing, and you will win. . . ." His first two words carried his real meaning.

Fighting alongside the Rough Riders and Teddy Roosevelt at San Juan Hill were units of the Ninth and Tenth cavalries. An eyewitness described how the Black troopers "started the charge, and, with the Rough Riders, routed the Spaniards, causing them to retreat in disorder, leaving their dead and wounded behind."

John "Blackjack" Pershing was in command of the Tenth Cavalry on the historic charge. He recalled it with pride:

> White regiments, black regiments, regulars and rough Riders, representing the young manhood of the North and South, fought shoulder to shoulder, unmindful of whether commanded by an ex-Confederate or not, and mindful only of their common duty as Americans.

Rough Rider Frank Knox, who served as secretary of war during World War II, recalled:

> I joined a troop of the Tenth Cavalry and for a time fought with them shoulder to shoulder, and in justice to the colored race I must say that I never saw braver men anywhere. Some of these who rushed up the hill will live in my memory forever.

In the battle at El Caney, African American units distinguished themselves. T. C. Butler, private in the Twenty-fifth Infantry, was the first to enter the blockhouse and capture the Spanish flag. But a white officer from another command who entered after Private Butler made him give it up. Butler tore off a piece of the flag to show his Black comrades.

For his actions in the battle, Sergeant Edward L. Baker won the Congressional Medal of Honor. He "gallantly assisted in the rescue of the wounded from in front of the lines and under heavy fire of the enemy."

Reaction to American Imperialism

The decisive defeat of the Spanish gave the United States a vast new empire of dark-skinned people. Despite American success in bringing modern health, sanitation, and education to the new possessions, many

Major Charles Young, the highest-ranking Black officer during the Spanish-American war.

"Buffalo Soldiers" rest after the Cuban campaign. Later they became America's first machine-gun experts, perfecting techniques of indirect and overhead fire.

resented American control. African American units were part of the U.S. occupation forces in the colonies that stretched from Puerto Rico in the Atlantic to the Philippines in the Pacific.

Americans were deeply divided over overseas expansion. An Anti-Imperialist League drew support from prominent Americans such as Mark Twain and former President Grover Cleveland. African Americans also formed a National Negro Anti-Imperialist League. The Black *Washington Bee* wrote, "A majority of the Negroes in this country are opposed to expansion. . . . Expansion is a fraud." Another Black paper thought it "deplorable" for Black people in "Cuba or Porto Rico to be ruled as the Negroes of the South had been ruled."

African American opposition to expansion increased after American troops landed in the Philippines to crush the revolt led by a young nationalist, Emilio Aguinaldo. Many Black Americans saw Aguinaldo as a dark-skinned liberator, fighting American greed. The Black *Illinois Record* complained, "We are asked to fight for . . . the almighty dollar, for commercial enterprises, coffee trusts, banana trusts, etc." The *Indianapolis Recorder* announced, "The war begun for humanity [in Cuba] is ending in a gratification of the greed for gain." Stanley Ruffin of Boston publicly asked his people "not to attempt or assist to uphold a country that cannot or does not protect us in life, liberty, and the pursuit of happiness. We shall neither fight for such a country or with such an army." Black scholar Kelly

Miller said, "The pill of imperialism may be sugar-coated to the taste, but the Negro swallows it to his own political damnation."

But America had taken up "the white man's burden" overseas as well as at home. Bigots gleefully applauded racism abroad and at home. Southern senators cheered their Northern colleagues who insisted Filipinos were unfit to govern themselves. South Carolina Senator Ben Tillman added:

> No Republican leader, not even Governor [Theodore] Roosevelt, will now dare to wave the bloody shirt and preach a crusade against the South's treatment of the Negro. The North has a bloody shirt of its own. Many thousands of them have been made into shrouds for murdered Filipinos, done to death because they were fighting for liberty.

Later Senator Tillman would ask "in the name of common sense . . . if the Filipinos are unfit [to vote] why are the Negroes fit?"

Professor Kelly Miller.

Claiming the North Pole

While there was disagreement among Americans about their nation becoming a colonial power, all rejoiced at news of the discovery of the North Pole by men of three races on April 6, 1909.

Matt Henson, first man to stand atop the world, reached the North Pole on 6 April 1909 and twice had saved Robert Peary's life. He won a hundred-dollar bet with a naval officer who claimed no African American could reach the pole and return with all his fingers and toes. However, Henson lost thirty-five pounds.

On a subzero arctic day, Matt Henson and three Eskimo guides of Commander Robert E. Peary's expedition reached the top of the world. The small party built an igloo and waited for the commander to arrive and confirm Henson's calculations indicating they were at the top of the world. In less than an hour an exhausted Peary arrived and confirmed the fact.

"Plant the Stars and Stripes over there, Matt—at the North Pole," directed Peary. It was a victory which the two men had tried to accomplish during seven previous expeditions. Peary had met Henson in a Washington clothing store, where the young man had been employed as a clerk. Henson became far more than a companion to Peary during their twenty-three years of joint exploration. Henson learned the Eskimo language and became an expert in the many skills needed for survival in the arctic. Donald MacMillan, another member of the Peary expedition, recalled that:

> He [Henson] was the most popular man aboard the ship with the Eskimos. He could talk their language like a native. He made all the sledges which went to the Pole. He made all the stoves. Henson, the colored man, went to the Pole with Peary because he was a better man than any of his white assistants. . . .

Inspired by Henson's courage, Herbert Frisby made twenty-one arctic trips in twenty-two years. He wanted to show up his teacher who said, "Henson was the first Negro to get to the Pole and you can bet he'll be the last!" Frisby devoted his life to securing recognition for the part Henson played in the Peary expeditions. Frisby's house, "The Igloo," sat on a quiet street in Baltimore, Maryland.

As Henson planted the American flag at the top of the world, he, Peary, and the three Eskimo guides gave three long cheers. But all the way home, Peary did not speak to Henson except to issue orders. He was furious because his Black companion, in reaching the North Pole ahead of him, had disobeyed orders. For years, Peary refused Henson permission to lecture or show slides of the trip.

Admiral Peary won important citations, promotions, and at least twenty-five trophies, medals, and honorary degrees. Henson worked as a porter, a carpenter, a blacksmith, and a messenger. At seventy, he retired with a pension of $1,020 a year. After his death, with the efforts of his friend Herbert Frisby, his state of Maryland placed a plaque in his honor in the statehouse—the first time a man of color was thus honored in the South.

The "Progressive Years"

A pistol shot ushered in the "progressive years" between the turn of the century and the First World War. A crazed assassin fired at President William McKinley as he stood smiling and shaking hands at the Pan-American Exposition in Buffalo, New York. The next man in line to shake hands, a six-foot-six, college-educated Black waiter named Parker seized the assassin before he could escape and turned him over to the police. In a week McKinley was dead and "Teddy" Roosevelt was sworn in as the new president. This energetic young reformer, who promised all Americans a "Square Deal," dominated American political life for the next dozen years.

Three months after he entered the White House, President Roosevelt invited Booker T. Washington to visit him. There was nothing unusual in this since the educator had often been consulted by presidents. At the White House the president and Washington had dinner. This meal made more history than any other since the first Thanksgiving. Southern newspapers exploded in anger. Wrote the *New Orleans Times Democrat,* "When Mr. Roosevelt sits down to dinner with a Negro he declares that the Negro is the social equal of the white man." Another paper screamed, "White men of the South, how do you like it? . . . White women of the South, how do YOU like it?"

For perhaps the only time in his life, the impulsive and fearless Roosevelt did not fight back. He said nothing. Later he wrote to a friend that the dinner "was a mistake." While Roosevelt and President Taft after him continued to meet with Booker T. Washington, neither of them ever ate with him again, and both presidents made greater efforts to win the support of white Southerners than Republicans had ever done before.

Both presidents said African Americans were, in the words of Theodore Roosevelt, "altogether inferior to the whites." In 1909, President Taft told graduates at a Black college in North Carolina, "Your race is meant to be a race of farmers, first, last, and always." Since Roosevelt and Taft appointed a number of Black people to minor or ceremonial posts, Republicans claimed at election time that they had "elevated the race."

The Democrats of the Progressive era offered Black America even less than the Republicans. Their three-time presidential candidate, William Jennings Bryan, summed up his views on racial relations: "Any one who will look at the subject without prejudice will know that white supremacy promotes the highest welfare of both races." In 1922 Bryan said a congressional bill to outlaw lynchings was "a grave mistake."

For African American men, women, and children of the South, the years of Roosevelt and Taft were not progressive. In 1903, the governor of North Carolina announced, "I am proud of my state" because "we have solved the Negro problem." He then explained: "We have taken him out of politics and have thereby secured good government. . . ." Governor James Vardaman of Mississippi told a cheering audience in Poplarville of his determination to keep Blacks from voting: "How is the white man going to control the government? . . . If it is necessary every Negro in the state will be lynched; it will be done to maintain white supremacy." He also suggested that the Fifteenth Amendment to the Constitution "ought to be wiped out. We all agree on that. Then why don't we do it?"

At the turn of the century, Southern states also sought to reduce Black education to a bare minimum. Governor Vardaman explained that "this education is ruining our Negroes. They're demanding equality." In 1912 a white school superintendent in the South reported:

> There has never been any serious attempt in this state to offer adequate educational facilities for the colored race. The average length of the term for the state is only four months. . . . [Some schools have] as many as 100 students to the teacher; no attempt is made to do more than teach the children to read, write, and figure, and these subjects are learned very imperfectly.

One year later, Senator Cole Blease of South Carolina announced, "God Almighty never intended he [the Negro] should be educated."

Blacks were losing faith in President Theodore Roosevelt. In 1906 President Roosevelt dishonorably discharged from the United States Army an entire battalion of Black troops stationed in Brownsville, Texas. The men, who had been insulted and even struck by the townspeople, were charged with shooting up the town and killing one man. Before this time the unit's military record had been superb. Senator Joseph B. Foraker of Ohio defended the troops, saying, "They ask no favors because they are Negroes, but only justice because they are men." The president discharged 167 men without trial, but in 1972 the army exonerated them. By then all but one, Dorsie Willis, eighty-seven, had died.

In the 1912 election, African American voters were deserting both Republican Taft and "Progressive" Roosevelt. Many Black leaders looked to the tall Princeton University president, Woodrow Wilson, as a more sympathetic leader—even though he was both a Southerner and a Democrat. Wilson was elected president of the United States when Taft and Roosevelt split the Republican vote. Black and white voters looked forward with enthusiasm to what Wilson called his "New Freedom."

Wilson and the New Freedom

Americans found Wilson to be a dynamic president. He convinced Congress to pass new laws to regulate interstate trade, control monopolies, and tax incomes. African Americans, however, found the New Freedom to be as empty as the Square Deal had been. President Wilson had even restored segregation to the Treasury and Post Office departments. Partitions were set up to separate Black from white clerks.

Booker T. Washington visited the capital in 1913 and remarked, "I have never seen the colored people so discouraged and bitter as they are at the present time." Those Black leaders who supported Wilson in 1912 were denounced by their followers.

Led by Monroe Trotter, the energetic editor of the Boston *Guardian,* a group of Black leaders visited President Wilson in 1913 to complain about his segregation of government employees. The president told them, "Segregation is not humiliating but a benefit, and ought to be so regarded by you gentlemen." When Trotter pointed out that Black and white clerks had worked side by side in the federal government for half a century, Wilson became angry. "Your manner offends me," he told the editor. "I was thunderstruck," recalled Trotter and replied, "You misinterpret my earnestness for passion." It was clear that the president would not alter his policy.

President Wilson further angered African Americans by endorsing the movie *Birth of a Nation.* This film pictured Black people as depraved animals and made heroes of the Ku Klux Klan. Wilson said the movie was "history written in lightning." At a special showing at the White House, Chief Justice of the Supreme Court Edward White proudly admitted he had been a Klan member.

World War I

When Congress declared war against the Central Powers in April 1917, African Americans were among the first to volunteer and serve. More than two hundred thousand went overseas as stevedores, artillerymen, machine gunners, and infantrymen. The first two Americans to win France's Croix de Guerre for bravery were Henry Johnson of Albany, New York, and Needham Roberts of Trenton, New Jersey. These two men smashed a German attack and virtually wiped out the raiding party.

At the outbreak of the war, Colonel Charles Young, the highest-ranking Black officer in the army, was forced into retirement by "high blood pressure." To establish his fitness for active duty, Young mounted his horse and rode from Ohio to Washington, D.C., and back. But he was not permitted to return to active duty until four days before the Armistice.

U.S. African American combat regiments were assigned to the French and fought in many of the important battles of the war, including the Marne defense and the Meuse-Argonne offensive. They captured important towns and strategic objectives and entered Germany as part of the French army of occupation. Despite German efforts to win them over by propaganda leaflets reminding them of the conditions they faced back home in the United States, not a single Black soldier deserted. Four entire Black regiments were awarded the Croix de Guerre, and the 369th spent 191 days on the firing line, more time than any other American regiment. A young white officer named Harry Truman observed that those units that were allowed to have Black officers were even more effective than those with white officers. In 1948 as president of the United States, he took steps to ensure that the armed forces were officially integrated.

On the home front as well as the fighting front African Americans backed the nation's war effort. Thousands of Southern Blacks poured into Northern industrial centers. Dr. George E. Haynes and Emmett J. Scott were brought to Washington by the Wilson administration to serve the nation's war effort. Dr. Haynes was made head of the Department of Negro Economics of the Department of Labor. Scott was a special assistant to the secretary of war, advising on matters affecting the morale of African Amer-

Sergeant Henry Johnson (holding flowers) receives a postwar New York ticker tape welcome honoring his bravery in fighting off a German unit of twenty men. His buddy, Private Needham Roberts, was in another car.

ican soldiers and civilians. He toured army camps and brought complaints to the attention of the government.

During the war to "make the world safe for democracy," people of color did not neglect their own fight for equality. Three months after the United States declared war, fifteen thousand African Americans conducted a silent parade in New York City. They carried signs to protest the continued lynchings and the race riots in American cities. One read MR. PRESIDENT, WHY NOT MAKE AMERICA SAFE FOR DEMOCRACY? The NAACP led a successful campaign to have the army train African Americans as officers—but the army insisted that they be trained separately from whites. By 1917, the African American officer-training center at Des Moines, Iowa, graduated more than six hundred captains and lieutenants.

Resistance of African American soldiers to discrimination brought about several dramatic incidents on the home front. When the Eighth Illinois Regiment, stationed in Newport News, Virginia, refused to accept segre-

A few soldiers who earned the French Croix de Guerre. Most African Americans in France, however, were assigned to service rather than fighting units.

New York City Silent Parade. Organized by the NAACP in 1917, it protested lynchings and race riots as the United States entered World War I "to make the world safe for democracy."

gation aboard the town's streetcars, it was quickly sent overseas. In Houston, Texas, soldiers of the famed Twenty-fourth Regiment faced the insulting jeers of the townspeople and the assaults of the local police. Some of the infantrymen seized arms and shot it out with the police and white citizens, killing seventeen. Thirteen of the soldiers were sentenced to death, forty others were given life imprisonment, and further prosecutions were planned. The condemned men were denied the right of appeal to the secretary of war or the president. Only the determined action of the NAACP halted further prosecution. James Weldon Johnson led other African American leaders in a delegation that convinced the president to halt other actions against the men.

After the Armistice, General Pershing addressed the much-decorated Ninety-second Division as it prepared to leave France. "I want you officers and soldiers of the Ninety-second Division to know that the Ninety-second Division stands second to none in the record you have made since your ar-

In 1917 some sixty-four members of the Twenty-fourth Infantry were tried for murder after a battle with Houston citizens.

rival in France. . . . The American public has every reason to be proud of that record. . . ." Earlier in the war Robert S. Abbott, Black owner of the *Chicago Defender,* told his readers, "The colored soldier who fights side by side with the white American in the titanic struggle now raging across the sea will hardly be begrudged a fair chance when the victorious armies return." Abbott had spoken too soon, too optimistically.

While President Woodrow Wilson was in Paris trying to bind the world together in a treaty that would end war forever, another American labored in Paris for the unity and peace of the world. William E. B. Du Bois orga-

The famous 369th Regiment, Harlem's "Hell Fighters," in the trenches in France. The regiment earned the French Croix de Guerre.

nized the first meeting of the world's colored peoples in 1919 in Paris. Delegates from fifteen countries and colonies attended. Blacks from Atlanta, Georgia, talked of peace and brotherhood with delegates from Capetown, South Africa. This "Pan-African" movement would grow to great power, uniting the many people of color throughout the world.

VOICE OF MILITANT NATIONALISM

Richard S. Abbott, editor of the *Chicago Defender.* He urged Black Southerners to flee North to jobs and freedom.

[From Reconstruction until World War I, one of twelve bishops of the African Methodist Episcopal Church, Henry M. Turner, was the leading spokesperson for Black nationalism and emigration to Africa. He founded and edited three newspapers and made four visits to Africa.]

. . . I believe that the Negroid race has been free long enough now to begin to think for himself and plan for better conditions than he can lay claim to in this country or ever will. *There is no manhood future in the United States for the Negro.* He may eke out an existence for generations to come, but he can never be a *man*—full, symmetrical and undwarfed. Upon this point I know thousands who make pretensions to scholarship, white and colored, will differ and may charge me with folly, while I in turn pity their ignorance of history and political and civil sociology. . . .

. . . Thousands of young men who are even educated by white teachers never have any respect for people of their own color and spend their days as devotees of white gods. Hundreds, if not thousands, of the terms employed by the white race in the English language are also degrading to the black man. Everything that is satanic, corrupt, base and infamous is denominated *black,* and all that constitutes virtue, purity, innocence, religion, and that which is divine and heavenly, is represented as *white.* . . . The Negro should, therefore, build up a nation of his own, and create a language in keeping with his color, as the whites have done. Nor will he ever respect himself until he does it.

John W. E. Bowen (ed.), *Africa and the American Negro* (Atlanta, 1896) 195–98.

THE SPANISH-AMERICAN WAR

Much has been said about fighting poor little Spain, the eighth power of the world, for the purpose of humanity, that the Spanish are cruel and brutal in their treatment toward the Cubans. . . . The United States puts more people to death without law than all the other nations of the earth combined. So our humanitarianism is too ridiculous to be made a count in the argument of justification.

The Negro will be exterminated soon enough at best, without being over-anxious to die in the defense of a country that is decimating his numbers daily.

Voice of Missions, July 1898.

GOD IS A NEGRO

We have as much right biblically and otherwise to believe that God is a Negro, as you buckra, or white, people have to believe that God is a fine looking, symmetrical and ornamented white man. For the bulk of you, and all the fool Negroes of the country, believe that God is white-skinned, blue-eyed, straight-haired, projecting-nosed, compressed-lipped and finely-robed *white* gentleman, sitting upon a throne somewhere in the heavens. . . .

Yet we are no stickler as to God's color, anyway, but if He has any we would prefer to believe that it is nearer symbolized in the blue sky above us and the blue water of the seas and oceans; but we certainly protest against God being a white man or against God being white *at all;* abstract as this theme must forever remain while we are in the flesh. This is one of the reasons we favor African emigration, or Negro nationalization, wherever we can find a domain . . .

Voice of Missions, February 1898.

[*Bishop Turner denounced the stars and stripes as "a dirty contemptible flag" and prayed he would not die under it. On 8 May 1915, he died in Ontario, Canada.*]

PAUL LAWRENCE DUNBAR, POET

[*One of America's most famous poets at the turn of the century was Paul Lawrence Dunbar, the son of fugitive slaves. Although most of his popular poems were light and amusing dialect stories, he was capable of writing serious poems about African American life in America, such as "We Wear The Mask."*]

We Wear The Mask

We wear the mask that grins and lies,
It hides our cheeks and shades our eyes,—
This debt we pay to human guile;
With torn and bleeding hearts we smile,
And mouth with myriad subtleties.

Why should the world be over-wise,
In counting all our tears and sighs?
Nay, let them only see us, while
   We wear the mask.

We smile, but, O great Christ, our cries
To thee from tortured souls arise.
We sing, but oh the clay is vile
Beneath our feet, and long the mile;
But let the world dream otherwise,
   We wear the mask!

Paul Lawrence Dunbar, *Lyrics of Lowly Life* (New York, 1899), 167.

UNITED STATES IMPERIALISM AND BLACK AMERICA

[*As the United States extended its power over darker peoples in other parts of the world, one voice of Black opposition was that of Kelly Miller, graduate of Harvard and dean of Howard University's College of Arts and Sciences.*]

The welfare of the Negro race is vitally involved in the impending policy of imperialism. . . .
   . . . The United States is attempting to force . . . an alien government upon a unanimously hostile and violently unwilling people. Acquiescence on the part of the Negro in the political rape upon the Filipino would give ground of justification to the assaults upon his rights at home. The Filipino is at least his equal in capacity for self-government. The Negro would show himself unworthy of the rights which he claims should he deny the same to a struggling people under another sky. He would not only forfeit his own weapon of defense, but his friends would lose theirs also. For how, with consistency, could the despoilers of the brown man's rights in Manila, upbraid the nullifiers of the black man's rights in Mississippi? The pill of im-

perialism may be sugar-coated to the taste, but the Negro swallows it to his own political damnation. . . .

The whole trend of imperial aggression is antagonistic to the feebler races. It is a revival of racial arrogance. It has ever been the boast of the proud and haughty race or nation that God has given them the heathen for their inheritance and the uttermost parts of the earth for their possession. . . . Will the Negro stultify himself and become part of the movement which must end in his own humiliation?

Whatever may happen, the Negro should adhere to the principles of the great Declaration [of Independence]. Of this instrument he has been the chief beneficiary; and whatever others may do, he should follow the light that has led him safe thus far on the road to American citizenship. Though all men should forsake it, yet should not he.

Kelly Miller, "The Effect of Imperialism Upon the Negro Race," *Howard's American Magazine* 5 (October 1900): 87–92.

FIRST MEN AT THE NORTH POLE

[*On 6 April 1909, America's flag was planted on another frontier. Matthew Henson, assistant to Commander Robert E. Peary, described the day.*]

We had been travelling eighteen to twenty hours out of every twenty-four. Man, that was killing work! Forced marches all the time. From all our other expeditions we had found out that we couldn't carry food for more than fifty days, fifty-five at a pinch. . . .

We used to travel by night and sleep in the warmest part of the day. I was ahead most of the time with two of the Eskimos. . . .

The morning of April sixth I found we were in the middle of hummock ice. I calculated about how far I had come, and I said to myself, "If I'm not on the Pole, I've crossed it, so I don't have to go no further." And I said to my Eskimos: "We're going top camp here. Make an igloo."

Commander Peary was forty-five minutes behind. He came up to us as we were building the igloo and says, "Well, my boy, how many miles have we made today?" And I answers, "Too many, Commander; I think we crossed the Pole." So the Commander got out his notebook and figured a bit and he says, "I guess you're right."

As a matter of fact, for about a mile or so I must have been going south instead of north. When you're up there, any direction you walk away from the Pole is south.

Lowell Thomas, "First at the Pole," *This Week*, 2 April 1939. Reprinted from *This Week* magazine. Copyright 1939 by the United Newspapers Magazine Corporation. Reprinted by permission of the author.

THE CREED OF MATTHEW HENSON

[*Matthew A. Henson kept this credo in his lecture notes.*]

Great ideals are the glory of man alone. No other creature can have them. Only man can get a vision and an inspiration that will lift him above the level of himself and send him forth against all opposition or any discouragement to do and to dare and to accomplish wonderful and great things for the world and for humanity. . . . There can be no conquest to the man who dwells in the narrow and small environment of a groveling life, and there can be no vision to the man the horizon of whose vision is limited by the bounds of self. But the great things of the world, the great accomplishments of the world, have been achieved by men who had high ideals and who have received great visions. The path is not easy, the climbing is rugged and hard, but the glory at the end is worth while. . . .

Lecture Notes of Matthew A. Henson (Baltimore, Henson Collection, Soper Library, Morgan State College).

MOVING NORTH TO JOBS, 1910–1920

[*The Great War in Europe brought prosperity to America's factories—located mostly in Northern cities. From 1910 to 1920 about half a million Southern Blacks moved northward, attracted by the opportunity for better jobs and homes. This letter from a Mississippi mechanic indicates the great desire to come north— and the Southern efforts to halt the exodus. The "Mr. Abbott" referred to is the publisher of the* Chicago Defender *who encouraged the migration.*]

Granville, Mississippi, May 16, 1917

Dear Sir: This letter is a letter of information of which you will find stamp envelop for reply. I want to come north some time soon but I do not want to leve here looking for a job where I would be in dorse all winter. Now the work I am doing here is running a guage edger in a saw mill. I know all about the grading of lumber. I have been working in lumber about 25 or 27 years. My wedges here is $3.00 a day 11 hours a day. I want to come North where I can educate my 3 little children also my wife. Now if you cannot fit me up at what I am doing down here I can learn anything any one els can. also there is a great deal of good women cooks here would leave any time all they want is to know where to go and some way to go. please write me at once just how I can get my people where they can get something for their work. There are women here cookeing for $1.50 and $2.00 a week. I would like to live in Chicago or Ohio or Philadelphia. Tell Mr. Abbott that our pepel are tole that they can not get anything to do up there and they are being snatched off the trains here in Greenville and a rested but in spite of all this, they are leaving every day and every night 100 or more is expecting to leave this week. Let me here from you at once.

Emmett J. Scott, "Letters of Negro Migrants of 1916–1918," *Journal of Negro History* 4 (July 1919): 435. Published by the Association for the Study of Negro Life and History, Inc. Reprinted by permission.

PRESIDENT WILSON AND SEGREGATION

[*Soon after he became president, Woodrow Wilson segregated Washington's federal employees. In November 1913, a Black delegation protested his action. A year later they returned to receive his answer. Monroe Trotter led the delegates.*]

[*Mr. Monroe Trotter.*] Mr. President, we are here to renew our protest against the segregation of colored employees in the departments of our National Government. We [had] appealed to you to undo this race segregation in accord with your duty as President and with your pre-election pledges to colored American voters. We stated that such segregation was a public humiliation and degradation, and entirely unmerited and far-reaching in its injurious effects. . . .

[*President Woodrow Wilson.*] The white people of the country, as well as I, wish to see the colored people progress, and admire the progress they have already made, and want to see them continue along independent lines. There is, however, a great prejudice against colored people. . . . It will take one hundred years to eradicate this prejudice, and we must deal with it as practical men. Segregation is not humiliating but a benefit, and ought to be so regarded by you gentlemen. If your organization goes out and tells the colored people of the country that it is a humiliation, they will so regard it, but if you do not tell them so, and regard it rather as a benefit, they will regard it the same. The only harm that will come will be if you cause them to think it is a humiliation.

[*Mr. Monroe Trotter.*] It is not in accord with the known facts to claim that the segregation was started because of race friction of white and colored [federal] clerks. The indisputable facts of the situation will not permit of the claim that the segregation is due to the friction. It is untenable, in view of the established facts, to maintain that the segregation is simply to avoid race friction, for the simple reason that for fifty years white and colored clerks have been working together in peace and harmony and friendliness, doing so even through two [President Grover Cleveland] Democratic administrations. Soon after your inauguration began, segregation was drastically introduced in the Treasury and Postal departments by your appointees.

[*President Woodrow Wilson.*] If this organization is ever to have another hearing before me it must have another spokesman. Your manner offends me. . . . Your tone, with its background of passion.

[*Mr. Monroe Trotter.*] But I have no passion in me, Mr. President, you are entirely mistaken; you misinterpret my earnestness for passion.

The Crisis 9 (January 1915): 119–20. Reprinted by permission.

TROUBLE WITH MEXICO, 1916

[*Prior to World War I, American-Mexican relations became strained. A famous incident of this time was the battle between U.S. Tenth Cavalry troops and Mexicans on 21 June 1916. Lance Corporal John A. Jeter, Jr., who took command when his white officers were killed or wounded, describes the scene.*]

. . . The [Mexican] General informed Captain Boyd [in charge of troops K and C of the Tenth Cavalry] that if he attempted to pass he would be compelled to fire upon him. Captain Boyd replied that "that made no difference as he intended to go through and was going to make the attempt." The General and his staff then returned to their troops; Captain Boyd returned to his troop. . . . After I joined the troop the command was given "Prepare to fight on foot, Action right." . . . We advanced between 25 and 50 yards toward the Mexican line when they opened fire upon us. We all fell prone and Captain Boyd gave the command "Commence firing." After two or three seconds, he gave the command to rush from the right. After the second rush, the Captain said he was shot. They opened on us at 200 yards with two machine guns. I shot one of the machine gun operators; this put the gun out of action. After the Captain said he was shot, he said, "jump them, boys, jump them." About the same time Sergeant Winrow remarked that he was shot but said it was not serious and for us to go ahead. . . . We drove practically everything in front of us up to the town. . . .

Deposition of Lance Corporal John Jeter, Jr. (Washington: National Archives, War Records Office, 27 June 1916). This deposition was recorded by Colonel Charles Young, highest ranking African American officer in the United States Army at the time.

AMERICAN INTERVENTION IN LATIN AMERICA

[In the early decades of the twentieth century, American economic interest in Latin America led to military occupation of various countries. The purpose of this "big stick" or "dollar diplomacy" was to protect American business interests or control the nations near our Panama Canal. United States control of the Republic of Haiti lasted from 1915 to 1934. It was investigated by poet and diplomat James Weldon Johnson. This is part of Johnson's report.]

To know the reasons for the present political situation in Haiti, to understand why the United States landed and has for five years maintained military forces in that country, why some three thousand Haitian men, women, and children have been shot down by American rifles and machine guns, it is necessary, among other things, to know that the National City Bank of New York is very much interested in Haiti. It is necessary to know that the National City Bank controls the National Bank of Haiti . . . and that Mr. R. L. Farnham, vice-president of the National City Bank, is virtually the representative of the State Department in matters relating to the island republic. . . .

. . . since July 28, 1915, American military forces have been in control of Haiti. These forces have been increased until there are now somewhere near three thousand Americans under arms in the republic. From the very first, the attitude of the Occupation has been that it was dealing with a conquered territory. Haitian forces were disarmed, military posts and barracks occupied, and the National Palace was taken as headquarters for the Occupation. After selecting a new and acceptable president for the country, steps were at once taken to compel the Haitian government to sign a convention in which it virtually foreswore its independence. . . .

. . . brutalities and atrocities on the part of American marines have occurred with sufficient frequency to be the cause of deep resentment and terror. Marines talk freely of what they "did" to some Haitians in the outly-ing districts. . . . I often sat at tables in the hotels and cafes in company with marine officers and they talked before me without restraint. I remem-ber the description of a "caco" hunt by one of them; he told how they fi-nally came upon a crowd of natives . . . and how they "let them have it" with machine guns and rifle fire. . . .

Perhaps the most serious aspect of American brutality [is shown in the remarks of an American officer who said] . . . "The trouble with this whole business is that some of these people with a little money and education think they are as good as we are," and this is the keynote of the attitude of every American to every Haitian. Americans have carried American hatred to Haiti. They have planted the feeling of caste and color prejudice where it never before existed. . . .

If the United States should leave Haiti today [1920], it would leave more than a thousand widows and orphans of its own making, more banditry than has existed for a century, resentment, hatred, and despair in the heart of a whole people, to say nothing of the irreparable injury to its own tradi-tion as the defender of the rights of man.

James Weldon Johnson, "Self-Determining Haiti," *The Nation* 3 (28 August 1920 and 4 September 1920): 236–37, 266–67. Reprinted by permission.

THE SILENT PARADE OF JULY 28, 1917

[*Soon after the United States entered World War I, fifteen thousand African Americans marched down Fifth Avenue to protest lynchings and discrimination. They marched in silence but their message was expressed in this leaflet distributed to crowds of spectators.*]

We march because by the grace of God and the force of truth the danger-ous, hampering walls of prejudice and inhuman injustices must fall.

We march because we want to make impossible a repetition of Waco, Memphis, and East St. Louis [anti-Black riots] by arousing the conscience of the country, and to bring the murderers of our brothers, sisters, and in-nocent children to justice.

We march because we deem it a crime to be silent in the face of such barbaric acts.

We march because we are thoroughly opposed to Jim Crow cars, segre-gation, discrimination, disfranchisement, lynching, and the host of evils that are forced on us. It is time that the spirit of Christ should be manifested in the making and execution of laws.

We march because we want our children to live in a better land and enjoy fairer conditions than have fallen to our lot.

Why We March, Leaflet.

Behind the Lines: Discrimination in France

[*Howard H. Long, an officer during the First World War, recalled the conditions imposed on himself and other African American soldiers by the United States Army in France.*]

. . . Many of the field officers seemed far more concerned with reminding their Negro subordinates that they were Negroes than they were with having an effective unit that would perform well in combat. There was extreme concern lest the Negro soldiers be on too friendly terms with the French people. An infamous order from division headquarters . . . made speaking to a French woman a disciplinary offense. . . .

We were billeted in Joneville, Haute Marne [France], for a period of training, where the men moved freely among the populace. For no obvious reason we were moved out on the drill ground a quarter of a mile away and even the officers were forbidden to return to the village. When the townspeople came out on the following Sunday they found that the Negro soldiers had been prohibited from meeting and talking with them. . . . One officer was put under arrest, guarded by a private with fixed bayonet, because the commanding officer saw him exchange a note with a French lady across the line. . . .

Howard H. Long, "The Negro Soldier in the Army of the United States," *Journal of Negro Education* 12 (Summer 1943): 311–12. Reprinted by permission.

The 369th and 371st Win the Croix de Guerre

[*During World War I the 369th Regiment set a record of 191 days on the firing line. The 371st won 121 French and 27 American Distinguished Service Crosses. Both entire units won the French Cross of War with these citations.*]

[*369th Infantry . . . French Croix de Guerre with silver star. . . .*]

Under the command of Colonel Hayward, who although wounded, insisted on leading his regiment into combat . . . and Major Little, a real leader of men, the 369th Regiment of American Infantry, under fire for the first time, captured some powerful and energetically defended enemy positions, took the village of Sechault by main force, and brought back six cannon, mainly machine guns, and a number of prisoners.

[*371st Infantry . . . French Croix de Guerre with palm. . . .*]

Under the command of Colonel Miles, this regiment, with superb spirit and admirable disregard for danger rushed to the assault of a strongly defended enemy position which it captured after a hard struggle under a violent machine-gun fire. It then continued its advance, in spite of the enemy artillery fire and heavy losses, taking numerous prisoners, capturing cannon, machine guns, and important material.

General Orders No. 11, United States War Department (Washington: National Archives, 27 March 1924), 22–23.

16 THE TWENTIES

In 1919, TRIUMPHANT ARMIES of khaki-clad soldiers passed in review down New York's Fifth Avenue to the cheers of thousands crowding the sidewalks. One of the most thrilling sights and sounds was that of the 369th Colored Infantry swinging up the avenue toward Harlem, marching to the syncopated beat of Jim Europe's blaring jazz band. Adults tapped their feet to the new sound and schoolchildren followed the solid ranks of marching men. Yet soon after the victory parades ended, soldiers like these, all over the country—in twenty-five cities—would be forced to defend their very lives.

The Growth of Intolerance

A fearful wave of lynchings and racist violence swept the nation. Hate-filled whites, afraid that Black returned soldiers would insist on fair treatment as citizens, decided that now was the time "to keep them from stepping out of their place." Discharged soldiers, some still in uniform, were among the victims of rampaging white mobs.

By the summer of 1919 bloody rioting had taken place in Chicago, Illinois; Omaha, Nebraska; Longview, Texas; Washington, D.C.; and Elaine,

Arkansas. African Americans were dragged from streetcars, beaten on the sidewalks, or attacked in their homes.

An investigator for the NAACP wrote from Arkansas, "The police and deputy sheriff either refuse to check the mobs or [they] join hands with the mobs." In Elaine, sixty-eight Black sharecroppers meeting in a church to form a union were fired on by sheriff's deputies. The sheriff claimed that the people in the church had fired first, but he was never able to explain why he and his men just happened to be outside the church on the particular night the meeting was being held. A dozen African American leaders were then arrested and afterward sentenced to death for firing back and killing one of the attackers, and sixty-seven of the farmers were sentenced to life or long terms in prison. The church was later burned down by lynch mobs and in the reign of terror that followed "men and women were shot down in the fields like wild beasts," numbers were rounded up and "penned in stockades in Little Rock." Two whites later ad-

The 369th Regiment marches up New York's Fifth Avenue in 1919. The men had learned their close-order march from the French.

mitted using torture to force confessions from the sharecroppers. Only after the NAACP provided lawyers and brought the facts to the public were all the defendants liberated.

"The land of liberty is in danger of becoming the land of lynchings," warned Kelly Miller of Howard University. The Ku Klux Klan enjoyed a spectacular rise in membership and power during and after the war. This growth had been partly stimulated by the 1915 movie *Birth of a Nation,* which showed columns of heroic Klansmen galloping off to save civilization.

By the time the war in Europe had ended, the Klan had extended its hate campaign to include Catholics, immigrants, Jews, Asians, union leaders, and "radicals" of all types. Klan officials claimed a membership of five million, and branches were set up in Northern cities and towns. The flaming cross—the Klan's warning to all those it opposed—burned from New York to Oregon as well as in Mississippi. Klan power stretched from Maine to California and from local sheriffs to the United States Senate. It was as influential in Indiana as in Georgia. D. C. Stephenson, Grand Dragon of the half-million-strong Indiana Klan, proclaimed, "I am the law in Indiana." Klan leaders became rich selling membership cards for ten dollars and special Klan regalia for six. Stephenson was said to have made two million dollars in one period of eighteen months.

James Weldon Johnson, first Black executive director of the NAACP, led its anti-lynching campaign.

In 1925, forty thousand Klansmen parade before the U.S. Capitol.

Klan floggings in Oklahoma in 1923 numbered 2,500. That year the governor of Oregon and mayor of Portland attended a dinner for the Grand Dragon of the Oregon Klan. The governor spoke on "Americanism."

By 8 August 1925, the KKK was able to assemble forty thousand members for a parade through Washington, D.C. From midafternoon to dusk, robed men and women marched, arms folded across their chests, past the Capitol. Grim-faced Washington African Americans stood in the crowds. One of them recalled, "We were ready to fight if they broke ranks. We didn't know anything about nonviolence in those days." In fact, the only violence that day was the thunderstorm that greeted the Klan effort to hold an outdoor meeting. No word came from the White House. President Calvin Coolidge was out of town that weekend. But no president in office during the entire period raised his voice against the Ku Klux Klan.

Racist violence and the rise in Klan popularity were part of a general climate of racial hatred that infected the country following World War I. The attorney general of the United States, A. Mitchell Palmer, said that the Communists planned some revolutionary actions for 1 May 1919. Although the date came and went peacefully, Palmer's fear remained.

In his search for "dangerous radicals," the attorney general investigated "Radicalism and Sedition Among the Negroes as Reflected in Their Publications." Magazines such as the *Messenger, Emancipator, Challenge,* and *Crusader* were found to have subversive purposes, including an "openly expressed demand for social equality." The attorney general also found something sinister in the fact that Black magazines were written in "fine, pure English, with a background of scholarship" by highly educated men.

Beginning in the 1920s a number of African Americans did join radical political groups. Ben Fletcher was the only one among 101 leaders of the fiercely radical "Wobblies," the Industrial Workers of the World (IWW), who were sentenced to long prison terms for opposing World War I. The Socialist party appealed to all workers and refused to see the African American as a special group. When their executive board was asked by a group of foreign Socialists what their solution to lynching was, they answered "*socialism.*" Some Socialists did not attempt to conceal their bias. Jack London, for example, said, "I am first of all a white man and only then a socialist." Yet the Socialists attracted Black intellectuals.

If people of color did not respond to the Socialist program, they felt great personal warmth for Eugene V. Debs, longtime leader of the party and five times its presidential candidate. Debs was one of those sentenced to prison for opposing American participation in World War I. Sam Morre, a Black life-termer he met in prison, said, "Gene Debs was the only Jesus Christ I ever knew." When Debs died in 1924, *Crisis* editor W. E. B. Du Bois wrote, "The death of so great a mind and so great a heart as that of

Eugene Debs is a calamity to this poor nation." All through his long career Debs had refused to speak to segregated audiences, and demanded that the labor movement treat Blacks as equals. But, like the other Socialist leaders, he did not feel that the oppression of African Americans was any worse than that experienced by all workers "under capitalism."

The Communist party advocated a special program designed to attract minorities. African Americans, they said, should have the right to form a separate republic in those sections of the South where they were a majority of the residents. By 1928, however, there were fewer than two hundred Black Communists. Blacks, pointed out some of their leaders, had enough trouble being Black without being "red" as well.

Marcus Garvey's Black Power Movement

"All the freedom movements that are taking place right here in America today were initiated by the work and teachings of Marcus Garvey," said Malcolm X. From the Congo to the Hudson and Mississippi, Blacks who call for separation from white society and ideals can trace their views to Marcus Garvey, a self-educated Black man who came to the United States from Jamaica during the First World War. From his headquarters in Harlem, Garvey attacked white racism, directed business enterprises, and told his followers to rejoice in their Blackness, study their heritage, and build a free and sturdy nation in Africa.

Four years after he arrived in America, his Universal Negro Improve-

Marcus Garvey.

ment Association claimed a million members in forty countries, and his newspaper, *Negro World,* sold two hundred thousand copies a week. He built the nation's first African American mass movement by offering racial pride and national identity to a people who had always been told they were inferior. Announcing himself as the Provisional President of Africa, Garvey toured thirty-eight states raising funds from Black ghettoes. Fifty thousand paraded in Harlem behind Garvey in 1920.

In New York's Madison Square Garden his twenty-five thousand followers cheered as he predicted a Black takeover of Africa. "It is in the wind. It is coming. One day, like a storm, it will be here."

But Garvey's African dream was doomed. The land he hoped to buy in Liberia was sold to an American company. J. Edgar Hoover, convinced Garvey was "the foremost radical of his race," had four Black agents follow him. Garvey was indicted and sent to jail in 1925 for mail fraud. It was Hoover's first "high-profile case," and he soon became head of the FBI.

Middle-class African Americans had little love for "this Jamaican Jack-ass." A flamboyant man, Garvey antagonized many by roundly condemning light-skinned Blacks, middle-class Blacks, and Blacks dependent upon white money and values. Integrationists felt Garvey was undermining progress, but he felt white society was hopelessly bigoted. He offered Blacks shares in his business enterprises and urged them to shun beauty preparations that tried to make them look white. "Up you mighty race, you can accomplish what you will." When he attracted support from the Ku Klux Klan, he was not concerned. At least they were whites who were not hypocrites about their racism, he said.

Although neither Garvey nor any of his followers ever emigrated to Africa, his message stirred the imagination of millions. The branch public library in Harlem reported "an intense interest in works on the Negro, his history, race achievements, and present problems." Garvey died poverty-stricken in London in 1940, but his message went marching on. "You know that Garvey is alive," Malcolm X used to tell his audiences.

He had appealed to his people's pride in their race and history as no one had ever done before. There has been no subsequent African American movement that has not drawn strength from Garvey's ideas and followers.

Gangster Days in Chicago

In the decade following the outbreak of the war in Europe, more than one million African Americans migrated from the South to Northern cities. Because they were just off the farms and nonwhite, they were restricted to the worst jobs, neighborhoods, and schools. Crime grew in all city slums, but Black crime was splashed over the front pages of the newspapers. Authorities noted that while African Americans were only 9 percent of the population, they represented 23 percent of the prison population. They ignored the part that discrimination in law enforcement played in piling up these statistics. "Negroes are more likely to be arrested on suspicion than white persons," stated Judge Kickham Scanlon of the Chicago courts. And his colleague Judge Hugo Pam said "the colored man starts with a great handicap" because there is "great prejudice" against him.

Those few people of color who did turn to crime found that whites had control of the most lucrative rackets. No Black crook ever had the money or the power of an Al Capone. John "Mushmouth" Johnson was one of the few African American racketeers to come anywhere near the "big time." He explained his career in crime in these words: "While my family went in for religion and all that, I didn't exactly fancy so much book learning and went out to see where the money grew. Some of those who know me say that I found it." By the time he died in 1907, his gambling establishments had become popular among whites, Blacks, and Asians.

Johnson's remark to losers is still remembered: "A man that gambles had better be without money anyway. I may put it to some good use; you wouldn't know how." He made a quarter of a million dollars from his various underworld operations. Along with other Chicago gangsters of the time, he contributed to both the Democratic and Republican parties and learned well in advance about police raids.

During Prohibition, Chicago racketeers of both races made and sold bootleg liquor, gunned down their competitors in the streets, and were carted off to prison by federal agents. Some ended up in Lake Michigan wearing "cement shoes." Only a rare few lived out normally long lives as "respectable citizens" and died natural deaths.

Dan Jackson, a graduate of Lincoln University, became the leading Black racketeer of the Roaring Twenties. He, like John "Mushmouth" Johnson, never made more than a quarter of a million dollars from his Chicago bootlegging and gambling syndicate. Jackson provided coal for the poor and often paid their rent bills. He contributed to charities and made donations to the NAACP. Along with Al Capone's representative, he sat on a local Republican committee that picked candidates for public office. The governor appointed Jackson to the Illinois Commerce Commission.

Jackson was himself a victim of as well as an overlord of Chicago crime. He was once held up on the steps of city hall and relieved of $25,000 in cash. It is unclear what he was doing at city hall with so much cash and whether he was going in or coming out. When he died in 1929 (of natural causes), he was sixty years old and under indictment. His friends on both sides of the law gave him "a grand funeral."

More than a hundred African Americans were part of Chicago's over-worked police force during this prolonged crime wave. Some were among those accused of "going around collecting graft money," but most did their best to foil crime, arrest criminals, and halt graft. Like most white police-men, they were hardworking, dedicated lawmen in a lawless city.

A Black Renaissance

While crimes of violence scarred the big cities, a movement of great importance to America was under way in New York, particularly in the ghetto of Harlem. In the decade of prosperity and easy money that followed World War I, the white population had enough cash in their pockets to make a pastime out of finding new ways in which to spend it. Plays and movies boomed as they rarely had before. The dance halls around Broad-way were packed to the doors by high school students and their grandpar-ents dancing afternoon and evening to the new jazz. Although the world

Bessie Smith, greatest blues singer of all time, drew immense crowds.

Jim Europe's army band brought American jazz music to France and back to New York. Vernon and Irene Castle credited Europe with teaching them the fox trot, which they taught to the world.

All-American football star Paul Robeson became a famous actor and singer.

credited the fox trot to the famous dance team of Vernon and Irene Castle, the Castles credited bandleader Jim Europe.

A new age had come to the American theater. At Greenwich Village's Provincetown Playhouse, a young man named Eugene O'Neill was writing plays which used the decks of oil tankers or tenements in Harlem as settings, rather than the fancy living rooms and gardens of the rich. Some of his plays called for Black actors in important roles, and Charles Gilpin made an astonishing success in O'Neill's *Emperor Jones*, which was first produced in 1920 and filled the theater for the next four years.

On Broadway the hit of the 1921 season was a sparkling musical with an all-Black cast, *Shuffle Along*. Its star, Florence Mills, was a tiny young lady of many talents. All America sang its lead song, *I'm Just Wild About Harry*. Virtually every year in the twenties saw another Broadway hit with either an all-Black cast or many African Americans featured in leading roles: *Liza, Running Wild* (which gave the world the Charleston dance), *Chocolate Dandies, Porgy,* and *Green Pastures*.

In 1924 at the Provincetown Playhouse in Greenwich Village, another young actor, a husky, former All-American football star named Paul Robeson, made history in O'Neill's *All God's Children Got Wings*. Robeson then won tremendous applause for his singing in the musical hit *Showboat* on Broadway. In 1930 his fame became worldwide when he starred in a London production of Shakespeare's *Othello*.

The significance of the African American contribution to the dramas of the twenties was stated by poet and critic James Weldon Johnson.

> In *Porgy* the Negro removed any lingering doubts as to his ability to do intelligent acting. In *Green Pastures* he established conclusively his capacity to get the utmost across the footlights, to convey the most delicate nuances of emotion, to create the atmosphere in which the seemingly unreal becomes for the audience the most real thing in life.

Soon whites seeking to see "Negro life," entertainers, or jazz bands began taking the short subway ride up to Harlem. They crowded the dance floors of the nightclubs and enjoyed the spectacular floor shows. The white owners of Harlem's night spots responded by offering new and bigger clubs. The best-known of these long excluded people of color. Even W. C. Handy, composer of the *St. Louis Blues* and hundreds of other songs, accompanied by the white director of the American Society of Composers, Authors and Publishers (ASCAP), could not get into one club where Handy's music was featured. "Harlem," complained poet Claude McKay, "is an all-white picnic ground with no apparent gain to the Blacks."

Alain L. Locke, first Black Rhodes Scholar, edited *The New Negro,* a book of verse, essays, and art that ushered in a "Harlem Renaissance."

But this was an exaggeration. While the average resident received no more money in his pay envelope as a result of all this white attention, talented African Americans found a new audience. Some of the whites who had come uptown for fun returned to study and learn. A few became patrons of Black poets, artists, novelists, and playwrights.

The three young poet-heroes of this Harlem Renaissance were Claude McKay from the West Indies, Langston Hughes from Missouri, and Countee Cullen from New York. All came to stay in Harlem—as did thousands pouring up from the South. Mainly in poetry, but also in short stories, novels, and essays, these three expressed the new mood of rugged determination to overcome the Jim Crow system. "We younger Negro artists who create intend to express our individual dark-skinned selves without fear or shame," wrote Langston Hughes. "If white people are pleased we are glad. If they are not, it doesn't matter."

Although the three had a sizable white audience unmatched by any African American since Paul Lawrence Dunbar, they faced limitations that angered them. "The more truthfully we write about ourselves," said Langston Hughes, "the more limited our market becomes."

Sometime after the 1929 stock market crash, the renaissance began to fade. "For how could a large and enthusiastic number of people be crazy about Negroes forever?" asked Langston Hughes. "The white people had

Countee Cullen.

Langston Hughes. He preferred the parties used by Harlem's poor to raise rent money to the fancy face Harlem put on for its white visitors.

much less money to spend on themselves, and practically none to spend on Negroes, for the depression had brought everybody down a peg or two. And the Negroes had but few pegs to fall." But between 1914 and 1924 no novels by African Americans had been published. In the next ten years twenty appeared.

The Frustrating Fight for Rights

During the 1920s African Americans battled against overwhelming odds to secure their rights, and there were some outstanding successes in business. By the mid-1920s there were twenty-five Black-owned insurance companies carrying policies amounting to two billion dollars. By 1928 African Americans owned fifty banks and twenty-five insurance companies. In New York the Black Swan Company sold seven thousand records a day. Walter H. Lee of Chicago ran a fleet of cabs.

Success in business, however, did not lead to civil rights victories, especially in the South. In Mobile, Alabama, only 135 of the city's 30,000 Black citizens were permitted to vote. In Birmingham it was 300 out of 80,000. Mrs. Indiana Little, a Birmingham schoolteacher, tried to organize a voter registration drive among her people in 1925. When she led them to the city hall to register, she was arrested and jailed for "disorderly conduct."

The battle for rights in the North achieved some success by 1930. In 1921 an antilynching bill passed the House of Representatives by a vote of 230 to 119, only to be filibustered to death in the Senate. But by 1930 an African American, Oscar DePriest, sat in the United States Congress and fourteen more were in state legislatures of five Northern states and two Southern border states. The NAACP successfully led a campaign to defeat a Supreme Court nomination. President Herbert Hoover had asked the Senate to confirm the nomination of Judge John J. Parker, who had once stated that Blacks should not vote for their own good and that of the country. Parker was defeated by a Senate vote of forty-one to thirty-nine and a Southern newspaper credited the NAACP as the force that "broke his back."

Congressman Oscar DePriest. In 1928 he became the first Black man to represent a Northern district in Congress.

In 1930 a Black Chicago newspaper, the *Whip,* led a boycott of stores that did not hire African Americans. By the end of its fifth month, the boycott had led to the hiring of one thousand people of color. Du Bois called the boycott "one tremendous and most effective weapon" and voiced the hope that "this is but the beginning."

The most dramatic affirmation of human rights took place in Detroit, shortly after Labor Day, 1925. Dr. Ossian Sweet, who had recently returned from Paris where he had studied the effect of radium with Madame Curie, purchased a home in a white neighborhood. He waited nine months for his neighbors-to-be to settle down before he moved in. During this time Mrs. Sweet received threatening calls predicting her death and the destruction of their new home.

On 8 September 1925, the Sweets moved in, bringing guns, ammunition, and a few relatives and friends to stand by them in case of trouble. The first night a small crowd gathered. The next night it grew menacing.

At 8:25 P.M. a car filled with relatives and friends to reinforce the Sweets arrived in front of the house. The mob charged to the door after the newcomers. "It looked like a human sea," Dr. Sweet later testified. "When I opened the door and saw the mob, I realized that I was facing the same mob that had hounded my people through its entire history. In my mind I was pretty confident of what I was up against. I had my back against the

A Washington, D.C., parade against the rise in postwar lynchings, part of the NAACP campaign to have Congress pass the Dyer antilynching bill. The House passed it by an overwhelming majority, but it was filibustered to death by Southern senators.

wall. I was filled with a peculiar fear, the fear of one who knows the history of my race. I knew what mobs had done to my race before."

Almost as soon as Dr. Sweet had let in his friends and shut the door on the mob, shots rang out from outside and from an upstairs window. A white man fell dead in the street. The police, who had done nothing to disperse the mob, arrested everyone in the house, including Mrs. Sweet. The entire group was charged with murder.

The NAACP hired Clarence Darrow to defend the Sweets. He faced many white witnesses who denied that there had even been a mob outside

White troops end the Chicago riot of 1919. As the number of white casualties reached the number of Black casualties, the whites decided they had had enough.

the Sweets' home that evening. Darrow pointed out that the prosecution had "put on enough witnesses who said they were there, to make a mob." He stressed that the man killed could not be "innocent," for no person in such a mob was innocent. His final point was simply that an African American had as much right to defend his home as a white. The jury agreed and the Sweets went free. It was a historic victory.

THE 369TH SWINGS *UP* FIFTH AVENUE

[Bernard Katz, a New York City high school student during World War I, tells of the memorable day the city welcomed home the 15th Infantry (Colored) National Guard of New York.]

I was strolling up Fifth Avenue on February 17, 1919, during lunchtime, with a lot of my buddies from school, when we heard the fanfare of the bugles and the booming drums of a marching band. I can't remember if the papers had said anything about a parade. There were lots of them before, during, and after the war and, it seems to me, generally without as much advance publicity and hullabaloo as is thought necessary nowadays to guarantee record-breaking crowds. Even before the troops appeared, the sidewalks were jammed from buildings to curbs with spectators, for there was something odd about this parade right from the start. Most of the other parades came *down* Fifth Avenue—this one was moving uptown!

We soon saw why. Back from the Rhine to get the applause of their city and of Harlem were the troops known in France as the 369th U.S. Infantry, but known in New York as the Harlem Hell Fighters. . . .

. . . The 369th was marching in a formation unfamiliar to most American troops, and certainly to the public until that day. Because the 369th had been segregated from the rest of the American forces and had served under the French command, they were marching in the extraordinarily dramatic Phalanx formation of the French Army. Shoulder to shoulder, from curb to curb, they stretched in great massed squares, thirty-five feet wide by thirty-five feet long, of men, helmets, and bayonets. Through the newly erected Victory Arch at 25th Street and Fifth, they tramped far up the Avenue in an endless mass of dark-skinned, grim-faced, heavy-booted veterans of many a French battlefield.

Then we heard the music! Somewhere in the line of march was Jim Europe and his band that the French had heard before we ever did. Major Little claims they played no jazz until they got to Harlem later that day— but if what we along the curbs heard was not jazz, it was the best substitute for it I've ever heard in my life. All I know is that my school friends and I stepped out into the middle of the street with great hordes of other spectators, and swung up Fifth Avenue behind the 369th and the fantastic sixty-piece band that was beating out those rhythms that could be heard all the way down at our end of the parade.

A VETERAN IS CHASED BY A MOB

[*In Chicago, during a 1920 race riot, a Black university student, working in a factory just outside the city, left work early, unaware of the riot that was in progress. As he was about to board a streetcar, he was attacked by about twenty young white men. He jumped into the car and they followed.*]

The motorman opened the door, and before they knew it I jumped out and ran up Fifty-first Street as fast as my feet could carry me. Gaining about thirty yards on them was a decided advantage, for one of them saw me and with the shout "There he goes!" the gang started after me. One, two, three, blocks went past in rapid succession. They came on, shouting, "Stop him! Stop him!" I ran on the sidewalk and someone tried to trip me, but fortunately I anticipated his intentions and jumped into the road. . . .

Then I came to a corner where a drug-store was open and a woman standing outside. I slowed down and asked her to let me go in there, that a gang was chasing me; but she said I would not be safe there, so I turned off Fifty-first Street and ran down the side street. Here the road had been freshly oiled and I nearly took a "header" as I stepped in the first pool, but fortunately no accident happened. My strength was fast failing; the suggestion came into my mind to stop and give up or try to fight it out with the two or three who were still chasing me, but this would never do, as the odds were too great, so I kept on. My legs began to wobble, my breath came harder, and my heart seemed to be pounding like a big pump, while the man nearest me began to creep up on me. It was then that an old athletic maxim came into my mind—"He's feeling as tired as you." Besides, I thought, perhaps he smokes and boozes and his wind is worse than mine. Often in the last hundred yards of a quarter-mile that thought of my opponent's condition had brought forth the last efforts necessary for the final spurt. There was more than a medal at stake this time, so I stuck, and in a few strides more they gave up the chase. . . .

This is no place for a minister's son, I thought, and crept behind a fence and lay down among some weeds. . . .

My problem was to get home and to avoid meeting hostile elements. Temporarily I was safe in hiding, but I could not stay there after daybreak So I decided to wait a couple of hours and then try to pass through "No Man's Land"—Halsted to Wentworth. I figured the time to be about 11:30 and so decided to wait until 1:30 or 2:00 A.M., before coming out of cover. Shots rang out intermittently; the sky became illumined; the fire bells rang, and I imagined riot and arson held sway as of the previous year. . . .

Then the injustice of the whole thing overwhelmed me—emotions ran riot. Had the ten months I spent in France been all in vain? Were those little white crosses over the dead bodies of those dark-skinned boys lying in Flanders fields for naught? Was democracy merely a hollow sentiment? What had I done to deserve such treatment? I lay there experiencing all the emotions I imagined the innocent victim of a southern mob must feel when being hunted for some supposed crime. Was this what I had given up my Canadian citizenship for, to become an American citizen and soldier? Was the risk of life in a country where such hatred existed worth while? Must a Negro always suffer merely because of the color of his skin? . . .

. . . with resources at an end, I picked up four rocks for ammunition and started out. . . .

At State and Thirty-seventh I saw two colored fellows waiting for a car and ran up to them. Putting my hands on their shoulders I said, "Gee! I'm glad to see a dark skin." . . . They assured me the "fun" was all over, and I was thankful. . . . A white man came along, and my first impulse was to jump on him and beat him up. But again reason told me he was not responsible for the actions of a gang of rowdies, and he was as innocent as I had been when set upon.

The Chicago Commission on Race Relations, *The Negro in Chicago, a Study of Race Relations and a Race Riot* (Chicago: The University of Chicago Press, 1922), 481–84. Reprinted by permission.

A BLACK WOMAN'S VIEW OF THE 1919 RIOTS

[*In this letter to the editor of* The Crisis, *an African American woman tells why she is happy that Black men fought back against their oppressors in the Washington, D.C., riot of 1919.*]

The Washington riot gave me the *thrill that comes once in a life time.* I . . . read between the lines of our morning paper that at last our men had stood like men, struck back, were no longer dumb driven cattle. When I could no longer read for my streaming tears, I stood up, alone in my room, held both hands high over my head and exclaimed aloud: "Oh I thank God, thank God." . . . Only colored women of the South know the extreme in suffering and humiliation.

We know how many insults we have borne silently, for we have hidden many of them from our men because we did not want them to die needlessly in our defense . . . , the deep humiliation of sitting in the Jim Crow part of a street car and hear the white men laugh and discuss us, point out the good and bad points of our bodies. . . .

And, too, a woman loves a strong man, she delights to feel that her man can protect her, fight for her if necessary, save her.

No woman loves a weakling, a coward be she white or black, and some of us have been near thinking our men cowards, but thank God for Washington colored men! All honor to them, for they first blazed the way and right swiftly did Chicago men follow [during the 1919 race riot]. They put new hope, a new vision into their almost despairing women.

God Grant that our men everywhere refrain from strife, provoke no quarrel, but that they protect their women and homes at any cost.

A Southern Colored Woman

The Crisis 19 (November 1919): 339. Reprinted by permission.

"The Negro Must Have a Country"

[*Marcus Garvey, who believed he was a Black Moses, explained his beliefs to white Americans.*]

The Negro must have a country, and a nation of his own. If you laugh at the idea, then you are selfish and wicked, for you and your children do not intend that the Negro shall discommode you in yours. If you do not want him to have a country and a nation of his own; if you do not intend to give him equal opportunities in yours; then it is plain to see that you mean that he must die, even as the Indian to make room for your generations.

Why should the Negro die? Has he not served America and the world? Has he not borne the burden of civilization in this Western world for three hundred years? Has he not contributed his best to America? Surely all this stands to his credit, but there will not be enough room and the one answer is "find a place." We have found a place, it is Africa and as black men for three centuries have helped white men build America, surely generous and grateful white men will help black men build Africa. . . .

Let the Negroes have a Government of their own. Don't encourage them to believe that they will become social equals and leaders of the whites in America, without first on their own account proving to the world that they are capable of evolving a civilization of their own. . . .

Marcus Garvey, *An Appeal to the Soul of White America* (Baltimore: Soper Library, Morgan State University, 1923), n.p.

The South During the 1920s

[*In 1929 Robert Bagnall, a Black investigator for the NAACP, toured the South and wrote this report.*]

It is Mississippi. "*The* River" is on its annual rampage. Wastes of water spread over the landscape. Houses are submerged up to the second story. Boats have replaced automobiles and buggies. . . . At any time, any and every Negro may be impressed to save the levees. . . . Everywhere there is unrest and an atmosphere of fear and suspense. . . .

The railroad embankment runs like a ribbon flanked by the flowing waters—but as we get away from Vicksburg we find fields above ground.

Looking out of my car window as my train scuttled across the state as if it feared the rising waters might engulf it, I was riveted by a scene in the field opposite me. A Negro was desperately fleeing. Behind him ran two white men. I saw the flashes of their pistols as they fired at him. All at once, he stumbled, threw up both arms and fell. In a moment he was on his feet once more. Again, the two whites running towards him blazed away, as he haltingly fled before them. My train whisked me out of sight and I shall never know whether the Negro was killed. He probably was. Who were the whites—officers or civilians? I shall never know. I scanned the papers for days afterwards but saw no word of what had happened. When I told my friend in Louisiana, he merely shrugged his shoulders and said—"Why, that was merely an incident"—a common one. "The world never hears of many things like that." In Baton Rouge they told me how Negroes dared not report whippings and lynchings. . . .

In the upper part of Louisiana—as in most places in the South—the whites believe that Chief Justice Taney's decision that "a Negro has no rights which a white man is bound to respect" yet holds. A Negro sued the parish for damages he had suffered. His was a good case. Therefore, persons close to the affairs of the parish determined to settle the matter out of court. They took him for a ride, flogged him until his clothing had been cut to ribbons and his back was in shreds, broke his arm, and ordered him never to return to the parish. The encouraging thing is that he has courage enough to continue his fight in court. I understand, too, action is to be started against his assailants whom he recognized, it is stated, as officers of the parish.

But it is "the magic city" of Birmingham which holds the prize for terrorism. There police and courts are run by that order of thugs—the Ku Klux Klan. Without provocation police shoot Negroes so frequently there, that it is no longer news. Negroes are beaten up daily for standing on the streets. Recently the police killed a schoolteacher because he was standing on a corner and didn't move with sufficient alacrity at their orders.

This is a black picture but there is another side. Here and there citizens are protesting and acting against these injustices. . . . Negroes dare not speak. But now and then . . . white men both speak and act. Their numbers steadily increase. . . . Down in a college town in Tennessee white and colored college students met regularly, ate, drank, discussed, and played together—even to the extent of dancing until a nasty newspaper article frightened the authorities in their schools. . . . I know southern whites who have given up father, mother, home, and hopes of inheritance, in order to cling to their beliefs, that men and women are to be made comrades on the basis of congeniality regardless of color, "My father died in my arms without forgiving me," said one of these to me, "because of my position on race matters, but I am happy, for I have found something worthwhile in life." . . .

The most hopeful thing in the South, however, is the growing realization of colored people that without organization destined to mould public opinion, to modify laws, and to gain justice in courts and safety of life, limb and property, Negroes can have no freedom nor ending of danger. . . .

Robert W. Bagnall, "The Present South," *The Crisis* 36 (September 1929): 303, 321–22. Reprinted by permission.

RETURN TO THE UNITED STATES CONGRESS

[In 1928 Oscar DePriest of Chicago became the first African American to be elected to Congress from the North and the first elected in the twentieth century. During his time in office, the Illinois Republican was America's only Black Congressman. He was always aware of the fact that he represented more than the people of his district. This was clear when he took part in the congressional debate about American occupation of Haiti.]

I . . . am very glad to see the gentlemen on the minority [Democratic] side of this House so solicitous about the condition of the black people of Haiti. I wish to God they were equally solicitous about the black people of America. We in America would like in some of the States of this country to have the right of self-determination also. The people of Haiti should have the right of self-determination under the broad principles laid down by our Constitution. . . .

This should apply to Haiti and also to every other class of people that God's sun shines on, and I am glad to see the gentlemen on the minority side of the House converted to the right way of thinking, for once in their lives, because I appreciate the condition of the black Americans, where they are denied the right of self-determination in almost every State south of the Mason and Dixon line, and I congratulate the gentlemen for starting in right in Haiti and conceding the common people the right of self-determination and hope it will spread to every State in America and that we will all enjoy the same rights and privileges.

The Congressional Record, part 1, 71st Cong., 2nd sess., 912–13.

THE "HARLEM RENAISSANCE"

[*Poet, dramatist, novelist, and historian Langston Hughes was in his twenties during the "Harlem Renaissance."*]

All of us know that the gay and sparkling life of the so-called Negro Renaissance of the 20s was not so gay and sparkling beneath the surface as it looked. . . .

It was a period when every season there was at least one hit play on Broadway acted by a Negro cast. And when books by Negro authors were being published with much greater frequency and much more publicity than ever before or since in history. It was a period when white writers wrote about Negroes more successfully (commercially speaking) than Negroes did about themselves. It was the period (God help us!) when Ethel Barrymore appeared in blackface in *Scarlet Sister Mary!* It was the period when the Negro was in vogue.

I was there. I had a swell time while it lasted. But I thought it wouldn't last long. . . . For how could a large and enthusiastic number of people be crazy about Negroes forever? But some Harlemites thought the millennium had come. They thought the race problem had at last been solved. . . . They were sure the New Negro would lead a new life from then on in green pastures of tolerance created by Countee Cullen, Ethel Waters, Claude McKay, Duke Ellington, Bojangles, and Alain Locke.

I don't know what made any Negroes think that—except that they were mostly intellectuals doing the thinking. The ordinary Negroes hadn't heard of the Negro Renaissance. And if they had, it hadn't raised their wages any. As for all those white folks in the speakeasies and night clubs of Harlem— well, maybe a colored man could find *some* place to have a drink that the tourists hadn't yet discovered.

Then it was that house-rent parties began to flourish—and not always to raise the rent either. But, as often as not, to have a get-together of one's own, where you could do the black-bottom with no stranger behind you trying to do it, too. . . .

The Saturday night rent parties that I attended were often more amusing than any night club, in small apartments where God knows who lived—because the guests seldom did—but where the piano would often be augmented by a guitar, or an odd cornet, or somebody with a pair of drums walking in off the street. And where awful bootleg whiskey and good fried fish or steaming chitterling were sold at very low prices. And the dancing and singing and impromptu entertaining went on until dawn came in at the windows. . . .

Almost every Saturday night when I was in Harlem I went to a house-rent party. I wrote lots of poems about house-rent parties, and ate thereat many a fried fish and pig's foot—with liquid refreshments on the side. I met ladies' maids and truck drivers, laundry workers and shoe shine boys, seamstresses and porters. I can still hear their laughter in my ears, hear the soft slow music, and feel the floor shaking as the dancers danced.

Langston Hughes, *The Big Sea, An Autobiography* (New York: Hill and Wang, 1963), 227, 228–29, 233.

TROUBLE WITH THE ANGELS

[*One of the hit shows of the twenties was Marc Connelly's* Green Pastures. *For the first time in the history of the American theater, a Black "Great God Almighty" and Black "Angels" were shown on stage in a nonreligious show with music. Blacks in Washington wrote to the show's management asking them to drop their discriminatory policies and allow them to purchase tickets. When the management turned them down and the actor who played God refused to interfere, the Angels, led by a young actor named Johnny Logan, decided to strike. Poet Langston Hughes tells of what followed.*]

Logan spent the whole day rallying the flagging spirits of his fellow actors. They were solid for the strike when he was around, and weak when he wasn't. . . .

"Listen here, you might as well get wise. Ain't nobody gonna strike tonight," one of the boys told him about six o'clock in the lobby of the colored Whitelaw Hotel. "You just as well give up. We ain't got no guts."

"I won't give up," said Logan.

When the actors reached the theatre, they found it surrounded by cops and the stage full of detectives. In the lobby there was a long line of people—white, of course—waiting to buy standing room. God arrived with motorcycle cops in front of his car. He had come a little early to address the cast. . . .

They called everybody together on the stage. The Lord wept as he spoke of all his race had borne to get where they were today. Of how they had struggled. Of how they sang. Of how they must keep on struggling and singing—until white folks saw the light. The strike would do no good. The strike would only hurt their cause. With sorrow in his heart—but more noble because of it—he would go on with the play. And he was sure his actors—his angels—his children—would, too.

The white men accompanying God were very solemn, also, as though hurt to their souls to think what their Negro employees were suffering—but far more hurt to think that they wanted to jeopardize a week's box office receipts by a strike! That would hurt everybody—*even white folks!*

All gave up but Logan. He went downstairs to fight . . . to carry through the strike. But he couldn't. Nobody really wanted to strike. . . .

The management sent two detectives downstairs to get Logan. They were taking no chances. Just as the curtain rose they dragged him off to jail—for disturbing the peace. All the other colored angels were massed in the wings for the opening spiritual when the police took the black boy out. They saw a line of tears running down his cheeks. Most of the actors thought he was crying because he was being arrested—and in their timid souls they were glad it wasn't them.

Langston Hughes, "Trouble with the Angels," *New Theatre* 11, no. 7 (July 1935): 7. Reprinted by permission of Harald Ober Associates.

DR. DU BOIS REVIEWS TWENTY YEARS OF PROGRESS

[In 1929, on the twentieth anniversary of the NAACP, Dr. Du Bois reviewed African American gains.]

Twenty years ago there was scarcely a reputable scientist who dared to assert the equality of the Negro race. . . . Africa was assumed to have no history and there was only one college in the United States that offered a course of study in Negro history and psychology. . . .

It was declared by all reputable authorities that the fate of the Negro race in the United States was extinction and death, and that what tuberculosis did not do, crime and inefficiency would finish. And finally, it was said by the Negroes themselves, almost unanimously, that real effective organization for the attainment of the rights of black men in America was impossible.

But we disregarded the advice of our friends. We went in for agitation. We pushed our way into the courts. We demanded the right to vote. We urged and pushed our children into college. We encouraged Negro art and literature. We studied African history and in season and out of season we declared that the colored races were destined at least to share in the heritage of the earth.

We stand today at the threshold of a new generation, with 12,000 of our children in college; with a recognized place in American literature and art; with the reappearance of the black man in Congress and, what is more important, with the emergence of an independent Negro vote. . . .

Keynote address, 20th Anniversary NAACP Conference (Washington: Library of Congress, Moorfield Storey Papers, Manuscript Collection, 27 June 1929).

17 DEPRESSION AND THE NEW DEAL

IN 1929 IT SEEMED as though the prosperity and good times of the 1920s would never end. Behind the secret doors of "speakeasies," jazz bands played on. And in spite of Prohibition, Americans consumed more liquor and beer than they ever had before.

The Great Depression

The stock market crash of 1929 brought America's most devastating depression to every doorstep. People were fired as factories closed. Across the nation Americans lined up for bread, milk, and jobs. Desperation born of hunger led some people to take matters into their own hands. By 1931 unemployed men of both races entered an Oklahoma City grocery store and seized all the food they could carry. In Greenville, South Carolina, two thousand African Americans and whites marched to a local construction site to demand work. Then they sat down together to plan other actions for their economic relief. Even hooded Klansmen did not shake their unity.

The most dramatic demand for relief was the march of from fifteen to twenty thousand veterans of World War I on Washington in the spring of 1932. This Bonus Expeditionary Force (BEF) as it called itself was composed of unemployed veterans demanding a bonus. *Crisis* reporter Roy

Wilkins toured the BEF tent camp in Washington and found no discrimination but he noticed that the white veterans were bitter while "disappointment and disillusionment are an old story to the Negroes." Though these veterans did not get their bonus, they notified the government that it could not stand by while Americans starved or had no work.

The common misery of the depression helped to build a new unity among farmers, especially the mistreated sharecroppers. On a July evening in 1934, the Southern Tenant Farmers' Union was started in a dingy Arkansas schoolhouse. Old and young farmers of both races debated whether to break tradition and build one union. An old, white-haired Black sharecropper, who had seen his union wiped out in the 1919 Elaine, Arkansas, massacre, rose to speak.

> We colored people can't organize without you and you white folks can't organize without us. Aren't we all brothers and ain't God the Father of us all? We live under the same sun, eat the same food, wear the same kind of clothes, work on the same land, raise the same crop for the same landlord who oppresses and cheats us both. For a long time now the white folks and the colored folks have been fighting each other and both of us has been getting whipped all the time. We don't have nothing against one another but we got plenty against the landlord. The same chain that holds my people holds your people too. If we're chained together on the outside, we ought to stay chained together in the

A government supervisor leads a discussion on home management with migratory workers. The New Deal took an interest in people who were ill clad, ill housed, and ill fed.

A meeting of an agricultural workers' union in 1936. The pain brought on by hunger cut across racial lines and united white and Black workers in the new CIO unions.

union. It won't do no good for us to divide because there's where the trouble has been all the time. The landlord is always betwixt us, beatin' us and starvin' us, and makin' us fight each other. There ain't but one way for us to get him where he can't help himself and that's fer us to get together and stay together.°

After the old man sat down the farmers voted for one union for all. The common misery of economic depression had brought about a new unity.

After eight months of organizing tenant farmers, Ward Rodgers, a white organizer, reported that the Arkansas union had ten thousand members "and practically no friction over the race question." Rodgers told how African Americans were able to run meetings "as they should be run" be-

---

°Mary White Ovington, *The Walls Came Tumbling Down* (New York: Harcourt, Brace & World, 1947), 163–64. Reprinted by permission of the publisher.

cause of the many clubs, burial societies, and organizations they had belonged to. But the white Southerners, complained the organizer, did not have this "training in correct procedures in meetings" because their only organization experience was as "members of the night-riding K.K.K." The depression had even united Klan members and African Americans!

However, when William Anderson, a Black nineteen-year-old janitor in a white junior high school, led a voter registration drive in Greenville, South Carolina, he met with determined Klan opposition. The local Klan leader stopped Anderson as he led his people to register. The two men argued and Anderson shook his finger in the Klan leader's face. Eleven days later Anderson was arrested by police and charged with calling a white student on the phone and trying to make a date with her. He was quickly tried, found guilty, and given thirty days in jail.

The depression struck the country's African Americans with a greater force than the whites. For example, in Pittsburgh they constituted 8 percent of the population but 38 percent of the unemployed in 1931. African Americans were the last to be hired, the first to be fired. They had less savings to fall back on than white workers. While all businesses suffered or went bankrupt during the depression, Black-owned businesses were particularly hard hit because African Americans had even less money.

A Farm Security Administration supervisor discusses cotton with a Louisiana farmer. One-eighth of those receiving loans from the FSA were African Americans.

President Roosevelt and the New Deal

During this period of worldwide depression, some European nations turned to dictatorship to solve the problems of economic and social unrest. But in America, President Franklin D. Roosevelt operated within the context of the American constitutional system as he charted a course of social and economic experimentation. The suffering of the depression would bring forth from Roosevelt a new and fresh approach to the role of the government during a severe crisis.

President Roosevelt understood the desperation of the times and the plight of the poor. He once said that if he were not a good president, he would be America's last president. Blacks came to feel that when the president spoke of "one-third of a nation ill fed, ill housed, and ill clad" he also meant them. His energetic wife Eleanor made an even deeper impression with her participation in African American causes and warm personal relationships with prominent people of color. The Republican party, the political home of the Black people since the Civil War, was abandoned for the Democratic party of FDR. By 1940, Harlem's Seventeenth Assembly District voted Democratic by a seven-to-one margin.

President Franklin D. Roosevelt greets Dr. George Washington Carver.

More than any other previous administration, the New Deal hired Black government workers, many as "racial advisers." The leading figures were called the "Black Brain Trust" or the "Black Cabinet." The two most prominent were Robert C. Weaver and Mary McLeod Bethune. A Harvard Ph.D., Dr. Weaver served in the Interior Department and Housing Authority. The "Black Cabinet" usually met in the basement of his house.

Mrs. Bethune, one of seventeen children born to ex-slaves, once had a book pulled out of her hand by a white child who said, "You can't read." With six students and $1.50 she established in Florida Bethune-Cookman College. Mrs. Bethune and Mrs. Roosevelt became close friends, and both tried to pressure the president into advancing equal rights. "I'm always glad to see you, Mrs. Bethune," the president told her, "for you always come asking for help for others—never for yourself."

William H. Hastie, a former chief counsel for the NAACP.

Two other young members of the Black Brain Trust were Dr. Ralph Bunche and William H. Hastie. After working for the State Department for years, Dr. Bunche became a high official at the United Nations, remaining there until his death in 1972. Dr. Hastie worked for the Interior Department. To protest segregation during World War II, he resigned a government post. Later he became a judge in the Virgin Islands, and ten years later its governor.

Mary McLeod Bethune with her students at Florida's Bethune-Cookman College. Mrs. Bethune refused to follow segregation laws and constantly prodded the White House on race relations.

The New Deal program meant more than just immediate relief or a job. "To the younger Negroes, the WPA and relief mean not only aid but a guaranty that no longer must they work at any salary given them, that they are entitled—they emphasize the word—to a living wage," wrote political analyst Samuel Lubell.

The WPA provided work for artists, musicians, actors, and playwrights during the 1930s. Artist Ernest Critchlow recalled how he and "many Negro artists were aided during those times by the work assigned them by the WPA. Without that aid many of today's important artists might never have made their contributions to the nation's art." Under government grants, African American scholars were able to research the history of their people in America. Federal funds provided salaries for Black actors who had been unable to find work for years. Soon impressive stage productions, under the best directors, were being shown free to city audiences.

When concert singer Marian Anderson was refused permission by the Daughters of the American Revolution to give a concert in their Constitution Hall in Washington, D.C., Secretary of the Interior Harold Ickes invited her to sing outdoors at the Lincoln Memorial. Before an audience of seventy-five thousand that included Supreme Court justices, cabinet officers, and congressmen, Miss Anderson began her historic 1939 concert. She recalled that "the crowd stretched in a great semicircle from the Lin-

A CCC worker handles a tractor.

A CCC worker helps to protect the nation's forests. Two hundred and fifty thousand African Americans were among the three million CCC workers.

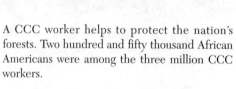

Marian Anderson sings at the Lincoln Memorial on Easter Sunday, 1939.

coln Memorial around the reflecting pool onto the shaft of the Washington Monument. I had a feeling that a great wave of goodwill poured out from these people, almost engulfing me." Her program included operatic arias and folk songs, and ended with *America the Beautiful.*

A New Deal for Labor

An important New Deal assault on the poverty produced by the depression was the attempt to raise wages in industry. For years the Black laborer had known the bitter truth that usually he could only get "any job that the white man cannot stand." And Black opportunities for promotion were severely limited. A Black worker in Pennsylvania who had trained many white employees said, "I have never been promoted. I am the oldest on my job and have never been advanced and have no chance. . . . Colored are seldom promoted." Secretary of Labor Frances Perkins, America's first woman cabinet member, indicated a new government interest in this issue in 1934, when she said, "A way must be found of gradually raising the living standards of the colored laborers. . . ."

The National Labor Relations Act of 1935 inspired unionization in mass production industries (steel, auto, rubber). A wave of union organization swept the country from coast to coast. John L. Lewis, president of the United Mine Workers Union, led a number of unions out of the American Federation of Labor (AFL) into the Congress of Industrial Organizations (CIO). Workers were welcomed into the CIO regardless of craft, sex, color, or the amount of their pay.

The CIO unions often introduced a new note of brotherhood among members. A white Chicago factory worker told how a Black organizer "woke a lot of us up by showing how the company built up race hatred by playing on our sense of superiority." Another white unionist found that "through union activity, white and colored have known each other better. . . . They are drawn closer together on the job." An African American worker in Pennsylvania said, "The union is breaking down prejudice and segregation. . . . There is no office in the union that is held from a colored man because of his color." In Birmingham, Alabama, as well as Chicago, Illinois, African Americans were elected to high posts in mixed unions.

Many Black laborers, long excluded from unions, were, at first, reluctant to support labor organizations. A difficult test of loyalty was met squarely in the 1941 Ford Motor Company strike. African American auto workers for Ford recalled that their employer had offered them jobs when few others did. When white unionists at Ford walked off the job, many Blacks remained at their posts. For a while it appeared that a labor dispute might turn into a racial conflict. But finally Black workers joined the strike and made it a success. An improved contract was worked out by African American and white union leaders and the Ford officials.

New Deal Failures

While the reforms of President Roosevelt lifted African American spirits and kept many from starving, they did not advance racial equality. Antilynching laws were filibustered to death by Southern senators. When Walter White of the NAACP asked the president to support such a bill, he refused. "If I come out for the antilynching bill now," he said, Southern congressmen "will block every bill I ask Congress to pass to keep America from collapsing. I just can't take that risk."

The record of New Deal agencies dealing with the Black communities reflected America's prejudice. Relief benefits for African Americans were less than those granted whites. The industrial code of the National Recovery Act allowed whites higher pay than African Americans. Its famous Blue

Throughout the New Deal Southern convict camps, such as this one in Green County, Georgia, provided Black slave labor under inhuman conditions.

Eagle emblem, one Black official said, was a nasty bird, not the harbinger of happiness. The TVA discriminated in job hiring against African Americans; and the Social Security Act, by excluding domestic and agricultural laborers, eliminated most working African Americans from its benefits.

Repeatedly people took matters into their own hands. In Harlem young Adam Clayton Powell, Jr., organized residents "Don't Buy Where You Can't Work" campaigns. He picketed stores refusing to hire Black salespeople. In 1935 a major riot exploded against the hold-out stores. Harlemites took to the streets to burn and loot white stores. As a result, each store hired at least one African American.

Southern African Americans intent on achieving justice met even more resistance. In Selma, Alabama, black sharecroppers struck for the right to sell their crop for cash, nine months of school for their children, the right to have their own gardens, and the right to food during the layover season. They formed a union and published a paper, "Sharecropper's Voice." At an outdoor meeting of three hundred, whites assassinated their two leaders.

African Americans were among those Americans ready to seek radical solutions and accept aid from Communists. In 1931 nine Black youths were arrested in Alabama and charged with attacking two white women on a freight train. When they were quickly convicted and sentenced to death, the Communist party came to their aid and carried the message of Southern injustice to twenty-eight countries. Even after Nancy Bates, one of their accusers, admitted that she and the other woman had lied, the nine "Scottsboro Boys" were again found guilty. After years of legal arguments by Communists, the NAACP, and others, the nine were released.

One of the leading spokesmen for the young men had been Angelo Herndon, nineteen years old and a Black Communist organizer in the South. When he led a thousand African American and white unemployed in Atlanta, Georgia, he was arrested under a law against slave rebellions. He was "placed in a cell, and was shown a large electric chair, and told to spill everything. I refused and was held incommunicado for 11 days." Sentenced to twenty years on the chain gang, he finally won his freedom.

Many African Americans found an outlet for ghetto conditions in religion. Harlem had almost one church for every block. During the 1930s the Muslim faith and a religion led by "Father Divine" attracted thousands. A judge who had sentenced Father Divine to four days in prison for singing too noisily in public suddenly died of a heart attack. "I hated to do it," Father Divine was reported to have said. This claim led to the rise in popularity of his cult, which included whites, particularly women.

Americans React to European Dictators

Soon after Hitler's rise to power in Germany, African Americans felt, as one expressed it, that "any individual who becomes a world menace on a doctrine of racial prejudice, bigotry, and oppression of minorities . . . is our concern." In 1933 Kelly Miller, Black educator and writer, compared Hitler's persecution of the Jews to Klan attacks on Blacks in an article called *Hitler—The German Ku Klux*.

The attack on the tiny kingdom of Ethiopia in 1935 aroused the world to the danger of Mussolini's fascism. Never had African American communities of the United States been so moved by a foreign event. They raised money and gathered medical supplies for the African nation. Emperor Haile Selassie said many years later, "We can never forget the help Ethiopia received from Negro Americans during the terrible crisis. . . . It moved me to know that Americans of African descent did not abandon their embattled brothers, but stood by us." Haile Selassie was loudly cheered by league members when he called for "collective security" against aggressors—but nothing was done.

In 1936, Mussolini and Hitler helped General Franco overthrow the Spanish republic. Almost ninety African Americans joined the Abraham Lincoln Brigade that tried to "make Madrid the tomb of world fascism." "This ain't Ethiopia," said one Black volunteer, "but it'll do."

As the war danger came closer to America in the late 1930s, African Americans bitterly protested their exclusion from the nation's defense industries. In New York City only 142 Blacks were among the 30,000 defense workers. Black leaders repeatedly asked the president to issue an executive order opening these jobs to all.

Meetings took place but no order was forthcoming. Labor leader Asa Philip Randolph concluded, "The Administration will never give the Negro justice until they see masses—ten, twenty, fifty thousand Negroes on the White House lawn." Randolph planned what he called a "nonviolent demonstration of Negro mass power"—a march on Washington. Four days before the march was to begin, its leaders were invited to the White House to meet with the president and members of his cabinet.

On 25 June 1941, President Franklin D. Roosevelt issued Executive Order 8802 banning discrimination in all plants working on national defense contracts. He signed this order "in the firm belief that the democratic way of life within the Nation can be defended successfully only with the help and support of all groups within its borders. . . ." For the first time since the Emancipation Proclamation, a president of the United States had issued an order protecting the rights of African Americans.

Congressman Arthur W. Mitchell defended Jewish rights against Nazi persecution in 1938, when few were interested.

A Chicago picket protests job discrimination in 1941.

Joe Louis, Detroit's "Brown Bomber," meets Brigadier General Benjamin O. Davis, highout ranking World War II Black officer in the United States Army. Louis became a hero to those opposing world fascism when he knocked out the German Max Schmeling in the first round in a 1938 fight. Nazis had claimed that Louis represented an "inferior race and country." World War II again found Louis and Schmeling in opposing corners: Louis was a sergeant in the United States Army; Schmeling was a Nazi paratrooper.

In less than six months every ounce of American manpower and patriotism would be needed to defend the very life of the nation.

ECONOMIC DEPRESSION HITS BLACK AMERICA

[A 1931 survey by the Urban League showed that Black unemployment soared above white unemployment. In Baltimore the Black 17 percent of the population was 31.5 percent of the unemployed. In Buffalo, the Black 3 percent of the population represented 25.8 percent of the unemployed; in Chicago the Black 4 percent of the population made up 16 percent of the unemployed; in Philadelphia the Black 7 percent of the population represented 25 percent of the unemployed; in Houston the Black 25 percent of the population represented 50 percent of the unemployed; in Little Rock the Black 20 percent of the population represented 54 percent of the unemployed; in Memphis the Black 38 percent of the population represented 75 percent of the unemployed. The plight of Black farmers was equally bad, as this letter from rural Arkansas to William Pickens of the NAACP reveals.]

Mr. Pickens, the conditions of some of our people in this part of the State or in Drew County, is exceedingly bad and absolutely deplorable. The gardens, the food and feed crops—the fruit crops, and in general, all crops have been absolutely burned up by the dry weather and hot sun . . . with no food and feed for the winter months.

We have some sick people, and old People, and Widow Women with from one to five Children School age, and no job by which to work for food and clothing during this winter. Those that have been put to work is alowed two and three days each month.

We have reported this matter, rather put in the Mail directed to Mr. Roosevelt, some one who would ancer and state that the matter have been referred back to the Emergency Relief Office at Little Rock. . . .

I was thinking whether I could handle said matters direct through you and then you take the matter up with Mr. Roosevelt direct. Our Case workers all is whites, when we should have Colored Caseworkers to see after our group.

Some of our People is loosing their homes by forclosure suits, from the fact their application for a loan from the Government was rejected.

May i have a letter from you advising me regarding how to handle such matters for my group.

I am Sincerely Yours
James Dodd

James Dodd, Wilmar, Arkansas, to W. M. Pickens (Washington, D.C., Library of Congress, NAACP files, 27 December 1934). Reprinted by permission of the NAACP.

THE UNEMPLOYED VETERANS MARCH ON WASHINGTON, 1932

[*In the spring of 1932 over fifteen thousand World War I veterans converged on Washington, D.C., to demand payment of a bonus. Reporter Roy Wilkins found that the Bonus Expeditionary Force (BEF) was integrated.*]

The men of the B.E.F. were come together on serious business; they had not time for North, East, South, West, black, and white divisions. The main problem was not to prove and maintain the superiority of a group, but to secure relief from the ills which beset them, black and white alike. . . .

Here they were, then, the brown and black men who had fought (some with their tongues in their cheeks) to save the world for democracy. They were scattered about in various state delegations or grouped in their own cluster of crude shelters. A lonely brownskin in the delegation from North Platte, Nebr.; one or two encamped with Seattle, Wash.; increasing numbers bivouacked with California and the northern states east of the Mississippi river; and, of course, the larger numbers with the state from below the Mason and Dixon line. . . .

At Anacostia some Negroes had their own shacks and some slept in with white boys. There was no residential segregation. . . . The Chicago group had several hundred Negroes in it and they worked, ate, slept, and played with their white comrades. The Negroes shared tasks with the whites from kitchen work to camp M.P. duty.

In gadding about I came across white toes and black toes sticking out from tent flaps and boxes as their owners sought to sleep away the day. . . .

All about were signs containing homely philosophy and sarcasm on the treatment of veterans by the country, such as: "The Heroes of 1918 Are the Bums of 1932." I believe many of the white campers were bitter and sarcastic. They meant what they said on those signs. But disappointment and disillusionment is an old story to Negroes. They were philosophic about this bonus business. . . . So, while the indifference of the government to the bonus agitation might be a bitter pill to the whites, it was nothing unusual to the Negroes. . . .

Over in one corner a white vet was playing a ukelele and singing what could have been the theme song of the camp: *In a Shanty in Old Shanty Town.* On a Sunday afternoon the camp piano was played alternately by a brown lad with a New York accent and a rednecked white boy from Florida, while a few rods away Elder Micheaux's visiting choir was giving voice, in stoptime, to a hymn, *God's Tomorrow Will Be Brighter Than Today.* Negroes and whites availed themselves of the free choice of patting their feet either outdoors to the piano or in the gospel tent to the choir. . . .

Captain A. B. Simmons, colored, who headed his company, hails from Houston, Tex. He and his men were loud in their declaration of the fair treatment they had received on the march to Washington. They were served meals in Southern towns, by Southern white waitresses, in Main Street Southern restaurants along with their white companions. They rode freights and trucks and hiked together. Never a sign of Jim Crow through Northern Texas, Arkansas, Tennessee, or Virginia. Captain Simmons attended the regular company commanders' councils and helped with the problems of administration. His fellow officers, all white Southerners, accorded him the same consideration given others of his rank.

His story was corroborated by others. A long, hard-boiled Negro from

West Virginia who had just stepped out of the mess line behind a white man from Florida said: "Shucks, they ain't got time for that stuff here and those that has we gets 'em told personally." And said a cook in the North Carolina mess kitchen (helping whites peel potatoes): "No, sir, things is different here than down home."

In general assemblies and in marches there were no special places "for Negroes." The black boys did not have to tag along at the end of the line of march; there was no "special" section reserved for them at assemblies. They were shot all through the B.E.F. In the rallies on the steps of the nation's capital they were in front, in the middle and in the rear.

Roy Wilkins, "The Bonuseers Ban Jim Crow," *The Crisis* 39 (October 1932): 316–17. Reprinted by permission.

SHARECROPPERS AND THE WHITE HOUSE DOOR

[*Will Alexander, a white Southerner who had been a leader in interracial organizations since 1907, was a director of the Farm Security Administration.*]

I recall so well the winter of 1935 with its sharecroppers' strike and whole-sale evictions from the cotton farms of southeast Missouri. Several hundred dispossessed families, white and Negro, squatted by the highway in severe winter weather, with all but no protection. One of the leaders was a Negro preacher, himself a sharecropper, a man of limited education but native initiative.

He decided to appeal to the White House and by writing to Mrs. Roosevelt, secured an appointment. He set out in a dilapidated Ford with his wife and the nineteen-year-old daughter of one of the evicted white families. The snow was deep in the Virginia mountains; their car broke down, but a free ride brought them to Washington on the day set.

As administrator of Farm Security, I was familiar with the situation in southeast Missouri, and Mrs. Roosevelt's secretary requested me to be present. Somewhat in advance of the hour, I was seated by an usher in one of the famous reception rooms on the first floor of the White House. Soon the visitors arrived. The couple was thinly clad in the shabby clothes of sharecroppers, and chilled to the bone. Their young white companion was bareheaded, and a thin cotton coat was her only outer wrap. They had scarcely sat down when a uniformed servant came in and lighted a crackling fire laid in the hearth.

There was to be a reception later that afternoon and already there was an air of festivity with uniformed musicians from the navy assembling outside our door. When Mrs. Roosevelt came in she greeted these special guests as naturally as if they belonged to the party. The Negro preacher told the story of the people by the roadside. He was perhaps forty—small, vigorous, if awkward, in his speech. With instant directness, Mrs. Roosevelt found out what lay back of the evictions and what the government was doing. She inquired of me what further could be done, and asked to be kept abreast of developments. In the few remaining minutes, her friendly overtures elicited from the wife the story of their eleven children, and she drew out the white girl's own story of herself and her folks.

There was still give and take, back and forth, as they left the room, threading their way through the navy's musicians and the bustle of activity for the reception. The visitors had been treated with dignity; they had been identified as individuals; their problems had been reviewed with practical directness. As they went out the front door of the White House, it was unmistakably with a sense of their own worth; new faith in their country, new hope for their kind.

Will W. Alexander, "The Negro in the Nation," *Survey Graphic* 36 (January 1947): 94.

LIGHT AND DARKNESS IN THE TENNESSEE VALLEY

[*In 1933 President Franklin D. Roosevelt proposed that the federal government go into the business of producing cheap electric power for a seven-state program in the Deep South. The Tennessee Valley Authority (TVA) provided jobs as well as electricity for the valley farmers. But all were not sharing the benefits equally.*]

A contrast of performance with promise shows that Negroes have never been given their proportionate share of jobs on TVA projects. In addition when payrolls of Negro and white workers are contrasted even greater inequities appear. . . .

It is in seeking a reason for these inequities that one discovers overt acts of discrimination on the part of TVA officials which nullify their every pretense of impartiality. For the most part skilled work is denied Negro workers. Employment of labor is done through the TVA personnel division. Negro workers are employed by Negro assistant personnel officers under the supervision of white officials. To the Negro assistants only requisitions for unskilled work are given. Thus the assistants cannot offer skilled work to any Negro applicants. Only by currying favor with white bosses, may a Negro worker once on the job hope to rise to a higher level of pay or skilled employment. Such instances are very few. Thus at Wheeler Dam where the largest number of Negroes were employed in June 1935, only eight Negro workmen out of 1,048 then employed received as much as $1.00 an hour. There were 300 white carpenters employed on the job there, but not a single Negro. Only 12 Negroes received as much as 75 cents an hour at Wheeler Dam. . . .

A basic concept put forward by TVA officials is that electric power may be used to remove many of the drudgeries of daily life, to effect many home and farm economies, and thus make possible a better life. It is on this basis that the policy of rural electrification was supposed to have been begun in the Valley. As first steps in putting this program into operation TVA successfully negotiated for the use of its power in Tupelo, Mississippi and Athens, Alabama. In Lee County in which Tupelo is located there are 11,225 Negroes or 31.8 per cent of the population. More than 50 per cent of the persons on relief are Negro. A rural county, a large share of the Negro population is engaged in sharecropping and tenant farming. In Tupelo the Negro population lives largely in grotesque rented slum dwellings.

For Negroes the introduction of cheaper electric rates into Lee county as [a] result of the TVA power policy has meant nothing. Landlords, whether of Negro slum dwellers in Tupelo or of Negro tenant farmers in the rural section of the county, have not found it to their advantage to wire their Negro tenants' homes at the cost of $15 to $25, when already they are squeezing all the rent possible from these tenants. . . .

[*According to a government agency the basic appliances for a family (range, water, heater, and refrigerator) could be purchased for $5.33 a month. The TVA electric rates amounted to $6.98 a month.*]

It is obvious that such rates are completely out of reach of the Negro resident of Lee County. The total sum represents more nearly his total monthly cash income than any amount which he would be able to spend for electricity. Thus so far as TVA's electrification program is concerned the Negro family is still in outer darkness.

John P. Davis, "The Plight of the Negro in the Tennessee Valley," *The Crisis* 42 (October 1935): 294, 314. Reprinted by permission.

"Belly Hunger" Erases the Color Line

[*Ward H. Rodgers, a white organizer for the Southern Tenant Farmers' Union, describes the success which the union had in uniting sharecroppers.*]

All too few have been the attempts in the South, or for that matter in the North, to organize labor unions which include both the Negro and white workers. The Southern Tenant Farmers' Union has from its beginning attempted to solve the difficulties of organizing across the race line. After eight months of work we now have 10,000 members, half of whom are Negro sharecroppers. During these months we have had practically no friction within the Union over the race question. Some of our best leaders are members of the Negro race. . . .

Because of his long experience in other organizations, such as churches, burial societies, fraternal organizations and the like, the Negro generally knows how to run meetings, as they should be run. Practically the only organization that the white sharecroppers have had experience in outside of the churches is the Ku Klux Klan, therefore they have not had training in correct procedures at meetings. The only explanation that I have for sharecroppers joining our interracial organization who used to show their race prejudice by being members of the night-riding K.K.K., is that they have learned that both white and Negro sharecroppers are the victims of the same system of exploitation, both Negro and white suffer from the same "belly hunger." The sharecroppers, regardless of color, have been deprived of a living which certainly they work hard enough to earn. Both races have been driven down to a low economic level of bare subexistence. The white sharecropper also is discriminated against and insulted. The word sharecropper itself has come to be used as a term of contempt. . . .

The argument against race prejudice which has been used by the organizers is: "If we organize only a Union of Negro sharecroppers then the Negroes will be evicted and white sharecroppers from the hill country or the unemployed in Memphis will take their places. If on the other hand we organize only a Union of white sharecroppers then the white men will be evicted and Negro sharecroppers from Mississippi and the unemployed in Memphis will take their places." . . .

In spite of increasing terror, the Union grows. Hundreds are joining, Negro and white sharecroppers. We now have 10,000 members, an increase of 35 per cent since January 15.

Ward H. Rodgers, "Sharecroppers Drop Color Line," *The Crisis* 24 (June 1935): 168, 178. Reprinted by permission.

AN AFRICAN AMERICAN IN THE CCC

[*The Civilian Conservation Corps offered jobs and hope to two million young people during the height of the depression. Luther C. Wandall, a New York African American, describes his life as a CCC worker in 1935.*]

According to instructions, I went Monday morning at 8 o'clock to Pier I, North River. There were, I suppose more than 1,000 boys standing about the pier. . . .

The colored boys were a goodly sprinkling of the whole. A few middle-aged men were in evidence. These, it turned out, were going as cooks. A good many Spaniards and Italians were about. A good-natured, lively, crowd, typical of New York. . . .

. . . we answered questions, and signed papers, and then a group of us marched over to U.S. Army headquarters on Whitehall Street in charge of an Army officer.

Here we stripped for a complete physical examination. Then we were grouped into busloads. . . .

We reached Camp Dix [New Jersey] about 7:30 that evening. As we rolled up in front of the headquarters an officer came out to the bus and told us: "You will double-time as you leave this bus, remove your hat when you hit the door, and when you are asked questions, answer 'Yes, sir,' and 'No, sir.'"

. . . when my record was taken at Pier I a "C" was placed on it. When the busloads were made up at Whitehall street an officer reported as follows: 35, 8 colored." But until now there had been no distinction made.

But before we left the bus the officer shouted emphatically: "Colored boys fall out in the rear." The colored from several buses were herded together, and stood in line until after the white boys had been registered and taken to their tents. This seemed to be the established order of procedure at Camp Dix.

This separation of the colored from the whites was complete and rigidly maintained at this camp. One Puerto Rican, who was darker than I, and who preferred to be with the colored, was regarded as pitifully uninformed by the officers. . . .

We stayed at Camp Dix eight days. We were never told officially where we were going. . . .

We were taken to permanent camp on a site rich in Colonial and Revolutionary history, in the upper South. This camp was a dream compared with Camp Dix. There [was] plenty to eat, and we slept in barracks instead of tents. An excellent recreation hall, playground, and other facilities.

I am still in this camp. At the "rec" we have a radio, a piano, a store called a "canteen," a rack of the leading New York papers, white and colored, as well as some from elsewhere. There is a little library with a variety of books and magazines. All sports are encouraged. We have a baseball team, boxing squad, etc. An orchestra has been formed, and classes in various arts and crafts. . . .

During the first week we did no work outside camp, but only hiked, drilled, and exercised. Since then we have worked five days a week, eight hours a day. Our bosses are local men, southerners, but on the whole I have found nothing to complain of. The work varies, but is always healthy, outdoor labor. As the saying goes, it's a great life, if only you don't weaken! . . .

Our officers who, of course, are white, are a captain, a first lieutenant, a doctor, and several sergeants. Our athletic director is colored, as is our vocational teacher. Discipline is maintained by imposing extra duty and fines on offenders. The fines are taken only from the $5 a month which the men receive directly [the rest of the money, about $30, being sent home].

On the whole, I was gratified rather than disappointed with the CCC. I had expected the worst. Of course it reflects, to some extent, all the practices and prejudices of the U.S. Army. But as a job and an experience, for a man who has no work, I can heartily recommend it.

Luther C. Wandall, "A Negro in the CCC," *The Crisis* 42 (August 1935): 244, 253–54. Reprinted by permission.

THE MEMORIAL DAY MASSACRE OF 1937

[*One of the most dramatic events for the CIO's United Steel Workers Union was the Memorial Day Massacre of Sunday, 30 May 1937. A parade of strikers was met by police bullets outside the Republic Steel plant of Chicago. Ten workers were killed.*]

[*A Black striker.*] On that Sunday we marched out of the plant with signs. Lots of us were singing songs and laughing. I was in the front line. All of a sudden the cops started shooting. When they started, I ran to my extreme right, then west, then I made an "L" turn to the south. All the time, bullets were going right past my face.

When I looked up I saw a guy right on top of the plant training his gun on us. I couldn't tell whether it was a machine gun, 'cause I was anxious to get out of the line of fire. I could see the police in my path, the way I was running, so I turned around toward Sam's Place. I ran to a car and started to duck into it. A bullet whizzed by and lodged right above the right fender. Boy, I shake now when I think that if I hadn't ducked I'd have been shot in the head. I finally made it into the car and was driven to Sam's Place.

[*The wife of the one Black killed that day.*] He was told to go to the meeting that Sunday. He was on the front line and was one of the first to get hurt. I have his clothes here. You can see where he was shot in the back. His hat is bloody. He sure was beat terrible. His life was really lost for the CIO, whether he understood it or not. I do hope his loss will help others who live.

St. Clair Drake and Horace R. Cayton, *Black Metropolis* (New York: Harcourt, Brace & Co., 1945), 322–23. Reprinted by permission.

A NEW DEAL CONGRESSMAN DEFEATS JIM CROW

[*Arthur W. Mitchell of Chicago was the first Black Democrat elected to Congress (1934–1942). When he was forced to leave a Pullman car because of his race, Congressman Mitchell took his case to the Supreme Court and won.*]

Mr. Speaker, on April 19, 1937, I purchased a first-class round-trip railroad ticket from Chicago, Ill., to and from Hot Springs, Ark., over the Illinois Central and Rock Island Railroads via Memphis, Tenn. While travelling on this ticket between Memphis, Tenn., and Little Rock, Ark., on the morning of April 21, 1937, I was ejected from the first-class car by the conductor of the Rock Island passenger train on which I was then travelling. The reason for ejecting me was that I was riding in the body of a Pullman car in which there were several white passengers, the conductor claiming that the law of the State of Arkansas prohibited such an act by statute. . . .

This fight for the rights of the Negro has been a hard and expensive one, covering a period of more than four years. All expenses incurred in this suit have been borne by me. I think it is well to note that I, with a Negro lawyer, Richard E. Westbrooks, of Chicago, Ill., have fought the case through all of the courts. We conducted the hearing in Chicago, argued the case before the Interstate Commerce Commission and before the United States district court in Chicago. We also argued the case before the Supreme Court of the United States, this being the first and only instance where a member of our race has argued his own case before that high tribunal.

. . . The case before the Supreme Court was heard by the full court, and their decision was unanimous for me, setting aside in strong language the findings of the Interstate Commerce Commission and the decision of the United States District Court of the Northern District of Illinois.

I think I should also call attention to the fact that the Attorney General's Office, whose duty it was to appear before the Supreme Court in behalf of the Interstate Commerce Commission, not only refused to appear and argue in favor of the findings of that commission, but through . . . Francis Biddle [later an attorney general], filed with the Supreme Court a very strong memorandum [in favor of Mitchell's complaint]. . . .

The Congressional Record, 77th Cong., 1st sess., A4294–97.

A Congressman Denounces Nazi Racism

[*Congressman Arthur W. Mitchell spoke out against the Nazi persecution of Jewish people in this letter to President Franklin D. Roosevelt of 12 October 1938. His plea came a month before the Nazis' infamous "week of broken glass" escalated an anti-Jewish campaign toward their "final solution"—mass murder.*]

As a representative of a minority group in America, an underprivileged group which has been subjected to prejudice and mistreatment from time to time, we are interested in the attitude of majority groups throughout the world toward minority groups. At the present time we are greatly disturbed because of the intolerance of certain major groups toward the Jewish people residing in European countries and wish to have our voice heard in the interest of justice and fair play for all racial groups. We believe that the same spirit of intolerance which is working so tremendously against the safety and sacred rights of the Jewish people, if permitted to go unchallenged, will manifest itself sooner or later against all minority groups, perhaps in all parts of the world. [We] request you, the highest representative of our Government, to use every reasonable and peaceable means at your command in securing protection for the Jewish people in this hour of sad calamity.

[*President Roosevelt answered Congressman Mitchell's telegram, saying, "I fully appreciate the concern expressed by you," and said that he would work for a national home for the Jews in Palestine.*]

The Congressional Record, 76th Cong., 1st sess., A4041.

18 WORLD LEADERSHIP IN WAR AND PEACE

IN THE EARLY MORNING OF 7 December 1941, Japanese planes swooped out of the clouds above Hawaii and rained destruction on the United States Naval Base at Pearl Harbor. Mess attendant Dorie Miller, a broad-shouldered young sailor who had battled his way to the boxing championship of the *West Virginia,* dropped the laundry he had been collecting and scampered on deck. In the midst of the crashing bombs and strafing by Japanese Zeros, he pulled his wounded captain to safety. Then he sprang to action behind a machine gun and fired away at the attacking aircraft. An officer finally had to order him to leave the sinking ship.

Dorie Miller reported that he shot down six Zeros. The navy gave him credit for four. Either way it was not a bad record for a man who never fired a machine gun until that morning. His victory was probably the only one credited to the United States that day, and Dorie Miller was America's first hero of World War II. He served as mess attendant because that, at the time, was the only position open to African Americans in the navy. On 7 May 1942, Fleet Admiral Chester Nimitz pinned the Navy Cross on Dorie Miller "for distinguished devotion to duty, extraordinary courage, and disregard for his own personal safety. . . ."

Miller was still a messman when he went down with his new ship, *Liscome Bay,* on 25 November 1944. But his courage would help pave the

Dorie Miller (right) is awarded the Navy Cross.

way for others who wished to do more for their country than serve as mess-men. And, before World War II had ended, three other African American sailors would win the Navy Cross.

World War II

The Japanese attack on Pearl Harbor united the American people against the Axis powers of Japan, Germany, and Italy. "If Hitler wins," wrote William E. B. Du Bois in 1941, "every single right we now possess, for which we have struggled here in America for more than three centuries, will be instantaneously wiped out. . . . If the Allies win, we shall at least have the right to continue fighting for a share of democracy for ourselves."

From home-front war factories to the fighting fronts of the world, African Americans contributed to Allied victories. More than a million entered the armed forces, and almost half of these served overseas. The men marched in every branch of the armed forces, and the women were army nurses, WACs, WAVEs, and SPARs. Seven thousand Blacks served as officers. Four commanded merchant marine ships, and thousands served

Troops guard Rhine River bridge.

Dr. Charles Drew.

in their crews. Paul Robeson, Louis Armstrong, and Lena Horne were among the many Black entertainers to tour with USO troops.

One of the most striking single contributions to Allied victory came from Dr. Charles Drew. A brilliant young surgeon, Dr. Drew was in charge of the Red Cross Blood Bank before the war began, and during the war organized a system that saved countless American and Allied lives. He worked to perfect a modern blood bank system despite the fact that his own blood, because he was an African American, would not be acceptable to an American blood bank for a long time to come. Continued criticism from Dr. Drew and others finally led to the acceptance of blood from people of color. But it was stored separately from the blood of whites.

The war also stimulated a vast migration that sent 5 million Southern Blacks to Northern cities by 1970. They were driven by injustice and lured by factory jobs that offered decent wages.

Military Campaigns: European Theater

Before American troops landed in Africa, African American engineers were sent into Liberia (a nation founded in 1819 by former American slaves) to prepare airstrips. Edward Taylor, the Black private who was the first American soldier to set foot in Africa, told the Liberians, "We are here to join hands and fight together until this world is free of tyrannical dictators." The 450th Anti-Aircraft Artillery Battalion, the first African American unit to land in the invasion of North Africa and the first to go into combat on European soil as well, was cited by General Mark W. Clark for "outstanding performance of duty." Among those wounded in the African campaign was "Kid Chocolate," famous for his many boxing victories before the war. He lost both of his legs.

In the invasions of Sicily, Italy, and Normandy (D Day) in France, African American troops were among the hard-hitting American forces. During a German night raid on ships in Naples Harbor, Black soldiers scampered on deck to man guns on the ship and on the trucks about to be unloaded. They brought down two Nazi planes and won praise from General Mark Clark, who said that "their conduct was excellent. . . . The Fifth Army welcomes such men." The Black battalion that landed at Normandy on D Day was commended by General Dwight D. Eisenhower because it "carried out its mission with courage and determination and proved an important element to the air-defense team."

From the battles on the African desert until the final surrender of the German forces, Black airmen struck at Axis land, sea, and air power. The

"Kid Chocolate." To his friends in Philadelphia, he was Travis Henry.

Members of the Ninety-second Division pushing northward in Italy toward the Arno River, 1944.

Benjamin O. Davis, Jr., (right) receives his third Legion of Merit award from Secretary of the Air Force Zukert. In 1965 Davis was made commander of all United States forces in Korea.

Sergeant Macon H. Johnson.

six hundred airmen trained at Tuskegee as pilots carried the war from Africa to France, Italy, Poland, Romania, and Germany. Eighty-eight of the pilots won the Distinguished Flying Cross in bombing and strafing missions. The 332nd Fighter Group won a Presidential Unit Citation. Together with the all-Black 99th Pursuit Squadron, they won eight hundred air medals and clusters.

The highest ranking African American officer was Colonel Benjamin O. Davis, a West Point graduate, who flew sixty missions himself and won a Silver Star, Legion of Merit, Distinguished Flying Cross, and Air Medal with four Oak Leaf clusters. One of his citations read:

> For: Extraordinary achievement—in an actual flight as a pilot of a P-47 type aircraft, led his Group on a penetration escort attack on industrial targets in the Munich area June 9, 1944. The bomber formation was attacked by more than one hundred enemy fighters near Udine, Italy. Faced with the problem of protecting the large bomber formation with the comparatively few fighters under his control, Colonel Davis so skillfully disposed his Squadron that in spite of the large number of enemy fighters, the bomber formation suffered only a few losses.

Just six months earlier, the 99th Pursuit Squadron, while protecting the Anzio beachhead, knocked down eight Nazi planes during one of the fiercest fights of the Italian campaign, a record superior to that of any other American squadron on that day.

Easter Eggs for delivery to Germany in 1945.

African American airmen, soldiers, truck drivers, and medical personnel moved across France with the liberating armies. Fifteen hundred African American drivers moved vital supplies along the Red Ball Highway to feed General George Patton's tanks and men. In all, twenty-two African American combat units served in the European theater. The 969th Field Artillery won a Distinguished Unit Citation for "outstanding courage and resourcefulness and undaunted determination. . . ." Private Ernest Jenkins of New York City won a Silver Star for knocking out an enemy gun position and capturing fifteen Germans. First Lieutenant Vernon Baker of Cheyenne, Wyoming, won the Distinguished Service Cross for "extraordinary heroism in action" when he knocked out three Nazi machine-gun nests and killed or wounded nine Germans.

Several African American GIs won foreign decorations. Macon H. Johnson was awarded the "Order of the Soviet Union" by a Russian general, and William Green won the "Partisan Medal for Heroism" from Marshal Tito's Yugoslav government.

The first Black Tank Battalion went into combat in Europe in 1944. This 761st Battalion of fifty-four tanks and 750 men served under General George S. Patton, who told them, "I don't care what color you are, so long as you go up there and kill" Germans. Patton reminded the men that "everyone has their eyes on you. . . . Don't let them down, and damn you, don't let me down." The 761st was in combat for 183 days from France through Austria and Germany. They won 391 battle awards and inflicted 129,540 casualties on the enemy. They captured a German radio station at Salz, seven enemy towns, knocked out 331 machine-gun nests, and helped liberate Nazi concentration-camp prisoners. They never let Patton down.

Until the Nazis counterattacked in the bloody Battle of the Bulge in December 1944, African Americans were confined to segregated units, many in service or noncombat units. When the Germans broke through the Bulge, the color bar was also broken. The United States Army asked for

After the Battle of the Bulge drove the Nazis back, smiling French soldiers fill the hands of American soldiers.

volunteers from among those serving behind the lines. "We've been giving a lot of sweat," remarked one Black GI. "Now I think we'll mix some blood with it." Fifty-five hundred African Americans volunteered, and twenty-five hundred were accepted to fight in the United States First Army. Black and white platoons fought side by side to drive back the fierce Nazi attack. They succeeded. After the battle, General Lanham told the volunteers, "I have never seen any soldiers who have performed better in combat than you." But segregation was restored to all units by the German surrender.

Military Campaigns: Pacific-Asiatic Theater

From 8 December 1941, when Private Robert Brooks, son of a Kentucky sharecropper, became the first American soldier of the armored force to lose his life in land warfare against the Japanese, until final victory, African Americans took part in the American victories in the Pacific.

United States troops in Bougainville patrol against the Japanese.

Machine gunners of the Ninety-third Infantry guard the Numa-Numa trail in the South Pacific.

In the Battle of the Solomon Islands, Mess Attendant Leonard Harmon of Texas won the Navy Cross but lost his life rescuing a fellow crewman of the U.S.S. *San Francisco*. The navy honored his memory by naming a destroyer escort after him.

On the Asian mainland ten thousand African American engineers built the road from India through Burma to China and called it "The Road to Tokyo." They worked day and night, through jungles, around cliffs, over the Himalayas—and fought off Japanese patrols as they worked. Others, as army engineers, helped build the Alcan Highway in Alaska.

During the historic May 1942 Battle of the Coral Sea, African American aviation engineers built the landing strips in New Caledonia from which American planes smashed Japanese targets. A few months later a Black machine-gun crew saved the vital airdrome at Milne Bay, New Guinea. Reginald Simonds and his crew manned unfamiliar machine guns as the Japanese came out of the jungle in attack formation. Simonds reported, "We knew enough to aim and keep them [the machine guns] shooting at the Japs. And I guess that's all we had to know."

African American servicemen were part of the vast offensive that rolled back the Japanese, island by island. The Ninety-third Division fought at Bougainville, Treasury Islands, and the Philippines. The United States Marines admitted African Americans in 1943, breaking a color bar that had lasted throughout marine history. Black marines served with distinction in the invasion of Saipan. Others as soldiers pushed into Guadalcanal and Okinawa and helped General Douglas MacArthur retake the Philippines. In April 1944 an African American gun crew aboard the U.S. *Intrepid* won the Bronze Star for bringing down Japanese Kamikaze planes.

As in the First World War, the second one had its share of racial clashes

During the Detroit riot, George Miller, a white ringleader, slaps a Black man guarded by police. Miller was not arrested for three weeks and then only after NAACP pressure.

behind the firing lines. Walter White of the NAACP and Lester Granger of the Urban League were hired by the government to investigate various racial incidents. Granger traveled fifty thousand miles to sixty-seven navy installations and talked with ten thousand men. "Some of the men I conferred with as individuals and in small groups. Sometimes I met with several dozen or several hundred, in recreation halls or open theatres." He reported many complaints and noted that "from month to month new progressive changes could be noted."

Walter White flew to Guam where white soldiers had hurled insults, cans, and even two grenades into Black army camps. After continued outrages, including the murder of one GI, some African American soldiers mounted an armed truck and headed for the white camp. They were arrested, and forty-four were given long prison terms. White reported that the NAACP had to "take the cases all the way to the Secretary of the Navy and the White House" to win release of the men.

In the spring of 1943 the most violent of civilian clashes exploded in Detroit, a center for war industries that had attracted many Southern Blacks and whites. In three days of rioting many African Americans were killed and injured. Federal troops had to be called in to restore order.

The Postwar Battle for Rights, 1945–1954

Most World War II veterans returned home to find too few jobs and too few homes to go around. In addition to facing these problems, African American veterans returned to face racial discrimination—something which they had often been told that they were fighting to destroy in Europe and Asia. It was difficult for men who had faced death to save their country to put up with the old patterns of discrimination once the foreign enemy had been defeated. Former officers bit their lips in anger when Southern police called them "boy" or abused them. Some did not bite their lips in anger, but fought back—and a few were killed.

Many whites also had returned from Europe and Asia believing that if the idea of a "master race" was wrong for our enemies, it was wrong for America too. During and after the war, the Congress of Racial Equality (CORE) opposed discrimination in the North by nonviolent resistance. CORE members first asked owners of eating places to allow people of color to enter. If persuasion failed, CORE members filed in, Black and white together, and did not leave until the issue was settled. Each Sunday during the summer of 1947, CORE members went out to picket against the segregated swimming pool at Palisades Amusement Park in New Jersey. Reported white member James Peck, "We knew in advance that we would be beaten, arrested, or both." But they finally won.

In Baltimore in 1949, Black and white Quakers, members of the Fellowship of Reconciliation, repeatedly entered Hutzler's department store and sat at its ground-floor lunch counter. White Thorne Shipley remembered that "we were not served, not beaten, and not arrested. We returned repeatedly until we got our story in the Baltimore newspapers."

Only a few months after the war had ended, more than one hundred African American war veterans marched on the courthouse in Birmingham, Alabama, to register to vote. They were turned away by white officials who claimed that they could not "interpret the United States Constitution."

For years Communists and others had demanded the integration of big-league baseball. Then, in 1947, it began to happen. Jackie Roosevelt Robinson, an athletic college graduate, was asked to play for the Brooklyn Dodgers baseball team but had to promise not to fight back against those

Jackie Robinson in a pivotal play at second base. In 1947 Robinson broke the color barrier in big league baseball—and became the National League's "Rookie of the Year." In his third season he earned the Most Valuable Player award.

who would hurl abuses at him on the diamond. For three hours Robinson and Branch Rickey of the Dodgers worked out a strategy for the baseball star that had nothing to do with playing ball. Robinson's hitting, running, and fielding soon won him a place in baseball history and the Baseball Hall of Fame as well as in the hearts of millions of Americans.

The federal government, Supreme Court, and many states moved steadily toward protecting equal rights. After an African American civilian group, in 1948, demanded that President Truman end segregation in the army, navy, and marines, the president issued an executive order to that effect. About a year earlier, President Truman had established the President's Committee on Civil Rights, to study the problem and issue recommendations for progress. Mrs. Sadie T. Alexander and Dr. Channing Tobias were the Black members of the group. Its report, *To Secure These Rights,* proposed "the elimination of segregation . . . from American life." By the time of the 1948 election the issue of civil rights had become a major issue dividing the Democratic party.

In cases brought by the NAACP, the Supreme Court of the United States, throughout the New Deal, war, and postwar periods, struck down laws that denied equality. In 1946, for example, it found unconstitutional a Virginia law that required a Black on an interstate bus to move to the rear to make way for a white passenger. In 1950 it ruled that an African American could not be denied a seat in the dining car of an interstate train. In 1953 the Court ruled that any "respectable well-behaved person" had a right to be served in any public place in Washington, D.C.

New York State became a leader in protecting equal rights. In 1945 it passed the first fair employment practices law in the nation's history. A State Commission against Discrimination was established to enforce equal job rights. By 1950 eight states had followed New York's example, and by 1963, twenty-two states, including Missouri (a former slave state), had passed fair employment practice laws. In 1949 Connecticut became the first state to ban discrimination in housing.

The full integration of the armed forces occurred during the Korean War. African American replacements were channeled into previously white units. Black men and white men fought side by side on all fronts to stem the advances of the Korean and Chinese forces. Two were among the Americans who won the Congressional Medal of Honor.

While important progress had been made toward securing equality in America, both silent and open opposition continued. On Christmas night, 1951, Harry T. Moore and his wife were killed by a bomb placed beneath their Florida home. Both had been leaders in the drive of the state NAACP to register African American voters.

Southern Blacks who fought in the integrated army in Korea knew that

Frederick F. Davis, a second lieutenant during the Korean War, mans a Sabre jet.

their hometowns would deny them a cup of coffee in a diner, or a bathroom for their children in a shopping center, or a home in a white neighborhood. Northern African Americans who returned from battle knew that segregation by custom to the worst slums and schools, and lowest-paying jobs, seemed just as strong as segregation by law in the South. The African Americans' growing pride and mounting anger with those who denied them rights were moving masses of people toward action by the 1950s.

Support for the United Nations and World Peace

Although President Franklin D. Roosevelt died before final victory over the Axis powers, he had helped to create an instrument of peace in the United Nations. America offered the world organization a home and played a key role in its formation and development. President Harry Truman selected Ralph Bunche as a United States delegate.

From its inception, African Americans followed the proceedings of the United Nations. They rejoiced in the Declaration of Human Rights because it struck at racial injustice. They also celebrated the new African nations emerging from European control.

Dr. Ralph Bunche, United Nations mediator, meets with his aides in Haifa, Palestine, in 1948. His peace plan earned him the Nobel Peace Prize in 1950.

The most important American contributions to the United Nations during the postwar period came from Ralph Bunche, grandson of a former slave. In 1948, Bunche was sent to Palestine to mediate the conflict between Arabs and Jews. His efforts were so successful that, in 1950, he was awarded the Nobel Peace Prize. In 1961 Bunche wrote, "I am proud of my ancestry just as I am proud of my nationality." He continued to work for world peace at the United Nations until his death in 1972.

As America became a world leader, the existence of discrimination within its borders hurt its world position. In 1963 Secretary of State Dean Rusk said, "The biggest burden we carry on our backs in our foreign relations in the 1960s is the problem of racial discrimination here at home."

President John F. Kennedy was shocked to discover that, because of their color, African ambassadors had been refused service in a restaurant on Route 40, outside Washington, D.C. The *Daily Times* of Nigeria was also angry: "By this disgraceful act of racial discrimination the United States forfeits its claim to world leadership." In the summer of 1961 the world was also told how three African American newsmen managed to get service in a Baltimore restaurant by dressing as delegates from "Goban," a mythical African nation. They had been refused service when they entered as African Americans. A nation that sought world leadership could not tolerate such discrimination.

Paul Robeson and W. E. B Du Bois shake hands at a Paris Peace Conference in 1949. Both men denounced United States intervention Korean.

However, officials tolerated a deadly forty-year secret experiment that used African American men. Beginning in 1932, an Alabama Public Health Service (PHS) diagnostic program denied a cure to 400 Black men with syphilis. As the disease painfully coursed through their bodies, PHS doctors told patients they were receiving treatment. Doctors prevented them from finding a cure elsewhere and refused to warn them that they could infect others. By the time it was exposed and halted in 1972, the experiment had killed an estimated twenty-eight to one hundred men.

After World War II, the State Department recognized that it had few African American representatives in foreign lands and that those few who were in foreign service were usually assigned to Black republics such as Liberia. In 1958, President Dwight D. Eisenhower assigned Clifton R. Wharton to be ambassador to communist Romania. In 1961 he was made ambassador to Norway by President John F. Kennedy. The president, shortly before his assassination, appointed veteran reporter and diplomat Carl T. Rowan as ambassador to Finland. President Lyndon B. Johnson made Rowan chief of the United States Information Service, which made him the first African American to sit on the National Security Council.

By 1973 African American ambassadors were serving their country at the United Nations, in the Middle East, in Europe, and in Africa. In May 1965, President Johnson appointed Mrs. Patricia Harris ambassador to

Ambassador Patricia R. Harris.

Luxembourg. She was a young Howard University professor of law whom newspapers referred to as "brainy and beautiful." Mrs. Harris was the second woman in American history to be named an ambassador.

THE HOME FRONT WAR AGAINST DISCRIMINATION

[*During World War II, Americans of both races formed the Congress of Racial Equality to battle for democracy at home. Writer Helen Buckler describes the group's use of "disciplined, nonviolent action" in its first "sit-in."*]

In Chicago, late one night in the spring of 1942, two men, one white, one Negro, entered a small, but well set-up coffee shop in a good residential neighborhood. They asked for a cup of coffee and were refused service.

Several ensuing interviews with the management failed to dislodge the policy of discrimination, which was said to be due to the unwillingness of patrons to eat beside Negroes. . . . It was suggested that the management try serving Negroes for a short period, and if the trial resulted in loss of business, the loss would be made good. The management refused to experiment.

After several weeks of such efforts, during which the management had put up a sign reading, "We reserve the right to seat our patrons where we choose," a group of twenty-one persons entered the coffee shop in the late afternoon. Among them were university students, business and professional people, men and women, a young minister or two. The majority were white, but included in the group were Negro men and women. . . .

The management immediately asked the Negro men, who had seated themselves at the counter, to descend to the basement where, it was said, Negroes were served. They refused, saying they wished to sit with their friends. . . . Whereupon the management telephoned for the police.

Meanwhile, though food had been placed before the whites in the group, they would not eat unless their Negro companions were served. All maintained an unruffled demeanor. . . . Two police officers arrived. . . . Asked by the management if they would not eject the group on the grounds that the coffee shop reserved the right to seat its patrons where it wished, the officers replied, "There is nothing in the law that permits us to do that," and they left. After an hour the management, seeing that this new style sit-down strike was costing business, capitulated and served the entire twenty-one.

. . . subsequent visits to the coffee shop found the management amiably serving all alike—nor did there appear to be any fall-off in business.

Helen Buckler, "The CORE Way," *Survey Graphic* (February 1946), 50. Reprinted by permission.

The Men Who Landed in France on D-Day

[General Dwight D. Eisenhower, commander of the D-Day invasion in June 1944, addressed an African American battalion that took part in the landings.]

Your battalion landed in France on June 6 under artillery, machine-gun, and rifle fire. Despite the losses sustained, the battalion carried out its mission with courage and determination and proved an important element to the air-defense team. The cheerfulness and devotion to duty of officers and men have been commented on by the personnel of other units.

. . . I commend you and the officers and men of your battalion for your fine effort, which has merited the praise of all who have observed it.

Helen Gahagan Douglas, "The Negro Soldier," *Remarks of Hon. Helen Gahagan Douglas* (Washington, 1946), 5. Reprinted from *The Congressional Record.*

WAR AND RACE IN SALINA, KANSAS

[*Lloyd L. Brown, an African American writer, recalled the days when he was stationed with the United States Army at Salina, Kansas.*]

One day at high noon several of us enlisted men from Squadron C went into a lunchroom on Santa Fe—Salina's main street—to see if the story we had heard was true. As we entered, the counterman hurried to the rear to get the owner, who hurried out front to tell us with urgent politeness: "You boys know we don't serve colored here."

Of course we knew it. They didn't serve "colored" anywhere in town when our all-black outfit first came to Salina in the fall of 1942 to open up the Smoky Hill Army Air Field just out of town. The best movie house did not admit Negroes and the other one admitted them only to the balcony. There was no room at the inn for any black visitor, and there was no place in town where he could get a cup of coffee.

"You know we don't serve colored here," the man repeated. He was still very polite, but he sounded aggrieved that we had not been polite enough to leave.

We ignored him and just stood there inside the door, staring at what we had come to see—the German prisoners of war who were having lunch at the counter. There were about ten of them. They were dressed in fatigues and wore the distinctive high-peaked caps of Rommel's Afrika Korps. No guard was with them.

We had seen platoons of such prisoners brought from nearby Camp Phillips to dig drainage ditches at our air base, and we had heard that because of the manpower shortage some P.O.W.'s came by bus each day to Salina to work at the grain elevators. Then when one of our men told us that he had seen those alien commuters come to this lunchroom for their meal, it was something we had to see with our own eyes.

We continued to stare. This was really happening. It was no jive talk. It was the Gospel truth. The people of Salina would serve these enemy soldiers and turn away black American G.I.'s. The Germans now had half-turned on their stools and were staring back at us, each man's cap at precisely the same cocky angle. Nothing further was said, and when the owner edged toward the phone on the wall, we knew it was time to go. The M.P.'s he would call would not treat us with his politeness.

As we left, I began thinking about the next session of the weekly orientation program I conducted for our squadron, giving lectures on why we fight and reporting on the progress of our war for the four freedoms. After this latest incident, what could I say?

The best thing I could come up with was this: If we were *untermenschen* in Nazi Germany, they would break our bones. As "colored" men in Salina, they only break our hearts.

Lloyd L. Brown, "Brown v. Salina, Kansas," *The New York Times,* 26 February 1973, 31.

THE 332ND WINS A CITATION

[*President Franklin D. Roosevelt awarded the 332nd Fighter Group a Distinguished Unit Citation in 1945. It read:*]

On March 24, 1945, fifty-nine P-51 type aircraft were airborne and set course for the rendezvous with the bomber formation. Through superior navigation and maintenance of strict flight discipline, the group formation reached the bomber formation at the designated time and place. Nearing the target approximately 25 enemy aircraft were encountered which included ME-252s which launched relentless attacks in a desperate effort to break up and destroy the bomber formation.

Displaying outstanding courage, aggressiveness, and combat technique, the group immediately engaged the enemy formation in aerial combat. In the ensuing engagement that continued over the target area, the gallant pilots of the 332nd Fighter Group battled against the enemy fighters to prevent the breaking up of the bomber formation. . . . Through their superior skill and determination, the group destroyed three enemy aircraft, probably destroyed three [more], and damaged three. Among their claims were eight of the highly rated enemy jet-propelled aircraft, with no loss sustained by the 332nd Fighter Group.

Leaving the target area and en route to base after completion of their primary task, aircraft of the group conducted strafing attacks against enemy ground installations and transportation with outstanding success. By the conspicuous gallantry, professional skill, and determination of the pilots, together with the outstanding technical skill and devotion to duty of the ground personnel, the 332nd Fighter Group has reflected great credit on itself and the armed forces of the United States.

United States Department of War, *Press Release,* 16 October 1945.

INTEGRATION DURING THE BATTLE OF THE BULGE

[*The Paris edition of the United States Army's* Stars and Stripes *reported the decisive Battle of the Bulge.*]

Negro doughboys are participating in the eastward sweep by General Hodges' forces. . . .

If comments of white personnel of these divisions are any indication, the plan of mixing white and colored troops in fighting units, a departure from previous United States Army practice, is operating successfully.

Negro reinforcements reported a sincere, friendly welcome everywhere. They also spoke of excellent relations with their white fellow-doughs, of the making of inter-racial friendships.

The integration of the Negro platoons into their units was accomplished quickly and quietly. There was no problem. . . .

"I was damned glad to get those boys," said the CO of K company, Capt. Wesley J. Simons, of Snow Hill, Md. "They fit into our company like any other platoon, and they fight like hell. Maybe that's because they were all volunteers and wanted to get into this."

Alan Morrison, *Stars and Stripes,* Paris Edition, 6 April 1945.

A Newsboy Strike in Alabama, 1944

[Black resistance to injustice marked the Jim Crow era, but news of it rarely reached the media. Jim McWilliams was twelve when he led a strike of newsboys in Fairfield, Alabama, a steel town six miles from Birmingham.]

It was a time when everything was segregated with signs all around saying "Whites Only" or "Colored Only." I was one of many Black and white *Birmingham News* delivery boys, many older than me. Each day the Black newsboys—but not the white—would have to unload the news delivery trucks and carry heavy bundles of one hundred papers into the delivery office. Mr. Morris, the white station manager, parceled papers out to all the newsboys, and we'd leave for our segregated neighborhoods.

One day when I arrived and saw the papers stacked in the street and the white newsboys waiting inside, I got angry. I told my buddies it was unfair for us to carry the papers inside and they agreed. When we told Mr. Morris, he told us to do like we always had. We said no, we would not deliver any papers until the white boys did, and then we went home.

No papers were delivered to the Black community that day, the next day and for two weeks. Meanwhile, each of us visited our customers—steelworkers, coal miners, retired laborers and schoolteachers and their families. Mr. Morris asked some customers to tell us to end the stoppage, but after we described our unfair treatment, they supported the strike.

Newspaper owners in Birmingham, furious that three thousand papers were not reaching Black customers, sent representatives to our minister, Reverend E. W. Williams, at Fairfield's First Baptist Church, to order us back to work. He knew all of us newsboys by first names, and I had taught in his Sunday school. But most important, his livelihood came from Fairfield's Black community, so he was a powerful and independent man.

He called together the *Birmingham News* officials, church members, newsboys and parents. He knew our answer before he asked us if we would return to work. We said unless things changed, we were on strike. Williams then told the representatives he could not order us back to work.

After two weeks, Mr. Morris agreed to our terms. From then on all the newsboys carried papers in from the street. So he wouldn't have to deal with us Black newsboys, Mr. Morris put me in charge of parceling out our papers, collecting our receipts, and he paid me extra for the work.

[James McWilliams graduated from the University of Wisconsin Law School and served as assistant attorney general of the Virgin Islands and as an official in the city government in Washington, D.C.]

James McWilliams to William Loren Katz, 15 November 1993.

ROBERT C. WEAVER, GOVERNMENT OFFICIAL

[*In January 1966 Robert C. Weaver became the first Black cabinet member in American history. A few years before this, after three decades of faithful government service, Weaver described his role as an official and an African American.*]

I happen to have been born a Negro and to have devoted a large part of my adult energies to the problem of the role of the Negro in America. But I am also a government administrator, and have devoted just as much energy—if not more—to the problems of government administration at the local, state, and national levels.

My responsibilities as a Negro and an American are part of the heritage I received from my parents—a heritage that included a wealth of moral and social values that do not have anything to do with my race. My responsibilities as a government administrator do not have too much to do with my race, either. My greatest difficulty in public life is combating the idea that somehow my responsibilities as a Negro conflict with my responsibilities as a government administrator: and this is a problem which is presented by those Negroes who feel that I represent them exclusively, as well as by those whites who doubt my capacity to represent all elements in the population. The fact is that my responsibilities as a Negro and a government administrator do not conflict: they complement each other. . . .

What are the responsibilities of Negro leadership? Certainly the first is to keep pressing for the status of first-class citizenship for all—an inevitable goal of those who accept the values of this nation. Another is to encourage and help Negroes to prepare for the opportunities that are now and will be open to them.

The ultimate responsibilities of Negro leaders, however, are to show results and to maintain a following. This means that they cannot be so "responsible" that they forget the trials and tribulations of those less fortunate or less recognized. They cannot stress progress—the emphasis that is so palatable to the majority group—without, at the same time, delineating the unsolved business of democracy. They cannot provide models that will have any meaning for their followers unless they can bring about social changes that will facilitate the emergence of these models from the *typical* environment of the Negro community. . . .

Most Negroes in leadership roles have made clear that they and those who follow them are part of America. They have striven for realization of the American dream. But they cannot succeed alone. Sophisticated whites realize that the status of Negroes in our society depends not only on what the Negro himself does to achieve his goals and to prepare himself for opportunities, but even more, on what all America does to expand these opportunities. The quality and character of future Negro leadership will be determined by how effective those leaders who relate to the *total* society can be in satisfying the yearnings for human dignity that lie in the hearts of all Americans.

The Negro as an American, Occasional Papers of the Fund for the Republic, 1963, 3–8.

DEFENDING THE FLAG IN GHANA

[*On 4 February 1964, Adger Emerson Player, of the American Embassy staff in Accra, Ghana, kept an anti-American mob from desecrating the American flag. His bravery received wide publicity and the special thanks of President Lyndon B. Johnson. Player explained his action in a letter to a California congressman.*]

Dear Sir: I have been the subject of much publicity since February 4, 1964. . . .

President Johnson wrote that I "have the gratitude of freemen everywhere who respect the principles and ideals for which our flag stands." The American dilemma is still the contradiction of racial bondage, injustice, and inequality as practiced by some Americans with the American principles of liberty, justice, and equality. I would like to set the record straight regarding what I consider the true meaning of my action.

My action was something that any American—black or white—would have done. However, my raising of the flag decreases in real significance when compared with the real acts of heroism and sacrifice by countless American Negroes who since August 1619 and continuing through today have lost their lives because they asserted their God-given rights as human beings and as Americans. I did only what American Negroes have been doing from the very beginning of the history of the United States—loyally defending the country that our ancestors made along with other Americans of all origins and races. This is our country in every respect. We have a perfect right to defend it. In addition, we must honor those Negro Americans of yesterday who sowed American and foreign soil with their lives so that generations of today and tomorrow may reap the rewards, benefits, duties, and responsibilities of free men and women. These—our ancestors—were real heroes and courageous American Negroes whose names have been hidden in American history far too long. . . .

I hope that all the words of praise for my deed in raising the American flag in Ghana will be translated now in the United States into respect and full acceptance of American Negroes. If this full respect and acceptance does not take place, then one must draw the sad conclusion—as many American Negroes and other people throughout the world will—that the American flag was raised once again in vain.

Sincerely yours,
Adger Emerson Player
American Embassy, Accra, Ghana.

The Congressional Record, 88th Cong., 2nd sess., A1041.

PRESSURE TO DESEGREGATE ARMED FORCES

[*In 1948 A. Philip Randolph testified before a congressional committee on his proposal that African American men refuse to serve in the military until it was desegregated. He is questioned by Senator Wayne Morse.*]

Mr. Randolph. . . . it is my deep conviction that in taking such a position we are doing our country a great service. Our country has come out before the world as the moral leader of democracy. . . .

Well, now, I consider that if this country does not develop the democratic process at home and make the democratic process work by giving the very people whom they propose to draft in the Army to fight for them democracy, democracy then is not the type of democracy that ought to be fought for. . . .

Senator Morse. But on the basis of the law . . . then the doctrine of treason would be applied to those people participating in that disobedience?

Mr. Randolph. Exactly. I would be willing to face that doctrine on the theory and on the grounds that we are serving a higher law than the law which applies the act of treason to us when we are attempting to win democracy in this country and to make the soul of America democratic. . . .

I want it thoroughly understood that we could certainly not be guilty of any kind of overt act against the country but we would not participate in any military operation as segregation and Jim Crow slaves in the Army.

Congressional Record, 80th Cong., 2nd sess., part 4, 4313–17.

Dr. Bunche Receives the Nobel Peace Prize

[*The Voice of America reported the day Ralph Bunche received the Nobel Peace Prize.*]

"I am flabbergasted!" said Ralph Bunche, when told he had been awarded the Nobel Peace Prize.

But his friends and co-workers in the United Nations, where Dr. Bunche directs the Department of Trusteeships, were not surprised. They and other international observers fully expected that Dr. Bunche's valiant efforts to end hostilities in the Holy Land would earn a just recognition.

Dr. Bunche acknowledged the praise:

"I wish to say that my peace efforts flowed from the strength of the United Nations."

But the legions of men and women who had followed his trials and triumphs were not satisfied with this explanation. In appreciation of Dr. Bunche's personal achievements as a U.N. mediator, they bestowed more than sixty awards and degrees on him.

Voice of America, English edition (July–August 1951), 15.

Integrating the Army in Korea

[*Thurgood Marshall, investigator for the NAACP, found that despite efforts at integration, the United States Army discriminated against African American GIs. In Korea and Japan he found that Black soldiers were "tried in an atmosphere making justice impossible, by officers who had contempt for them."*]

The men of these outfits told me repeatedly that many of the white officers sneered at their troops, who were about to go forth to fight and, if necessary, to die for their country. They openly announced: "I despise 'nigger' troops and I don't want to command you and the regiment is no good and you are lousy. You don't know how to fight."

While this was not true of all the officers, it was a prevalent attitude and created lack of confidence between the men and their assigned leaders. As a consequence, the casualty rates among the enlisted men and officers were disproportionately high. Neither had confidence in the other and neither offered the maximum protection to the other.

I believe this condition was the cause of the court martials. The high rate of casualties among officers made it necessary to blame someone. The Negro soldier was the convenient scapegoat. . . .

Under these circumstances it was natural that the men were seized with despair. Some who had perfect alibis and airtight excuses failed to offer them. Others neglected to testify in their own behalf. Repeatedly I asked the men:

"Why didn't you tell your lawyer that? Why didn't you speak up in court?"

The answer was invariably the same:

"It wasn't worth it. We knew when we went to trial that we would be convicted—and we were hoping and praying that we would only get life. They gave the officer death solely because he was a Negro. What could we expect? We know the score."

Thurgood Marshall, *Report on Korea* (New York, 1951), 13–15.

19 THE CIVIL RIGHTS DECADE

GREAT SOCIAL REVOLUTIONS are not born in a day, a year, or even a decade. When they do happen, people begin to realize they come from long-ignored smoldering fires. The civil rights crisis of the 1960s had its roots deep in America's struggle for freedom and justice. It was born in the fierce resistance of Africans aboard the ships of the slave trade and on the plantations of the New World. The descendants of Africans gained renewed hope and courage from the ringing words of the Declaration of Independence and from the efforts of fearless abolitionists of both races.

The civil rights revolution can trace its demands for equality to the fiery words hammered out by William E. B. Du Bois. "The problem of the twentieth century," wrote this gentle scholar in 1903, "is the problem of the color-line." Only equality, he pointed out during most of his ninety-five years on earth, would make the dream of America a reality for all. On the day he died in 1963, hundreds of thousands of Americans were moving toward Washington, D.C., to voice their protest against all color lines in the United States. They were taking part in a long historic process, deeply embedded in their nation's history. And they were contributing to the fulfillment of America's commitment to equal justice for all.

Congratulating themselves on the 1954 Supreme Court decision are the three NAACP lawyers, including Thurgood Marshall (center), in 1967 appointed a justice of the Supreme Court.

The Supreme Court Decision of 1954

Shortly after high noon on Monday, 17 May 1954, members of the Supreme Court, spectators, and reporters sat solemnly listening to Chief Justice Earl Warren read the Court's unanimous decision in the *Brown* case. High above the entrance to the building is the motto "Equal Justice Under Law." Inside the marble meeting room more than a half century of legal segregation was being overturned by the unanimous decision of the nine justices. The heart of the decision was in the sentence: "Separate educational facilities are inherently unequal." One year later the Court ruled that all school districts must desegregate "with all deliberate speed."

Within a year after the 1954 decision more than five hundred school districts in the North and upper South had quietly desegregated. In the cities of Baltimore and Washington, D.C., Black and white children sat side by side for the first time in history. Virginia, leader of the South, appeared calm and thoughtful after the *Brown* decision. Governor Thomas Stanley commented, "We will consider the matter and work toward a plan which will be acceptable to our citizens and in keeping with the edict."

Everywhere in the upper South the pattern was the same. Children and parents of both races accepted the change more easily than anyone would have predicted. Only where there was organized opposition by white "segregationists" was there trouble. In Hoxie, Tennessee, twenty-six African Americans were enrolled in a white school system of eight hundred. There was no opposition until a few white parents began to stir others with fears of interracial marriages. When a group of white parents demanded that the board of education halt integration, the board held firm, and peaceful integration continued. The issue died.

In the Deep South, open defiance of the Supreme Court decision began to develop as soon as it was announced. Georgia's Governor Herman Talmadge declared that his state would "not tolerate the mixing of the races in the public schools or any other tax-supported institutions." Except for a few districts in Texas, no Blacks were admitted to schools in the Deep South until districts had been compelled to admit by federal court orders.

In many places, White Citizens Councils battled school integration by threatening loss of business to persons employing those who supported compliance with the court decision. The Ku Klux Klan became more active, using terror and violence to silence the voices that called for peaceful acceptance of the *Brown* decision.

Defiance of the Supreme Court was spurred by a "Southern Manifesto" issued by ninety-six Southern congressmen in March 1956. It denounced the *Brown* ruling and called for "all lawful means to bring about a reversal of this decision which is contrary to the Constitution. . . ." The pace of integration began to slow down. While two hundred new school districts had integrated in 1956, only thirty-eight had done so a year later.

The first important test of federal power for integration came in September 1957. Governor Orval Faubus of Arkansas interfered with a court order directing Central High School in Little Rock to admit nine qualified Black pupils. Faubus warned of bloodshed if the nine entered the high school and called out National Guard troops to protect the school.

The governor's fearful announcements brought out large crowds of segregationists in front of the high school. When one of the nine students, fifteen-year-old Elizabeth Eckford, tried to enter the school, she was halted by a National Guardsman. "When I tried to squeeze past him he raised his bayonet and then the other guards closed in and they raised their bayonets." A jeering crowd ("Lynch her!") followed her as she walked bravely to the bus stop. A white Northern reporter put his arm around her and whispered, "Don't let them see you cry." A white woman placed her aboard a bus. Elizabeth Eckford's heroism in the face of both the National Guard and the mob was carried to the far corners of the earth by radio and television. News of Governor Faubus's defiance of federal court orders was also heard around the world.

President Dwight D. Eisenhower, reluctant to use federal force to compel a state to cooperate with court orders, had often said, "I do not believe you can change the hearts of men with laws and decisions." But in September 1957 he ordered one thousand of the 101st Airborne Division into Little Rock to protect the nine students and to enforce the court order.

Paratroopers guarded the entrances to Central High School, and twenty-four were stationed in hallways. The nine students were brought to school by the United States Army. When some white students called for a "walkout," less than 60 out of the 1,800 students left school. Others invited the new students to join the Glee Club or sat with them at lunch.

An angry white Arkansas crowd followed Elizabeth Eckford to the bus stop.

The 101st Airborne Division escorts Black students into Central High School in Little Rock, Arkansas.

But the troublemakers did not quit. They singled out Minnejean Brown, sixteen, and cursed, tripped, or pushed her at every opportunity. After five months of this abuse, her patience came to an end. When another girl spilled hot soup on her in the school cafeteria, she struck back. The principal suspended both pupils. Minnejean Brown entered the private New Lincoln School in New York City and graduated a year later, high in her class.

Governor Faubus's interference continued. He closed the Little Rock schools for more than a year. But when the board of education forced the opening of the schools again, small "token" groups of African American pupils were present in several of the city's schools.

The Montgomery, Alabama, Bus Boycott

On 1 December 1955, Mrs. Rosa Parks boarded a bus in Montgomery, Alabama, the first capital of the Confederacy, and took a seat near the front. When a white man entered the bus and found no empty seats, the bus driver asked Mrs. Parks to move to the rear so that he could have her seat. There was nothing unusual in this request, for African Americans were expected to give up their seats and follow bus drivers' orders. But

Mrs. Parks refused. "I don't really know why I wouldn't move. There was no plan at all. I was just tired from shopping." Mrs. Parks was arrested on the spot for breaking the segregation law and taken to police headquarters to be fingerprinted.

The night after Mrs. Parks's arrest, the Reverend Martin Luther King, Jr., twenty-seven, called a meeting of church leaders in his Baptist church. The entire group agreed to ask all people of color to stay off the buses the day Mrs. Parks came to trial. On that fateful December 5, Dr. King got up early and went to check on the progress of the boycott. He wrote of this incident in *Stride Toward Freedom.*

> I jumped in my car and for almost an hour I cruised down every major street and examined every passing bus. During this hour, at the peak of the morning traffic, I saw no more than eight Negro passengers riding the buses. By this time I was jubilant. . . . A miracle had taken place.

And a new, powerful American movement and leader had been born!

Ninety-six percent of the African Americans stayed off the Montgomery buses that day and continued to stay off them month after month, for more than a year. People organized carpools; others walked great distances to work. The bus company lost 65 percent of its business and had to cut schedules, lay off drivers, and raise fares. The businesses of the white merchants suffered.

The city in which Jefferson Davis took the oath of office as president of the Southern Confederacy had become a nonviolent battleground for human rights. Southern whites learned again that their picture of Black people as content under segregation and happy without equal rights was a lie. African Americans discovered the economic boycott weapon used so effectively by American colonists against the British.

After the boycott had been under way for eighty days, a desperate city administration ordered the arrest of Dr. King and one hundred other boycott leaders. Dr. King told a packed meeting the next night that the boycott would continue no matter how many of its leaders went to jail. The conflict, he pointed out, was not "between the white and the Negro" but "between justice and injustice." He called upon his followers to love rather than to hate those who opposed them.

> If we are arrested every day, if we are exploited every day, if we are trampled over every day, don't ever let anyone pull you so low as to hate them. . . . We must realize so many people are taught to hate us that they are not totally responsible for their hate.

The bus boycott went on until final victory. In November 1956, the Supreme Court ruled that bus segregation violated the United States Constitution. The Montgomery bus company agreed to end segregation and hire African American drivers.

As the day approached for the integration of the buses, Black churches instructed their members to sit where they pleased but not to strike back if beaten. At 5:55 in the morning of 21 December 1956, Dr. King and Reverend Glen Smiley, a white friend, boarded the bus near Dr. King's house. As Dr. King paid his fare, the bus driver said, "We are glad to have you this morning." Dr. King and Reverend Smiley rode into history, sitting side by side. During that 1956 season of "peace on earth and goodwill toward men," a new day had begun to dawn in Alabama. The city of Montgomery had produced the most important civil rights leader of the day and the most effective weapon of protest yet devised.

But all was not peaceful. That same year Alabama outlawed the NAACP. And on the Christmas Eve after the boycott ended, a bomb exploded under the bed of Reverend Fred Shuttlesworth, Dr. King's assistant. He escaped unharmed.

Dr. Martin Luther King, Jr., speaks to a group of young people.

The Sit-Ins: Beginning of Mass Resistance

Although progress was being made by 1958, desegregation of the schools had not even begun in five Southern states. In most schools "tokenism," the admission of a very few Black students, was the rule. African American anger grew faster than this snail-pace progress. In 1958, students in Kansas and Oklahoma began to "sit-in" in lunch counters, demanding the right to be served like any other customers.

The technique of nonviolence was used most effectively by college students staging "sit-ins." On 1 February 1960, the manager of a five-and-ten-cent store in Greensboro, North Carolina, watched four Black college students who sat on the stools at his lunch counter and who insisted on each being served a cup of coffee. He turned to a reporter and said, "They can just sit there. It's nothing to me." The students continued to sit, returned the next day, and sat some more. By the fourth day whites joined the "sit-in." After several months, the lunch counter was opened to all.

The sit-ins immediately spread to hundreds of other Southern cities, almost always led by students from high schools or colleges. In the first six months of the new campaign, over sixteen hundred young men and women, Black and white, were arrested at lunch counter sit-ins. But it was

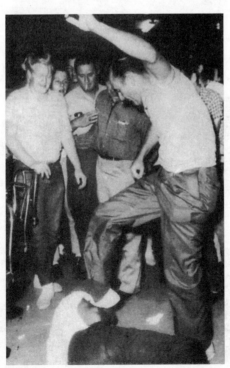

A Mississippi college student is dragged from a lunch counter stool and kicked by a former Jackson policeman.

now possible for people of color to sit on the stools of more and more Southern lunch counters and order whatever they pleased.

Many of the sit-ins were led by members of the Congress of Racial Equality (CORE), an interracial organization that had used nonviolent techniques to smash racial bars during World War II. As a reminder of their nonviolent purpose CORE members carried cards which read:

> Don't strike back or curse if abused;
> Don't laugh out;
> Don't hold conversations with floor workers;
> Don't block entrances to the stores or aisles;
> Show yourself courteous and friendly at all times;
> Sit straight and always face the counter;
> Remember love and non-violence;
> May God bless you.

While demonstrators were often abused by segregationists, by not fighting back they increasingly won sympathy and support for the justice of their cause across the country. Led by young Black students, these sit-ins were successful. By the end of 1961, Woolworth and other chain stores in 114 cities had agreed to serve all customers on an equal basis.

Integration of Ole Miss

In the spring of 1961 the Kennedy administration had been in office only a few months when it was presented with its first civil rights crisis. James Farmer, director of CORE, led a mixed group of "Freedom Riders" into the South. They began a series of bus rides to make sure that bus terminals in the Deep South were not segregated. One bus was set afire. On Mother's Day, 1961, James Peck, a white Freedom Rider, was almost beaten to death in Birmingham. He said that as he stepped from a bus "six of them started swinging at me with fists and pipes. . . . Within seconds I was unconscious on the ground." His head wounds required fifty-three stitches. Attorney General Robert Kennedy sent United States marshals to protect other riders and personally planned some of the trips through the South to prevent further violence.

The next great test for the federal government came on 30 September 1962, when James Meredith, son of a Mississippi farmer, entered the University of Mississippi to complete his studies. Meredith was brought onto the campus protected by five hundred U.S. marshals.

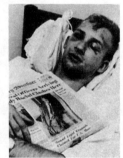

White "Freedom Rider," James Zwer, twenty-one, was beaten by a white mob in Montgomery, Alabama, in 1961.

That night, as President Kennedy addressed the country on television and radio, calling for peace and order, the marshals were holding off a mob of 2,500 Mississippians determined to drive off Meredith or kill him. Meredith, however, reported, "I think I read a newspaper and went to bed around 10 o'clock. . . ." He added, "And I slept pretty well all night."

By morning two men lay dead, shot by the rioters, scores of marshals and citizens had been injured, and many cars and buildings had been damaged. But James Meredith was enrolled at "Ole Miss" despite the violence and the estimated cost of almost half a million dollars. Student Meredith ignored some nasty pranks and said of the students, "Most, I'd say—have been courteous, and the faculty members certainly have been."

On 18 August 1963, James Meredith lined up with his fellow classmates to receive his diploma. It was a bright, sunny Southern day.

James Meredith graduates from "Ole Miss."

1963: *The Year of Decision*

On the one-hundredth anniversary of the Emancipation Proclamation, the civil rights drive was picking up momentum. For many progress was slow, too slow. Ten years after the *Brown* decision of the Supreme Court had ordered the integration of the schools, only 1.06 percent of the South's African American schoolchildren sat in classes with whites. The strategy of the civil rights movement, now led by Martin Luther King, Jr., was to strike at the most segregated city in America: Birmingham, Alabama.

This Southern steel city has had a long history of racial injustice, unequaled in the nation. It has been the scene of sixty unsolved racial bombings since the end of World War II. Birmingham officials had banned a children's book that showed Black and white rabbits playing together. Its leading law enforcement official, Eugene "Bull" Connor, readied his weapons for the demonstrators and said, "I got plenty of room in the jail." As it turned out, he would need every bit of jail space.

On 3 April 1963, Dr. Martin Luther King and his aides arrived in Birmingham to plan their most ambitious program of resistance to segregation and discrimination. Fearing their phones were tapped, they used code names—King was called "JFK" and demonstrators were "baptismal candidates." Arrests of demonstrators began with the first demonstrations. Orderly, well-dressed Black women and men were loaded into patrol wagons when they tried to march into downtown Birmingham. The charge was "parading without a permit."

As more people joined the marching, singing groups into Birmingham, the shopping area suffered a severe drop in sales. To stem this mounting tide of humanity, Connor ordered the police to use their trained dogs against the paraders. Dogs were first used on Palm Sunday.

Next the city secured a court order banning further marches. For the first time Reverend King and his group decided to disobey a court order. "We did not hide our intentions," King wrote in *Why We Can't Wait.* "In fact, I announced our plan to the press, pointing out that we were not anarchists advocating lawlessness, but that it was obvious to us that the courts of Alabama had misused the judicial process in order to perpetuate injustice and segregation." On Good Friday, Dr. King and Reverend Abernathy were arrested for leading a march into Birmingham.

A concerned President Kennedy called Mrs. King to promise whatever help was possible, and Attorney General Robert Kennedy called Birmingham and had Dr. King released from solitary confinement. In eight days Dr. King was free, and the marches continued. So did the arrests. Before the crisis ended with the surrender of the Birmingham officials, 3,300 others, many of them schoolchildren, had been jailed.

On May 7, a stunned nationwide television audience watched high-pressure hoses shoot powerful jets of water on neatly attired demonstrators. Men and women were swept into the gutter or struck down. One jet tore the bark off a tree, and another sent Reverend Fred Shuttlesworth crashing into the side of a building. Birmingham police then clubbed their way into demonstrators.

A few days later the home of Dr. King's brother was bombed, and the parents and their five children narrowly escaped death. A series of bomb blasts rocked the African American areas of the city a few days after that. As the infuriated inhabitants moved into the streets, police sealed off the African American sections and drove the people off the streets. On a few

Reverend Martin Luther King, Jr. (right), and Reverend Ralph Abernathy (at his side) lead a Birmingham march in violation of a court order. They and fifty-one other demonstrators were arrested.

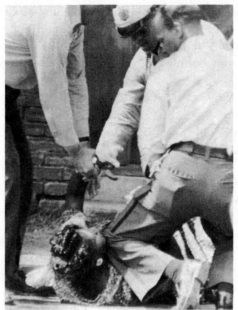

Three Birmingham, Alabama, policemen subdue a female demonstrator.

occasions, such as this one, African Americans responded to violence with violence. But it was their restraint, when contrasted with the violence launched by "Bull" Connor, that made Dr. King's Birmingham campaign a success. President Kennedy later told King that Connor's police dogs and fire hoses had done as much to advance the cause of freedom as had Lincoln's Emancipation Proclamation.

Segregation in Birmingham was dying despite the violence. A white businessman asked, "Are the Negroes I see around town walking a little straighter these days?" Birmingham, wrote Dr. King, "was a fuse—it detonated a revolution that went on to win scores of other victories."

In the months following the events in Birmingham, eight hundred civil rights demonstrations took place in cities and towns of the South and North. Increasingly, white clergymen and citizens of all faiths joined in the civil rights campaign. Dr. Eugene Carson Blake, head of the United Presbyterian Church, was quoted as saying, "Some time or other, we are all going to have to stand and be on the receiving end of a fire hose." Then he joined other clergymen in a protest march and was arrested.

The events in Birmingham brought a demand from President Kennedy for Congress to pass a civil rights law which would open public facilities to all Americans. Our people, the president told the nation, "for all its hopes and all its boasts, will not be fully free until all its citizens are free. . . . Now the time has come for this nation to fulfill its promises." The urgency of his

Birmingham's police dogs in action. Photographs like this carried the story of Southern racial injustice to the world.

demand for action was underscored by the assassination of Medgar Evers, a veteran of World War II and a Mississippi civil rights leader. He was shot in the back just twenty-four hours after the president's talk.

Congress responded to the civil rights crusade with weak laws in 1957 and 1960 and stronger ones in 1964 and 1965. The 1964 law aimed to eliminate segregation and discrimination in broad areas of American life: employment, education, public accommodations, and voting rights. The Twenty-fourth Amendment to the Constitution (ratified 1964), which eliminated the poll tax in federal elections, and the 1965 Civil Rights Law, which eliminated literacy tests and other devices that prohibited the exercise of Black voting power, led to an immediate increase in Black voters. The great test for these laws, in light of history, was whether they would be enforced. African Americans had long insisted that the key issue was not new laws but enforcement of laws that already existed. This bitter truth was reflected in the very subtitle of the 1965 Civil Rights Law—"An act to enforce the Fifteenth Amendment to the Constitution of the United States." The Fifteenth Amendment had been ratified in 1870.

America's Largest Protest March

Beginning in the 1960s a determined young army of college students of all races and religions entered the South to teach a new freedom to long-oppressed people. These new "carpetbaggers" were trained in nonviolence and came armed with thick books and high ideals. They helped local African Americans establish libraries, community centers, and "freedom schools." Their classes met under trees until rooms could be found. Children learned to read and write, to understand the rights of American citizens, and about the role African Americans played in U.S. history.

The schools and teachers lived under a reign of terror similar to that of the Reconstruction period. Buildings were bombed and civil rights workers beaten or murdered. But every act of violence only seemed to convince these young men and women of the rightness of their cause. As his deputies tried to intimidate a 1962 meeting of Georgia Blacks, Sheriff Z. T. Mathews told a reporter, "We want our colored people to go on living like they have for the last hundred years." But African Americans had no intention of doing that, no matter what the cost. As one Southern Black woman said, "I'm afraid, but I'm not terrorized."

Throughout the South and the nation Black men, women, and children drew strength from the civil rights movement. Increasingly, the South produced its own leaders for "freedom schools" and voter registration drives. Most of them were young, and some were white. While not all believed in the theory of nonviolence, even those who believed in meeting violence with violence left their guns at home during demonstrations and meetings. But in case of night attack, many kept guns in readiness.

To dramatize their demand for equality, civil rights leaders planned a gigantic march on Washington for 28 August 1963. The idea of Asa Philip Randolph, seventy-five, it won the support of Martin Luther King's Southern Christian Leadership Conference, Roy Wilkins's NAACP, James Farmer's CORE, Whitney Young's Urban League, and John Lewis's Student Non-Violent Coordinating Committee. Additional aid came from Catholic, Protestant, and Jewish leaders and ordinary citizens.

On the day of the march, buses, trains, cars, and planes brought Washington its greatest crowd in history. Housewives and congressmen, sharecroppers and celebrities, civil rights workers and clergymen were among the quarter of a million people who gathered before the Lincoln Memorial that day. Television cameras brought the story to the world.

The crowd listened to Dr. King's vision of an America free from bigotry: "I have a dream that my four little children will one day live in a nation where they will not be judged by the color of their skin but by the content of their character." They listened to men who long had been on the racial firing line such as Randolph, Wilkins, and Young. (James Farmer was in a Louisiana jail for having led the civil rights drive there.) They heard from John Lewis, twenty-three, whose SNCC had brought hundreds of young people into the South, new "carpetbaggers" who had come to build schools and to encourage people to register for voting. His speech struck so hard at racism that moderate Black leaders toned it down.

Although some fearful voices had predicted violence that day, the mood in Washington was far different. Emily Rock, fifteen, of Woodlands High School, New York, recorded her thoughts:

> I have never seen such a crowd of people as there were that day. There was a special feeling of closeness. I have never felt so small and yet a part of something so immense, wonderful, and grand.
>
> I had a feeling of pride for my race and for the whites who thought enough to come. And there was a sense of triumph. We had proved by being orderly,

A smiling President Kennedy congratulates leaders of the 1963 March on Washington. From left to right: Whitney Young, Jr. (National Urban League), Reverend Martin Luther King, Jr. (Southern Christian Leadership Conference), Rabbi Joachim Prinz (American Jewish Congress), A. Philip Randolph (director of the march), President Kennedy, Walter Reuther (president of the United Auto Workers), Roy Wilkins (NAACP). America's largest protest march was without incident.

nonviolent, and determined that we were not the kind of people our enemies said we were.

All around, in the faces of everyone, there was this sense of hope for the future—the belief that this march was the *big* step in the right direction. It could be heard in the voices of the people singing and seen in the way they talked. It poured out into smiles.

The battle for equality did not end on that August afternoon. There were other marches—and other murders. But Emily Rock was right. The "hope for the future" present that day had never been brighter.

The Last Message of Dr. Du Bois

Emily Rock. At graduation she was chosen school valedictorian.

[On 26 August 1963 Dr. William E. B. Du Bois died in Ghana, an exile from his native land and a Communist. On the day after, Roy Wilkins of the NAACP told the huge march on Washington "at the dawn of the twentieth century his was the voice that was calling you to gather here today in this cause." In 1957 Dr. Du Bois wrote this "last message" which was released after his death.]

I have loved my work, I have loved people and my play, but always I have been uplifted by the thought that what I have done well—will live long and justify my life; that what I have done ill or never finished can now be handed on to others for endless days to be finished, perhaps better than I could have done.

And that peace will be my applause.

One thing alone I charge you. As you live, believe in life. Always human beings will live and profess to a greater, broader, and fuller life.

The only possible death is to lose belief in this truth simply because the great end comes slowly, because time is long.

Goodbye.

Elizabeth Eckford, Sixteen, Tries to Go to School

[*When she left for Central High School in Little Rock, Elizabeth Eckford did not know that the governor of Arkansas, to prevent her entrance to the school, had disobeyed a federal court order. This is her story.*]

Before I left home Mother called us into the living-room. She said we should have a word of prayer. Then I caught the bus and got off a block from the school. I saw a large crowd of people standing across the street from the soldiers guarding Central. As I walked on, the crowd suddenly got very quiet. Superintendent Blossom had told us to enter by the front door. I looked at all the people and thought, "Maybe I will be safer if I walk down the block to the front entrance behind the guards."

At the corner I tried to pass through the long line of guards around the school so as to enter the grounds behind them. One of the guards pointed across the street. So I pointed in the same direction and asked whether he meant for me to cross the street and walk down. He nodded "yes." So, I walked across the street conscious of the crowd that stood there, but they moved away from me.

For a moment all I could hear was the shuffling of their feet. Then someone shouted, "Here she comes, get ready!" I moved away from the crowd on the sidewalk and into the street. If the mob came at me, I could then cross back over so the guards could protect me.

The crowd moved in closer and then began to follow me, calling me names. I still wasn't afraid. Just a little bit nervous. Then my knees started to shake all of a sudden and I wondered whether I could make it to the center entrance a block away. It was the longest block I ever walked in my whole life.

Even so, I still wasn't too scared because all the time I kept thinking that the guards would protect me.

When I got right in front of the school, I went up to a guard again. But this time he just looked straight ahead and didn't move to let me pass him. I didn't know what to do. Then I looked and saw that the path leading to the front entrance was a little further ahead. So I walked until I was right in front of the path to the front door.

I stood looking at the school—it looked so big! Just then the guards let some white students go through.

The crowd was quiet. I guess they were waiting to see what was going to happen. When I was able to steady my knees, I walked up to the guard who had let the white students in. He too didn't move. When I tried to squeeze past him, he raised his bayonet and then the other guards closed in and they raised their bayonets.

They glared at me with a mean look and I was very frightened and didn't know what to do. I turned around and the crowd came toward me.

They moved closer and closer. Somebody started yelling, "Lynch her! Lynch her!"

I tried to see a friendly face somewhere in the mob—someone who maybe would help. I looked into the face of an old woman and it seemed a kind face, but when I looked at her again, she spat on me.

They came closer, shouting, "No nigger bitch is going to get in our school. Get out of here!"

I turned back to the guards but their faces told me I wouldn't get help from them. Then I looked down the block and saw a bench at the bus stop. I thought, "If I can only get there I will be safe." I don't know why the bench seemed a safe place to me, but I started walking toward it. I tried to close my mind to what they were shouting, and kept saying to myself, "If I can only make it to the bench I will be safe."

When I finally got there, I don't think I could have gone another step. I sat down and the mob crowded up and began shouting all over again. Someone hollered, "Drag her over to this tree! Let's take care of the nigger." Just then a white man sat down beside me, put his arm around me and patted my shoulder. He raised my chin and said, "Don't let them see you cry."

Then, a white lady—she was very nice—she came over to me on the bench. She spoke to me but I don't remember now what she said. She put me on the bus and sat next to me. She asked me my name and tried to talk to me but I don't think I answered. I can't remember much about the bus ride, but the next thing I remember I was standing in front of the School for the Blind, where Mother works.

I thought, "Maybe she isn't here. But she has to be here!" So I ran upstairs, and I think some teachers tried to talk to me, but I kept running until I reached Mother's classroom.

Mother was standing at the window with her head bowed, but she must have sensed I was there because she turned around. She looked as if she had been crying, and I wanted to tell her I was all right. But I couldn't speak. She put her arms around me and I cried.

Daisy Bates, *The Long Shadow of Little Rock* (New York: David McKay, 1962), 73–76. Reprinted by permission.

A Presidential Aide Recalls the 1960 Election

[In 1956, E. Frederick Morrow became the first Black presidential aide in history. He was appointed by President Dwight D. Eisenhower, and he later served in the 1960 presidential campaign of Richard Nixon.]

Late in the campaign I joined the Nixon entourage on the road. Unlike the Eisenhower campaigns of '52 and '56, I was never seen with the Vice-President. I rode in caravans in a rear car and was never called into parleys or strategy meetings.

In the closing days of the campaign, Reverend Martin Luther King, Negro idol and civil rights leader, was thrown in jail in Atlanta on a trivial charge. It was an international sensation. It was the moment for American leadership to speak.

I begged the Nixon managers, by memo and in person, to have the Vice-President make a statement deploring the situation under which King was jailed. They demurred. They thought it bad strategy.

The next day I joined the Nixon campaign train in Illinois. I urged his press secretary to have him take some action. I even drafted a telegram for the Vice-President to send to the mayor of Atlanta. The press secretary put the draft in his pocket to "think about it."

Twenty-four hours later, King was freed from jail. His freedom came after the intercession of the Democratic presidential candidate, John F. Kennedy. He had scored tremendously, not only by wiring the mayor of Atlanta, but by phoning King's wife to express his concern and ask if he could be of assistance. And his brother Robert had apparently talked to other Atlanta officials.

This action won the election. Kennedy's action electrified the entire Negro community and resulted in tens of thousands of Negro voters going over to the Democrats' banner. . . .

The results of this campaign should hold many valuable lessons for Republican leaders and politicians. The strategy of wooing the solid South and ignoring the available Negro vote was a costly blunder. . . .

E. Frederick Morrow, *Black Man in the White House* (New York: McFadden Books, 1963), 213–14.

A "FREEDOM RIDE" REACHES BIRMINGHAM

[*On 4 May 1961, Freedom Riders sought to test the South's compliance with federal court orders which forbid segregation on buses or in terminals. James Peck, white, and Charles Person, African American, were among the group that arrived in Birmingham, Alabama, on Mother's Day, 1961. Peck wrote the story.*]

Upon my arrival in Birmingham, I could see a mob lined up on the sidewalk only a few feet from the loading platform. Most of them were young—in their twenties. Some were carrying ill-concealed iron-bars. A few were older men. All had hate showing on their faces.

I looked at them and then I looked at Charles Person, who had been designated as my team mate to test the lunch counter. Person, a slim youth, quiet and determined, had been jailed-in for sixteen days during the campaign to desegregate Atlanta lunch counters. . . .

Now we stood on the Birmingham unloading platform with the segregationist mob only a few feet away. I did not want to put Person in a position of being forced to proceed if he thought the situation too dangerous. When I looked at him, he responded by saying simply, "Let's go."

As we entered the white waiting room and approached the lunch counter, we were grabbed bodily and pushed toward the alleyway leading to the loading platform. As soon as we got into the alleyway and out of sight of onlookers in the waiting room, six of them started swinging at me with fists and pipes. Five others attacked Persons a few feet ahead. Within seconds, I was unconscious on the ground.

I learned only later that the mob went on to assault Tom Langston of the *Birmingham Post-Herald* and smashed his camera. Langston had been sufficiently quick-witted to remove his film, and the photo of my beating, clearly showing the hate-filled expression of my assailants, appeared in the next morning's *Post-Herald* and in many newspapers throughout the country. Then, Clancy Lake, a radio newsman, was attacked as he sat in his car, broadcasting an account of the onslaught.

When I regained consciousness, the alleyway was empty. Blood was flowing down my face. . . .

. . . I did not realize how seriously I had been hurt. My head required fifty-three stitches. [Person did not require hospitalization.]

James Peck, *Freedom Ride* (New York: Grove Press, 1962), 98–99.

JAMES MEREDITH ATTENDS "OLE MISS"

*[James Meredith, twenty-nine and an air force veteran, entered the University of
Mississippi in the fall of 1962. The night after the riot, he began attending classes
with the all-white student body and faculty.]*

Monday morning at eight o'clock I registered, and at nine I went to class in
Colonial American History. I was a few minutes late, and I took a seat at
the back of the room. The professor was lecturing on the background in
England, conditions there at the time of the colonization of America, and
he paid no special attention when I entered. I think there were about a
dozen students in the class. One said hello to me, and the others were
silent. I remember a girl—the only girl there, I think—and she was crying,
but it might have been from the tear gas [used by the United States marshals the night before] in the room. I was crying from it myself.

I had three classes scheduled that day. I went to two, and the third
didn't meet because there was too much gas in the room. No marshals
were in the classrooms with me, nor were they all week. . . .

As far as my relations with the students go, I make it a practice to be
courteous. I don't force myself on them, but that's not my nature anyway.
Many of them—most, I'd say—have been courteous, and the faculty members certainly have been. When I hear the jeers and the catcalls . . . I don't
consider it personal. I get the idea people are just having a little fun. I
think it's tragic that they have to have this kind of fun about me, but many
of them are children of the men who lead Mississippi today, and I wouldn't
expect them to act any other way. . . .

It hasn't been all bad. Many students have spoken to me very pleas-
antly. They have stopped banging doors and throwing bottles into my dormitory now.

One fellow from my home town sat down at my table in the cafeteria. "If
you're here to get an education, I'm for you," he said. "If you're here to
cause trouble, I'm against you." That seemed fair enough to me.

James Meredith, "I'll Know Victory or Defeat," *The Saturday Evening Post* 235 (10 November 1962): 17. Reprinted by permission of James Meredith.

BIRMINGHAM IN 1963

[Mary Hamilton, eighteen, was one of many young Black civil rights workers who led groups marching into downtown Birmingham in 1963. She describes her arrest.]

I had been helping out with the demonstrations in one way or another. And on Monday I was asked to help clear the sidewalks of the pedestrians so the Freedom march—so the demonstrators—could walk on the sidewalk without interference. . . . Generally the case is when they [the police] see an organizer around, they, if they can, they will arrest you. So I had been ordered by the police to stay off the sidewalk.

I had really stepped up on the ledge as the demonstrators were walking towards us. And I lost my balance. It was really this simple. I had lost my balance and stepped down to gain my balance. And the minute I stepped down on the sidewalk I was nabbed—and placed in a police car. I was arrested.

At that time about eighty people were arrested. Two groups were placed in two different buses. We were taken to the city jail. These demonstrators were—the average age range I would say was about, um, seventeen. . . .

All, all of the girls were placed in the downstairs cell block. It then began to rain and so we all climbed up and looked out the window. And here were these children—a good two hundred children out in the rain—just being drenched. The rain was coming down in torrents. And people were milling about and the police were out trying to drive people away. There was plenty of room in the cell block which I was in, to put these children. But instead the police preferred to leave them out. And it rained on those children two hours.

So we began banging on the—there were steel doors. So a mob of policemen came in. One of them said, "Well, we know what to do with the whole group." So they herded us all into solitary confinement cells, which were about two by two. You could take two steps, two short steps, in both directions. . . . There were from twelve to fifteen of us in these cells. We were left in there a good two hours. . . . We were uncomfortable . . . and so after about three hours we began banging on the walls of the cell. And of course there was a big noise and everything.

Policemen crowded in again—suddenly. There seemed to be a characteristic about these cops—they can never be alone by themselves and they must always come with their guns, their clubs, and their helmets. Anyway, they all herded into the cell and wanted to know what was up. And I told them, I said, "The girls have been in here for five hours without bathroom facilities and without water—and you can't treat people this way." And I just went on like this. So they took all the girls out except me. . . .

"Freedom Now" presented on *Pacifica Radio* (WBAI in New York). Reprinted by permission.

President Kennedy Calls for Equal Rights

[*In June of 1963 President John F. Kennedy spoke to a nationwide television and radio audience using terms never before used by an American president.*]

. . . This Nation was founded by men of many nations and backgrounds. It was founded on the principle that all men are created equal, and that the rights of every man are diminished when the rights of one man are threatened.

Today we are committed to a worldwide struggle to promote and protect the rights of all who wish to be free. And when Americans are sent to Vietnam or West Berlin, we do not ask for whites only. It ought to be possible, therefore, for American students of any color to attend any public institution they select without having to be backed up by troops. . . . In short, every American ought to have the right to be treated as he would wish to be treated, as one would wish his children to be treated. But this is not the case.

The Negro baby born in America today, regardless of the section of the Nation in which he is born, has about one-half as much chance of completing a high school education as a white baby born in the same place on the same day, one-third as much chance of completing college, one-third as much chance of becoming a professional man, twice as much chance of becoming unemployed, about one-seventh as much chance of earning $10,000 a year, a life expectancy which is 7 years shorter, and the prospects of earning only half as much.

This is not a sectional issue. Difficulties over segregation and discrimination exist in every city, in every State of the Union, producing in many cities a rising tide of discontent that threatens the public safety. Nor is this a partisan issue.

We are confronted primarily with a moral issue. It is as old as the scriptures and is as clear as the American Constitution.

The heart of the question is whether all Americans are to be afforded equal rights and equal opportunities, whether we are going to treat our fellow Americans as we want to be treated. If an American, because his skin is dark, cannot eat lunch in a restaurant open to the public, if he cannot send his children to the best public school available, if he cannot vote for the public officials who represent him, if, in short, he cannot enjoy the full and free life which all of us want, then who among us would be content to have the color of his skin changed and stand in his place? Who among us would then be content with the counsels of patience and delay?

One hundred years of delay have passed since President Lincoln freed the slaves, yet their heirs, their grandsons, are not fully free. They are not yet freed from the bonds of injustice. They are not yet freed from social and economic oppression. And this Nation, for all its hopes and all its boasts, will not be fully free until all its citizens are free.

We preach freedom around the world, and we mean it, and we cherish our freedom here at home, but are we to say to the world, and much more importantly, to each other that this is a land of the free except for the Negroes; that we have no second-class citizens except Negroes; that we have no class or cast[e] system, no ghettoes, no master race except with respect to Negroes?

Now the time has come for this Nation to fulfill its promise. The events in Birmingham and elsewhere have so increased the cries for equality that no city or State or legislative body can prudently choose to ignore them.

The fires of frustration and discord are burning in every city, North and South, where legal remedies are not at hand. Redress is sought in the streets, in demonstrations, parades, and protests which create tensions and threaten violence and threaten lives.

We face, therefore, a moral crisis as a country and as a people. It cannot be met by repressive police action. It cannot be left to increased demonstrations in the streets. It cannot be quieted by token moves or talk. It is a time to act in the Congress, in your State and local legislative body and, above all, in all of our daily lives.

It is not enough to pin the blame on others, to say this is a problem of one section of the country or another, or deplore it. A great change is at hand, and our task, our obligation, is to make that revolution, that change, peaceful and constructive for all.

Those who do nothing are inviting shame as well as violence. Those who act boldly are recognizing right as well as reality.

Next week I shall ask the Congress of the United States to act, to make a commitment it has not fully made in this century to the proposition that race has no place in American life or law. . . .

John F. Kennedy in *Public Papers of the Presidents of the United States* 3 (Washington, 1964): 236–37.

THE MIND OF THE KU KLUX KLAN

[In the summer of 1964, shortly after the bodies of Michael Schwerner, James Chaney, and Andrew Goodman were found, the Klan issued a newsletter, written in question (Q) and answer (A) form.]

Q. What is your explanation of why there have been so many National Police Agents [F.B.I.?] involved in the case of the "missing civil rights workers"?

A. First, I must correct you on your terms. Schwerner, Chaney and Goodman were not civil rights workers. They were Communist Revolutionaries, actively working to undermine and destroy Christian Civilization. The blatant and outlandish National Police activity surrounding their case merely points up the political overtones of the entire affair. . . .

Q. By "political overtones" do you mean that the case has a bearing on the forthcoming elections?

A. It is doubtful that the case itself will be made an issue in the election. However, the incumbent in the White House [Lyndon B. Johnson] is a communist sympathizer, as proven by his numerous acts of treason, and his sole chance of victory in the November election will depend upon his being able to hold his communist-liberal bloc together by continuing to support and protect all Domestic Communists. . . .

Q. Isn't it unlikely that the Communists would do that [kill the three civil rights workers themselves] in this case? Schwerner was a valuable man?

A. Not at all. The Communists never hesitate to murder one of their own if it will benefit the party. Communism is pure, refined, scientific Cannibalism in action. A case in point is the murdered Kennedy. Certainly, no President could have been a more willing tool to the Communists than was the late and unlamented "Red Jack." He cooperated with them at every turn. Yet . . . he was callously given up for execution by those whom he had served so well. . . .

Q. Do the White Knights of the KU KLUX KLAN advocate or engage in unlawful violence?

A. We are absolutely opposed to street riots and public demonstrations of all kinds. Our work is largely educational in nature. . . . All of our work is carried on in a dignified and reverent manner. . . . We are all *Americans* in the White Knights of the KU KLUX KLAN of Mississippi.

The Klan-Ledger, Special Neshoba County Fair Edition.

LANGSTON HUGHES VIEWS A HARLEM RIOT

[During the summers of 1964 and 1965, riots erupted in many Northern ghettos. Langston Hughes takes a satirical look at the Harlem riot of 1964.]

Opinion in Harlem is divided as to whether or not riots do any good. Some say *yes,* they achieve concrete results in community improvements. Others say *no,* they set the Negro race back 50 years. Those who disagree say, in effect, "But Negroes are always being set back 50 years by something or another, so what difference does a riot make?"

Old-timers who remember former riots in Harlem say, "White folks respect us more when they find out we mean business. When they only listen to our speeches or read our writing—if they ever do—they think we are just blowing off steam. But when rioters smash the plate glass windows of their stores, they know the steam has some force behind it. Then they say, 'Those Negroes are mad! What do they want?' And for a little while they will try to give you a little of what you want.

"After every riot in Harlem, the whites respect you more. After that big riot in 1935, the white-owned shops all along 125th Street that would not hire Negro clerks, began to hire at least one. We got a great many jobs out of that riot that we couldn't get before in our own community because the clerks, cashiers and everything were all white."

The big riot in 1943, which grew out of a white policeman shooting a black soldier at 126th Street and 8th Avenue during a period of much police brutality in the area, produced remarkable changes in police attitudes in Harlem, and resulted in a number of additional Negro officers being added to the force.

Chocolate and vanilla teams of policemen appeared on uptown streets walking together. Squad cars became integrated. And a white policeman would often grant his Negro colleague the courtesy of making the arrest, if an arrest had to be made. And for a long time, after the '43 riots, seldom did Negro or white cops beat a culprit's head in public—as they frequently did before the riots. . . .

After the 1943 riots, one night on Lenox Avenue, I saw two white policemen attempting to push a young Negro into a squad car. The man refused to get in. Each time the police tried to force him, he would spread out his arms and legs or twist his body so that they could not get him through the door. With a crowd of Negroes all around, the white cops seemingly did not dare hit the Negro. But, to their fortune a colored policeman on foot arrived. He simply said, "Get in that car fellow!" The Negro got in, and the car sped away with its prisoner.

Folks in the crowd said, "You see—since the riots, they sure do arrest you politely. Now his head won't be cracked, till they get him down to the precinct house." The riots of 1943 almost ended *public* police brutality on the streets in Harlem.

Out of our 1964 riot this week I do not know what concrete results will come but certainly its repercussions have already reached into high places. No less an authority than President Johnson has spoken from the capital saying grandiloquently, "Violence and lawlessness cannot, must not, and will not be tolerated." Some Harlemites interpret this to mean that there will be no more head-bustings on the part of the police, or shooting of adolescents, black, white, or Puerto Rican by men representing New York's Finest. "American citizens have a right to protection of life and limb," continued the President, "whether driving along a highway in Georgia, a road in Mississippi, or a street in New York City."

. . . Negroes have been asking for years that Georgia and Mississippi be made safe—and getting no results from federal or state governments. But now, after a weekend of rioting in Harlem, you see what the President says! The riots have already produced one good result. . . .

Langston Hughes, "Harlem III," *New York Post,* 23 July 1964, 29. Reprinted by permission of Harold Ober Associates.

Mrs. Hamer Registers to Vote

[Sharecropper Mrs. Fannie Lou Hamer of Ruleville, Mississippi, registered to vote. She told a committee in Washington, D.C., what happened.]

. . . I will begin from the first beginning, August 31, in 1962.

I travelled 26 miles to the county courthouse to try to register to become a first-class citizen. I was fired the 31st of August in 1962 from a plantation where I had worked as a timekeeper and a sharecropper for 18 years. My husband had worked there 30 years.

I was met by my children when I returned from the courthouse, and my girl and my husband's cousin told me that this man my husband worked for was raising a lot of Cain. I went on in the house, and it wasn't long before my husband came and said this plantation owner said I would have to leave if I didn't go down and withdraw.

. . . [The plantation owner] said, "Fannie Lou, you have been to the courthouse to try to register," and he said, "We are not ready for this in Mississippi."

I said, "I didn't register for you, I tried to register for myself."

He said, "We are not going to have this in Mississippi, and you will have to withdraw. I am looking for your answer, yea or nay."

I just looked. He said, "I will give you until tomorrow morning. . . ." So I left the same night.

On the 10th of September, they fired into the home of Mr. and Mrs. Robert Tucker 16 times for me. That same night, two girls were shot at Mr. Herman Sissel's. Also, they shot [into] Mr. Joe Maglon's house. I was fired that day and haven't had a job since. . . .

[*In 1963 Mrs. Hamer was arrested and beaten by the state police after returning from a voter registration workshop. In 1964, "my husband was fired the day after I qualified to run as a Congresswoman." That year she headed a delegation of sixty Mississippi Black and white delegates to the Democratic National Convention. But she and only one other were seated as delegates.*]

Hearing Before a Select Panel on Mississippi and Civil Rights at the National Theatre, . . . Washington, D.C., Monday, June 8, 1964. Reprinted in *The Congressional Record*, 16 June 1964.

"I Shall Cast My Lot"

[*As the Civil Rights Law of 1964 speeded toward passage on 2 July 1964, Congressman Charles Longstreet Weltner of Atlanta, Georgia, rose to speak. "His fellow Southerners sat stunned," wrote a reporter, as the white representative told why he had changed his mind.*]

Mr. Speaker, over 4 months ago, the civil rights bill came to this floor. Its stated purpose, equality of opportunity for all Americans, is a proper goal. But I questioned its means, and voted against passage. Now, after the most thorough and sifting examination in legislative history this measure returns for final consideration. It returns with the overwhelming approval of both Houses of Congress.

Manifestly, the issue is already decided, and approval is assured. By the time my name is called, votes sufficient for passage will have been recorded.

What, then, is the proper course? Is it to vote "no," with tradition, safety—and futility?

I believe a greater cause can be served. Change, swift and certain, is upon us, and we in the South face some difficult decisions.

We can offer resistance and defiance, with their harvest of strife and tumult. We can suffer continued demonstrations, with their wake of violence and disorder.

Or, we can acknowledge this measure as the law of the land. We can accept the verdict of the Nation.

Already, the responsible elements of my community are counseling this latter course. And, most assuredly, moderation, tranquillity, and orderly processes combine as a cause greater than conformity.

Mr. Speaker, I shall cast my lot with the leadership of my community. I shall cast my vote with that greater cause they serve. I will add my voice to those who seek reasoned and conciliatory adjustment to a new reality.

And finally, I would urge that we at home now move on to the unfinished task of building a new South. We must not remain forever bound to another lost cause.

Representative Charles Longstreet Weltner, *Report from Washington* (Washington, 24 July 1964). Reprinted from *The Congressional Record*.

A PRESIDENT ANNOUNCES "WE SHALL OVERCOME"

[*In 1965, when a march in Selma of African Americans demanding the right to vote was attacked by Alabama state troopers, President Lyndon B. Johnson called on Congress to enact a voting rights law.*]

I speak tonight for the dignity of man and the destiny of democracy. . . .

There is no Negro problem. There is no Southern problem. There is no Northern problem. There is only an American problem. And we are met here tonight as Americans, not as Democrats or Republicans, we are met here as Americans to solve that problem. . . .

Every device of which human ingenuity is capable has been used to deny this right [to vote]. The Negro citizen may go to register only to be told that the day is wrong, or the hour is late, or the official in charge is absent. And if he persists and if he manages to present himself to the registrar, he may be disqualified because he did not spell out his middle name or because he abbreviated a word on the application. And if he manages to fill out the application he is given a test. The registrar is the sole judge of whether he passes this test. He may be asked to recite the entire constitution, or explain the most complex provisions of state laws. And even a college degree cannot be used to prove that he can read and write.

For the fact is that the only way to pass these barriers is to show a white skin. . . .

Wednesday I will send to Congress a law designed to eliminate illegal barriers to the right to vote. . . .

But even if we pass this bill, the battle will not be over. What happened in Selma is part of a far larger movement which reaches into every section and state of America. It is the effort of American Negroes to secure for themselves the full blessings of American life.

Their cause must be our cause too. Because it is not just Negroes, but really it is all of us, who must overcome the crippling legacy of bigotry and injustice. And we shall overcome. . . .

The real hero of this struggle is the American Negro. His actions and protests, his courage to risk safety and even to risk his life, have awakened the conscience of this nation. His demonstrations have been designed to call attention to injustice, designed to make good the promise of America. And who among us can say that we would have made the same progress were it not for his persistent bravery, and his faith in American democracy.

Lyndon B. Johnson, Remarks of the President to a Joint Session of Congress (Washington: Office of the White House Press Secretary, 15 March 1965), 1–5.

DR. KING EXPLAINS NONVIOLENT RESISTANCE

[In an essay written for this volume, Dr. King explains nonviolent resistance.]

During my freshman days in 1944 at Atlanta's Morehouse College I read Henry David Thoreau's essay *On Civil Disobedience* for the first time. Here, in this courageous New Englander's refusal to pay his taxes and his choice of jail rather than support a war that would spread slavery's territory into Mexico, I made my first contact with the theory of nonviolent resistance. Fascinated by Thoreau's idea of refusing to cooperate with an evil system, I was so deeply moved that I reread the work several times.

A few years later I heard a lecture by Dr. Mordecai Johnson, President of Howard University. Dr. Johnson had just returned from a trip to India and he spoke of the life and teachings of Mahatma Gandhi. His message was so profound and electrifying that I left the meeting and bought a half-dozen books on Gandhi's life and works.

Before reading Gandhi, I had believed that Jesus' "turn the other cheek" philosophy and the "love your enemies" philosophy could only be useful when individuals were in conflict with other individuals—when racial groups and nations were in conflict, a more realistic approach seemed necessary. But after reading Gandhi, I saw how utterly mistaken I was.

During the days of the Montgomery bus boycott, I came to see the power of nonviolence more and more. As I lived through the actual experience of this protest, nonviolence became more than a useful method; it became a way of life.

Nonresistance attacks the forces of evil rather than the persons who happen to be doing the evil. As I said to the people of Montgomery: "The tension in this city is not between white people and Negro people. The tension is at bottom, between justice and injustice, between the forces of light and the forces of darkness. And if there is a victory, it will be a victory not merely for fifty thousand Negroes but a victory for justice and the forces of light. We are out to defeat injustice and not white persons who may be unjust."

It must be emphasized that nonviolent resistance is not for cowards. *Nonviolent resistance does resist.* If one uses this method because he is afraid or merely because he lacks the weapons of violence, he is not truly nonviolent. That is why Gandhi often said that if cowardice is the only alternative to violence, it is better to fight. He made this statement knowing that there is always another choice we can make: There is the way of nonviolent resistance. No individual or group need submit to any wrong, nor need they use violence to right a wrong. This is ultimately the way of the strong man.

The nonviolent resistance of the early Christians shook the Roman Empire. The nonviolence of Mahatma Gandhi and his followers had muzzled the guns of the British Empire in India and freed more than three hundred and fifty million people from colonialism. It brought victory in the Montgomery bus boycott.

The phrase "passive resistance" often gives the false impression that this is a sort of "do-nothing method" in which the resister quietly and passively accepts evil. But nothing is further from the truth. For while the nonviolent resister is not physically aggressive toward his opponent, his mind and emotions are always active, constantly seeking to persuade his opponent that he is wrong—constantly seeking to open the eyes of blind prejudice. This is not passive nonresistance to evil, it is active nonviolent resistance to evil.

Nonviolence does not seek to defeat or humiliate the opponent, but to win his friendship and understanding. The nonviolent resister not only refuses to shoot his opponent but he also refuses to hate him. To strike back in the same way as his opponent would do nothing but increase the existence of hate in the universe. Along the way of life, someone must have sense enough and morality enough to cut off the chain of hate.

In the final analysis all life is interrelated. All humanity is involved in a single process, and all men are brothers. To the degree that I harm my brother, no matter what he is doing to me, to that extent I am harming myself. Why is this? Because men are brothers. If you harm me, you harm yourself.

20 THE BLACK REVOLUTION

On Sunday morning two weeks after the march on Washington in 1963, a bomb exploded in Birmingham, Alabama. It caved in the floors and shattered the walls of the black Sixteenth Street Baptist Church. In the wreckage searchers found the bodies of four Black girls. The girls had just finished singing "The Love That Forgives." Within the next few hours, two other Black Birmingham youths were shot in the back and killed. For many African American people, these senseless crimes were proof that white society would stop at nothing to halt the march to equality. This type of violent white resistance came to be known as "the white backlash." During the 1960s the white backlash would take a heavy toll in lives and crushed hopes, and it would spark a new movement that aimed to use power rather than argument and nonviolent persuasion to attain its goals.

The White Backlash

There was absolutely nothing new about white opposition, and especially violent opposition, to the advance of equal rights. What was new was its strength despite a decade of civil rights activity, new laws, and repeated pledges from the federal government to protect Black people.

A cotton worker and a voter registration worker discuss voting.

In compliance with the 1965 Civil Rights Law, a federal registrar helps a Mississippi voter fill out the proper form.

The racist violence that marked the end of 1963 accelerated after passage of the 1964 Civil Rights Law. That summer of 1964, the Student Non-Violent Coordinating Committee (SNCC) organized Mississippi's "Freedom Summer." Thousands of white and Black students went to Mississippi to organize "freedom schools" and voter registration drives. SNCC had foreseen that a substantial white presence in Mississippi would focus national attention on their crusade. National attention grew after the murder of two white Jewish New Yorkers, Michael Schwerner and Andrew Goodman, and one Black Mississippian, James Chaney, in Philadelphia, Mississippi, in June 1964.

That summer violence in Mississippi became commonplace. In the course of the search for the bodies of the three civil rights workers, numerous African American bodies were discovered. Before the year was over in Mississippi, fifteen African Americans had died, thirty-three African American churches had been bombed, and countless civil rights workers, Black and white, had been beaten and jailed.

In March of 1965, Martin Luther King, Jr., seeing voting power as crucial, planned a march from Selma to Montgomery, Alabama, to spur voter registration. Even before the march began, an African American youth, Jimmy Lee Jackson, and a white Boston minister, Reverend James Reeb, who had been helping in the voter registration drive, had been murdered. Alabama state troopers first used tear gas on the lead column of the Selma march, then beat down the marchers with clubs. Finally it took a federal armed force, including helicopters, to escort the marchers to Montgomery. The last day of the march, a Detroit housewife, Mrs. Viola Liuzzo, was assassinated as she drove marchers back from Selma. That same summer of 1965 in Alabama, a Protestant seminarian was killed and a Catholic priest mortally wounded by a shotgun blast. The accused murderer was acquitted. By the end of 1965, at least 108 men, women, and children had met violent death during a decade of civil rights activity. And it was still not safe for a Black man to walk down a road in Mississippi.

To "march against fear" and spur voter registration, in June 1966, James Meredith began a one-man walk across Mississippi. On the second day, while surrounded by FBI men, he was shot from ambush. Major civil rights leaders immediately took up his march. Dr. Martin Luther King, conducting a prayer service for slain civil rights workers Goodman, Chaney, and Schwerner on the steps of the Neshoba County, Mississippi,

Alabama state troopers use tear gas and clubs to smash the first Selma march.

Local African Americans wave to the "Selma to Montgomery" marchers.

Courthouse, said, "Before I will be a slave, I will be dead in my grave." White onlookers shouted, "We'll help you." As Dr. King and the marchers left, they were pelted with rocks and bottles and then charged by knife-swinging whites. At Canton City, Mississippi, state troopers used tear gas to smash the march. It regrouped and marched on.

At Greenwood, Mississippi, and other points along the way, a new and important leader emerged in young Stokely Carmichael, chairman of SNCC. Instead of leading local African American residents in singing "We Shall Overcome," he urged them to think and chant "Black power." Born of white violence and Black frustration, a new phase of the African American revolution was emerging.

Northern Racism

By 1964, civil rights leaders found a white backlash in the North to match the hate they faced in the South. When African American and white parents boycotted New York City schools to protest de facto segregation, white groups organized counter-boycotts. One group called itself SPONGE—"Society for the Prevention of Negroes Getting Everything." "The North," said one Harlem resident, "is one big white blank wall."

Repeatedly, whites vetoed integration by walking out of integrated schools and moving out of integrated neighborhoods. Between 1950 and 1960, Detroit gained 185,000 Black citizens and lost 361,000 whites. In 1961, Dr. James E. Allen, Jr., New York State commissioner of education, deplored the fact that 41 percent of the state's public schools were segregated. By 1966, the figure had soared to 69 percent. Faced with city school integration, many whites fled to the suburbs. Few people of color could afford to follow them.

In the summer of 1966, Dr. King's "open-housing" drive in Chicago unmasked a violent racism. It took two thousand police to hold back screaming, bottle-throwing white crowds as Dr. King led several hundred followers to Marquette Park. At the park Dr. King was struck by a rock. Some whites carried signs reading, "KKK, We Need a Ku Klux Klan" and "King Would Look Good with a Knife in His Back." King said of the day:

> I have seen many demonstrations in the South but I have never seen any so hostile and so hateful as I have seen here today. I have to do this—to expose myself—to bring this hate into the open.

Most of the hate-filled whites were young men, descendants of European immigrants who had made enough money to move to the suburbs. They viewed people of color both as carriers of the poverty that they had recently fled and as "inferiors."

In Milwaukee, Wisconsin, Father James Groppi, son of an Italian immigrant, led African Americans in "open-housing" marches daily for three weeks. White violence grew. Before the National Guard arrived to hold back white mobs, the American Nazi party had convinced many rioters to wear swastika armbands or join their "White Guard." Said Father Groppi, "How can you tell a Black man not to be violent. I can't."

There were new civil rights laws and President Johnson's promise that "We Shall Overcome." But against a snail-like movement toward acceptance of more African Americans in schools, jobs, and housing, Black fury began to build.

The mounting Black rage also stemmed from a more subtle kind of racism that a decade of civil rights efforts had not erased. In Connecticut, a white businessman told an African American friend, "Jim, I've got a colored boy from Harvard working in my office, and he's holding down a white man's job." In Florida, a white school principal reported on progress toward integration in his school, "My staff is integrated. I've got eight Negroes—three janitors, four cooks and a washroom attendant." In 1965 Cleveland's police chief Richard Wagner insisted the Ohio legislature retain the death penalty "to keep the Negro in line."

African Americans also found their very claim of equality under constant attack. In California, a school board member told a Black delegation that demanded inclusion of prominent African Americans in the history courses, "If you people had a history, it would be in the books."

In 1968, a white novelist, William Styron, won the Pulitzer Prize for *The Confessions of Nat Turner*. It portrayed Turner as a slave rebel driven to revolt by an unfulfilled sex urge and lust for a white-skinned woman rather than by a desire for liberty. The book, said one Black critic, "was the worst thing to happen to Nat Turner since his execution." And in 1969, Professors Jensen and Shockley claimed "proof" that in some kinds of intelligence African Americans were inferior to whites. Their theories were published in the *Harvard Educational Review* and in *The New York Times*.

By April 1968, the African American community was developing two distinct responses to mounting white racism. A significant, if small, number favored separatism from white society and the use of any means necessary to gain and protect their rights. On the other hand, Dr. Martin Luther King, Jr., was planning a giant, nonviolent Poor People's March on Washington that would unite poor whites, Blacks, Indians, Puerto Ricans, and Chicanos. But many of Dr. King's supporters had become tired of meeting violence with nonviolence. When Dr. King led a march in Memphis for striking garbage collectors, his followers became violent for the first time. On 4 April 1968, Dr. King returned to Memphis to prove that he

Dr. King said, "I think the people of Mississippi ought to come to Chicago to learn to hate." The year he won the Nobel Peace Prize, FBI Director J. Edgar Hoover called him "the most notorious liar in the country."

could control his marchers and win through nonviolence. He was assassinated.

Within hours of the murder, many ghettos erupted. In 172 cities, people took to the streets to loot and destroy. By the time a simple mule cart had carried Dr. King's body to its final resting place, 32 black people had died, 3,500 had been injured, and 27,000 had been arrested. President Johnson ordered 4,000 troops to Baltimore, 5,000 to Chicago, and 11,000 to Washington, D.C. An age of African American nonviolence had ended.

A sad and fatherless Poor People's March limped into Washington. Its "Resurrection City" of tents spread out near the Lincoln Memorial. Soon heavy rain reduced grassy streets and tent floors to thick mud. Congressmen, more concerned with "violence in the streets" than the needs of the poor, ignored Resurrection City. But thousands of poor had erased color lines to unite behind a crusade. It was an important beginning.

Black Power

The cry of "Black power" was born of anger and despair. It was a response to unfulfilled promises and to white violence. It was no accident that it first arose after the attempted assassination of James Meredith. Its voice was Stokely Carmichael, chairman of the Student Non-Violent Coordinating Committee. For years he had been a nonviolent civil rights worker. At nineteen he had been a Freedom Rider, and at twenty-three he ran the voter registration drive in Lowndes County, Alabama, that raised the number of African American voters from 0 to 3,900. But he had seen enough white violence to shake his faith in a nonviolent response. The white backlash, he explained, was driving people from nonviolence.

> Each time the people in those cities saw Martin Luther King get slapped, they became angry; when they saw four little black girls bombed to death, they were angrier; and when nothing happened, they were steaming.

The first important spokesman of Black power was Malcolm X. He grew up believing that his father had been murdered by white men. As a young man he came to Harlem, and as "Big Red," began "making it" as a hustler, dope peddler, and thief. While serving a sentence for robbery, he learned of the Honorable Elijah Muhammad and his Black Muslim sect. His conversion to the Muslim faith changed the course of his life. In prison, he educated himself by reading every book he could find. Released in 1952, he changed his last name, becoming Malcolm X. For twelve years, he served as chief assistant to Elijah Muhammad.

While a follower of Elijah Muhammad, Malcolm X became the most articulate spokesman for Black separatism. He called white men "devils" and insisted, "I'd rather be dead than integrate into the American nightmare." Repeatedly, he told his audiences that they had "a right to resist oppression" and "by any means necessary."

After he had broken from the influence of Elijah Muhammad in 1963, Malcolm X left the Black Muslims and charted a new course for himself. He visited African and Asian nations, praying and talking with Muslims of every color. He "began to see things on a broader scale." "Hating white men," he reasoned, "didn't bring us anything." He refused to attack whites: "If you attack him because he is white, you give him no out. He can't stop being white. We've got to give the man a chance."

Malcolm X had been threatened with death several times, and once his home had been bombed. On 21 February 1965, before he could carry his new ideas much further, he was assassinated. As he began to address a New York City audience that included his wife and their four young daughters, three Black gunmen fired sixteen shots into him.

Malcolm X addresses a Harlem rally in 1963, supporting efforts to integrate Birmingham, Alabama.

At the funeral, actor Ossie Davis eulogized Malcolm X as "our own Black shining prince, Malcolm was our manhood, our living black manhood! This was his meaning to his people." At his grave, African Americans refused to let white gravediggers bury their leader. His followers, some with shovels and others with handfuls of earth, buried Malcolm X.

But Malcolm X's legacy of self-assertion and pride in being Black inspired many young men and women. Taking up his cause, they challenged their people to end their lethargy and abandon their fear. Increasingly, they spoke of "Black self-defense" and "Black retaliation" against white violence. By the summer of 1966, the spiritual heirs of Malcolm X had chosen the rallying cry of "Black power."

The "Black power" slogan captured newspaper headlines and frightened most Americans. They associated it with Black rifle clubs, Molotov cocktails, and H. Rap Brown's bitter truth, "Violence is as American as cherry pie." Its advocates, however, defined it as the right of African Americans to organize along any lines necessary to control those political, economic, and educational institutions that shaped their lives. Floyd McKissick of CORE described its application:

Black militants H. Rap Brown and Stokely Carmichael. Said Brown, "The only politics relevant to Black people is the politics of revolution."

> We'll have Black Power when every cop in Harlem is black, every building and every business is owned by blacks, the schools are black, there's an all-black university, and the whole city of Harlem is run by blacks.

Some challenged the "Black power" slogan as dangerous to America and harmful to Black communities. Roy Wilkins of the NAACP predicted it would "lead to black death," and psychologist Dr. Kenneth W. Clark insisted it would accomplish "the very segregation we have been fighting all these years." Above all, warned opponents, "Black power" would lead to an isolated Black community without power and to violent retaliation of white extremists. Many urban and suburban whites began to purchase guns.

But soon even the SCLC (Southern Christian Leadership Conference) and the Urban League accepted the idea of "Black power." The NAACP continued to oppose it, as it had "all forms of racial separatism" and "invitations to violence." African American organizations that accepted "Black power" changed. Some rejected integration as a goal, white involvement as a method, and nonviolence as a tactic. These replaced older and white leaders with young Black militants who spoke in words of defiance.

Whites who had worked in these organizations were asked to leave. "Your role is not in the Black movement," insisted H. Rap Brown of SNCC. "If you're white, your role is in Appalachia, your role is with the poor white people." Sad, confused, and angry, white people left SNCC and

CORE. Many joined the anti–Vietnam war movement. Few took Brown's advice to fight poverty in Appalachia or bigotry in white communities.

The Black Panthers

The most significant organization to emerge from the "Black power" movement was the Black Panther party. It was created after the Watts riot to provide information to Black residents picked up by the police. The Black Panthers soon armed themselves. Huey Newton, Panther minister of defense, explained that the Panthers wanted to make "Black people aware that they have the right to carry guns." "Armed ghetto citizens," said Panther chairman Bobby Seale, "will stop police brutality on the streets." Their flamboyant display of weapons and their willingness to meet police brutality with force made headlines from coast to coast. Rarely mentioned was their campaign to provide breakfast for ghetto schoolchildren or their legal aid to ghetto residents.

The Panthers were soon fighting for their lives. Vice President Spiro Agnew called them "anarchistic criminals" and FBI Director Hoover said they among all Black groups were "the greatest threat to the internal security of the country." From Connecticut to California police raids and arrests aimed at crippling the organization. By 1967 FBI agents had infiltrated Panther offices in major cities and disrupted their activities throughout the country.

Faced with constant harassment because they were Black, radical, and defiant, Panther leaders' internal disputes tore the organization apart. Angela Davis, a philosophy instructor at UCLA and a Communist, championed their cause and led a campaign to aid Panthers such as George Jackson who were in prison. Davis was arrested for aiding a prison breakout, but an all-white jury found her innocent.

James Baldwin wrote an open letter to Ms. Davis that expressed the fears of many African Americans: ". . . if they take you in the morning, they will be coming for us that night." Prison authorities later killed George Jackson "while [he was] attempting to escape."

Symbol of the Black Panther party.

The Enduring Ghetto

One hundred years after the Civil War most African Americans were no longer living in the rural regions of the South but in cities throughout the

Professor Angela Davis enters the California courtroom where she was charged with murder and kidnapping. An all-white jury found her not guilty.

nation. In giant, sprawling ghettos they shared their nights with poverty, hunger, filth, disease and, on occasion, terror. Created and controlled by white power, the ghetto limped along with less transportation, crime control, garbage collection, educational and recreational facilities than the rest of the city. Yet its residents paid higher food prices and rents, held poorer jobs, and had fewer opportunities than white neighbors. "There is power in our community," noted Eldridge Cleaver, "but it is held by outsiders— or by traitors. They drain the prosperity out of our communities and take it home with them to the suburbs."

Lacking the economic and political power to change their community, ghetto dwellers looked on helplessly as conditions worsened. In a nation of abundance they were part of "the other America" that lived without decent homes, jobs—or hope. Many found escape in drugs or alcohol. Some died young. In the six square miles of New York City called Harlem, James Baldwin grew to manhood. He recalled:

Everything was falling down and going to pieces. And no one cared. And it spelled out to me with brutal clarity and in every possible way that I was a worthless human being.

He found the schools "terribly overcrowded." Ghetto life left him "caged like an animal." Like other residents, Baldwin suffered from police brutality: "I wished I had a machine gun to kill them."

Two or three times a week, young Baldwin read at the famous Schomburg Library of African American history and literature: "I knew I was Black but I knew I was bright." At fourteen, he decided to become a writer and eventually became an eloquent spokesman for his fellow citizens.

Beginning with Harlem during the summer of 1964, the African American ghettos in the East burst into flames. Civil rights laws had not improved their conditions. The "War on Poverty" came too late with too little. Government expenditure in Harlem for all poverty programs, for example, amounted to twenty-five dollars per person, and most of this paid for "administrative costs." From Harlem, rioting spread to the huge Brooklyn ghetto of Bedford Stuyvesant. Two weeks later, it erupted in Rochester, New York, and Jersey City, New Jersey. "Riots like this will occur again and again and again," insisted one social worker, "until discrimination stops and we Negroes are allowed to be men."

By the summer of 1965, rioting had spread to the West Coast. In Watts, California, poor transportation and an unemployment rate three times higher than the white average led to six days of urban guerrilla warfare. Rioting left 34 dead, more than 1,000 injured, and 4,000 arrested. H. Rap Brown lauded the Watts violence as "our Declaration of Independence."

In 1967, rioting reached 164 cities, leaving 82 dead, 3,400 injured, and 18,800 arrested. An African American antipoverty worker insisted, "The problem is the way people live. We have to change the way people live. All the rest is Band-Aids and lollipops." After full-scale revolts in Newark and Detroit (which required federal troops), President Johnson appointed a Commission on Civil Disorders to investigate the violence.

This commission, headed by Governor Otto Kerner of Illinois, issued a report which surprised most Americans. "Our nation," it warned, "is moving toward two societies, one Black, one white—separate and unequal." It identified the root cause of the riots as "white racism" and urged immediate government and private action to rebuild the ghettos. Never had a federal commission pointed out so clearly the guilt of white America. Never had one painted such a bleak picture of the nation's future.

The Kerner Report found that typical rioters were neither criminals, drifters, nor newcomers from the South:

Newark, 1967. "Finally the neighborhood is integrated," said one resident. "If you're Black," said another, "the National Guard treats you the same whether you're violent or not."

The typical rioter was a teenager or young adult, a lifelong resident of the city in which he rioted, a high school dropout; he was, nevertheless, somewhat better educated than his nonrioting Negro neighbor, and was usually underemployed or employed in a menial job. He was proud of his race, extremely hostile to both whites and middle-class Negroes and, although informed about politics, highly distrustful of the political system.

Despite the widespread belief that the disorders were planned and led by African American extremists or white Communists, the Kerner Commission found this was not true. The riots were triggered by police actions that residents considered "brutality." These communities considered the police "an army of occupation" and viewed all police activity with suspicion.

The main targets of rioters were police and white-owned stores, both symbols of the foreign power that ruled ghetto life. Most Black residents did not take part in the disorders and many tried "to cool it," but few in the ghetto would condemn those who did riot. The Kerner Commission found that much of the violence had stemmed from National Guard troops who were 99 percent white and inexperienced in handling riots. Often the looting had been interracial, with poor whites and Puerto Ricans participating. In all riot areas, unemployment or underemployment was high; school, housing, health, and other facilities were woefully inadequate.

The Kerner Report drew little support and scant praise from the white community. Presidents Johnson and Nixon did not endorse it or carry out its many recommendations. Some critics of the report claimed that the disorders were caused by extravagant government promises to the Black poor rather than white racism. They insisted the "War on Poverty" had convinced Black people that something was going to be done. When these rising expectations were frustrated, ghettos had erupted in violence. Some critics denied that there was any police brutality in the ghettos. Others admitted that police brutality existed, but, since it had always been present, discounted its role as a cause of riots. White "law and order" candidates denounced the report for encouraging rioting. They promised greater armed control of the ghettos, and this promise won many elections. Police departments ordered new and powerful weapons to meet ghetto "trouble."

Challenge to United States Foreign Policy

African Americans played a crucial part in the peace movement that helped to bring America's seven-year undeclared war in Vietnam to an end in 1973. In 1965 the Mississippi Freedom Democratic Party in McComb issued the first organizational denunciation of the war. It rejected "fighting in Vietnam for the White Man's Freedom" and urged Black men "not to honor the draft here in Mississippi. Mothers should encourage their sons not to go."

As in previous wars, African American soldiers, almost a fourth of the frontline troops in Vietnam, established a record for bravery under fire. However, Black officers accounted for only 5 percent of the total. The Black reenlistment rate was triple the white rate. In the army people of color found fewer barriers and more pay than civilian life could offer. One Black soldier joked, "It's the kind of integration that could kill you."

African American leaders repeatedly drew a connection between racism in Vietnam and at home. "There is no reason for a Black man to be fighting in Vietnam when he can't walk the streets of our cities without being shot down," said Stokely Carmichael. Bobby Seale denounced the "imperialist war against a colonial people" in Vietnam and drew this comparison: "I view the Black people in America as a colonial people. Therefore we have to arm ourselves and make the colonial power give us our freedom."

The most dramatic confrontation with United States foreign policy was posed by Muhammad Ali, world heavyweight champion. He refused to report for the draft, saying, "No, I am not going ten thousand miles to help murder and kill and burn other people simply to help continue the domination of white slavemasters over the dark people the world over." Ali was stripped of his boxing crown and lost a fortune for his stand against the war.

Opposition to the war increased dramatically in 1967 when Dr. Martin Luther King, Jr., called the American government "the greatest purveyor of violence in the world today" and urged young men to refuse to answer draft calls. Dr. King and Stokely Carmichael led thousands of marchers to a rally for peace before the United Nations. "Hell no, we won't go!" Carmichael shouted into the microphone. The crowd made it a chant. After Dr. King's death, his widow and Dr. Ralph Abernathy, Dick Gregory, and a host of Black figures continued to lead the antiwar movement.

Black Muslim leader Muhammad Ali. For his refusal to be drafted into the army, his world heavyweight boxing crown was taken away.

The African American challenge to United States foreign policy aimed at more than ending the Vietnam War. It criticized American aid to white governments opposing colonial liberation in Africa and Asia. It urged self-determination for African nations and an end to European control in Rhodesia and the Union of South Africa. Each year hundreds of U.S. Black students visited African nations to seek cultural exchange with their Black brothers and sisters.

A Separate Black Path?

Four days before the death of Dr. King, a survey of fifteen cities showed that 6 percent of the African Americans favored a "separate Black nation" in the United States. A year later, a *Newsweek* survey disclosed that the percentage had risen to 21 (with another 10 percent not answering the question). Many had been shaken by the assassination of the major spokesperson of nonviolence and integration.

But separatism also sprang from the growing self-pride and "Black awareness" of many young people. They maintained that Black people had "soul," whites were "irrelevant," and the world's darker-skinned people were their "soul brothers and sisters." They sometimes rejected their white friends, called those who failed to do so "Uncle Toms," and sought the company of other Black people. There was much to talk over—a new Black culture.

This attitude was most clearly expressed by college students. During the "student revolution" of the 1960s, Black students often demanded separate dormitories, African American studies courses taught by Black profes-

After breaking the existing world record in the four-hundred-meter run and coming in first, second, and third at the Mexico City Olympics in 1968, Larry James, Lee Evans, and Ron Freeman give the Black Power salute.

Cleveland Donald and Dr. Gloria I. Joseph of Cornell. Young people began an "African Renaissance" that brought many changes to the community.

sors and open only to Black students, and recreational facilities apart from white students. To emphasize their demands they, like the white students, seized buildings, blocked entrances, and sometimes disrupted classes or college offices. Television and newspapers from coast to coast showed armed Black students at Cornell University leaving a campus building after they had forced concessions from the Cornell president. But, as Dr. Gloria Joseph, assistant dean of students, pointed out, the news media failed to emphasize that seizure of this building took place after a Klan cross-burning in front of a Black women's dormitory. The guns were brought to the Black students at 3:00 in the morning, after a dozen white fraternity members entered their building and injured several male and female students, reported Cleveland Donald.

Some separatists insisted that African American people be given their own land area in the United States. The "Republic of New Africa" group demanded "Mississippi, Alabama, Louisiana, South Carolina and Georgia—right now." *Liberator* editor Daniel Watts laughed at whites. "When we get our free state in Southern California, we'll let you honkies in with a passport, but you can't live there. Nothing discriminatory—you'll just be happier among your own kind."

Young Black audiences often thrilled to flaming rhetoric and sometimes to threatened violence, such as that suggested by H. Rap Brown of SNCC when he said, "President Johnson says every day if Vietnam don't come 'round, Vietnam will be burnt down. I say if America don't come 'round, America should be burnt down." At Cornell, Black students demanded as part of their African American studies program Physical Education Course 300c: "Theory and practice in the use of small arms and hand-to-hand combat. Discussion sessions in the proper use of force." By 1974 a small Black radical group called the Symbionese Liberation Army was using assassination and kidnapping to force white compliance with its demands. Such tactics were roundly denounced by Black and white alike.

Black Pride, Black Progress

By 1967, despite many differences of opinion, Black people were as united as they had been when they opposed slavery a hundred years before. Many young people proudly sported "Afro" hairstyles, wore African dashikis, and insisted they be called "Black" or "Afro-American." They developed a massive campaign for cultural awareness that celebrated Black playwrights, poets, authors, and artists. Unlike the 1920s Harlem Renaissance, which depended on white financial support, this new cultural movement was independent and aimed at African American cultural liberation. White America began to take an interest in African and Black styles in cooking, literature, history, and culture. African American models found jobs as did Black historians and writers.

To provide information long ignored about African America, white universities offered important positions to Black scholars and poets. After repeated demands by many students and Black leaders, public schools began to teach children about African American heroes in American and world history. Black movie and TV actors were finally hired to play cowboys, spies, crooks, or heroes. Previously, comedian Godfrey Cambridge pointed out, Black "good guys" in the movies always died saving the white hero:

I don't want to be Jesus; it's very painful for my palms. Why do I always have to die? Why can't the white guy just turn to me and say, "Hey, I was wrong."

"Black is Beautiful" became an important slogan among the young. For centuries African Americans had been told that white was attractive and Black ugly, and many had accepted this myth. Beginning in 1968, a "Miss Black America" was chosen to counter the all-white Miss America Pageant. The first winner, Saundra Williams, said, "With my title, I can show Black women they too are beautiful, even though they do have large noses and thick lips. There is a need to keep saying this over and over. . . ."

Pearl Bailey and Cab Calloway starred in the hit musical "Hello Dolly!"

One of the most persistent demands of African American leaders had been for the improvement of ghetto schools. As white districts resisted attempts toward integration, Black educators demanded improved education in ghetto schools. They insisted on "community control" of these schools. Principal Kenneth W. Haskins of Washington, D.C.'s Morgan Community School explained:

Up until now the education of Black children has been in the hands of whites. They have done a poor job. Community control assures education will be in the hands of those most vitally concerned with their children's education. We demand the responsibility for our children's education.

The Morgan Community School became a model of community control and improved education.

But in New York, a battle between community control groups and the United Federation of Teachers in 1968 resulted in prolonged teacher strikes. The UFT claimed the community control groups were antiunion, antiwhite, and anti-Semitic. In Ocean Hill–Brownsville, where a community board of education ran the schools, the board refuted these charges by pointing out that 70 percent of its teachers were white, including 40 percent who were Jewish. Although only a few people had made anti-Semitic statements, these statements were displayed by the UFT as examples of rampant Black anti-Semitism. Blithely ignoring the charges of both sides, hundreds of Harlem's Black Jews proudly marched in the annual Israel Independence Day Parade and received the warmest ovations.

Principal Kenneth W. Haskins and a few of his students. Mr. Haskins said, "Those who don't like Black adults are not the ones to teach Black children."

A democratic revolution began to unfold nationally. By 1967 there had been a Black cabinet member, Robert C. Weaver; a Federal Reserve Board member, Andrew Brimmer; and a United Nations leader, Ralph Bunche. That year there were 1,702 African American elected or appointed officials, with 385 elected by the Southern states and 96 state legislators nationally.

Black and white students found it easier to get along than many of their parents did, but had less chance. Since 1954, school segregation increased in the nation.

A teacher and student at the Morgan Community School. Student academic accomplishments rose when the community became involved.

There were eleven African American federal judges. Edward Brooke, a Republican from Massachusetts, sat in the Senate, and seven other African Americans were in Congress. NAACP attorney Thurgood Marshall, "Mr. Civil Rights," was a Supreme Court justice.

President Johnson had appointed Justice Marshall to the Supreme Court, saying, "He's the best qualified by training and by very valuable service to the courts." Marshall's major training and service had occurred in the service of the NAACP, from Mississippi to Korea. In thirty-two cases before the high court, Marshall had won twenty-nine, his most significant victory being the 1954 *Brown* vs. *Board of Education* decision outlawing school segregation.

A rise in Black power thinking in ghetto communities by 1967 led to the election of African American mayors in seven cities. Representative Carl Stokes defeated Cleveland's mayor in a primary and then went on to defeat a white opponent in a city where African Americans were outnumbered two to one. Richard Hatcher carried the industrial city of Gary, Indiana. Though both relied on their African American base, they also campaigned in white communities and promised to represent everyone. That year

Senator Edward E. Brooke of Massachusetts, who turned down an invitation to serve in President Nixon's cabinet.

President Lyndon Johnson also announced he would appoint Walter Washington as mayor of the nation's capital.

But political gains still had not changed the level of Black poverty. Although a Black man, Percy Sutton, was borough president of Manhattan, the conditions of most Black people in Manhattan had worsened. "Practically all of the gains have been made by the growing Negro middle class," reported *Time*. The poor became still poorer, their schools and facilities more run-down. Automation replaced Black workers faster than they could be retrained. The Black unemployment rate was three times higher than the white rate.

The main theme of Black history was summarized at this time by educator Kenneth W. Haskins:

> We want to be free. Whether we joined the Indians and fought the cavalry or joined the cavalry and fought the Indians, whether we protest against the war in Vietnam or bravely fight in Vietnam, whether we shouted for freedom from the mountain tops like Frederick Douglass, Martin Luther King, Jr., and Malcolm X, or, like Booker T. Washington, bent our knees to try to win concessions from the white man, whether we threw rocks at police or took a "token" job in a white

Black members of the U.S. House of Representatives formed a "Black Caucus" to pressure for legislation important to minorities.

Congresswoman Shirley Chisholm was elected from the Bedford-Stuyvesant ghetto in New York, and later ran for president.

Julian Bond, Georgia state senator, and civil rights leader Bayard Rustin at the 1968 Democratic National Convention. Bond, at twenty-eight, was nominated for vice president, but withdrew because he was too young.

firm—each was a *tactic* we used to become free, to assert our manhood, to live as human beings. That is the theme of Afro-American history—to be free.

THE PSYCHOLOGICAL BRUTALITY OF WHITE RACISM

[Dr. Alvin F. Poussaint, an African American psychiatrist, had risen high in the medical and academic world—but not high enough to escape white racism. He describes an incident in the capital of Mississippi in 1966.]

Once last year as I was leaving my office in Jackson, Miss., with my Negro secretary, a white policeman yelled, "Hey, boy! come here!" Somewhat bothered, I retorted: "I'm no boy!" He then rushed at me, inflamed, and stood towering over me, snorting, "What d'ja say, boy?" Quickly he frisked me and demanded, "What's your name, boy?" Frightened, I replied, "Dr. Poussaint, I'm a physician." He angrily chuckled and hissed, "What's your first name, boy?" When I hesitated he assumed a threatening stance and clenched his fists. As my heart palpitated, I muttered in profound humiliation, "Alvin."

He continued his psychological brutality, bellowing, "Alvin, the next time I call you, you come right away, you hear? You hear?" I hesitated. "You hear me, boy?" My voice trembling with helplessness, but following my instincts of self-preservation, I murmured, "Yes, sir." Now fully satisfied that I had performed and acquiesced to my "boy status," he dismissed me with, "Now, boy, go on and get out of here, or next time we'll take you for a little ride down to the station house!"

No amount of self-love could have salvaged my pride or preserved my integrity. In fact, the slightest show of self-respect or resistance might have cost me my life. For the moment my manhood had been ripped from me—and in the presence of a Negro woman for whom I, a "man," was supposed to be the "protector." In addition, this had occurred on a public street for all the local black people to witness, reminding them that *no* black man was as good as *any* white man. All of us—doctor, lawyer, postman, field hand and shoeshine boy—had been psychologically "put in our place."

The self-hate that I felt at that time was generated by the fact that I and my people were completely helpless and powerless to destroy that white bigot and all that he represented. Suppose I had decided, as a man should, to be forceful? What crippling price would I have paid for a few moments of assertive manhood? What was I to do with my rage?

And if I, a physician in middle-class dress, was vulnerable to this treatment, imagine the brutality to which "ordinary" black people are subjected—not only in the South but also in the North, where the brutality is likely to be more psychological than physical. . . .

Alvin F. Poussaint, "A Negro Psychiatrist Explains the Negro Psyche," *The New York Sunday Times Magazine,* 20 August 1967, 53. © 1967–68–69 by The New York Times Company. Reprinted by permission.

MALCOLM X EXPLAINS BLACK NATIONALISM

[*Malcolm Little left high school at fifteen and was jailed at twenty-one for bur-glary. After his release from prison in 1952, he became the most articulate Ameri-can spokesman for Black nationalism. A year before his assassination, he outlined his views in these words.*]

The political philosophy of black nationalism means: we must control the politics and the politicians of our community. They must no longer take or-ders from outside forces. We will organize, and sweep out of office all Ne-gro politicians who are puppets for the outside forces. . . .

. . . Whites can help us, but they can't join us. There can be no black-white unity until there is first black unity. There can be no workers' solidar-ity until there is first some racial solidarity. We cannot think of uniting with others, until after we have first united among ourselves. . . .

Concerning nonviolence: it is criminal to teach a man not to defend himself when he is the constant victim of brutal attacks. It is legal and law-ful to own a shotgun or a rifle. We believe in obeying the law.

In areas where our people are the constant victims of brutality, and the government seems unable or unwilling to protect them, we should form ri-fle clubs that can be used to defend our lives and our property in times of emergency. . . . When our people are being bitten by dogs, they are within their rights to kill those dogs.

We should be peaceful, law-abiding—but the time has come for the American Negro to fight back in self-defense whenever and wherever he is being unjustly and unlawfully attacked.

If the government thinks I am wrong for saying this, then let the govern-ment start doing its job.

Statement by Malcolm X delivered to a New York press conference, 12 March 1964.

ERNIE CHAMBERS TELLS IT LIKE IT IS

[*Ernie W. Chambers, a lifelong resident of Omaha, Nebraska, appeared before the Kerner Commission to explain the new mood in the nation's ghettos. His verbatim testimony is searing, direct, and eloquent—and constitutes one of the most astute analyses of racial problems offered during the 1960s.*]

. . . we have marched, we have cried, we have prayed, we have voted, we have petitioned, we have been good little boys and girls. We have gone out to Vietnam as doves and come back hawks. We have done every possible thing to make this white man recognize us as human beings, and he refuses. . . .

You can understand why Jews who were burned by the Nazis hate Germans, but you can't understand why black people who have been systematically murdered by the government and its agents, by private citizens, by the police department, you can't understand why they hate white people. . . .

July 4th you celebrate as Independence Day because you stood up against the British Empire and told them to go to hell. Your ancestors committed treason and you celebrate it now, and you were not treated nearly as badly as black people in this country.

As Malcolm X said, we are catching more hell than Patrick Henry ever saw or thought of. He wouldn't have been able to take it. . . .

A policeman is an object of contempt. A policeman is a paid and hired murderer and you never find the policeman guilty of a crime no matter what violence he commits against a black person.

In Detroit you were shooting snipers, so you mounted a .50 caliber machine gun on a tank and shot into an apartment and killed a four-year-old sniper. . . .

Yet black people doing ordinary, reasonable, peaceful things in this country are attacked by the police and the police are praised for it. And you talk about giving the police more money and more power. You have got them walking arsenals now—pistols, guns, . . . clubs, some of them carry knives, cattle prods, the new tear gas canister, high-powered rifles. They will be giving them hand grenades. They can call in tanks with .50 caliber machine guns. In the United States of America in 1967, when you are raising hell in Vietnam killing people, and then you can't straighten out what is happening in this country and you wonder why I would tell a black boy, Don't go fight for this racist country, and it is a racist country. . . .

And do you know why I think they [the U.S. Congress] voted against that rat control bill? . . .

. . . They fear black people more than they do the Bubonic plague and other diseases that rats carry, because you wouldn't appropriate $40 million to control rats, but you will appropriate all kinds of money to give the National Guard increased training in how to wipe us out, and it is a funny thing that in all these so-called riots the police and the National Guard kill far more people than the so-called rioters.

And as for the sniping, don't you believe that. If all of you were sitting in this room I could just shoot at random and I would hit somebody. Why are no cops killed? They ought to be killed. I think the cops should be killed. I believe the National Guard should be fought like they are telling us we should fight in Vietnam.

When a man comes into my community and he is going to endanger the life of my wife and my children, he should die, and if it is within my power, I will kill him. We are tired of sitting around with white people and saying we have to die for what we believe. We have been dying ever since we have been in this country for what you believe and what you have taught us. . . .

Here is what you are going to give my little kid. I am going to send him to school and teach him to respect authority. So here is a cracker teacher standing in front of my child making him listen to Little Black Sambo. See, that is the image that the school gives him when he is young to teach him his place. A caricature, wearing outlandish clothing that even the animals in the forest don't want to wear. His name is Sambo. His mother's name is Mumbo. And his father's name is Jumbo. . . .

I sat through Little Black Sambo, and since I was the only black face in the room, I became Little Black Sambo. . . .

And there is brutality in Omaha schools. A junior high school teacher named ———— had beaten, kicked, and cut little black children. We took these children with their parents to the Mayor's office. He would take no action. . . .

Why do we have to take each individual case of brutality and handle it personally like this? The school system is terrible. It is rotten. They have incompetent teachers. There is discrimination in the placement of teachers and the placement of pupils. They spent $5 million to just complete a white high school and arguing about whether they should have a planetarium in it, yet in Technical High, where most of the Negroes go, they can't even get blackboards, and again I had to go personally to the Board of Education and tell them they had better put some blackboards in there or some of these other schools that have got them are not going to have them, but Tech is going to have everything they need.

Then the blackboards found their way over there.

Some books that my little boy didn't have in his classroom this semester came there only after I made a personal visit to the school, and here was water leaking through the roof, buckets all over, and I have pictures of it with me, running through the light fixtures, dripping in the cafeteria onto the table where sandwiches were being made. Then when I went over there the principal, instead of wanting to correct this, wanted to know why in the hell they didn't come to get him and let him know I was in there. . . .

By the way, before the Legislature killed open housing, they passed— they authorized the Governor to use $500,000 to put down riots as they call them in our area. We can't buy a house. They refused to pass the legislation necessary to help relieve these tensions, but they will pass, they will authorize this man $500,000, and he made some threats about his little 1800-man National Guard is going to come into our community and do something to us.

When they come, something is going to be waiting for them. And it is not singing "We Shall Overcome." And it is not playing these little footsy games we have been playing all these years. . . .

. . . some people there [in Omaha] call me militant. How can you call me militant when in view of all these things I have mentioned to you I haven't started a riot. I haven't burned a building. I haven't killed a cop.

You are looking at somebody who is more rational than any of you, or some of you, because some of you support the war in Vietnam but you wouldn't support us if we burned down Omaha. . . .

We have to show that every other means that we have tried to employ has been taken away from us and it won't work, so the only thing left is violence because that is the only thing this government understands. . . .

Official Transcript of Proceedings before the National Advisory Commission on Civil Disorders (Washington, D.C., 21 September 1967), Remarks of Ernie W. Chambers, Omaha, Nebraska, 1533–96.

"THROUGH HIS BRAVERY . . ."

[*In Vietnam Private Milton Olive III earned the Medal of Honor by throwing himself on an enemy grenade to save the lives of his platoon. His citation read:*]

Private First Class *Milton L. Olive III* RA16810165, United States Army, who distinguished himself by conspicuous gallantry and intrepidity at the risk of his own life above and beyond the call of duty while participating in a search and destroy operation in the vicinity of Phu Cuong, Republic of Vietnam, on 22 October 1965. Private *Olive* was a member of the 3d Platoon of Company B, 2nd Battalion (Airborne), 503d Infantry, as it moved through the jungle to find the Viet Cong operating in the area. Although the Platoon was subjected to a heavy volume of enemy gunfire and pinned down temporarily, it retaliated by assaulting the Viet Cong positions, causing the enemy to flee. As the Platoon pursued the insurgents, Private *Olive* and four other soldiers were moving through the jungle together when a grenade was thrown into their midst. Private *Olive* saw the grenade, and then saved the lives of his fellow soldiers at the sacrifice of his own by grabbing the grenade in his hand and falling on it to absorb the blast with his body. Through his bravery, unhesitating actions, and complete disregard for his own safety, he prevented additional loss of life or injury to the members of his Platoon. Private *Olive*'s conspicuous gallantry, extraordinary heroism, and intrepidity at the risk of his own life above and beyond the call of duty are in the highest traditions of the United States Army and reflect great credit upon himself and the Armed Forces of his country.

General Orders, No. 18, Headquarters Department of the Army, Washington, D.C., 26 April 1966.

SHOULD BLACK AND WHITE UNITE: TWO BLACK VIEWS

[*Following the Meredith March, many Black leaders challenged traditional Black dependence on white support. Stokely Carmichael, was interviewed in Stockholm, Sweden, by Vera Pegna, an Italian journalist.*]

Carmichael. . . . there is no organization among poor whites. I mean there's no revolutionary white organization in the U.S.

Pegna. And there are no revolutionary whites? I think you are wrong.

Carmichael. Yes, there are revolutionary whites, but you don't form political links with individuals.

Pegna. But you draw them inside the black organizations.

Carmichael. No, no, no. Not at this point. That has to do with a lot of psychological impact of whites always leading movements in the U.S., and the psychological defeat of blacks not feeling that they can lead their own movements.

Pegna. Well, what's going to happen now? Will you just wait and see what happens with the poor whites?

Carmichael. There's nothing we can do except to urge people to organize poor whites.

Pegna. White people to organize poor whites?

Carmichael. That's a reality. Our organization has tried to organize poor whites. . . . The project failed. In 1964 we tried again with some white students in the U.S., and that failed too.

Pegna. Why did this fail?

Carmichael. It failed because of the students mainly, I think. And also because of our philosophy—the people who were leading the movement were trying to organize these people around integration, rather than organizing them around their own self-interest. I mean, if you tell a poor white person to integrate, he's not going to do anything. Why should he integrate, given his own racism? So they didn't organize around their own self-interest. . . .

Guardian, independent radical newsweekly, 16 December 1967, 1, 14. Tape-recorded by John Duffert of the *Guardian* staff. Reprinted by permission.

[*Fannie Lou Hamer, a Mississippi field worker, who led the Mississippi Freedom Democratic Party (MFDP) delegation to the 1964 Democratic Convention, gives her views on Black-white unity.*]

. . . let's face it, man, what's hurtin' the black folks that's without, is hurtin' the white folks that's without. You see, I'm 100 per cent in the same way that I felt when I started working, and I say now, if the white folk fight for theyself and black folk fight for theyself, we gonna crumble apart. These are kinds of things that we gonna have to fight together.

. . . There's white people that suffer, there's Indian people that suffer, there's Mexican American people that suffer, there's Chinese people that suffer, so as black people, we not the only one that suffer, and I'm perfectly willing to make this country what it have to be. We gonna fight these battles together.

. . . Now what could we build by you hating me and me hating you? We would be two miserable creeps, you know, really! You have to think about the problem and we all have to do something about it.

. . . But let me tell you one thing—Stokely Carmichael and people like Rap Brown, let's face it, I worked with those kids and they tells a whole lotta truth that America don't want to face. I'm not kiddin' with you.

Fannie Lou Hamer, "We Have to Fight These Battles Together," *The Movement* (October 1967), 10. Reprinted by permission.

DR. CLARK DENOUNCES SEPARATISM

[*Dr. Kenneth Clark, who had exposed the harm inflicted on young people by segregation, also opposed any segregation advocated by Black students. He resigned as a trustee of Antioch College when the college initiated an Afro-American Studies program and dormitories open to Black students only. His resignation included the following.*]

To exclude someone of one race—or to admit that it would be appropriate to do so—on the grounds that his background or experience are irrelevant, that they render him unable to achieve, is precisely what white segregationists have been doing to blacks for centuries.

Yet this seems to be the burden of rationalization at Antioch for a black separatist policy. Yet it is whites who need a black studies program most of all.

The white liberal who concedes black separatism so hastily and benevolently must look to his own reasons, not the least of them perhaps an exquisite relief.

To encourage or endorse a separate black program not academically equivalent to the college curriculum generally, indeed to endorse any such program, is to reinforce the Negro's inability to compete with whites for the real power of the real world. It is no excuse to justify the deed by citing the demand. . . .

I do not believe that Antioch, in permitting the more hostile Negro students to coerce and intimidate other Negroes and whites by quashing vocal dissent, has showed the courage necessary to maintain that type of academic climate which permits man that freedom of inquiry, freedom of thought and freedom of dissent which are essential to the life of the intellect. . . .

In permitting a group of students to inflict their dogmatism and ideology on other students and on the total college community, and in being silent while some students intimidate, threaten and in some cases physically assault Negro students who disagree with them, the administration at Antioch has not only defaulted in its responsibilities but I believe has made a mockery of its concern for the protection and development of human dignity without regard to cost.

Peter Kihss, "Clark Scores 'Separation' at Antioch," *The New York Times,* May 1969, © 1967–68–69 by The New York Times Company. Reprinted by permission.

STILL A BROTHER

[*During the Newark riot of 1967, Horace Morris, a director of the National Urban League in Washington, found that despite being middle-class he was still a Black man to the National Guard.*]

Last summer the entire nation was made aware of the violence that erupted in Newark. I happened to be attending a National Urban League conference in New York. My family still lives in Newark, and so I decided to visit them on my way back to Washington. I visited with my stepfather for about a half-hour or so, and then we decided to visit a sister of mine.

As we were about to get into the car, about three carloads of police came around the corner. Without warning and, to my knowledge, without any provocation from us, they opened fire on us and a group of about 40 or 50 people who were standing on the stoop. My stepfather was mortally wounded. One of my brothers was wounded twice and required an operation and extensive hospital care. We were under fire, I would say, for approximately 10 minutes by the Newark police. They said they were looking for a sniper on the roof or the upper floors of the apartment building, but they were still firing at ground-level range.

And once I had an opportunity to collect my senses and really evaluate and think this thing through, it came through to me in stark reality that regardless of how far up the economic ladder any Negro goes, there's still this oppressive thing of prejudice that he is subjected to from the point of the white man here in America. And I realized that I was extremely fortunate not to be killed myself. And that even though I possessed two degrees, even though I had played football for Syracuse, even though I was an elementary school principal who had educated white children, even though I work with white people in the Washington Urban League, even though there are white people that I consider close friends, I realized that—as the boys say—when it gets down to the nitty gritty, right down to where it really matters, you're still a Negro and you're still identified with every other Negro in America, be he in a ghetto or in a suburban neighborhood. You're still a brother.

Horace Morris, "Still a Brother: Inside the Negro Middle Class," program on National Educational Television, Channel 13, New York.

RACISM AND GUNS AT CORNELL UNIVERSITY

[*On 20 April 1969, a shocked nation watched on TV as more than a hundred African American Cornell students, some carrying rifles at the ready, left a campus building they had occupied the day before. Dr. Gloria I. Joseph, assistant dean of students, explains what led to this.*]

The Black guns at Cornell emerged only after many threats to Black male and female students. Events began with the university's unfulfilled promise to give Black students the use of the Wade Avenue building. When Black students staged a takeover there to prod the university, they were tried for breach of discipline by an all-white student court. Hostility toward Black women on campus, including myself, took the form of white males yelling "Nigger" and other obscenities at us.

Then Wari, the Black co-ed living quarters at Cornell, began receiving phone calls threatening to burn down the Wade Avenue building or Wari or both. University officials only gave this routine notice. One midnight I received a frantic call from the Head Resident at Wari. She told me a rock had crashed through her window and she awoke to find a fiery cross burning on Wari's wooden porch. The Fire Department arrived to douse the fire and left without taking any notes. "The cross is still smouldering and the girls are afraid," she told me. The Fire Department never came back, claiming they had "11 false alarms that night" to keep them busy. When neither local police nor the campus patrol officials offered protection, the co-eds called some "Black brothers" who came unarmed to guard Wari.

About 24 hours later, 120 Black students took over the campus building to protest these mounting threats and violence and the failure of the university to do anything about them.

Dr. Gloria I. Joseph to William Loren Katz, 8 August 1969.

[Graduate student Cleveland Donald was among those who seized the building.]

On Saturday, April 19th the Afro-American Society began its occupation of Willard Straight Hall, the Student Union building at Cornell University. We entered the building at approximately 5:30 A.M. and proceeded to secure our position there. . . .

Our initial manner was one of urgency, but also one of nonviolence. However, at approximately 10:30 A.M. about 12 fraternity boys from Delta Upsilon broke into the building through the campus radio station office and proceeded upstairs at which point they were asked to leave the building. They refused and proceeded to assault several people (including some Black women). They were armed with sticks and crowbars. After the scuffle one brother had been wounded.

We Black students, totally unprepared to deal with such an assault, began to improvise weapons for our defense. After we had successfully driven the fraternity boys out of our building, we addressed ourselves to using whatever resources we possessed to prevent further surprise entrances. The Cornell campus police permitted these students to enter and attack us. They later stated that they did not know about the fraternity boys' forcible entry, although they had surrounded the building. Later on that night we received reports from our people on the outside of the building that Delta Upsilon had organized over 100 armed fraternity boys to forcibly evict us from the building.

We responded to this threat on our lives by requesting that arms be brought in for our protection. However, the fraternity boys, cognizant of the fact that we were armed, did not confront us. We later learned that eight carloads of fraternity boys were armed with rifles and shotguns and were on their way over to the building.

Subsequently, we made our agreement with the University administration and left the building in good faith, expecting that the University would honor its agreement. Several hours later, however, we learned that the administration was trying to confuse the issues once more and had refused to deal with the issues involved. They had raised the emotional issue of Black students being armed and had suppressed the relevant issue of the demands which had precipitated the entire incident.

Cleveland Donald, "The Occupation," *Cornell Daily Sun*, 7 May 1969, 5.

"SCHOOLS SHOULD RELATE TO THE PEOPLE"

[In the late 1960s Black people increasingly sought control of schools in their neighborhoods. A leading spokesperson for this movement was Kenneth W. Haskins, principal of a Washington, D.C., elementary school. He explains how it worked.]

Community control means only one thing: the public institutions that serve a particular community should be controlled by it. In education this movement has grown out of the failure of existing institutions to meet the needs of the children of the black community. . . .

I am the principal of the Morgan Community School in Washington, D.C., a school that is now community controlled. Four years ago, before I came, the school had four classes in the auditorium. It is a very old building, and the auditorium was the only extra facility. Parents could no longer register their children in kindergarten because it was overcrowded, and the first, second, and third grades were on half-day sessions. Textbooks were poor and in bad condition, and the school had very little equipment. It wasn't until the parents really got concerned and organized that things began to change.

If a community school is to have any meaning, it must take its character from the nature of the people living in the community and from the children utilizing the school—rather than rigidly defining itself as an institution that accepts only those people who fit into a preconceived definition. This would mean that there would be a minimum of social problems in the school because what is socially acceptable in the community would be worked with and tolerated within the school setting. Such terms as "uneducable" or "unteachable" must be separated from forms of social behavior.

For example: I live in a community where children fight in the street. It doesn't bother me particularly; that is the way they get their reputations. I grew up in the same kind of neighborhood, and I don't believe that children who fight at the age of five, six, or seven necessarily grow up to be criminals. But because there are a few middle-class children in my school whose parents don't want their children exposed to fighting, should I call every child who fights a criminal and force him into a pattern of conformity that is alien to him? If the child is not a problem at home or in the community, but he fights in school, should I consider the fighting in itself a problem? If so, I become obligated to solve it, and that usually means calling in a psychologist and giving the child labels such as "emotionally disturbed" or "aggressive." This gives the school ammunition to push the child further away.

I have found that once you stop fighting with children about fighting, the incidence of fighting diminishes because you no longer have teachers and students acting like prison guards and inmates. You don't condone fighting, but you don't stop it simply because someone labels it a problem; you stop it because young people should be taught that there are better ways of handling social relationships.

In a sense, schools should relate to the people who use them in much the same way that any other producer relates to a consumer. I would like to see schools in Spanish-speaking neighborhoods be forced, because of their relationship to the community, to put up signs saying SE HABLA ESPANOL as quickly as every store in the community had to put one up in order to stay in business. I have seen stores do this in one or two days, but schools spend fifteen years in a Spanish-speaking neighborhood without one Spanish-speaking teacher in the school. The teachers merely speak English louder, and the louder they talk the less the pupils understand them—so the more ignorant the pupils are.

When you talk about community control, questions are always raised about who is asking for control—about making certain that the militants don't take over. The people of the black community can take care of their own militants. They really don't need anybody else to define for them who are militants, particularly not those who three or four years ago were calling Roy Wilkins a militant. People learn by their mistakes. The right to vote means that you can vote again in two or three years; if someone doesn't represent you, you can get rid of him. You don't need people from outside to make definitions and selections for you, unless, of course, you really feel you are not capable of making decisions for yourself.

Kenneth W. Haskins, "The Case for Local Control," *Saturday Review,* 11 January 1969, a special issue produced in cooperation with the Committee for Economic Development, 52–54. Reprinted by permission of the author and publisher.

[*At a Harvard University conference on 25 January 1968, Rhody McCoy, Kenneth Haskins, and thirty other Black educators issued their demand for community control. In part it read as follows.*]

Black people in American cities are in the process of developing the power to assume control of these public and private institutions in our community. The single institution which carries the heaviest responsibility for dispensing or promulgating those values which identifies a group's consciousness of itself is the educational system. To leave the education of black children in the hands of people who are white and who are racist is tantamount to suicide. . . .

In sum, we demand the responsibility for what happens to our children. We consider it an insult to be asked to prove whether we can do a better job in order to be granted the necessary resources and support. We should not be forced into answering the question, "Can you do it better?" to those who have failed miserably in the past despite their control over substantial resources.

Our vision for control by the community is not on a demonstration basis for one or two years, but indefinitely.

[Rhody McCoy, Kenneth Haskins, et al.] *Position Statement: Five-State Organizing Committee for Community Control,* 25 January 1968 (mimeographed at Harvard University, copy provided by Kenneth Haskins).

21 THE BACKLASH TRIUMPHANT

Nineteen sixty-eight was a tumultuous year. In the first six months, 221 upheavals disrupted 101 colleges. Some U.S. Army intelligence officers felt Dr. King was leading a revolution. FBI agents increased surveillance of major civil rights organizations.

Leadership was in disarray. President Johnson quit the presidential race, and Chief Justice Earl Warren left the Supreme Court. In April, Dr. Martin Luther King, Jr., was assassinated, and riots and looting broke out in 125 ghettos that left 46 dead and over 3,500 injured. In Washington, D.C., 7 people died, 1,166 were injured, and 7,370 were arrested. It took 15,000 troops and army tanks to restore order to the city. By June Robert Kennedy had also been assassinated.

Nixon: From Candidate to Watergate

The Democratic National Convention in Chicago put violence on display. Mayor Richard Daley denied permits to demonstrators and told his police to crack down. Protesters, reported an eyewitness, were not the only ones "beaten, gassed, and maced. No one was safe from the policemen's frenzy. Their sergeants lost control of them repeatedly, and they beat reporters, bystanders, and yippies with equal abandon." Inside the convention hall security forces responded to any commotion on the floor by roughing up delegates and even journalists. Democrat Hubert Humphrey faced two candidates appealing to the white backlash. George Wallace had a reputation for stirring racial animosity. As governor of Alabama, he proclaimed, "Segregation now, segregation tomorrow, segregation forever." At the University of Alabama, he had "stood in the schoolhouse door" and defied a federal court order to admit two African Americans. "Haters don't need to join a Klan when they have George Wallace," wrote the Birmingham *Post-Herald*. "If you want something to hate, just name it—he'll hate it for you."

Wallace's racist appeal was confirmed in the primaries. He won 30 percent of Wisconsin's vote, 30 percent of Indiana, and 45 percent of Maryland.

To outflank Wallace and draw his white vote, Republican Richard Nixon crafted a "Southern strategy." He claimed the Democrat's "Great Society" stimulated unrealistic expectations in African Americans. Unless he was elected, he also hinted, ghetto looters soon might invade white, middle-class suburbia.

On election day 73 million Americans went to the polls, and Nixon, by stealing Wallace's thunder, defeated Humphrey by half a million votes. However, Wallace's 45 electoral votes and 10,000,000 popular votes also proved something. Though many whites sympathized with the goal of desegregation, millions of others had voted for a pugnacious racism.

The National Commission on the Causes and Prevention of Violence announced that "a police riot" had taken place outside the Democratic National Convention. However, Judge Julius Hoffman's Chicago court tried eight radical leaders—"the Chicago Seven" and Bobby Seale, who insisted on being tried separately—for what the court called "conspiracy to riot."

Demonstrators outside Judge Hoffman's court grew in numbers, and by the third week of the trial National Guard troops arrived to control unruly crowds. Inside, the judge traded barbs with the defendants and their radical lawyers and eventually sentenced some lawyers and defendants to jail for contempt of court.

Judge Hoffman lost patience with Black Panther leader Bobby Seale, the only African American among the riot leaders. In the trial's fifth week, he had him gagged and shackled to a chair. Later Hoffman sentenced him to four years for contempt. Bobby Seale muzzled and bound to a chair in an American court seemed to symbolize the fate of the Black revolution.

A week after his inauguration in 1969, Nixon's "Southern strategy" became policy when he postponed a federal cutoff of funds to five Southern districts that had failed to desegregate schools. By April the chair of the Equal Employment Opportunity Commission, saying he lacked presidential support, resigned. After nine months the Civil Rights Commission declared the White House was in retreat on civil rights and no longer enforced school desegregation.

For a Supreme Court post, Nixon picked a conservative Southerner who withdrew, then a Southern believer in "white supremacy" who was rejected by the Senate after strong objections by the AFL-CIO and the NAACP. The president pointedly had stuck to his "Southern strategy."

In 1970, on the recommendation of Democrat Daniel Patrick Moynihan, Nixon adopted a policy of "benign neglect" toward African Americans. This meant the federal government would soft-pedal or ignore African American needs. Congressman John Conyers saw this as "a calculated, aggressive, systematic effort" to "wipe out civil rights progress of the past twenty years." If ghetto economic and social conditions were like cancer, said Black leaders, they could not be ignored.

By 1970 Nixon began to denounce "forced bussing" to achieve school integration. He proposed instead to improve ghetto schools. School bussing used for a variety of goals, including segregation, suddenly became unfair to whites.

The most persuasive antibussing argument for parents was that it undermined "the neighborhood school." However, social psychologist Dr. Kenneth Clark presented evidence that segregation was more damaging to white than Black children.

In 1970 the NAACP denounced the president for abandoning equality as a goal. Nixon encouraged defense contracts with firms that discriminated and tried to ignore the Voting Rights Law. By the September term, school desegregation triggered violent clashes in Pontiac, Michigan, and Trenton, New Jersey. In 1971 the Civil Rights Commission found the White House guilty of a "major breakdown" in civil rights enforcement three times.

Inside the Oval Office, Nixon revealed his bigotry and his racial strategy to H. R. Haldeman, saying, "The whole problem is really the Blacks. The key is to devise a system that recognizes this while not appearing to." Another time he told his top aides, "The Democrats have the Jews and the Blacks and let them have them. In fact, tie them around their necks." This approach would become the Republicans' "Southern strategy" and win one election after another.

Though smaller meetings had been held in 1966, 1967, 1968, and 1970, in 1972 the first National Black Political Convention met in Gary, Indiana. Gary's mayor, Richard Hatcher, was host to eight thousand people, including elected officials. Panther Bobby Seale and Coretta Scott King sat together on the platform. The "Black Agenda" demanded reparations for enslavement, more representatives in Congress, cutting military funds, a guaranteed family income of $6,500, and local control of public schools.

In 1972, when Nixon ran for reelection, he proposed a moratorium on all court-ordered school desegregation. He renewed his offer to increase funds for ghetto schools by $1.5 billion. African American leaders again rejected this as a return to "separate but equal" education.

In May, George Wallace again entered the presidential race seeking the Democratic nomination. But during a speaking appearance at a Laurel, Maryland, shopping center, he was shot by Arthur Bremer, left partly paralyzed, and withdrew from the race. Nixon easily won a second term against George McGovern.

The president undercut affirmative action by recommending a merit system, denounced "forced bussing," and had his Justice Department declare that before it could act in a case, racial discrimination had to be proven. Father Theodore Hesburgh, chairman of the Civil Rights Commission since 1957, resigned to protest what he called a White House surrender to inequality.

Desperate to improve African American education, Atlanta's Black superintendent of schools, Alonzo Crim, implemented a plan that would leave 80 of the city's 140 schools all Black and limit bussing to 3 percent of students. The NAACP denounced his plan as a dangerous precedent, but Crim and his staff felt in the current climate they had no other way to improve inner-city education.

The Equal Employment Opportunity Commission (EEOC) became a battleground after Nixon increased its budget from $12 to $42 million and its staff from 250 to 2,500. Despite these increases, the president knew EEOC had a backlog of sixty thousand cases, it lacked power to sue, and it was chaired by his appointee, William Brown III.

Finally, Congress voted EEOC power to take cases to court, and in 1974 EEOC began a series of class action suits against companies with records of systematic discrimination. Chairman Brown abandoned his conservative viewpoint. He hired public-interest lawyers to track discriminatory companies. Brown now held the upper hand, and EEOC demanded compliance with fair hiring practices.

Major businesses once had fought discrimination cases until officials ran out of funds and patience. This time companies learned they could face damaging publicity and began to comply with the law. The first to surrender was American Telephone and Telegraph (AT&T), America's largest corporation. EEOC asked for $4 billion but accepted AT&T's $15 million in reparations and $23 million each year to increase the paychecks of women and minorities. AT&T also admitted past discrimination and promised reforms. EEOC filed eighty more suits, and soon New York Telephone, Detroit Edison, steel firms, and labor unions had capitulated.

Brown was not the only public figure to change his views. After George Wallace left the presidential race, he rejected segregation. He met with the National Conference of Black Mayors in Tuskegee and the next year shook hands with SCLC chair Reverend Ralph Abernathy. He soon hired African American advisers and publicly kissed a Black beauty queen.

Before Nixon left office in 1974, the Supreme Court, with three of his appointments, Harry Blackmun, Warren Burger, and Lewis Powell, set the stage for a return to school desegregation. In 1973 in the Rodriguez case in Texas, a high court majority ruled a state did not have to spend as much for education in poor as in rich districts. Justice Powell wrote for the majority, which included Burger and Blackmun, that poor children were being educated even if given "a poorer quality education" than richer children. Wealth was the issue rather than "equal protection" under the Constitution, said the majority. This ended any chance to equalize educational opportunities. Justice Thurgood Marshall strongly disagreed, saying education was "a right which must be made available to all on equal terms."

In the Milliken case a U.S. district court in Detroit found the city's quarter of a million schoolchildren were given a "separate" and "unequal" edu-

The 1967 Newark, New Jersey, Black Power conference opened in July, and included Dick Gregory (left), Ron Karenga, Rap Brown, and (not shown) Jesse Jackson.

cation and ordered a merger with the 500,000 pupils of nearby suburban school districts. In 1974 Chief Justice Burger wrote for the Supreme Court majority, that also included Powell and Blackmun, and reversed the order as one that would punish white suburbs. Justice Marshall wrote that after "twenty years of small, difficult steps . . . the Court today takes a giant step backwards [toward] separate and unequal education."

This decision eliminated the hope of desegregating urban schools or of ending white flight to the suburbs to avoid integration. In 1994 the *New York Times* noted, "Two-thirds of America's Black children know few, if any, white people."

The Milliken decision also ignored an important bussing study. In Hartford, Connecticut, several hundred children began a bussing program in 1966 that took them to wealthier suburbs. Over the next sixteen years the males bussed, compared to those left behind, were more likely to graduate high school, attend college longer, and have fewer difficulties with police.

By the mid-1970s African American children increasingly were confined to schools with lower-paid teachers, fewer books and materials, and less of a chance to enter college. One father who dropped out of school in the South and came north seeking a better education for his daughter confronted the New York City Board of Education at an open meeting. He was saddened that each school year she fell further behind in studies.

> You people operate a goddam monopoly, like the phone company. I got no choice where I send my child to school. I can only send her where it's free. And she's not learning. Damn it, that's your responsibility that she's not learning. When you fail, what happens: Nothing. Nobody gets fired. Nothing happens to nobody except my child.

In 1975, after Ford replaced Nixon in the White House, he took two new steps for a Republican president. He addressed an NAACP convention and he picked an African American cabinet member, William Coleman, secretary of Housing and Urban Development.

The economic picture did not change for African Americans from the administrations of Nixon to Ford. Some 31 percent lived in poverty compared to 8.9 percent of whites. The national jobless rate was 9 percent, but for African Americans it stood at 15 percent and the Urban League claimed the real rate was 26 percent.

In 1974, a federal court in Boston ordered school desegregation through bussing. Whites rioted. Rocks were heaved at school busses and Black children. The Civil Rights Commission blamed the violence on Nixon's and Ford's public antagonism to bussing. On 5 April 1976, a white mob at

The January 1971 cover of *The Negro History Bulletin* illustrates a renewed focus on education and the school curriculum in social studies.

'OPEN UP, MAN—I PUT IN 300 YEARS HELPING WRITE IT'

Boston's city hall attacked Theodore Landsmark, a Black attorney. One rioter used the pole from an American flag to stab Landsmark in the face. In Roxbury, soon after, a white man was pulled from his car by Black teenagers and beaten to death.

The Carter Administration

A former segregationist governor of Georgia, a born-again Christian, Jimmy Carter owed his election to the Voting Rights Act. Under it, millions of African American voters gave Carter 94 percent of their vote. A majority of whites voted for Ford, but that was not enough.

Black hopes began to climb as Carter appointed African Americans to top administration posts. He named nine African Americans as ambassadors, and in four years he appointed more as federal judges than Presidents Nixon, Ford, Kennedy, and Johnson combined. Nine of his appointees went to the court of appeals and twenty-one to lower courts.

For the first time, an African American represented the United States to the world: Andrew Young, a leading assistant to Dr. King, became the chief U.S. delegate to the UN. Patricia Harris, a seasoned diplomat, became secretary of Housing and Urban Development, and later, secretary of Health, Education, and Welfare, a cabinet post never before held by an African American.

Carter and Harris visited the South Bronx in New York, a neighborhood of burned-out buildings and empty lots. Surrounded by the media, the president promised urban renewal programs to revitalize the area. But nothing happened. Carter soon had a "credibility gap"—promises unfulfilled and problems unsolved. Congress would not follow his leadership. The Humphrey-Hawkins bill sought to reduce unemployment to 4 percent, but Congress did not vote funds to carry out its mandate.

During the Carter term, the jobless rate failed to go down, and then edged upward. In a Democratic administration the African American unemployment rate remained double the white rate, and a third of Black families remained below the poverty line. To most whites and people of color, the administration's pledges of reform appeared empty.

Carter appointed Eleanor Holmes Norton, a former civil rights activist, as chair of EEOC. However, EEOC's backlog of cases rose from 130,000 to 340,000 in 1978, and Norton had to consolidate cases and hope her legal victories would have a ripple effect.

Eleanor Holmes Norton.

Money pledged to ghetto areas like the South Bronx never arrived. Soaring inflation cut down family incomes, and so did rising interest rates. Carter reduced funding for the poor, but not the military. The termination of federal services usually associated with the Reagan era began with President Carter.

The Supreme Court's conservative trend did not diminish under the Democrats. In the Bakke case, the high court limited the impact and scope of affirmative action programs. It also declared intentional discrimination had to be proven in elections in order for government to act. It was almost impossible to prove legislators intended to reduce Black voters even when this was in fact their goal.

African Americans also found the president unfair to refugees fleeing the brutal Duvalier dictatorship in Haiti. As a committed anti-Communist, Carter eagerly welcomed people from Castro's Cuba and saw they had federal aid and found jobs. But refugees from the Black nation of Haiti were another matter. By the end of 1980 the administration had accepted 125,000 Cubans (almost all white), but the 12,400 Haitians admitted to the United States represented only a small percentage of those who fled.

In 1980 this discrimination set the stage for a Florida riot. African Americans saw more and more jobless people in their community, but newly arrived Cuban refugees received government help and work. Four

Freedomways' cartoonist Brandon assailed President Carter's discriminatory policy toward Haitian refugees in 1980.

white officers stopped a Black businessman on his motorcycle. Though he had no arrest record, he was beaten to death. When the four were acquitted by a white jury, Liberty City exploded in mayhem, looting, and fire. When the smoke cleared, 9 were dead and 163 injured.

In the Middle East, Ambassador Andrew Young tried to make a change. He secretly met with the UN observer of the Palestine Liberation Organization (PLO). But since Young had ignored U.S. policy of unqualified support of Israel and opposition to Palestinians, President Carter had him resign. Infuriated at Young's dismissal, Reverend Joseph Lowery led an SCLC delegation to Lebanon where, with Yasir Arafat, they sang "We Shall Overcome." Jesse Jackson also traveled to the Middle East, where he met with the president of Syria and urged political rights for Palestinians. Although he embraced Yasir Arafat and recommended the PLO be included in any peace initiatives, he also urged Arafat to halt PLO attacks on Israel and create an atmosphere conducive to peace talks. Like Young, some American Jewish leaders never forgave Jackson for taking this approach to peace in the Middle East. Those who attacked Jackson did not mention that he twice visited with Egypt's president Anwar Sadat, who earlier had signed a historic peace agreement with Israel.

In 1993, Arafat and the PLO signed a peace accord with Israel, but Young was not invited to the White House ceremony celebrating the goal he had tried to advance. After the signing a smiling Arafat visited the Jackson family at their Washington home.

By 1980 the Congressional Black Caucus noted its serious disappointment with Carter's failure to create jobs, help the poor, or cut back on military spending. The caucus charged that the White House overfed the military and starved society's needy.

Voting Rights Victories

Mayor Charles Evers of Fayette, Mississippi, at his inaugural ball.

Jimmy Carter was not the first or last beneficiary of the Voting Rights Act of 1965. It ended the restrictions and terror that denied African Americans political participation in the South. In a ten-year period, over a million people registered to vote. Men and women who marched for justice filed for office. In 1965, seventy African Americans were elected officials, and in 1968 the figure was four hundred. By 1968 the United States had seven African American mayors and ninety-seven state legislators. There was a 14 percent annual increase of African American elected officials in the early 1970s.

It was revolution without fury. In 1969 in Fayette, Mississippi, Charles Evers was elected mayor. Six years earlier his brother Medgar Evers had been assassinated by Klansmen.

In 1972 Barbara Jordan became Texas's first Black representative in Congress. Andrew Young was elected to Congress in Georgia. The Black congressional delegation increased from twelve to fifteen, all Democrats. Republican Senator Edward Brooke also won reelection in Massachusetts.

Urban voting also rose. Until 1968 the Bedford-Stuyvesant ghetto of Brooklyn had not sent an African American to Congress. Teacher Shirley Chisholm became the first—and the first woman of color in Congress. In 1972 she announced her candidacy for the Democratic presidential nomination and ran a spirited if brief campaign.

In 1973 African Americans had elected 2,991 officials nationwide, including 108 mayors. Tom Bradley, son of Texas sharecroppers, was elected mayor of Los Angeles. In a city where less than one in five voters were African Americans, he was reelected four more times before retiring from office in 1992.

In 1974 voters elected African Americans as lieutenant governors in Colorado and California. Others ran city halls in Detroit, Michigan (Coleman Young), Gary, Indiana (Richard Hatcher), and Atlanta, Georgia (Maynard Jackson).

By 1976 six hundred African Americans held office in Southern states. Half of the city councils of Charleston, South Carolina, and Montgomery,

In 1985 Tom Bradley won a fourth term as mayor of Los Angeles with the greatest margin of votes in the city's history.

Alabama, were African Americans. In 1961 McComb, Mississippi, was "the bombing capital of the world" run by Klansmen. By 1978 a third of the police department was Black, schools were desegregated, and African Americans served as clerks in downtown stores and banks. Said C. C. Bryant, "Now Blacks can vote, go were they want to go. Once we got a number of Blacks registered, this brought about the necessary change."

However, no people of color in McComb had been elected to office. The average Black income was 60 percent of the white income, and the Black joblessness rate was double the white rate. Blacks and whites attended the same schools but sat in different classrooms.

In 1979 Birmingham, Alabama, was no longer "the citadel of segregation." Richard Arrington, born to Alabama sharecroppers, had a doctorate in zoology and sat on the city council. Then one night African American citizen Bonita Carter, twenty, was shot three times in the back by a policeman. The white mayor refused to fire the white officer, and a night of rioting erupted.

Black politicians warned Arrington not to mention police brutality, but his constituents said, "We have invested in you. You are the Black political leader in this town and we want you to pay off on the investment." Arrington ran for mayor, took 98 percent of the Black vote, 12 percent of the

Birmingham Mayor Richard Arrington.

white vote, and won city hall with 51.1 percent. His inauguration was attended by Governor George Wallace, two delegates from the Carter administration, and Birmingham's two previous mayors. Four years later Arrington won reelection with 20 percent of the white vote.

Fighting the KKK

Civil rights laws did not end the Ku Klux Klan or its potential for violence. But a weakened KKK could no longer act like an arm of the state and keep people from voting. By the time Nixon left office in 1974, its membership had fallen to a new low of 1,500. But a steep rise began under Carter until in 1980 it had reached 11,000. About 75,000 others read KKK literature and attended meetings.

As the Carter administration floundered in foreign policy and retreated from civil rights and aid for the poor, Klansmen picked up phrases from Republican speeches. Who, it asked, was better equipped to defend white people from what it called "reverse discrimination" and to fight bussing for integration?

But a decade of struggle in the South also prepared Black and white people to unite against Klan hatred when it appeared. In 1977 in Tallahassee, Florida, 110 robed Klansmen began a recruitment march through town, only to be challenged by 1,500 young people of both races. Shouting

Florida youths in the 1970s taunt a marching Klansman.

"Down with the Klan," they charged the Klansmen, who were finally rescued by the police. During a July Fourth KKK rally on the steps of the Columbus, Ohio, statehouse, a Klan Grand Dragon sprayed Mace on protesting Black youths. In turn, they charged, ripped off the Klan sheets, and ended the rally.

In 1979 in the Greensboro, North Carolina, ghetto, radicals organized a "Death to the Klan" rally. Four TV news crews captured the scene as armed Klansmen drove in, unpacked guns from car trunks, and opened fire. Five radicals were killed. Two government agents riding with the assailants did not warn anyone of the impending violence. A white jury acquitted the accused.

Klan activities could no longer halt African American gains. In 1977, after Benjamin Hooks took over, the NAACP grew by fifty thousand new members, three hundred new branches, and $1.5 million more in its treasury. However, one critic, Harold Cruse, called the NAACP stalled because "it failed to realize that the problems Blacks have been experiencing are also economic, not just racial. There isn't much it can do with respect to economics. We'll have to look to new organizations for that."

Astronaut Guy Bluford.

Some individuals became heroes. In 1974 Hank Aaron, despite death threats, passed Babe Ruth's 714 career home runs and went on to enter the Baseball Hall of Fame as a legend in his own time. In 1975 General Chappie James was promoted to become the first four-star African American U.S. general.

In 1977 Alex Haley's *Roots* enthralled millions of American readers and won a Pulitzer Prize. As a TV miniseries, *Roots* reached tens of millions more. Its tale of family survival and redemption during and after slavery added light and luster to a side of America's story often ignored. Above all, *Roots* sent African Americans in hot pursuit of family histories.

By 1978 Major Guion Bluford, Jr., Major Frederick Gregory, and Dr. Ronald McNair joined NASA's space program as the first African American astronauts. The next year Judge Amalya Kearse became the first woman appointed to the U.S. Court of Appeals, and after Thurgood Marshall, the second African American.

Beginning in the late 1960s Black history departments were established at universities such as Harvard, Yale, Columbia, and the University of California, and courses were first offered in high schools. The civil rights campaign had lost momentum, but activists were determined to see young people in schools and colleges learn about an African heritage. "If you believe someone has no history worth mentioning," said one historian, "it's easy to assume he or she has no humanity worth defending." The 1970s ended with the Schomburg Center for Research in Black Cul-

General Daniel
"Chappie" James.

ture in New York City dedicating a $3.8-million building to preserve a courageous past.

The Hidden Backlash

The civil rights struggle was secretly undermined from inside the federal government. J. Edgar Hoover was a man obsessed with two fears: "the Communist conspiracy" and a Black messiah who might lead his people to revolution. Among enemies of civil rights few were as well placed for sabotage as Hoover. In his forty-eight years in high federal office he served during ten presidents and four wars—from Woodrow Wilson to Richard Nixon, from World War I to Vietnam.

Hoover saw deadly peril in atheists, radicals, liberals, or those who opposed segregation and racial injustice. A bigot, he once referred to Dr. King as a "burr head." In 1947 the FBI opened a file on college student Martin Luther King, Jr., as it earlier had opened files on his father and grandfather. The bureau also tracked boxer Joe Louis, scholar W. E. B. Du Bois, and actor/activist Paul Robeson. Using the Freedom of Information Act, Paul Robeson, Jr., found his father had been tracked by many government spies:

> For twenty-five years Paul Robeson was investigated by, among others, the Federal Bureau of Investigation, the Central Intelligence Agency, the State Department, the Criminal Division of the Department of Justice, the Internal Revenue Service, the U.S. Immigration Service, naval intelligence, army intelligence, the National Security Council, the White House, the office of the attorney general, the Secret Service, and quite a few more.

Hoover's uncontrolled power stemmed in part from his large secret files on presidents, senators, judges, and prominent citizens. These were hidden from the public, the president, the attorney general, and Congress. To hide his treasures from scrutiny, Hoover kept such special files as "June Files" and "Do Not File" files.

FBI power also stemmed from presidents who quietly approved Hoover's illegalities. Presidents Kennedy and Johnson urged him to keep illegal surveillance of King and other activists.

Civil rights worker Virginia Durr remembered FBI agents asking about Communists but not protecting workers. When school desegregation led to conflict in the 1950s, Hoover told President Eisenhower's cabinet that NAACP leaders and Communists were turning crises into revolution. "Our experience with the FBI was that no matter what kind of brutality . . . all the FBI agents did was stand over on the corner and take notes," recalled Andrew Young. Another volunteer recalled FBI agents watching "out of the courthouse windows while you were being chased down the street."

By 1963 army intelligence and the FBI were tracking those they considered part of the civil rights revolution. In January the army's 113th Intelligence Detachment recorded King at a dinner discussion in Chicago's Edgewater Beach Hotel about his marches in Birmingham. Major General William P. Yarborough, the army's spymaster, was convinced King and other leaders received cash from China or the USSR funneled through Cuba. Top army officers said King's efforts gave "aid and comfort to the enemy in time of war."

When King marched children into downtown Birmingham in May 1963, the FBI supplied Bull Connor's police with his plans. From the supersecret "Site 98" in Nevada, U.S. Army U-2 planes spied on the marchers. In Alabama, Green Berets of the Twentieth Special Forces Group relied on Klan members to monitor civil rights workers. In 1993 a former army sergeant told how Mississippi Klansmen informed the Twentieth's officers "where nigger troublemakers might meet, and we'd go there and then file a report. It wasn't any big deal."

As King's activities intensified in 1963, some army brass wanted to recall troops from the Seventh Army in Europe or from Vietnam. Hoover began a new file, "Communist Influence Racial Matters" and ordered assistant

Dr. Martin Luther King, Jr. (left), with Jack O'Dell at his side discusses civil rights issues.

William Sullivan to come up with proof King was a Communist. Sullivan later revealed how his men concocted "a lot of nonsense [on King] which we ourselves did not believe." Hoover then labeled King "most dangerous" from "the standpoint of communism and national security."

Hoover insisted that President Kennedy have King fire two of his trusted assistants, Stan Levison and Jack O'Dell, whom Hoover considered but could not prove were Communists. After a talk with Kennedy at the White House, King felt he had no choice and fired the two men.

At the 1964 Democratic National Convention, President Johnson asked Hoover to wiretap the phones of Fanny Lou Hamer and the Mississippi Freedom Democratic Party. Between 1963 and 1970 U.S. Army commanders ordered surveillance of civil rights demonstrations in twenty-six U-2 spy flights from Site 98 and other sites.

Hoover also blocked the prosecution of four Klansmen who in 1963 had bombed Birmingham's Sixteenth Street Baptist Church and killed four girls. The FBI's Birmingham office twice sent Hoover evidence and twice recommended prosecution of the guilty. In 1977, fourteen years after the crime, Robert Chambliss finally was convicted of the bombing. Hoover's refusal to prosecute was not discovered until 1980—eight years after his death—in a Justice Department report.

By 1964, Hoover called his assault on the Black Revolution COINTEL-PRO, or "counter intelligence program." His aims went beyond surveillance to the disruption of legal political activities. In 1975 the Church Senate Committee on abuses by Secret Service agencies found this COINTELPRO memo on FBI goals:

Fannie Lou Hamer of Mississippi helped lead the fight for voting rights, school integration, and racial justice in her state. She was tracked by the FBI.

1. Prevent a coalition of militant Black nationalist groups. . . .
2. Prevent the rise of a messiah who could unify and electrify the militant nationalist movement . . . Martin Luther King, Stokely Carmichael, and Elijah Muhammad all aspire to this position.
3. Prevent violence on the part of Black nationalist groups. . . .
4. Prevent militant Black nationalist groups and leaders from gaining respectability by discrediting them.
5. . . . prevent the long-range growth of militant Black nationalist organizations, especially among youth.

By the early 1960s, FBI agents infiltrated the Black Muslims and spied on Malcolm X, whose personal bodyguard, Eugene Roberts, was an undercover New York City police agent.

The urban riots of 1964 to 1968 caught the FBI by surprise, but Hoover soon announced these riots had united "Moscow-directed revolutionaries" with "vicious, hate filled . . . Black extremists." The army continued to play

Voices for Black Power who met in March 1964 were Malcolm X (right), representative Adam Clayton Powell, and educator Milton Gilamisos. Each was tracked by the FBI.

a role in espionage at home. In the 1967 Detroit riot, 496 African American men, arrested for firing guns, were detained at a warehouse and interviewed by agents of the army's Psychological Operations Group, dressed as civilians.

In 1967 Hoover's COINTELPRO aimed at "Black Hate Groups," the Black Panthers and Black Muslims. In 1968, another COINTELPRO operation called "Ghetto Informant Program" recruited 3,248 FBI informers in dozens of cities. New York's FBI office ordered its agents to find "Subversive and/or Communist Links Between Harlem and Africa."

Activists were disrupted in ingenious ways. The FBI "bad-jacketed" individuals by leaving notes for friends claiming they were secret agents. It mailed harmful data on individuals to the media. When comedian/activist Dick Gregory criticized the Mafia, the FBI saw that his words reached Mafia leaders. The bureau also urged the arrest of Black nationalists "on every possible charge until they could no longer make bail."

After King denounced the Vietnam War in 1967, surveillance of him intensified. U.S. Army agents taped conversations between King, Stokely Carmichael, and H. Rap Brown as they planned the Poor People's March. King was taped when he addressed six hundred people at the Vermont Avenue Baptist Church. The FBI placed hidden microphones in fifteen of King's hotel rooms. Hoover sent some tapes to King's wife in an effort to destroy their marriage or perhaps edge King toward suicide.

In April 1968 when King arrived in Memphis he was tracked by the U.S. Army's 111th Military Intelligence Group from a sedan stuffed with elec-

Black Panther announcements often featured guns.

tronic equipment. A top-secret "Operation Detachment Alpha 184 Team" also served in Memphis that week.

By spring, army intelligence had devised plans to protect 124 cities from potential summer violence. Landing sites for planes were plotted and files were kept on "troublemakers." In November, after Peace and Freedom party presidential candidate, Panther Eldridge Cleaver, polled 200,000 votes, Hoover labeled the Panthers "the greatest threat to the internal security of the country." He warned Attorney General John Mitchell of "an armed [Panther] Black revolution."

Hoover escalated COINTELPRO to "exploit all avenues of creating . . . dissension" within the Panthers. To provoke violent confrontations among Panthers or against their rivals, the bureau used forged and anonymous letters and phone calls. Though some leading Panther supporters were Jewish, the FBI forged notes and documents claiming the party was anti-Semitic and pro-Nazi.

In December 1969, William O'Neal, an FBI informant inside the BPP, supplied Chicago police with a layout of the Monroe Street apartment of Fred Hampton, a dynamic Panther figure, and his staff. In the early morning of 4 December 1969, fourteen police officers with twenty-seven guns besieged the apartment and fired about a hundred rounds. Fred Hampton died with two bullets in his head fired at close range. Mark Clark also died.

The FBI rewarded O'Neal with a three-hundred-dollar bonus. Victims' parents and survivors brought suit for damages, and William Hampton, Fred Hampton's brother, told how families and survivors, despite adverse rulings, kept going to the trial almost daily:

> But we in the family knew we were right and that the police were wrong, so we kept praying and kept fighting.
> Now that it is about over, we feel a sense of relief. The settlement won't bring back those lives but it does show that people should continue to fight injustices regardless of how long it takes.

In 1982 the court awarded a $1.85-million settlement to nine plaintiffs. Attorney G. Flint Taylor, who represented the families, called it "an admission of the assassination conspiracy between the FBI" and Chicago police.

> The case may be almost over in the legal sense but it will live on as a reminder to people of how far the government can and will go to suppress those whose philosophies it does not like.

The bureau continued to wiretap Panther offices from Oakland to the Bronx and to monitor calls to mothers, dentists, and wives. In California, bureau disruptions kept the Blackstone Rangers and the Panthers from uniting and provoked armed BPP confrontations with Ron Karenga's US. By 1969, 28 Panthers had been slain, 750 had been jailed, and some leaders had fled the country. The party was finished as a political force.

The FBI was also secretly investigating the Urban League, the Civil Rights Commission, the Ford Foundation, and top Black elected officials. By 1972 the FBI had files on 2,873 African American groups and 8,585 individuals. This included a sixteen-page report on a North Carolina strike by blind African Americans.

Hoover died in 1972, but his secret war did not. In 1978 President Carter's National Security Council's Memorandum 46 detailed CIA efforts "to generate mistrust and hostility . . . and cause division among" African leaders and their African American friends.

Speaking of the government's long war, Ron Karenga said,

Hoover took his paranoia and imposed that as public policy. We knew it wasn't going to be a tea party, but we didn't anticipate how violent the U.S. government would get.

SPYING ON AFRICAN AMERICANS

[*For sixteen months journalist Stephen Tompkins of the Memphis* Commercial Appeal *studied public and U.S. classified documents, and interviewed two hundred people to uncover "the army's largest-ever espionage operation within the United States."*]

The intelligence branch of the United States Army spied on the family of Dr. Martin Luther King, Jr., for three generations.

Top-secret, often illegal, intrusions into the lives of black Americans began more than 75 years ago and often focused on the black churches in the South and their ministers.

The spying system was born of a conviction by top Army intelligence officers that black Americans were ripe for subversion—first by agents of the German Kaiser, then by Communists, later by the Japanese and eventually by those opposed to the Vietnam War.

At first, the Army used a reporting network of private citizens that included church members, black businessmen . . . and black educators. . . . It later employed cadres of infiltrators, wiretaps and aerial photography by U2 spy planes.

As the civil rights movement merged with the anti-war protests in the late 1960s, some Army units began supplying sniper rifles and other weapons of war to civilian police departments. Army Intelligence officers began planning for what some officers believed would soon be armed rebellion.

By March, 1968, King was preparing to lead a march in Memphis in support of striking sanitation workers and another march a few weeks later that would swamp Washington with people demanding less attention to Vietnam and more resources for America's poor.

By then the Army's Intelligence system was keenly focused on King and desperately searching for a way to stop him.

On April 4, 1968, King was killed by a sniper's bullet at the Lorraine Motel in Memphis.

In the 25 years since, investigators have focused on the role the FBI and other police agencies played in King's life. Few have paid any attention to the Army's activities. . . .

Portions of the month-long Birmingham disturbances [in May 1963] were recorded by U2 spy planes taking off from the supersecret "Site 98" outside Nellis Air Force Base in Nevada. Over the next seven years, at least 26 other such domestic spy flights by U2s and at least two involving the more advanced SR71 were requested by Army commanders and flown by the Air Force, according to classified documents reviewed by The Commercial Appeal. . . .

When King turned against the war in mid-1965, it merely made him that much more dangerous to some Army officers. . . .

Army Security Agency microphones [in early 1967 in King's office] recorded [Stokley] Carmichael trying to warn King that he was making powerful enemies. . . .

Carmichael: You making a lot of new enemies. . . . The man don't care you call ghettos concentration camps, but when you tell him his war machine is nothing but hired killers, you got trouble.

King: I told you in Los Angeles I can do nothing else. . . .

After the [1967 Detroit] riot, 496 black males arrested for firing rifles and shotguns at Army troops were herded into a warehouse north of Detroit. They were interviewed by agents of the Army's Psychological Operations Group, dressed as civilians, in conjunction with the Behavior Research Institute of Detroit.

The arrested men were asked dozens of questions, but the responses 363 of them gave to the question, "Who is your favorite Negro leader?" stunned Army Intelligence.

Dr. Martin Luther King Jr. was the clear favorite—178 of the men named him. Men considered more radical, such as Carmichael and Malcolm X came in a distant second and fourth.

Army Intelligence leaders repeatedly used this survey to signify the danger King represented to national security.

King really scared top Army commanders on December 4, 1967 when he announced his intent to lead a poor people's march on Washington the next spring to focus public attention on "total, direct and immediate abolition of poverty."

King's call for a "Poor People's Campaign" came on the heels of the nation's worst summer of violence in three years and an October anti-war protest in which 200,000 demonstrators had besieged the Pentagon as alarmed Army brass watched from the roof. . . .

Memos obtained by *The Commercial Appeal* reveal Army leaders were increasingly frustrated with top civilian Pentagon officials who ignored warnings that black unrest was Communist-inspired, damaging morale in Vietnam and leading to armed revolt at home.

By December, 1967 some officers felt desperate. Among them were [William] Yarborough, who had been named assistant chief of staff for intelligence in 1966, and Maj. Gen. William Blakefield, chief of U.S. Army Intelligence Command who reported to Yarborough. . . .

"You couldn't expect people to be rational and look at this in a cool way," he [Yarborough] said. "We were trying to fight a war at the same time when the home base was being eroded."

. . . Army Intelligence intensified its surveillance of King and covertly dispatched Green Beret teams to make street maps, identify landing zones for riot troops and scour sniper sites in 39 potential racially explosive cities. . . .

Green Berets from the 20th [Special Forces Group in Alabama] spied on King and other black Americans during the 1960s, military records and interviews show. . . .

In return for paramilitary training at a farm in Cullman, Alabama, Klansmen soon became the 20ths Intelligence network, whose information was passed on to the Pentagon. . . .

On April 3 [1968] King returned to Memphis. Army agents from the 111th Military Intelligence Group shadowed his movements and monitored radio traffic from a sedan crammed with electronic equipment.

Eight Green Beret soldiers from an "Operation Detachment Alpha 184 Team" were also in Memphis carrying out an unknown mission. Such "A-teams" usually contained 12 members.

On April 4 at 6:01 P.M. a bullet from a 30.05 rifle equipped with a scope struck King down on the balcony of the Lorraine Motel.

Stephen G. Tompkins, "Army Feared King, Secretly Watched Him," *The Commercial Appeal*, 21 March 1983, A1, 8–9, 47. Copyright 1993, *The Commercial Appeal*, and reprinted with the permission of Henry A. Stokes, managing editor.

THE RADICALISM OF DR. DU BOIS

[*In 1968 Dr. King had adopted a more radical philosophy as he opposed the war in Vietnam and began to organize a multiracial Poor People's March on Washington. At a Carnegie Hall tribute to mark the one hundredth anniversary of Dr. W. E. B. Du Bois's birth that February, King spoke warmly of the scholar's radical activism.*]

History had taught him it is not enough for people to be angry—the supreme task is to organize and unite people so that their anger becomes a transforming force. It was never possible to know where the scholar Du Bois ended and the organizer Du Bois began. The two qualities in him were a single united force.

The life style of Dr. Du Bois is the most important quality this generation of Negroes needs to emulate. The educated Negro who is not really part of us, and the angry militant who fails to organize us have nothing in common with Dr. Du Bois. He exemplified black power in achievement and he organized black power in action. It was no abstract slogan to him.

We cannot talk of Dr. Du Bois without recognizing that he was a radical all of his life. Some people would like to ignore the fact that he was a Communist in his later years. . . . It is time to cease muting the fact that Dr. Du Bois was a genius and chose to be a Communist. Our irrational obsessive anti-communism has led us into too many quagmires to be retained as if it were a mode of scientific thinking.

Dr. Martin Luther King, Jr., "Honoring Dr. Du Bois," Carnegie Hall Tribute, 23 February 1968. *Freedomways,* 8, No. 2, 1968. Reprinted with the permission of Esther Jackson, editor.

THE NIXON ADMINISTRATION

[*Congresswoman Shirley Chisholm of New York evaluated the Nixon administration for Radio Station WLIB in New York City, 26 March 1969.*]

On the same day President Nixon announced he had decided the United States will not be safe unless we start to build a defense system against missiles, the Head Start program in the District of Columbia was cut back for the lack of money.

As a teacher, and as a woman, I do not think I will ever understand what kind of values can be involved in spending nine billion dollars—and more, I am sure—on elaborate, unnecessary and impractical weapons when several thousand disadvantaged children in the nation's capital get nothing.

When the new administration took office, I was one of the many Americans who hoped it would mean that our country would benefit from the fresh perspectives, the new ideas, the different priorities of a leader who had no part in its mistakes of the past. Mr. Nixon had said things like this: "If our cities are to be livable for the next generation, we can delay no longer in launching new approaches to the problems that beset them and to the tensions that tear them apart." And he said, "When you cut expenditures for education, what you are doing is short-changing the American future."

But frankly, I have never cared too much what people say. What I am interested in is what they do. We have waited to see what the new administration is going to do. The pattern now is becoming clear.

Apparently launching those new programs can be delayed for a while, after all. It seems we have to get some missiles launched first. . . .

Two more years, two more years of hunger for Americans, of death for our best young men, of children here at home suffering the lifelong handicap of not having a good education when they are young. Two more years of high taxes, collected to feed the cancerous growth of a Defense Department budget that now consumes two-thirds of our federal income.

Two more years of too little being done to fight our greatest enemies, poverty, prejudice and neglect here in our own country. Two more years of fantastic waste in the Defense Department and of penny-pinching on social programs. Our country cannot survive two more years, or four, of these kinds of policies. It must stop—this year—now.

Now I am not a pacifist. I am, deeply, unalterably, opposed to this war in Vietnam. Apart from all the other considerations, and they are many, the main fact is that we cannot squander there the lives, the money, the energy that we need desperately here, in our cities, in our schools.

I wonder whether we cannot reverse our whole approach to spending. For years, we have given the military, the defense industry, a blank check. New weapons systems are dreamed up, billions are spent, and many times they are found to be impractical, inefficient, unsatisfactory, even worthless. What do we do then? We spend more money on them. But with social programs, what do we do? Take the Job Corps. Its failures have been mercilessly exposed and criticized. If it had been a military research and development project, they would have been covered up or explained away, and Congress would have been ready to pour more billions after those that had been wasted on it.

The case of Pride, Inc., is interesting. This vigorous, successful black organization, here in Washington, conceived and built by young inner-city men, has been ruthlessly attacked by its enemies in the government, in this Congress. At least six auditors from the General Accounting Office were put to work investigating Pride. They worked seven months and spent more than $100,000. They uncovered a fraud. It was something less than $2,100. Meanwhile millions of dollars—billions of dollars, in fact—were being spent by the Department of Defense, and how many auditors and investigators were checking into their negotiated contracts? Five.

We Americans have come to feel that it is our mission to make the world free. We believe that we are the good guys, everywhere, in Vietnam, in Latin America, wherever we go. We believe we are the good guys at home, too. When the Kerner Commission told white America what black America has always known, that prejudice and hatred built the nation's slums, maintains them and profits by them, white America would not believe it. But it is true. Unless we start to fight, and defeat, the enemies of poverty and racism in our own country and make our talk of equality and opportunity ring true, we are exposed as hypocrites in the eyes of the world when we talk about making other people free.

Courtesy of The Honorable Shirley Chisholm, Congresswoman 12th District, Brooklyn, New York.

PRISON REVOLT, 1970

[*In October 1970, Black and Puerto Rican prisoners in three New York jails revolted against inhuman conditions. Newspapers immediately charged the Black Panthers had led the revolt, although Panther prisoners had been segregated from the other prisoners. One unidentified Black, paroled prisoner was interviewed on radio station WBAI during rioting at the Queens County House of Detention.*]

. . . This is the people's problem, not the Mayor's problem, you understand, not the Governor's problem, this is the people's problem. Because you have the authority to tell them what to do; you don't let that Mayor go flashing-dashing around New York City talking that he ain't going to bargain with us. We don't want to bargain. We don't want to bargain. We're *demanding* because this is rightfully ours—our rights that we are speaking about, our right to live, you understand. . . . We don't want to live in health violation; we don't want our rights abused in the courts, we don't want bails we can't meet, you understand. Just treat us as *men*. That is what we are demanding, that is *all* we are demanding.

Those hostages are not going to be let go until your Mayor comes in there and sits down and makes commitments which you, the people of this city, make him keep, and the people of this country make these people keep these commitments they make, you understand. Because they owe that to you. That is your right as well as my right.

You never know when you will be put in this position, or another one similar to it, I mean the same purpose, it's the same thing, only different forms and different ways happen to all of us. What you've got to watch [is] who it's happening to because you don't want it to happen to you. You had better learn to support your brothers and sisters wherever they are. Wherever you are, don't be afraid to speak up if you see wrong being done. Insofar as that and everything is concerned, we've got to become more outspoken as people and support wherever support is needed. Don't let the news media and the establishment dupe you into indoctrination and to turning against yourself. Know yourself. Know yourself. And learn about yourself.

. . . The news media seems to be trying to throw all the weight on the Black Panther Party for what happened in Branch Queens. But I want to make it very clear that them brothers was completely isolated . . . [and] there was no way of us getting to them unless we broke through bars and everything else.

Now, as soon as we took our hostages and had them pretty well controlled, we broke into the area where the Black Panthers was at and asked them, we *asked* them to represent us, to speak for us. The brothers was kind of skeptical at first being that they was on trial and everything else, but we practically forced them into the position of talking for us and representing us. . . . They was in there and we asked them, and by all means being a brother they would serve a brother, and they served us, and we owe them all our thanks and gratitude.

Right on!

THE COALITION'S THE THING

*[Congressman Ronald Dellums of California expressed the theme of interracial
unity in a 1972 speech honoring Dr. Martin Luther King, Jr.]*

. . . I've got good news for all the black people from the bottom floor to the
top row: We no longer have a monopoly on "niggerism" in America.

You no longer have to be black to be a "nigger." You can be a Chicano—
you're a "nigger;" a woman in a white, male-chauvinist, sexist society that
sees women as bed-makers, broom-pushers, bottle-makers and bed partners—they're "niggers" in this society! You've got long hair and a beard, sir,
you're a "nigger" in this society. You believe that the war in Indochina is illegal, immoral and insane; you believe that corporate presidents ought to
be put behind bars for polluting the air, and polluting the water, you're a
"nigger" in this society. So what I'm trying to stand here and say is, since us
black folks have got so much experience at being "niggers," then let's assume the leadership of all the "niggers" in the country and change America. "Nigger" power! Because when you put the black "niggers," the
brown, red, yellow, and white, and the women "niggers," the young, the
anti-war and the ecology "niggers" together, you don't have a microscopic
minority in this country, you have the *majority* of America. We can turn
this country around.

And we also have got to help the white silent majority understand that
when they do an objective assessment of their misery, they'll wake up at
four o'clock in the morning and say, "Hey, y'all—I'm a 'nigger,' too!"

. . . But most important, we're standing side by side, unified; unified for
freedom in this country in 1972. We may not be uniform, but we're unified. Because there's a strange, weird thing about freedom. Once you take
that first step toward freedom, all slaves have got to be free. So when the
black people stood up and said "Freedom," so did the Chicanos, the Indians, the Orientals, the young and the women. And when the people outside of prison said there must be freedom, the brothers and sisters inside
the prisons said there must be freedom. That's the strange, weird thing
about freedom.

Ronald V. Dellums, *Speech at the Third Annual Du Bois Cultural Evening*, at Carnegie
Hall, New York City, 30 January 1972. Reprinted by permission of *Freedomways* and
Esther Jackson, editor.

TEXTBOOKS AND MINORITIES

[In 1973 the Michigan Department of Education evaluated seventy-five textbooks used in its secondary schools for fair treatment of minorities. Only eight (11 percent) received "very good" as a rating and "69 percent were on the negative side." The quotes below are either by the reviewers or appear within the texts.]

[Reviewer]

Reading the text would lead one to believe that the United States is a benevolent god watching over his children.

[Reviewer]

The tone of this book is an optimistic one. It is best expressed by the phrase, "Things are getting better." ... Most minority group students know that this statement is untrue and are turned off by this kind of hypocrisy. Students not only need to be aware of the problems within this society regarding ethnic groups, but they also need to learn effective strategies for change.

[Text]

People who owned large numbers of slaves were rich and became important leaders in the southern states.

[Reviewer]

One picture of blacks dealing with slavery shows a slave reclining on a wagon filled with hay; a few other slaves are standing around talking. ... This picture could lead a student to conclude that slaves had a significant amount of freedom, and that slavery wasn't particularly harsh.

[Reviewer]

Frankly, I wish the authors had not said anything about America's minorities. If they had entirely left them out, instead of token and often distorted inclusion, there could be no mistaking the fact that this book belongs on the ash pile of tired and irrelevant texts.

[Reviewer]

This text if used in the schools will succeed in perpetuating the arrogant racist beliefs in the white students, and may even make some of them capable of participating in another My Lai or Wounded Knee.

[Reviewer]

We are virtually unaware that minorities exist until near the end of the text.

[*Finally, one text described Ku Klux Klan members in the 1920s as "honest and hardworking Americans" who opposed gangsters, favored Prohibition, and "pledged themselves to lead virtuous lives and protect the 'American way.' "*]

Cited in William L. Katz, "Minorities in American History Textbooks," *Equal Opportunity Review* (June 1973), Teachers College, Columbia University.

INTEGRATING THE SCHOOL CURRICULUM

[*In what would be called the "curriculum of inclusion" in the 1980s, and "a history of multicultural America" in the 1990s, in 1970 the NAACP issued* American Majorities and Minorities, *"the first comprehensive and fully representative syllabus for teaching U.S. history in secondary schools ever to be developed."*]

Teachers, for the first time, will now have available an entire course in U.S. history that deals adequately and accurately with Indians, Negroes, Puerto Ricans, Mexican Americans, and other minorities that have helped shape the nation. At the same time *American Majorities and Minorities* is perfectly inclusive as regards the traditional events and developments in American history. It is, in other words, a complete course of study in American history for secondary schools, not a supplement to the regular course.

The syllabus is not an effort to replace white history with black history, to substitute George Washington Carver for George Washington. It does place in perspective, as no other treatment has ever done, the many and varied contributions of racial and ethnic minorities along with those usually included in the regular school syllabus. For most American schoolchildren it will mean a first chance to learn about the great Indian nations that ruled the land before Columbus, of the Mexican American and Black cowboys who drove cattle up the Chisholm Trail, of the inventors of every race and nationality that helped make America an industrial giant. It also offers neglected information on the roles prejudice and racism have played in our nation's history.

Now, school systems that have insisted they would integrate their teaching of U.S. history if only they had a plan, have one. The students who insisted that history as now taught is not relevant have an opportunity to learn some history they never knew about. All of us, as citizens, can find a fully dimensioned picture of our nation's history.

. . . [This syllabus] has as much applicability to Maine as California, and has enough flexibility to stimulate good teaching from Florida to Oregon, from ghetto to suburb, from slow learners to fast. Since this is the first published multi-ethnic and multi-racial syllabus in U.S. history, this is an historic occasion. We hope it will mark a turning point for our schools.

[American Majorities and Minorities *received some media coverage but quickly faded from view. It was used in few school districts. In 1995 thousands remained stored at a New Hampshire warehouse.*]

Statement of Roy Wilkins, NAACP executive director, 21 September 1970.

A BICENTENNIAL EVALUATION

[*In January 1976 the National Urban League issued its report on the "State of Black America." It stated, "There was no escaping in 1975 the fact that the Second Reconstruction had indeed come to an end, and it, like the First Reconstruction that followed the Civil War, was uncompleted." Black family income was 58 percent of white family income, down from 61 percent in 1969.*]

As the nation enters its Bicentennial Year, Black America is in a state of crisis. By any of the accepted indicators of progress—employment, housing, education, etc.—many of the gains made over the past decade were either wiped out or badly eroded in 1975, and the portents for the future are not encouraging.

True, on a limited and individual basis there were exception to this downward trend in 1975, but the growing number of blacks without jobs, the increasing gap between white and black income, new public displays of racism and the negative attitude of policy-makers toward programs that aid the poor, marked the year as one of increasing hardships for Black America.

With violence breaking out in Boston and Louisville in 1975 over the implementation of court ordered desegregation the President [Gerald Ford] himself gave encouragement to the mobs by criticizing the courts and expressing opposition to bussing. . . .

The revelations of how the late J. Edgar Hoover used the FBI to harass civil rights groups and their leaders, most notably the late Dr. Martin Luther King, Jr., demonstrated to blacks the precarious status of their civil rights and further eroded their confidence in the impartiality of law enforcement agencies.

White women are expected to live to be 76.7 years old and black women 71.3 years. Black males have a life expectancy of 62.9 years as against the 68.9 average for white males.

The infant mortality rate for nonwhites in the U.S. is nearly twice the rate of whites.

Almost 24 million Americans, 12 percent of the population, are black, but only 2 percent of the nation's physicians are black. About 2.6 percent of the dentists are black and 5.7 percent of the professional nurses.

Not only were black children not being educated by the schools, a fact attested to by declining test scores, but they were also being thrown out of the institutions in disproportionate numbers for alleged infractions, the majority of which had nothing to do with offenses connected with school safety or protecting property.

Statistics collected by the Children's Defense Fund revealed that about two million school-age children, about half of them under the age of 13, are not enrolled in school. There is evidence that the figures are conservative and that the number is even higher than this, especially in some states and among black children.

Blacks were four times as likely to be robbed as whites, twice as likely to be assaulted, and four times as likely to be raped. Of the nation's murder victims last year, 51 percent were black.

[*Black law enforcement officers in forty-two states amounted to only 1.5 percent of the total.*]

CONCLUSION

In the context of the recent past, no year has been more destructive to the progress of blacks than 1975. . . .

To be remembered is that other societies have disintegrated when they ignored signs of spreading poverty and disenchantment among their people. It can happen in America, but it does not have to. The hour is late but there is yet time to set the American house in order.

"The State of Black America 1976," *The National Urban League*, 28 January 1976, New York City. Reprinted by permission of the National Urban League.

[In 1978, two years later, Professor Al Pinkney, chair of the Hunter College Sociology Department, found little change.]

Ten years after publication of the Report of the National Advisory Commission on Civil Disorders in 1968, in which the Commission concluded that "Our nation is moving toward two societies, one black, one white—separate and unequal," there have been minor changes in the citizenship status of Afro-Americans, but these changes have been so minuscule as to be hardly recognizable. The euphoria of the late 1960s and early 1970s appears to have given way to despair. . . .

    In sum, it seems fair to say that the decade of 1968–1978 was one of minor gains for black Americans. And just as it seemed that some progress was being made in the struggle for equity, the Bakke decision will probably mean that the next decade will be characterized by intense struggle. . . .

Al Pinkney, "Civil Rights: Gains Minimal," *Bill of Rights Journal* (December 1978), 5–6. Reprinted by permission of Al Pinkney.

AFRICAN AMERICANS: A COLONIZED PEOPLE?

[In 1852 Martin R. Delany had said, "We are a nation within a nation," and compared Black people to the Poles within Russia and the Irish under British rule. In 1962 writer Harold Cruse returned to this theme.]

From the beginning, the American Negro has existed as a colonial being. His enslavement coincided with the colonial expansion of European powers and was nothing more or less than a condition of domestic colonialism. Instead of the United States establishing a colonial empire in Africa, it brought the colonial system home and installed it in the Southern states. When the Civil War broke up the slave system and the Negro was emancipated, he gained only partial freedom. Emancipation elevated him to the position of a semidependent man, not to that of an equal or independent being.

Harold Cruse, "Revolutionary Nationalism and the Afro-American," *Studies on the Left,* 1962. Cited in Harold Cruse, *Rebellion or Revolution?* (New York: Morrow, 1968), 76.

[In 1976 Professor Alfonso Pinkney expounded on the idea.]

There are obvious differences between the internal colonialism of blacks in the United States and classical colonialism of European powers in Africa, Asia and Latin America. However, if colonialism is defined broadly as the subordination of a people, nation or country by another, with power for administration of life chances of the subordinate group vested in the hands of the dominant group for purposes of exploitation, the concept is applicable to both internal and external colonialism. . . .

. . . Furthermore, from the point of view of the colonized, the consequences of the system are similar. Indeed, in many ways internal colonialism is more destructive of human beings than external colonialism. In the former, the colonized are forced into direct contact with the colonizer, thereby leading to greater psychic damage in the form of self-hatred, which leads to confused identities. In external colonialism few of the colonized are forced into situations of interaction with the colonizers. Hence, except for lower-level bureaucrats and service workers, most of the indigenous people are spared the destructive effects that result from close personal interaction with those who consider themselves superior.

Alfonso Pinkney, *Red, Black and Green: Black Nationalism in the United States* (New York: Cambridge University Press, 1976), 8–10. Reprinted by permission of Alfonso Pinkney.

Electoral Gains, 1976

[*In 1976 Eddie N. Williams, president of the Joint Center for Political Studies, summarized recent political trends.*]

We're electing blacks at a rate of 464 a year. At that rate, by the year 2000 there will be 15,000 blacks in public office, but that figure will be only 3 percent of the total. . . .

It's sad to note that 200 years after the Revolution the percentage of black public officials is less than 1 percent but the potential for immense power is there. That potential is an indication that black political power has not peaked, as some believe, but needs only to be mobilized.

Blacks make up 10 percent of the legislatures of Alabama, Maryland and Michigan, but the representation is not proportionate to the black population of those states.

Blacks make up 25 percent of the population in Georgia, Louisiana,

Mississippi, North Carolina and South Carolina, but hold less than 10 percent of the seats in their respective legislatures.

THE NEW SHERIFF

[*Before he was elected sheriff in Greene County, Alabama, in 1970, Tom Gilmore had been mistaken for a civil rights agitator and stopped by an Alabama state trooper in 1965.*]

He put me up against a gas pump and frisked me and unbuckled his gun. He said, "I'm going to be in Selma tonight and I'll see you again, I'm going to blow your brains out." That's really how I decided to stay in Alabama. He made up my mind for me.

[*Gilmore became field director for the Southern Christian Leadership Conference. During a sit-in, the sheriff cane-whipped him. By 1970 Gilmore, elected sheriff, replaced the man who caned him. In 1978 Sheriff Gilmore evaluated the changes:*]

Whites are appealing to blacks for votes in a respectable manner now. Ain't nobody in Alabama trying to out-nigger the other one. Ain't nobody in the South playing those nigger games anymore.

Many of us have committed the rest of our lives to making Dr. King's dream come true. We've tried to do another kind of politicking, to appeal to the goodness in men and the honesty in men. A lot of us who were in the civil rights movement are politicking in this way, like we did in the old mass meetings.

Thurgood Marshall: The Bakke Dissent

[Justice Thurgood Marshall, in his dissent in the Bakke case, defended a university program that set aside places for minority applicants in a medical school.]

. . . it must be remembered that, during most of the past 200 years, the Constitution as interpreted by this Court did not prohibit the most ingenious and pervasive forms of discrimination against the Negro. Now, when a State acts to remedy the effects of that legacy of discrimination, I cannot believe that this same Constitution stands as a barrier. . . .

The position of the Negro today in America is the tragic but inevitable consequence of centuries of unequal treatment. Measured by any benchmark of comfort and achievement, meaningful equality remains a distant dream for the Negro.

A Negro child today has a life expectancy which is shorter by more than five years of a white child. The Negro child's mother is over three times more likely to die of complications of childbirth, and the infant mortality rate for Negroes is nearly twice that for whites. The median income of the Negro family is only 60% of the median of a white family, and the percentage of Negroes who live in families with incomes below the poverty line is nearly four times greater than that of whites.

. . . Although Negroes represent 11.5% of the population, they are only 1.2% of the lawyers and judges, 2% of the physicians, 2.3% of the dentists, 1.1% of the engineers and 2.6% of the college and university professors. . . .

In light of the sorry history of discrimination and its devastating impact on the lives of Negroes, bringing the Negro into the mainstream of American life should be a state interest of the highest order. To fail to do so is to ensure that America will forever remain a divided society.

I do not believe that the Fourteenth Amendment requires us to accept that fate. Neither its history or past cases lend any support to the conclusion that a University may not remedy the cumulative effects of society's discrimination by giving consideration to race in an effort to increase the number and percentage of Negro doctors.

. . . it is more than a little ironic that, after several hundred years of class-based discrimination against Negroes, the Court is unwilling to hold that a class-based remedy for that discrimination is permissible. In declining to so hold, today's judgement ignores the fact that for several hundred years Negroes have been discriminated against, not as individuals, but solely because of the color of their skins. It is unnecessary in [the] 20th century to have individual Negroes demonstrate that they have been victims of racial discrimination; the racism of our society has been so pervasive that none, regardless of wealth or position, had managed to escape its impact. The experience of Negroes in America has been different in kind, not just in degree, from that of other ethnic groups. It is not merely the history of slavery alone but also that a whole people were marked as inferior by law. And that mark has endured. The dream of America as the great melting pot has not been realized for the Negro; because of his skin color he never even made it into the pot. . . .

It is because of a legacy of unequal treatment that we must now permit the institutions of this society to give consideration to race in making decisions about who will hold positions of influence, affluence and prestige in America. For far too long, the doors to those positions have been shut to Negroes. If we are ever to become a fully integrated society, one in which the color of a person's skin will not determine the opportunities available to him or her, we must be willing to take steps to open those doors. . . .

I fear that we have come full circle. After the Civil War our government started several "affirmative action" programs. This Court in the Civil Rights Cases and Plessy v. Ferguson destroyed the movement toward complete equality. For almost a century no action was taken, and this nonaction was with the tacit approval of the courts. Then we had Brown v. Board of Education and the Civil Rights Acts of Congress, followed by numerous affirmative action programs. Now, we have this Court again stepping in, this time to stop affirmative action programs. . . .

Justice Thurgood Marshall, "Dissent in the Bakke case," Supreme Court, 1978. Cited in *Freedomways* 18, no. 3 (1978): 127–34. Reprinted by permission of Esther Jackson, editor.

JEWS, BLACKS, AND CONFLICT, 1979

[*Relations among civil rights allies soured as Jewish groups denounced quotas and affirmative action. A 1979* Village Voice *symposium was published.*]

[*Roger Wilkins, former* New York Times *columnist and professor*]

You do not have to be anti-Semitic to think that Palestinians have some rights; you do not have to be stupid to know that Israel cannot forever be protected by American bombs. . . .

That, really, is all Andy [Young] was saying. But for a long time we could not even say that because we were scared to be called anti-Semites.

[*William Strickland, professor of political science at Amherst*]

Now, for the white world the Holocaust stands unique in history, but there have been other holocausts. The Caribs, and the Arawaks, the Congolese killed by [Belgian King] Leopold, the native Americans in this country, black people in this country—although it is not in your history books—have all been victims of a holocaust. . . .

People say we must never forget the Holocaust because it was an experience unparalleled in history. But that's not quite true. What is unique about the Holocaust is that white people killed other white people on a scale unprecedented in history. But whites have been killing nonwhites on the same scale throughout the history of the West. . . .

The associated relationship to the Holocaust is the notion of shock. How could it have happened? You had only to ask black people about what your white brothers were capable of doing. Blacks—perhaps alone in Western society—understand white society's capacity to commit holocaust. For blacks, that experience is an inextricable part of Western history.

Village Voice, 5 November 1979, 70–74. Reprinted by permission.

Progress for the Few, 1980

[*A journalist who interviewed African Americans leaders around the country in 1980 quoted two of them at length.*]

[*Robert Williams, Jr., executive director Fort Wayne Urban League:*]

There's been significant progress by a few black people—those who were in a position to take advantage of the benefits of the civil rights movement. The masses of black people have been largely unaffected.

Despair and disillusionment and anger is surfacing. . . .

Today the coalitions that were so successful in the 60s are falling apart, partly because civil rights just moved off the national agenda. . . . Because of the illusion of black progress, white people no longer feel that programs should be targeted toward black people. . . .

We've also seen a tip of the centers of power really away from large urban areas, where there's a concentration of blacks, into basically suburban areas.

[*Peggy Cooper, chair, Commission on the Arts and Humanities, Washington, D.C.*]

Through history, progress has been directly related to education, in all ethnic groups. You're talking about a school system that is not working and hasn't worked for a long time.

A whole generation that is by no means dumb is being allowed to remain untaught, and in a state of depression.

That's really frightening. . . . Having no way to vent their anger, the kids have turned it inward. They're laconic. Their faces look empty. . . .

Kids are as cynical as we were in the 60s, but their cynicism has turned inward and augmented their depression. . . .

These kids, no matter how untutored they are in articulating their feelings, have sophisticated feelings. They really don't think black leaders have any power.

Paul Delaney, "Rights Has Moved Off the National Agenda," *New York Times*, 6 July 1980, E5. Copyright 1980, The New York Times Company. Reprinted by permission.

22 SURVIVING REAGANOMICS, 1980–1992

RONALD REAGAN was a master of communication. As an actor and politician he had learned to deliver words in an affable, down-home manner. In projecting a "Southern strategy," he was also a master of symbolism. His race for the presidency in 1980 began in Philadelphia, Mississippi, where in 1964 Klansmen had murdered three civil rights workers. The candidate was a smiling, jaunty, gracious presence; not only did he not condemn the triple murder . . . he didn't even mention it.

Klan leader Bill Wilkinson was one of the first to endorse Reagan. The candidate repeatedly repudiated Wilkinson's support. Then, a month before election, Reagan aimed this message at voters: "I see affirmative action becoming a kind of quota system . . . a kind of reverse discrimination."

The President and Reaganomics

Reagan's 489 electoral votes swept him into the White House. Except for Carter's Georgia, he carried the entire South. Only a quarter of registered voters elected him because half of those qualified did not vote.

The president believed that "government is the problem." His solution

Freedomways' cartoonist Brandon spoke out against Reaganomics.

was "deregulation," and he began to curtail the federal regulatory role. In June, his administration cut back on civil rights enforcement in jobs, education, and electoral rights. Addressing the annual NAACP convention, Reagan insisted that federal programs had created "a new kind of bondage for blacks" and argued that only private enterprise led to "economic emancipation." Delegates greeted his analysis coldly.

As a candidate Reagan promised to place African Americans in high office. But this promise was largely unmet. His one African American cabinet member was Samuel Pierce, Jr. Reagan's White House also replaced half of Carter's Black ambassadors. Seasoned diplomats were assigned to dull desk jobs at the State Department. Black foreign service appointments fell from 8.4 percent under Carter to 6.3 percent under Reagan.

In September 1981, at the outset of the Reagan era, NBC-TV News reported that there were 182 African American mayors and 18 in Congress, more than ever before. In ten years African American college enrollment doubled. Of the 502 attending Harvard, 20 were women.

Civil rights laws created small miracles. In 1964, 7 percent of Southern African Americans were registered to vote, and by 1980 it was 67 percent. Mississippi, once the most segregated state, had more African American elected officials than any other. NBC-TV producers focused on a growing African American middle class living in suburbia on tree-lined streets.

TV journalists also found bad news. African Americans were 46 percent of prison inmates. Few areas devastated by the 1960s riots had been rebuilt. In Watts, California Assemblywoman Maxine Waters said 57 percent of her constituents were on welfare, 40 percent of youths were jobless, and as many lived below the poverty line as in 1965. There was, she said, "not enough money to turn things around."

In Detroit, NBC reporters found 60 percent of the city signed up for public assistance and 70 percent of sixteen-to-nineteen-year-olds without jobs. "You just exist . . . or you die young," said graduate student Clark White. Another resident said young people had the choice of "shooting basketball, bullets or dope," and he warned, "Time is running out." A youth of twenty said, "You got to keep the faith within yourself." But without a job, security, or much hope for either life was hard. NBC writers concluded America still had "two nations—Black and white" unequal in opportunity and wealth.

African Americans increasingly saw political participation as a solution for many problems. In August 1981 a first Black Women's Summit, summoned by sixty-eight organizations and attended by 700 delegates, met in Washington, D.C. Congressman Parren J. Mitchell called it "the convulsive expression of an agonized Black America saying, 'We have retreated to this point and we will retreat no further.' "

Congresswoman Shirley Chisholm urged delegates to combine their power and resources, and make "their voices heard."

> The reason Black women have not been a powerful political force is that they have always borne the brunt of the twin jeopardy of racism and sexism. Their big job was just to survive. But they're now beginning to realize the necessity of politicalization.

Ronald Reagan proceeded with his own agenda, which included his fight against "world communism." By 1982 the administration arms shipments to foreign buyers amounted to 21 billion dollars. This, said the Black Congressional Caucus, amounted to "an entitlement program" for U.S. arms makers, the U.S. military and anti-Communist dictators.

Reagan reduced taxes for the poor by 8 percent, for the wealthy by 35 percent and for corporations by 40 percent. These cuts then became excuses to trim programs such as food stamps, Medicare, student loans, child nutrition, legal services for the poor, and Aid to Families with Dependent Children.

By 1982 the administration had eliminated 80 percent of the funds for the Youth Employment Demonstrations Project, 20 percent of funds from the Summer Youth Program, 27 percent of funds for day care centers for children of working parents. A job-training program that had aided five hundred thousand people the previous year was ended. For the poor, including many people of color, life became more grim.

In 1982 the Black unemployment rate reached 18.9 percent, more than double the white 8.4-percent rate. Chicago had 616,000 people at work in 1970 and only 277,000 in 1982. Entry-level jobs dried up. "Now you can't find any job," said a Black male of twenty. A Chicago man of thirty said, "There just aren't any starting companies here."

The nation's economic picture improved over the next three years, and the white jobless rate fell to 6.2 percent. But the African American rate hovered at 16.3 percent. Half of Black teenagers had no jobs. In 1983 Americans living in poverty increased by almost a million a year, and the total rose to 35,300,000, the highest in eighteen years. On average African American workers consistently made less than whites of the same age, education, talent, and occupations.

To sell his cuts in social programs to the country, Reagan publicly denounced "welfare cheats." He told quaint anecdotes about recipients who used food stamps to buy liquor, or "welfare queens" who lived a life of ease at taxpayer expense.

Few learned that the average yearly family welfare check was $4,000, and that it cost taxpayers little. The federal share of the cost for Aid to Families with Dependent Children (AFDC) was only 1 percent of the federal budget. The average state share was 3.4 percent of state budgets.

Most recipients were women and children, many were people of color, and AFDC was designed to humiliate and offer beneficiaries too little. Chairwoman Johnnie Tillmon of the National Welfare Rights Organization termed welfare "a woman's issue . . . a matter of survival." Tillmon said:

> . . . male society tells [a lot of lies] about welfare mothers; that AFDC mothers are immoral, that AFDC mothers are lazy, misuse their welfare checks, spend it all on booze and are stupid and incompetent.
>
> If people are willing to believe these lies, it's partly because they're just special versions of lies that society tells about all women.

The president's words impacted on many citizens who were unemployed, underemployed, or unable to realize their dreams. Americans fearful of not being able to meet mortgage payments or afford health care saw a welfare system on TV that featured inner cities and people of color. The media falsely conveyed the idea that most recipients were unwed teen mothers of color who had children to gain additional benefits. It was true many people of color had landed on welfare rolls. It was also true, but rarely stated, that two-thirds of welfare recipients were white.

White House warnings about "reverse discrimination" told the public that people of color menaced democratic rights and principles. The president's harping on "welfare queens" called poor women and people of color a major U.S. economic threat.

Individuals rarely chose to be jobless or live on government money. But most starting and unskilled jobs paid little, and few offered health insurance. By 1984 unmarried women headed 20 percent of white and 50 percent of African American households. More than half of Black and more than a fourth of white children lived in poverty.

Before Caryn Johnson became Whoopi Goldberg and won an Academy Award, she lived poor in New York City. Divorced and with her daughter, Alexandrea, to raise for five years, she had to depend on welfare.

> I wasn't raised in a welfare household, so this was a tough thing to do. But I'm glad they were there, although it's a system I've come to see, in hindsight, that's devised for you not to get off. It's demeaning and dehumanizing.

Reaganomics also hurt family farming. Huge agricultural conglomerates had driven many small farmers from their lands. The U.S. Department of Agriculture (USDA) favored the richest 10 percent of farmers with more than two-thirds of benefits. In Louisiana only 5 percent of USDA funds reached family farmers. Only a fourth of African American farmers received any USDA assistance.

In 1910 Black Southern farmers numbered more than a million and owned fifteen million acres. In 1980 they were a dying breed of less than a million and were losing their land at the rate of one thousand acres a day. Most owned forty to eighty acres, far less than whites and, on average, were twenty years older than white farmers.

Reverend A. J. McKnight left Brooklyn, New York, for Louisiana and became president of a National Black Survival Fund to aid Black farmers. "When I first came to St. Landry's Parish in 1953, there were more than six thousand Black farmers. But today," he said in 1983, "you have difficulty finding more than sixty." In St. Landry's Parish, unemployment for people of color stood at 30 percent.

Reversing Civil Rights Gains

President Reagan moved quickly to end the federal role in civil rights enforcement. In 1982 he did not support renewal of the Voting Rights Law until inundated with public demands. He also announced plans to reverse an eleven-year federal policy that denied tax exemption to private colleges which discriminated on racial grounds. Public uproar persuaded Reagan to abandon this policy.

In North Carolina, Attorney General Ed Meese sued in court to oppose a voting plan recommended by the Carter White House to increase African American voters. Federal attorneys insisted the Carter plan discriminated against white voters. Julius Chambers, head of the NAACP Legal Defense Fund (LDF), witnessed many policy changes:

> LDF used to be able to count on the federal government as an active partner in civil rights enforcement. Since 1981, the department is more often than not fighting us every step of the way in voting rights, school desegregation, equal opportunity, and affirmative action. I felt the weight of the burden of this change. Battling the federal government is both disheartening and expensive.

The White House also developed strategies to divide foes and develop allies in the Black middle class. Protest leaders, Reagan claimed, held power largely by fanning discontent among members. "Think tanks" such as the Lincoln Institute for Research and Education in Washington, D.C., encouraged African Americans to challenge liberal arguments.

A Lincoln Institute report in 1980 blamed African American unemployment on a lack of education or skills for the job market. However, in 1983 and using government reports, Professor Manning Marable found, "Black males and females at all ages and in almost all sectors of employment have been overqualified. In 1976 the high school overqualification rate for Black males and females was 52 percent and 27 percent higher than the rate for whites." But Black conservatives who denounced affirmative action and welfare were often able to capture media attention.

In *Reversing Discrimination: The Case for Affirmative Action* (1992), Dr. Gerald Horne described how whites benefited from special treatment. Children of alumni had long been given preference in admission to college, and for years labor unions admitted sons of members over others, particularly people of color. The United States traditionally offered veterans preferences, subsidized farmers, and gave special discounts to senior citizens. Horne summarized such programs in the 1980s:

> Affirmative action was the name given a set of policies designed to compensate minorities and women for past and present discrimination. Contrary to popular opinion, women by dint of their preponderance in the population are the largest beneficiary of affirmative action—not African Americans.

Utilizing white anger over bussing, affirmative action, and welfare, the Ku Klux Klan tried to regain its slipping power. "The Republican platform reads as if it were written by a Klansman," Klan leader Bill Wilkinson said in 1980. However, when the Klan burned a cross in front of the home of a

BALLOTS BULLETS AND BLOOD

How Blacks Have Died for the Right to Vote

An NAACP brochure on the fight for voting rights in the South as a continuing campaign.

Surviving Reaganomics, 1980–1992

President and Nancy Reagan in 1982 visited with African American Phillip Bulter (right), whose home had been the scene of a cross burning.

Maryland African American family, Ronald and Nancy Reagan arrived to stand with them on their lawn and to denounce racist violence. A rise in KKK membership from 1978 to 1982 finally began to wane.

For his second term, President Reagan promised "You ain't seen nothing yet!" The White House further reduced programs for the poor, curtailed aid to small businesses, loans, and set-asides for minority contractors. It even ended self-help programs it once had sponsored. But with military costs rising, the national debt soared to a new high.

The crisis of American education grew as public schools lost white pupils and with this, financial support. Between 1979 and 1989, federal money for schools fell from 2.5 percent of the federal budget to 1.7 percent. By 1990 thirty million people were functionally illiterate.

Segregation had returned to classrooms. In Illinois, African Americans were 19 percent of the population, but more than 82 percent attended segregated schools. In California, African Americans were 9 percent of the population, and in Michigan they were 20 percent of the population, but in both states 76 percent of Black students attended segregated schools. In his book *Savage Inequalities,* educational investigator Jonathan Kozol found that African American educators no longer discussed how to integrate schools, but how to make segregated schools work.

The dropout rate for people of color soared above that for whites. In 1988 California reported that only half of Black children entering kindergarten would graduate high school.

In the decade ending in 1987 white college enrollment increased by a million, but African American enrollment fell by one hundred thousand. Chicago with a 30 percent Black population gave the University of Chicago a 4 percent Black enrollment. Although 12.3 percent of the U.S. population, African Americans received only 4 percent of doctoral degrees.

Ghetto life was marked by economic erosion and punctuated by desperation. By 1985 the 16 percent jobless rate for African Americans was more than two and a half times the white rate. Fewer young men and women of color entered the labor force each year. Between 1973 and 1986 the real wages of young Black men fell by one-half.

Freedomways' Brandon cartoons on the Reagan policy on school bussing to achieve racial integration.

During Reagan's second term, prosperity returned to white America: the median white income rose to a record $31,435. For African Americans it stood at $19,758. Black communities also suffered singularly high rates of crime, drug abuse, and AIDS.

The Reagan policies impacted on federal courts. Of his eighty-three appeals court appointments, only one, Lawrence Pierce, was African American. In 1987, when the president nominated Robert Bork to the Supreme Court, a vigorous campaign by African Americans, trade unionists, and women's groups lobbied against Bork. He was defeated in a close senate vote. Two months later Justice Thurgood Marshall said Attorney General Meese had tried "to undermine the Supreme Court itself."

Marshall was increasingly isolated on the court. In 1987 in a death penalty case, he and Justice William Brennan agreed:

> The capital sentencing rate for all-white victim cases was almost 11 times greater than the rate for Black victim cases. . . . Furthermore, Blacks who kill whites are sentenced to death at nearly 22 times the rate of Blacks who kill Blacks and more than 7 times the rate of whites who kill Blacks.

However, a solid court majority upheld the death penalty.

Bigotry put on a new face. David Duke had marched in a Nazi uniform during his college days and then become a KKK leader. In the late 1980s he had a face-lift and was courted by the media. In 1987 a Forsyth county, Georgia, King Day march was disrupted when Klansmen and others threw bottles and stones. It resumed a few days later with 12,000 activists from all over the country. Duke arrived with Klansmen from twenty states. To avoid bloodshed, Governor Joe Harris summoned 2,200 state troops, "the greatest show of force the state has ever marshaled." Duke was one of 55 men arrested, but his star was rising, his career far from over.

George Bush and Clarence Thomas

George Bush had opposed the 1964 Civil Rights Act and had called Jesse Jackson "a street hustler from Chicago." In 1988 Bush was groomed to follow Reagan as president and easily won the Republican nomination. The Democratic nominee was Massachusetts Governor Michael Dukakis.

Republican managers unfurled a dramatic TV commercial that targeted Dukakis's parole program. While on parole, Willie Horton, a convicted murderer, allegedly seized a white couple and committed a brutal rape. The Bush ad, said Kings Features columnist Christopher Matthews, was an effort to "stampede" conservative Northern ethnic and Southern white voters. Matthews described the ad's impact:

> Race is the fault line in American politics. It is for us what language is to Canada, what nationality is to the Soviet Union. Making a Black man who raped a white woman the symbol of an American political campaign is like placing a nuclear reactor in downtown San Francisco.

Bush swamped Dukakis by more than eight million votes and carried forty states to the Democrat's ten.

Violent racism rose during the election year. Skinheads were alienated white youths who bore a violent hatred of people of color and Jews and celebrated Hitler's birthday. One night in Portland, Oregon, three skinheads committed a cold-blooded murder. Ethiopian student Mulugeta Seraw, twenty-seven, was talking to friends on the street when he was beaten to death with baseball bats. The skinheads then went off to celebrate.

Tom Metzger of the White Aryan Resistance (WAR) had instigated the murder. But in 1990 a Klanwatch attorney won a twelve-million-dollar damage judgment for the Seraw family against Metzger, which put his WAR out of business.

As president, Bush promised a "kinder and gentler" reign. He appointed an African American, Louis Sullivan, as secretary of the Department of Health and Human Services. General Colin Powell, appointed by Reagan,

Portland, Washington, SWAT teams guarded witnesses during the trial of Tom Metzger for instigating the murder of Mulugeta Seraw by skinheads.

U.S. secretary of Health and Human Services, Dr. Louis Sullivan served in the Bush administration.

continued as chief of the Joint Chiefs of Staff, the first African American U.S. armed forces commander. In 1990 Gary Franks, representing a white Connecticut district, became the first Black Republican to serve in the House in more than half a century.

Though President Bush called himself "the education president," he continued plans that starved public schools. Ghettos continued to suffer a flight of leadership and of capital. As middle-class people and money left, neighborhoods became weaker, more isolated, and despairing.

In racially divided America, Bush continued to use the same coded rhetoric as his predecessor. For two years he denounced civil rights legislation as a "quota bill" even though his supporters assured him it had no quotas. In 1991 Bush finally signed the bill.

As early as 1989 the Center for Democratic Renewal found "A racist insurgency is in the process of birth, even as we declare that the laws of the land are 'color-blind.'" That year Duke ran for the Louisiana state legislature as a Republican. Though his election was opposed by former president Reagan and President Bush, he won with only a 234-vote margin, because in an off-year election, in heavy rain, a striking 78 percent of voters turned out. Within two years racist and anti-Semitic groups grew from 69 to 97 and neo-Nazi, skinhead, and Aryan race clubs increased from 160 to 203. Skinheads boasted clubs in thirty-four states.

Chantee Charles, thirteen, at a White House ceremony in 1989 to mark President Bush's signing an antidrug law, surprised the president by also attacking capital punishment.

David Duke had higher ambitions. In 1991 he entered the race for Governor of Louisiana. In a three-cornered contest he first defeated the incumbent governor and then in a runoff faced a former Governor who had a reputation as an incompetent.

Commentators said Duke would be lucky to win a tenth of the vote. Media stars such as Dan Rather and Phil Donahue saw Duke as a celebrity who could increase their ratings. In order to interview him, some agreed not to ask questions about his Nazi and Klan past. After Duke's free media exposure, people from fifty states donated money to his campaign.

Duke lost the election with 39 percent of the vote, and the media called his defeat a solid triumph over racism. The facts did not support this conclusion: 55 percent of whites voted for Duke. Determined campaigning among African Americans and patriotic appeals to reject a Nazi defeated Duke. Louisiana's Jews, a leading Duke target, were also important in his defeat. That year the Justice Department found hate crimes had risen by 550 percent in the previous decade.

The rise of Duke was more than matched by African Americans in positions of power. Ron Brown, who grew up poor in Harlem, became chairman of the Democratic National Committee. Kansas City elected its first

African American mayor and first congressman. More and more cities elected Black mayors.

In 1989 Virginia had a quiet revolution. Douglas Wilder, the grandson of slaves, born poor in segregated Richmond, became governor. In the land of Jefferson and Madison, African Americans were less than a fifth of the population. Wilder won, he believed, as a moderate, conservative voice. He had specifically asked Jesse Jackson not to campaign in his state.

At his inauguration, Wilder said, his voice rising, "I am a son of Virginia." A journalist noted, "Blacks and whites sat side by side in the bleachers reserved for dignitaries. They cheered side by side, fought off the chill wind side by side." To an elderly African American woman it was a "great day, and I don't think things will ever be the same again."

Through their strong representation in the U.S. armed forces, African Americans were involved in the overseas interventions of the Bush admin-

Virginia governor Douglas Wilder (second from right) received the 1990 Springain Medal from the NAACP. Los Angeles mayor Tom Bradley is to his right, and Judge Veronica McBeth is on his left.

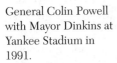
General Colin Powell
with Mayor Dinkins at
Yankee Stadium in
1991.

istration. In 1990 they comprised about 30 percent of the 24,000 U.S. soldiers who invaded Panama. The next year the United States was at war in the Persian Gulf, again with a former ally, Iraq's Saddam Hussein, who had received billions in U.S. aid during a war with Iraq. "Operation Desert Storm" stirred both soaring patriotism and somber reflection.

African Americans were strikingly represented by Colin Powell, chief of the Joint Chiefs of Staff, and 30 percent of the 470,000-strong armed forces. This figure included 12,400 African American women. Reverend Ben Chavis, Congressman Louis Stokes, and others had called for continuation of economic sanctions, not war.

In 1991 a political firestorm ignited over a Supreme Court nomination. In twelve years Presidents Reagan and Bush chose 115 high-judicial candidates, and only two were people of color. Bush appointed one, Clarence Thomas, to a federal court.

Then, to replace Justice Marshall, Bush chose Thomas, whom he called "the best man for the job." As an appeals court judge for less than two years, Thomas had written only 20 opinions in his career. (By contrast, Ruth Bader Ginsburg, who joined the Supreme Court in 1993, wrote 405 opinions on the same court.)

Suddenly Thomas, still in his forties, and the all-male, all-white Judiciary Committee that examined his fitness for the post, heard startling charges. Anita Hill, a college professor, said that as her boss in two federal agencies, Thomas repeatedly demanded sexual favors. Thomas angrily called the hearings "a high-tech lynching for uppity Blacks who in any way deign to think for themselves, to do for themselves, to have different ideas." Stunned, the men of the Judiciary Committee did not rigorously cross-examine the controversial nominee.

For a weekend TV audiences sat in silent wonder as a quiet, composed professor challenged a president's high court choice. Hill's testimony focused public attention on a crime rarely discussed. "I don't know a woman who watched those hearings whose life hasn't been changed," said Jewell Jackson McCabe, founder of the National Coalition of 100 Black Women. "I have not been so wrenched since Dr. King was shot."

In October 1991, by a vote of 52–48, the Senate confirmed Thomas. Across from the Supreme Court building, someone had scribbled on a Capitol Hill sidewall, "Anita Told the Truth." It marked a sense of many that the male senators did not really understand and so could not pursue Hill's serious charges.

For all Americans, the hearings opened a dialogue over a buried, discomforting issue. Some people of color, including women, resented Hill for leveling her charges in public. Others were thankful she had been brave enough to expose the issue.

Thomas reacted to his ordeal by identifying himself with the extremist groups he credited with helping him gain confirmation. He also repudiated everything Marshall stood for. On the day after Marshall died, Thomas expressed his support for death penalty laws Marshall had always vigorously opposed.

Journalist Jeffrey Toobin wrote, "Thomas's every vote—even his every public utterance, written or spoken—seems designed to outrage the liberal establishment that so venerated Marshall." In his first two years on the court, Thomas engaged in a degree of political activity, Toobin found, "unprecedented for a Supreme Court justice." His decisions marked him, said Toobin, as "one of the most conservative Justices of the late twentieth century." In a Louisiana case, a trial judge found white guards had badly beaten a shackled Black convict. The man had suffered bruises and swellings in the face, mouth, and lip, loosened teeth, and a cracked dental plate. Seven justices agreed he had been a victim of cruel and unusual punishment, a violation of the Eighth Amendment. Thomas said he suffered "minor" injuries and voted to deny his claim.

Poverty's Legacy

By the 1990s the national debt reached a historic high, and American business debts stood at a trillion dollars. For many the American dream seemed very distant. Fourteen percent of Americans, mostly women and children, lived below the poverty line.

In the 1930s President Franklin Roosevelt warned citizens about "economic royalists." By the 1990s they held power. The poor 20 percent of citizens owned 3.8 percent of national income. Poverty was not evenly distributed. A quarter of white children and half of Black children lived below the federal poverty line. People of color were more likely to be unemployed, underemployed, underpaid, less educated, out of school, in jail, on welfare, or in trouble.

In 1990, sociologist Dr. William J. Wilson found since the ghetto riots of the late 1960s poor neighborhoods not only had not been rebuilt but suffered further deterioration. Children played in playgrounds of rubble near burned-out buildings. Inner-city have-nots struggled to gain some measure of control of their lives but were losing again. Wilson attributed the failure to joblessness, crime, lack of education, and few real chances. The underclass Wilson wrote about a decade earlier was angrier, larger, more despondent. Hopelessness among the young led to a casual recklessness—teen pregnancies, guns, and violent disputes.

Wilson uncovered a growing remorse among young men who desired to work but could only find marginal positions. Many blamed themselves for their plight. A McDonald's worker of nineteen told him, "I cheated myself of an education. It'll be harder." Locked into a single-class environment, ghetto youths were more vulnerable, without jobs or a future.

Manufacturing jobs were replaced by service work requiring special skills and training. Unemployment rose and with it personal misery. Jobs often moved to the suburbs. But transportation from the ghetto areas to jobs in suburbia was usually expensive and not always available.

Black teenagers, Wilson discovered, encountered huge job obstacles. He found "most inner-city applicants are screened out based on racial stereotypes." Few appeared at employment offices with the necessary recommendations. Employers rarely hired African American males for anything but jobs at the bottom of the wage scale. Many ghetto young people had not worked steadily in years. Some lived in families where joblessness had become a tradition, an inescapable way of life.

Wilson uncovered large numbers who accepted a culture based on joblessness. This class shared a weak, spiritless attachment to the labor force and had little expectation of change. A flimsy hold on work ruined any chance for a disciplined framework for daily behavior, hindered logical organization of each day, and undermined sensible planning for the future. "Don't anybody getting up early in the morning," a jobless man told him.

Ghettos provided few decent role models, so the jobless fed on community negatives such as crime, drugs, and guns. For many people a cumulative self-doubt replaced any likelihood of a better day. Wilson also discovered that whites needed federal aid as much as people of color did.

Marian Wright Edelman was a young civil rights worker the day Dr. King was assassinated in 1968. She confronted a group of teens about to loot a store. "Think about your future," she told them. One looked at her and said, "Lady, why should I listen to you? Lady, I ain't got no future." In 1989, as Children's Defense Fund (CDF) director, Edelman found they "had a better future twenty-two years ago than they do today."

Marian Wright Edelman.

> Today a Black boy has 1 in 684 chances of becoming a doctor, 1 in 2700 chances of becoming a dentist. But the same Black boy has a 1 in 10 chance of being unemployed as an adult and a 1 in 45 chance of becoming a cocaine abuser.

Edelman's CDF was one of many efforts to rescue ghetto children from the domination of poverty. Communities developed varied strategies to keep families intact, build their churches, and reach out to children. Men moved to suburbia but returned to teach young boys self-respect, important values, and useful skills. Black ministers led marches into the streets to retake neighborhoods dominated by gangsters and drug lords. In Washington, D.C., Black Muslims protected local children and convinced drug dealers to leave one particular community.

In Harlem Mother Clara M. Hale raised private funds to support her treatment home for babies of mothers suffering from AIDS or drug dependency. President Reagan interrupted a speech to Congress to introduce her to the American public. But during the Reagan-Bush years federal funds were not used to duplicate her effort in other cities. When she died at eighty-seven in 1992, her daughter continued Hale House and its work with abandoned and HIV-infected children. They relied on donations from neighbors and corporations.

To teach empowerment, Willie Brown, Speaker of the California House of Representatives in Sacramento, welcomed delegations of poor women who came to lobby their representatives. He sat them in the empty chamber's chairs reserved for their lawmakers and spoke to them about power:

Mother Hale of Harlem.

> The people who sit in these seats during most days decide legislation for the state. You must vote. You too can sit here as elected representatives, but you have to organize at the community level with your neighbors.

In many neighborhoods people united to fight illiteracy. In 1990 volunteers enrolled 2,500 nonreaders, largely people of color, in a Brooklyn Public Library course. Congressman Ed Towns visited a reading center and wrote, "They just can't read. But they want to, desperately, and we as a nation must give them the opportunity."

In Houston, Texas, the Fifth Ward Enrichment Program trained boys to become healthy, independent, responsible men. To this end, it coordinated efforts by teachers, parents, and community members. "Positive reinforcement" was its slogan.

African American adult men made weekend visits to ghetto boys without fathers. In Baltimore, Maryland, the Afrikan Men's Leadership Council matched young boys with adult male role models on a one-to-one basis. The council acted on the belief that "no Black boy has ever succeeded who did not believe in himself." The boys learned self-discipline and pride in their culture from people they came to trust and admire.

In prison Muslim leaders tried to help young prisoners learn to read and write. In 1930 more than three-quarters of American prisoners were white, but by the 1980s 45 percent of those behind bars were African American, and 15 percent were Hispanic or Native American. Whites comprised less than 40 percent of the prison population. Many young African American men ended up in the armed forces or in prison because there were few other choices.

Ripples from a Revolution

The revolution begun by Dr. King and Malcolm X survived to change the world. Inspired by the fight against Southern segregation, in the 1960s college students found their own voice. They demanded courses in multicultural America, and the hiring of minority professors.

The African American campaign for voting rights helped win public approval for constitutional amendments such as the Twenty-third which allowed residents of Washington, D.C. (largely African American) to vote in federal elections, the Twenty-fourth ending poll tax restrictions on voting, and the Twenty-sixth that extended the suffrage to eighteen-year-olds.

In 1968 Dr. King's Poor People's March charted a new direction when it united the poor across lines of race and creed. Jesse Jackson's "Rainbow Coalition" advanced this multicultural unification to the political arena.

By 1969 the King campaigns had inspired Native Americans, who formed the American Indian Movement (AIM). Puerto Ricans and Mexican Americans announced "Venceremos" ("We shall overcome"). San

In 1968 the Poor People's March united Chicano leader Reies Tijerina (left), American Indian Al Bridges, and Reverend Ralph Abernathy of Dr. King's SCLC.

Antonio's Chicano mayor Henry Cisneros told the 1984 Democratic Convention how King's efforts benefited "countless thousands of women, Hispanics, Asian Americans, disabled persons, Native Americans, and working people."

Later campaigns for women, people with disabilities, and gay and lesbian rights drew courage from King's ideals and also employed his nonviolent methods to fight societal injustices. In 1989 Chinese students of the prodemocracy movement in Tiananmen Square sang "We Shall Overcome." People who demanded liberty in Moscow, Bucharest, and Prague were spurred by the civil rights drive in the United States.

From all over the world visitors came to the Martin Luther King, Jr., Center in Atlanta to pay tribute to his vision and heroism. Speaking at the King Center, Nelson Mandela said, "In our prison cells we felt a kinship and an affinity with him and were inspired by his indomitable spirit."

The women's movement of the 1970s had its wake-up call during the campaign to rid the South of racist violence. Women who taught in freedom schools became aware of their own oppression when they tried—not always successfully—to convince male volunteers women also could manage political campaigns.

Brave and resourceful women such as Rosa Parks, Fannie Lou Hamer, and Coretta Scott King inspired generations of women of all colors. It did not take highly educated, middle-class, confident young women too much time to learn to fight for themselves. In 1964 the Civil Rights Act also included a provision that granted equal rights to women.

Teacher Shirley Chisholm and feminist Faye Wattleton made outstanding contributions to racial and sexual equality. Chisholm was the first

Civil rights marchers led by Coretta Scott King (right), Councilman John Lewis, Reverend Joseph Lowry, and Jesse Jackson commemorate the twentieth anniversary in 1985 of the Selma March of 1965.

In early 1972, Congresswoman Shirley Chisholm campaigned for the U.S. presidency in the Massachusetts Democratic primary.

African American woman elected to Congress. In 1971, with Betty Friedan, Bella Abzug, and Gloria Steinem, she helped found the National Women's Political Caucus.

In 1972 Chisholm became the first woman of color to run for president in a major party. She faced a new kind of intolerance:

> The harshest discrimination that I have encountered in the political arena is antifeminism both from males and brainwashed, Uncle Tom females. When I first announced that I was running for the United States Congress, both males and females advised me . . . to get back to teaching—a woman's vocation—and leave politics to men.

Faye Wattleton was a daring voice for Planned Parenthood (PP). She was elected to a high office in PP in 1975 while she was in labor with her first child, Felicia. In 1978, as PP director, she launched a vast educational crusade to reduce teen pregnancies.

Even as her clinics were bombed and set afire by fanatical foes of abortion across the country, Wattleton spoke out for family planning on nationwide TV. In 1991, she received the Tom Paine award of the Emergency Civil Liberties Committee and said:

> The battle of our lives is about whether we will control our lives! It's about whether our role in society will remain a secondary one, and whether our bodies will be controlled by the government in order to keep us in check!
> . . . Our issues are not trivial because our lives are not trivial. Reproductive freedom is not a single issue—it's a fundamental issue—as fundamental as freedom of speech, freedom of the press, freedom of religion, freedom to assemble here today!

White Flight in Boston

[*In 1982 Boston's school superintendent, after eight years and four hundred court rulings against segregation, admitted failure. Justice Julian Houston of Roxbury wrote in the* Boston Observer:]

The ironies abound. After a long, agonizing, bitter struggle to achieve racial equality in the public schools, Boston schools are now predominantly black and, not surprisingly, the majority of the students responsible for the violence in the school are black.

They have survived the political exploitation and outright corruption of the political process [and] literally tens of thousands of the local electorate. They have survived, for the most part, the protracted trauma of adjustment to court-ordered desegregation . . . and a tragicomic parade of superintendents worthy of Gilbert and Sullivan.

But now the black students are becoming violent. It is as if they have recently discovered, long after the previous owner and tenants have disappeared into the night, that the system is mortgaged to the eyeballs, that the bills have not been paid in years, and that the goods are badly damaged.

[David Tatel, former director of President Carter's Office of Civil Rights, stated:]

Boston is a great example of how desegregation can be frustrated by public officials. If the school board and the Mayor and newspaper support desegregation, it often works—as in St. Louis.

Dudley Cleveliner, *New York Times*, 6 June 1982, 22. Copyright 1982, The New York Times Company. Reprinted by permission.

EDUCATIONAL TESTS AND RACE

[In 1982 Scholastic Aptitude Tests showed Black students scored on average one hundred points less than whites. This, said Dr. Kenneth B. Clark, the psychologist and New York State regent, "should not be surprising."]

Black children are educationally retarded because the public schools they are required to attend are polluted by racism. Their low scores reflect the racial segregation and inferiority of these schools. These children are perceived and treated as if they were uneducable. From the earliest grades, they are programmed for failure. Throughout their lives, they are classic examples of the validity of the concept of victimization by self-fulfilling prophecy. . . .

Those who have successfully resisted school desegregation under the guise of opposing busing, or who insist upon finding ways of publicly supporting private schools as havens of escape from multiracial public schools, directly contribute to the educational retardation of black children.

The enormity of the problem illustrated by the S.A.T. scores becomes even graver when one faces the fact that the reported scores reflect only the performance of a select group of black students who were motivated to apply to college and presumably took the necessary academic courses toward this objective. . . .

The continued academic retardation of black children is linked to such problems as the rising crime rate, increasing dependency on welfare and the total cycle of social pathology that afflicts inner cities. Attempts to solve these problems by piecemeal and simplistic approaches, while continuing to deny the core problem of racially determined segregated and inferior education for black children, cannot work. If crime is to be controlled, it cannot be done by building more prisons and reinstating the death penalty; if welfare rolls are to be reduced, it cannot be done by identifying the "welfare cheats" and punishing them. The functional illiterates spawned by academically and morally inferior segregated schools contribute to growing urban problems and the instability of democracy.

Kenneth B. Clark, "Blacks' S.A.T. Scores," *New York Times*, 21 October 1982. Copyright 1982, The New York Times Company. Reprinted by permission.

BLACK UNEMPLOYMENT, 1983

[*In 1983 the* Wall Street Journal *found a 50-percent jobless rate for Black youths, triple the white rate. Interviewing Black leaders, it found a fear that "the economic gains of the past two decades are fast evaporating—casualties of the recession, of federal budget cuts, of a president viewed as insensitive to minorities. . . ."*]

[*George Walker, thirty-seven, business consultant and Reagan voter:*]

[W]e were going nowhere fast under Jimmy Carter and I felt, "How can it get any worse?"

I didn't think he'd turn out the way he has. He's failing as a president. He's taken the rich man's viewpoint. He's creating depression conditions for many Americans, and in 1982 that's immoral.

We're moving back toward slavery. Not with chains and shackles, because that's illegal. But it's the same racist frame of mind: if you can keep a group of people ignorant, you can control them.

[*Barbara Hampton, forty-one, mother of five in a housing project:*]

Whoever is putting their foot on our neck, we try to get it off. These are the worst times I've witnessed. Never have we had a president who has done so much damage in such a short period of time.

[*Floyd Norfleet, thirty-two, a carpenter who was laid off and feels the Black community "is at a standstill."*]

Reagan's hurting a lot of small people. A lot of my friends are in the same boat I'm in. It's upsetting because I figured that by gaining a skill, I'd be better off economically and eventually could use my knowledge to make the community a better place.

[*Loretta Lever, part-owner of an office-supply company that suffered government cutbacks in assistance:*]

If we can just survive Reaganomics, we can enjoy a profit. But the economy is getting worse, and interest rates are still sky-high. Most black businesses are undercapitalized and can't weather the storm. Everywhere you look, small minority businesses are going under because of Reaganomics.

[*Brenda Hill, director of the Carver YMCA Day Care Center, reported mothers asking staff members to toilet train children earlier so they could save on diapers.*]

Some mothers are snatching baby bottles from their infants earlier to cut down on milk purchases, and others are bringing children sick to the center because they can't afford the medicine prescribed by their doctors.

Wall Street Journal, 7 July 1983, 1, 16. Reprinted by permission of the *Wall Street Journal.* © 1983, Dow Jones and Co. All rights reserved worldwide.

The Unease of a Novelist

[*David Bradley, author of* The Chaneysville Incident, *in 1982:*]

There is an uneasiness in our hearts, an irritation in our guts; somehow, we sense that even the most well-meaning and fairminded of our white fellow citizens do not understand us, do not believe in us, have of us subtly diminished expectations, vaguely demeaning opinions; that those of us who achieve some measure of greatness are seen as sports, or mutants; that all the horrors of past decades are gone—but not beyond recall. This is oppressive. And it is not a delusion.

David Bradley, "Ads on TV Carry Subtle Message," *Boston Globe,* 28 June 1982, 18. Copyright by and reprinted courtesy of Alfred Larkin, Jr., editor, the *Boston Globe.*

CONSERVATIVE IN 1980

[*Conservative African Americans attacked federal programs for their people as paternalistic, ineffective, and divisive. Basic to this view was a belief racism no longer held anyone back.*]

[*Gloria Toote, a senior Reagan adviser:*]

Governor Reagan's approach, our approach, is the economic approach. We talk in terms of entrepreneurship, and reducing welfare rolls simultaneously with increasing work opportunities and full employment. Democrats, blacks as well as whites, still think in terms of social benefit program from government, the handout, the dole.

[*Walter E. Williams, professor of economics, Temple University:*]

I ask what kind of assumptions are being made about the mental competence of blacks, saying they need the paternalism of the state when other ethnic groups did not. All we need is for government to get off our backs.

[*Dr. Nathan Wright, Jr., former State of New York professor at Albany:*]

Black people cannot be subsidized into self-sufficiency. They cannot get on with the business of life and make contributions to society by being kept on a wall-to-wall covered life raft completely equipped with coal or plumbing.

[*Thomas Sowell of the Stanford University Hoover Institution:*]

It is truly frightening. Affirmative action and busing are stirring up such enormous resentment among whites, even though there are no real benefits to blacks.

[*Other leaders in this movement were Professor Glenn Loury of Harvard University's Kennedy School of Government and Roy Ennis, head of the Congress of Racial Equality.*]

Sheila Rule, "Black Conservatives Seeking New Approach," *New York Times*, 3 November 1980. Copyright 1980, The New York Times Company. Reprinted by permission.

THE HOMELESS

[On 28 December 1989, two Black law students, David A. Singleton of Harvard and C. Benjie Louis of Cornell, wrote of their work with the homeless at Boston's Legal Action Center for the Homeless.]

From our first day on the job, we learned that the ranks of the homeless are filled with capable people overwhelmed by larger-than-life problems.

We met individuals with extraordinary backgrounds: a Broadway playwright who fell on hard times, a highly decorated World War II veteran who lost a battle with alcoholism and an ex–professional basketball player who gambled his money away. Each day we spoke to pregnant women who lost the race to stay one step ahead of the housing marshal, students trying to study in noisy shelters and average families working diligently to save enough money for an apartment. . . .

Fundamentally, there is no difference between the shocking racism that blacks experience and the prejudice that the homeless face daily. Like victims of racism, the homeless are dehumanized, and their struggle for self-worth is undermined every time someone stereotypes them as worthless, characterizes them as shiftless bums, avoids them or averts their eyes as they pass.

David A. Singleton and C. Benjie Louis, "The Homeless: Victims of Prejudice," *New York Times*, 28 December 1989, A21. Copyright 1989, The New York Times Company. Reprinted by permission.

THE DR. MARTIN LUTHER KING, JR., HOLIDAY

[On 2 November 1983, with Mrs. King looking on, President Ronald Reagan signed the bill to designate January 15, Dr. King's birthday, a national holiday. First Reagan, then Mrs. King, spoke.]

Martin Luther King was born in 1929, in an America where, because of the color of their skin, nearly one in ten lived lives that were separate and unequal.

In a nation that proclaimed liberty and justice for all, too many Black Americans were living with neither. . . .

In the years after the bus boycott, Dr. King made equality of rights his life's work. Across the country, he organized boycotts, rallies and marches.

Often he was beaten, imprisoned, but he never stopped teaching nonviolence.

In 1964 Dr. King became the youngest man in history to win the Nobel Peace Prize. . . .

Now our nation has decided to honor Dr. Martin Luther King, Jr., by setting aside a day each year to remember him and the just cause he stood for. . . .

. . . So each year on Martin Luther King Day, let us not only recall Dr. King, but rededicate ourselves to the commandments he believed in and sought to live every day. . . .

Thank you, God bless you, and I will sign it.

[*Mrs. King*]

All right-thinking people, all right-thinking Americans, are joined in spirit with us this day as the highest recognition which this nation gives is bestowed upon Martin Luther King, Jr.

In his own life example, he symbolized what was right about America, what was noblest and best, what human beings have pursued since the beginning of history.

He was in constant pursuit of truth and when he discovered it, he embraced it. His nonviolent campaigns brought about redemption, reconciliation and justice.

May we make ourselves worthy to carry on his dream and create the love community.

White House transcript of remarks by the president and Mrs. King.

JUSTICE MARSHALL ON THE CONSTITUTION

[*In 1987, during celebration of the bicentennial year of the U.S. Constitution, Justice Thurgood Marshall offered an evaluation.*]

I do not believe that the meaning of the Constitution was forever "fixed" at the Philadelphia Convention. Nor do I find the wisdom, foresight and sense of justice exhibited by the framers particularly profound. To the contrary, the government they devised was defective from the start, requiring several amendments, a civil war and momentous social transformation to attain the system of constitutional government, and its respect for the individual freedoms and human rights, we hold as fundamental today. . . .

They could not have imagined, nor would they have accepted, that the document they were drafting would one day be construed by a Supreme Court to which had been appointed a woman and the descendant of an African slave. "We the people" no longer enslave, but the credit does not belong to the framers. It belongs to those who refused to acquiesce in outdated notions of "liberty," "justice," and "equality," and who strived to better them. . . .

Thus, in this bicentennial year, we may not all participate in the festivities with flag-waving fervor. Some may more quietly commemorate the suffering, struggle and sacrifice that has triumphed over much of what was wrong with the original document, and observe the anniversary with hopes not realized and promises not fulfilled.

THE CRISIS IN EDUCATION

[*In 1989, California congressman Gus Hawkins urged a reverse of Reagan-Bush policies on federal aid to education.*]

Our national education crisis is growing in magnitude each passing day, and will continue to worsen unless we assert the necessary leadership and provide realistic budgetary resources to improve current trends. If we want to straighten out our nation's economic muscle, we must provide all sectors of our economy and indeed, all avenues of society, with the best and brightest minds. . . .

It is time for the President [Bush] to wake up to present realities and observe the dramatic changes in America's population profile. . . .

1) 1 out of 4 will come from a family living in poverty. 2) 14 percent will be the children of teenage mothers. 3) 15 percent will be physically or mentally handicapped. 4) As many as 15 percent will be immigrants who speak a language other than English. 5) 40 percent will live in a broken home before they reach eighteen. 6) 10 percent will have poorly educated,

even illiterate parents. 7) Between one-quarter and one-third will be latchkey children with no one to greet them when they come home from school. 8) One-quarter or more of them will not finish school. . . .

One way we can begin to change the present course is by investing in children early. Everything we know tells us that a child's predisposition to learn is largely formed in the first few years of life.

Congressman Gus Hawkins, *Daily Challenge*, 21 December 1989, 6. Reprinted by permission of the *Daily Challenge*.

SPEAKING TRUTH TO POWER

[In 1989, Reverend Bill Howard, former head of the National Council of Churches, Professor William Strickland, and Dr. Malauna Karenga, chairman of US, a cultural organization, addressed the issue of Black liberation.]

[*Howard*] Unless we understand freedom in terms other than achieving, materially, what our oppressors have achieved, we may be guilty of actively working for our own demise. What we may spend a whole history struggling to obtain may prove to have little ultimate meaning.

[*Strickland*] Without a job the young Black male cannot provide for himself or his family; without a moral struggle to reorient him, he becomes a misguided warrior who slays his own people; and without opportunities for real manhood, he falls back on a counterfeit virility that expresses itself in making babies but not in caring for them. (*Essence* [November 1985])

[*Karenga*] . . . I am a cultural nationalist, and I argue that the key crisis and challenge in African life is the crisis and challenge of culture, i.e., the struggle to break the monopoly that the oppressor has on our minds and redefine our world in our own image and interest. Because until we break the monopoly that the oppressor has on our minds, liberation is not only impossible, it is unthinkable, because what you can't conceive, you can't achieve. The key battle, I say, is to win the hearts and minds of our people, to redefine the world in our own image and interests, to grasp self, society and the world in a more radical way and to break with the established order.

African Commentary 1 (October 1989): 19, 20, 62. Reprinted by permission.

MANDELA AND AFRICAN AMERICANS

[Dr. Gerald Horne, chair of Black Studies, University of California at Santa Barbara, compared differences in tactics and results in the fight for civil rights in South Africa and the United States.]

In 1990, as the cold war recedes and Pretoria finds it more difficult to pose as the lonely bastion against Communism in Africa, Nelson Mandela is released, and in his first public words, he gives thanks not only to the A.N.C. but also to the South African Communist party and its leader, Joe Slovo. In the United States, however, the leading black organization, the National Association for the Advancement of Colored People, fired W. E. B. Du Bois in 1948 in a capitulation to cold war pressures, shunned Paul Robeson and other domestic equivalents of Mr. Mandela, precisely because they were perceived as too far to the left.

Only recently, because of wariness about ties to the left of groups like the A.N.C., have the N.A.A.C.P. and other civil rights organizations taken up the anti-apartheid cause. The cold war has come and the cold war has gone while many civil rights organizations still act as if global developments have no impact in this country, while interest rates and economic growth are increasingly influenced by developments in Bonn, Tokyo and elsewhere.

Mr. Mandela, on the other hand, pointed to international solidarity as a major reason for his release. Our left allergy has hampered our movement, has provided fertile ground for the anti-Semitic allusions of Louis Farrakhan, Public Enemy and others, and so in 1990 it is possible to be more optimistic about the situation of blacks in South Africa than their American counterparts.

This helps account for the emotional outpouring among African Americans at Mr. Mandela's release. We were subliminally mourning our own lost opportunities.

Gerald Horne, letter to the *New York Times*, 2 March 1990. Reprinted by permission.

[Dr. Horne also made this criticism of leftist groups:]

The left and liberal movements in the U.S., the environmental movement, journals like *The Nation* and *Mother Jones,* think tanks like the Institute for Policy Studies have less Blacks and people of color proportionally from top to bottom than the U.S. military; the Joint Chiefs of Staff [after

General Colin Powell] will probably have another Black leader before any of these aforementioned entities have Black leadership of any kind.

Gerald Horne, "Parting with Illusions," *ILIMU*, Black Studies Department Newsletter (Fall 1990), 2, University of California, Santa Barbara. Reprinted by permission.

RON BROWN, CHAIRMAN, DEMOCRATIC NATIONAL COMMITTEE

[*Ron Brown, born poor in Harlem, attended college on a scholarship, worked his way through school as a waiter, and attended law school at night. In this 1990 letter to African American voters, he assesses the progress of a race.*]

Dear Friend,

In 1964, Fannie Lou Hamer, a determined black woman from Ruleville, Mississippi, fought to get a single seat at the Democratic National Convention in Atlantic City.

Twenty-six years later, I am the Chairman of the Party, Doug Wilder is the nation's first black elected Governor, and Congressman Bill Gray is the third-highest-ranking official in the U.S. Congress.

That's a long way in a short time.

We've made real progress. You and I have opportunities that were out of reach for our parents and grandparents.

But, remarkable and morally intolerable disparities still exist between white and black Americans.

One in three blacks still live in poverty. And, many more live in neighborhoods with poor schools, high crime, drug abuse, too few jobs, and too little hope. . . .

A recent Urban League study made the disadvantages facing black Americans perfectly clear.

At current rates of progress, it will be the year 2058 before black males earn as much as their white counterparts.

It will take until 2154 before the percentage of blacks living below the poverty line matches that of whites.

Precisely because of the success you and I have achieved, we have a special responsibility to carry on the struggle for true equality.

Ron Brown, Chairman, signed letter from Democratic National Committee, 1990.

The KKK Still Rides

[*Daniel Levitas, executive director of the Center for Democratic Renewal, investigated an active Klan chapter in Blakely, Georgia, in 1990 and 1991.*]

Until recently, Blakely's African American community—which comprises fully half the town's population—had been completely disenfranchised by decades of segregation and at-large voting. It took a federal voting rights lawsuit to force the city council to create single-member districts. Further courageous organizing by a handful of black activists helped ensure an end to more than 100 years of all-white government. . . .

Cross burnings were frequent in the town and surrounding county. The targets were usually white families who socialized with blacks. The local police chief refused to investigate.

In 1990 and 1991, I made that 3 1/2 hour trip [from Atlanta] more times than I care to remember. On one of those visits, I interviewed Charles Weatherford, the regional Klan organizer. Dissatisfied with the administration of the local Klavern, he was eager to spill the beans on the fire chief [and his department which was filled with Klansmen]. . . .

I had the luxury of leaving Blakely before sundown, but for millions of people of color who must endure racism's debilitating and oftentimes deadly effects, there is no escape. And, unlike Blakely, their struggles usually do not reach the federal courts, the pages of the *New York Times,* or network television.

Daniel Levitas, *Poverty and Race* 2, no. 6 (November/December 1993): 3–4. Reprinted with permission of the Poverty and Race Research Action Council, 1711 Connecticut Ave., NW, Washington, D.C. 20009.

The Persian Gulf War

[*The Gulf War reminded Reverend Ben Chavis of another war that had an enormous impact on the poor and unfortunate.*]

We recall back in the 1960s when there was the declaration of a "war on poverty." But the reality was not a war on poverty, but an immoral war on Vietnam. . . .

We wonder aloud why neither the United States nor Great Britain opposed South Africa's 1975 invasion of Angola. At that time the United

States was getting more oil from Angola than Kuwait. Yet, there was no sense of "crisis" or emergency in America. In fact, South Africa "occupied" southern Angola until 1988. We question these apparent contradictions.

In addition, since the 1960s the U.S. military has become more and more multiracial in character. African Americans are disproportionately today deployed on the front lines of the present U.S. military presence in the Persian Gulf. For many families, they are proud to see their sons and daughters serving in the nation's armed forces to defend democracy and U.S. strategic interests. But for many other African American families, there is a sense of anxiety and hypocrisy. African Americans question why they are called to fight abroad for democracy and freedom and yet still be denied full democratic rights here in the United States.

Daily Challenge, 27 September 1990, 4. Reprinted by permission of the *Daily Challenge*.

[*Congressman Louis Stokes gave his reaction.*]

When I think of these young Black men and women stationed in Saudi Arabia, I am both proud and disturbed. Proud to know why they are so willing to serve their nation even when our reasons for being over there are ambiguous at best. Disturbed because I recognize that after risking both life and limb, these young people will not return to freedoms they defended abroad.

Just a couple of weeks ago, President Bush vetoed the 1990 Civil Rights bill. The president's veto was a blatant slap in the face to the personnel sent to the Persian Gulf to fight and possibly die for human rights of people in another part of the world. How does he explain to them that while fighting for the human rights of foreigners they are not entitled to their civil rights at home?

[*Hazel Dukes offered her view:*]

I believe that this is a senseless war for all persons that have to be involved in it. I had joined many Americans praying that we would have allowed sanctions time to prevail. . . . And for all those men and women of color returning back home, they will be faced with what seems to be an never ending war—the denial of the basic rights under the Constitution such as employment, affordable housing, quality education and a fair and just criminal justice system.

"The Gulf War: Where We Stand," *Daily Challenge*, 28 January 1991, 2. Reprinted with permission of the *Daily Challenge*.

Mr. Harvey Gantt of North Carolina

[*Harvey Gantt, born to parents who did not finish high school, got his first start in public housing. Government scholarships sent him and his four sisters to college. As mayor of Charlotte, North Carolina, he challenged Senator Jesse Helms.*]

I ran last year as a proud Democrat against Jesse Helms in North Carolina. We waged a campaign full of hope and, while we fell short on election day, we learned some important lessons. . . .

The first and most important lesson is this one: We progressive Democrats have to got to stop hiding from our own beliefs. We've got to be ourselves.

The promise of America was made real to my parents with the assistance of government, and the belief they had—deep down—that they could make it. Government didn't give them that belief, but it certainly helped make things happen in their lives.

Government can be bad, wasteful and bureaucratic—but it can also be good and uplifting. It can make a difference. We can use government to face the challenges here at home. . . .

Two thousand kids drop out of high school every day—the equivalent of forty bus loads of kids being consigned to the junk heaps of society every 24 hours. People know we can do better than that. . . .

In my campaign, we refused to allow Jesse [Helms] to define the value I represented.

Sure, he tried. He said I would destroy unborn babies. He said I would allow drug dealers to go free. He said I would promote quotas which inhibit advancement.

This type of demagoguery must be stopped.

I campaigned not by responding to every attack or by backing away from my beliefs. Rather, I vigorously defended who I am—and I openly attacked Jesse Helms's hate-and-fear-based politics. . . .

As the campaign drew to a close, we had Jesse Helms on the defensive. By standing up proudly for progressive values and by talking about those values in plain, everyday language, we put our campaign on the road to victory. . . . [Then] Jesse Helms and the Republicans played the race card. They skillfully manipulated economic fears and the quota issue to scare and divide my state.

Harvey Gantt, *Daily Challenge*, 1 August 1991, 5. Reprinted by permission of the *Daily Challenge*.

BLACK WOMEN AND CLARENCE THOMAS

[In 1991, 1,603 women of African descent signed this letter entitled "African American Women in Defense of Ourselves."]

As women of African descent, we are deeply troubled by the recent nomination, confirmation and seating of Clarence Thomas as an Associate Justice of the U.S. Supreme Court. We know the presence of Clarence Thomas on the Court will be continually used to divert attention from historic struggles for social justice through suggestions that the presence of a Black man on the Supreme Court constitutes an assurance that the rights of African Americans will be protected. Clarence Thomas' public record is ample evidence this will not be true. . . . The seating of Clarence Thomas is an affront not only to African American women and men, but to all people concerned with social justice.

We are particularly outraged by the racist and sexist treatment of Professor Anita Hill, an African American woman who was maligned and castigated for daring to speak publicly of her own experience of sexual abuse. The malicious defamation of Professor Hill insulted all women of African descent and sent a dangerous message to any woman who might contemplate a sexual harassment complaint. . . .

Many have erroneously portrayed the allegations against Clarence Thomas as an issue of either gender or race. As women of African descent, we understand sexual harassment as both. We further understand that Clarence Thomas outrageously manipulated the legacy of lynching in order to shelter himself from Anita Hill's allegations. To deflect attention away from the reality of sexual abuse in African American women's lives, he trivialized and misrepresented this painful part of African American people's history. This country, which has a long legacy of racism and sexism, has never taken the sexual abuse of Black women seriously. . . .

As women of African descent, we express our vehement opposition to the policies represented by the placement of Clarence Thomas on the Supreme Court. The Bush administration, having obstructed the passage of civil rights legislation, impeded the extension of unemployment compensation, cut student aid and dismantled social welfare programs, has continually demonstrated that it is not operating in our best interests. Nor is this appointee. We pledge ourselves to continue to speak out in defense of one another, in defense of the African American community and against those who are hostile to social justice no matter what color they are. No one will speak for us but ourselves.

"African American Women in Defense of Ourselves," *New York Times,* 17 November 1991, 53 (Campus Life section, paid advertisement).

23 URBAN POLITICS IN THE REAGAN-BUSH ERA

In 1957, Little Rock, Arkansas, witnessed a celebrated constitutional confrontation over the desegregation of Central High School. A quarter century later the city had an African American mayor and city manager. Local banks had Black vice presidents. The state legislature's 135 members included five African Americans. Nathaniel Hill, the African American director of human resources for the city, said the 1964 Civil Rights Law helped people of color "move into the business world and into better jobs. If it weren't for that, I wouldn't be here today." Central High School, 53 percent African American, sent its graduates into a different world.

To Win City Hall

By the 1980s cities were dangerous places to live. Rich and middle classes felt outnumbered by the poor and threatened by the homeless. Ghetto residents had to contend with less work, worse housing, and more crime than other areas. To James Baldwin, police officers had always been "an occupying soldier in a bitterly hostile country."

Mayor Lottie H. Shackleford was both the first woman and first African American to be elected in Little Rock, Arkansas.

Rare, indeed, is the Harlem citizen, from the most circumspect church member to the most shiftless adolescent, who does not have a long tale to tell of police incompetence, injustice, or brutality. I myself have witnessed and endured it more than once.

In 1982 Los Angeles Police Chief Daryl Gates tried to explain why a Black man had died from a police "choke hold." Blacks might be more vulnerable to choke hold injuries, Gates told the *LA Times,* because their "veins and arteries do not open up as fast as they do on normal people." In 1993, and many deaths later, New York City ordered an end to police use of choke holds. But choke holds by police continued to kill people of color.

Education had been the pathway to the American dream, but urban schools now failed to educate children of color. Compared to suburban schools, inner-city schools had older, more run-down buildings, less experienced teachers, and dated books and instructional materials. Suburban schools averaged $6,200 per pupil costs, but the largest forty-seven urban school systems—educating only 5 percent of whites in school but 37 percent of African Americans—spent $5,200.

In 1993 Harvard University issued a report that showed segregation entrenched in U.S. classrooms. "The civil rights impulse from the 1960s is dead in the water and the ship is floating backward toward the shoals of racial segregation," said its author Professor Gary Orfield. NAACP education director Dr. Beverly Cole said while the NAACP supports integration "at the present time, we are more concerned with the quality of education and this had to take precedence over whether schools are integrated."

Of the 42 million students enrolled in school from 1991–1992, 16.4 percent were African American and 67.4 percent white. However, in inner cities fifteen of sixteen Black students were in schools largely with other students of color, and in middle-size cities the figure for African Americans was 63 percent. The report found that school budgets and administrative practices perpetuate "the educational inequality of minority students."

Many of the brightest pupils of color reported their teachers treated them as poor learners, talked down to them, and guidance counselors did not recommend they go on to college. Guy Bluford, the first African American astronaut, was told by a guidance counselor he was only smart enough for a trade school.

States routinely voted city schools less funds than wealthier suburban districts. In 1993 Johns Hopkins University education professor Robert Slavin returned from the Netherlands and said, "For every gilder they spend on a middle-class child, they spend 1.25 on a lower-class child and 1.90 on a minority child." He added, "No industrialized countries give the poorest children the least, except the U.S. and South Africa, perhaps for the same reason."

Each day thousands of children were afraid to walk to school and afraid to walk in school hallways. By 1992 New York City schools had had 5,761 violent incidents. One in five high school students regularly carried a weapon to class.

Under these conditions urban politics began to change color. In 1974 African American mayors numbered 108, and by 1982 the figure had soared to 206.

Nineteen eighty-three was a turning point. Tom Bradley, the popular mayor of Los Angeles and the only African American then governing a major city, ran for governor of California. The most populous state in the Union had a Black population of less than 9 percent, but Bradley lost by less than fifty thousand votes. Some said prejudice had caused his defeat. Others saw a strong showing in his vote and a new vision for the country.

Chicago was the scene of a portentous primary triumph. Harold Washington defeated the Democratic political machine and its Mayor, Jane Byrne. Washington described a glacial change for his people:

> We were slow to move from the protest movement into politics. We were lulled to sleep thinking that passing a few laws was enough. But we've got to be involved in mainstream political activity. That's what's happening here in Chicago. And that's the lesson that's going out across the country.

Elected to a second term as Chicago's mayor in April 1987, Harold Washington greets his cheering supporters.

Washington, with a 51 percent vote, won Chicago's city hall. His inaugural speech celebrated "a multiethnic, multiracial, multilanguage city" as "a source of our stability and strength." Solving Chicago's immense problems, he said, was like "wrestling an alligator" . . . then he wrestled the beast. Beginning with himself, he reduced the salaries of top officials. He also opened city records to the public. In 1987 he easily won reelection with 20 percent of the white and 57 percent of the Hispanic vote.

Black electoral strength was expressed in other places. Mayor Richard Hatcher won his fourth term in Gary, Indiana, Thirman Milner won his second term in Hartford, Connecticut, and Richard Arrington won his second term in Birmingham, this time gaining 20 percent of the white vote. Harvey Gantt became the first Black mayor of Charlotte, North Carolina, and James Sharp, Jr., won in Flint, Michigan. In both cities whites formed a huge electoral majority.

In Cleveland ten of twenty-one council posts were won by Blacks. Melvin King, who became the first African American to win a mayoral primary in Boston, became its Democratic nominee. By the end of 1983, thirty-one African Americans had been elected to city halls, more than in any previous year. Most had significant white support.

By the year's end, more than 5,400 African Americans held elective office, 240 as mayors and 350 in state legislatures. Reversing an eight-year decline, the number of Black elected officials rose by 8.6 percent. African Americans governed four of America's largest city halls.

To Eddie N. Williams, president of the Joint Center for Political Studies, Reaganomics had mobilized people. "Blacks," he said, "were being ignored and felt their backs were against the wall. Therefore they felt they had to come out and vote and be politically active. The alternative was to throw bricks." He continued, "With major victories in numerous places, the attitude became, 'We can do it.' " That upbeat phrase, he said, had come from a dynamic Jesse Jackson.

"Run, Jesse, Run!"

Jesse Jackson was a man who had tried various jobs and demonstrated many talents when he decided to run for president. He had never held office, but he had worked alongside Dr. King, run his own civil rights organization, "Operation Push," and had built the Democratic party in Chicago. By 1982 the Gallup Poll placed him ninth in popularity among Americans, by 1983 he was sixth, and by 1984 he rated third, trailing only President Reagan and Pope John Paul II.

In 1983 he increasingly addressed youthful crowds who shouted, "Run, Jesse, Run!" In August, at the twentieth anniversary of the march on Washington, Jackson told how Reagan won New York, Massachusetts, and nine Southern states by less than the number of unregistered African American voters. He became enthusiastic: "Hands that picked cotton in 1884," he concluded, "will pick the president in 1984."

> The Rainbow Coalition [Jackson's organization] represents promise and power, but we must focus on the strength and courage of David, not just on the tyranny of Goliath. The repressive Reagan regime won because David did not use all of his political rocks . . . Little David, your time has come.

A week before the 1983 election, Jackson announced his candidacy. He favored drastic cuts in war spending and promised to unite voters across lines of race and religion and to fight big business interests for a fairer distribution of America's rich resources.

> This nation needs a new industrial policy. Workers must share in policy making, profits, and risks. We can't allow the corporations to take our tax dollars and put dioxin in the earth and pollute the ground.

Jackson's first action was, with Minister Louis Farrakhan of the Nation of Islam, to fly to Syria, where he convinced President Hassad to release Lt. Robert Goodman, a U.S. flyer it had shot down and imprisoned. President Reagan welcomed Jackson and Goodman at the White House. But to some Jackson's dramatic feat was less an act of diplomacy than "grandstanding"—playing to the crowd.

Jackson's candidacy was not well received among Black leaders. Benjamin Hooks and others feared he might lose "our voice in selecting the white candidate who will be the Democratic choice." However, in debates with other nominees, senators, and governors, Jackson demonstrated a strong command of world issues and a fiery brand of oratory. His Rainbow Coalition, he said, sought to find people's economic "common ground" and a moral "higher ground."

Jackson also introduced a new issue to U.S. politics: imposing sanctions on South Africa until it ended apartheid and released jailed freedom fighter Nelson Mandela. The other candidates and the Democratic platform adopted the demand for sanctions.

On the twentieth anniversary of the 1963 March on Washington, thousands celebrated in Washington led by Jesse Jackson (right), D.C. congressman Walter Fountroy, Coretta Scott King, and Reverend Joseph Lowry.

With a tireless fervor, Jackson increased voter registration and brought out a record three million African Americans, 18 percent of Democratic primary voters. In Illinois and New York, Jackson placed second behind Mondale, and he carried Louisiana and the District of Columbia. In New York his campaign brought out the largest Black vote in state history.

Jackson also stumbled badly. He offhandedly characterized New York City as "Hymietown," a derogatory reference to its Jews. Though he immediately and repeatedly apologized, he had damaged his credibility about maintaining a moral higher ground. His foes harped on his remark, tied it to his embrace of Yasir Arafat and to Reverend Farrakhan. Jackson denounced anti-Semitism. But he refused to renounce Farrakhan, who supplied a corps of Nation of Islam bodyguards to protect Jackson's family after death threats were made.

The white media kept reminding the public of Jackson's "Hymietown" remark. But press criticism solidified support from his African American base of support. Reported Michael Robinson, director of the Media Center at George Washington University:

In an apparent paradox of press power, Jackson seemed to do better in the campaign as his press got worse. Jackson's best press preceded his worst showing at the polls, his worst press preceded his best electoral performance.

Jackson finally ended his ties to Farrakhan after a speech in which Farrakhan assailed Israel's birth as "an outlaw act." Jackson had only three hundred delegates at the Democratic Convention, but his speech was its high point:

Our time has come. We must leave the racial battleground and find the economic common ground and moral higher ground. Americans, our time has come.

He again apologized for errors: "God is not yet finished with me."

At the polls, Reagan won with 59 percent of the vote, forty-nine states, and 525 electoral votes. Jackson had registered millions, solidified ten million African American voters behind his party, and had helped in the election of more than six thousand Black officials. However, his Rainbow Coalition did not become a permanent organization in each state and city. It had a Chicago national office that grew few local roots, and Jackson was its voice.

Under Reaganomics, urban life became worse. In 1988 Urban League president John Jacob summarized the previous seven years: "While America was riding an economic boom, Black poverty rose and we've slipped further from our goal of parity with white citizens." By 1986 African Americans' political clout rose to new heights, with 6,370 elected officials out of 490,000, or 1.3 percent of the total.

In 1988 when Jackson again ran, his new slogan, "Keep hope alive," was a measure of ghetto desperation. Another measure was the solid support he received from African American officials and public figures who had opposed his 1984 effort.

Jackson picked up steam quickly with spectacular gains in early primaries. He carried Alabama, Georgia, Mississippi, Louisiana, and Virginia and placed second in Massachusetts, Missouri, North Carolina, and Texas. Then he carried Michigan with its white voting majority. For a moment many thought America had changed enough that a Jesse Jackson might run for president. Vermont and Alaska, states with few people of color, dropped into his column.

By March, Jackson, Albert Gore, and Michael Dukakis were locked in a battle. But in New York City Mayor Ed Koch personally attacked Jackson, saying any Jews who voted for him were "crazy."

Jackson lost the state, and Dukakis gained enough delegates for the nomination. But even in defeat Jackson had altered the course of history. He had carried New York City, paving the way for Koch's defeat in 1989 and the election of the Big Apple's first African American mayor.

Jackson entered the Democratic Convention with a delegate count close behind Dukakis. His speech, seen by millions on TV, again was a dull convention's high point. Though Jackson saw himself as a logical choice for the vice presidential nomination, he was ignored. When Dukakis virtually treated him as a liability, Jackson's effort waned. Dukakis, a weak campaigner, unwilling to counterpunch when attacked, was trounced by George Bush.

The Big Apple

The Reagan Revolution, especially its cutbacks in financial aid impacted all of American life, especially cities. New York City was marked by crime, drug use, police brutality, unemployment, deteriorating housing, schools, and public transportation. Mayor Ed Koch had taken part in civil rights activities in Mississippi in the 1960s. But in the 1980s the Koch who ruled the Big Apple was a conservative whose policies did not markedly differ from Reagan's. He had little to offer people of color.

Journalist Peter Noel found police brutality on the rise in ghettos with officers often violating the law or writing their own. In 1983 a delegation of ministers and community leaders arrived in Washington to complain to Congressmen Peter Rodino and John Conyers. Their report revealed:

> A series of questionable arrests and allegations of police beatings of arrestees, including those of a young black minister, had pushed tension levels between the black community and the New York City Police Department to a new high. Efforts to deal with the problem locally had been unsuccessful; and doubts [were] expressed by Mayor Edward Koch as to the existence of a problem. . . .

Rodino, chair of the House Judiciary Committee, asked Conyers, chair of his Criminal Justice Subcommittee, to investigate.

The Conyers hearings that September heard many charges of officers using racial epithets and sometimes excessive force. The final report by Conyers included the following:

> Stories were related of black officers working plainclothes being subjected to racial epithets and attacks by white uniformed officers before, and even after identifying themselves as police. A list was shared of black plainclothes officers killed in the line of duty by white officers who mistook them for lawbreakers. Ugly confrontations between the black police organizations and the [white-controlled] Policeman's Benevolent Association were related. "We can't help the black community," the officers stated, "because we are still hard-pressed to help ourselves."

Attorney Colin Moore (second from right, holding sign) and demonstrators at the Manhattan entrance to the Brooklyn Bridge protesting the cover-up of murders of Black youths.

Less than one month after the hearings began, the mayor hired the city's first Black police commissioner, Benjamin Ward, an old friend. But police abuse of their authority did not end.

By the mid-1980s, some citizens made their own law. Bernhard Goetz was a white New Yorker who had once been robbed and beaten at a subway station. He carried an unlicensed gun and rode the subways ready for trouble. One afternoon in December 1984, four African American youths approached Goetz and asked for money. Goetz drew his gun, and without words or warning, fired, wounding all four. As Caryl Gabbey lay on the subway floor, Goetz said, "You seem to need another," and fired again.

Goetz fled into a tunnel but later agreed to face trial. By this time the media hailed him as "the subway vigilante." When police were not around, he had suitably dealt with young hoodlums. Goetz pleaded self-defense, and a jury that included two African Americans acquitted him of all charges except carrying an unlicensed weapon.

One survey showed 90 percent of the public approved the verdict. That included 52 percent of Blacks and 83 percent of Hispanics. White New Yorkers had responded to the Goetz verdict on racial lines, equating young African American men with crime. As potential victims who had to live in high-crime areas, half of African Americans in New York saw Goetz as a man who "fought back."

Four nights before Christmas 1986, Michael Griffith, twenty-three, and two companions were in a car that broke down in Howard Beach, New York. The three went to look for a phone or tow truck. Suddenly they were surrounded by white youths with baseball bats who attacked them. One escaped, another was severely beaten, and Griffith was chased by the mob onto a busy highway and killed by an oncoming car.

Police first treated the beaten, bleeding victims as suspects. Few Howard Beach residents stepped forward to help identify individuals in the mob, and those arrested were soon out on bail. Black rage rose with each humiliating step of the case. Though few listened, Jesse Jackson tried to put the tragedy in perspective:

> The White House is more segregated than Howard Beach. . . . There is, in fact, more integration in Queens County than in the boardrooms of our major newspapers, or any television network or any Wall Street firm.

Reverend Al Sharpton, a smooth-talking man who had met and been inspired by Reverend Adam Clayton Powell and Martin Luther King, Jr., organized protest marches through Howard Beach. Each march required a strong police presence to restrain racists.

In protest over police mishandling of the case, the victims refused to

A New York demonstration in the wake of the attack on Michael Griffith.

testify. Some suspects in the case were convicted of lesser crimes than murder, and all served short sentences.

In August 1989, the city witnessed another racial murder. Yusuf Hawkins and three other African American teens emerged from a subway in Bensonhurst, Brooklyn, to seek a man selling a used car. Suddenly the four were surrounded by thirty whites armed with bats. Hawkins and his friends had been mistaken for Black youths invited to visit a white teen. Before anyone could explain, a boy stepped from the mob and fired two shots into Hawkins's chest, killing him.

Except for the shooter, the assailants were granted bail, and Black New Yorkers were furious. Keith Cormier angrily wrote:

> The bloodstains on the sidewalk of Bensonhurst will be forever etched in my mind. . . . In Bensonhurst, they have a set of morals straight from hell.

Within eleven days of the murder, Reverend Sharpton led a "Day of Outrage and Mourning," and then three Saturday marches into Bensonhurst. About five hundred marchers shouted and chanted, "What do we want? Justice! When do we want it? Now!" Long lines of police kept matters peaceful. But marchers were jeered by residents shouting, "You savages," "Long Live South Africa," and "Nigger, Go Home." Bensonhurst resident Joseph Bono, twenty-two, felt justified:

> We don't go to Harlem; the kids were in the wrong spot. This is Bensonhurst. It is all Italian. We don't need these niggers.

When the leading suspects made bail, Sharpton exploded:

> For them to allow two of the murderers to go home shows you today that there is an imbalance of justice. . . . Now, with murder, we find the assailants are sent home to enjoy Labor Day weekend. Well, they are not going to enjoy Labor Day.

The shooter, Joseph Fama, and three others who had surrounded Hawkins that fateful night finally went to prison.

In 1991, as Sharpton prepared to lead a Brooklyn march honoring Dr.

Activists Al Vann (left) and Elombé Brath are greeted by Julius Garvey, the son of Marcus Garvey, at a New York rally.

Reverend Al Sharpton was stabbed as he prepared to lead a march into Bensonhurst, Brooklyn. He is helped into a car and taken to Coney Island Hospital, where he recovered. His assailant was arrested and jailed.

King's birthday, a white man plunged a knife into his chest. The minister quickly recovered, and the assailant was jailed. In 1992 Sharpton entered the Democratic primary race for U.S. senator. He placed third in a field of four well-known candidates and polled 20 percent of the vote. By then he had moderated his tone and become a formidable community voice.

The 106th Mayor

In 1989, African Americans ruled three of the largest American cities—Los Angeles, Philadelphia, and Chicago. That year the boiling racial cauldron of New York tipped in a new direction. David Dinkins, the great-grandson of a slave, a mild-mannered former marine who was devoted to his party and interracial harmony, defeated Mayor Ed Koch in the Democratic primary.

Dinkins then squared off against a popular Italian-American Republican, Rudy Giuliani, and city politics became polarized. A 5 percent increase in African American voters placed Dinkins in city hall. But a Republican had won the white vote by more than two to one in an overwhelmingly Democratic city. Before Dinkins, however, first-time African American mayoral candidates never rolled up more than a quarter of white voters. Dinkins polled 30 percent. Would the Big Apple lead the United States toward a new interracialism?

The city's huge economic and social problems, including a massive debt inherited from Koch, were not to be solved quickly. Dinkins ruled city hall, but people of color did not gain equality. City Consumer Affairs Commissioner Mark Green filed suits against five agencies who coded job applications by race. Insurance companies, he found, assigned car owners higher rates based not on driving records but on their neighborhoods.

Bank ghetto branches since the 1960s, Green found, "have been shuttered." Many banks required applicants to live or work within ten blocks of a branch but waived the policy for whites. This policy virtually denied people of color mortgages and checking accounts. Green also found African Americans were rejected for mortgages twice as often as whites. In 1990 Green wrote:

> Until the day arrives when minorities can open a checking account at any bank, successfully hail a medallion cab, have mortgage applications fairly evaluated and get equitably priced insurance, there will be a steady and generous supply of grist for the mill of racial anger.

Mayor Dinkins and Lee Brown, his Black police commissioner, had little impact on police brutality. In the summer of 1992, Mrs. Annie B. Dodds summoned police to her Brooklyn home to break up a brawl between her two sons. The police struck down the sons and the mother. Mrs. Dodds, however, was a community leader and took her complaint to the district attorney who had a grand jury indict one officer. To African American congressman Ed Towns the incident proved "that all of us are potential victims of police brutality."

Perhaps the emotional high point of Dinkins's term came in June 1990 with the triumphant arrival of Nelson Mandela, the South African freedom fighter. Following a huge ticker tape parade, Mandela was received at city hall by Governor Mario Cuomo and other dignitaries. Dinkins proudly presented him the key to the city.

In Harlem Mandela received a tumultuous ovation. When Winnie Mandela found that the woman who introduced her, Dr. Betty Shabazz, was the wife of Malcolm X, she threw her arms around her. At Yankee Stadium Dinkins and Mandela spoke to tens of thousands of cheering citizens of every age and color. Mandela waved a New York baseball cap, laughed, and shouted, "You can see I'm a Yankee."

People of color in New York City, not always able to protect the living,

Winnie and Nelson Mandela are welcomed to New York City by Governor Mario Cuomo and Mayor David Dinkins (right) and his wife (left).

found they were able to defend their ancient dead. In 1991 during excavation for a federal building in lower Manhattan, bulldozers unearthed a vast and important African American burial ground dating to colonial times.

State senator David Patterson and Dr. Howard Dodson of the Schomburg Center for the Study of African American Culture led picket lines to prevent further excavations. New Yorkers of every race joined in daily marches, chants, and vigils. In 1993 Patterson announced that the General Services Administration agreed, he said, that "a world-class museum be erected to commemorate the history of the archaeological dig uncovered; that landmark status be granted by the national and city agencies, and that the remains be reinterred on the site."

High Hopes and Urban Blight

In a political development that seemed impossible before 1964, African American mayors had been elected to dozens of American metropolises in one generation. By 1993 people of color had ruled city halls in Atlanta and Birmingham, Chicago and New York, Kansas City and Seattle, Denver and Memphis, New Orleans and Los Angeles.

However, these successes unfolded as urban life sank beneath over-

West Indian Day celebration in Brooklyn, New York.

whelming economic and social weights. Mayors inherited collapsing infrastructures, dysfunctional school systems, rising poverty, rampant drug use, and escalating crime rates. It was a terrible time to run a big city.

Black candidates had to persuade white voters they were public servants first and foremost and posed no threat to whites. African American candidates were carefully scrutinized by white voters fearful they might slight duty and suspend fairness for racial advantage.

Some African Americans leaned over backward to win white votes. In New York City, Mayor David Dinkins, a career politician, repudiated Reverend Louis Farrakhan. He also proved his pro-Israeli stance during the Gulf War by visiting Israel. African Americans saw his visit as unnecessary, and many citizens thought the mayor had more urgent work at home.

Mayor Wilson Goode, elected in 1983 in overwhelmingly white Philadelphia by 53.2 percent of the vote, had to make a terrible choice. In 1985 he confronted an abrasive African American radical group called MOVE. In their West Philadelphia building, MOVE members did not pay utility bills, violated housing codes, and antagonized neighbors. Goode and heavily armed state and local lawmen finally appeared in front of the MOVE building and demanded surrender. No one waved a white flag.

Goode authorized use of tear gas and water cannons. Then, on orders Goode later denied issuing, state police dropped a powerful explosive on the MOVE roof. Landing near a gasoline can, it triggered a raging fire. For ninety minutes, stated fire department officials later, they did not douse the flames because they feared being fired on. Two city blocks, sixty-one homes, were reduced to rubble, and eleven MOVE members, including four children, died.

Mayor Wilson Goode claimed he had no knowledge of the bomb. Louise James of MOVE, who lost her family, claimed that Goode "ok'd the bomb, and he's been lying about it ever since." "The fact is," she said, "eleven people are dead, he's responsible for their dying, and denying it won't change it." In 1988 Goode was cleared of criminal responsibility.

The new mayors arrived in city hall at a time when lawlessness had raised new fears and desperation among middle-class voters of every race. They took office amid high constituent hopes they would curb crime, keep taxes low, and rebuild city superstructures. They had inherited huge debts, blighted economies, and a tax base that was moving to the suburbs. The new mayors were expected to tackle and solve inner-city poverty, provide for the homeless, uplift the rootless, and revive the despairing.

Their awesome task required a massive transfusion, and neither party promised strong federal help. State legislators from suburbia increasingly held life-and-death power over cities. Elected officials were more willing to vote state and federal subsidies for suburbs than cities. It took millions and miracles to save a metropolis, and money was no longer available.

The Reagan and Bush initiatives undercut the efforts of state governments to aid cities. Thirty states provided a general assistance that enabled one and a half million adults who were not elderly or physically challenged to survive economically. By 1992 fourteen had cut funding and thirteen froze levels of benefits. In Michigan 82,000 people lost all cash and medical assistance. Illinois reduced its coverage to six months. Ohio cut its program in half, granting single adults only $100 a month. Massachusetts removed ten thousand poor men, women and children from its program and cut benefits by $56 million.

From coast to coast urban centers lost when states cut back on aid programs. California reduced payments to families with dependent children by 4.5 percent and froze funding levels for five years. Maine reduced funds for low-cost housing by 90 percent. Washington, D.C., slashed housing aid for the homeless by 43 percent.

The federal government spent millions for nuclear and conventional weapons even after the cold war ended. An F-16 jet fighter cost as much as a thousand teacher salaries for a year. A billion dollars spent on guided missiles produced 20,700 jobs, but if spent on education would create

71,500 jobs, wrote Columbia University professor Manning Marable. Each 1 percent rise in unemployment, said Johns Hopkins University professor Harvey Brenner, led to 920 more suicides, 650 more homicides, 500 more patients in mental hospitals.

No matter who ruled city hall, the justice system was infected with racism. In 1991 a New York judicial commission of seventeen legal experts spent a million dollars, three years, and half a million words to find the state's system was "infested with racism." Headed by former secretary of state Cyrus Vance, the panel uncovered "two justice systems at work in the courts of New York State, one for whites and a very different one for minorities and the poor."

Of 1,129 state judges, the commission found 93 people of color, including 71 African Americans. Court officials often allowed whites to use racial slurs against Black attorneys. Vance called the findings "a terrible condemnation of our society."

Scholar Cornel West believed that most African American politicians also shared a major shortcoming, "the tame and genteel face of the Black middle class." He found leaders of courage and principle such as Chicago mayor Harold Washington. Of most others, West was highly critical:

> . . . Black political leaders appear too hungry for status to be angry, too eager for acceptance to be bold, too self-interested in advancement to be defiant. And when they do drop their masks and try to get mad (usually in the presence of Black audiences), their bold rhetoric is more performance than personal, more play-acting than heartfelt. . . . Black political leaders' oratory appeals to Black people's sense of the sentimental and sensational.

By the end of the Reagan-Bush era, many people of color had begun to believe that the federal government conspired against them. In 1990, in a CBS-TV/*New York Times* poll in New York City, a quarter of African Americans said the government "deliberately" made drugs available to poor Black communities and another 35 percent said this might possibly be true. Almost a third of interviewees said that it was either true or might possibly be true that "AIDS was deliberately created" to "infect Black people." Harvard psychiatrist Dr. Alvin Poussaint saw matters differently:

> When you put out theories like genocide you make victims think they have no power, they can't help themselves. It gives one more excuse for not taking responsibility.

Three-quarters of those interviewed said it was true or might be true that Black elected officials had been deliberately singled out by government investigations and discredited. When world heavyweight champion

New York police stand between Hassidic Jews and African Americans who clashed in Crown Heights, Brooklyn, in 1991.

Michael Tyson was jailed for rape, Michael Jackson was tried in the press for sexually abusing a young boy, and O. J. Simpson was charged with the murder of his former wife and a male companion, many saw these steps as part of a government effort to remove Black role models.

During the early 1990s, African Americans lost their hold on the city halls of Los Angeles, Chicago, Philadelphia, and New York. For the first time in two decades none of these metropolises had an African American at the helm. White politicians returned to power. There were even losses in smaller cities. In Hartford, Connecticut, three-term mayor Carrie Saxon Perry, the first African American woman mayor of a large city, was defeated by a white candidate.

In New York City, David Dinkins became the first Black mayor of one of the five largest cities to fail to win reelection. Democrats outnumbered Republicans five to one in 1993, but out of two million votes cast, Dinkins lost to Giuliani by forty-four thousand. Only ninety-two thousand votes had shifted between Dinkins's victory in 1989 and his defeat in 1993.

Giuliani was a Republican who served in Reagan's Justice Department and never held elective office. Though serious crimes (according to FBI statistics) fell dramatically during Dinkins's term, Giuliani labeled the mayor as indifferent to crime and a foe of his own police department. Queens College professor Andrew Hacker said Giuliani's supporters knew he stood for

> turning the city back to white New Yorkers. He doesn't even have to say it. When he talks about crime and the like, white people know what he means.

Columbia University professor Manning Marable said Giuliani won through "a white united front." In 1994, citizen Dinkins found that on the street he was just another Black man. Taxicab drivers ignored him, but stopped to pick-up whites.

However, 1993 was not all losses. Minneapolis voters, 78 percent of whom were white, rejected white candidate John Derus, who harped on the traditional white code words promising law and order, warning about gang violence and crime, and demanding more police. Derus, who also changed parties from Democrat to Republican, was defeated by city council president Ms. Sharon Sayles Belton. For ten years a city council member, at forty-two Belton became the city's first African American and woman mayor. She stitched together a coalition of liberal whites and abortion rights advocates. After her victory, she said, "A lot of people said it couldn't be done. A lot of people said Minneapolis wasn't ready."

Norman Rice, who in 1989 was Seattle's first African American mayor, in 1993 was reelected by a two-to-one majority in a city with a 10-percent African American population. His opponent ran a law-and-order campaign aimed at the white backlash, promising to impose curfews and to hire two hundred more police. In victory Rice said, "I think people understand that there aren't simplistic answers to these questions."

The Black Muslims

Urban African Americans during the Reagan era increasingly turned to Islamic religions that had once provided solace for their slave ancestors. By 1993 almost three million African Americans had joined seventeen Muslim congregations and accounted for most of America's native-born Muslims and 42 percent of Muslims in America. They were from all classes, from college professors and bus drivers to nurses and cosmeticians. One was the mayor of Kountze, Texas, whose twenty-seven hundred residents included 30 percent African Americans and two Muslim families. Classes in Islamic culture, algebra, and U.S. history were held in modern buildings and rickety wooden shacks.

By 1993 Islamic religions had eleven hundred mosques in the United

States, one in almost every state, and the vast majority built since 1980.

Muslims opposed abortion and premarital sex and forbade gambling, eating pork, or drinking alcohol. In urban mosques women prayed in back of men and were not permitted to join the church hierarchy. Women wore scarves, and did not shake hands with strangers.

Islam's American origins can be traced to D. W. Fard (Muhammad), who in 1930, in Detroit, claimed that Allah had touched him with his message. His disciple, Elijah Muhammad, led the Nation of Islam for forty years and argued that "the Black man is the first and last maker and owner of the universe." He recruited Malcolm X as his spokesman, who recruited Louis Farrakhan. Muhammad died a millionaire in 1975, hoping to leave this organization to his son, Wallace Deen Muhammad.

Wallace Deen Muhammad guided this largest African American Muslim sect in the 1990s, a quarter of a million people, toward a traditional Sunni Islam, "a religion for all people." He supported President Bush and the Persian Gulf War and opposed the welfare system. "His stance is always pro-American," said one critic.

In order to build five mosques, Muhammad accepted more than eight million dollars from Saudi Arabia. In 1992 he became the first Muslim to recite the invocation before the U.S. Senate.

Minister Louis Farrakhan broke with Wallace Deen Muhammad and instead followed Elijah Muhammad's Nation of Islam traditions. A fiery, compelling orator, he began his career excoriating whites as devils and say-

A special education class listens in rapt attention to a Black history storyteller.

ing racism was incurable. After a dressing-down by Elijah Muhammad, he moderated his strident talk about "white devils" and "Satan."

In 1978 Farrakhan started his own Nation of Islam. In a break from the Islamic past, Farrakhan chose five women as ministers. Many non-Muslim African Americans saw him as a charismatic political figure fully devoted to his people. His paramilitary Fruit of Islam were noted for their strict dress code—neat white suits and bow ties—and iron discipline. The Fruit of Islam not only acted as bodyguards for leaders but served as street patrols in some drug-infested neighborhoods.

From his Chicago office, Farrakhan commanded a growing and highly disciplined organization with a treasury in the millions. It not only rehabilitated former convicts but issued popular newspapers, audiotapes, videos, and books. The Nation of Islam gained a reputation as a champion of African Americans and a foe of whites in general and Jews in particular.

Farrakhan and other Nation of Islam leaders hurled harsh and abusive invective at their Black foes and sometimes threatened violence. The white media treated the Nation of Islam not as a religion offering salvation but as a dangerous force to be reckoned with. His political role increasingly brought Farrakhan public attention and sharp criticism from most whites. Reverend Farrakhan seemed to relish using the soapbox as much as he did the pulpit, and his intense, fervent oratory were well suited to religious and secular forums.

Civil rights activist H. Rap Brown became Jamil Abdullah Al-Amin and an independent Muslim leader. From a poor section of Atlanta, Al-Amin extended his influence to thirty other cities. Some of his disciples patrolled against drug pushers, and others ran a school for three hundred students. His male followers wore beards and long shirts, and the women wore long dresses and scarves. Women and men were separated because, he believed, "We're turning away from the natural roles of men and women, and producing monsters. . . . We're trying to build a model community," he said. "It's hard to do in America with a liquor store on every corner."

THE POLICE IN NEW YORK

[*As a New York journalist, Peter Noel, who covered many cases of police brutality in the 1980s and 1990s, in 1993 spoke of his experiences.*]

The police have had an adversarial relationship to the black community historically. They have been viewed as an "occupying force." They don't live in the City, they don't live in African American communities, they don't even live in New York City but in Nassau County and upstate. Some of them belong to the KKK or white supremacist groups, bring all the stereotypes of blacks as lazy and shiftless, and come in ready to "kick ass."

Police are here to protect. Ed Koch denied that he had a brutal police department. Police act like Black residents are intruders, but it is they who come guns and nightsticks, shoot up the night and bust heads.

A lot of whites were aghast at the [1993] Mollen Commission hearings. "How could these white cops do this?" But Officer Bernard Cawley had the nickname "the mechanic" because he would go into black communities and indiscriminately beat up black women, black men and teenagers. The Mollen commission focused on this but it goes on every day.

With [the] advent of Reaganism came a resurgence of racism. Police officers at the time thought they had carte blanche to stop black people. There was an erosion of civil liberties. The police played Judge, Jury, executioner on the street.

Now in the subways around September 1983, there was a graffiti problem. Michael Stewart wore dreadlocks, looked like a Rastafarian and he was writing RAF at the Union Square station. Cops, coming in from different parts of the state, thought this was a secret code and it called on black people to rebel. Michael Stewart's was the most vicious attack. He died still in a coma in Bellevue hospital.

Alton Maddox, C. Vernon Mason, Sonny Carson [community activists] were searching for something to bring forth the issue of police brutality, and that case more than any other focused attention on the issue in black neighborhoods.

The Stewart case more than any other brought the Conyers Congressional Committee investigation in October 1984 to the city. But there were other cases. By then police had beaten up a black minister and also the son of the owners of "Sylvia's," a famous restaurant in Harlem.

The Eleanor Bumpers case at the end of 1984 showed how bold white police are, they can go into projects and say, "We're going to kill you, if you don't pay your rent." Mrs. Bumpers was 66, a grandmother, a three-hundred-pound woman, and according to a cop she had a knife. But the police are trained to disarm people—but no, her life was worth nothing. The first shotgun blast tore her finger off—so why was another shot necessary to kill her?—but that is what happened. The cop with the shotgun asked for a nonjury trial knowing that judges can be lenient, and he was let off. It sent the wrong message.

In the Bronx in December 1986, Larry Davis fought an army of cops because he allegedly shot four drug dealers to death. But this was just a pretext to "get" Davis who had been dealing drugs for certain police officers and had his army of people helping him deal. Cops heard he was going to spill the beans about the police officers he worked for. They shot up the place and Davis just fired back. When they finally captured Davis people looked out of their project windows and were cheering not the fact that Larry Davis was captured. They were cheering Larry Davis as a hero—because of the relationship they had with police officers. They cheered Davis and they jeered the police officers.

Taped interview with Peter Noel, 1 November 1993, in NYC, with the permission of Peter Noel.

The Roots Learning Center

[*Founded in 1977 in Washington, D.C., the Roots Activity Learning Center instructed more than one hundred children each year from prekindergarten to eighth grade. Marian Wright Edelman described its program and impact.*]

The teachers, addressed by African names and titles of Mama and Baba rather than Ms. or Mrs., go the extra mile to make sure that their students do prepare original creations for the yearly science fair or leading them in the celebration of leaders from throughout the African diaspora. The teachers encourage every child to strive for success.

The result of their efforts are seen every year in the Roots students' consistently high test scores on the Comprehensive Test of Basic Skills (CTBS), a nationally administered exam of academic achievement. Michelle Sweeny, Executive Administrative Assistant to the Director explains. "The majority of our test scores are in the 90th percentile. Unlike public schools that give the CTBS only once per year for every other grade, Roots administers the test twice per year to every student. . . ."

The African cultural component which is incorporated into every aspect of Roots' programming insulates the children from society's negative stereotypes and messages. Each day at Roots begins with teachers and students forming a circle of love where teachers tell stories, children sing, and they celebrate their heritage. As the day continues the students work together in multi-grade teams to change the learning process of younger children and promote a sense of maturity and responsibility in older children. Through team efforts, teachers try to instill the importance of the African value system, which emphasizes citizenship, into their future leaders.

As with any successful educational program, Roots parents are deeply involved in the school and in their children's educational development.

Through the Roots Parents' Advisory Council, parents donate supplies as well as their time and resources to fund-raising, school maintenance and classroom assistance. . . .

To accommodate working parents, Roots is open from 7 A.M. to 6 P.M. year round. . . .

Marian Wright Edelman, *Daily Challenge*, 14 December 1993, 4. Reprinted by permission of the *Daily Challenge*.

WHOOPI ON WELFARE

[*In October 1992, Caryn Johnson, known as Whoopi Goldberg, who won an Oscar in 1991 for* Ghost, *spoke about her experience with the welfare system.*]

I grew up in a time of great hope coming through the sixties. I never grew up with racism in New York. I didn't find racism until I came to California. Back then, kids had hope.

As kids, my mom instilled in both my brother and me an ideal of what life could and should be, and how we could participate in it. It was never intimated to me that I couldn't be exactly what I want to be. . . .

[*In the 1970s she married, had a child, and had to go on welfare.*] I wasn't raised in a welfare household, so this was a tough thing to do. But I'm glad they were there, although it's a system I've come to see, in hindsight, that's devised for you not to get off. It's demeaning and dehumanizing. I was on it for four or five years.

Daily Challenge, 28 October 1992, 16. Reprinted by permission of the *Daily Challenge*.

MAYOR HAROLD WASHINGTON

[*In April 1983, Harold Washington was inaugurated as mayor in what he called "the greatest grassroots effort in the history of the city of Chicago." His speech celebrated Chicago's diversity.*]

One of the ideals that held us together said that neighborhood involvement has to replace the ancient, decrepit and creaking machine. City government, for once in our lifetime, must be equitable and fair. . . .

. . . I want you to know that the situation is serious, but not desperate. I am optimistic about our future. . . .

We are a multiethnic, multiracial, multilanguage city and that is a source of stability and strength.

Our minorities are ambitious, and this is a sign of a prosperous city on the move. . . .

Most of our problems can be solved. Some of them will take brains, and some of them will take patience, but all of them will have to be wrestled with like an alligator in the swamp.

But there is a fine new spirit that seems to be taking root. I call it the spirit of renewal. It's like spring coming here after a long winter, this renewal. It refreshes us and gives us a new faith that we can go on. . . .

In our ethnic and racial diversity, we are all brothers and sisters in a quest for greatness.

Mayor Harold Washington, Inaugural speech press release, 29 April 1993.

How Many More of Us Must Die?

[*Moved by the murders of Michael Griffith and Yusuf Hawkins, in 1990 high school student Chsauna Jenkins wrote this editorial for a Brooklyn, New York, newspaper.*]

We cannot wait for another Michael Griffith or Yusuf Hawkins to be killed by whites before we act our outrage. We can't wait until another Eleanor Bumpers is shot and killed by a cop before we continue to protest.

How many more of us must die before we realize that the only way to get justice is by being vigilant and militant? We should be grieving the unfortunate deaths of these innocent citizens every day. And each time that we feel this grief we should start protesting. . . .

I agree with the need for Black militancy. For it appears that the only time the authorities really try to deal with injustices is when we protest and fight for rights which have been denied. This action also shows unity. It also sends a signal that more or other actions would be taken if we don't get justice. This is why the authorities are more afraid of anything else than African Americans uniting. I feel that if everyone united all the time instead of only after a tragedy we will overcome.

Chsauna Jenkins, "How many more must die?" *Daily Challenge*, 23 May 1990, 12. Reprinted by permission of the *Daily Challenge*.

ATTEMPTED ASSASSINATION

[On Martin Luther King's birthday in 1991 Reverend Al Sharpton's friends and admirers visited him in the hospital. As he had prepared to lead a protest march from PS 205 in Bensonhurst the previous Saturday—surrounded by police and his followers—he was stabbed in the chest. Moses Stewart was an eyewitness:]

As we stood there getting ready in the schoolyard to join the front of the march, Reverend Stokley noticed a dirty-looking white man passing through the ring of policemen around us. The police line actually opened up so this white man could get in. Reverend Stokley said to Al, "Here comes an undercover cop to talk to you." As Al turned to face the oncoming white man, this white man said, "Al Sharpton!" and stabbed Brother Al in his chest with a 4–5-inch knife. The man turned around and walked away. Reverend Al pulled the knife out of his chest and fell to the ground. . . . Henry Johns, Reverend Stokley and I ran after this white man and cops started to beat all three of us. Later, the cops took this white man into custody.

   [Two days later, as Sharpton was interviewed by telephone over WLIB:]
"I am just like a lightning rod! Therefore I expect to be hit by lightning."

Dr. Jack Felder interviews, *Daily Challenge,* 15 January 1991, 3. Reprinted by permission of the *Daily Challenge.*

VIOLENCE IN CROWN HEIGHTS, 1991

[In August 1991 Hassidic Jews and African Americans clashed in Crown Heights after Yosef Lifsh, driving a car in a Hassidic motorcade, ran a light at the corner of President Street and Utica Avenue, leaped the curb, and ran over Gavin Cato, seven, and Angela, his younger cousin. Cato died, and his cousin suffered serious injuries that left her maimed for life. A Hassidic ambulance picked up the driver, who had minor cuts, and left the children.
   Later that day Yankel Rosenbaum was surrounded by a group of Black youths, some of whom yelled anti-Semitic slogans and stabbed him to death. Three days of rioting by African Americans followed, police responded slowly, and damage was considerable. After the second night of rioting, two Black leaders, Alton Mad-

dox and Reverend Al Sharpton, speaking from the steps of city hall, announced that if the police failed to arrest Lifsh, they would seize him.

In his Inside the Storm: My Role in Crown Heights, *Reverend Herbert Daughtry told of how he and other community leaders tried to halt the rioting. One youth told them, "We are tired of marching and all that stuff. We got our own plans."]*

I knew I had been talking to the wind. I said, even more wearily for I knew what they meant, "Well, I share your anger and frustration. . . . But I hope, however, that you vent your rage through constructive channels." They smiled at me and at each other. I shook my head and sadly moved away. I knew there would be another night of violence.

[Daughtry found that he knew few rioters and that two-thirds were jobless. The riot caused him "a painful admission of failure":]

We did not start it and we could not stop it. . . . Everybody agreed that these youths, mostly of Caribbean background, were alienated, angry and fearless. . . . I have criticized Black leadership, myself included, for allowing such a large segment of our community to be unattached.

Cited in Peter Noel, *Village Voice*, 18 August 1992, 32. Reprinted by permission.

[The next year the annual West Indian Day carnival in Brooklyn featured the Mighty Sparrow, the Grenada-born father of modern calypso. He returned after seventeen years to celebrate the festival's twenty-fifth anniversary, and he had composed a special song for Crown Heights.]

> Preacher man, rabbi or priest
> We must learn to live in peace, live in peace.
> Both of us suffered loss—history will show
> From slavery to Holocaust, the whole world know.
> So we have to live in peace
> No reason to fight like beasts.
> Live in peace.

New York Times, 6 September 1992, 51. Copyright 1992, The New York Times Company. Reprinted by permission.

White Press, Black Candidates

[*Two University of Michigan professors, Vincent Price and Michael Traugott, reported on the* New York Times *coverage of the 1989 Dinkins election in New York City.*]

. . . we found that three-quarters of campaign-related articles contained at least one paragraph mentioning "race," "white," or "black." Many days, there was substantial coverage (more than twenty paragraphs) referring to race or ethnicity. This increased toward Election Day.

About one-third of these articles contained at least one reference to polls and candidate standing. Of these, one in five contained a reference to white voters and one in seven to black voters. By the end of the campaign, virtually every article contained a reference to candidate standing and racial preferences.

Similar coverage returned last spring with "New York's Blacks Back Dinkins, but Whites Don't, Poll Indicates" [news article, 19 May 1993]. The article reported "deep cleavage along racial lines" and predicted that the Mayor "has consolidated his support slightly among white voters who may have feared that he would favor blacks if elected." Mayor Dinkins's advantage is attributed to his "cast-iron support among black voters."

The results of our continuing study echo an analysis of a recent mayoral vote in Chicago: campaign coverage typically deals with race and ethnicity not as substantive social concerns but as matters of practical electioneering—buttons to push to get out the vote. That social and economic differences might underlie what appears on the surface to be a racial or partisanship division is not reflected in the polls or the articles, most of which focus simplistically on race as a source of political conflict. (The same could be said, incidentally, about gender.)

The well-documented phenomenon of the shrinking of white support for minority candidates as Election Day draws near suggests that news coverage emphasizing racial conflict can activate negative racial attitudes and stereotypes among white voters. Clearly, some whites are moved to alter their preferences. The undecided may shift in disproportionate numbers to support a white candidate. And those who had made up their minds but weren't motivated to go to the polls may be stimulated to vote in unusually large numbers.

Letter to *New York Times*, 10 October 1993. Reprinted by permission.

DINKINS: VICTORY SPEECH

[The 106th mayor of New York City was elected in 1989, and in the midst of cele-brating recalled that he came from slaves.]

My father remembers when he was young, talking with neighbors who themselves remembered the days of slavery. Tonight, we've forged a new link in that chain of memory. . . .

Tonight is special in our city for another reason. No matter how tough things got in this campaign, we refused to yield the moral high ground. We held to the high road, and we proved that it is the right road to victory.

. . . we never forgot that the proper purpose of politics is to defeat our opponents, not to destroy them. . . .

I intend to be the mayor of all of the people—not just those who voted for me.

. . . I stand here now as your next mayor because of the fairmindedness and decent instincts of the people of New York.

David Dinkins Speech, TV broadcast, 7 November 1989.

[A few days before Election Day in 1993, David Dinkins spoke to three hundred students and faculty at Hostos Community College in the Bronx. He hardly sounded like a candidate.]

I was born in Trenton, New Jersey, in the old days. My mother and father separated when I was six years old. My mother came to New York to live with her mother. They cooked and cleaned and worked for other people as domestics for a dollar a day. I was poor but I didn't know it. They put their arms around me and they loved me.

I have friends of mine this day, some who have gone, some who have been in prison, some who have become drug addicts. And I know that there but for the grace of God go I. Instead, I am the 106th mayor of the city of New York. . . .

And so we have to understand that if we help our young people and if we will be superior role models for them, they, too, can achieve. And I tell young people you can be anybody you want to be if you learn to reason. And you can. You can be mayor, no doubt about that.

Speech of Mayor Dinkins, 30 October 1993.

POVERTY IN WASHINGTON, D.C.

[*In 1989 Marian Wright Edelman was director of the Children's Defense Fund when it issued a report,* Bright Futures or Broken Dreams.]

Only 43 percent of all District two-year-olds are fully immunized against preventable childhood diseases, a rate no better than Third World countries—such as Haiti.

Each night 1,300 homeless children sleep in shelters across the city while grown men, some of them fathers, sleep in rags on sidewalks near the White House and Lincoln Memorial.

Children are the poorest residents of the District of Columbia. One in three District children is poor a child poverty rate exceeding that of 48 states. Yet the District's median income is higher than that of four-fifths of all states. . . .

What I can't understand is why in the midst of all this privilege, Americans tolerate so much suffering and official neglect, especially among children, in the very shadow of the White House.

Marian Wright Edelman, "Bright Futures or Broken Dreams," *Daily Challenge,* 12 January 1989. Reprinted by permission of the *Daily Challenge.*

THE MANDELA VISIT, 1990

[*In June 1990, Nelson and Winnie Mandela were greeted by a huge ticker tape parade and New York City mayor David Dinkins with the symbolic key to the city. But the Mandelas first stopped at a high school in Brooklyn. Jitu Weusi, community activist and teacher, described their reception.*]

The day was perfect. Sunshine, warmth and ocean breeze. . . .

Mandela's hectic world tour, in which he is visiting more than 15 nations in a period of 45 days, is an ambitious schedule for a young, energetic and healthy individual. You can imagine the toll this tour must exact on the 71-year-old who has recently had minor surgery and just spent 27 1/2 years behind bars.

But Mandela is on a mission. . . .

The turnout was fabulous.

Mandela was due by 11 A.M. but by 10 A.M. people had flooded the field at Boys and Girls High School. . . .

The arrival was swift and sudden: And then Mandela was on stage.

. . . He spoke of colonial education and the white control of education experienced by Africans in South Africa. Many of us, parents and educators, sighed in agreement with his statements as the conditions applied to African American communities facing the same kind of apartheid education here in New York.

Mandela spoke of the need for educational cooperation between the masses in South Africa and the masses in the United States. Finally, toward the end of his speech, the audience cheering his every word, Mandela used the word "love" to describe the relationship between African American and South African communities. The crowd roared in approval. . . .

Winnie Mandela was outspoken and strong. She started off by immediately raising her fist and calling for power. And she electrified the crowd. . . .

The visit of Nelson and Winnie Mandela to Central Brooklyn will not cure all of our ills: there is still far too much homelessness, unemployment, drugs, senseless acts of criminality, miseducation and a myriad of social and economic crises plaguing our community. But the visit gave us hope: Hope that we can solve our problems.

If Mr. Mandela, by spending more than 27 productive years in prison, can change the conditions under which his people live in South Africa, we, by affirming and dedicating our lives to the struggle, can change the conditions under which we live here in America. The Struggle Continues.

Jitu Weusi, "Mandelas' Brooklyn Visit Historic," *Daily Challenge*, 21 June 1990, 7. Reprinted by permission of the *Daily Challenge*.

NEW YORK CITY AND ITS "TWO WORLDS"

[*In a 1991* Daily News *and WNYC-TV forum, former Manhattan borough president Percy Sutton described life in the city.*]

We live in two worlds. You live in your world and I live in my own world.

I live on 135th Street in Harlem, and when it is mentioned that a number of opportunities have been offered for blacks, we are grateful that there is a black Mayor of the city of New York, we are grateful there is a black Police Commissioner, and we suffer any time there is an injury to either of them. We know they are being judged all the time.

We are glad to see breakthroughs, but we don't want the television audience, society in general, to think that a few blacks making it can excuse all of the indignities for all the rest of the blacks. The fact that Percy Sutton may be sitting on this panel with you eminent persons does not mean that my neighbors are resting any better today.

I wish I could wake up one day and not know that somebody is going to remind me of who I am, remind me that I am black. It doesn't make any difference how many opportunities I get, how many jobs I can get for others. It doesn't make any difference what money I gather.

[*Said Dr. Betty Shabazz:*] I'm not a follower of Al Sharpton or some of the other leaders. But let me just say to you that in the various inlets of our city, there are people—adults, children—who are ignored, who are abused, who are treated badly even in the stores. Even in the stores where they have green money to spend. They are not listened to. They have to pay more for a little efficiency than some of us pay for mortgages in one of the best areas and they are individuals who find Sharpton and the rest of them because nobody else will listen.

Sam Roberts, "Metro Matters," *New York Times,* 30 September 1991, B1. Copyright 1991, The New York Times Company. Reprinted by permission.

POLICE RIOT, POLICE REVIEW BOARD

[*On 16 September 1992, ten thousand off-duty police at city hall protested hearings on an all-civilian police review board. About four thousand became unruly and, shouting racial epithets, tried to storm city hall and were barely restrained. For nearly an hour part of this mob blocked the nearby Brooklyn Bridge. City council member Una Clark, trying to enter city hall, was called "nigger."*

Mayoral candidate Rudolph Giuliani arrived to address the police in the street. He stood with his jacket off and heaped verbal abuse on the Mayor. One eight-letter word he used repeatedly had to be bleeped from the evening TV news.

The next day Mayor Dinkins had his say about the event.]

Some [police] were calling out "nigger," for instance. Why would the people in our communities have the confidence in them, that they have the sensitivity to handle a tense situation in the minority community.

[Reverend Herbert Daughtry, who testified for an all-civilian review board, referred pointedly to the police riot.]

I cannot leave this hearing without reflecting on what we witnessed yesterday. As a religious man, it is easy for me to believe that the Almighty was sending us a warning by exposing before us the true mindset and character of those in the police department who rallied yesterday. This unruly, racist—and I would venture to say unlawful—behavior on the part of police officers yesterday argues even more persuasively and eloquently that I ever could against the current system.

After observing this incredibly raucous behavior by police officers, no impartial citizen would not want the strongest measure to ensure civility, justice and peace. One cannot help but wonder if the mayor of this city was treated this way what would—and often does—happen to the ordinary citizen in the hands of these people? It is not the first time, but I pray it is the last. Likewise if citizens had acted in this manner, surely there would have been arrests and possibly blood on the pavement.

Both cited in the *Daily Challenge*, 23 September 1992, 8. Reprinted by permission of the *Daily Challenge*.

THE DINKINS DEFEAT, 1993

[Director of the Child Welfare Administration Robert Little, the brother of Malcolm X, spoke about Giuliani's defeat of Dinkins.]

I listened to the way he played the crime game. I listened to him talk about how dirty the city was and about the homeless. He used a lot of code words that catered to people to say, "I wish they'd go back to Africa or the Dominican Republic or wherever they came from."

[Asked if he would stay on under Giuliani, Little said,]

I'm not about to be a shuffler. I don't know if that's what they expect of black men, but that's not me. I've always been proud of my blackness. And I'm not going to be talked down to by anybody.

New York Times, 18 November 1993, B11. Copyright 1993, The New York Times Company. Reprinted by permission.

A MOTHER SPEAKS OUT

[*Writer Jean Carey Bond's two children graduated from private schools and Ivy League colleges. When the* New York Times *published an editorial by an African American claiming that the only Black people who had something to fear from the police were criminals, she responded.*]

Don't tell any African American mother in this nation that the only Black men who have something to fear from the police are those who have committed crimes. When my son, who is in his 20s, was a teenager attending the Dalton School, he was standing one night at the bus stop at Madison Avenue and 89th Street after leaving a school event. Suddenly, a police car screeched to a halt in front of him, its doors flew open and four white cops jumped out with guns drawn. They threw him up against a wall, patted him down and grilled him, a gun at his head all the while. Fortunately for my son, he didn't flinch; then, along came a white classmate who, peering through the small crowd that had gathered, saw my son and identified him to the cops. It seems a mugging had occurred in the area and, according to the cops, my son fit the description of the perpetrator—meaning my son is Black. On another occasion, my son was in a taxi that was turning onto our block in Washington Heights late one night when he made the mistake of making eye contact with a white cop in a patrol car that had pulled up beside the taxi. The cops stopped the cab, yanked both my son and the cabbie out and frisked them with guns drawn. Given the chronic nature of police misconduct, either of these encounters could just as easily as not have ended in my entirely law-abiding son's death.

Jean Carey Bond, (unpublished) letter to the *New York Times,* 27 May 1994. Reprinted by permission of Jean Carey Bond.

24 THE CLINTON ADMINISTRATION

African Americans had often claimed the police were an enemy. Few whites believed them until the night in late March 1992 when Rodney King, twenty-five, a Black motorist who had been stopped for drunkenness and speeding by Los Angeles police, was beaten by four officers as many others watched. A man with a video camera recorded King being beaten. The minute-and-a-quarter videotape showed King trying to crawl away as police nightsticks landed on him eighty-two times.

Less than two months later three officers tried for the crime were exonerated by a suburban jury of ten whites, a Hispanic, an Asian American, but no African Americans. Before night fell, South Central Los Angeles was in flames. Stores were looted and burned, and drivers were dragged from their cars and beaten. Destruction spread rapidly in the outbreak's first few hours when Chief Daryl Gates withdrew his police from the riot zone. TV viewers had a choice between watching LA burning or the last episode of the Bill Cosby show, a saga of Black upper-class progress.

Rebellion and Aftermath

South Central Los Angeles experienced the largest American urban rebellion of the century. In a presidential election year, voters tried to understand why fellow citizens would set fire to their neighborhoods. Everyone in politics accused someone else. Democrats pointed to heartless Republican policies. The Bush White House blamed Lyndon Johnson's Great Society programs of 1965, but did not name which ones. Vice President Dan Quayle believed criminal elements and declining family values were the cause. Bush administration drug czar William Bennett said:

> The road to disaster has been paved by a corrosive popular culture, educational failure, moral and spiritual depletion and the breakdown of our critical institution—the family.

Others saw it differently. The "seeds of the rebellion," said James Johnson, director of the Center for the Study of Urban Poverty at the University of California in Los Angeles, were economic. Between 1973 and 1986 the average yearly income of Los Angeles African American high school graduates fell 44 percent, and the average income of Hispanic Americans fell 35 percent. Black teenage joblessness stood at 44 percent. The local high school dropout rate soared to between 60 percent and 80 percent. And there were no jobs. Between 1978 and 1989, Johnson said,

> about 200,000 jobs disappeared from the Los Angeles economy, most of them centered in South Central Los Angeles. These were high-paying, highly unionized jobs in manufacturing, jobs that were the lifeblood of the communities in South Central Los Angeles, providing stable employment and livable wages that allowed people to maintain stable families.
>
> What you have . . . is a large population of mostly males who are neither at work nor in school, and that is the lethal combination.

Crack and guns were sold on street corners, and LA had the largest number of street gang members of any city, about one hundred thousand. In the two dominant gangs, the Crips and the Bloods, despair and virile self-assertion fused into a murderous mayhem. Gang slayings the previous year had reached 771. But during the riot, for the first time, the Crips and Bloods observed a truce.

To Professor Cornel West, the Los Angeles explosion was

> a multiracial, trans-class and largely male display of justified social rage. For all its ugly, xenophobic resentment, its air of adolescent carnival and its downright barbaric behavior, it signified the sense of powerlessness in American society.

One in seven arrested during the riot were whites, and more Hispanic Americans were taken into custody than African Americans. Most of the arrested were not criminals or jobless. West found "only 36 percent were Black, more than a third had full-time jobs, and most claimed to shun political affiliation."

The LA rebellion exposed the plight of new immigrants who groped for an elusive American dream. The Urban League's John Jacob said Los Angeles was "a reminder that . . . anger based on economic inequality cuts across racial and ethnic lines." A billion dollars in property was destroyed, and of the fifty-one who died, almost all were people of color.

Minor rioting shook other cities. However, wrote Jacob:

> What is remarkable about those disorders is not that they took place but that there were so few of them, for the conditions of despairing anger that drove so many Los Angelenos into the streets were duplicated in virtually every city in this nation.

TV news cameras captured the scene as rioters pulled Reginald Denny from his truck, and kicked and stoned him until he was rescued by other African Americans. The media were incensed by the assault on Denny. However, Northwestern University professor Adolph Reed made this comparison:

> The people who beat the truck driver was a mob. The people who beat Rodney King were public officials. In principle, if the truck driver had 25 cents and somehow could have gotten to a phone, he could have called 911 and gotten help. If Rodney King had a bag full of quarters in his pocket, he couldn't call 911 because it was the cops beating him up.

Henry Watson, Denny's chief assailant, pleaded guilty to minor charges, and a jury acquitted him of more serious ones. In court Watson apologized to Denny. The two then appeared on the Donahue show, Watson again apologized, and they shook hands. Denny said he had "just walked into the mess that somebody had created a long time ago."

President Bush toured the devastated area, and in a visit to a Black church, he slipped to his knees to ask God's help in solving urban unrest. For many citizens, the president seeking heavenly guidance indicated not religious faith but an inability to understand ghetto problems.

Eventually officers Stacey Koon and Laurence Powell were found guilty of beating Rodney King, expressed no remorse, and were released on bail. District judge John Davies chose to ignore federal guidelines of five to seven years for the offense and sentenced the two officers to only thirty months.

Rodney King, who eventually won a $3.8-million judgment from the city, urges citizens, on 1 May 1992, to remain calm and not riot after police officers were found not guilty of beating him.

Judge Davies found the first sixty-three seconds of the King beating to be lawful. Louise James of Philadelphia wrote angrily about the decision:

> Rodney King was beaten over every inch of his body for 82 seconds. Ask him if it was right. Ask him if his body was able to separate the 63 seconds that is so-called lawful, from the "unlawful" 19 seconds.

Watson, who had spent more time behind bars than the convicted police officers did, was finally sentenced to eight years in prison. King won a $3.8-million damage award from the city of Los Angeles. And a higher court sharply assailed the leniency of Judge Davies.

When South Central Los Angeles tried to rebuild, problems were compounded when white laborers were hired. On August 18, jobless African Americans shouted at white men erecting a shopping center in the riot area. Jake Bellamy of the Black Carpenters Association said:

> You white guys won't give us Black people a chance. You aren't fair. You don't know nothing about fair. Black men can do this work, too. They need to do this work to give their children a better future.

Three days later Bellamy, Danny Blackwell, and one hundred Black workers would not leave the work site. Said Blackwell, "We are saying to the people operating in our community, 'You have an obligation and a responsibility to hire the people who live here.'"

Noted Californians called for a massive restoration effort and 75,000 to 90,000 new jobs. Sixty-eight firms publicly promised a billion in investments. But nothing happened. Riding past the LA's ruins a year later, *Nation* writer Eric Mann found:

dashed expectations, outright misrepresentation and chaos. Drive through South LA on any afternoon, and you will see thousands of unemployed men and women.

The Clinton Road to the White House

Lyndon Johnson in 1964 was the last Democrat to gain the White House with a majority of white voters. By 1980 the Republican party had established itself as the white party. No Republican crudely said anything so offensive, but voters knew it.

Anyone with a TV set saw that people of color were a highly visible presence at Democratic conventions—actually 20 percent of Democratic delegates—and a token handful among Republicans. Each time TV news cameras pointed to the Democrats' most loyal constituents, Republicans gained white support. Further, Democrats were accused of "throwing money" at minorities for programs Republicans said were wasteful or stirred false expectations for people of color. This "careless spending," claimed Republicans, would raise middle-class taxes.

Republican and some Democratic strategists found that presidential contests could be won through a careful stretch for white votes. Americans were gravely worried about their livelihoods in a shrinking economy facing mounting foreign competition. Politicians could not solve the problem and would not accept their culpability. But they could target others for blame, especially those dependent on government aid. And it was no secret that many of the poor and needy were people of color.

Republicans stood on a racial record that was both open and hidden. In 1964 Barry Goldwater, Ronald Reagan, and George Bush had opposed the civil rights bill. To line up whites behind their candidates, Republican "spin doctors" learned to weave a fabric of subtle and unsubtle racial code words and images. The idea was to persuade whites their real interests did not lie with Democrats.

In 1988 Bush captured the White House with a TV Willie Horton scare. In 1990 Senator Jesse Helms faced a formidable and highly respected African American candidate in Charlotte's mayor, Harvey Gantt. A Helms TV commercial showed a white man being rejected for a job as a voice-over said, "You needed that job, and you were the best qualified. But it had to go to a minority because of a racial quota." Gantt opposed racial quotas, but he was a Black man challenging a white man. Helms's manipulation of white fears helped him edge out his first serious threat in years.

In 1992 the Democratic party chose two centrist candidates from the

Harvey Gantt emerges from a polling booth in his 1990 effort to unseat Senator Jesse Helms. He was narrowly defeated by Helms.

upper South, Bill Clinton and Albert Gore. Clinton was a founder of the Democratic Leadership Council (DLC), which in 1990 said of equality, "We believe in equal opportunity, not equal outcomes." Equal opportunities did not automatically produce equal outcomes, but this approach offered no other remedies.

The DLC devised an electoral blueprint that favored "crossover candidates" who sounded like Republicans and relied on such phrases as "race neutral remedies." Democratic policy made no special appeal to African Americans, but national chair Ron Brown and other Black politicians endorsed it. Had the DLC shaped a winning strategy or fashioned a betrayal of its most loyal members? Jesse Jackson did not run and found himself largely isolated within his party. For him worse was on the way.

Candidate Clinton chose his speech at Jackson's Operation Push convention to send a special message. He accused rap singer Sister Souljah, an invited guest, of lyrics that condoned violence: "If Black people kill Black people every day, why not have a week to kill white people?" Clinton's choice of place and issue proved he could "stand up" to Jackson and proved he was tough enough for the White House. His message to white voters was that he was as committed to law and order as any Republican.

Bill Clinton did not mention the Rodney King beating or discuss rampant police brutality in the ghetto. He addressed Jackson's organization, but his target audience were frightened whites. White violence toward people of color had been a consistent part of U.S. history, and so too was a white fear of retaliation. Clinton knew many whites watched rising Black-on-Black crime in that context.

Clinton hammered at twelve years of Republican "trickle-down economics" that had made the rich richer, the poor poorer, and created fewer jobs and more homeless people.

By Election Day Bush's military victories in Panama and Iraq seemed like ancient history. Many civilians had died, but little had changed. "Saddam Hussein still has his job, do you have yours?" was a popular Democratic bumper sticker. Bush also appeared "out of touch" with common people and unable to reverse a steep economic decline at home or the soaring national debt. Without a Willie Horton TV add, President Bush had to run on his record.

At the polls, Ross Perot garnered 19 percent of the vote, a barometer of public repudiation of old parties and solutions. For the first time since 1932 and the Great Depression a Republican who sat in the White House had been turned out of office.

The Democratic Administration

The chair of the Democratic National Committee was Ron Brown, and the cochair of Clinton's campaign was representative Maxine Waters. Some 82 percent of African Americans voted for Clinton, many in key electoral states. "By the Grace of God and your help, last year I was elected president," President Clinton said. The Clinton transition team cochair was former Urban League president, Vernon Jordan. Dr. Johnetta Cole, president of Spelman College, helped recommend cabinet members.

For their preinauguration religious service, the Clintons prayed at an African American church. At the inauguration, fellow Arkansas poet and actress Maya Angelou recited her inspiring poem for the new administration, *On the Pulse of Morning*.

Congresswoman
Maxine Waters.

Bill and Hillary Clinton enjoyed long friendships with Marian Wright Edelman, Lani Guinier, Dr. Joycelyn Elders, Ron Brown, Dr. Cole, Mr. Jordan, and others. It was clear the new first family personally felt at ease with African Americans. Clinton's cabinet choices included four African Americans. Ron Brown became secretary of commerce. Mike Espy, Mississippi's first African American in Congress since Reconstruction, became secretary of agriculture. He resigned in 1994.

Jesse Brown, at forty-eight, became secretary for Veterans Affairs. In Vietnam he survived a gunshot wound in the right arm. He later served as the executive director of the Disabled American Veterans Association, earning a reputation as a fierce advocate for veterans. Brown's agency employed 220,000 employees and served 27 million veterans. His particular interest was in aiding homeless and drug-dependent veterans.

The fourth cabinet member, Hazel O'Leary, secretary of energy, demonstrated independence and daring. "Openness is an affirmative obligation of the government," she said, "not simply a limitation on secrecy." She revealed that in the past her agency had secretly conducted 204 nuclear tests, and some of these endangered the public needlessly.

O'Leary insisted the public was entitled to the truth. "Repression" of this information, she said, left her "appalled and shocked and it just gave me an ache in my gut and my heart." By 1994 she had reduced the number of documents her agency classified as secret by 57 percent.

Never before had African Americans held these cabinet posts. To Ron Brown it was "nothing short of a miracle." He added, "But that's not enough. The president is committed to having African Americans at all levels of government, in all departments."

Lee Brown, a former New York police commissioner, became director of the Office of National Drug Control Policy. Dr. Joycelyn Elders, a committed and opinionated public health authority who ran the Arkansas health program, became U.S. surgeon general, directing an agency of six thousand doctors, nurses, and scientists responsible for the country's physical and mental health. The outspoken Elders told an interviewer for *Emerge,* "It's far better to pay for college, than it is to pay for prison." She continued:

> . . . it's time to begin to discuss issues that are making people poor, ignorant and slaves . . . and allow them the opportunity to grow up and reach their full potential. . . .
>
> If we think education is expensive, try ignorance. And we've tried ignorance a very long time. We've sacrificed our children.

The president appointed Mary Francis Berry, for twelve years a member of the commission, to serve as the chair of the Federal Civil Rights Commission. Berry believed the political debate of the 1990s would be over the creation of voting districts that allowed people of color to send their own representatives to Congress.

In September 1993, the White House listed 329 African Americans in "top political positions." These included Margaret Williams, chief of staff for Hillary Rodham Clinton, who guided her campaign for national health care. Scholar William Julius Wilson became a presidential adviser on domestic issues. But many others were at the level of assistants and confidential secretaries.

The Clinton cabinet.

However, when Clinton nominated and withdrew Lani Guinier as assistant attorney general for civil rights, he stumbled badly. He and Hillary had befriended Guinier at Yale Law School and had attended her wedding. She had served as a Civil Rights Division attorney in the Carter administration's Justice Department, worked for years at the NAACP Legal Defense and Educational Fund (LDEF), and had been a appointed a University of Pennsylvania professor of law.

Some authorities said Guinier's record showed that she "had trained for the job all her life." She based her legal arguments on the writings of founding fathers James Madison and Alexander Hamilton. She also was warmly recommended by Attorney General Janet Reno.

Guinier had angered foes of affirmative action. Once she had said, "Substantive equality should be measured by equality in fact. . . . The process must be equal, but the results must also reflect the effort to remedy the effects of a century of official discrimination." Though some of her views had been policy during the Bush administration, conservatives in Congress and the media trashed her record as radical and called her antidemocratic. Though Guinier opposed any kind of numerical racial quotas, the media labeled her a "quota queen." She eagerly looked forward to answering her critics before the Senate Judiciary Committee.

That did not happen. Clinton, who said he had not read her writings,

Professor Lani Guinier

later said he read them "again" and found her views clashed with his policies. He then withdrew the Guinier nomination. Mary Francis Berry spoke angrily of Clinton's decision:

> . . . The slap at Lani Guinier was just another reminder of the racial problems that demand our attention.
> . . . The Senate Judiciary Committee, even with the addition of women senators, including Carol Mosely Braun, since the Anita Hill–Clarence Thomas debacle, is still arrogant and out of control when it comes to race. The senators cared little for the appearance of unfairness to Guinier. They, like the president, saw that it was in their best political interest to avoid a discussion of the institutional and individual racial discrimination that still pollutes this country.

Scholar, author, and activist Dr. Mary Francis Berry.

Guinier's fate left many African Americans with a feeling of betrayal. Congressional Black Caucus chair Kweisi Mfume curtly canceled a scheduled meeting with the president. Not all African American officials, Berry said, expressed such outrage, noting those in Clinton's cabinet "maintained a deafening silence."

In January, when Clinton was inaugurated, polls showed only 1 percent of the public believed crime was the country's leading problem. But by November 1993, when President Clinton visited the Memphis' Church of God and spoke from the same pulpit where Dr. King gave his last sermon, the figure had increased to 16 percent. The president talked about "the great crisis of the spirit that is gripping America today." King, he said, "did not fight for the right of Black people to murder other Black people with reckless abandonment" or the "freedom to die before you're a teenager."

Not since the 1960s had a president so dramatically addressed problems of African Americans, and his words on crime were widely applauded. Some critics said his speech failed to address issues of police brutality and lax law enforcement in ghetto communities or the media that cast people of color as potential criminals. He did not mention white-collar crime or the savings and loan scandal in which white financiers aided by five senators stole more money than the United States spent on World War II. The president mentioned joblessness as a cause of crime but not the failure of his and other administrations to stem the flow of ghetto jobs.

A New Political Map

As Clinton entered the White House, dramatic changes unfolded for Black America. The most solid demonstration of African American power was the Black Congressional Caucus, founded in 1970 by thirteen members.

President Clinton embraced by Bishop Ford after his speech at the Church of God in Memphis, Tennessee.

The caucus's motto was "no permanent friends, no permanent enemies, just permanent interests." Missouri representative William Clay recalled the caucus's record of standing up to presidents.

> We fought publicly with Jimmy Carter almost every day of his administration. It's no different, Democrat or Republican. We will challenge anybody who seeks to undermine the basic interests of our people.

By 1990 the Caucus had twenty-six members, all Democrats. In 1993, as a result of changes in the Voting Rights Law that created new minority districts, it boasted forty members. These included thirty-eight Black congressional Democrats, a woman senator, and a lone Republican, Connecticut congressman Gary Franks. Many new members came to Congress after having previously served in state legislatures.

The caucus's increased numbers also meant more African Americans would serve on congressional subcommittees. After years in the caucus some had earned seniority. For example, Ron Dellums, long a critic of bloated Pentagon budgets, chaired the House Armed Services Committee.

In the wake of the Clarence Thomas and Anita Hill hearings, six women were elected to the Senate and forty-seven to the House. In Illinois Senator Carol Mosely Braun had been a former federal prosecutor and state representative. Her early life had been harsh. She had survived beatings by her father, a divorce, the death of a brother from drugs, and had had to raise her son alone. She defeated the popular senator Alan Dixon in a primary and then barnstormed Illinois, gathering voters from both parties. In the Senate she was assigned to the powerful Judiciary Committee.

The caucus's new strength also created opportunities for alliances. In 1993 the Hispanic Congressional Caucus discussed a coalition with the Black caucus. Congressman Jose Serrano said, "The Hispanic caucus continues to work closer and closer to achieve the goal of having an extremely good working relationship with the Black caucus." Chair Mfume listed as logical subjects for cooperation civil rights, social policies, and minority businesses.

Senator Carol Mosley Braun.

Some 75 percent of African Americans were represented by whites, and the idea of Black majority voting districts had won important adherents in both races. Such districts, said Mary Francis Berry, were important since "they are represented by people of color who have a determined constituency they must answer to."

The Democratic party favored Black districts, knowing they would probably send Democrats to Congress. The Reagan and Bush Justice Departments favored Black-majority districts, but for different reasons. Each district shaped to ensure an African American representative meant one that drew Democrats from neighboring districts. By simple mathematics this increased Republican chances for victory in races they usually lost. If the Democrats became more visibly Black, this also highlighted the Republicans as the white party.

In some U.S. farming areas, African American political success was followed by economic defeat. By 1993 almost a fifth of African American elected officials were in Mississippi and Alabama alone. But as whites left the area, jobs disappeared and crime rose. Rural ghettos developed. "You're in charge, but how much can you do?" said Jonestown's Black former mayor Bobbie Walker.

We have 1,476 people, but we may have 100 who actually work. Almost all the stores have closed. The town is basically broke. People expect miracles because there are Black people in office, but this town is so strapped, and the tax base is so small, you can barely stay afloat.

Jonestown's Black population, largely elderly people and young women with children, had little work. The Delta Oil Mill, a farmers' cooperative that produced $22 million in cottonseed oil a year, was the major business. It hired whites for clerical and supervisory jobs and most of the laboring jobs. More than a few towns in the rural delta region had moved from a 50 percent Black population in the 1950s to 90 percent by the 1990s, and many had lost their economic power in the process.

Washington, D.C., the nation's capital and showplace of American democracy, had African American mayors since the administration of Lyndon Johnson. Other cities suffered various degrees of blight, but Washington had urban cancer. It was known as the murder capital and averaged a homicide for each day of the 1990s. In October 1993 Mayor Sharon Pratt Kelly asked President Clinton to send National Guard troops to fight crime. "We've got . . . to get real and do whatever it takes to provide safety." Clinton refused the request.

Despite its shortcomings, the election process had opened new prospects for African Americans. In 1992 Jackie Barrett, forty-one, became sheriff of Fulton County, Georgia, which includes Atlanta. Barrett, with sixteen years in law enforcement and a master's degree in sociology, first defeated the incumbent sheriff in a primary election and then swept past her opponent with 73 percent of the vote as the first African American woman to become a U.S. sheriff. "You don't set out to make history, it just happens," she said on election night. "We have a tough road to plow."

In 1965 Joe Smitherman was mayor of Selma, Alabama, when it was the scene of a bloody state trooper assault on voting rights marchers. The violence led Congress to pass the Voting Rights Act of that year. By 1978, of the four African Americans who sat on Selma's council, some had been among the clubbed. Black councilman F. D. Reese described how Mayor Smitherman had changed:

> Of course, we tamed him. He is actually engaged now in looking after the rights of blacks in the town; because of the voting strength that we have. Sometimes that vote can make them smile when they want to frown.

In 1993 Smitherman was in his eighth term, and African Americans held five of the nine council seats. "It's going to be fine. Selma will survive," said the mayor.

Not all African American activists focused on the polling booth. When Nelson Mandela arrived for a triumphal tour of the United States in 1990, Dade County, Florida, officials withdrew their invitation. Mandela had praised Fidel Castro for standing by him during his years in prison, and county officials were influenced by angry anti-Castro Cubans.

African Americans in the county then organized an economic boy-

Nelson Mandela is greeted by Mayor David Dinkins and Jesse Jackson.

cott that kept 50 million in tourist and convention dollars from reaching Dade. In 1993 boycott leaders and the county signed an agreement that provided thirty-one training scholarships in hotel management and a job-training program for African American youths. Hispanic, white, and African American leaders formed a "Partners for Progress." Said boycott leader and attorney H. T. Smith:

> The Mandela snub is what sparked the boycott but it went way beyond Mandela. The reason Mandela was snubbed is because the African American community was powerless politically and economically so we empowered ourselves politically by electing three African Americans to Congress. We empowered ourselves politically with four members of the County Commission, including chairman Arthur Teele, and we made them respect us with Miami Beach issuing a proclamation declaring Mandela Day and giving him a medallion of honor and Dade County voting to give a proclamation to Mandela.

New Challenges and Leaders

The two oldest civil rights organizations in the country were the NAACP, founded in 1909, and the National Urban League, founded the next year. In 1993 Benjamin Hooks retired as executive director of the NAACP and was replaced by Reverend Benjamin Chavis. John Jacob retired as president of the National Urban League and was replaced by Hugh B. Price. Each new leader began to steer his organization in divergent directions.

Price pointed out that in poor neighborhoods pupils suffer not only from weak schools and but no after-school activities or safe places to play. Fearful of the street environment, parents kept their children inside tiny apartments. Girl and Boy Scout troops had closed down and no school-based programs replaced them due to lack of funds. Gangs, said Price, "filled the void left by adults and have built their own antisocial infrastructure." He called for a vast array of "youth services after school" in schools, churches, community centers, museums, and National Guard armories.

Chavis, forty-five, became the NAACP's youngest executive director. At twelve in Oxford, North Carolina, he joined the NAACP and at fourteen, he led a drive that desegregated the library. In 1971 he was one of the "Wilmington Ten"—wrongfully accused of a firebombing and imprisoned for four years. Before he was exonerated and released, Chavis had earned a master's degree at Duke University.

Two days after assuming office, he visited the ruins of the LA rebellion, slept in a project, and met with gang leaders. "I'm an activist, . . . I believe in going to the source of the problem," he explained. He felt the NAACP's middle-class leadership had ignored its working-class membership. By the end of May, Chavis organized and sponsored a gang-leadership summit. Later he held a special meeting with Dr. Angela Davis, Dr. Cornel West, and other radical thinkers and activists the NAACP had shunned.

Chavis was among the seventy-five thousand people who gathered at the Lincoln Memorial to celebrate the thirtieth anniversary of the 1963 March on Washington. Leaders who attended represented a wide range of political viewpoints that had been stirred by the movement Dr. King led: President Lane Kirkland of the AFL-CIO, Patricia Ireland, president of NOW, Jose Velez of the League of United Latin American Citizens, James Zogby of the Arab American Institute, Lillian Kimura of the Japanese American Citizens League, Reverend Joseph Lowery of the Southern Christian Leadership Conference, John Jacob of the Urban League, and Galashki-bos of the National Congress of American Indians.

Among famous figures were Bill Cosby, Kris Kristofferson, Harry Belafonte, Governor Doug Wilder, Rabbi David Saperstein, Lani Guinier, Senator Carol Moseley Braun, and Coretta Scott King. Jesse Jackson marched arm in arm with Attorney General Janet Reno. "The civil rights movement in the United States is alive, well, expanding, building and growing," commented Chavis.

Jackson told the audience, "Thirty years later, there are more poor people. The ghettos and barrios of our cities are more abandoned, more endangered." C. T. Vivian, president of the Center for Democratic Renewal, remembered the first march. He said. "It's plain to me that people are tired of seeing things the way they are. They want something done."

However, even the sharp growth in the Black Congressional Caucus seemed precarious. That June a five-to-four Supreme Court ruling in *Shaw* v. *Reno* sent a North Carolina redistricting case back for trial as possible "racial gerrymandering." Speaking for the court majority, Justice Sandra O'Connor called these districts "racial apartheid," a phrase no Justice had ever used to describe decades of legal slavery, segregation, and discrimination. There had been a 75 percent increase in African American legislators in Mississippi. In Louisiana the increase in the legislature was 60 percent and the number of African American judges more than doubled from nineteen to forty-two. But now that all seemed threatened.

By the year's end similar white legal challenges to newly created minority districts came from Louisiana, Georgia, Florida, and Texas. Critics pointed out that the new districts had odd shapes—an inkblot in Houston, a long worm in central North Carolina, or a shaggy letter N in northern Florida. "Democracy is not defined by the symmetry of political district lines," answered Jesse Jackson. "It is determined by function."

Reverend C. T. Vivian, director of the Center for Democratic Renewal.

A racial double standard seemed at work. Texas legislator, Eddie B. Johnson, described how those in Congress "practically draw their own districts. Not practically, they have." And no court objected as state legislatures created oddly shaped "encumbancy protection" districts for those in Congress. Yet these districts posed a clear threat to fair elections.

"This is Southern white resistance," said Representative Cynthia McKinney of Georgia, whose district was among those challenged. Reagan and Bush nominees dominated the federal courts, and the future of the Voting Rights Act appeared uncertain. "We began this century with no Black representation in Congress, and the prospect is we could end it that way," added McKinney.

In June 1994, with the support of the Democratic National Committee, Jesse Jackson's Rainbow Coalition financed two busloads of people for a ten-day tour from Texas to Virginia to marshall support for the endangered districts. Jackson told audiences how federal courts that had eliminated discrimination also once had protected it. "Throughout our history, it seems that the black robes have been more devastating than white sheets," Jackson said, alluding to the former power of the Ku Klux Klan.

Catching Cold: America in the 1990s

During the early Clinton years, Americans lived in a troubled society, one that had not come to terms with its diversity, preferred myth to reality, and was sharply divided into rich and poor. The richest 1 percent of people, including eighty-three billionaires, owned 37 percent of the wealth, and this amounted to more than the financial worth of 90 percent of the rest of the people.

The average American standard of living fell. A generation earlier, the United States was first in wages and benefits in the world, but in 1994 it was twelfth. In a generation millions of jobs had vanished, and real wages dropped by 20 percent. Labor union membership fell to 11 percent of the workforce.

In his two years of chairing the Armed Services Committee, fellow Congressmen asked Ron Dellums to increase the military budget by ten billion dollars. "Their constituents desperately needed jobs," he explained, "There are too few jobs out there and no federal plan to increase jobs."

What had happened to that icon of solidity, economic health, and national stability, middle-class America? On Labor Day, 1994, Secretary of Labor Robert Reich looked at "the old middle class" and found it splintered into three parts. There was "an underclass, largely trapped in inner cities, increasingly isolated from the core economy," and an "overclass" able "to ride the waves of change." The largest portion, said Reich, was "an anxious class, most of whom hold jobs but are justifiably uneasy about their own standing and fearful for their children's futures."

In 1992 the number of individuals who filed for bankruptcy rose to over nine hundred thousand, more than triple the number in 1984. More than a third of families, 35.7 percent, lived below the federal government's poverty line, and half were white. Two-thirds of welfare recipients were children. In 1994 the Department of Health and Human Services reported that about 14 million children under eighteen lived in poverty in 1991, half a million more than the previous year, and two and a half million more than in 1980. Reich noted that "America is in danger of splitting into a two-tiered society. This is not anyone's idea of progress." He added, "America has the most unequal distribution of income of any industrialized nation in the world. We cannot have a prosperous society if these trends continue."

Thirty-nine million people under the age of sixty-five (17 percent of the population) had no medical insurance. Nine million children, one in three, were not covered by health care insurance. For African Americans the rate of the uninsured was 25 percent, for Hispanic Americans it was 35 percent. The United States in the early 1990s was the only industrialized country without a national health care system.

Economic malaise was only a part of the problem. Between 1970 and 1990 the marriage rate fell by 7.5 percent and the divorce rate rose 34 percent. For married couples between ages twenty-five and twenty-nine, divorces increased fivefold. Sociologists described these failures with a new term—"starter marriages." The divorce rate stood at 50 percent, and half of fathers responsible for child support made no payments to mothers. By contrast only 3 percent of people carrying car loans defaulted on their payments. The results of divorce were immediate and severe: 10 percent of families became homeless, half faced a serious housing crisis, and nearly a third reported their children went hungry during the first year.

Each day 1,500 students dropped out of U.S. high schools. New York City high schools graduated 34,000 in 1994; its class of 1994 had begun four years earlier with 80,000 students. In September 1993, the U.S. Department of Education reported an estimated 5 million Americans could not read or write. Some 90 million, almost half of America's population, could barely read a simple magazine article or bus schedule. Some high schools sent graduates to Harvard, Yale, and Columbia, but the graduates of others lacked competence in reading and writing. In addition, efforts to

Uniting to combat violence in New York schools in 1992 are actor Bill Cosby (second from left), Mayor David Dinkins (right), and clergymen and educators.

ban books considered controversial from classrooms began to rise sharply.

The school atmosphere often was not conducive to learning. 14 million children sat in schools badly in need of repair. Each day an estimated 135,000 guns were carried into primary and secondary schools. To stop the flow of weapons, an increasing number of pupils had to pass through metal detectors. Fear of violence kept thousands of children each day from attending the country's 85,000 schools.

From 1982 to 1994 the number of doctorates awarded in the United States rose and immigrants accounted for the entire increase. With so many people arriving with higher learning, the American business community had little incentive to improve public schools or curriculum in poor neighborhoods. This ended hope for many youths.

A 1994 CBS-TV nationwide poll of teenagers found "many lead lives shadowed by adult concerns like violence, drinking, and getting a good job, but these are worries that many say they cannot share with adults." Thirty-one percent of white and 70 percent of African American youths knew someone who had been shot in the last five years.

The American youth experience had changed dramatically in a few decades. In the 1990s each year five thousand people under twenty-five committed suicide, including two thousand teenagers. For every suicide there were an estimated 350 attempted suicides, 60 percent of high school students had contemplated suicide, and the figures were rising.

More than a million people owned guns. In 1990 handguns killed 22 people in England, 87 in Japan, 68 in Canada, and 10,567 in the United States. Between 1980 and 1990, the Centers for Disease Control reported that death by gunfire increased by 14 percent, became the fourth leading cause of death in America, and rose faster than any other cause except AIDS. *New York Times* reporter Isabel Wilkerson wrote of a United States "where many citizens lead a frightened, paranoid existence, where every stranger is suspect, where people think twice before venturing out at night and avoid some neighborhoods altogether."

"Guns in the hands of teenagers are more a threat today by far than . . . even cholera in the drinking water," announced the Centers for Disease Control in Atlanta. Nine out of ten children who died violently in the industrialized world were Americans. By 1994, thirteen children in the United States died every day from gunfire, and thirty more were wounded. Homicide was the second leading cause of death among teens fifteen to nineteen, third among children ten to fourteen, and fourth among children nine and under. The Centers discovered that the annual teen homicide rate between 1985 and 1991 rose by 154 percent, far higher than any other category. "It's a national problem," the study said, "with the same trends for whites and Blacks."

One fearful measure of the 1990s was a rise in crimes such as murder, rape, and violent assaults by children. About thirty children each year were arrested for homicides. On the last Sunday in August, 1994, on Chicago's Far South Side, eleven-year-old Robert Sandifer, Jr., four feet eight inches, asked to prove himself to fellow gang members, fired a semiautomatic pistol into teenagers playing football, killing a girl of fourteen and wounding a boy. Three days later Sandifer was found dead, shot in the head.

That day a boy of thirteen was charged with murder in a firebombing of a Bronx, New York, grocery that killed four people. The next day in High Bridge, New Jersey, Jacob Tracy, eleven, was shot to death in his home after an argument with a friend, a boy of thirteen. "It's an arms race on the streets of America," reported Kathleen Kostelny of Chicago's Erikson Institute of Child Development. In a survey conducted with nine- and ten-year olds, to the question "What would make you feel safer?" Kostelny found the overwhelming response was "a gun." Some children saved money to pay for their funerals.

Fearful citizens increasingly purchased guns against "intruders" they saw through such media images as the Willie Horton TV ad. However, the real crime problem was closer to home. Three out of every four people who died by gunfire in their homes were murdered by a relative or someone they knew. Each year 2 million women were beaten by husbands or friends, and 1,400 of these women died. In 1991 15,745 women were killed, and 60 percent were slain by someone they knew or lived with.

For women fifteen to forty-four the Department of Health and Human Services reported domestic violence was the leading cause of injuries, surpassing car accidents, muggings, and rapes combined. And most domestic injuries to women went unreported.

"Black violence" was so commonly featured by the media that some used it to mask crimes of their own. In 1989 Charles Stuart killed his wife for her insurance in Boston, wounded himself, and blamed an African American assailant. Police swept through a ghetto randomly rounding up men, and Stuart picked "the assailant" out of a police lineup. As the net of evidence finally closed around him, Stuart took his own life. For nine days in 1994, Susan Smith, a young South Carolina mother, tearfully told a believing nationwide audience about how a Black man had stolen her car and her two infants. Then she admitted she had rolled the car with her children inside into a river.

A growth in police crime was one sign of the time. In 1994 the Mollen Commission found widespread corruption throughout the New York City Police Department, particularly in minority neighborhoods. On-duty officers provided protection for drug dealers. Cops stormed drug locations to seize money, drugs, and guns. Some established narcotics distribution networks. Police illegalities, said the commission, were "far more criminal, violent and premeditated" than before and were condoned by "willfully blind" precinct commanders. "Warnings don't get much louder than this," wrote columnist Bob Herbert.

Politicians ignored the warning. Instead, they vied to be the toughest on crime. They urged more police and jails, less leniency, longer mandatory sentences, and a return of the death penalty. "All across the country we're building more prisons and closing schools," said Janette Wilson, a Chicago social worker. Between 1980 and 1993 the prison population increased by 200 percent.

By 1990, prison construction had increased 612 percent in twenty years, and had become a major growth industry, providing jobs largely for rural whites. Crime statistics showed a downward trend, but this was not the public perception nor the one offered by politicians seeking jobs for their constituents.

A million and a half Americans went to bed each night in jail cells, the highest percentage for any industrialized country. In 1992, 62,936 women and 452,453 men were arrested for serious felonies. Between 1980 and 1990, the number of women in jail increased by 256 percent, from 12,331 to 48,845 inmates. For thousands of young men, jail time was a rite of passage, a measure of manhood, and led to more lucrative criminal work.

Jails were rarely designed to reform, rehabilitate, or train men and women. Time in crowded prisons often taught convicts new criminal skills, and they reentered a society offering fewer jobs than before. Pariahs to society, their only hope came from people who valued their time in prison. When they committed new crimes, this reinforced public fears and led to cries for more and stiffer sentences and more prisons. By 1994 "restore the death penalty" elected people to governorships and Congress.

The news media preferred entertainment to education. Between 1980 and 1990, children's educational program hours fell by 80 percent. Newsman Dan Rather told the Radio and Television News Directors Association that commercial TV was "putting good ratings ahead of responsible journalism. They've got us putting more and more fuzz and wuzz on the air, cop-shop stuff, so as to compete not with other news programs, but those posing as news programs, for dead bodies, mayhem, and lurid tales."

In June 1994, President Clinton told a St. Louis talk radio program that certain media voices offered "a constant, unremitting drumbeat of negativism and cynicism." The result was, he said, "too much cynicism and too much intolerance." In 1994 half of the voters asked in a poll did not know who their representative in Congress was, and a third who said they knew guessed wrong.

Julian Bond opens a 1988 Harvard University conference on the impact of anti-communist hysteria on U.S. life.

In 1988 Roger Ailes was responsible for the Willie Horton ad that helped put George Bush in the White House. In 1995 he was a media expert responsible for thirty-two hours of original TV programming each day, more than any other individual. "Politics is nothing compared to this," he said with sparkle in his eye.

Catching Pneumonia

"If America catches cold, we get pneumonia," was an expression heard in American ghetto communities. In the "post–civil rights era" the distance between the races had widened.

The law was color-blind, but America was not. Whites made up 70 percent of those arrested but only 50 percent of those jailed. Although the National Institute for Drug Abuse reported 64 percent of crack users were white, 91.5 percent of those jailed for crack offenses were African American, and only 3 percent were white.

Three-fourths of federal drug arrests were of whites. However, under the 1988 "drug kingpin law," where the federal government had sought the death penalty, nine out of ten defendants were African American or Hispanic. Of thirty-seven charged under the law all but four were African American or Hispanic. African American columnist Bob Herbert wrote:

> Too many whites have tried to portray violent crime as strictly a Black problem. Too many Blacks have been unwilling to discuss crime honestly.

Now is the time to get past the polarization. Violence is a huge *American* problem.

Despair over few entry-level jobs created more than street crime. The sluggish economy also created what some called "a reverse draft" that drove a disproportionate number of African Americans into the U.S. armed forces. By the 1990s African Americans were "overrepresented" in all branches of the U.S. military, which became the nation's largest equal opportunity employer.

By 1994, 23 percent of young African Americans were in jail, on parole, or on probation. Of the 2.2 million African Americans arrested every year, most were unemployed or had salaries that averaged $8,000 a year. They were 48 percent of the federal prison population and 41 percent of those on death row. Since only 2 percent of people executed by states had slain people of color, the message the American justice system sent forth was that African American lives did not matter.

In 1990 the average prison sentence for African Americans convicted of drug and firearm crimes was 49 percent longer than the white average. Whites who stole millions from Savings and Loan Institutions received short sentences and glamorous publicity. People of color arrested for petty theft or on drug charges often spent years in jail.

Crimes of hate rose sharply in America. In 1993, law enforcement agencies representing 56 percent of the U.S. population reported there had been 6,746 criminal acts based on hatred, and the largest number of victims, 37 percent, were African Americans. Connecticut's hate crimes, for example, rose from 69 in 1990 to 137 in 1993, and 42 percent of the victims were African Americans.

"In the 1960s," said Harvard's Dr. Price Cobb, "our rage was directed outward. In the eighties and nineties it is directed inward." In 1955 Rosa Parks began the Montgomery Bus Boycott when she refused to move to the back of the bus. In 1994, at eighty-one, she was assaulted by a Black robber in her Detroit home. Black-on-Black violence became a major focus of African American leaders.

In the 1990s Jesse Jackson campaigned not for the White House but to save young people from cynicism and gunfire. In a New York high school, a student told Jackson, "I'm sorry, this is 1993 not 1963, I don't know where you've been." Jackson put his hand on the young man's shoulder and said, "I've been to a lot of teenage funerals."

Jackson claimed grinding poverty, poor housing, and joblessness created a quiet violence and set the stage for despair. Statistics supported his words. In 1994 a *USA Today* survey found the average net worth of white

Gabe Grosz and Candace Mills began *Interrace Magazine* in 1989 for people born to parents of different races.

households was $44,408, and for African American households the average was $4,406. At the Ida B. Wells housing project in Chicago, of the 5,660 residents, 90 percent received public assistance. More project children landed in jail or on welfare than graduated high school.

The dropout rate in the nation's fifty-one largest city school systems continued to rise each year for minority children, reported the Council of the Great City Schools in 1994. It found that the backlog of maintenance for the fifty-one districts was $13 billion, and termed "patently unfair" that suburbs spend $437 more per student than big cities.

Reverend Louis Farrakhan and Reverend Jesse Jackson urged coalitions to end the disastrous mayhem and murder in communities, but to no avail. From Boston to LA, men and women whose parents demanded civil rights in the 1960s marched through neighborhoods to protest the daily toll taken by violence.

In 1994 a *New York Times* editorial wrote of a striking change in racial relations throughout the country: "Many educated and affluent people now feel a heightened sense of permission to express bigoted opinions and to do so in language that is either flagrantly or marginally racist." It cited Richard Kraft, a New York Yankees vice president for public relations, who referred to Bronx children as "little colored boys" and "monkeys."

Overt expressions of racism were merely a clanging alarm for a larger problem. Part of America could not even find the other part. Government statisticians for the Clinton administration revealed that during the 1980s, the Reagan and Bush years, federal officials counted only six hundred thousand homeless when they actually numbered more than six million. In 1970, 1980, and 1990, the U.S. Census Bureau had admitted that each decade it had failed to count more than a million African Americans.

A PRESIDENT SPEAKS OF BLACK CRIME

[In November 1993, President Bill Clinton spoke in Memphis, Tennessee, from the same pulpit that Dr. King in 1968 delivered his last sermon before his assassination. His subject was crime.]

By the grace of God and your help, last year I was elected president of this great country. I never dreamed that I would ever have a chance to come to this hallowed place where Martin Luther King gave his last sermon.

Thirteen percent of all my presidential appointments are African Americans, and there are five African Americans in the Cabinet of the United States—two and a half times as many as have ever served in the history of this great land.

If Martin Luther King, who said, "Like Moses, I am on the mountaintop and I can see the promised land, but I'm not going to be able to get there with you, but we will get there,"—if he were to reappear by my side today and give us a report card on the last twenty-five years, what would he say? You did a good job, he would say, voting and electing people who formerly were not electable because of the color of their skin. You have more political power, and that is good. You did a good job, he would say, letting people who have the ability to do so live wherever they want to live, go wherever they want to go in this great country. You did a good job, he would say, elevating people of color into the ranks of the United States armed forces to the very top, or into the very top of our government. You did a very good job, he would say. He would say, you did a good job creating a Black middle class of people who really are doing well; and the middle class is growing more among African Americans than among non-African Americans. You did a good job. You did a good job in opening opportunity.

But he would say, I did not live and die to see the American family destroyed. I did not live and die to see thirteen-year-old boys get automatic weapons and gun down nine-year-olds just for the kick of it. I did not live and die to see young people destroy their own lives with drugs and then build fortunes destroying the lives of others. That is not what I came here to do.

My fellow Americans, he would say, I fought to stop white people from being so filled with hate that they would wreak violence on Black people. I did not fight for the right of Black people to murder other Black people with reckless abandon.

More than thirty-seven thousand people die from gunshot wounds in this country every year. Gunfire is the leading cause of death in young men. And now that we've all gotten so cool that everybody can get a semi-automatic weapon, a person shot now is three times more likely to die than fifteen years ago, because they're likely to have three bullets in them. One hundred and sixty thousand children stay home from school every day because they are scared they will be hurt in their school.

The freedom to do that kind of thing is not what Martin Luther King lived and died for. It's not what people gathered in this hallowed church for, the night before he was assassinated in April of 1968. If you had told anybody who was here in that church on that night that we would abuse our freedom in that way, they would have found it hard to believe. And I tell you it is our moral duty to turn it around . . .

So I say to you, we have to make a partnership—all the government agencies, all the business folks—but where there are no families, where there is no order, where there is no hope, where we are reducing the size of our armed services because we have won the cold war—who will be there to give structure, discipline and love to these children? You must do that. And we must help you.

So in this pulpit, on this day, let me ask all of you in your heart to say we will honor the life and the work of Martin Luther King; we will honor the meaning of our church; we will somehow, by God's grace, we will turn this around. We will give these children a future. We will take away their guns and give them books. We will take away their despair and give them hope. We will rebuild the families and the neighborhoods and the communities. We won't make all the work that has gone on here benefit just a few. We will do it together by the grace of God.

Excerpts from remarks by the president to the 86th Annual Holy Convocation of the Church of God in Christ, Memphis, Tennessee, 13 November 1993. The White House.

THE OUTSPOKEN SURGEON GENERAL

[Dr. Joycelyn Elders, fifty-nine, the daughter of rural Schaal, Arkansas, share-croppers, in 1993 became the first African American female U.S. surgeon general. She held a degree in biochemistry and a medical degree and had published 138 papers on medical problems.]

I really feel we must put our children first and I'm willing to do whatever we have to do to save the children.

Condoms are not the government's solution to the teenage pregnancy crisis. But we want to make condoms available to those who choose to be sexually active. I am not of the opinion that just because you have a condom, you are going to go out and have sex. There is not a person in this room that doesn't have car insurance, but you're not going to go out and have a wreck because of it.

I feel that denying them the availability of contraceptives, and saying to them that you have to take this kind of risk, is almost child abuse.

[She referred to driver education programs for teenagers and then made this statement about sex education:]

We taught them what to do in the front seat of a car. Now it's time to teach them what to do in the backseat.

New York Times, 14 September 1993, C9.

[Talking about America's drug epidemic, Dr. Elders said:]

There are a lot of things that are sensitive subjects, and just because they're sensitive subjects does not mean that we should ignore them when they are destroying the very fabric of our country.

[By the end of 1994, Dr. Elders's outspoken remarks led to her being asked to resign by the president.]

New York Times, 8 December 1993, A23. Copyright 1993, The New York Times Company. Reprinted by permission.

"My Critics Drove Me from Washington"

[After Lani Guinier's nomination as assistant attorney general was withdrawn, the NAACP's Crisis *magazine gave Guinier its "Torch of Courage" award. This was her acceptance speech.]*

It is a wonderful honor to be among real friends—to be recognized by the president of the *Crisis* magazine and to be given a chance to address a plenary session of the NAACP. When I was an attorney for the NAACP Legal Defense Fund, I represented many NAACP plaintiffs, and with the support of the NAACP local branches, I won legal victories in thirty-one of approximately thirty-three voting cases I litigated.

In the most recent civil rights case in which I was involved, I followed the example set by these NAACP plaintiffs and other Black people who refused to suffer quietly the indignity of unfairness. I endured the personal humiliation of being vilified as the "madwoman" with the strange name, strange hair—and with strange ideas. Those ideas being that all people deserve equal representation.

The national media condemned me, my critics drove me from Washington as a "race-obsessed radical" whose views were so out of the mainstream that I did not even deserve the fundamental fairness of being allowed to defend myself and my reputation under oath before a Senate hearing.

But lest any of you feel sorry for me, according to the press reports, the president still loves me. He just won't give me a job. But don't worry. The same press reports that Reverend Chavis has offered me a job with the NAACP; and I can understand Reverend Chavis's desire to have me work for him again. After all, when I was at the Justice Department in the Carter administration, I helped write the brief that ultimately persuaded the court to overturn Reverend Chavis's conviction.

But the issue here is not about a job. I have a job for life as a tenured law professor. My nomination was merely a metaphor. It was a metaphor for the way Black people and the issue of race and racism are being defined and characterized by others who are not sympathetic to the cause of civil rights.

Unless we want to be considered race-obsessed radicals, we are no longer permitted to discuss race in polite conversation or in Law Review articles.

Lani Guinier, *Crisis* (August/September 1993), 52. Reprinted with permission of the *Crisis* magazine.

[*In 1994 Guinier spoke on radio about her book,* The Tyranny of The Majority, *and answered those who called her a "quota queen."*]

I never advocated quotas because my father was a victim of quotas. He was turned down as the second Black man to apply to a college which had filled its quota of one.

We have become a marketplace of emotions rather than a marketplace of ideas. We demonize our enemies. We in this country are in a state of denial about issues of race. We have a drive-by debate instead of a conversation. The American people want to move beyond our differences without becoming entrenched in them, and find common ground. Silence won't make the problems go away.

Our friendship has been sacrificed to politics [*she said of her friendship with President Clinton, who had been a guest at her wedding*].

Radio station WBAI, New York, 2 May 1994. Reprinted by permission of WBAI.

"A STATE OF EMERGENCY EXISTS"

[*Dr. Ronald Daniels, a civil rights advocate, served as campaign manager to Jesse Jackson in 1988 when he was a presidential candidate. In 1992 Daniels ran as an independent candidate for the White House. In 1993 he called for military budget cuts of 50 percent to 75 percent, and then spending 50 billion dollars a year on a "Marshall Plan" to save American cities.*]

While some African Americans are comfortably nestled in the quietude of suburbia, life is not just bleak for the masses of Black poor and working people in the inner cities, life is a disaster. Black unemployment is officially listed at nearly 15 percent, but in reality it is much higher because so many Black people have lost hope of ever finding a job. Unemployment among Black people hovers in the range of 40–60 percent. And underemployment, the confinement to part-time jobs and jobs with pitifully low wages, condemns a disproportionate number of Black folks to be among this nation's working poor. . . .

Many inner-city areas look like bombed-out war zones with countless blocks of dilapidated houses, pothole-marked streets and trash-filled alleyways and vacant lots. Tuberculosis, AIDS and other life-threatening diseases have reached epidemic proportions in many Black communities as health care centers and hospitals have shut down in Black neighborhoods. Drugs, crime, violence and fratricide have become the scourge of the urban ghettos. Devastation, death and despair is the state of the Black poor. A state of emergency exists for the Black masses under what can only be described as a callous, racist system of brutal exploitation and oppression. . . .

Unless we as Black people are educated to the need to unapologetically promote and protect our interests, then we will always be betrayed by politicians who may mean well, but are beholden to the rich and the super-rich, the corporations and the military-industrial complex. If this nation can squander billions of dollars in the S&L [*savings and loan bank*] scandal and other scandals and waste untold billions in unnecessary military/war spending, then it can and must find the money to alleviate the state of emergency which afflicts the Black masses of this country. . . .

The masses of Black poor and working people are suffering, and we don't need to be polite about expressing our determination that "it will either be freedom for everybody or freedom for nobody."

Ron Daniels, "A State of Emergency Exists for Black Masses in U.S," *Daily Challenge,* 9 March 1993. Reprinted by permission of the *Daily Challenge.*

A WOMAN TURNS THE SENATE AROUND

[*On 22 July 1993 the Senate voted fifty-two to forty-eight to approve a white Southern women's society use of the Confederate flag as their symbol. Senator Carol Mosley Braun challenged this, and after her remarks senators voted again and defeated the amendment seventy-five to twenty-five.*]

On this issue there can be no consensus. It is an outrage. It is an insult.

It is absolutely unacceptable to me and to millions of Americans, black or white, that we would put the imprimatur of the United States Senate on a symbol of this kind of idea. . . .

This flag is the real flag of the Confederacy. [*The Civil War was*] fought to try to preserve our nation, to keep the states from separating themselves over the issue of whether or not my ancestors could be held as property, as chattel, as objects of trade and commerce in this country.

This is no small matter. This is not a matter of little old ladies walking around doing good deeds. There is no reason why these little old ladies cannot do good deeds anyway. If they choose to wave the Confederate flag, that certainly is their right.

[*Native American Senator Ben Nighthorse Campbell chimed in.*]

. . . there are some places in this country where American Indians are called "prairie niggers," which is the most vulgar term I can think of. . . .

I would point out . . . that slavery was once a tradition, like killing Indians like animals was once a tradition.

Senator Carol Mosley Braun, *New York Times,* 23 June 1993. Copyright 1993, The New York Times Company. Reprinted by permission.

New Stars in Orbit

[*In 1983 Guion Bluford, Jr., became the first of four African Americans to soar into space as an astronaut. Nine years later, on 12 September 1992, Mae Carol Jemison, thirty-five, a doctor and engineer, became the first Black woman to do so with* Endeavor's *seven-member crew. These were her comments:*]

I'm extremely excited to be on the flight because it's something that I wanted to do since I was a small child.

It's important not only for a little Black girl growing up to know, yeah, you can become an astronaut because there's Mae Jemison. But it's important for older white males who sometimes make decisions on those careers of those little Black girls.

Warren E. Leary, "A Determined Breaker of Boundaries," *New York Times,* 13 September 1992. Copyright 1992, The New York Times Company. Reprinted by permission.

Guns and Children

[*Marian Wright Edelman of the Children's Defense Fund wrote in 1993 of the impact of guns on American children.*]

Every four hours in America a Black child is murdered, a young Black adult is murdered, and a white child dies from firearms.

Every six hours in America, a Black child dies from firearms, a white child is murdered and a young white adult is murdered.

In 1990, two out of five Black male high school students reported carrying a weapon—more than half of them firearms—in the previous month. . . .

We're in danger of becoming our own worst enemy: more young Black men die from homicide each year than we lost in all of the horrible decades of lynching. . . .

How bad is it? The Harris survey tells us that:

Eighteen percent of all adults, 20 percent of all parents, and 30 percent of all Blacks report having had or knowing someone who had "a child who was wounded or killed by another child who had a gun."

Marian Wright Edelman, "Fed Up With Guns," *Daily Challenge*, 18–20 June 1993, 4. Reprinted by permission of the *Daily Challenge*.

"Doing Pretty Well"

[*In 1993 Jackson State University's economist Dr. David Swinton, surveying African American economic conditions in the previous decade, found "Blacks have lost ground." But from a legal point of view, he wrote, "It is almost impossible to prove that anybody is discriminating intentionally."*]

My notion is that African Americans are doing pretty well, given the circumstances that they confront. African Americans are having a very difficult time getting that connection to the labor market. They are having a difficult time getting the resources that are necessary to have a stable family over the years. This is my view of the major part of the reason for a decline of the family structures in the African American community.

The middle is shrinking because the bottom is growing fairly dramatically. There are Blacks with incomes under $5,000. Since the middle 1970s, their number more than doubled from 5.3 percent in 1976 to 11.4 percent in 1991. At the same time there has been some modest increase from 11 percent to 15 percent of those with incomes over $50,000. . . . We have roughly three times the poverty level.

David Swinton, *Emerge* magazine (October 1993), 18–20. Reprinted with the permission of George E. Curry, editor.

A JOURNALIST VIEWS AFFIRMATIVE ACTION

[*Gregory Freeman served as "national diversity chairman" of the Society of Professional Journalists.*]

I suspect there are many people—especially white males—who find the whole idea of diversity threatening. Actually, that's understandable, particularly at a time when the job situation in the United States looks scary, a time when our economy seem to be shrinking, a time when work seems more difficult than ever to find.

But I also suspect that in their haste to oppose the concept, some critics have not taken the time to examine the full issue.

Let's look at my own profession—print journalism—as an example.

According to the American Society of Newspaper Editors, minority professionals make up 10.25 percent of the newsrooms of daily newspapers. On the face of it, that looks pretty good, especially when you consider that in 1978, when the organization began its annual newsroom survey, minorities made up 4 percent of those newsrooms.

Obviously, strides have been made.

But looking at it a little closer, that 10.25 percent really isn't very high at all. The term "minorities" as defined by the newspaper society includes Blacks, Hispanics, Asians, and Native Americans. When you consider that the most recent census figures show that these groups make up nearly a quarter of the population, 10.25 percent is considerably less impressive.

It also means that whites hold nearly 90 percent of the jobs in newspaper newsrooms.

The concept behind diversity is not to discriminate against white males or anyone else. The idea is to try to make businesses—including newspapers—look a bit more like this country. That's not a bad goal for any business and ultimately should help that business.

"Diversity: Friend or Foe," *Crisis* (October 1993), 11. Reprinted with the permission of the *Crisis* magazine.

Justice for Haitian Refugees

[*U.S. presidents from Carter to Clinton have turned back refugees from Haiti while accepting white refugees from communism. In 1992, Congressman Major Owens spoke about the Bush administration, but he was just as critical of other presidents.*]

Every day thousands of Haitians risk their lives to flee from their country's oppressive military regime. They take their life's savings to book passage on badly constructed, leaky boats and try to make that perilous trip to Florida. Many do not survive the trip. Now the administration is telling the Coast Guard to simply stand by and watch as these boats topple and sink while their passengers drown before their eyes.

It is the U.S. policy toward Haiti that is largely responsible for political conditions in that country in the first place. For years a succession of administrations looked the other way, as the Duvalier regime, and the military dictatorships that came after it, exploited the people and looted the country of its few resources, all because they claimed to be "anticommunist."

When Haiti's popularly elected president, Jean Bertrand Aristide, was overthrown by yet another military coup last September 30 [1991], the Bush administration gave him little support, and sent numerous signals to the new regime that it tacitly approved the coup.

. . . The U.S. policy toward the Haitians is clearly racist; they would not be treated so coldly if they were white.

Daily Challenge, 1 June 1992, 3. Reprinted by permission of the *Daily Challenge.*

WOMEN REDEFINE THEMSELVES

[Audre Lorde had reached her forties and had a cancer that would later prove fatal when she wrote Sister Outsider, *a series of brilliant essays on relationships in the United States. This excerpt is from "Age, Race, Class and Sex: Women Redefining Difference."]*

Much of Western European history conditions us to see human differences in simplistic opposition to each other: dominant/subordinate, good/bad, up/down, superior/inferior. In a society where the good is defined in terms of profit rather than in terms of human need, there must always be some group of people who, through systematized oppression, can be made to feel surplus, to occupy the place of the dehumanized inferior. Within this society, that group is made up of Black and Third World people, working-class people, older people, and women.

As a forty-nine-year-old Black lesbian feminist socialist mother of two, including one boy, and a member of an interracial couple, I usually find myself a part of some group defined as other, deviant, inferior, or just plain wrong. Traditionally, in american society, it is the members of oppressed, objectified groups who are expected to stretch out and bridge the gap between the actualities of our lives and the consciousness of our oppressor. For in order to survive, those of us for whom oppression is as american as apple pie have always had to be watchers, to become familiar with the language and manners of the oppressor, even sometimes adopting them for some illusion of protection. Whenever the need for some pretense of communication arises, those who profit from our oppression call upon us to share our knowledge with them. In other words, it is the responsibility of the oppressed to teach the oppressors their mistakes. I am responsible for educating teachers who dismiss my children's culture in school. Black and Third World people are expected to educate white people as to our humanity. Women are expected to educate men. Lesbians and gay men are expected to educate the heterosexual world. The oppressors maintain their position and evade responsibility for their own actions. There is a constant drain of energy which might be better used in redefining ourselves and devising realistic scenarios for altering the present and constructing the future.

Institutionalized rejection of difference is an absolute necessity in a profit economy which needs outsiders as surplus people. As members of such an economy, we have *all* been programmed to respond to the human differences between us with fear and loathing and to handle that difference in one of three ways: ignore it, and if that is not possible, copy it if we think it is dominant, or destroy it if we think it is subordinate. But we have no patterns for relating across our human differences as equals. As a result, those differences have been misnamed and misused in the service of separation and confusion.

Certainly there are very real differences between us of race, age, and sex. But it is not those differences between us that are separating us. It is rather our refusal to recognize those differences, and to examine the distortions which result from our misnaming them and their effects upon human behavior and expectation.

Racism, the belief in the inherent superiority of one race over all others and thereby the right to dominance. Sexism, the belief in the inherent superiority of one sex over the other and thereby the right to dominance. Ageism. Heterosexism. Elitism. Classism.

It is a lifetime pursuit for each one of us to extract these distortions from our living at the same time as we recognize, reclaim, and define those differences upon which they are imposed. For we have all been raised in a society where those distortions were endemic within our living. Too often, we pour the energy needed for recognizing and exploring difference into pretending those differences are insurmountable barriers, or that they do not exist at all. This results in a voluntary isolation, or false and treacherous connections. Either way, we do not develop tools for using human difference as a springboard for creative change within our lives. We speak not of human difference, but human deviance.

Somewhere, on the edge of consciousness, there is what I call a *mythical norm*, which each one of us within our hearts knows "that is not me." In america, this norm is usually defined as white, thin, male, young, heterosexual, christian, and financially secure. It is with this mythical norm that the trappings of power reside within this society. Those of us who stand outside that power often identify one way in which we are different, and we assume that to be the primary cause of all oppression, forgetting other distortions around difference, some of which we ourselves may be practising. By and large within the women's movement today, white women focus upon their oppression as women and ignore differences of race, sexual preference, class, and age. There is a pretense to a homogeneity of experience covered by the word *sisterhood* that does not in fact exist.

Unacknowledged class differences rob women of each others' energy and creative insight. Recently a women's magazine collective made the decision for one issue to print only prose, saying poetry was a less "rigorous" or "serious" art form. Yet even the form our creativity takes is often a class issue. Of all the art forms, poetry is the most economical. It is the one which is the most secret, which requires the least physical labor, the least material, and the one which can be done between shifts, in the hospital pantry, on the subway, and on scraps of surplus paper. Over the last few years, writing a novel on tight finances, I came to appreciate the enormous differences in the material demands between poetry and prose. As we reclaim our literature, poetry has been the major voice of poor, working class, and Colored women. A room of one's own may be a necessity for writing prose, but so are reams of paper, a typewriter, and plenty of time. The actual requirements to produce the visual arts also help determine, along class lines, whose art is whose. In this day of inflated prices for material, who are our sculptors, our painters, our photographers? When we speak of a broadly based women's culture, we need to be aware of the effect of class and economic differences on the supplies available for producing art.

As we move toward creating a society within which we can each flourish, ageism is another distortion of relationship which interferes without vision. By ignoring the past, we are encouraged to repeat its mistakes. The "generation gap" is an important social tool for any repressive society. If the younger members of a community view the older members as contemptible or suspect or excess, they will never be able to join hands and examine the living memories of the community, nor ask the all important question, "Why?" This gives rise to a historical amnesia that keeps us working to invent the wheel every time we have to go to the store for bread.

We find ourselves having to repeat and relearn the same old lessons over and over that our mothers did because we do not pass on what we have learned, or because we are unable to listen. For instance, how many times has this all been said before? For another, who would have believed that once again our daughters are allowing their bodies to be hampered and purgatoried by girdles and high heels and hobble skirts?

Ignoring the differences of race between women and the implications of those differences presents the most serious threat to the mobilization of women's joint power.

As white women ignore their built-in privilege of whiteness and define *woman* in terms of their own experience alone, then women of Color become "other," the outsider whose experience and tradition is too "alien" to comprehend. An example of this is the signal absence of the experience of women of Color as a resource for women's studies courses. The literature of women of Color is seldom included in women's literature courses and almost never in other literature courses, nor in women's studies as a whole. All too often, the excuse given is that the literatures of women of Color can only be taught by Colored women, or that they are too difficult to understand, or that classes cannot "get into" them because they come out of experiences that are "too different." I have heard this argument presented by white women of otherwise quite clear intelligence, women who seem to have no trouble at all teaching and reviewing work that comes out of the vastly different experiences of Shakespeare, Molière, Dostoyevsky, and Aristophanes. Surely there must be some other explanation.

This is a very complex question, but I believe one of the reasons white women have such difficulty reading Black women's work is because of their reluctance to see Black women as women and different from themselves. To examine Black women's literature effectively requires that we be seen as whole people in our actual complexities—as individuals, as women, as human—rather than as one of those problematic but familiar stereotypes provided in this society in place of genuine images of Black women. And I believe this holds true for the literatures of other women of Color who are not Black.

The literatures of all women of Color recreate the textures of our lives, and many white women are heavily invested in ignoring the real differences. For as long as any difference between us means one of us must be inferior, then the recognition of any difference must be fraught with guilt. To allow women of Color to step out of stereotypes is too guilt provoking, for it threatens the complacency of those women who view oppression only in terms of sex.

Refusing to recognize difference makes it impossible to see the different problems and pitfalls facing us as women.

Thus, in a patriarchal power system where whiteskin privilege is a major prop, the entrapments used to neutralize Black women and white women are not the same. For example, it is easy for Black women to be used by the power structure against Black men, not because they are men, but because they are Black. Therefore, for Black women, it is necessary at all times to separate the needs of the oppressor from our own legitimate conflicts within our communities. This same problem does not exist for white women. Black women and men have shared racist oppression and still share it, although in different ways. Out of that shared oppression we have developed joint defenses and joint vulnerabilities to each other that are not duplicated in the white community, with the exception of the relationship between Jewish women and Jewish men.

On the other hand, white women face the pitfall of being seduced into joining the oppressor under the pretense of sharing power. This possibility does not exist in the same way for women of color. The tokenism that is sometimes extended to us is not an invitation to join power; our racial "otherness" is a visible reality that makes that quite clear. For white women there is a wider range of pretended choices and rewards for identifying with patriarchal power and its tools.

Today, with the defeat of ERA, the tightening economy, and increased conservatism, it is easier once again for white women to believe the dangerous fantasy that if you are good enough, pretty enough, sweet enough, quiet enough, teach the children to behave, hate the right people, and marry the right men, then you will be allowed to coexist with patriarchy in relative peace, at least until a man needs your job or the neighborhood rapist happens along. And true, unless one lives and loves in the trenches it is difficult to remember that the war against dehumanization is ceaseless.

But Black women and our children know the fabric of our lives is stitched with violence and with hatred, that there is no rest. We do not deal with it only on the picket lines, or in dark midnight alleys, or in the places where we dare to verbalize our resistance. For us, increasingly, violence weaves through the daily tissues of our living—in the supermarket, in the classroom, in the elevator, in the clinic and the schoolyard, from the plumber, the baker, the saleswoman, the bus driver, the bank teller, the waitress who does not serve us.

Some problems we share as women, some we do not. You fear your children will grow up to join the patriarchy and testify against you, we fear our children will be dragged from a car and shot down in the street, and you will turn your backs upon the reasons they are dying.

The threat of difference has been no less blinding to people of Color. Those of us who are Black must see that the reality of our lives and our struggle does not make us immune to the errors of ignoring and misnaming difference. Within Black communities where racism is a living reality, differences among us often seem dangerous and suspect. The need for unity is often misnamed as a need for homogeneity, and a Black feminist vision mistaken for betrayal of our common interests as a people. Because of the continuous battle against racial erasure that Black women and Black men share, some Black women still refuse to recognize that we are also oppressed as women, and that sexual hostility against Black women is practiced not only by the white racist society, but implemented within our Black communities as well. It is a disease striking the heart of Black nationhood, and silence will not make it disappear. Exacerbated by racism and the pressures of powerlessness, violence against Black women and children often becomes a standard within our communities, one by which manliness can be measured. But these woman-hating acts are rarely discussed as crimes against Black women.

As a group, women of color are the lowest-paid wage earners in america. We are the primary targets of abortion and sterilization abuse, here and abroad. In certain parts of Africa, small girls are still being sewed shut between their legs to keep them docile and for men's pleasure. This is known as female circumcision, and it is not a cultural affair as the late Jomo Kenyatta insisted, it is a crime against Black women.

Black women's literature is full of the pain of frequent assault, not only by a racist patriarchy, but also by Black men. Yet the necessity for and history of shared battle have made us, Black women, particularly vulnerable to the false accusation that antisexist is anti-Black. Meanwhile, woman hating as a recourse of the powerless is sapping strength from Black communities, and our very lives. Rape is on the increase, reported and unreported, and rape is not aggressive sexuality, it is sexualized aggression. As Kalamu ya Salaam, a Black male writer points out, "As long as male domination exists, rape will exist. Only women revolting and men made conscious of their responsibility to fight sexism can collectively stop rape."

Differences between ourselves as Black women are also being misnamed and used to separate us from one another. As a Black lesbian feminist comfortable with the many different ingredients of my identity, and a woman committed to racial and sexual freedom from oppression, I find I am constantly being encouraged to pluck out some one aspect of myself and present this as the meaningful whole, eclipsing or denying the other parts of self. But this is a destructive and fragmenting way to live. My fullest concentration of energy is available to me only when I integrate all the parts of who I am, openly, allowing power from particular sources of my living to flow back and forth freely through all my different selves, without the restrictions of externally imposed definition. Only then can I bring myself and my energies as a whole to the service of those struggles which I embrace as part of my living. . . .

What are the particular details within each of our lives that can be scrutinized and altered to help bring about change? How do we redefine difference for all women? It is not our differences which separate women, but our reluctance to recognize those differences and to deal effectively with the distortions which have resulted from the ignoring and misnaming of those differences.

As a tool of social control, women have been encouraged to recognize only one area of human difference as legitimate, those differences which exist between women and men. And we have learned to deal across those differences with the urgency of all oppressed subordinates. All of us have had to learn to live or work or coexist with men, from our fathers on. We have recognized and negotiated these differences, even when this recognition only continued the old dominant/subordinate mode of human relationship, where the oppressed must recognize the masters' difference in order to survive.

But our future survival is predicated upon our ability to relate within equality. As women, we must root out internalized patterns of oppression within ourselves if we are to move beyond the most superficial aspects of social change. Now we must recognize differences among women who are our equals, neither inferior nor superior, and devise ways to use each others' difference to enrich our visions and our joint struggles.

The future of our earth may depend upon the ability of all women to identify and develop new definitions of power and new patterns of relating across difference. The old definitions have not served us, nor the earth that supports us. The old patterns, no matter how cleverly rearranged to imitate progress, still condemn us to cosmetically altered repetitions of the same old exchanges, the same old guilt, hatred, recrimination, lamentation, and suspicion.

For we have, built into all of us, old blueprints of expectation and response, old structures of oppression, and these must be altered at the same time as we alter the living conditions which are a result of those structures. For the master's tools will never dismantle the master's house.

As Paulo Freire shows so well in *The Pedagogy of the Oppressed,* the true focus of revolutionary change is never merely the oppressive situations which we seek to escape, but that piece of the oppressor which is planted deep within each of us, and which knows only the oppressors' tactics, the oppressors' relationships.

Change means growth, and growth can be painful. But we sharpen self-definition by exposing the self in work and struggle together with those whom we define as different from ourselves, although sharing the same goals. For Black and white, old and young, lesbian and heterosexual women alike, this can mean new paths to our survival.

> We have chosen each other
> and the edge of each others' battles
> the war is the same
> if we lose
> someday women's blood will congeal
> upon a dead planet
> if we win
> there is no telling

we seek beyond history
for a new and more possible meeting.

25 TOWARD A NEW CENTURY

Approaching the end of the twentieth century, African Americans are not very optimistic. Poverty, unemployment, homelessness, teenage pregnancy, premature death, and school dropout rates are dangerously high. Ghetto residents spend only three cents of every dollar in their communities, causing a daily drain of vital capital that could build jobs, stabilize homes, and raise family esteem.

There is also good news. Black consumers, with a spending income of 300 billion dollars a year, increasingly talk of "keeping it in the family." Fourteen million Black people are part of the labor force.

In 1994 the top one hundred African American firms boasted two-year sales figures that climbed 8 percent, with employees rising 22 percent. Their share of the market, however, $46.2 billion in sales, amounted to less than Kellogg's, a white company that ranked in eighty-sixth place in the Fortune 500 corporations. The Fortune 500 made $2.3 trillion and African American–owned companies, representing more than 12 percent of the population, had only 3 percent of the pie. Some 44 percent of whites had assets over $50,000, compared to only 13 percent of African Americans.

The Past and Its Presence

In the 1990s the African American community has begun a careful examination of its legacy, the better to understand its present and chart its future. Black publishers abound, bookstores have sprouted in cities, and African American books, some more than a century old, are eagerly hawked by street-corner vendors.

By the end of the 1960s African American leaders had taken aim at a new foe: public school courses and a curriculum that buried the African American heritage. This was an ancient battle, since they were building on research by W. E. B. Du Bois in the last century and Carter G. Woodson early in this century. Books by John Hope Franklin, Ivan Van Sertima, and John Henrik Clarke detailed a virtually unknown African world legacy. Some scholars sought to establish a special "Afrocentric" approach with accompanying instructional materials and teaching methods.

In the 1980s these efforts became part of "The Curriculum of Inclusion." Pupils learned for the first time that Africans reached the Americas before Columbus, that African American cowhands rode the Chisholm Trail or joined the Indians, and others served heroically in the American Revolution, the Civil War, and America's global conflicts.

This look at the past stimulated new holidays and celebrations. After his assassination in 1968, many wanted to honor Dr. Martin Luther King, Jr., and his devotion to peace. Persistence led to success. President Reagan first ignored a bill submitted by Indiana congresswoman Katie Hall to make Dr. King's birthday a national holiday. After he said FBI data might show King was a Communist, Reagan apologized to the King family for his tasteless remark.

In November 1983, at a Rose Garden ceremony attended by Coretta Scott King, Vice President Bush, Congresswoman Hall, and civil rights leaders, the president made January fifteenth the King holiday. States officially celebrated the day, some more enthusiastically than others.

In 1986, in a simple ceremony near Bruneté, Spain, veterans of the Lincoln Brigade paused to honor their African American commander, Captain Oliver Law. In 1937, the year General Colin Powell was born and when the U.S. Army was rigidly segregated, Law became the first of his race to command fellow Americans into battle. On a hill near where Commander Law died leading his men, Steve Nelson, his comrade and successor, and other brigade veterans and families proudly marked Law's pioneer contribution.

Captain Oliver Law, commander of the Abraham Lincoln Brigade in 1937.

In 1988 a southwestern holiday, Juneteenth, was introduced to eastern states. It celebrated the day in 1865 that news of emancipation finally reached slaves in Texas. Juneteenth was on its way to becoming another

Documentary TV movie "Eyes on the Prize" recaptured the toil, pain, and struggle of the civil rights era, and aimed its message at a new generation in schools.

Black national holiday. In 1994 a Queens, New York, Juneteenth holiday celebrated Nelson Mandela, president of the New South Africa, Father's Day, and heard a "Positive Rap Concert."

More than 5 million African Americans also adopted a new holiday born of African and African American aspirations. Kwanzaa, created in 1966 by political activist and professor Ron Karenga, was celebrated during the last seven days of December. In Swahili, Kwanzaa meant "first fruits of the harvest" and the holiday fused traditional African cultural, spiritual, and moral values, and community, family strength, and learning.

Each day emphasized a different African cultural principle, such as family unity, self-determination, economic cooperation, creativity, collective work, responsibility, restoration of historic greatness, sense of purpose, and renewed faith "in our people, our parents, our teachers, our leaders." Marian Wright Edelman said, "With a child's face as our beacon and a child's needs as our guideposts, let us live up to Kwanzaa's potential as an affirmation of family, of community, and of life."

By 1992, millions of people of color had reached the conclusion that Columbus symbolized not the discovery but the invasion of the Americas. A Black student said, "Columbus set the precedent for the genocide of Indians and then carried it over to Africans." That year a student of African and Indian ancestry carried a sign that read, "In 1492 the Native Americans Discovered Columbus Invading Their Territory."

Recent scholarship uncovered historic links between African Americans and Native Americans. Raul Dennis wrote, "Faced with a common oppressor and linked by shared values, Africans and Indians often came together in brotherhood, and in resistance." On Columbus Day starting in the 1980s New York's leading African American–owned radio station, WLIB, raised funds—sometimes as much as a fourth of its entire yearly operating budget—for KILI in South Dakota, the country's only Native American radio station.

In 1992 noted political campaign manager Ron Daniels, an indepen-

Comedian, author, and performer Dick Gregory was arrested many times for defending the rights of Native Americans and African Americans.

dent presidential candidate, revived these links when he chose Asiba Tubahache, a Mattinecock Indian, as his vice presidential nominee.

In 1993 Pope John Paul II renounced the Catholic Church's part in the enslavement of Africans. He stated, "The immensity of their suffering corresponds to the enormity of the crime committed against them." The Catholic church, profoundly influenced by the civil rights revolution, welcomed African American members. Black Catholics numbered 600,000 in 1960, and 2.3 million in 1992.

The federal government began to issue stamps to honor such figures as Jean Baptiste Pointe du Sable, founder of Chicago; Ida Wells, antilynching crusader; scientist Percy Julian; boxing champion Joe Louis; scholar W.E.B. Du Bois; and the Buffalo Soldiers. Fascination with this legacy also led to hours of family reading as young and old learned their cultural identity.

Given the vital role of remembrance for people of color, 1994 became a year to recall the pain of struggles and to cherish some victories. On the fiftieth anniversary of D-Day, the Allied invasion that led to the liberation of Europe, people of color had their own recollections. Paul Parks of the

This 1994 ad for a doll shows how Black enterprises made use of historical materials for children of color.

MEET ADDY WALKER

Bring Black history alive with books, dolls, dresses, and other delights!

ADDY · 1864

Addy was named for her great-grandmother, Aduke, a brave African woman whose name means "much loved" in Yoruba and whose memory brought Addy great strength and comfort.

First Army's 365th Engineer Regiment was one of three to four thousand African Americans who stormed ashore on Omaha Beach on D Day. He recalled racial bias before, during, and after the landing. Stationed in England with the Eighty-second Airborne, he said, "It got nasty. We had nine or ten guys killed." Black soldiers were tied to trees overnight for eating too slow, he remembered, or locked in a barbed-wire cage and forced to sleep in the mud for returning a few minutes late from leave.

For his bravery fighting across Europe, Parks was recommended for a battlefield commission by his superior, but rejected by a white colonel who said, "No Black soldier could be the leader of men." Parks felt the celebration of D Day "has opened some old wounds." Parks described the "contradiction, doing what we did, fighting an evil empire, only to come home and still be treated as second-class citizens."

Some recollections led to victories. In 1923 an armed mob of three hundred whites surged through Rosewood, Florida, an African American community forty miles southwest of Gainesville. At least six people of color and two whites died in four days of violence. Every home, business, and church was burned down, and several hundred had to flee. Officials from the sher-

A White House ceremony in 1993 honoring the famed Buffalo Soldiers included Black veterans in their nineties.

iff to Governor Caley Hardee had failed to protect residents, and no one was indicted or punished. In 1993 eleven survivors demanded justice and $7 million in reparations.

In March 1994, the Florida legislature voted survivors 1.5 million dollars, and half a million for descendants of deceased Rosewood residents. Some seventy-five to one hundred Black people filed claims.

This victory in Florida increased the number of voices clamoring for reparations for centuries of unpaid service as slaves. In 1994 the fifth annual Conference on Reparations met in Detroit with a thousand delegates. Some pointed to Congress's cash award in 1991 of $20,000 for sixty thousand Japanese Americans who had been sent to concentration camps during World War II. Others cited the 1980 Supreme Court decision that awarded $105 million to Native-American nations whose land had been seized by Congress in 1877. The reparations demand was supported by Jesse Jackson, Spike Lee, the rap group Public Enemy, and twenty members of the U.S. Congress. Conference coordinator Ray Jenkins, who had worked for reparations for twenty-seven years, said, "We mean business. There is no statute of limitations on injustice. The delegates did not expect the government to capitulate on the issue quickly or easily."

Nineteen ninety-four was also the fortieth anniversary of the Supreme Court decision in the Brown case that ended legal school segregation. It was celebrated with mixed emotions. Professor Roger Wilkins said the "decision challenged core values in our society," but admitted he and others were shortsighted in thinking it would lead to profound changes. Recalling 1954, when he worked for the NAACP, Wilkins said:

> We thought the only thing really wrong with America was that we were not allowed in. Black poverty was largely hidden. The denial of racism was deeper in the North than the South.

Wilkins concluded, "Slavery lasted from 1619 to 1863, and legal subordination until 1954, totalling 335 years, so something else has reigned only forty years."

Mrs. Leola Brown sued in the original desegregation case for her daughter Linda. In 1994 she recalled her motivation:

> There was nothing specific. It was everything. We were discriminated against in all phases of life. We couldn't go to restaurants or the shows, or if we did, we had to sit in a certain place, we had to go through a certain door to get there. . . . It wasn't only about the schools, you see, it was about all of the things that were against us, all the rejection and neglect, all the things we could not do here.

Linda Brown, whose case had changed America, was a mother in 1979 when she also brought suit against the Topeka Board of Education for segregating her child. In 1994 she said, "It makes you wonder when, if ever, we will achieve integration."

Judge Robert Carter, who worked on the case for the NAACP, told an NYU audience that today more students of color attend "all- or virtually all-Black schools." Columbia University Professor Manning Marable pointed out that in the United States whites and people of color inhabit "two parallel universes" and in schools this had led to a Black "educational underclass."

The Media Image

In 1993 basketball star Charles Barkley said, "Every time you talk to a group of reporters, you're talking to ninety-nine white guys and one Black guy. . ." The media included a sprinkling of people of color on camera, but the message behind its images had changed little since early movies portrayed nonwhites as either dangerous or foolish. The media's new movies paraded as a gritty "realism."

"As long as it's in the ghetto and people are carrying guns and even the dog speaks in four-letter words," said director Robert Townsend, "they'll

Dramatic breakthroughs in the media were made by Spike Lee (left), TV's Ed Bradley (center), and Robert Townsend (right).

give it four thumbs-up and nine stars." TV actors in college student roles used street language, slapped each other around or threatened to. HBO produced "Strapped," in which a Black teenager sold semiautomatic weapons from his stoop in the ghetto to bail out his pregnant girlfriend jailed for selling crack.

In "Laurel Avenue," an unwed mother and recovering drug addict tried to keep her son, a crack dealer, from a murderous rendezvous with her abusive lover. *Times* journalist Isabel Wilkerson found these films featured high production values and African American characters immersed in "crack . . . violence and pathology." Though more Blacks were, she found, "in front of and behind the camera," none had the power "to green-light a project and get it to the public." Director Marlon Riggs explained one reason racial distortions continued as realism:

> Black folks have played the role of absorbing and reflecting all that is wrong with America. There is this sense that we can be used because we're so elastic, so empty in our identity that society can project upon us its fantasies and phobias.

White executives, said Wilkerson, "obsess about ratings and box office" and were convinced pathology "sells." "To people who may know few Blacks personally, television or movie stereotypes reinforce widely held notions about black sexual prowess, criminality or laziness," she wrote.

African American stars fought against media distortions. Malcolm-Jamal Warner, asked on "Here and Now" to slap a buddy on the side of the head, refused. For a scene in Harlem, producers told director Kevin Hooks to litter the streets "so it would look more like Harlem." He refused. In his 1992 induction speech to the Television Hall of Fame, Bill Cosby told an audience of producers:

> I'm begging to you all, stop this horrible massacre of images that are being put on the screen. It isn't fair. It isn't fair to your children watching, because that isn't us. It isn't us. It isn't us.

Some African Americans commanded their own independent film companies. In 1991 these men and women produced nineteen movies, more than in the previous ten years. By then director and actor Spike Lee's name had become a household word.

In the early 1990s rap captured the field of popular music and stirred furious debate in the African American community. It had an insistent, loud beat, abrasive lyrics, catchy tunes, and was danceable. Words were stitched together with complex drumbeats and language from older songs and recent commercials.

Demonstrating a potential for crosscultural exchange, rap swept the world with imitators in Bombay, Tokyo, Berlin, Beijing, Moscow, London, Paris, Prague, Mexico City, and the Caribbean. In 1988 L L Cool J brought rap to Abidjan, Ivory Coast, in West Africa.

Some rappers saw their music as part of a revolution. For rapper Ice Cube, people of color needed a revolution.

> The [ghetto] kids want to separate from this culture. People started wearing different hairstyles. People started wearing their clothes baggy, so hey can let the system know that we ain't with this. We're our own people. And we gonna stand on our own; and we gonna try to get some of the fire that was given off in those times [1960s demonstrations] for today.

Some artists—"gangsta rappers"—through outrageous behavior, an uninhibited lifestyle, and self-destructive imagery, stirred a backlash. When the Beatnuts sang, "It ain't nothing you should laugh to I'll shoot your mom if I have to," debate became steamy, rancorous, and uncompromising. To protest rap songs that degraded Black women, glorified violence, and suggested shooting police, women of color, Black ministers, and parents took their protests into the streets.

In a community-wide debate young and old were often pitted against each other. In Los Angeles Black-owned radio station KACE refused to air morally offensive lyrics, and Inner City Broadcasting, owner of Black radio stations in New York and other cities, banned vulgar rap songs, followed by stations in San Antonio and St Louis. ICE T, who claimed to be the "Original Gangsta," turned against any who used rap to insult Black people.

Adults were aghast at rap's amorality and hostility toward women—characterized as "hos and trix" (whores and tricks) in "gangsta rap" lyrics. "Such records are the sonic equivalent of a drive-by shooting," wrote columnist Playthell Benjamin. He particularly denounced white record company owners who made a fortune passing "these creatures off as exemplars of black culture [when] this amounts to psychological warfare against the Black community." A scholar compared rap to crack: "It gives people a false sense of agency. It gives them a sense that they have power over their lives when they don't."

The music had its defenders. Congresswoman Maxine Waters called rappers "our poets." Ice Cube blamed not rappers but a violent culture for America's problems, saying "There are more weapons in Toys "Я" Us than there are at the gun shop." *Washington Post* columnist William Raspberry

Rap artists (from left) Chuck D., Flavor Flav, Ecstasy of Whodini, and LL Cool J.

pointed out that Black youths reject middle-class existence "not because it is hopelessly square, but because they believe it is unattainable." Yo-Yo, rapper Yolanda Whitaker, told a congressional committee:

> Attack the world rappers live in, not the words they use to describe it. Being from the 'hood, I can tell you that violence didn't start from a cassette tape that . . . popped into a home or car stereo system.

Dr. Charles W. Faulkner saw rap musicians as rising against the mounting victimization of young Black men and using unequivocal lyrics to highlight police abuses.

> Even though most Black males were aware of police brutality and [the] injustice of the legal system, it was the rap groups that led the way to publicizing the problem and raising it as an issue in America. Rap artists are the new leaders who are replacing a decadent Black philosophy that allowed things to go unchanged with a new philosophy of anger and the elements of social revolution. Most rap artists do not support the abuse and disrespect of the Black woman. Many rap artists are legitimate leaders.

University of California professor Gerald Horne pointed out that rappers, most of whom come from "staid, middle-class" homes, were not reflecting poor backgrounds, but the criminality of the corporations who sell music to the public. "Some of the attention that has been devoted to the puppets," he wrote, "needs to be accorded to the puppeteer."

The rap debate sounded a wake-up call on violence. As rap increasingly found white fans and financial success, positive rap and gentle lyrics lost out to brutal and harsh ones. Love became loveless love, drug habits became excitement, and daring was measured by felonies. "White youngsters want the vicarious thrills and exhilaration, without the real danger, of the free-fire zones in black ghettos of America," wrote Dr. Donald Suggs.

William Raspberry said rap is "about degradation."

> Listeners become desensitized to . . . gratuitous violence, rape, gay-bashing, sexual objectification—become, well, speakable.

A Role in Foreign Affairs

In the 1990s African Americans increasingly sought a role in foreign affairs. Many were shocked to learn that the U.S. CIA had played a key role in the assassination of the Congo's first prime minister Patrice Lamumba in 1961, Nelson Mandela's arrest by South African police in 1964, and the overthrow of Ghana's president Kwame Nkrumah in 1966.

This awareness led to a desire to protect and aid people of color the world over. In the 1980s Randall Robinson's Trans-Africa mobilized protests against apartheid South Africa and its imprisonment of Nelson Mandela. Pickets demanded Mandela's release and U.S. economic sanctions to force an end to apartheid. When Robinson and others blocked the South African embassy in Washington, D.C., and were jailed, protest meetings took place across the country. Finally, in 1985, Congressman Ronald Dellums's sanctions bill overwhelmingly passed Congress, and Congress easily overrode President Reagan's veto.

African Americans demanded increased trade relations with African nations, and some mobilized to send aid to Africa's hungry millions. In 1989 Congressman Mickey Leland died in a plane crash as he flew food and supplies to starving Ethiopians.

Since the Carter administration, American presidents have turned back people fleeing brutal dictatorships in Haiti. The Reagan and Bush State Departments called Haitians ineligible for admission to the United States,

Congressman Mickey Leland carries a hundred-pound sack of grain bound for starving people in Ethiopia in April 1989. In August he died while bringing more supplies to Africa.

Leading an antiapartheid rally are Arthur Ashe (left) and Harry Belafonte (center).

since they were not "political" but "economic" refugees. As a candidate Clinton denounced Bush's policy as "heartless."

In 1990 Jean Bertrand Aristide was elected president of Haiti with 67 percent of the vote, the highest plurality of any leader in the Americas. The flow of refugees halted. However, in September 1991, a military junta drove out Aristide and his government and began a slaughter that took upwards of three thousand lives.

Haitians again set out in boats for the United States, only to be turned back by the U.S. Coast Guard. At Governor's Island, New York, the junta agreed to return Aristide, but it failed to honor its word. Next President Clinton imposed sanctions that failed to deter the junta, its rich supporters, or halt their trade with the United States. He ordered Haiti ringed with American warships to turn back refugees.

U.S. supporters of Haitian democracy protested anew. In 1994 four Democratic members of Congress chained themselves to the White House fence and were arrested. Randall Robinson, calling U.S. policies "cruel, patently discriminatory . . . and profoundly racist," began a hunger strike of forty-seven days, until Clinton changed his policy. President Clinton said of Robinson; "I understand and respect what he's doing. And we ought to change our policy. It hasn't worked."

Finally, Clinton prepared an invasion of Haiti. With U.S. troops in the air heading toward Haiti in September, the junta agreed to a surrender of power. Aristide returned in triumph.

Farrakhan and the Leadership Crisis

In September 1993, during the Black Caucus's twenty-third annual week-end, Reverend Louis Farrakhan of the Nation of Islam participated in a panel discussion. Ben Chavis denounced Farrakhan's exclusion—at the insistence of white groups—from the thirtieth anniversary of the march on Washington. Farrakhan firmly said:

> When we have this meeting in closed session, may we iron out whatever differences we may have and make a pledge to each other that we can say in public that we will never let somebody outside of our family determine what goes on inside of our family. And, we will tell those who wish to exclude a member of the family from participating with the family to keep their mouth out of our family business.

Farrakhan, trim in a white suit and bright bow tie, had become the most controversial figure in America, and a leading voice among Black Americans. He proudly said, "There has not been a Black man in the history of America that has been so repudiated as Brother Farrakhan." He was a magnetic, spellbinding orator who shifted easily from sly innuendo to lethal warnings. In a 1990 speech he prophesized the death of a white way of life.

> We are looking at the setting sun of the rule and dominance of the peoples of the earth by Caucasian influence or Eurocentric thought or white supremacy doctrine. . . .
> As a white person you have to change your way of thinking . . . or you will not only lose power to rule, but you will lose your life. . . .
> Sometimes we can get caught up in what Anglos did to us, but we can put a stop to what they are doing if we put a stop to what we are doing to ourselves. We have become our own worst enemy.
> I'm coming to separate the people, I didn't come to unify them. Unity with hypocrites is not valid, unity with devils is not accepted, unity with the evildoer is not accepted. So I want those who want righteousness to be in unity and those who choose evil to also be in unity and I will bring a clash about between the right and wrong.

Born Louis Eugene Walcott in the Bronx in 1933 to a "very poor" family, Farrakhan at sixteen began a successful ($500-a-week) career on stage billed as "Calypso Gene" or "The Charmer." Baptized an Episcopalian, he served as a choirboy, an altar boy and then found himself segregated in Christian churches. His first response was to compose a calypso song, "Why America is no Democracy."

Farrakhan was recruited into the Nation of Islam by Malcolm X, but then, when Malcolm left, Farrakhan wrote in *Mohammad Speaks* on 4 December 1964, "The die is set, and Malcolm shall not escape. Such a man as Malcolm is worthy of death." Less than ninety days later, Malcolm X was assassinated.

Bowie Professor Zak Kondo wanted to prove people of color were not involved in Malcolm's death. But instead research for his 1994 book, *Conspiracies*, showed the opposite: Farrakhan and the Muslim Newark Mosque were deeply implicated and "Malcolm's assassination came all the way from the top" of the Nation of Islam. In 1994 a video showed Farrakhan shouting to a Chicago Nation of Islam audience:

Was Malcolm your traitor, or was he ours? And if we dealt with him like a nation deals with a traitor, what the hell business is it of yours?

After viewing the video, Dr Betty Shabazz, Malcolm's widow, said she always believed Farrakhan created the atmosphere that led to her husband's murder.

Farrakhan often directed his harshest invective at his own people. In 1990 he told the ultraconservative Liberty Lobby that African Americans were like people with a "communicable disease" and suggested whites remove them "from the house" and keep them "in a place which is separate"

Reverend Louis Farrakhan addresses a Nation of Islam meeting in Chicago in the 1980s.

until they "come back to health." In Farrakhan's reading of history, "African Americans after slavery did not have the mentality of a free people to go and do for themselves." On a Phil Donahue TV program he said Black people still suffer from a slave's dependent, welfare mentality.

On the issue of race, Farrakhan was a firebrand, but on other issues he was very conservative. His commitment to Black self-help, entrepreneurship, and capitalism placed him somewhere between Booker T. Washington and Richard Nixon. His approach to family values, feminism, and homosexuality made him sound as old-fashioned as Dan Quayle, Jerry Falwell, or Pat Robertson.

Farrakhan's critics saw him as a master of double messages, a demagogue whose bigotry undercut the high moral ground attained by the civil rights movement. How could a man who harbored hostility to so many, some asked, participate in the grand alliance necessary to achieve Black goals?

To his supporters Farrakhan was an avenging angel building Black institutions and pride, defying white structures, and restoring the faith of the urban poor. His Nation of Islam also rehabilitated hopeless men, including dangerous former convicts. These men were taught to respect themselves, mend their ways, and pledge their loyalty to the Nation of Islam. In drug-ridden neighborhoods in Washington, Philadelphia, Cleveland, Chicago, Pittsburgh, and Baltimore, Fruit of Islam unarmed street patrols protected residents from drug dealers. Critics believed they also formed Farrakhan's armed personal bodyguard and hit men.

The Nation of Islam, its critics noted, always talked tough about whites, but reserved its use of violence for its own people. Farrakhan said of Milton Coleman, the Black journalist who released Jesse Jackson's "Hymie-town" remark to the media, "One day we will punish you with death." Farrakhan denied he meant a death threat, and no jury ever indicted him for his statement.

In 1994 five Christian African American ministers in Boston wrote an open letter to Farrakhan entitled "A Question of Morality." Some had received death threats after disagreements with the Nation of Islam. They asked about his knowledge of or participation in acts of intimidation, beatings, and murders over a thirty-year period.

> For many years you have called for unity and development in the black community and an end to black-on-black violence. Many have rushed to embrace you. To our amazement, few if any have sought a clear account of your connection with, and statements concerning, episodes of black-on-black violence, which are ultimate betrayals of the black community. . . .
>
> It is hypocritical for the black community and black leadership . . . to de-

nounce the brutality of white police, soldiers, governments or hooded Klansmen while remaining silent about the brutal assassination of Black men, women, and children by other black people. We will not participate in this conspiracy of silence.

The white media feasted on Farrakhan's anti-Jewish rhetoric. In 1984 he was accused of referring to Judaism as "a gutter religion." He offered a $10,000 reward to anyone who could prove he used that phrase. A tape of his speech showed he referred to it as a "dirty religion." For centuries racist rhetoric by white Americans had echoed freely in the land—even in Congress—and no one had been censured. This time, by a vote of 95–0, the U.S. Senate unanimously condemned Farrakhan for "racist sentiments."

When Jesse Jackson publicly apologized for his "Hymietown" remark, Farrakhan was furious. Jews, he said, never apologized for their part in the slave trade and their other crimes:

You didn't apologize for putting my brothers and sisters to live in homes and apartments, charging them the highest rent for nothing. You don't apologize for setting up liquor stores, though you don't drink too much yourself, feeding my brothers and sisters alcohol.

So very humbly, I'm saying to you: Back off my brother Jesse Jackson. . . . Get up off those Black men who don't have the strength because you're paying them.

African Americans and Jews in the 1990s tried to cross the "broken bridge" that once had united them through forums, exhibitions, and this theatrical production in New York called "Crossing the Broken Bridge."

To Farrakhan Israel was based on the violent seizure of Palestinian land, and he charged a Jewish media conspiracy covered this up. In 1985 he told twenty-five thousand people in Madison Square Garden, "The Jewish lobby has a stranglehold on the government. The president himself is actively punking out to the Jewish lobby."

Two months after Farrakhan was accepted under the amity tent spread by the Black Caucus and the NAACP in 1993, his leading spokesman, Khallid Mohammad, ignited a media firestorm. At Kean College in New Jersey in November, Mohammad unleashed a harsh diatribe against whites, homosexuals, Jews, the pope, and "Uncle Tom Negroes." He urged Black South Africans to kill all whites, then "dig them up and kill them all over again." Jews were called the "bloodsuckers" of the African American community, and he caricatured a "Jewish" accent.

In January 1994, the Anti-Defamation League (ADL) entered the picture. Once the Jewish ADL had been a civil rights advocacy group, but more recently it had been exposed in court for spying on African Americans and other Jewish Americans it claimed harbored radical beliefs. In a full-page ad the ADL reprinted key sections of Mohammad's speech and demanded its repudiation by Black leaders.

Most civil rights figures were outraged by Mohammad's words, but there was another question. Should African American leaders denounce a hateful speech because the ADL demanded it? Some were so appalled by Mohammad's language, they immediately spoke out. One commentator slyly suggested that the Nation of Islam and ADL were "engaged in a joint fund raising effort."

At about the same time Senator Ernest Hollings said African leaders might attend European conferences for "a good square meal" instead of "eating each other." His charge of cannibalism by Africa's most distinguished figures created quiet smiles rather than a furor. No media or political groundswell demanded a Hollings apology.

However, the U.S. House of Representatives responded to Mohammad's speech with a unanimous resolution of denunciation. For the second time in history the U.S. Congress had condemned hate speech in America, and again it was the Nation of Islam which was singled out. If nothing else, the citation of Mohammad and not Hollings was an example of a racial double standard.

Farrakhan blamed the furor on "Jewish manipulation of the media." He gave a Harlem audience his view of the media and Jews:

> They don't want Farrakhan to do what he's doing. They're plotting as we speak. They want to use some of our brothers and some of our brothers are willing to

California University professor Angela Davis dedicated her life to scholarship and political action against all forms of bigotry.

be used to curry favor. . . . They want to use my brother Khallid's words against me to divide the house.

Jesse Jackson, Kweisi Mfume, Ben Chavis, and other prominent leaders condemned what Chavis called Mohammad's "violence-prone and anti-Semitic comments." Farrakhan then held a rambling TV press conference. He admiringly characterized Mohammad as a "young stallion" who had uttered "many truths," chastised him for a tone inappropriate for an Islamic representative, and suspended him as a Nation of Islam spokesman. Farrakhan condemned the ADL and said he was ready to work with "responsible" Jewish and other white leaders. Jackson and others were wrong to listen to their white foes, he said, reminding them of their agreement to discuss differences within "the family."

Farrakhan scored heavily in the Black media, and his meetings overflowed with enthusiastic supporters. The Nation of Islam's numerical strength was calculated unofficially between thirty and three hundred thousand, but Farrakhan now swayed millions. In the post–civil rights era he was the only African American figure who could attract an audience of thousands whenever he spoke. His ability to fill an auditorium did not go unnoticed by civil rights leaders.

In early June 1994, after Khallid Mohammad spoke in Riverside, California, a former Nation of Islam minister opened fire, wounding him and four bodyguards. "We live in such a dangerous hour," Farrakhan said a few days later in Las Vegas. He told his audience of four thousand supporters:

> Anything you want in America, you will get not because America wants to give it to you, but because you're powerful enough to take it. . . .
>
> America seems to want to be a country of white people, by white people, and for white people. As for people of color, we have to get our house in order.

Mohammad recovered from leg wounds, stepped up his public appearances, and called himself a "Truth Terrorist," "Knowledge Gangsta," and "Black History Hit Man." His tone only became more raucous: he called Nelson Mandela "the Jesse Jackson of South Africa" and said Jewish Americans were not only "bloodsuckers" but "bagel eating, hooknose . . . Jews."

In June, Farrakhan was one of a hundred leaders Chavis invited to an NAACP summit conference in Baltimore. Chavis explained:

> Almost half of all African American children live in poverty. Black unemployment is twice that of whites. The infant mortality rate in many black communities is equal to that of many third world nations. The statistics for housing, crime, and education deliver a tragic statement of despair and inequality. Yet in

the polls, more than 60 percent of whites say blacks now have equal opportunity.

The focus in Baltimore often was on the young and for good reason. Chicago's Paul Robeson High School that month symbolized a shocking national problem. The Class of 1994 began with 500 students and by graduation it had only 150 young men and women. They called themselves not graduates but "survivors." Some failed to graduate because they had been slain or disabled by gunfire, or were in jail. Others dropped out to have babies or to find work. Robeson High was similar to hundreds of others.

The media focused on Farrakhan's presence, but columnist Playthell Benjamin found "the audience was inspired not by Farrakhan's views but what many regarded as a long overdue declaration of independence by Black leadership." Any coalition excluding Farrakhan, said Benjamin, would lose credibility among African Americans. At the conference, Farrakhan admitted that he "did not appreciate the value of Dr. Martin Luther King, Jr., as an integrationist . . . when I was preaching separatism. But I matured in the struggle." He continued:

I have begun to see the value of each component of this struggle. The potential and challenge of this summit, of pulling all of the ideologies and philosophies together under one umbrella, in order to develop a common strategy to uplift our people.

Chavis ended the summit on a note of unity and resolve:

Never again will we allow any external force to the African American community to dictate who we can meet with, where we can meet, and what we can meet about. . . . We have locked arms and our circle will not be broken.

Questions remained. Would Farrakhan heed criticism from those he called "my family"? What would he contribute to, and whose principles would dominate the new coalition?

Farrakhan's message of black pride and self-help during a rising tide of racism and his fiery oratory struck a responsive chord in poor communities. Not all were impressed. Black columnist Stanley Crouch called Farrakhan "a live wire in a swimming pool."

Before he could preside over another scheduled summit with Farrakhan, Chavis was charged with using $332,400 from an NAACP three million dollars in debt to pay off a suit for sexual discrimination. Repeatedly he had ignored his own board of directors. In sixteen stormy months at the helm, Chavis, without their approval, had embraced radicals, street gangs, and Farrakhan.

When Chavis defended himself before fifty-seven NAACP board members, one reported, "The more he talked the worse it got." With only five dissenting votes, he was fired. Chavis called his ouster "a crucifixion." The NAACP vowed to carry on, find a new leader, and to resume its historic eighty-five-year quest for equality in America.

In 1995 the NAACP, more than 4 million dollars in debt, elected Merylie Evers-Williams its new Board chair. She was the wife and co-worker of civil rights leader Medgar Evers, who in 1963 was gunned down and died in her arms outside their Mississippi home. "I'm going to make who ever did this pay," she vowed. She raised three children, graduated college, relentlessly pursued the murderer, and in 1994 finally saw him convicted and jailed.

A Rising Middle Class

The rise of an articulate, smiling, African American middle class was as sure a sign of the 1990s as the sullen face of Black poverty. Two million African Americans were college graduates, 1.5 million families had incomes over $50,000 and 2 million individuals served as managers and professionals.

Advertisers began to act on the trend. J.C. Penney opened an Afrocentric boutique, and Black advertising agencies became a busy if small part of the market. African American models sold fashions by Ralph Lauren, the Gap, and Banana Republic.

McDonald's, Kmart, Ford, Pepsi, and Cola-Cola were among fifty companies *Emerge* magazine found in 1993 to be "aggressively showing African Americans as consumers." *Emerge* made another discovery: "Not only are the ads targeting the Black community, but what is new is that they also are being used to sell to mainstream America." On TV Michael Jordan's image sold underwear, James Brown's music sold laxatives, rappers sold sneakers, and Ray Charles sold sodas.

A higher income and improved status did not automatically entitle one to a home on a tree-lined street in suburbia. Some families found the bony hand of bigotry still raised against them. In 1992 9 percent of whites but 23 percent of African Americans who applied for home loans were rejected. Wrote Scott Minerbrook,

> For the black middle class, exclusion from better housing is the bitter fruit of a legacy of racial prejudice. In what scholars call the "inertia of segregation," millions of African Americans who have climbed into the security of the middle and upper classes . . . only to find that the dream of buying a home is a night-

mare of miscues and obstacles. Nowhere is this fact of greater consequence than in the field of housing. Buying a home is not only part of the American dream, it is essential to grasping it. But study after study reveals that those in the middle class are restricted in their choice of where to live and what to buy. They are treated differently by lending and insurance institutions simply because of the color of their skin. This has a profound impact on the wealth of generations to come.

An associate editor of *U.S. News and World Report,* Minerbook found barriers when he sought a family home.

> Despite the fact that I was working for one of the largest and most prestigious newspapers in the country [Long Island's *Newsday*], I found it almost impossible to find a place to live that was not in the ghetto. We found that real estate agents were showing us rental and sale properties that were always in so-called black neighborhoods.

Many who achieved success aided those less fortunate. The Harlem Little League's "Dream Team" was sponsored and managed by bankers, corporate attorneys, and investment counselors. A host of Black men returned as father-helpers to boys in ghetto neighborhoods. Oprah Winfrey's "A Better Chance" guided poor children through schools to a college education. Ossie Davis and Ruby Dee volunteered their talents for the United Negro College Fund and a host of Black charities. Bill and Camille Cosby educational projects included a $20-million gift to Spelman College. Some celebrities remained focused on their own needs. Superstar O. J. Simpson told writer Robert Lypsyte, "What I'm doing is not for principles or Black people. No, I'm dealing first for O. J."

Many successful African Americans looked beyond upper-class values. In 1993 the National Association of Black Scuba Divers (NABSD) carried out a project to memorialize their ancestors. In 1701 the *Henrietta Marie,* a slave ship, had sunk in the Gulf of Mexico, thirty-five miles from Key West, Florida. It was found and still carried leg shackles, seven thousand artifacts, and what NABSD members called "a powerful presence." In 1993 a dozen NABSD divers plunged thirty feet to plant a plaque honoring "our early ancestors" and planned a museum based on the ship's artifacts. In 1994 NABSD members found another slave ship and began a new educational project.

Black Women Writers

Maya Angelou's inspired lyricism at the Clinton inauguration focused attention on the dazzling African American contributions to literature. Alice

Author Maya Angelou shakes hands with Mayor David Dinkins of New York City in 1993.

Walker won a Pulitzer Prize for her stunning book *The Color Purple,* which also became a major Hollywood film. Walker had taught in Mississippi freedom schools in the 1960s and remained a political activist who used her talents to expose racism and sexism. Along with those of Terry Macmillan, Gloria Naylor, and Ntozake Shange, her views about the personal relationships between men and women of color stirred controversy.

Audre Lorde (she often used her African name Gamba Adisa), the poet laureate of New York State and a brilliant essayist, wrote seventeen books and received three honorary college degrees and a National Book Award. She was an outspoken lesbian, served on the board of the Feminist Press, and became a leader in the fight for interracial democracy in South Africa. In the *Cancer Journals,* Lorde traced the first stages of her battle against the disease that finally took her life in 1992 at 58. In 1993 Rita Dove, forty, became the youngest person and first African American chosen as the U.S. poet laureate.

Princeton professor Toni Morrison, born in a steel town in Ohio, earned a Pulitzer Prize for her novel *Beloved,* a story about slavery. In 1993 she became the first African American awarded the Nobel Prize in Literature, the world's highest literary honor. "What is curious to me is that bestial treatment of human beings never produces a race of beasts," Morrison once said. Her works, said the Nobel Committee, capture the African American experience, "give life to an essential aspect of American reality," and are "characterized by visionary force and poetic import."

Morrison's eloquent half-hour speech to the Swedish Academy brought a standing ovation. In the United States, she said, "Children have bitten their tongues off and use bullets instead" as "the voice of the speechless." She connected language to liberty:

Oppressive language does more than represent violence; it is violence; does more than represent the limits of knowledge; it limits knowledge.

Facing the Twenty-first Century

As they approach a new century, individual African Americans have made undeniable and even striking progress on many fronts. They have defeated the fear and terror that denied them the right to vote and to hold office. They live under laws that promised them access to public facilities and equal opportunity in the professions, schools, and the workplace.

The 280 African American elected officials in 1965 rose to more than 8,000 in 1993. "But," cautioned Columbia professor Manning Marable, "that is only 2.5 percent of elected officials." He also pointed out that these officials "have responsibility without authority," and "little connection to the Black community." *Emerge* magazine reported in 1994 that new Black mayors in Seattle, Denver, and St. Louis led efforts "to replace bussing with school choice." To Professor Ron Walters, this stance was wrong, and he warned, "We're headed down a very scary road."

One African American man became a governor of Virginia, one woman a Senator from Illinois, and forty men and women served in the Congress. Two were appointed to the Supreme Court, four sat in the president's cabinet, one served as head of the Joint Chiefs of Staff, and two represented their country as U.S. ambassadors to the United Nations. The Miss America Beauty Pageant in the 1990s was as likely to crown a Black woman as a white.

Some African American men and women won their place in sports, and others became media superstars. A handful won Pulitzer prizes, one won the Nobel Prize in Literature, and two won the Nobel Peace Prize. A few became millionaires, and hundreds of thousands of others have used a combination of brains, education, and sweat to lift their families into the middle class and find homes on quiet suburban streets. Since 1964 the number of Black doctors has risen 350 percent and the number of Black lawyers has quadrupled.

But the vast majority are not so lucky. The average white male lives to be 75.3 years, but the average African American male dies by 64.8—so they do not live to cash their first social security check. Blacks are twice as likely as whites to die before their first birthday, and three times as likely as whites to die of AIDS. Compared to whites, Black men under forty-five have a 45-percent higher lung cancer rate, a 33-percent higher diabetes rate, and are ten times more likely to die of hypertension.

Many African Americans, through no choice of their own, lead a more dangerous life than other citizens. In 1990 two doctors found New York City's Harlem had "extremely high mortality rates" amounting to a "natural disaster." Harlem's death rate exceeded that of impoverished Bangladesh, India. Nationally, twelve thousand Black men die a violent death each year.

In rural areas people of color are more likely than others to live close to hazardous waste. Environmental Protection Agency chief Carol M. Brauner said, "I don't think that there is any doubt that low income and minority communities have borne the brunt of our industrial lifestyle."

Despite changes in the law and the opening of opportunities, white attitudes have not changed. Marcus Alexis, an investment banker in Manhattan, found a more subtle racism from what his parents and grandparents experienced. "It's inflection, it's body language, it's all the nuances people feel that suggest 'you're not welcome here.'" Alexis also found the civil rights crusade had opened doors for him. "My world is a bigger place. It doesn't always welcome me, but it's a bigger place. And I like that, even with all the baggage that comes along with it."

Many white citizens still choose to see the average African American as lazy and irresponsible, dangerous, or on welfare. When homicide became the greatest killer of African American men and women under forty in the 1990s, this was not treated as a national calamity but a "Black problem."

Whites often believe nonwhites vote on racial lines, but this is rarely the case. For example, in Maryland Senator Barbara Mukulski won 85 percent of the African American vote against a Black candidate. Statistics have proved it is whites who largely vote on racial lines.

Gross white racial stereotypes are still alive. In Teaneck, New Jersey, a school board meeting in September 1993 was interrupted by a man in a gorilla costume who handed bananas, a stuffed monkey, and a message to Mel Henderson, the only Black member of the board. In a cartoon showing people from all over the world making phone calls, AT&T used a gorilla to represent Africa.

In October 1993, Black marines with long and honorable service records accused the Marine Corps of failing to promote minority officers. Marine Corps commandant, General Carl E. Mundy, Jr., interviewed on "60 Minutes," said members of minority groups did not shoot, swim, or use compasses as well as whites. After protests, he apologized for "any offense that may have been taken."

Racist hatred can still ignite cross burnings and other fires. On 1 January 1993, three whites kidnapped Christopher Wilson, a New York stockbroker clerk visiting Tampa, Florida. They drove to a remote field, doused him with gas, set him afire—and yelled "nigger!" Wilson lived to identify his assailants in court, and two were given life sentences. Wilson made a request of those jailed: "I would like them to get counseling in prison. I hope that they will learn never to hurt someone because of their color."

Despite a Supreme Court ruling in 1967 that outlawed state bans on interracial marriages, "racial purity" has its defenders. Revonda Bowen, sixteen, junior class vice president and chair of the prom committee at Randolph County High School in Alabama, was born to a white father and African American mother. She burst into tears in 1994 when her high school principal, Hulond Humphries, told her he did not want any interracial couples to attend the prom. Who should she attend with? she asked him.

Humphries said her parents had "made a mistake" and called a special assembly to tell students he would cancel the prom if any interracial couples planned to attend. The high school endured months of marches and boycotts, Ms. Bowen eventually won a $25,000 lawsuit, and the U.S. Justice Department entered the case.

Officials of Stratford High School in South Carolina allowed white students to wear T-shirts emblazoned with the Confederate battle flag. But when Shellmira Green, seventeen and a Black honor student, wore a T-shirt with a Confederate flag dominated by the red, black, and green colors of African liberation, she was suspended from school. She and the NAACP filed a federal lawsuit.

Inequality in America remains a fact of life. In 1994 Thelma Roby, a metalworker for the U.S. Navy, and thirty-one other people of color filed a $130-million suit charging discrimination in Pensacola, Florida, in promotion, hiring, and training policies. In Detroit a survey found that salesmen sold a car worth $11,000 to white males for $11,352 and to Black males for $11,783.

In 1994 Denny's restaurant chain, part of a Fortune 500 company, settled a discrimination suit for $54 million. The case was initially brought in Maryland by six U.S. Secret Service agents (assigned to guard President Clinton) who had been denied service. The six were soon joined by 4,300 other customers.

Former California manager Robert Norton testified Denny's managers used the term "Blackout" to announce "too many Black customers were in the restaurant," and issued instructions to close down during a "Blackout." His district manager told him "to limit or discourage Black patronage."

The Denny's case was settled. But in 1995 the Equal Employment Opportunity Commission had a backlog of 100,000 unresolved job-discrimination cases—double the number since the Democrats took office in 1993.

There have been enormous economic gains for individuals and political advances for African Americans since 1960. But barriers to equality remain. The civil rights movement has slowed to a crawl, but not many of the injustices that sparked it. Jesse Jackson transformed presidential politics and became a global presence, but his effort is increasingly devoted to helping the young end violence and combat cynicism.

At the end of 1994 *The Bell Curve* became a best-seller and was widely praised by conservatives and liberals. However, its argument that people of color were genetically inferior intellectually to other ethnic groups, rested on old, refuted studies, some written by pro-Nazis and other racists. Its thesis and popularity were welcomed by those who sought to reduce federal aid to the poor and disadvantaged.

The 1994 elections swept Republicans (after forty years as a minority) back into control of Congress. The results also brought a new approach to race. Only 38 percent of eligible voters went to the polls, and one in three identified themselves as white Christian conservatives. Republicans fielded forty conservative Black Congressional candidates, and elected two.

Voters had been taught to respond to a new vocabulary. In the 1970s and 1980s white politicians transmitted racist appeals through "buzz words" such as "forced bussing," "racial quotas," and "reverse discrimination." By 1995 more common words—"crime," "welfare system," "public schools," "death penalty," and "teen pregnancies"—served the same racist purpose.

Senator Robert Dole, insisting that "the race counting game has gone too far," called for an end to affirmative action and a "return to a merit system." But the United States has never been a meritocracy. White males, some with little merit, were hired for the best jobs. In 1995 little had changed. White men were 29 percent of workers, but held 95 percent of senior management jobs. Among lawyers, doctors, and professors, African Americans comprised less than 5 percent. White women were the main beneficiaries of affirmative action, but they still had a way to go.

Affirmative action was an effort to pry open doors that locked out merit when it was not white nor male. Richmond, Virginia, with a 55 percent

Black population, finally made rules to insure that 30 percent of city construction contracts went to minority businesses. Whites objected, the rules were terminated, and in 1993 the 55 percent of Richmond landed only 5 percent of city contracts.

Noting that "two-thirds of white males voted Republican," Senator Robert Dole said "slavery" should no longer be an excuse for affirmative-action programs. In California two college professors launched a voter ballot initiative to replace affirmative action with "true color-blind fairness in the United States." The movement spread to other states. New York *Daily News* columnist and former New York construction worker Playthell Benjamin was one of many to remember "bosses who, except for affirmative action, would have only hired their white cronies."

Capitol Hill quickly reflected the changed racial climate. Charles Murray, one of the authors of *The Bell Curve*, was asked by Republican leaders to address newly elected senators and representatives. The new chair of the House Rules Committee, New York's Gerald Solomon, prominently displayed in his hearing room a photograph of former chair Howard Smith, for decades a leading Southern racist. Only after nine Black Caucus members vigorously objected was it removed.

House Speaker Newt Gingrich forcefully pushed his party's "Contract with America." It called federal funds for welfare, child nutrition, and Medicaid "burdens." Though only 1 percent of the federal budget, welfare became the national scapegoat. Recipients were caricatured as women of color who had children in order to increase their benefits. Actually the average welfare family received less than $400 monthly, and only 38 percent of recipients were African Americans. Also, only 8 percent of welfare mothers were under the age of twenty, and most had only one or two children. Felicia Smith, eleven, thought the proposed cuts would undermine her family. In 1995 she told a reporter, "My mother and I are very smart and she is a wonderful cook. But with welfare no matter how hard we try, my brother, my mother, and I don't have enough to eat."

The "Contract with America" aimed to swiftly and substantially reduce taxes on corporations and the rich, and offer much smaller middle-class tax reductions. Though no major power threatened the United States, conservatives advocated billions more be added to the military budget, and some sought to renew the $30 billion Star Wars antimissile defense program. To pay for tax reductions and increased military spending, fiscal conservatives of both parties targeted drug- and crime-prevention and rehabilitation programs, as well as rent subsidies and legal services for the poor. "Something is a burden," concluded economist John Kenneth Galbraith, "when it is not for the rich, not for the merely affluent, but for the poor." Representative John Lewis infuriated Republicans when he said of the Contract,

"They are coming for the children. They are coming for the poor. They are coming for the sick, the elderly, and the disabled."

Racist bigotry remains deeply embedded in America's psyche and its institutions. Racism no longer permeates flagrant laws and has jettisoned its vulgar rhetoric. It has developed a pattern of broken field running that makes it harder to tackle. With a public barely interested in the plight of Black people, old white allies have left the fight for equality. Politicians routinely speak of racial tolerance and practice tokenism, but staunch white foes of racism are hard to find.

At the end of the twentieth century, African Americans are grappling with an old dragon that has sprouted new heads. Professor Manning Marable said,

> The issue now is Black survival in an era when the number of Black people who are in prisons doubles every seven years. It's a brave new world where the old political rules no longer fit. What is required is a breakthrough in the political imagination of today's Black political leadership. The problems facing African Americans today require a whole new set of political skills.

Ron Daniels, director of the Center for Constitutional Rights, saw a rising tide among his people:

> There is a new sense of militancy surfacing again in Black America and the power elite is deathly afraid that if Black people unite, we will lead a movement that will shake this racist and oppressive society to its foundation. Those who rule America are well aware that historically when Black America wakes up from its slumber, and moves, other oppressed people will also be stirred to act.

SKINHEAD PLOT

[*In July 1993 federal agents arrested six white supremacists, including three women and two minors. They had planned to blow up the First African Methodist Episcopal Church in South Central Los Angeles and assassinate Rodney King, Reverend Louis Farrakhan, and several Jewish leaders. Their aim was to provoke "a holy war" against both groups. Those arrested were members of the Church of the Creator in Florida, White Aryan Resistance in Southern California, and the Fourth Reich Skinheads in Huntington Beach, California.*]

In July, two loosely affiliated bands of white supremacists plotted to ignite a race war in the United States with a series of carefully planned assassinations and bombings on the West Coast.

Neo-Nazi Skinheads—long noted for their violence and their eagerness to act out the race-war fantasies of older white supremacists—played a major role in the uncovered plots.

Their targets—selected for their potential to provoke maximum racial conflict—included Los Angeles police beating victim Rodney King and a prominent church whose members included such celebrities as Arsenio Hall and Oprah Winfrey.

Days after the arrests in Southern California, a second band of white supremacist terrorists bombed an NAACP office in Tacoma, Washington, and were plotting other bombings. Military bases, synagogues and rap singers were on the hit lists of both groups.

While most of the key figures in the bombing and assassination schemes have now been arrested and the latest white supremacist plot to start a bloody racial conflict has been foiled, these events underscore an alarming trend toward large-scale violence by neo-Nazi Skinheads in the organized hate movement, according to Klanwatch Director Danny Welch.

"If law enforcement hadn't been diligent in their efforts to infiltrate these groups, we could have seen a repeat of the LA riots or worse, much worse," Welch said. "These individuals picked their target well, and we can only be grateful that they were stopped."

The breadth of the conspiracy of violence suggests a degree of organization not previously seen among neo-Nazi Skinheads in the U.S. . . .

According to Welch, "There has always been a fear that if the Skinheads ever got organized, they would cause a lot of trouble. What has just been uncovered on the West Coast may be a wake-up call for law enforcement all over the country. These young Nazis are ready and willing to act and, next time, we might not be so fortunate."

[*A year later Klanwatch reported that white supremacists had infiltrated the antigovernment "militia movement" underway in eighteen states, and had succeeded in six states.*]

"Neo-Nazi Skinheads Plot Bombings, Assassinations," *Southern Poverty Law Center Report* (October 1993), 1, 3. Reprinted by permission.

AFROCENTRICS AND LEARNING

[*Precious Duncan, sixteen and in a Brooklyn high school, added her voice to the debate over "the curriculum of inclusion."*]

I am of the opinion that if a child is given something he or she can relate to he will not only accept it, but he or she will thirst for even more. For myself, it was a book on El Hajj Malik Shabazz (Malcolm X) at the age of 9 that sparked an interest not only in him, but in who I was and my place in society. From that time on I was determined to learn all I could. Now, at 16, I can see why my brothers are in such a state of desperation, we need something to aspire to.

The history curriculum is killing us. We are lost, not because of self-esteem alone, but because we are a generation cut off from our past and have been satisfied with what we're given. Most of our men are fighting the wrong revolution. Instead of fighting the enemy, they're doing his job.

Precious Duncan, "Afrocentrics," *Daily Challenge,* 15 October 1990. Reprinted with permission of the *Daily Challenge.*

CRISIS AND SELF-HELP IN RURAL MISSISSIPPI

[*In the 1990s urban blight captured the media eye, but rural African Americans also faced an economic crisis. In Quitman County, in 1994, a survey of housing conditions for 230 families found 163 had leaky roofs, 150 had holes in the side, 129 had holes in the floor, 143 had unsound foundations, and 140 had windows broken out. Tom Bailey, Jr. of the Memphis* Commercial Appeal, *interviewed residents.*]

"This thing may fall at any time," Willie Mae Reed said of her house on Cutrer Avenue in nearby Lambert. "If a bad storm comes through here you can forget it."

The unemployed nurse's house even looks dangerous. A floor beam has broken at the northwest corner, so the living room floor slopes severely.

Pails and buckets are scattered throughout the house to catch the rain that comes through the roof.

Tom Bailey, Jr. "The Commercial Appeal." Reprinted in a Quitman County Development Organization 1994 report.

[*Robert Jackson, thirty-four, director of the Quitman County Development Organization, a self-help organization founded in 1982, announced he no longer waited for aid from the federal, state, and county governments.*]

"The churches are the only hope here," said Jackson, who is a [county supervisor and a] deacon at New Hope Missionary Baptist Church in Vance. "We've been trying to get churches more involved in the community, as opposed to just religious services on Sunday."

He has signed up about 20 black churches for the Housing Development Corporation, which will provide low-interest loans and grants to help people rehabilitate their houses and build new ones. The money would come from private sources.

Quitman County Development Organization, *1994 Newsletter*, 1.

ASSESSING MINISTER LOUIS FARRAKHAN

[*Yale University professor of political science Adolph Reed, Jr., made this assessment of Reverend Louis Farrakhan and his white critics:*]

Farrakhan has been attacked so vigorously and singularly in part because he is black. He is seen by whites as a symbol embodying, and therefore justifying, their fears of a black peril. Blacks have come to his defense mainly because he is black and perceived to be a victim of racially inspired defamation; he gets points in principle for saying things that antagonize whites. Few who rally to vindicate him know or have anything substantive to say about his program; most defend his as a strong black voice that whites want to silence. Farrakhan's wager is that he can build a personal following by asserting his apparent victimization as *de facto* evidence of political legitimacy. . . .

Indeed, Farrakhan has reproduced the contradiction within the old Nation of Islam, the tension between militant posture and conservative program. But that contradiction fits the ambivalent position of the student audience. Their racial militancy often rests atop basically conventional, if not conservative, aspirations. . . .

The combination of cathartic, feel-good militancy and conservative substance is the source as well of whatever comparable following Farrakhan may have generated among the older population. It is also what makes him a dangerous force in American life—quite apart from what he thinks of whites in general or Jews in particular. He weds a radical, oppositional style to a program that proposes private and individual responses to social problems; he endorses moral repressiveness; he asserts racial essentialism; he affirms male authority; and he lauds bootstrap capitalism.

Adolph Reed, Jr., "False Prophet—II," *Nation*, 28 January 1991, 86–87. Reprinted by permission of *The Nation*. Reprinted by permission.

[*Michael Lerner, a leading Jewish intellectual and editor of* Tikkun, *gave three reasons why he did not get worked up about Farrakhan's "obnoxious lies" and anti-Semitism.*]

First, I can't stand the hypocrisy from a white media and white establishment that does everything it can to exploit and degrade blacks, then looks on in pretended horror when pathologies start to develop in the black community.

Second, I can't stand the hypocrisy coming from some in the Jewish world who for decades have used the Holocaust and the history of our very real oppression as an excuse to deny our own racism toward blacks or Palestinians. In our frantic attempts to make it in America, we not only fixed our noses and straightened our hair and learned to talk more softly and genteelly to be accepted by WASP culture, but we also began to buy the racist assumptions of this society, and to forget our own history of oppression. . . .

But the third and most important reason I can't get exercised about Farrakhan is because to do so distracts us from the deep underlying crisis of meaning in American society that is central to why people are in so much pain that they are willing to seek any kind of anesthetic, from drugs and alcohol to communities based on fascism and racism. . . .

To explain why their lives don't feel better, these communities pick a demonized Other who is supposedly responsible. Typically, Christian-based societies have chosen the Jews, though in the U.S. it has been African Americans, and more recently, homosexuals and feminists, who become the demonized Other.

. . . One tragic irony of black anti-Semitism is how easily it becomes yet another justification for some Americans to declare themselves "disillusioned" with the oppressed. So they succumb to the allures of American selfishness, lower their taxes by cutting social programs for the poor, and shut their eyes to the suffering of others.

Time magazine, 28 February 1994, 33–34. Reprinted by permission of Michael Lerner.

[*Columnist Playthell Benjamin saw Farrakhan's popularity stemming from the "desperate [Black] economic crisis."*]

While the response to economic crisis takes its specific character from the time and place of its occurrence, it generally manifests certain common characteristics. Among these are a militant nationalism or class consciousness and a willingness to sacrifice personal freedom and compromise moral principles to achieve quick solutions. This explains the rise of the radical movements [*such as Vladimir Zhirinovsky in Russia, Jean-Marie Le Pen in France and the Chiapas revolt in Mexico*] and the present popularity of Farrakhan.

. . . But unless those who govern devise a strategy that will address long-term unemployment, disillusioned black men will continue to turn to the

Nation of Islam, just as disillusioned white men are increasingly turning to white-power organizations in search of economic salvation.

Daily News, 1 February 1994. Permission granted by the Claudia Menger Literary Agency for Playthell Benjamin. Copyright 1994 by Playthell Benjamin.

[*Writer and editor Jean Carey Bond wondered if the media focus on Farrakhan did not have a sinister goal. Her analysis began with a quote from President Nixon: "You have to face the fact that the whole problem is really the blacks. The key is to devise a system that recognizes this while not appearing to."*]

Might that "system" be what we're looking at today in the steady media drumbeat on "black anti-Semitism" and black crime?

While "not appearing to" attack the entire black community in that their attacks focus only on a handful of black demagogues, some media nevertheless tar the entire black community with the anti-Semitic brush. Op-ed pieces and feature articles, while not appearing to suggest that the fundamental nature of black people is revealed in the unruly and criminal behavior of some blacks, these media nonetheless sow the seeds of that idea by lavishly and uncritically reporting white perceptions to that effect, and by trotting out black people who imply as much by their own public expressions of concern about inner-city violence.

My question is, given this white approach: If black people are the problem, as Jews were "the problem" in Germany, what is the solution?

Jean Carey Bond, 2 June 1994 fax to William Loren Katz. Reprinted by permission.

RAP MUSIC: THE DEBATE

[*As rap swept the world, it stirred intense controversy within the African American community about the importance of culture and self-respect. Columbia University professor Manning Marable saw the music as a product of its age.*]

The "Hip-Hop" generation's primary experience in politics can be characterized by one word—defeat. This generation's most dominant and influential national political figure was Ronald Reagan. Reaganism came to power in 1981, destroying the concept of liberal government and social welfare, and undermining affirmative action programs.

The generation which produced the dynamic cultural expression of rap music came to maturity in a context of rising Black-on-Black violence, symbolized by the Crips. vs. the Bloods in South Central Los Angeles. . . .

Hip-Hop emerged in the context of widespread unemployment, homelessness, and in the context of fear and social alienation. For many of our young people, there is no sense or expectation that a future is worth living for—or that it even exists.

Daily Challenge, 26 May 1994, 5. Reprinted by permission of the *Daily Challenge.*

[Jesse Jackson scolded some rappers for undermining their people.]

The successful rap artists are ignoring the uplifting messages found in some hip-hop music and doing what the money people tell them to do. This is a tragic misuse of our intellectual and musical talent.

Through the years, our artists have used music to convey joy, sorrow, pain and protest, but never to promote the degradation of our race and our women or as a promotion for self-destructive violence. Demeaning and degrading each other while on the oppressor's payroll, and while the hearse wheels roll through our communities like jitney cabs, is not defiance. It is fear and cowardice covering up as tough. It is spiritual surrender. It is bowing to the worst, most perverse desires of our enemies.

The victims are not responsible for going down, but they must be responsible for getting up.

Jesse Jackson, *Crisis* (March 1994). Reprinted by permission of *Crisis* magazine.

"I COULD BE NEXT"

[Konate Lilas was a journalism major at Kingsborough Community College who had lost more than one close friend to violence, and vengeance was on his mind. As an intern for a Black Brooklyn paper, he was assigned to cover a local march against violence, and he found it changed him.]

The inspirational walk in Bedford Stuyvesant last Friday was much more of a personal experience than I could have ever anticipated. I quite frankly expected it to be one of those quiet "We Shall Overcome" walks that nobody really paid attention to, or took seriously. It was, however, anything but that.

One of the most powerful things about the walk was that everyone who participated or just happened to be a bystander definitely got the message. And the message was: *We're sick and tired of our children, sons and daughters, brothers and sisters, boyfriends, and the fathers of our babies, being killed senselessly.*

I expected to see about maybe 25 to 30 people, mostly adults, attend the walk. My expectations were, however, far from accurate. There were about 250 walkers easy.

But what struck me most was the presence of young people—young ladies pushing carriages not accompanied by a father, particularly. It saddened me to think that perhaps these teenage girls were carrying the babies of slain fathers. I was saddened by the thought that not only will these infants not have a father to guide and provide for them, but they will never get to see, much less know, their fathers.

And it's a shame because these children have been robbed of their greatest natural resource, which is a father.

As the marchers shouted, "Stop the violence, Increase the peace, Stop the violence, Increase the peace"—demanding, but at the same time begging for the violence to stop—I found it difficult to maintain my position as a reporter.

As members of the Khalifah Mosque stopped on street corners in Bedford Stuyvesant and called off name after name of slain young victims, all I kept thinking about is that I could be next on that list. As I looked into the crowd and saw the mothers of slain youths begging for the violence to stop I thought to myself that any one of them could be my mother.

Many of these young men who have lost their lives are a lot like me. Many of them walk the same streets as I do, dress like me, talk like me, spend their free time like me, listen to the same music as me, and are young Black males living in America—like me.

Sometimes, I get a little worried, because it would not be unusual if my life was suddenly aborted. I am presently at an age where, according to the Centers for Disease Control, homicide is the leading cause of death among Black males.

During the walk I thought about a scene in the movie "Menace to Society" that penetrated me like a spear. Charles S. Dutton, who played a father in the movie, says to a Black teenager, "The hunt is on, and you're the prey."

As I was taking notes during the march I kept thinking about close friends who have passed away as a result of homicides, one of them buried just three weeks ago.

I thought too about Black men all across America dying in mass numbers every day. I thought about my brothers and sisters in Africa, who live in places like Rwanda that are dying in phenomenal numbers at the hands of other Black men.

Konate Lilas, "Eyewitness to Grim Harvest of Urban Youth," *Daily Challenge,* 13 May 1994, 3. Reprinted by permission of the *Daily Challenge.*

"THE WORST CRISIS . . . SINCE SLAVERY"

[In June 1994, on behalf of the Children's Defense Fund, president and founder Marian Wright Edelman wrote of the crisis confronting children.]

I write you today about a crisis more urgent, heartbreaking, and important than anything Black Americans have ever had to face.

Quite simply, we are losing our children. . . .

I fear that today we face the worst crisis for Black Americans since slavery—the loss of our children to a world of violence, poverty, drugs, despair, school failure, family and community breakdown, and fear of the future. . . .

Consider what will take place *today*—and each and every day this year.

Before today is over, 5 Black teenagers will be murdered, 6 Black children will die from guns, and 1,118 Black teenagers will be victims of violent crimes.

Another 3,494 Black children will be suspended from school and 1,451 will be arrested for a crime. In addition, 907 Black teenagers will become pregnant, 1,271 Black babies will be born to unmarried women, and 1,019 Black infants will be born into poverty.

[Ms. Edelman insisted, "We can reverse this course," and announced coordination of a Black Community Crusade for Children for which she solicited funds.]

Marian Wright Edelman, undated letter (June 1994?), Children's Defense Fund, Washington, D.C.

ACTION ON THE LEGAL FRONT

[One measure of the road still to be traveled toward racial justice is the NAACP Legal Defense and Educational Fund's "1995 Action Agenda."]
(LDF is moving simultaneously on many fronts to redeem the guarantees of equal treatment under the law assured to all citizens by the Constitution. Following is a brief status report on some of the leading cases in LDF's aggressive civil rights docket as well as other innovative programs.)

HEALTH CARE.   The persistence of poverty and racism has life and death impact—from the targeting of minority communities for hazardous toxic waste dumps to the removal of preventive services and acute care facilities from poor communities.

Matthews v. *Cove*—According to recent estimates, fully two-thirds of inner-city black children have dangerously high levels of toxic lead in their bloodstream! In 1991, LDF achieved a landmark settlement which forced the state of California to screen nearly 500,000 poor children for lead poisoning and prospectively to offer testing to all one-year-olds. This case serves as a critical model as advocates around the nation address the unconscionable health-care neglect of children in inner cities.

Latimore v. *Contra Costa County*—LDF has sued to prevent the discriminatory siting of a public hospital in a virtually all-white area of the County that is inaccessible to poor and minority county residents. The district court's order granting our clients' motion for preliminary relief has been sustained by the federal appellate court.

EDUCATIONAL EQUITY.   In the 40 years since the Supreme Court unanimously ruled in *Brown* v. *Board of Education* that intentionally segregated public schools violate the Constitution's guarantee of equal protection of the law, LDF has played the principal role in working to insure the promise of *Brown*.

Jenkins v. *Missouri*—Earlier this year, LDF argued this landmark case in the U.S. Supreme Court, which reaffirms the critical principles of *Brown*, involving the Kansas City, Missouri, school district to determine if the massive remedial measures ordered by the court must continue until the black-white academic achievement gap is eliminated. While steps have been taken to improve educational opportunities for this majority black school district, African-American achievement scores have not improved. We expect a decision later this spring.

Sheff v. *O'Neill*—In Hartford, Connecticut, LDF has joined with others to challenge the racial and economic isolation of this overwhelmingly segregated school system where seven out of ten children fall below minimum level reading skill by the fourth grade. We have brought the case under Connecticut state constitutional and statutory law guaranteeing adequate education. The case has been tried; we are awaiting a decision.

VOTING RIGHTS.   LDF has been a central player in defending Congressional districts drawn pursuant to the Voting Rights Act to guarantee meaningful political participation for African-American voters. The attacks on these districts threaten to erode the diversity in Congress that has made it truly more representative of America in pluralism. The Supreme Court will review cases from Georgia, Louisiana, North Carolina and Texas this spring. At stake is the most fundamental right—the right to vote and meaningfully participate in the political process.

POVERTY AND JUSTICE.   Lack of financial resources all too often precludes equality and limits access to public resources. LDF continues to fight so that lack of wealth does not translate into an absence of justice.

Labor/Community Strategy Center v. *MTA*—LDF represents poor and minority residents of Los Angeles who have challenged the Metropolitan Transit Authority's (MTA) plans to raise bus fares and eliminate passes on the bus lines serving their communities while it continues to heavily subsidize underutilized rail lines serving affluent and predominately white suburbs. There is a history of discriminatory allocation of transportation services provided by the MTA and its predecessor agencies. The district court has preliminarily enjoined the proposed fare hike and termination of the bus pass program. We are preparing for trial.

EMPLOYMENT DISCRIMINATION.   As long as the average income of African Americans remains well below that of whites, and as long as the African-American unemployment rate is double that of whites, LDF will battle employment practices that shut people of color out of America's economic mainstream.

McKennon v. *Nashville Banner*—LDF won a landmark victory in the Supreme Court, which held unanimously that employers could not evade responsibility for unlawful discrimination by claiming that they would have fired an employee for another reason discovered *after* the illegal discrimination occurred.

Greenwood v. *Secretary of the Army*—The United States Army Corps of Engineers in Pittsburgh, Pennsylvania, is charged with being a hotbed of racist activities, influenced by the local chapter of the Ku Klux Klan. African-American civilian employees are charging discrimination in hiring, job assignments, and promotions, as well as acts of harassment and intimidation directed at anyone who challenges the discriminatory practices.

HOUSING DISCRIMINATION.   According to a report by the federal Department of Housing and Urban Development, African Americans face overt discrimination in rentals and home sales more than 50% of the time. LDF's Fair Housing Program uses the courts to aid the victims of pernicious housing discrimination and exploitation.

Comer v. *Kemp*—The Buffalo metropolitan area is the fourth most segregated area in the United States. LDF is challenging segregation in Buffalo housing projects, where 23 of 26 sites are occupied almost exclusively by either minority or white residents. Minorities have been told that they don't qualify for federal vouchers that would supplement their rent payments and permit them to move to predominantly white, suburban neighborhoods. We won our appeal in August, and are working towards a settlement that will open up the entire metropolitan area to low-income, minority residents.

ANTI-VIOLENCE INITIATIVE.   LDF is working to deliver the message that the Second Amendment's "right to bear arms" does not require Americans to passively watch as a generation of African-American and other children is decimated. LDF is leveraging its vantage point as a respected and highly accomplished civil rights law firm to help end the madness that is ravaging our communities and threatening progress.

Gang Truce—In one violence-plagued Los Angeles neighborhood, LDF worked with community members to maintain a truce between gangs even while we are continuing to address the lack of employment and educational opportunities that underlies urban violence.

"1995 Action Agenda," NAACP Legal Defense and Educational Fund, New York, NY. Reprinted by permission.

THE STATE OF BLACK AMERICA, 1994

[In 1963 the National Urban League first proposed a "Domestic Marshall Plan for America" to rebuild the economy much as the U.S. Marshall Plan for Europe rebuilt the economies of European countries after World War II. In the 1990s John Jacob renewed the league's proposal each time he issued annual reports on African Americans. This excerpt is from the 1994 report.]

More equitable national economic policies are required to arrest the relentless rise in poverty and in unemployment. In October, the Census Bureau reported that the number of people living in poverty rose in 1992 for the third straight year, to 36.9 million, or 14.7 percent of the population. The poverty rate among African Americans was a staggering 33 percent; for Hispanics, 29.3 percent. One of every four American children was poor. Forty percent of all poor people worked, and almost a fourth of those worked full-time. Even those devastating figures understate the true amount of poverty, since they are based on outdated and unsatisfactory measures of what constitutes poverty-level income.

What should set alarm bells ringing, though, is not the extent of poverty, enormous as it is, but the fact that poverty is in a long-range upward trend that started in the 1970s and accelerated in the 1980s. Breaking that trend will take determined national policies along the lines of our Marshall Plan for America, because even a brisk economic recovery will not reach enough of the poor. The experience of the 1980s definitively proved that a rising tide does not lift all boats; that some sink deeper into the mud. The negative poverty trend line is supported by state cutbacks in assistance to the poor, eroding wages and blue-collar job opportunities, and limited work opportunities for single-parent family heads. So even if the economy picks up in 1994, the most we can expect is that poverty does not increase.

The same holds for unemployment. In the third quarter of 1993, the national unemployment rate was 6.6 percent; for African Americans, it was 12.6 percent. As with the poverty figures, these official unemployment figures are seriously understated. The National Urban League's Hidden Unemployment Index, which uses official government figures to count discouraged workers and involuntary part-time workers, measured total unemployment at 13.1 percent, while putting African American unemployment at 23.2 percent.

In the past, such figures were associated with recessions, but now they are accepted as inevitable—a sign of social callousness fostered by a general mood of helplessness in the face of the inevitable. But, again, there is nothing inevitable about either poverty or unemployment. The levels of both can be changed with the right mix of government policies and private initiatives. This suggests the nature of the task that lies before the Clinton administration which came to office last January, pledged to restore the economy and to make government an effective force for progress.

John Jacob, "Black America, 1993: An Overview," in *The State of Black America, 1994*, published by the National Urban League.

DIRECTOR JOHN SINGLETON

[John Singleton's "Boyz N the Hood" showed the lethal threat of random violence in LA and was nominated for an Academy Award. He told of his experience in Hollywood.]

I have two sides. The positive side realizes that I'm in America, I can do anything I want, I couldn't have done it anywhere else. My cynical side says, "I can direct movies. I can win an Oscar. I can affect so many people with a movie. But I can go down the street right now and a cop can stop me and shoot me in the back of the head, and no fuss will be made of it because that person is an authority figure. . . . So I'm always looking over my shoulder, always expecting someone to try to get the drop on me."

"Singleton on Hollywood Racism," *Daily Challenge,* 11 August 1993, 2. Reprinted by permission of the *Daily Challenge.*

FOUR VOICES ON RACE AND AMERICA'S FUTURE

[Four authorities give their assessments of racial relations as America closes out the twentieth century.]

HARRY BELAFONTE:

We're in a struggle for the soul of this country. We're in a struggle for America's moral center. And unless that can be made straight, I'm not sure any of the other battles are winnable.

How do you end racism in the midst of a place that is so morally collapsed? How do you end poverty in a place so spiritually poor? How do you end hunger in a place so driven by greed and avarice? If one does not attend to this moral question, how can you lead this country if you're morally weak, like Clinton is? . .

We will ultimately arrive at a place, I think, where there will just be an explosion, because despair will be so vast among so many.

New York Times, 9 September 1993, C6. Copyright 1993, The New York Times Company. Reprinted by permission.

PROFESSOR DERRICK BELL:

Black people will never gain full equality in this country. Even those Herculean efforts we hail as successful will produce no more than temporary "peaks of progress," short-lived victories that slide into irrelevance as racial patterns adapt in ways that maintain white dominance. This is a hard-to-accept fact that all history verifies. We must acknowledge it, not as a sign of submission, but as an act of ultimate defiance.

Faces at the Bottom of the Well, 1992, Basic Books. Reprinted by permission.

DR. KENNETH B. CLARK:

Reluctantly, I am forced to face the likely possibility that the United States will never rid itself of racism and reach true integration. I look back and shudder at how naive we all were in our belief in the steady progress racial minorities would make through programs of litigation and education, and while I very much hope for the emergence of a revived civil rights movement with innovative programs and educated leaders, I am forced to recognize that my life has, in fact, been a series of glorious defeats.

Cited in Herbert Hill and James E. Jones, Jr., Editors, *Race in America: The Struggle for Equality,* 1993. Reprinted by permission of the University of Wisconsin Press.

[*Harry Hampton, president of his own production company, Blackside, Inc., produced the acclaimed television series "Eyes on the Prize," a history of the civil rights movement.*]

. . . our greatest failure as a nation remains our inability to deal with racism and poverty. It is under pressure that the weaknesses can destroy the whole. We are at great risk. and need to move quickly toward cures. . . .

. . . it seems clear that, in 1992, we are faced with a situation that threatens our future because of the problems of racism, drug abuse, poor education, unemployment, crime, horrific violence. These problems seem insurmountable, but for anyone who watched and resonated to the history of the American civil rights movement it is clear that challenges faced in the segregated South were equally daunting, and that success was gained through discipline, creativity, courage, intelligence, and faith. . . .

There are powerful lessons, and instruction can be taken from the miracle of the civil rights movement that is directly applicable to the problems of today. Lessons like the impact of coalitions. The role that government—municipal, state, federal—can appropriately play. The role of the law. Political options that can be used to propel a movement forward. The multiple strategies—people seem to think the movement was a single act of impulse, almost, to stand up and move into the streets. They ignore the intelligence and strategic awareness that was in play, which allowed the movement to succeed.

Why did it work? It worked because it was accessible: you could go to your church, you could go someplace and get into the movement. It had achievable objectives: you didn't have to wait for the whole thing to come down to find some wins. And it cut across class lines, in part because the jeopardy was common to all blacks. . . .

. . . People without hope are dangerous people, and we must renew our commitment to see that all have opportunity and access. Many will be surprised that, out of a sustained assault on poverty and racism, we will free America and truly make it the powerful, humane, prosperous country that we know it can be.

. . . Most of us understand the diagnosis of what ails our nation; the issue now is to chart a course and a vision, for shared dreams are at the very core of rebuilding public trust.

Henry Hampton, "Social History: Our Rudder in the Midst of Storms," *Poverty and Race* 1, no. 5 (November 1992). Reprinted by permission of the Poverty and Race Research Action Council, 1711 Connecticut Avenue, NW, Washington, D.C. 20009.

TIME FOR REPARATIONS FOR BLACK AMERICANS?

[*Economist Richard America, a long and ardent champion of reparations for years of slavery, explained his ideas in these words.*]

Reparations isn't the issue. It's a conceptual framework, a way of looking at a set of related issues. The issues are economic, political and social dysfunction and the management of a large complex multiracial society that's competing internationally less than optimally.

Unjust enrichment based on slavery and discrimination causes this dysfunction. The country will not have a bright future if the problems stemming from past economic injustice and inequity aren't solved. . . .

The real question is, what is the present value and distribution of the stream of income that has been coercively and wrongfully diverted from blacks to whites through slavery and discrimination to produce lopsided income and wealth distributions by race, and, in doing so, has robbed too many blacks of skills they need to perform effectively?

The top 20%, disproportionately white, received 42% of earned income. The bottom 20%, disproportionately blacks, received 5% of earned income. Wealth is even more maldistributed. A major reason for this skewed outcome is past injustice—slave labor in agriculture, manufacturing, many services and in infrastructure development—followed by exclusion, discrimination and exploitation. Common resource pools, produced by everyone's labor, were maldistributed, by white decision makers, overwhelmingly to whites, primarily in the form of education and training.

Richard America, *Poverty and Race* (July/August 1994), 1. Reprinted with permission of the Poverty and Race Research Action Council, 1711 Connecticut Avenue, NW, Washington, D.C. 20009.

HUGH B. PRICE: "GET ON WITH OUR CALLING"

[*Calling it "a thrilling moment for me," the new President Hugh B. Price addressed the 1994 annual convention of the National Urban League.*]

. . . Yes, racism is still abroad in the land. Though subtler and somewhat less pervasive now, it's still a well-documented and undeniable reality in employment, housing, lending and the like.

Even so, we must not let ourselves and, especially, our children fall into the paranoid trap of thinking that racism accounts for all that plagues us. The global realignment of work and wealth is, if anything, the bigger culprit. We who serve must be clear-eyed about these color-blind economic trends if we're to be genuinely helpful to our folk.

Lest we and our children forget, the civil rights movement was a huge success in many respects. It unquestionably placed those of us with solid educations, ample family support, personal drive and a healthy dose of luck on the up escalator economically.

Yet millions of our people remain stuck on the down escalator, headed nowhere or worse. Their dire circumstances must dwell in our consciences because of the tragic loss of human potential and the mounting drain on societal resources and compassion.

It is their fate, then, that must be the primary focus of the Urban League movement. This renewed emphasis on our sisters and brothers and children in greatest need honors our original mission. . . .

Most urban school systems are too strapped financially to provide the rich array of extracurricular clubs that many of us enjoyed as teenagers. Many inner-city settlement houses, assuming they're even still on the scene, are too underfunded and dilapidated physically to provide safe havens and constructive activities for all the children who need them. Municipal park and recreation departments are but a shadow programmatically of their former selves.

But I'll tell you who is well financed and omnipresent, however. The gangs that are growing everywhere. They've filled the void left by we supposedly responsible adults and have built their own antisocial developmental structure which ensnares youngsters in search of identity and companionship. . . .

Politicians talk incessantly these days about taking back the streets from criminals. I say we take back our children from the streets and from the gangs, and the streets will take care of themselves. . . .

Let's get right down to cases. I propose that each Urban League affiliate establish a Youth Development Fund and formulate, in conjunction with others in the community, a master plan for delivering youth services after school and over the summer in churches, schools, settlement houses, community centers, safe homes, museums, even National Guard armories.

. . . for a mere $1,000 annually per child, we can put a caring adult in the daily life of a youngster during the school year. Given the frightening realities facing our kids today, how can we afford not to make certain this happens? . . .

Which anticrime strategy—100,000 cops [*proposed by the 1994 crime bill before Congress*] or 2 million inner-city kids tended by a caring adult every day—do you think would work best?

[*Price next addressed the issue of separatism.*]

I fully understand the instinct to separate when we are incessantly under economic siege, when we're still discriminated against some forty years after the Brown decision. And when, thanks to those recurring images on the evening newscasts of black youngsters being hauled off to jail, even our honor students are trailed like common thieves when they enter stores.

Even so, it is suicidal economically to become so bitter that we isolate ourselves from others. America is a robustly multicultural society. So is its labor market. . . .

For all our suffering, we cannot become so fixated on our problems that we ignore our commonality of interest with others. All of the problems I've addressed this evening—inadequate schooling, idle and alienated youngsters, and chronic unemployment—cut across racial lines. If we're ever to deal with them on a scale remotely equal to their size, we must coalesce with people of other complexions who feel the same pain, even if it isn't yet as acute. . . .

Whites of all religions have oppressed us at one time or another. Mormons, Catholics, Jews, Episcopalians, Baptists. We've been oppressed by our own on occasion. It's a form of reverse discrimination to single out any specific group of whites for vilification. . . .

What constructive purpose is served by driving deeper wedges between races? Of course we must root out any vestiges of racism. But let's not wallow forever in real or perceived grievances lest we become Bosnia someday.

I say, let's get on with making our gloriously multicultural society work. If Nelson Mandela and F. W. DeKlerk can bury the hatchets of hatred and oppression in the sand, instead of one another's heads, and get on with South Africa's future, then surely so can we.

Hugh B. Price, *Keynote Address*, National Urban League Convention, Indianapolis, Indiana, 24 July 1994. Reprinted by permission of the New York Urban League.

"The Black Nation Was Not Deceived"

[In 1995 when Qubilah Shabazz, daughter of Malcolm X, was indicted in a plot against Minister Louis Farrakhan, Black leaders, including Farrakhan, saw a frame-up. Activist Ron Daniels spoke to this response and the future.]

The Black Nation was not deceived. It soon became clear that an unsuspecting Qubilah Shabazz was/is the victim of a U.S. Government Counter Intelligence Program (Cointelpro)–style sting operation. Her accuser, the purported hitman, is an FBI informant, a renegade entrapment artist who has been in and out of the government's witness protection program for nearly two decades; a shadowy, shakey snitch who has a history of being used by the FBI to carry out a variety of dirty assignments. . . .

There is no more potentially divisive and explosive issue internal to the National Black Community than the controversy surrounding the assassination of Malcolm X. As is evident in the attempted frame-up of Qubilah Shabazz, the U.S. government is anxious to exploit any real or perceived divisions in the Black community to disrupt movements and discredit/destroy leaders who have the potential to mount serious opposition to this racist/oppressive system. We cannot allow old wounds to fester and explode into conflict thereby doing the government's dirty work for them. . . .

Minister Farrakhan must acknowledge and accept responsibility for the role he played in the assassination of Malcolm X. In this regard Farrakhan has on occasion forthrightly conceded that he contributed to the climate that led to the assassination of Malcolm. . . . Recently, Minister Farrakhan has been saying that Black people would be better off if Malcolm were alive. Consistently maintaining this kind of positive posture would be helpful in the healing process.

Minister Farrakhan and the NOI must also be open to accepting criticism without resorting to intimidation and the threat of violence against its critics. . . . Elombe Brath of the Patrice Lumumba Coalition in New York [among others] is also reported to have been threatened by an official of the NOI because he criticized Farrakhan. . . .

Last year I had the privilege of participating in a Gang Peace Summit in Pittsburgh . . . that grew out of the Rebellion in South Central Los Angeles. I rode through the streets of the city with two leaders of different factions of the Crips. These leaders told a grim and grisly story of having both been involved in hits against members of their respective families—brothers, cousins. It took the rebellion for them to realize that the deadly game of fratricide that they were engaged in was playing into the hands of the real enemies—the authorities and the system. Former enemies were not riding the streets of Pittsburgh preaching the gospel of reconciliation and peace in the interest of fighting for justice and liberation of the race.

Ron Daniels, "The Assassination of Malcolm X," 1, 7–8, 1995. Reprinted with the permission of Dr. Ron Daniels.

Children and a "Perfect World"

[*In 1993 the* Amsterdam News's *"Children's Express," edited by teenagers, asked readers to describe their "perfect world."*]

Sam, 9 (New Haven, Conn.):

A perfect world is when no drug needles are on the ground. And no paper on the ground, just clear grass and houses, beautiful houses. . . . And they [*children*] would be fed nice. They would be respected. A big world with no guns, no drugs and everybody getting along. Like if you walk out at night, nobody will try to stick you up with a gun. . . . No one would rob you.

Monica, 16 (Chicago Ill.):

Definition of a perfect world? I never thought of it. There couldn't be because of the violence, the drugs, the power trips.

Molly, 14 (Missoula, Mont.):

I'd change welfare. You can only be on it for a little while, maybe six months, and only while you're looking for a job, or something. My mom, she was on welfare for 14 years. She's still on it. It's like a trap.

Latoya, 9 (New Haven, Conn.):

Mostly, I dream about a better place and a nice environment. . . . First, I'd want to get the world clean, so we'll go around picking up trash. . . . The best thing would be to live with my parents and be happy, make them all happy.

"Children's Express," *Amsterdam News,* 11 December 1993, 24. Reprinted by permission.

BIBLIOGRAPHY

Aptheker, Herbert. *American Negro Slave Revolts*. New York, 1963.

———— *Abolitionism: A Revolutionary Movement*. Boston, 1989.

————, ed. *A Documentary History of the Negro People in the United States*. New York, 7 volumes, 1951–1992.

Bell, Derrick. *Faces at the Bottom of the Well*. New York, 1992.

Bennett, Lerone, Jr. *Black Power, U.S.A.: The Human Side of Reconstruction*. Chicago, 1969.

Berlin, Ira, et al., eds. *The Black Military Experience*. New York, 1982.

————. *The Destruction of Slavery*. New York, 1985.

Berry, Mary Francis. *Black Resistance/White Law*. New York, 1971.

Blassingame, John W. *The Slave Community: Plantation Life in the Antebellum South*. New York, 1974.

————. *Slave Testimony, Two Centuries of Letters, Speeches, Interviews, and Autobiographies*. Baton Rouge, 1977.

Boyd, Herb and Robert L. Allen, eds. *Brotherman: The Odyssey of Black Men in America*. New York, 1995.

Branch, Taylor. *Parting the Waters: America in the King Years: 1954–1963*. New York, 1988.

Clark, Kenneth. *Dark Ghetto*. New York, 1955.

Cone, James H. *For My People: Black Theology and the Black Church*. New York, 1984.

Crockett, Norman L. *The Black Towns*. Lawrence, Kansas, 1979.

Cruse, Harold. *The Crisis of the Negro Intellectual*. New York, 1967.

Davidson, Basil. *The African Slave Trade*. Boston, 1961.

————. *Africa in History*. New York, 1969.

Davis, Angela Y. *Women, Race and Class*. New York, 1983.

Davis, Charles T., and Henry L. Gates. *The Slave's Narrative*. New York, 1985.

Douglass, Frederick. *My Bondage and My Freedom*. New York, 1969.

Du Bois, W. E. B. *Black Folk Then and Now*. New York, 1939.

————. *The Souls of Black Folk*. New York, 1903.

————. *Black Reconstruction in America.* New York, 1962.

Durham, Philip, and Everett L. Jones. *The Negro Cowboys.* New York, 1965.

Foner, Philip S. *Organized Labor and the Black Worker, 1619–1973.* New York, 1974.

Franklin, John Hope. *From Slavery to Freedom.* New York, 1988.

Gatewood, William B. *"Smoked Yankees" and the Struggle for Empire.* Urbana, 1971.

Giddings, Paula. *When and Where I Enter: The Impact of Black Women on Race and Sex in America.* New York, 1985.

Greene, Lorenzo J. *The Negro in Colonial New England.* New York, 1942.

Guinier, Lani. *The Tyranny of the Majority.* New York, 1994.

Gutman, Herbert H. *The Black Family in Slavery and Freedom: 1750–1925.* New York, 1976.

Hacker, Andrew. *Two Nations, Black and White, Separate, Hostile, Unequal.* New York, 1992.

Harding, Vincent. *There Is a River: The Black Struggle for Freedom in America.* New York, 1981.

Herskovits, Melville J. *The Myth of the Negro Past.* New York, 1941.

Higgenbotham, A. Leon, Jr. *In the Matter of Color: Race and the American Legal Process.* New York, 1978.

Higginson, Thomas Wentworth. *Army Life in a Black Regiment.* Boston, 1870.

Hill, Herbert, and James Jones. *Race in America.* Madison, 1993.

Horne, Gerald. *Black Liberation—Red Scare: Ben Davis and the Communist Party.* New York, 1994.

Johnson, James Weldon. *Black Manhattan.* New York, 1930.

Jones, Jacqueline. *Labor of Love, Labor of Sorrow: Black Women, Work, and the Family from Slavery to the Present.* New York, 1985.

Kaplan, Sidney. *The Black Presence in the Era of the American Revolution 1770–1800.* New York, 1973.

Katz, William Loren. *Black Indians: A Hidden Heritage.* New York, 1986.

————. *Breaking the Chains: African American Slave Resistance.* New York, 1990.

Kelley, Robin D. G. *Hammer and Hoe.* Chapel Hill, 1990.

King, Martin Luther, Jr. *Stride Toward Freedom.* New York, 1968.

————. *Why We Can't Wait.* New York, 1964.

Kluger, Richard. *Simple Justice.* New York, 1976.

Kozol, Jonathan. *Savage Inequalities.* New York, 1991.

Lapp, Rudolph M. *Blacks in Gold Rush California.* New Haven, 1977.

Leckie, William. *The Buffalo Soldiers.* Norman, Oklahoma, 1967.

Lerner, Gerda, ed. *Black Women in White America.* New York, 1972.

Lewis, David Levering. *W. E. B. Du Bois: 1868–1919, Biography of a Race.* New York, vol. I, 1993.

————. *When Harlem Was in Vogue.* New York, 1981.

Lincoln, C. Eric. *The Black Muslims in America.* Boston, 1973.

Litwack, Leon F. *Been in the Storm So Long: The Aftermath of Slavery.* New York, 1979.

Logan, Rayford W. *The Betrayal of the Negro.* New York, 1965.

————, and Michael R. Winston, eds. *Dictionary of American Negro Biography.* New York, 1982.

Lorde, Audre. *Sister Outsider.* Freedom, CA, 1984.

Lovell, John. *Black Song: The Forge and the Flame.* New York, 1972.

McPherson, James M. *The Negro's Civil War.* New York, 1965.

Malcolm X and Alex Haley, *The Autobiography of Malcolm X.* New York, 1966.

Bibliography

Marable, Manning. *How Capitalism Underdeveloped Black America.* Boston, 1993.

Marks, George P,. ed. *The Black Press Views American Imperialism: 1898–1901.* New York, 1971.

Meier, August. *Negro Thought in America, 1880–1915.* Ann Arbor, 1963.

Miller, Loren. *The Petitioners: The Story of the Supreme Court of the United States and the Negro.* New York, 1966.

Mumford, Esther Hall. *Seattle's Black Victorians, 1852–1901.* Seattle, 1980.

Myrdal, Gunnar. *An American Dilemma: The Negro Problem and Modern Democracy.* New York, 1944.

Nelson, Jill. *Volunteer Slavery.* New York, 1993.

O'Reilly, Kenneth. *"Racial Matters": The FBI's Secret File on Black America, 1960–1972.* New York, 1989.

————. *Black Americans: The FBI Files,* New York, 1994.

Painter, Nell Irvin. *Exodusters.* New York, 1976.

Porter, Kenneth W. *The Negro on the American Frontier.* New York, 1971.

Price, Richard, ed. *Maroon Societies.* Baltimore, 1979.

Quarles, Benjamin. *Black Abolitionists.* New York, 1969.

————. *The Negro in the American Revolution.* Chapel Hill, North Carolina, 1961.

Rampersad, Arnold. *The Life of Langston Hughes.* New York, 1986. 2 vols.

Reed, Adolph Jr. *The Jesse Jackson Phenomenon: The Crisis in Afro-American Politics.* New Haven, 1986.

Rogers, J. A. *World's Great Men of Color.* New York, 1972.

Rose, Willie Lee. *Rehearsal for Reconstruction.* New York, 1966.

Stampp, Kenneth M. *The Peculiar Institution.* New York, 1956.

Sterling, Dorothy, ed. *We Are Your Sisters: Black Women in the Nineteenth Century.* New York, 1984.

Still, William. *The Underground Railroad.* New York, 1872.

Strickland, William. *Malcolm X: Make It Plain.* New York, 1994.

Van Sertima, Ivan. *They Came before Columbus.* New York, 1976.

Vincent, Theodore. *Black Power and the Garvey Movement.* Berkeley, 1971.

Wade, Wyn Craig. *The Fiery Cross: The Ku Klux Klan in America.* New York, 1987.

West, Cornel. *Race Matters.* Boston, 1993.

White, Walter. *Rope and Faggot: A Biography of Judge Lynch.* New York, 1929.

Winch, Julie. *Philadelphia's Black Elite.* Philadelphia, 1988.

Woodson, Carter G. *The Education of the Negro Prior to 1861.* New York, 1969.

Woodward, C. Vann. *The Strange Career of Jim Crow.* New York, 1974.

INDEX

Index

Index

Index

Index

Index

Index